M000159693

The Preacher's Demons

Sano di Pietro (1406–81). *San Bernardino Preaching in Piazza del Campo.* Duomo, Siena. Photograph courtesy Scala/Art Resource, New York.

The Preacher's Demons

Bernardino of Siena and the Social Underworld of Early Renaissance Italy

Franco Mormando

The University of Chicago Press
Chicago and London

Franco Mormando is assistant professor of Italian in the Department of Romance Languages and Literatures at Boston College.

This publication was assisted by a grant from the Trustees of Boston College.

The University of Chicago Press, Chicago 60637
The University of Chicago Press, Ltd., London
 Published 1999
08 07 06 05 04 03 02 01 00 99 1 2 3 4 5
ISBN: 0-226-53854-0 (cloth)

Library of Congress Cataloging-in-Publication Data

Mormando, Franco.
The preacher's demons : Bernardino of Siena and the social underworld of early Renaissance Italy / Franco Mormando.
p. cm.
Includes bibliographical references and index.
ISBN 0-226-53854-0 (alk. paper)
1. Bernardino, da Siena, Saint, 1380–1444. I. Title.
BX4700.S55M67 1999
282'.092—dc21
[B] 98-40505
CIP

⊗ The paper used in this publication meets the minimum requirements of the American National Standard for Information Sciences—Permanence of Paper for Printed Library Materials, ANSI Z39.48-1992.

For
Lori Ohliger,
in memoriam

"dolente di non potere
a più splendido
e
a più durevole monumento
raccomandare
il caro nome
e
la memoria
di
tanta virtù"

(*Manzoni*, Adelchi)

CONTENTS

PREFACE

The subject of this book is the response of an enormously popular public figure of early-fifteenth-century Italy, Franciscan preacher Bernardino of Siena (1380–1444), to three critical moral-social issues of that society: witchcraft, sodomy, and Judaism. As such, this is the first book-length study in English—and, indeed, one of very few in any language—of Bernardino since Iris Origo's 1962 portrait, *The World of San Bernardino.* It is also the first in-depth study, in any language and of any genre, of the friar's words and deeds with respect to the witch, the sodomite, and the Jew, three prominent categories of the problematic "Other" in late medieval and early Renaissance Italian society. In examining these figures, we will also be encountering along the way other problematic figures—the Devil, the heretic, the prostitute, and women in general—and other problematic issues—intolerance and persecution, sexuality and gender, moneylending and poverty—troubling the people of that time and place.

I will have more to say about the structure and content of this study in chapter 1, sections 6 and 7, but it behooves me to here alert the reader to what he or she will or will not find in the pages that follow. Since the topics with which it deals are significant issues of enduring moral and social relevance into our own day, I have written *The Preacher's Demons* so that it can be read with both profit and, I hope, delight, not only by the scholar-specialists of the various fields it embraces, but also by the literate general public. Hence, I have included introductory background information—especially, but not only, in chapter 1—in order to help the reader make sense of what Bernardino is saying and doing, within the larger realm of the historical period and the theoretical issues in question. Since this book covers so wide a range of issues, even the scholar-specialist may appreciate, at one point or another, this contextualizing material. In any case, the reader can simply skip those passages or pages that prove either too elementary or too technical for his or her level of interest.

At the same time, however, *The Preacher's Demons* is not an introductory work, nor a broad historical synthesis, nor a narrative portrait of the fifteenth-century Italian witch, sodomite, and Jew. It focuses with great concentration and depth on specifically one man, one body of texts, one time and place in history. Frequent reference is, of course, made as necessary, beyond Bernardino, beyond his lifetime (in both directions), and beyond Italy; but the reader should not expect extensive coverage thereof. I have limited this study in this way to give Bernardino the center-stage attention he merits (and to which he was accustomed in his own day!), and, more pragmatically, to ensure that this book would finally see the light of day and not be a thousand pages long. However, though it is not a narrative portrait of the witch, the sodomite, or the Jew, the present study contributes in no small way to the ongoing compilation of such a portrait through a presentation and analysis of texts that had considerable influence on the fate of these three classes of people in Italy, if not elsewhere. Finally, even though the principal subject of this book is Bernardino, the producer of "persecuting" texts, and not his audience, the "consumers" of those texts, I have recorded and commented on the response of his listeners whenever and to whatever extent that response is known. It is my hope that the present book will inspire other scholars to continue the search for further concrete traces of Bernardino and his influence amid the abundant but unexplored documentation that survives from Quattrocento Italy.

A Note on the Translations

All translations from Bernardino and other non-English sources, primary or secondary, are my own, unless otherwise indicated. In translating Bernardino, I have tried to keep as close to the original text as possible in syntax, register, and tone. Some of the Bernardino texts come from secondhand transcriptions that vary greatly in completeness and polish. Some are, indeed, telegraphically laconic, crude, incomplete, or otherwise defective in capturing what Bernardino said (see chapter 1, section 5). When necessary to render Bernardino's thought more clearly, I have filled in the missing pieces (duly noted), but have not tried to give the text the completeness and polish it does not possess in the original; hence the occasional awkwardness one might encounter in the English translations. I have, however, modernized punctuation in certain cases for greater clarity and ease of reading.

Bernardino's speech is at once both learned and colloquial, constantly oscillating in its syntax and idiom between the language of the marketplace and that of the medieval classroom. I have tried to convey both of these levels of Bernardino's style and tone. The *marchesa* Iris Origo's translations of Bernardino—which, by default, have come to represent the preacher's voice for most non-Italian-speaking English readers—are expressively elegant, but make the preacher at times sound like a nineteenth-century British gentleman. This he decidedly was not; like Dante in his *Inferno,* Bernardino did not hesitate to call a spade a spade in rather direct and at times wonderfully earthy fashion.

I have supplied in the notes the original text for every citation from Bernardino and the other primary sources, except for a few brief ones. You will observe that the Italian of Bernardino and his scribes was not yet standardized in its orthography: the same word may be spelled differently even within the same text (such as *esempio* and *essempio*). Other differences from contemporary Italian represent standard features of fifteenth-century Tuscan speech in its local varieties (such as *dei* for *devi, ma'* for *mali, grolia* for *gloria, essare* for *essere*). Because such cases are so frequent, I have had to forgo the customary "[*sic*]" alerting the reader to them, except in rare cases. The reader will also encounter the usual differences in orthography between classical and medieval Latin, for example, *Iudei* for *Iudaei.*

ACKNOWLEDGMENTS

I began studying Bernardino long ago in 1981 as a doctoral student at Harvard, and have since then accumulated many debts in my pursuit of Bernardino that I am here happy to acknowledge. Thanks, to begin with, go to Professor Nicolae Iliescu, who first introduced me to Bernardino and under whose guidance I wrote my dissertation, a literary analysis of the friar's oratory. My love of Italian studies, however, was nurtured and encouraged, years previously, as an undergraduate at Columbia, especially by my senior thesis adviser, Olga Ragusa, whose kindness and scholarly example I would be remiss not to acknowledge here. I would also like to gratefully record my debt to the work of the late *marchesa* Iris Origo, whom I was fortunate to visit in her Roman home in 1986 and who helped me to come to know better Bernardino and his world.

In Italy, many teachers and friends have lent much help, inspiration, and *appoggio morale* in my studies, especially Stefano Tani and Francesca Avezzano-Comes of Florence. I am deeply grateful to the Tani and Avezzano-Comes families as well for years of warm, generous hospitality, along with that of Pietro and Virginia Crovetto of Milan and that of my cousins, Enzo and Nella Bitonto, Vittoria and Cosimo Blandamura, and Rosetta and Pino Vitelli.

At the Graduate Theological Union in Berkeley, California, several people were of vital help in the first stages of this book, whom I here thank most gratefully: John Baldovin, David Biale, Christopher Ocker, and William Short. Thanks go as well to John H. Wright, who, for four patient years, guided me through the challenges of medieval and humanist Latin. Several other people have read and commented on all or parts of this work over the years, thus earning my gratitude: Frances Barna, Mary

Ann Donovan, Corrie Norman, John W. O'Malley, Dana Kramer Rolls, Thomas W. Worcester, and especially Mark Jordan and Larissa Taylor. A word of appreciation is owed to the Boston College Graduate School of Arts and Sciences and to the Jesuit Community at Boston College for making available the resources necessary for finishing this book. At the University of Chicago Press, my heartfelt thanks go to Doug Mitchell, Matt Howard, Leslie Keros, and Salena Fuller Krug, whose expertise helped guide this work, so efficiently and so pleasantly, from manuscript to published book. And for the many different and crucial ways in which they helped me reach this moment, my heartfelt thanks to Jim Boland, Franz Xaver Brandmayr, Deborah Contrada, Leonard Duhl, Jane Ferdon, Professor Joseph and Mary Figurito, Brian French, Tom Gallagher, Donal Godfrey, Pino Gulia, Walter Hildner, Jim Keenan, Rena Lamparska, Ann and Kay Macdonald, Andrea Malvezzi, Connie Mazella, George Murphy, Tom Powers, Denis Reidy, Laurie Shepard, Kathy Short, Shirley and Giacomo Smith, Helen Swartz, Marta Vides, Sam Yin, and Michael Zampelli. Of course, to my family, especially my mother, Maria, my father, Antonio, and my sister, Julie, my debt is too great for words.

Portions of chapters 1, 2, and 3 appeared as "'To Persuade Is a Victory': Rhetoric and Moral Reasoning in the Sermons of Bernardino of Siena," in *The Context of Casuistry*, ed. James F. Keenan and Thomas A. Shannon (Washington, D.C.: Georgetown University Press, 1995), 55–84; "Bernardino of Siena, Popular Preacher and Witch-Hunter: A 1426 Witch Trial in Rome," *Fifteenth-Century Studies* 24 (1998); and "Bernardino of Siena's Campaign against Sodomy: Emasculating Mothers as Culprits," *NEMLA Italian Studies* 19 (1995): 17–32. Reprinted with permission.

ABBREVIATIONS

All citations from Bernardino's sermons and treatises are from the following editions:

OOH	*Opera omnia*. Ed. Johannis De la Haye. 5 vols. (Venice: Poletti, 1745). Cited by volume, page and column: e.g., OOH.III.217b.
OOQ	*Opera omnia*. 9 vols. (Quaracchi: Collegio San Bonaventura, 1950–65).
A, B	*Le prediche volgari (Firenze 1424)*. Ed. Ciro Cannarozzi. 2 vols. (Pistoia: Pacinotti, 1934).
C, D, E	*Le prediche volgari (Firenze 1425)*. Ed. Ciro Cannarozzi. 3 vols. (Florence: Libreria Editrice Fiorentina, 1940).
F, G	*Le prediche volgari (Siena 1425)*. Ed. Ciro Cannarozzi. 2 vols. (Florence: Rinaldi, 1958).
R	*Prediche volgari sul Campo di Siena 1427*. Ed. Carlo Delcorno. 2 vols. (Milan: Rusconi, 1989).

In addition, the following abbreviations are used:

AASS	*Acta Sanctorum*, Paris and Rome: V. Palme, 1866. (The Bernardino material is in *Maii tomus V, die vigesima.*)
AB	*Analecta Bollandiana*
AFH	*Archivum franciscanum historicum*
Atti-Aquila	*Atti del convegno storico bernardiniano in occasione del sesto centenario della nascita di S. Bernardino da Siena (L'Aquila, 7–9 maggio 1980)*. L'Aquila: Comitato aquilano del sesto centenario della nascita di S. Bernardino da Siena, 1982.
Atti-Assisi	*Il rinnovamento del francescanesimo: l'Osservanza. Atti dell'XI Convegno Internazionale, Assisi, 20–21–22 ottobre 1983*. Perugia: Università di Perugia, Centro di studi francescani, 1985.
Atti-Maiori	*S. Bernardino da Siena predicatore e pellegrino: Atti del convegno nazionale di studi bernardiniani (Maiori, 20–22 giugno 1980)*. Ed. Francesco D'Episcopo. Galatina (Lecce): Congedo Editore, 1985.

Atti-Siena	*Atti del simposio internazionale cateriniano-bernardiniano (Siena, 17–20 aprile 1980).* Ed. Domenico Maffei and Paolo Nardi. Siena: Accademia Senese degli Intronati, 1982.
Atti-Todi	*Bernardino predicatore nella società del suo tempo.* Convegni del Centro di Studi sulla Spiritualità Medievale, XVI, 9–12 ottobre 1975. Todi: L'Accademia Tudertina, 1976.
Atti-Vicenza	*San Bernardino: storia, cultura, spiritualità. Atti delle celebrazioni organizzate a Vicenza in occasione del VI centenario della nascita di San Bernardino da Siena.* Vicenza: L.I.E.F., 1982.
BSB	*Bullettino di studi bernardiniani*
CF	*Collectanea franciscana*
MF	*Miscellanea franciscana*
SBSSR	*S. Bernardino da Siena: Saggi e ricerche pubblicati nel quinto centenario della morte (1444–1944).* Milan: Vita e Pensiero, 1945.
SF	*Studi francescani*
Vita anonima	*Vita sancti Bernardini edita per quendam fratrem et aliqua miracula,* published by Franciscus van Ortroy, "Vie inédite de S. Bernardin de Sienne par un frère mineur, son contemporain," *AB* 25 (1906): 304–38.

CHAPTER ONE

"The Voice Most Eagerly Listened To"

THE PUBLIC CAREER AND CRITICAL FORTUNE OF BERNARDINO OF SIENA

1. Popular Preaching in Early-Fifteenth-Century Italian Society

In the late summer of 1427, popular preacher Bernardino of Siena (1380–1444) arrived in the town whose name he now bears to deliver yet another eagerly awaited course of daily sermons to the people of both town and countryside.[1] Each day, for forty-five days, people in the thousands—forty thousand, says one contemporary chronicler with some exaggeration—gathered just before the break of dawn in the dimly lit arena of the town's main square, the Piazza del Campo.[2] There, for two, three, or more hours, they sat listening to the "soft, clear, sonorous, distinct, explicit, solid, penetrating, full, rounded, elevated and efficacious" voice of friar Bernardino.[3]

Though they might still be struggling to shake off the heavy vapors of sleep and had another long hot day of hard labor ahead of them, even the less pious citizens of Siena would have paid attention to what the Franciscan said and did. Not only were they in the presence of an esteemed native son and genuine curiosity-rousing celebrity—"there was no one in Italy more famous at the time"—they also had an excellent chance of seeing a miracle performed by the wonder-working "prophet."[4] In addition, with no demands made upon their purses, they could also count on a good dose of expert storytelling and theatrical entertainment, both comic and tragic. On an especially good day, they could also catch some intriguing bit of the latest world news and gossip that the preacher had picked up from his own constant journeys and from the far-flung international Franciscan network of communication. "In our times," Pierre Dubois, lawyer and adviser to the French king, remarked in 1300, "the Dominicans and Franciscans are better informed than anyone else on the current state of society."[5] What was true of the fourteenth century was also true of the fifteenth. Even such an unlikely person as the famous and decidedly unpious "merchant of Prato," Francesco di Marco Datini, was, according to his biographer Iris Origo, "an assiduous attender of sermons." As Origo reminds us, "this pastime, if a duty, was also often a pleasure. Books, even for the educated, were few and dear; but sermons were frequent and often extremely entertaining."[6] Datini may also have been heeding the advice of the popular middle-class manual of good manners, the *Libro di buoni costumi*, by another Tuscan merchant (of the fourteenth century), Paolo da Certaldo, who reminds his readers that, by attending sermons, one becomes "wise and astute, both in action and in speech."[7]

Naturally, the real aim of Bernardino's preaching was evangelization, moral-spiritual instruction, and penitential exhortation, and this—"gratefully free from the bombast of the humanists and delivered in the honest dialect of shop and market"[8]—would also have commanded their attention to varying degrees. The world in 1427 was a confusing, frightening place: as Bernardino and his audience firmly believed, the Devil was omnipresent and frequently had the upper hand; humankind was still largely at the mercy of the mysterious and capricious forces of mother nature, and, to add insult to injury, death by famine, plague, war, marauders, unjust lords, or absurd accident threatened to carry one off at any given moment.

Friar Bernardino's preaching, he promised, would shed light on this fearful darkness; his instruction and advice, despite the fire-and-brimstone cast in which they were often delivered, would offer the people another mantle of protection against the evil, threatening world, teach them how to escape the eternal fires of that place he called "la casa calda" ("the hot house"), and, on occasion, console them with Dantesque visions of a happier existence on the farther banks of that celestial river dividing time from eternity. In fact, they were told, listening to his—or any—sermon was one of the most important things they could do in their lives. Life was, above all, a constant moral test: who will pass, who will fail? Most decisions in daily life seemed to represent a dramatic choice between good and evil, salvation and damnation, heaven and hell. The possibility of mortal sin lurked at every corner. How would they know how to choose? The preacher would help them:

> Oh! How many will there be here today who will say: "I didn't know what I was really doing. I thought I was doing good and instead I was doing evil."

> And then, remembering this sermon, they will say to themselves: "Oh! Now my mind is clear about what I have to do." . . . And when you go to draw up a contract, you will first do some thinking and say to yourself: "Now what did friar Bernardino say? He said such and such: this is evil and mustn't be done; this is good; this is what I'm going to choose." And this takes place inside you only through the word that you hear in the sermon. But tell me: what would happen to the world, that is, to the Christian faith, if there were no preaching? In a little while, our faith would disappear, because we wouldn't believe in anything of what we believe. That's why Holy Church has ordered us to preach every Sunday, a little or a lot, as long as we preach. And to you she has given the command to go and hear Mass.[9]

Bernardino then goes on to state outright this piece of advice:

> And if, between these two things—either to hear Mass or hear a sermon—you can only do one, you must miss Mass rather than the sermon; the reason for this is that there is less danger to your soul in not hearing Mass than there is in not hearing the sermon. . . . Tell me: how would you believe in the Blessed Sacrament on the altar if it weren't for the sacred preaching which you heard? Your faith in the Mass comes to you only through preaching. Also: what would you know about sin if it weren't for preaching? What would you know about hell if it weren't for preaching? How would you know about any good act, and how you must go about it, if you didn't learn it through sermons?[10]

Yet mere physical presence at the sermon is not enough: since the preacher's message is so crucial for the salvation of their souls, it is, the friar warns his audience, no less than a mortal sin to fall asleep or to otherwise let one's attention wander during the sermon (R.162).

What occurred in Siena in the summer of 1427 took place nearly every season in all of the greater and lesser towns of Christian Europe for centuries following the rise of the major preaching orders, the Franciscans and the Dominicans. The phenomenon lasted well into modern times. "The important role preaching played in the life of these eras," John O'Malley has stated, " . . . needs no proving to anybody who has studied them even superficially."[11] Of the centuries and the countries here in question, Denys Hay reminds us, there is one century and one region that stand out in prominence:

> In one field of religious activity there is no doubt that fifteenth-century Italy was pre-eminent: preaching. The competition to get famous preachers occupied governments all over the peninsula, especially for the Lenten

sermons. It was in this field that the [Franciscan] Observants were pre-eminent, led by San Bernardino da Siena.[12]

Over a century ago, in his landmark study of the Italian Renaissance, Jacob Burckhardt had already alerted scholars to this fact, underscoring "the power exercised over the nation by its great Preachers of Repentance," among whom he included Bernardino:

> No prejudice of the day was stronger than that against the mendicant friar, and this they overcame. They were criticized and ridiculed by a scornful humanism; but when they raised their voices, no one gave heed to the humanists. . . . Men kept on laughing at the ordinary monkish sermons, with their spurious miracles and manufactured relics; but did not cease to honor the great and genuine preachers. These are a true speciality of the fifteenth century.[13]

More recently, in his overview of the religious culture of late medieval Italy, Daniel Bornstein has spoken of "the voracious appetite for sermons" that "made the fifteenth century one of the great ages of homiletics."[14]

In Italy, the fifteenth century opens with "the Saint Paul of Saint Francis our Patriarch's Order," Bernardino degli Albizzeschi—during his lifetime (1380–1444) "perhaps the most influential religious force in Italy" and the "voice most eagerly listened to"—and closes with Savonarola (1452–98), the apocalyptic Dominican who singlehandedly brought proud Renaissance Florence to its feet before his brandished crucifix.[15] In that age before the triumph of printing, preaching was the most important means of mass communication and mass persuasion: successful popular preachers like Bernardino and his many disciples in this "golden age of Franciscan preaching"[16] were thus the influential information disseminators, opinion makers, and power wielders of the day, perhaps far more so than any other category of ecclesiastical officeholder.

During the forty years of his preaching career, Bernardino combed the cities, towns, and villages of central and northern Italy, from Venice to Genoa, from Milan to Rome, with numerous stops in between, crisscrossing several times the upper half of the peninsula. The preacher even made brief excursions farther north into the Canton Ticino (and hence the Alpine pass bearing his name) and farther south into the Kingdom of Naples, to L'Aquila, where he died on the eve of the Ascension, May 20, 1444, and where his body is still preserved, on display in a splendid Renaissance church built in his honor. Once fame reached him—this turning point is usually dated at 1417, coinciding with a successful mission to Milan—towns competed with each other to play host to the friar and the usual small retinue of confreres who assisted him in the various attendant components of a typical Bernardino town mission, especially that of hearing confessions. For instance, on May 2, 1425, the "Magnifica Signoria" of Siena sent an urgent letter to Cardinal Antonio Corraro (Correr) of Perugia, begging him to temporarily release Bernardino from his prior commitment to Perugia so that the friar might extend his stay in Siena. Bernardino's preaching in Siena has excited such enthusiasm, the letter states, and is fulfilling such a desperate need in the city, that the people are threatening to besiege the convent of San Francesco where Bernardino is residing and to close the city gates in order to prevent the friar's departure. Fortunately, the Cardinal granted their request.[17]

Since the popular sermon was considered a public civic event that directly contributed to the welfare of the entire town, frequently it was the local civil—not ecclesiastical—authorities who invited Bernardino to come as their official guest and paid for all the expenses involved. Even when he was not an official guest, the town still extended "alms" to Bernardino and his companions, as we learn from the January 12, 1427, decree of the Umbrian town of Orvieto.[18] Sometimes the hosting town actually made a profit from the visit of the friar: as Bernardino himself reported to the people of Assisi (in an attempt to persuade them to spend some public money on his preaching mission there), Siena earned 30,000 florins from those who journeyed to the town to hear him preach.[19] One official letter of invitation to Bernardino still extant is that sent by the city of Florence, written by humanist chancellor Leonardo Bruni in florid terms of great respect and deep affection:

> Reverend Sir and most beloved Father,
>
> There is no need to tell you what great devotion and what immense love the people of Florence bear for you, just as there is no need to tell you with how much delight and how much joy they listen to your admonitions and your counsel. For you have already been able to note this from the most frequent marvelous crowds and assemblies [at your sermons].
>
> The ears of our citizens are still overflowing with your divine and mellifluous eloquence, and however full they may be, they are still desirous of more of the same sweetness, as if completely empty. Indeed, divine banquets never satiate, but even after the meal, leave a hunger perhaps even greater than that which was felt before.[20]

Naturally, there is hyperbole in the chancellor's praise of Bernardino, such as we find in much Quattrocento humanist civic rhetoric. We know, furthermore, that not everyone was as eager to listen to the friar's "admonitions" as, according to Bruni, were the Florentines. In Siena, four irate sodomites almost succeeded in their plot to beat Bernardino with clubs right after his sermon against sodomy; in Padua, "many traps were prepared by a certain man" who, as he later confessed, had wanted to kill Bernardino; another assassination plot was uncovered in Vicenza, while in Viterbo, Bernardino was publicly slapped in the face, this humiliating act of violence occasioned no doubt by the bold frankness of the friar's sermonizing. In the Abbruzzese capital of L'Aquila, some of Bernardino's enemies even sawed the legs of the pulpit in which he was to preach in such a way that during the sermon, the friar fell right onto the crowd of people in front of him, losing several teeth and much blood as a result of this prank.[21] No less bitter to him must have been the animosity directed at him by his own Observant Franciscan brothers, resentful of his having deprived many of them of the right to hear confessions (because of their lack of education) when he was vicar of the Observants of Tuscany and Umbria (1421–42) and of his adamant opposition to any formal division of the Franciscan family.[22] Indeed, of the thirty-three articles presented at Bernardino's canonization trial as grounds for his induction into the rank and file of official saints, Article 27 is entirely devoted to his silent, patient, and humble suffering in the face of bodily infirmities and "magnas persecutiones" over various issues and from various quarters, including Franciscan ones.[23] In the chapters that follow, we will encounter other, no less violent, sources of opposition to the friar, most notably those surrounding Bernardino's "idolatrous" new cult of the Holy Name of Jesus.

Though the most celebrated, Bernardino was only one of many itinerant preachers working the Italian peninsula in the same decades, many of whose names and works are still to be rescued from the oblivion of unpublished archival material and library manuscripts. Most closely associated with and most similar in spirit to Bernardino was a small band of other Observant friars—John of Capistrano, Giacomo (Jacopo) della Marca (James of the March), and Alberto da Sarteano—all of whom are important ecclesiastical figures of influence in their own right. These men, together with Bernardino, are traditionally called "the four pillars of the Franciscan Observance," the spiritually vibrant, though theologically and politically cautious, reform movement that, out of modest hermit beginnings with Paoluccio de' Trinci of Foligno in the second half of the fourteenth century, grew to great magnitude, prestige, and power in the first half of the fifteenth century.[24] This phenomenal growth was in large part due to Bernardino, who has even been called "second founder of the Franciscan Order."[25]

The similarity in doctrine and modus operandi and the nature of the presumed collaboration or continuity among these men and the other Franciscan preachers often styled disciples of Bernardino (Cherubino da Spoleto, Michele Carcano, Bernardino of Feltre, and Roberto Caracciolo) have never been adequately studied. These preachers of course had their own differing personalities and life experiences that colored their rhetorical styles and message; although they sometimes traveled together, they also pursued largely different itineraries. Capistrano (1386–1456) is a good case in point. He was already an "old" man of thirty when he joined the Franciscans, having previously been a lawyer, a husband, and governor of Perugia. By the time he met Bernardino (most likely in 1420), Capistrano's preaching style had already matured on its own, and he had accrued an intellectual-spiritual reputation independent of Bernardino. Indeed, in one of his letters Capistrano wrote of Bernardino, "He was my superior [as Vicar General of the Observants]; but I was his teacher."[26] Hence, when hearing or speaking of Bernardino of Siena as head of a "school" of preachers, we should not form too strict an image of uniformity of thought, oratorical style, or public behavior.

2. The Medieval Popular Franciscan Sermon

Though the focus of this study is on *what* Bernardino taught—that is, its moral-doctrinal-social content—a word is in order about *how* he taught (the mechanics, if you will, of his preaching), since, as we are becoming increasingly aware, form often, if not always, determines content. Bernardino's message was communicated through the medium of the medieval popular Franciscan sermon, a carefully and self-consciously constructed product of centuries of rhetorical theory and practice.[27] Each of the three adjectives, *medieval, popular,* and *Franciscan,* is significant and implies a different set of attributes.

Bernardino, Medieval Preacher

Though his lifetime coincided with the beginnings and affirmation of the Renaissance in Italy, Bernardino the rhetorician is decidedly a personality of the Middle Ages. The spirit and form of the friar's oratory derive, not from the humanists' discussions of classical eloquence, which was becoming the new fashion of his day, but rather from the medieval preaching manuals, the *artes praedicandi*. In both their organic structure and their characteristic content, Bernardino's sermons clearly derive from a mind trained according to the rhetorical principles of the Middle Ages. They are also the product of a preacher who was extremely conscious of his own role and goals as public teacher of the masses and the methods best suited to fulfilling that role and achieving those goals. Indeed, to the Sienese in 1427, Bernardino delivered an entire sermon on the office and duties of the preacher and on the concomitant role and responsibilities of the audience listening to that preaching.[28]

In their construction, the friar's sermons faithfully reproduce the form of the medieval sermon, also called the "thematic" sermon, from the *thema*, the scriptural verse that opens the sermon and upon which, according to John of Wales's *De arte praedicatoria*, "the entire edifice of the sermon is built."[29] In the typical medieval and, thus, Bernardinian sermon, the "theme" is announced and, having invoked divine assistance (the *prothema*, in Bernardino usually a Hail Mary), the preacher, in the *corpus sermonis*, divides and subdivides the verse into smaller propositions of a theological, spiritual, or, as most often in Bernardino's case, moral or catechetical nature. Each of these propositions is then meticulously explained and proven (the *dilatatio*) by multiple means of demonstration, usually involving linguistic analysis (definition and etymology), syllogistic or other forms of logical argumentation, *auctoritates concordantes*, and concrete examples drawn from nature, history, and the everyday world of human affairs.

The initial metaproposition of the *thema* having been amply and methodically, if at times laboriously, dismantled and demonstrated, the preacher then brings his discourse to an end, the *conclusio* being a clear, neat summary of the various parts of the sermon.[30] All along, the object of the preacher is to teach (hence the use of explicit mnemonic devices), to delight (hence the recourse to the theatrical and the narrative), and to persuade (hence a major appeal to the emotions). As Bernardino most likely read for himself in Augustine's *De doctrina christiana* (IV, XII, 27): "Therefore a certain eloquent man said, and said truly, that he who is eloquent should speak in such a way that he teaches, delights and moves. Then he added: 'To teach is a necessity, to please is a sweetness, to persuade is a victory.' "[31]

The thematic sermon was often called in the past the "scholastic sermon," since it was thought to have originated in the university *disputatio*.[32] Although this is no longer scholarly belief, this *forma praedicandi* nonetheless has much in common with the dialectic of the medieval schools, with its love for meticulous exactitude and finely articulated order. Whatever its precise origins, the thematic sermon and the body of theory that produced it in the High Middle Ages were essentially a new creation in the realm of European rhetorical art, distinct from the forms of oratory practiced by the ancient Romans and the Fathers of the Church. The Church Fathers, in supplying the needs of the new institution, had not concerned themselves with matters of the form and method of preaching. The two patristic texts most consulted by preachers, Augustine's *De doctrina christiana* and Gregory's *Cura pastoralis,* contained influential, enduring, but limited instruction on the preaching task. This may seem curious to us, but not to the medieval theoreticians: the orators of the Church in its first centuries, they believed, preached under the direct inspiration of the Holy Spirit and thus paid no attention to and had no need of "a method."[33] But the Spirit was "quenched" over time—again, so the medieval rhetoricians believed—and the preachers found themselves struggling for words. Hence, after 1200 years of virtual silence came the birth of the *ars praedicandi,* in which preaching is treated as a serious, elaborate, highly formal rhetorical art. With individual extant treatises numbering more than three hundred, the *ars praedicandi* is so distinct, so self-conscious, and so thorough a body of literature that it has rightly been called "the medieval analogue to the oratory of ancient pagan Rome."[34]

To be sure, the medieval sermon had its defects and proves an easy target of ridicule—for instance, in the allegorical acrobatics it performs with scriptural texts, the naïveté and farfetchedness of its "true" stories of the supernatural, and its obsessive-compulsive hairsplitting division of texts. Bernardino himself frequently falls into such excess: to cite just one of many instances, in a 1425 sermon (D.92–107) analyzing "the *fifth* type of ignorance" (namely, to believe oneself in the state of grace when actually in mortal sin), the friar distinguishes and discourses on *three* separate "states" therein, each of which is then further segmented into respectively *seven* distinct "grades"! Even so, as Gilson reminds us, "no period of history was more aware than the Middle Ages of the goals it pursued and of the means required for reaching them."[35] The medieval rhetoricians had clearly identified their task and accomplished it thoroughly, efficiently, and in harmony with the aesthetic tastes and cognitive capacities of their audiences. The "scholastic" preaching method eventually was to collapse of its own dead weight, but in its better days, it succeeded in producing "an artistic, well-worked, grammatically and stylistically finished sermon . . . treating a definite subject with logical unity and to its fullest extent."[36] Even more important, it succeeded in "moving the will to do the good," the prime objective of the art of rhetoric. Even the antischolastic, anticlerical Ciceronian humanists of Renaissance Florence were obliged to acknowledge that this product was as effective as anything to have emanated from the forums of classical Rome.[37]

The principles of classical oratory were by no means unknown in the Middle Ages. The theoretical treatises and the orations of the ancients had survived and were studied as part of the trivium, the tripartite foundation of the medieval curriculum, consisting of grammar, rhetoric, and dialectic, that is, logic. Bernardino studied rhetoric both as an adolescent and again as an adult in the winter of 1422–23 at the school of famed humanist educator Guarino Veronese.[38] Yet despite these studies, Bernardino's oratory shows little trace of the classical; even after his 1423 "sabbatical" at Guarino's school, the friar's preaching was unchanged in its fundamental medieval character. The choice was deliberate: ancient oratory may have been appropriate for its tasks in its pagan world; Christianity, by contrast, represents a new dispensation, a new, fuller, truth, and hence the adoption of a new rhetoric:

> And here you see how this warmth [of the word of the Lord] is life-giving, it gives life to both soul and body. And mind you, this is a different kind of teaching and knowledge, it is not the rhetoric of Tullio [i.e., Cicero]. This rhetoric of the word of God is better. What does it say? It says: "*Qui sitit veniat ad me et bibat*. Whoever is thirsty, come to me and drink." And in order that this word be announced to the peoples, that the doctrine be preached, Isaiah tells us in chapter 58: "*Clama, ne cesses, quasi tuba exalta vocem tuam, et annuntia populo meo scelera eorum*. Call out and shout, and never silence your voice, and just like a trumpet . . . you too, shout high and low, and announce to my people their wickedness and their sins."[39]

Again, Bernardino is neither ignorant of nor opposed to classical models of eloquence. Classical eloquence, however, is for use in secular affairs—for instance, in the world of diplomacy, as implied in Bernardino's complaint to the Sienese: "And these young people who study Cicero do well in learning how to become public speakers, but I don't hear that there are many of them. It's a great shame for this city that there isn't a band of talented young men who would know how to put two decent sentences together when the need arises."[40]

We might point out that in such remarks Bernardino does not seem to distinguish form from content. It did not occur to him that perhaps the "pagan" form of classical rhetoric could be adopted by Christians to transmit a Christian message and to teach Christian values with as much of the success as he was experiencing with his own "Christian" brand of rhetoric. Little did he know that within a few decades after his own death, precisely this transformation was to begin to occur in sacred oratory, even among his fellow Franciscans, as in the preaching of friar Lorenzo Traversagni (1425–1505).[41] Though he did not oppose the humanist revival of antiquity, Bernardino saw a moral abyss between the two civilizations, the ancient and the Christian. The "pagans" wallowed in a shadowy moral world of, at best, only partially glimpsed truth; with Christ, the new and full revelation of the clear, distinct, and salvation-gaining truth had finally been bestowed upon humanity. Repeating this *locus communis* of Christian apology in his comment on Psalm 119:130 ("The proclamation of your words illuminates and gives understanding to the simple"), Bernardino declares to the Sienese:

> [I]t doesn't say the proclamation of Plato, or of Aristotle, or of Galen or of Hippocrates, or of many other philosophers—not that I am condemning this either, not at all—however, I do not want to praise the latter as much as one should do of the former. Just as one can draw water either through a channel made of polished, clean stone or through one of clay, which, unlike the first, will cause the water to become muddy, I am saying that there are some teachings that speak of the health of the soul and those that speak of the health of the body. The latter speak of the earthly goods, the former speak of the spiritual, and here you can see why the *eloquia Domini* [the proclamations of the Lord] are better than any other kind of speech.[42]

Unlike the Christians, who believed their Scripture to be of divine dictation and hence the repository of absolute moral proof, the "pagans" had no sacred text they could use apodeictically in their moral arguments. Hence, as James Murphy reminds us, all the classical rhetorician-moralist could hope to achieve in his own moral reasoning and persuasion were probabilities: "No ancient pagan rhetorician ever conceived of any single mode of proof as being conclusive or binding."[43] Instead, the Christian preacher-moralist such as Bernardino could quote Scripture with confidence, knowing that its veracity was guaranteed by the all-knowing, all-powerful, wise, truthful God. Of course, the human task was to penetrate the at times inscrutable, allegorical surface of the text, but Bernardino was confident that the *dottori* had mastered this challenge for all of Christian posterity.

To think that Scripture or Christian doctrine derived from Scripture was anything less than a reliable, apodeictic moral authority would be to suggest that God is inadequate, deceitful, and unloving. This equation Bernardino openly asserts in the final item in his long exposition of the *firmitas* (veracity) of the Christian faith, entitled "That God would appear callous and unjust, if the Christian faith were not true":

> The . . . last proof of the truth of the Christian faith is the justice and fidelity of divine providence. If our Lord Jesus Christ had been in error, then . . . the providence of God would be callous and unfair, since, through His own example, He would have given and would have permitted to be given the highest occasion of absolute error. Moreover, in no way is it believable that God has not provided humankind with a trustworthy way to salvation.[44]

The certainty of the Scriptures, then, provides the foundation for a moral logic in preaching that begins with absolute, unchanging premises.

Bernardino, Popular Preacher

By "popular," I mean that Bernardino's preaching was intended not for small, restricted audiences of fellow preachers, theologians, and other university masters, but for the general public of minimally lettered laypeople. Since his words were most likely to fall upon the ears of the rudimentarily catechized and the philosophically unsophisticated, one of Bernardino's foremost concerns was simply to be understood. This meant, of course, tailoring his subject matter and vocabulary to the level of his audience's understanding. With respect to the needs of the audience and the responsibilities of the preacher, Bernardino was an entirely self-conscious professional. He makes this abundantly clear in his third sermon to the Sienese populace in 1427, entitled "This sermon treats of the roles of the preacher and his listeners," in which he underscores comprehensibility and utility as among the primary qualities of a good sermon (R.140–73).

Aiming for these qualities, Bernardino is obliged to reduce the complexity of issues and moral cases to a linguistic and conceptual form that can be readily absorbed by his listeners. Though we should not exaggerate the extent of this process of reduction and simplification (many of his sermons are still remarkably intricate in the treatment of their respective subjects), it is, nonetheless, a constant reality of his popular preaching. For example, Bernardino shows himself ever eager to furnish his audience with clear, concrete rules that they can apply directly to the moral decisions of their everyday lives. Thus, expressions such as "Take this as a general rule" (A.295) abound in the friar's sermons, as Bernardino reduces yet another complicated moral discourse to a single, easily remembered sentence.

The friar does, on occasion, exhort his audience to seek out and shop around for a good, holy, and, above all, wise confessor ("even if you have to travel many miles to find one") with whom to discuss the specifics of moral questions and one's moral actions (OOQ.I.174, A.44). However, Bernardino was well aware that confessors of this type were sadly and scandalously rare; he bluntly laments this on several occasions (for example, OOQ.I.171, IV.10, OOH.III.207b). Hence he tries to fill the void with as precise and tangible a form of moral instruction as possible, even if this means leaving audiences with the impression that moral decision-making is simply a technique of applying general rules to particular cases. Therefore, what has been said of the state of moral theology of a much later period, that is, after the rise of high casuistry, may also have been true in the early fifteenth century as well:

> [I]n some historical periods formal casuistry was replaced by more structured, abbreviated expressions of moral reasoning. Dependency on the wise personnel evolved into a dependency on formulated methods and rules. On those occasions, a shortage of teachers led to the formulation of such rules to guide the judgments of the less skilled and the less experienced.[45]

Bernardino, Franciscan Preacher

Bernardino is thoroughly a product and one of the greatest exemplars of the Franciscan preaching tradition. "[O]ur apostolic life," Bernardino reminds his listeners, quoting chapter 9 of the *Regula bullata*, "we have taken under the seraphic Francis, who commands us in his Rule, among other things, 'preach to the people of vice and virtue and of reward and punishment,' and I have promised to observe it."[46] Two of the features of the "Franciscanism" of Bernardino's sermons most pertinent to his approach to moral teaching and persuasion, and hence most relevant to the concerns of this study, are first, its penitential character, and second, its ready exploitation of the emotional and the dramatic.

Franciscan preaching was meant, above all, to be penitential; that is, its goal was to move the hearts of the faithful to reform their lives. Much of the friars' preaching, Bernardino's included, occurred during Lent and was intended to be preparatory to the annual reception of the sacrament of confession required of the faithful. Even when it occurred, as often was the case, outside the season of Lent, the friars' preaching never lost its fundamentally penitential character, which determines to a large extent both Bernardino's subject matter and his style. Though Francis commands the Franciscan preacher to speak of *both* virtue *and* vice, of *both* reward *and* punishment, in reality, it was the latter terms of those two couplets that received far more attention, at least in the sermonizing of Bernardino. Bernardino sees sin everywhere, with the possibility of damnation due to unrecognized or unconfessed mortal sin lurking in all corners. "Our entire life is a spider's web of sins spun by the Devil," he warns his listeners in 1424, while elsewhere reminding them that ignorance of the law does not excuse a sinner before God, and that omitting to confess even one sin invalidates the entire sacrament.[47] Hence listeners are left with the distressing impression that hardly a day goes by in which they have not committed grave sin, either actively, through their own behavior, or passively, by permitting sin to be committed in their homes or towns. Moreover, since Bernardino's aim is to move people to repentance, he will not hesitate to make use of attention-getting, emotion-stirring hyperbole in describing either the sins in question or their consequences and punishments. As we shall see time and time again, our preacher was not always a man of careful, sober speech, measuring his every word for its literal accuracy and its logical consistency with what he had previously uttered. Though a person of integrity, Bernardino could be somewhat of a rhetorical grandstander, using inflated language in the heat of the moment to win the implicit debate being conducted between him and the unbelieving or lukewarm soul. For this reason, therefore, we must always exercise caution in using Bernardino's accounts to construct a picture of the state of Quattrocento Italian mores, especially in the absence of other corroborating evidence from reliable contemporary sources.

In recent years, Jean Delumeau's monumental but controversial work, *Sin and Fear: The Emergence of a Western Guilt Culture, 13th–18th Centuries*,[48] has brought to scholarly debate the role that guilt, sin, and fear of a terrifying, vengeful God have played in the pastoral practice and literature of premodern and early modern Christianity. All of this, according to the author, was to the detriment of the original "good news" of Jesus of Nazareth—love, mercy, and forgiveness. According to Delumeau, Bernardino of Siena is one of those Christian ministers of the Word guilty of what Delumeau calls "culpabilisation," of having "inflated the dimensions of sin over and against those of forgiveness," of having preached, not a salutary "fear of God," but instead a harmful "dread" of God.[49] In fact, Bernardino is one of the most frequently cited sources in *Sin and Fear*. Since the publication of his book, the French scholar has been criticized for exaggerating the role of sin, guilt, and fear in Christian pastoral literature by what has been seen as a distortingly narrow and self-serving selection of texts.[50] Yet my examination of a mass of evidence far larger than that presented in *Sin and Fear* only confirms Delumeau's judgment of the friar.[51]

Bernardino certainly preaches at length on such "reassuring" or encouraging topics as the love of God and the reward of paradise, including a ten-sermon Latin treatise on the latter subject (*De gloria paradisi*, OOQ.II.308–471). However, such material is far outweighed by the sermons, treatises, and numerous *obiter dicta* remarks communicating the opposite message of guilt and fear. Indeed, in light of what he says in his sermons on sin, death, judgment, and hell, any statements of Bernardino's about a compassionate God and humankind's hope of salvation end up ringing hollow. In the final analysis, how reassuring and encouraging, for instance, can a wonderfully evoked vision of heaven and the glorified resurrected body be when, as the preacher declares with complete certitude, the multitude of the damned shall vastly outnumber the saved?[52]

Furthermore, if anyone had pointed out to Bernardino that he spent more time in his sermonizing on guilt, sin, and punishment than virtue, forgiveness, and reward, he simply would have agreed, replying that this was precisely his job as preacher of repentance as defined by Scripture itself, specifically Isaiah 58:1. In the same passage in which he defends the superiority of Christian "eloquence" over that of pagan "eloquence," Bernardino calls himself, and every preacher, the "trumpet of God" (a traditional image), whose whole task consists especially in identifying and condemning evil:

> And in order that this word [of God] be announced to the peoples, that doctrine be preached, Isaiah tells us in chapter 58: " . . . Call out and shout, and never silence your voice, and just like a trumpet . . . you too, shout high and low, and announce to my people their wickedness and their sins." . . . In this way, listening [to the preacher], you will cleanse yourself of your sins.

For Bernardino, the emphasis on "wickedness" (and hence guilt and fear) is a salutary pastoral procedure, leading, in his mind, to conversion in this world and, he hopes, salvation in the next.

A second characteristically Franciscan feature of Bernardino's popular oratory, exacerbating this tendency toward hyperbolic descriptions of sin and fear-inspiring punishment, is its thorough predilection for the emotional and the theatrical. From Francis onward, Franciscan piety was, above all, affective and "imaginative," that is, appealing to the imagination. From the start, the Friars Minor had been intent on moving people to repentance and conversion as much (if not more) by a "deliberate and skillful appeal to crude emotion,"[53] especially in the form of vivid narrative and other word-pictures, as by any of the more subtle tools and techniques of rational persuasion. This is the hallmark of the "pervasive and durable 'Franciscan' style," which transformed European Catholicism in the late Middle Ages, and, through the written or spoken word, theater, and the plastic arts, permeated Europe with those "large and gripping pathetic images, painted with the panchromatic variety of rouged bruises and carmined blood."[54]

Even humanist Poggio Bracciolini, no friend of the clergy, admitted in his anti-Mendicant treatise *De avaritia:* "In one thing [Bernardino] greatly excels: by persuading and exciting the emotions, he manipulates the people and leads them wherever he desires, moving them to tears and, when the subject matter allows it, to laughter."[55] The realm of affect plays as important a role as the intellect in the friar's moral persuasion. Persuading his audience of the evil of a particular act, or simply to hate sin and love virtue, Bernardino never fails to paint for them an appropriately emotional, touching picture or fantasy-stirring story. Especially vivid examples of this Franciscan-affective approach to moral persuasion are the friar's Good Friday sermons on the Passion of Christ, in which he evokes exquisitely detailed images of the physical and "mental" sufferings of Christ and his Mother, the underlying message of such sermons being: Look how much your sins have caused these innocent victims to suffer!

Other excellent examples are the friar's vernacular sermons (the *prediche volgari*) on usury, transcribed by various tachygraphers during their live performance. In these sermons, preached before an audience of merchants, housewives, farm folk, and youth, Bernardino devotes most of his energy to evoking horror-inspiring images of the restless, tortured life, the gruesome, painful death, and the eternal punishment of the usurer. This is not so in the friar's so-called *sermones latini* on the same topic but intended for a different audience. In these formal Latin treatises, composed as reference works for fellow preachers, most of the friar's treatment of usury consists of explanations of the rational whys and wherefores of that sin as contained in Scripture and canon law. On the opposite side of the emotional spectrum are Bernardino's appeals to a more positive, uplifting affect, such as in *De gloria Paradisi,* where he delights and encourages his audience with visions of heavenly bliss. Such soothing moments, however, are less frequent in the Bernardinian sermon.

Bernardino's characteristically Franciscan taste for the emotional and dramatic represents yet another reason for caution in evaluating the preacher's statements on any given question. At times they proceed not from the scrupulously circumspect, guarded speech of a cloistered philosophizing theologian, but rather from the often quick-fire, crowd-rousing, heartstring-pulling rhetorical opportunism of a marketplace orator. Accordingly, we must be careful in using any given statement of Bernardino's as apodeictic and as a reliable representation, not only of the contemporary social reality he is describing, but also of his own mind on the matter. On those matters in which it is possible to know the friar's mind, such knowledge will not be achieved by the quoting of one or two provocative statements or "purple passages" in isolation and out of context, as too many scholars have been wont to do with Bernardino. What is necessary is a comparative analysis of the wider body of Bernardino's utterances on a given question, both public and private, and an examination of his actual behavior in both his public and his private life, as documented in contemporary sources.

Moral Instruction and Argumentation: "Ratio, Auctoritas, Exemplum"

In addition to being penitential, Bernardino's oratory was also catechetical, that is, aimed at instructing the masses in fundamental matters of faith and morals, teaching them what they were to believe and how they were to act. This moral content represents a sizable portion of any given Bernardino sermon. Since, therefore, much of his preaching is concerned with moral instruction, Bernardino has the task of proving to his audience the validity of the moral precept or other morally prescriptive statement he has announced. How does he go about this task? The answer, in most cases, is by a formulaic appeal to "ratio-auctoritas-exemplum," another hallmark of the medieval thematic sermon, representing at the same time a further technique of moral persuasion aimed not at the heart, but at the intellect.[56] Introductory announcements such as "Twelve propositions we will touch upon this morning concerning these [political] factions, and for each proposition we will see the evidence of reason, authority, and example" are omnipresent in Bernardino.[57] Recognizing the importance of these three components, even the scribe who recorded Bernardino's Siena 1427 preaching cycle notes in several of the titles he supplies to the sermon that the topic in question is treated with "bellissimi esempi" or "bellissime ragioni" or "bellissime autorità."

To demonstrate the truth of his proposition, Bernardino first makes an appeal to reason, *ratio*. He carries his listeners through a rational explanation of the proposition's meaning and implications, employing whatever tools and forms of logic seem most appropriate to him at the moment. It is impossible to summarize or illustrate all of the various ways the friar goes about this; the important point here is his emphasis on rational analysis, logic, and, frequently, utilitarian common sense. One favorite technique of his is to engage one of his listeners in an imaginary dialogue, leading him or her through a step-by-step, question-and-answer process of logical demonstration. For instance, in arguing against those who say that the planetary influence abolishes our free will and hence our moral responsibility, he says:

> But, you there, I want to debate this point with you. Answer me like a reasonable man. Do you believe in the goodness of God? Yes, you say. Okay, now tell me: do you believe that these constellations have more power than your own free will? If you consent and do what they make you do, you're saying that you are forced to do so and couldn't resist. Okay, answer me then, who is worse? You who do the evil or the planet that forces you to do the evil? If you answer that the planet is more evil because it forces you to do evil, then I say to you that God is even more evil than either you or that planet because He created that planet that is forcing you to do evil. Since God is the first cause, He is the worst of all. Look at this again step by step: if you do evil, you're evil; if you say "I was forced to do it," then the one who is forcing you is even more evil, and the one who created it [i.e., the thing that is forcing you to do evil] has to be the worst of all.[58]

Shortly thereafter in the same sermon, we find Bernardino involved in this "conversation" on the absolute authority of Church teaching:

> Who do you think is greater, God or an angel?—God is greater.—Who is greater, an angel or the soul?—An angel.—What is greater, the soul or the constellations?—The soul.—What is greater, the constellations or the body?—The body.—What is greater, reason or the senses?—Reason.—What is greater, the Holy Church with her doctors or your own opinion?—The Holy Church.—Well, then, stick to what the Holy Church says and believes and holds and forget about your own opinion.[59]

Despite the appearance of utter methodical logic and cohesion on the microscopic level in Bernardino's moral argumentation and demonstration, on the macroscopic level, things can be at times quite different; when we amass the sum total of the friar's utterances on any given topic, we at times discover not only lacunae and ambiguity in his logic, but also outright contradiction.[60] This should not surprise us. Again, Bernardino is not a systematic philosopher or theologian, but rather a popular preacher; that is, his ultimate goal is not to build an impressive, watertight logical edifice—even though he does believe he is doing so—but rather to move the hearts of his listeners to reform their lives through the most expedient means available. Hence, I suspect, the friar's choice of statements is frequently determined not by careful, inexorable logic, but rather by sheer immediate rhetorical and emotional effect, such a choice being justified, Bernardino would explain, I daresay, by the higher end of saving souls from eternal damnation.

Be that as it may, this first ratiocinative step of the friar's three-pronged method of argumentation is followed by a procession of corroborating *dicta* from the *auctoritates*, that is, from Scripture, from canon law, or from *un dottore*, "a doctor." In Bernardino, the latter term designates not only an official "doctor" or Father of the Church, but also any other ecclesiastically recognized *magister*. There is little originality of thought in the friar's teachings. With scarce interest in original speculation, Bernardino saw his pedagogical task primarily as that of summarizing and transmitting to the people in understandable terms the teachings of the "doctors": "the doctors teach us [preachers] and we make a bouquet of them and pass it on to you."[61] Accordingly, Bernardino's sermons are crowded with quotations from Scripture and citations from the friar's numerous "doctoral" sources. The friar frequently prefaces these citations with an imperative such as "Listen to Albert the Great, our solemn doctor" or "Hear what saint Augustine says in his book, *On Free Will*," but just as frequently his introduction is no more than a vague, generic "The doctors say . . ." Bernardino places great importance on his use of "the doctors" in preaching: "Do you know why [I had so much success in Lombardy]?" he asks. "Because I was constantly armed with the sayings of the doctors" (R.325). Though the *dottori* may disagree—but only in matters irrelevant to salvation—they are, nonetheless, the revered, Spirit-inspired, seemingly infallible source of truth, equal in authority to Scripture itself. In other words, *auctoritas locuta, causa finita*, the friar often appears to imply.

Bernardino's "arming himself" with the *auctoritas* of the doctors was not only a gesture of fidelity to the prescribed method of the medieval *ars praedicandi*, but also an act of self-protection against the dreaded and sometimes fatal charge of heresy. Bernardino's was an age of enormous ecclesiastical upheaval and at times violent challenges to the doctrinal authority of the Church; the memory of the Great Western Schism and the Hussite and other heretical uprisings was fresh in everyone's mind. The

Church in Italy may not have known heretical dissent of the same kind, dimensions, or intensity as the Church in Bohemia, southern France, or England, but this does not mean that it felt secure in its status quo, or that it did not have to do regular battle with smaller pockets of radical and at times militant heterodoxy in the form of the *fraticelli,* the Waldensians, and other nameless groups believed to be hiding out in the remote highlands of the north. Pointing to the multiplication of heresy in Europe as one of the signs of the imminent approach of the Antichrist, Bernardino specifically mentions the Wycliffites in England and the Hussites in Bohemia, adding that their heresies "have already been sown in the minds of very many in Italy." He expects Italy, and indeed the entire world, "mundus totus," to be soon filled with them.[62] In such a climate, orthodoxy was of prime concern for the Church, and certainly no less for Bernardino, who himself was denounced as a "heresiarch" for his propagation of the "novel" cult of the Holy Name of Jesus.[63] As we shall later see, in 1426 the friar was even brought to trial in Rome for these charges, though he successfully acquitted himself.

After rehearsing the pronouncements of the "authorities," the friar then arrives at the *exempla,* the "examples," the third and final step of the typical Bernardinian *dilatatio:* "Hey! Take this nice big example . . . Listen now to the example . . . Here's a great example for you." These are the friar's constant exhortations, as he prods his audience to pay close attention to the story he is about to relate. On this single element—the masterfully executed, vivid, entertaining *exemplum* recounted in an agile, vivacious Tuscan vernacular—a great deal of the friar's enduring reputation depends. The term *exemplum,* in its widest sense, described any narrative, long or short, used to illustrate a moral or catechetical precept. Of historical, legendary, or fantastic provenance, these narratives range in length from rapid sketches of four or five lines to well-developed short stories covering one, two, or even three printed pages of sermon text. Modern audiences familiar with the didactic tales of Aesop or Phaedrus would readily recognize the basic plots of many of these preacher's *exempla,* since they often are the very same tales refit in medieval garb. The *exemplum* played a most useful role within the economy of the thematic sermon because it both translated into concrete, familiar, vivid imagery the preacher's abstract notions, and provided a refreshing pause from an often lengthy and perhaps monotonous discourse. With its direct roots in the New Testament parable, the *exemplum* was widely recognized throughout the Middle Ages for its value as a pedagogical tool, and therefore, for centuries received widespread attention from the theorists and anthologists responsible for the numerous *artes praedicandi.*

Bernardino, himself endowed with a natural gift for storytelling, states that the preacher, in teaching his flock about "the lofty matters of the heavens and the stars and sacred theology," must make abstract notions concrete and readily comprehensible; he must work "to make [his audience] able to touch them with their hands, that is to say, to speak of them in such a fashion and with complete clarity for our understanding so that [those who hear] can almost touch them and stroke them."[64] Therefore, Bernardino concludes,

> You should not criticize those speakers [*dicitori*] who, in order to show you the lofty things that exist above us, do so by means of down-to-earth, palpable examples, because that is what the art of good clear speaking is about. Jesus, font of eloquence, always used parables and concrete things in order to explain the kingdom of heaven; that is to say, through these human things we come to understand clearly divine things.[65]

The spirited, apologetic tone of his defense of the practice leads us to suspect that Bernardino may himself have been one of those "speakers" criticized for using "examples":

> These down-to-earth examples are retained more easily by the mind than rational explanations or the other things. Jesus Christ himself spoke through the analogies of examples. . . . Since there are a lot of people here today, I will give you examples so clear that I will be understood and my talk will be useful to all of you.[66]

Clear, useful, and entertaining, Bernardino's *exempla* have indeed proven, for many, to be the element of most enduring interest in all of his oratory.

3. The Audience and the Setting: Christendom in Crisis

The souls whom Bernardino was trying to save from eternal damnation, to move to repentance, and to instruct in the faith embraced the entire spectrum of society. In attendance at his sermons at one point or another were popes (Martin V), emperors (Sigismund of Luxembourg), kings (René of Anjou), dukes (Filippo Maria Visconti), feudal lords and ladies, communal chancellors, rectors and other civic leaders, university faculty and students, humanist scholars, priests and nuns, merchants and shopkeepers and their families, the urban patriciate (old and new), and the poor, as well as farmers and other *contadini* who made the trip from the countryside into the nearest city, town, village, or castle in which Bernardino was scheduled to preach. Occasionally Bernardino preached private sermons to specialized audiences, such as political leaders and the clergy, but as a rule, the crowd before him in the church, cathedral, or open square in which he normally preached counted representatives from all social classes and walks of life.[67]

Judging, however, from the topics he typically broaches, the imagery he usually employs, and the language he most readily speaks, one has the impression that the specific world Bernardino is above all addressing is that of the urban middle class, the merchants, the shopkeepers, the craftsmen, and the more skilled, more affluent employees of the various industries of the Italian city-states of his time. This impression may simply be a function of the fact that many of Bernardino's surviving sermons were those preached in major urban centers—that is, Siena, Florence, and Padua; yet on the other hand, this is the very world that Bernardino himself knew best from his own childhood, and to which the largest segment of his audience belonged.

Because he "spoke their language," with its utterly blunt and at times earthy realism, and addressed the concrete, practical moral-theological-spiritual needs of their everyday lives, Bernardino commanded the ears of his listeners. At the height of his career, he was "perhaps the most influential religious force" in Italy, even if the results he obtained were not always long-lasting.[68] Bernardino's great public stature, however, was not only due to his own charismatic style, intelligence, and reputedly thaumaturgic sanctity; there was another factor, large, complex, and external to the preacher, favoring his success. This factor was the multifaceted crisis of Italian society of the late fourteenth and early fifteenth centuries. These were times of great trouble, distress, and upheaval; and in the midst of their tribulations, many people appeared to be well disposed to listen to and place their trust in Bernardino, the self-assured friar with the captivating voice and awe-inspiring "odor of sanctity," who seemed to have ready explanations and solutions for the troubles that beset them.

Although documentation is scarce and scholarly opinion divided as to how the masses of "ordinary" women and men in the street responded, emotionally or otherwise, to the crises and upheavals (such as the Great Western Schism) surrounding them, there is no doubt whatsoever about Bernardino's response. This he reveals in his own sermons: His response was one of profound anxiety, an anxiety that only his deep, unquestioned faith kept from becoming despair. Although we shall have further occasion to hear many expressions of Bernardino's anxiety, perhaps the best example is his sermon on the "end times," "De seminatione daemonii," delivered in Padua in 1423. The preacher imagines for his audience Satan seated before his infernal court, conducting a detailed review of the political, social, and ecclesiastical conflicts and crises of the age. Among the many afflictions brought upon the world by his own diabolical inspiration, Satan specifically includes the Great Schism and what today is called the Hundred Years War between France and England. Conjured up, in the end, is a vast apocalyptic picture of a world on the brink of complete dissolution. Sin, strife, heresy, sedition, and upheaval, the friar says, are running rampant, and all of this, he warns, portends a not-too-distant arrival of the end times.[69] Indeed, Bernardino announces confidently that the world—as men of the Church then generally believed—is now well into the penultimate of the seven ages of history, one of inexorable moral decay and institutional crisis, a prelude to the coming of the great Antichrist and the Apocalypse.[70] Giving expression to his anxiety in such open, direct, and emotionally vivid terms, Bernardino inevitably transmitted it—if they had not felt it already—to the masses of people seated at his feet listening to the every word of someone they considered a learned, worldly-wise, and saintly teacher. It is difficult to imagine how a member of Bernardino's audience could sit through the two or three hours of such an apocalyptic sermon and not feel, by its conclusion, some anxiety over the state of his or her world.[71]

Bernardino's anxiety, though apocalyptically extreme, was not unwarranted, for his lifetime coincided with a period of great dislocation in both Church and society. In fact, Bernardino first reached notoriety as a public preacher in 1417, the year of the election by the Council of Constance of the Colonna pope, Martin V. This election marked the definitive end of the forty-year Great Western Schism, yet the collective European psyche would remain troubled for some time. There was no guarantee that schism or some other institutional crisis would not strike again; the Church would take years to regain its composure, only to be shaken again in the early sixteenth century with the Protestant Reformation. The Great Schism represented a major disruption of temporal and spiritual governance at all levels throughout the continent. It was a calamity with few counterparts in the history of the Western Church: "For nearly forty years there [were] two and sometimes three Popes on the papal throne, and two or three Bishops in the same diocese; two or three Superiors . . . in a single monastery, and two or three rival priests in the same parish."[72]

The struggle for power within the Church mirrored the state of secular Italian politics, in which, of course, it was deeply entangled. The republics, duchies, and city-states of northern and central Italy continued to be true to their long history of chronic warfare, some measure of peace coming only later in the century (and temporarily) through the person of Lorenzo de' Medici. The Papal States were no exception to this rule, the turmoil of the papacy-in-schism exacerbating what had been already considerable political disarray; they would remain that way until 1429, when Martin V succeeded in crushing the revolt of Bologna, an upheaval that ended up involving in some way or another a great many of the northern Italian states.[73] Moreover, although their support shrank with each passing year, antipope Benedict XIII and his successor Clement VIII stubbornly persisted in their claims to the papacy for many years after Martin's election. Indeed, Clement formally renounced the papal (or rather, antipapal) tiara only in 1429.

Ten years later, in 1439, yet another schism broke out with the election by the renegade Council of Basel of Duke Amadeus VIII of Savoy as antipope Felix V. Although this ten-year schism ended up not stirring the socioecclesiastical waters in any significant way, Amadeus's election nonetheless must have been a source of renewed anxiety to those who had lived through the earlier decades of strife. It certainly was so for Bernardino, for whom the schism redivivus was "so horrible and so scandalous a monster":

> I know many people who have been deceived over the papacy. And although some of them have insisted that they had this [their claim to the papacy] as a result of extraordinary revelations, nonetheless, I am of the opinion that all of them have been deceived and deluded, as they have, in fact, shown themselves to be. And how much of a peril this be, unfortunate Christendom is now experiencing in our own times, in the unfortunate Infelix, since, because of this kind of delusion, as all signs clearly show it to be, the deluded antipope has given birth to so horrible and so scandalous a monster in the Church; this "is the greatest iniquity and an act of denial of the Most High God."[74]

The schism had followed the even longer and likewise disruptive seventy-year exile in Avignon of the papacy, which had fled Italy in order to escape the hostile and menacing environment of Rome and the Papal States. Even after the schism was healed, the climate of Rome turned mortally hostile once again for Martin's successor, Eugene IV, who in 1434 had to flee to Florence, where he and his court remained until 1443. In the long run, the papacy was victorious in the restoration of its monarchical powers, but that outcome was still far from guaranteed or obvious during Bernardino's lifetime.

In his sermons and treatises Bernardino only rarely speaks in any direct way of these ecclesiastical troubles. Lest ecclesiastical authority be further undermined, Bernardino refrains, as a rule, from drawing attention to the institutional ills of the Church and from criticizing its prelates before a general audience of laypeople.[75] Yet on one occasion he does break his self-imposed rule and comments, if only parenthetically and generically, on the sorry conditions of the Church. He acknowledges the current grave problems besetting the Church—it is filled with "every kind of lust, avarice, and heresy"—while bemoaning the scandalous, calamitous "papal schisms."[76] On another occasion, he even admits: "If we got rid of all the bad priests, there would be few good ones remaining, [but] it is better to have priests who are not good than not to have any at all."[77] As for those who naively think that all it will take is one good pope to "clean up" the Church, Bernardino makes a long reply that may perhaps be an oblique allusion to the "angelic pope" expectations of Joachimite eschatology. In his reply, Bernardino seems to imply that no truly "holy pope" has occupied the chair of St. Peter for a long while:

> There are some who say: "When will God send us a holy pope who will get rid of these evil [priests]!" For your information, let me tell you that even if you had the holy pope you want, he could not get rid of these bad prelates and priests. Some will have to be kept in order to maintain friendship with the emperor, or others in order to maintain friendship with kings or barons or other temporal lords, and others to maintain friendship with cardinals or other lords and prelates of the Holy Church. And even if some could be eliminated, it is impossible for a pope to live long enough to have the time to replace all of the benefice holders and start over again. So he could do only little or nothing of what you think he can. The local lords will want bishops to their own liking, and the pope will have to let them have their way for the good of the Holy Church. It is impossible to reform the Holy Church if first the head and members are not in agreement. The head must be good, the members must be good, that is, all Christian peoples and lords. I don't say this to let the evildoers off the hook, but to encourage the good and resist the bad. The Church has never been reformed from the top, only from the bottom in its individual members. This is the only way reform happens. Increase and encourage the good individuals, and the rest will take care of itself.[78]

Bernardino's attitude is one of pragmatic (if pessimistic) realism, recognizing the inescapable influence of pure politics on the Church. Yet apart from these few *obiter dicta* remarks, Bernardino is silent on the ecclesiological topics of schism, conciliarism, and institutional reform, problems that had so vexed his generation of churchmen.

Bernardino's silence has led Walter Brandmüller to conclude that "the great mass of the population in San Bernardino's field of activity had remained detached . . . from all of these [institutional] problems."[79] In other words, Bernardino did not preach on these topics because, supposedly, they did not concern or affect his constituency. Given the intimate presence and involvement of the Church in his audience's daily lives on so many different levels, private and public, individual and collective, I am reluctant to subscribe to such a conclusion, despite the admitted scarcity of evidence to the contrary. To begin with, Brandmüller forgets that all of Bernardino's extant sermons date from after 1417, that is, after the resolution of the schism. We do not know what the friar was preaching about while the schism was still raging, apart from some indications that it was highly apocalyptic, as would befit those troubled times.[80] Furthermore, if Bernardino did not preach to the people of conciliarism and other ecclesiological topics, it was more likely due to a belief that the popular marketplace sermon was simply not an appropriate venue for discussing such technically abstruse and controversial questions. Nonetheless, the preacher makes it abundantly clear in his sermonizing that he is gravely concerned over the moral state of the Church; if, in doing so, Bernardino was not mirroring the feelings of his audience, it would certainly seem that he was attempting to move them to feel likewise.

Daniel Bornstein has likewise argued in *The Bianchi of 1399* that "the schism was merely an affair of the ecclesiastical hierarchy" and that "[r]eligious belief, like religious practice, remained unshaken by the disputes at the summit of the ecclesiastical hierarchy."[81] Yet, elsewhere in the same study, Bornstein admits that the schism did "provoke feelings of uneasiness among believers," that "people [were] disturbed by the Schism," and that "[t]ensions resulting from the Great Schism and the concomitant desire for a reformed and reunited church headed by one true pope" were contributing elements to the explosion of the Bianchi Flagellant movement of 1399, an extravagant, though nonheterodox, expression of popular piety. Although the troubles of the Church may not have driven the Christian masses of Bernardino's lifetime to apostasy and rebellion—what viable alternative was there for them, after all?—it is hard to believe that the prolonged ecclesiastical disturbances made no difference in their lives and left no mark on their psyches. How could the presence of two rival bishops have failed to register its effects on the populace of a town in which traditionally the bishop, for better or worse, was one of the most powerful moral, political, and social arbiters of daily life? True, sufficient documentation has not yet surfaced to allow us to determine precisely what this difference and this mark may have been, but evidence is always lacking when we attempt to reconstruct the lives and mentalities of the lower classes of society.

In any case, the troubles afflicting the institutional Church were by no means the only problems facing society in Bernardino's lifetime. The picture of early-fifteenth-century Europe that the historical facts and contemporary eyewitness accounts convey is one of upheaval, confusion, and apprehension on a massive scale, affecting all realms of society. "Those whose lives spanned the latter part of the fourteenth century and the beginning of the fifteenth were conscious of living in a period of disaster. . . . [D]isorder and disobedience were endemic in every part of Christendom."[82] It is a landscape of chronic catastrophic warfare between nations, towns, political factions, and rival families; widespread economic depression; chronic famine; the constant threat of invasion by the Islamic Ottoman Turks; and, above all, repeated traumatizing outbreaks of the unconquerable "Black Death." The latter struck Italian cities repeatedly during Bernardino's lifetime, including his hometown, Siena; Florence experienced this merciless, unpredictable scourge seven times between the years 1350 and 1430. What Gene Brucker remarks of the Florentines was no doubt true of every population hit by the plague: "In addition to rebuilding their private worlds shattered by the loss of parents, children, relatives, and friends, they also had to restore those collective institutions—commune, guild, church, confraternity—which were threatened with disintegration. Perhaps the most demoralizing aspect of this reconstruction was the realization that pestilence would recur, that the struggles to rebuild might be futile."[83] "Small wonder, then," we say with Francis Oakley, "that it was an era during which . . . religious feelings [were] frequently expressed in extreme and violent form" and "that religious phenomena that smack to us of the pathological periodically surfaced."[84] Small wonder, as well, that fear and intolerance of the "enemies" of Christendom, which we witness in the preaching of Bernardino and in the response of his audiences, experienced a sudden dramatic increase beginning in the second decade of the fifteenth century.

We shall see in the chapters that follow the precise ways in which Bernardino's audience responded to his calls for the penitential cleansing of Italian society, specifically with respect to the witch, the sodomite, and the Jew. Another form of positive response to the preacher that it behooves us to note here was the dramatic increase in vocations to Bernardino's Observant movement. Inspired by the word and example of this unkempt, emaciated, "simple" friar, multitudes of young men—to borrow an image from Dante—"threw off their shoes and ran" to follow Bernardino within the discalced ranks of the Franciscan Observance.[85] During his lifetime, the number of Observant houses grew from approximately 15 to 230, with membership swelling to nearly 4,000 from an initial 130, a phenomenal pattern of growth and yet another indication of the impact of Bernardino's preaching on contemporary society.[86] Bernardino had his enemies, but their opposition never succeeded in neutralizing his popular appeal or moral authority. One episode he briefly recounted is emblematic of the kind of moral authority vested in him by the "ordinary" people of his time: The parishioners of an unspecified parish in an unspecified town that Bernardino visited "got rid of" (*cacciare*) their unpopular parish priest and installed another, who, unfortunately, was an excommunicate. So they appealed to Bernardino, asking him to restore the priest to legitimate canonical status. Bernardino protested that he did not have the authority to do so, for he was not their bishop. To this protestation, one of them responded: "It seems to me that you're not only our bishop, you're our pope and emperor as well."[87]

According to his younger contemporary and biographer, the humanist Maffeo Vegio, the friar himself would, in a spirit of jest (and perhaps self-satisfaction as well), answer those questioning his repeated rejection of the various episcopal sees offered him with the rejoinder: Why should he agree to become bishop of just one city, when he was already "considered the bishop of all of the cities of Italy"? On one occasion, according to the same source, Bernardino is supposed to have retorted "that it didn't seem right to him to be made bishop since he was already pope," for, as Vegio comments, "whenever he entered any city or town, he was welcomed, celebrated, and honored with the same veneration as that accorded the pope."[88] Indeed, according to Andrea da Cascia, in his anti-Bernardino treatise entitled "Sermo contra imaginem nominis tabulellae, quae est imago et signum antichristi," when Bernardino entered the Umbrian town of Spoleto in 1426, the people were lined up along the sides of the roads, ready to greet him with olive branches in their hands. The local bishop, not pleased by this attempted restaging of Christ's triumphal entry into Jerusalem, tried to stop it; to the bishop's objections, Bernardino is supposed to have defiantly replied: "What is it to the bishop if these people, out of the devotion they bear toward me, wanted to receive me with olive branches?"[89]

4. Bernardino of Siena: The Making of a Preacher-Celebrity

The process by which Bernardino reached such celebrity as a public preacher was a slow one; fame did not come until he was about thirty-seven years old. This turning point in his career is usually seen as coinciding with a particularly successful 1417 mission to Milan. A look at Bernardino's life before this point will be useful for understanding the man whose later teachings and opinions we shall be examining in the rest of this book.

Bernardino, "so steeped in the history of his times," is not another shadowy medieval figure constructed of legend and lore; he is, on the contrary, one of the best-documented saints of the first fifteen centuries of ecclesiastical history.[90] The first works to be produced about Bernardino right after his death were biographical: by the year 1480, there were already over a dozen written accounts of the preacher's life. Not surprisingly, all of these are hagiographic in nature to some degree, selecting and interpreting their data according to the conventional norms of that literary genre, the *vita sanctorum*. Nonetheless, these early *vitae* convey a great deal of reliable, useful information about the bare facts of the saint's life, work, and character, transmitted by close friends or other contemporaries of respectable intellectual stature, such as Sienese statesman Leonardo Benvoglienti and humanist Maffeo Vegio. There is, of course, still much we would like to know about the formation of the young Bernardino's mind and heart, and we must always handle what we do learn from these hagiographic sources with due caution.

Born in 1380, Bernardino was the much-prayed-for and only child of Tollo (Albertollo) degli Albizzeschi, governor of the Sienese territory of Massa Marittima, and Nera (Raniera) degli Avveduti.[91] Bernardino was born with the proverbial silver spoon in his mouth: the Albizzeschi were a Sienese family of minor aristocracy—"an ancient house of nobility," as one witness at Bernardino's canonization trials was later to describe the preacher's lineage.[92] However, that silver spoon was soon snatched away. In 1383, at the age of twenty-two, Bernardino's mother, Nera, died.[93] She was followed three years later by his father, Tollo, age thirty-nine.[94] Thus, at the age of six, Bernardino found himself an orphan.

The deaths of his parents were not the only significant losses of Bernardino's early life. Five years after the death of his father, in 1391, Bernardino's maternal aunt, Diana, who had raised the boy since the death of his mother, died as well. The early *vitae* assure us that all those responsible for Bernardino's welfare were, without exception, good, loving, generous Christians. If this is true, then Diana's death would have been yet another painful experience of maternal abandonment for the boy, although the adult Bernardino was never to mention it.[95] With no family left in Massa Marittima to take care of the eleven-year-old orphan, Bernardino was obliged to leave behind the familiar faces and landscape of his boyhood home as he was sent off to the strange, big "city" of Siena, to be placed in the custody of Tollo's brother, Cristoforo (Cristofano), and his wife, Pia, a childless couple. Although Cristoforo and Pia, we are assured by the hagiographers, were also upright and loving persons, it is reasonable to assume that their care could not adequately compensate for Bernardino's traumatic loss of parents, surrogate mother (Diana), and childhood hometown. Combined with the other threats and horrors of life—"nasty, brutish, and short"—in fifteenth-century Italy, these emotional traumas could not have left the child with the impression that he lived safe and secure in a stable and trustworthy universe. Indeed, it is reasonable to conjecture that these experiences instilled in him a certain, perhaps even a deep, sense of fear, anxiety, and insecurity, deeper than that felt by many of his contemporaries.

The love of his relatives and his family's financial resources were a protective cushion to him to some degree, but it seems that his real security, his truly safe haven, was his faith, a deeply pious, orthodox, unquestioned Catholic faith, "the one and only true faith," which had a self-confident answer for every question and every doubt about existence. Given the crucial psychic function that Bernardino's faith thus fulfilled—it was his defensive barrier against the yawning abyss of fear, anxiety, and insecurity—it is no wonder that he was to cling to it with such zealous, perfectionistic tenacity and could not tolerate those who diluted, violated, corrupted, questioned, or denied it, as did the witches, sodomites, and Jews. This is not to say that Bernardino's faith was not genuine or was merely a psychological reaction to trauma. It is simply to say that the series of childhood losses he experienced necessarily left their mark on his unconscious. That mark was the intensely intransigent nature of Bernardino's fear- and anxiety-ridden faith and of his treatment of sinners, the enemies and violators of that faith and its precepts.

Bernardino's "Petticoat Government"

According to the earliest biographers, Bernardino owed his faith and character to, above all, the series of four women who assumed his care after his mother's death. These were all exceptionally devout, virtuous, matronly

as plagues, famines, and warfare as punishment for the sins of humankind. "If you do not turn to repentance for your sin," Bernardino warns his audience, with Scripture in hand to prove it, "you will all be executed by the accursed Destroyer [i.e., Abaddon/Apollyon of Revelation 9:11] and even greater troubles will come upon you."[112] Having tasted the bitterness of life in his own earliest years, Bernardino speaks poignantly on the subject of *contemptus mundi:*

> Do you not see, when you have an infant who is nursing, how when he has become too big to nurse anymore, but is used to that milk, you, his mother, in order to wean him, mix something bitter in with the sweet, that is, you put a little bit of absinthe there? So that when the child wants to suck, he tastes the bitterness, and as soon as he tastes it, he immediately turns his face away from the breast and does "tpu, tpu, tpu!" and spits hard, because he finds it bitter; and so it is that the tiny little tot begins to experience the bitterness of life. And what is true about children, is also true of all of us; we have sweet things in this life, but mixed in with them is much bitterness. Look how many dangers there are in these delights, how many scandals! These are the stings of the world. And when you have meditated on them, you will say: "O treacherous world, I no longer believe in you!" You have seen that this man who was once big and tall is now puny and hunched over; that man was once rich, now he's poor, and so forth, for there is nothing stable in this world. Oh! Believe you me, the world deceives you in every direction.[113]

Observant Franciscan Vocation

Recovering from the long postplague illness that kept him hovering between life and death, and having decided on a Mendicant vocation, Bernardino found himself unable to decide between the Order of Preachers and the Order of Friars Minor. His choice ultimately fell to the latter group, "because its greater contempt for the world, humility, and poverty pleased him more."[114] The decision having been made, heavenly ratification opportunely came to the young man in the form of "this vision, which appeared to him in sleep":

> He saw himself in some great uncultivated field, in the midst of which was a lofty tower, and in the tower, a window. Through the window great flames were issuing forth, and in the midst of the flames, a woman [appeared], with her hair all unbound and her arms raised up and apart, who shouted three times, "Francis."[115]

The reporter of this dream, Maffeo Vegio, adds that Bernardino "used to say that he held the dream as vividly in his memory as if it had just occurred," a remark that adds a ring of authenticity to the account.[116] According to Bernardino's own interpretation of this symbolic vision, "the field meant this world; the tower, God; the fire, the Holy Spirit; the woman, religious life or the Church."[117] Modern psychologists, I daresay, will have other interpretations.

In joining the Franciscans, Bernardino seems to have found his heart's fulfillment; it was to be his family for the remaining forty-two years of his life. The blood family and childhood friends he left behind, however, felt differently. The author of the Surius *Vita* tells us of their reaction to Bernardino's new life as a Franciscan novice: "He gave himself so zealously to those works which to the world seem lowly and worthy of contempt, holding his and his family's noble stature in complete disdain, so that the common people who had known him before considered him no otherwise than insane and foolish."[118] Bernardino occasionally makes reference to the loathing he personally experienced as a wandering Mendicant, as when a woman responded to his request for food by throwing a loaf of bread from her window that, Bernardino reports, "struck me on the finger and hurt me very much."[119] Closer to home, Bernardino found that some family members were none too enthusiastic about his choice of vocation: this had entailed giving away his considerable inheritance to the poor, much to the vexation of his family.[120] Upon a visit of the neophyte friar to his relatives in Siena, one of them, "quite angry that he had taken the religious habit," assaulted Bernardino with the following tirade:

> We had hoped that you would lead an honorable life in the world and take a fertile wife and produce joyful children so that your house (*domus*), increased by offspring, could be exalted in its wealth, and your family (*genus*) could grow even more renowned. But, tell me, what is a friar if not a pig, since he lives in complete leisure and idleness [and] eats off the labors of others, thinking of nothing else but food so that he can grow nice and fat?[121]

Though there were many "nice and fat" Franciscans at the time, they were, in reality, not to be found in Bernardino's branch of the order. The Franciscan Observant reform was an ascetically radical yet politically temperate, unpolemical Franciscanism directly descended from that of the thirteenth- and fourteenth-century "Spirituals," who had made absolute poverty the cornerstone of their charism. The Franciscans, we might add, were not unique in having a reform wing within their fold; a similar reform spirit was sweeping through most of the major orders at this time.

Since the Observants lived and worked separately from the rest of the order, being governed by their own Vicar General, Bernardino's Franciscan formation—theological, spiritual, and otherwise—took place outside the usual academic setting of the order's *studia*. Indeed, in the hermitage of Il Colombaio, where he completed his two years of novitiate, Bernardino seems to have been largely self-taught, presumably concentrating on Scripture, canon law, and the works of his "Spiritual" Franciscan forefathers.[122] Most important among the latter were Peter John Olivi and Ubertino of Casale, author of Bernardino's *vademecum*, the *Arbor vitae crucifixae Iesu*. The *Arbor vitae*, together with all of Olivi's works available to him, was assiduously studied, copied, paraphrased, and quoted verbatim time and time again by our friar.[123] Bernardino felt great spiritual and emotional affinity with the passionate ascetic and reformist zeal of Olivi and Ubertino; it is no exaggeration to say that their presence is discernible in some way in Bernardino's every sermon, treatise, and gloss. At the same time, however, our friar neither mentions the names of these two men in his writings or preaching nor otherwise publicly acknowledges his debt to them; this silence is most probably due to prudence, since the names of the long-dead Olivi and Ubertino were still shrouded in suspicion of heterodoxy and schism.[124]

Bernardino would have also begun the study of the usual panoply of medieval preaching and confessional manuals and reference works, the *artes praedicandi*, *summae confessorum*, and *summae theologiae*. Among the latter, especially important to Bernardino was that of Alexander of Hales, which had been designated the official theological textbook of the Franciscan Order. Bernardino continued to consult these works his entire life; indeed, the friar, it would seem, never ceased to be an avid student, leaving at his death a fairly substantial personal library.[125] (Moreover, in the winter of 1422–23, as already mentioned, he even took time off from his preaching duties to audit classes in rhetoric in Guarino Veronese's famed school of humanistic studies.)[126] After his ordination to the priesthood in 1404, Bernardino began his itinerant preaching career, focusing on the cities and towns of northern and central Italy. Unfortunately, this period of Bernardino's life is not well documented; suffice it to say that, quietly and unspectacularly, through trial and error, he eventually gained the practice and self-confidence that resulted in his becoming the "voice most eagerly listened to" of early Quattrocento Italy. Although this study is not biographical, much of what subsequently transpires in Bernardino's career between the beginning of his fame in 1417 and his death in 1444 will be encountered in one form or another in the chapters that follow.

Canonization and Posthumous Reputation

Death did not put an end to Bernardino's celebrity status, power, and influence. His sermons and treatises found immediate and ready dissemination throughout the well-organized international Franciscan network, and began to be cited as respectable *auctoritates* by preachers and compilers of moral treatises.[127] At least this is what John of Capistrano, one of Bernardino's closest followers, tells us: after Bernardino's death, copies of his works were reportedly requested by all branches of the wide-flung Franciscan family, including those in the "Holy Land, Cyprus, Asia," and "even . . . barbarian nations."[128] Bernardino's message and method also lived on, in some degree and form, in the men who were moved to follow his style and example, although sufficient study of this influence has yet to be carried out. In a sermon in praise of Bernardino, Roberto Caracciolo (da Lecce), another accomplished Franciscan Observant preacher of the second half of the fifteenth century, lists twenty other "famous" Italian preachers who "endeavored to imitate the mode, rule and style of Saint Bernardino." Caracciolo even adds himself, through modest circumlocution, to this list of "praedicatores clari" working in the Bernardinian style: although he never heard Bernardino preach, Caracciolo says, he has studied the works he left behind.[129]

It was not only Bernardino's preaching that made him the object of continuing attention and fame; it was his miracles as well. Already a wonder-worker during his earthly life, he became, after death, an even more prodigious thaumaturge: miracles in the thousands were attributed to him.[130] From Milan and from England came letters from Filippo Maria Visconti and Henry VI seeking relics to cure them of their ailments; and from France, in gratitude for Bernardino's miraculous deliverance of his son from death, Louis XI sent a magnificent silver sarcophagus to contain the body of the by then canonized friar.[131] In Siena, the donkey upon which Bernardino had traveled so many miles was literally and thoroughly depilated in the mad rush for miracle-working relics.[132]

It took fewer than six years for Bernardino's canonization to become a reality, so overwhelming had been the signs of his sanctity and so great the clamor of those demanding its official recognition—including, as the papal bull of canonization notes, that of "our most distinguished son in Christ, Alphonsus, illustrious king of Aragon."[133] Bernardino's much beloved companion, Giacomo della Marca, eventually to be sainted himself, boasted (inaccurately) of his master's rapid rise to officially proclaimed sainthood: "There hasn't been a saint since St. Peter until today who didn't have to wait twenty or thirty or sometimes a hundred years before being canonized."[134] In Rome, the triumphal ceremony itself, on Pentecost Sunday in the Jubilee year of 1450, was an event of lavish proportions: "innumerable hordes" attended—40,000 people in all, we are told—"French, German, Spanish, Portuguese, Greek, Armenian, Dalmatian and Italian, all singing hymns in their own tongue." The procession of Franciscans was so long that, one eyewitness reports, by the time the head of the line was entering St. Peter's Basilica across the Tiber, its "tail" was still leaving Santa Maria in Aracoeli, the Franciscan convent in the center of town on the Capitoline Hill.[135] Soon thereafter, the faithful began crowding their votive candles before his familiar, easily recognizable, gaunt face with its delicate, angular features, toothless mouth, and sparkling eyes gazing out upon them from numerous altarpieces, statues, and frescoes decorating the basilicas, churches, and chapels of Christendom, many of them bearing his name.[136]

For reasons unknown, Bernardino's popularity seems to have waned somewhat in the late fifteenth century and in the first half of the sixteenth, judging from the number of extant copies of the printed editions of his works, which are few in comparison to those of preachers of lesser stature of his century, such as Caracciolo.[137] However, it was never fully extinguished even during this period, especially in the realm of iconography. In the 1480s, Pinturicchio was commissioned by the Bufalini family to fresco their chapel in the Aracoeli, dedicated to Bernardino, with scenes of his life, miracles, and apotheosis.[138] In the following century, on May 19, 1518—the vigil of Bernardino's feast day—in the Franciscan Church of Santa Maria Gloriosa dei Frari, the *Serenissima* Republic of Venice unveiled one of the most exquisite paintings of the Italian Renaissance, Titian's *Assumption of Mary,* in honor of the preacher-saint, whom they had already elected co-patron of their proud homeland.[139]

In the late sixteenth century and throughout the seventeenth—that is, in the post-Tridentine era—Bernardino's star began once again to shine brightly. New, more widely diffused editions of his *opera omnia* were put into print in Venice (1591), Paris (1635), and Lyons (1650); the famed Jesuit exegete Cornelius a Lapide (1567–1637) cites Bernardino's "pious and erudite" sermons in his own monumental, best-selling commentary on Scripture, while Bernardino returned as one of the most widely depicted Franciscan saints in art, including that of El Greco.[140] In 1625, Bernardino was honored with a church of his own in the center of Rome, on the present-day Via Panisperna, adding to the already considerable number of churches, oratories, monasteries, convents, confraternities, and other religious houses dedicated to his memory in other parts of Italy. Rigorous reform was the order of the day in the post-Tridentine Church, and it comes as no surprise that the words and deeds of Bernardino, rigorous reformer of the post-schismatic Church, would once again resonate in the hearts of Roman Catholics.

From then on, Bernardino's light continued to burn steadily in the firmament of Roman Catholic sanctity. His cult soon spread beyond Europe to the New World, where, in California and South America, Franciscan missionaries attached his name to newly founded cities and other localities. In the nineteenth century, the Franciscan Order began to press the Vatican to have its beloved son Bernardino named official "doctor" of the Church. After many decades of agitation and promotion, Bernardino came within a hair's breadth of obtaining his "doctorate": On April 3, 1966, Monsignor Nicola Ferrari, "Promoter of the Faith" of the Apostolic See, signed a *declaratio* favorable to the nomination of Bernardino as "Doctor of the Church." "The whole matter, however, got swept up into the vortex following the Second Vatican Council," and the nomination was never officially proclaimed.[141] Nonetheless, the fact that Bernardino's cause had advanced that far—and as recently as 1966—attests to his continuing importance in the eyes of the official Catholic magisterium as an ever-relevant teacher and role model for Catholics, as well as to the complete approbation by the Church of the specific content of his teaching.

5. The Sources: Bernardino's Extant Works

Bernardino's extant works can be divided between those which come directly from the friar's own pen and those which were transcribed during actual public delivery by unofficial scribes.[142] The scribes in question—most, but not all, anonymous—were men of varying talent, scrupulosity, and personal interest, and this has resulted in transcriptions, or *reportationes*, differing conspicuously in length and quality. The works from Bernardino himself are contained in the nine volumes of the Quaracchi critical edition and are all in Latin. These collective works are often referred to as the *sermones latini*, a misnomer inasmuch as they do not represent readymade sermons for the general public; they are, for the most part, scholastic treatises written in a formal (non-oral) style for the benefit and convenience of fellow preachers, summarizing the scriptural and doctrinal content of a multitude of "preachable" topics. The Quaracchi volumes also include Bernardino's detailed outline for a year's worth of preaching, known as the *Itinerarium anni;* many rough sermon sketches and drafts; scriptural glosses (mostly copied from other sources); and twenty-two brief letters, representing, for the most part, business-related matters.[143]

As for the rest of the friar's production, the secondhand sermon *reportationes,* most of the extant cycles—Florence 1424, Florence 1425, Siena 1425, and Siena 1427—are in Italian (hence their collective name, the *prediche volgari,* "vernacular sermons") and have been published over the years by Ciro Cannarozzi and Carlo Delcorno.[144] There is also a Latin transcription of the 1423 Padua cycle published only in the now antiquated edition of Bernardino's *opera omnia* compiled by Johannis de la Haye (last edition, Venice 1745). Among the major sermon cycles still unpublished are those preached in Perugia and Assisi in 1425, copied down (in Latin) by John of Capistrano, and that of Padua 1443, "reported" (also in Latin) by the same jurist-scribe responsible for the 1423 Padua *reportatio,* Daniele de Purzillis.[145] Disparate remaining fragments of further cycles or occasional sermons also have survived: many of these have been published in various books and journals (particularly in the *Bullettino di studi bernardiniani*) as new discoveries have been made. The latest discovery was published in the 1986 volume, *Abbozzi (inediti) di Sermoni,* edited by Floro di Zenzo and Siggillino (Naples: Massimo, 1986).

All of this amounts to a considerable mass of printed material, about which two general observations must be made. First, there exists no critical edition of any of the just mentioned vernacular cycles or of any significant portion thereof. The closest we get to such a work is Delcorno's expertly and generously annotated edition of the Siena 1427 cycle, based on a far wider selection of manuscripts than previous editions, but still falling short of a complete census of all surviving manuscripts.[146] The second observation concerns the existence of double *reportationes.* Not only do there exist multiple, nonidentical manuscript copies of the same transcription (more than twenty for Siena 1427, for example), there are as well in some cases at least two separate transcriptions produced by two scribes working independently at the same sermon. This is true for the Padua 1423 cycle, the Florence 1424 cycle, and the Siena 1425 cycle, the latter of which comes down to us in both an anonymous Italian version (published by Cannarozzi) and an unpublished Latin version produced by a certain Iacobus Nannis de Griffulis (excerpted by Cannarozzi in the notes to his edition of this cycle). For the Florentine sermon *corso* of 1425, we possess not two but three separate *reportationes.* In addition to these, there exists, as well, an unpublished manuscript, codex 28 of the Convent of the "Osservanza," Siena, corresponding closely to the friar's Florence 1425 cycle but not a *reportatio,* which may have been composed in advance of its actual delivery by Bernardino himself, if it is not the reworking of Bernardinian sermons by another hand. Over the years, these double textual witnesses have been described, compared, and contrasted to a limited degree, but none has been published in its entirety.[147]

It is difficult to capture in a general statement the differences between the two simultaneous transcriptions. Some merely summarize the friar's expositions, while others appear to capture it more fully in what we assume was its original discursive form. Some scribes are more interested in the scriptural and doctrinal content of the preaching, while others are more interested in its more entertaining narrative elements—his didactic tales (the *exempla*), his colloquial asides, and his digressions. Even where there is no discernible prejudice, one scribe may grasp one portion of a lengthy exposition or of a set of *exempla* recounted on the same theme, while the other may have caught a different portion of the same exposition or the same set of tales. At times, the same point or the same *exemplum* is captured by both scribes, but in differing words.

Even with the collation of all extant *reportationes,* a fully faithful, total reconstruction of any one of the friar's sermons would never be achieved—not even in the case of the Siena 1427 *corso,* transmitted to us by an extraordinarily scrupulous transcription. Bernardino's message was communicated to his audience by elements simply beyond reconstruction—for example, the tone and volume of his voice, the changing expressions of his face, and the posturing of his body. How all of the nonverbal elements of his "performance" were manipulated and how his audiences responded to and interpreted them, we shall never know. Moreover, even if captured with accuracy in writing, the original spoken word, carrying with it layers of meanings and nuances, had a cognitive-emotional resonance within its first audience that, five hundred years later, we can hope to recover only in small part. In addition to these issues of transcription and performance, there is the further problem of what is lost in translating Bernardino's fifteenth-century Italian or Latin into twentieth-century English.

The present state of the printed editions of these secondhand *reportationes* necessarily imposes some restraint on their use as sources of the friar's thought and examples of his craft. This is not to say, however, that they are without great value: despite the differences between these dual transcriptions and the multiple manuscripts, thus far none of the scholars who have compared them has come across instances of open contradiction between the two versions, a consoling thought to Bernardino scholars. Indeed, the degree of actual consistency is remarkable. Another consoling thought is that Bernardino returns to the same topic repeatedly in his preaching career, not only in the various cycles of the *prediche volgari,* but also in his personally composed *sermones latini.* The overlap in subject matter is considerable, since Bernardino had what appears to be a fixed and limited, albeit large, repertoire of *materia praedicabilis;* hence most, if not all, of the vernacular sermon topics are represented in the reliable Latin *opera omnia* as well. Thus, any given assertion or *exemplum* from one of the imperfect *reportationes* can often be verified with its counterpart in another transcription, Latin treatise, sermon draft, outline, or postilla. Occasionally, such verification can also be found in independent descriptions of the friar's doctrine contained in the several contemporary biographies written soon after his death and in the many pages of canonization trial testimony, as well as in the many panegyrics and polemical treatises written for or against Bernardino during and shortly after his lifetime. In those few cases where this system of checks and balances is not possible, we can content ourselves with the thought that even if Bernardino did not make a specific assertion or expressed it otherwise, it nonetheless represents what was transmitted to posterity as his opinion, and thus what influenced subsequent "consumers" of that text.

Among the transcriptions of Bernardino's vernacular preaching, however, the forty-five sermons of the Siena 1427 cycle stand in a class by themselves. Through circumstances that even the modern reader is tempted to call miraculous, we possess an utterly scrupulous reproduction of Bernardino's words—scrupulous in its attempt to capture on paper every word the friar uttered. The curious tale of how this was accomplished is related in the prologue to this collection of sermons:

> And therefore the great and mighty God inspired a certain man called Benedetto di maestro Bartolomeo, citizen of Siena and a textile cutter who had a wife and several children, few possessions, and much virtue, [who,] setting aside his work for the necessary time, recorded and wrote down the present sermons *word for word,* not omitting to write a single word that [Bernardino] preached. . . .
>
> And note the virtue and grace of the aforementioned cutter, Benedetto: as he listened to the sermon, he would write down [what he heard] on waxed

> tablets with a stylus [presumably in stenographic form, a common procedure at the time]; and after the sermon was finished, he would return to his shop and rewrite on paper all of what he had copied down on the said tablets of wax, so that, on the same day, before beginning his own work, he had written down the sermon two times. Anyone who takes note will find this to be a miraculous thing for a human being to have accomplished, that in so short a time he had written down so many things not once but twice, and not failing to write down the least little word from all of those which came from that holy mouth, just as is clear from the present book.[148]

It seems incredible that, a poor, humble (but evidently stenographically talented), patient, and not unintelligent textile worker should have undertaken such a toilsome and time-consuming enterprise—and brought it to successful completion—for forty-five successive summer days. But such apparently was the extent of his devotion to the friar, and such was the reputation of Bernardino, by then already a living legend.[149] "[A]s is clear from the present book," the concrete printed results of his toil decidedly overcome all the disbelief that such an otherwise uncorroborated tale might incite. Scholarly prudence, however, restrains us from calling it an "utterly faithful" or "perfect" reconstruction of the friar's discourse.

Benedetto's text is as close as we can ever hope to come to the spoken words of Bernardino, recorded *de verbo ad verbum,* with all of his characteristic mannerisms and idiosyncrasies. The nearly 1,400 pages are an incomparable masterpiece of oral prose, with all of the vivid immediacy and agile expressiveness of the justifiably renowned Tuscan vernacular speech. Without the testimony of this *reportatio,* our image of Bernardino's oratory would be greatly impoverished. These pages are, furthermore, an invaluable guide to Bernardino's thought as communicated, not to fellow friars and preachers (as in the more somber *sermones latini*), but before a live audience of mixed, largely plebeian humanity. Nearly every sermon is registered in its structural entirety: introduction, body, and conclusion, along with all the further divisions and subdivisions, digressions, asides, parentheses, and exclamations with which the friar developed and colored his speech. Even long passages of the preacher's Latin, frequently quoted from Scripture and the "doctors," are reproduced, with surprisingly few errors. Did the scribe, we wonder, receive help from Bernardino or one of his associates in correcting his text?

As for verbal exactitude, Benedetto seems to have at least attempted to capture every syllable uttered by the friar. If Bernardino stumbles and gropes for his word, Benedetto copies down this hesitation: "Oh! oh! oh!

aspetta, doh, aspetta un poco, ch'elli m'occorre un detto di Gregorio a nostro proposito" ("Oh, oh, oh, wait, uh, wait a minute, it seems to me that Gregory has said something on this subject," R.283). If Bernardino moans and groans to add a tone of foreboding to his speech, Benedetto registers these "special effects": "guarda se tu ve 'l vedi: . . . ooh! se tu ve 'l vedi, uuuh! . . . male sta" ("Look to see if you see it there: . . . uh oh! if you see it there, ooo, ooo . . . that's a bad sign," R.283). When he imitates the cackle of a goose ("ca ca ca ca") or the buzzing of a fly ("us, us, us, us"), his faithful scribe is careful to reproduce this humorous mimicry (R.417, 667). Bernardino occasionally interrupts his speech to reprimand those who are causing a disturbance in the vicinity—"Oh, you people near the fountain, conducting business, go do it somewhere else! Oh you by the fountain, don't you hear me?"—or to address the scribe himself—"And therefore, you who are writing this down, be sure to write it well so that you don't make a mistake"—and Benedetto dutifully sets down even these parenthetical remarks.[150] Now and then Benedetto even annotates the text for his readers, such as when he tells us: "At this point, it began to rain and [Bernardino] stopped the sermon and didn't preach anymore today" (R.361). In view of all of this, it is reasonable to accept Benedetto's work as a reliable source of Bernardino's thought and as an authentic reflection of the art and craft of his "live performance" oratory, especially when corroborated with the other above-described documents at our disposal.

6. Bernardino and the History of the "Persecuting Society"

The humble layman and textile cutter Benedetto di Bartolommeo endured his forty-five days of intense scribal labor because he was convinced that what Bernardino had to say to him and his contemporaries was of vital importance to a deeper understanding and successful conduct of their lives. Scholars, however, have thought otherwise: outside of Italy the work of Bernardino and of popular preachers in general was for centuries simply ignored by historians, who deemed it irrelevant to or of scarce value in their attempt at reconstructing the Italian past. This all changed dramatically just a couple of decades ago, at which time scholars came finally to realize what Benedetto and his peers had known very well: to understand the people and events of the Quattrocento, one must listen to its popular preachers.

This new appreciation for sermon texts as gold mines of information about and insight into the past was itself a consequence of an earlier revolution in this century in the field of historiography: the birth of a "new history."[151] Historians came to recognize the gross lacunae in our picture of the past contained in textbooks and monographs that concentrated on the lives of the few and famous elite; they also came to understand that the course of human destiny has not been shaped merely or even primarily by the external political-military machinations of the privileged few at the top of the social pyramid. Hence, scholars began to write what is variously described as "social history," "history from below," the history of "the everyday world of ordinary people," or, to cite the title of a well-known series emanating from France (the center of this "new history"), the "history of private life." First inspired by Marxist ideology, the historiographical downward shift in its early stages meant that the focus of history dropped from the narrow top of the social pyramid—the rarefied, managerial, and moneyed domain of kings, princes, and landowners—to its massive proletarian base, the crowded, little-charted world of peasants and workers.

More recently, however, in the study of premodern and early modern Europe, an even deeper "plunge" has been taken. Exemplified by a work such as Bronislaw Geremek's *The Margins of Society in Late Medieval Paris,*[152] the scholarly spotlight has now been made to shine on those tenebrous, long-neglected classes of the social riffraff and the moral outcast: pimps and prostitutes, lepers, sodomites, thieves, and heretics. To this list we need to add the Jews and witches (putative or otherwise) of Christian Europe, who suffered the same or worse treatment at the hands of their contemporaries, though their historiographical destiny has been different—that is, slightly more "fortunate" in the amount of scholarship devoted to them. In a history largely and until very recently written by the winners, these "losers" (again, with the exception of witches and Jews) have been, for all intents and purposes, invisible and all but forgotten.[153]

These are the groups or individuals whom medieval and early modern Christendom deemed unworthy of a secure, public, and respectable place in its tightly constructed pyramid of humanity. To be sure, in certain cases, such as those of thieves and pimps, marginalization, most of us would agree today, represented a healthy and necessary mechanism of defense against truly destructive elements. But in other cases, Christendom was doing battle with enemies that were, in fact, largely the product of "scientific" misinformation, ancient polemical stereotypes transmitted unquestioningly from one generation to another, or its own fearful, traumatized imagination.

This, of course, the Christians of these centuries could not recognize, instead believing themselves to be acting "in good faith" and with logical coherence, given what they were taught by Scripture and the official ecclesiastical *auctoritates,* both considered divinely inspired and utterly trustworthy sources of moral guidance.

Whatever the differences among them, these marginalized men and women were alike in their "otherness," in their nonconformity to the prevailing social-moral code of Christian Europe. As a result, slowly over the centuries they became increasingly the objects of at times grotesque stereotypes, and were widely publicized as enemies of society. Because they were "other," they were also feared. Being feared, they were also persecuted, and, in certain cases, persecuted with intensifying ferocity as time wore on. The beginnings of this persecution phenomenon can be traced back to the twelfth century, to the triumph that Christianity achieved over European society in all its dimensions. With the pagan Roman empire no more, the "barbarians" at least superficially converted, and civil stability restored, "Christianity" became "Christendom" and reigned supreme. That is, by the twelfth century, Europe had become a theocracy—the social-political order had become completely identified with the religious order—and hence, any dissent with or departure from the spiritual code of behavior amounted to social subversion, if not outright treason (as in the case of heresy). This theocracy was never as complete or as powerful as certain popes imagined it to be—it was imperfect and embattled on all sides—but it was real nonetheless. As ecclesiastical hegemony grew stronger, more confident, and better organized, intolerance grew proportionately. Indeed, intolerance seemed a logical and inevitable response for the sake of survival, being justified by Scripture itself (e.g., John 15:6).[154]

This brings us to Bernardino and the present study. The citizens of Christian Europe did not come into the world already knowing who their enemies were; this they had to be taught, and in this, as in all other social-moral subjects, their primary and most authoritative instructor was the preacher. Bernardino rose willingly and energetically to the task. During his long, wide-flung, and indefatigable career of public instruction, the friar had much to say about who was acceptable in decent, respectable Christian society and who was not. In doing so, he contributed greatly to the slow but steady crystallization of negative, alienating stereotypes of the "enemies of the faith" and to the rising climate of intolerance. Moral unacceptability, of course, meant persecution, ostracism, and, at times, even death. The ultimate and unspoken goal of Bernardino's public mission was the furtherance of the great medieval dream of a total Christian theocracy, that morally and socially homogeneous society in which Christian doctrine had the first and final word. Such a dream had never been and would never be fulfilled, even though many—including Bernardino and the Church hierarchy—behaved as if it had. The pursuit of this goal meant the elimination or at least the drastic isolation of those subversive "foreign" elements within the "Body of Christ."

Isolation or elimination (through execution) are measures bluntly, strenuously, and continuously advised by the intransigent friar in his forty years of zealously evangelical campaigns throughout northern, central, and southern Italy from the Alps to the Abruzzi. One readily visible sign of this successful and far-reaching dissemination of Bernardino's word is his "signature," the omnipresent "Holy Name of Jesus" (IHS) monogram in Gothic letters surrounded by a sunburst across a blue field, the product of his own design. Even the less attentive traveler cannot help noticing the Bernardinian monogram everywhere in Western Europe, especially Italy, on the façades of private and public buildings in cities, towns, and villages.[155] Another concrete sign of the effectiveness of Bernardino's public mission is the specific legislation passed in several Italian towns incorporating the ideas and, in some cases, the specific dictates of the preaching friar. Even where no legislation was passed—or, if passed, was not enforced—emotions were nonetheless stirred up and attitudes were formed or confirmed against those "enemies of society" that Bernardino identified.

Bernardino's word had an impact, a calamitous one for many individuals. Indeed, reading the at times gruesome Bernardino-inspired civic legislation and the considerable body of "fire and brimstone" sermons that motivated it, it is difficult to understand how hagiographers and even secular critics of the past (including some of the stature of Eugenio Garin) could have so successfully and for so long portrayed Bernardino as "the sweet Saint of Siena" and "the genuine and cheerful soul [who] by nature eschewed visions of sorrow."[156] We find even in Origo, the most recent and most judicious of Bernardino's biographers, a tendency to minimize this dark, unpleasant side of the saint's personality and to repeat the hagiographic commonplaces about Bernardino's "humor and acceptance of the weakness of human nature," his "equanimity," "his moderation, his natural sense of balance, his personal humility and warm humanity."[157] The gentle, soft-featured, smiling face of the many contemporary painted portraits of the saint and his famous, frequently anthologized comic parables can be deceiving!

7. The Witch, the Sodomite, the Jew, and Bernardino

In the course of the fifteenth century there were three groups in particular that became, in dramatic fashion and ever-increasing numbers, the object of collective fear and persecution by Italian society. They are the "witches," the "sodomites," and the Jews.[158] In the chapters that follow, we shall hear what Bernardino has to say about each of these categories of people while we assess his contribution to this marked and unprecedented crescendo of fear and persecution.[159] This examination of Bernardino's utterances and public efforts concerning these three groups will involve us in further important and related issues, such as the question of heresy and attitudes toward women and sexuality in general. At the same time, it will give us the opportunity to review some more of the major events and people in Bernardino's life, as well as to further appreciate the social role and power of rhetoric—that is, formal public oratory designed to persuade through eloquence, one of the most ancient of literary arts, to which present-day Madison Avenue mass-media advertising can trace its roots.[160]

Each of the three central chapters (2, 3, and 4) engages the same areas of inquiry, to varying degrees: (*a*) Bernardino's conceptual understanding and visual image of the figure in question; (*b*) the sources of his information and judgments pertaining to them; (*c*) his use and transformation of these sources; (*d*) the tactics he uses to persuade his contemporaries of the truth of his message and move them to specific action; and (*e*) the response of his audiences—both leaders and populace—in the various towns he visited. In each case, we will find that Bernardino disseminates a fear-inspiring, demonized portrait of the individual involved and of his or her activity, manipulating for his purposes Sacred Scripture, "scientific" observation, "true" historical data, and, above all, the emotions of his audience. The response of his audiences, however, was varied and uneven: Bernardino had his successes and his failures, but there is sufficient evidence to conclude that the ultimate effect of his preaching was to make life more difficult and more precarious for the witch, the sodomite, and the Jew.

Bernardino was not alone in this endeavor. Since the early centuries of Christianity, in the various parts of Europe and in various hands, the witch, the sodomite, and the Jew increasingly had been made the object of slowly crystallizing, hatred-rousing stereotypes. Bernardino represents only a link, though an important one, in a great chain of antiwitch, antisodomite, and anti-Jew propaganda that was to continue for centuries, indeed into our own. Although legally sanctioned persecution of these three groups was by no means at its worst in the fifteenth century, this century nonetheless can be considered a watershed in their collective fortunes, inasmuch as it was then that the tide began a noticeably sharp upward rise, at least in Italy. I conclude that this marked rise in intolerance of these groups at this juncture of history can be at least partially traced to the specific influence of Bernardino and his ample company of preaching disciples and emulators, dispersed throughout Italy, and indeed, throughout Europe. However, our focus is exclusively on the one man, Bernardino, and the one country, Italy. Not only are the words and activities of the latter group of fellow preachers working in Italy or beyond too vast to be covered in one volume, but much more preliminary scholarship is also necessary before we can proceed to a synthetic account and analysis: we are still lacking the edited primary texts and monographic studies upon which such a global assessment must necessarily be constructed.

Having emphasized Bernardino's role in the rise of persecution of these three marginalized classes, I hasten to add a qualification about the Jews. Until very recently Bernardino's name has been conspicuously absent from studies of how "the persecuting society" treated witches and sodomites, but this is not the case for the Jews. Scholars have long noted Bernardino's role in Jewish marginalization and oppression. Yet, though frequently mentioned in studies of European anti-Semitism, Bernardino's word and activity have been only superficially examined; the same is generally true of most of the history of Mendicant hostility toward the Jews, as Léon Poliakov observes at the beginning of chapter 4. This, unfortunately, has led to hasty, inaccurate, exaggerated evaluations of the friar's anti-Semitism and its place in the overall economy of his life and *opera omnia*. The present work on Bernardino and the Jew represents the first attempt at a more thorough investigation and more accurate assessment of the friar's anti-Semitism. In fact, in order to arrive at this more accurate assessment, I have deliberately placed the discussion of Bernardino and the Jews *after* the two chapters on the witches and the sodomites. It is only after we have become acquainted with Bernardino's treatment of these other marginalized groups or "enemies" of Christian society, and with the broader context of his life, utterances, and general modus operandi as popular preacher, that we can more accurately assess what Bernardino has to say about the Jews. I leave the details of this reassessment of Bernardino's anti-Semitism for the conclusion to chapter 4. Here, suffice it to say that the conclusions therein contradict some of the hitherto unquestioned judgments of many decades of scholarly generalization.

Throughout the discussion that follows, I try to place the friar's remarks and his behavior in the broader context of both his historical, psychosocial setting and the Judeo-Christian, Greco-Roman tradition, which he inherited, modified, and transmitted to yet another generation. However, this book does not provide exhaustive historical and theoretical discussions of the complex and age-old issues of witchcraft and witch hunting, Christian anti-Semitism, and what has now come to be termed *homophobia*, that is, the fear of same-sex love and genital activity. In addition to the three general surveys by Moore, Richards, and McCall listed in the bibliography, there are already many fine studies on all of these larger problems, which are identified as we come to each topic.[161] The goal of this study is to bring to light and evaluate the specific nature and extent of Bernardino's contribution to these three areas of the Western European tradition, by sifting out, collating, and analyzing all available evidence scattered amid the numerous volumes of sermons, treatises, and other historical documents.

Now, in doing so, we may find some or much of what the friar asserts and counsels frankly unpalatable. My task here is not to excoriate him for speaking or acting so, nor is it to pretend that he does not. My task is rather to describe his teaching and behavior and render them understandable in the context of the theological-intellectual premises, "scientific" information, and social-historical-psychological milieu in which Bernardino and his contemporaries lived.

In the end, however, what we do not know about the man and his times perhaps amounts to more than what we do know. But is this not the case for many, if not most, areas of scholarly pursuit? As a searcher for knowledge remarked long before Bernardino's lifetime:

> For although a researcher must toil through many vigils and keep vigils over his toils, there is hardly anything so cheap and easy that a man can understand it fully and clearly, unless perhaps he knows for sure that *nothing* is known for sure. This may seem an unresolvable contradiction. But why? "For the corruptible body is a load upon the soul, and the earthly habitation presses down upon the mind that muses on many things." [Eccles. 8:16–17.] Hear what Solomon says about this: "All things are hard; man cannot explain them by word." [Ps. 63:7–8.][162]

CHAPTER TWO

"Let's Send up to the Lord God Some of the Same Incense"

PREPARING THE GREAT WITCH CONFLAGRATION

> I don't know how better to tell you: To the fire! To the fire! To the fire! *Oimmè!* Do you want to know what happened in Rome when I preached there? If I could only make the same thing happen here in Siena! Oh, let's send up to the Lord God some of the same incense right here in Siena![1]

The "incense" that Bernardino is encouraging his Sienese audience to raise to the heavenly courts is not the fragrant resin usually found in church censers, but rather the earthly remains of a condemned witch burned at the stake. The events in Rome to which the preacher refers concern the bringing to "justice" of a large number of witches and sorcerers routed by the Franciscan and his incendiary oratory. In Siena, a year later, still flushed with victory, Bernardino was attempting to duplicate the same purging of the community. The friar did not achieve the same spectacular results in Siena as he had in Rome, but, judging from the extant sermons preached there, we know that he certainly tried his strenuous best to do so. We also know that he met with success in other localities in his campaign to bring to justice other supposed practitioners of witchcraft and to eradicate completely what he considered devil-inspired subversion.[2]

Bernardino reports with disgust that he has encountered witchcraft in every place he has visited in the course of his wide and frequent journeying throughout Italy: "There is neither town nor castle nor state," he claims, "that is not filled with seers, sorcerers, diviners, and witches."[3] His response was an outpouring of sermons and treatises on the topic and closely allied topics, such as superstition,[4] heresy, and the Devil. Bernardino includes witchcraft in his "Top Twelve" list of egregiously heinous crimes "for which God frequently condemns and punishes states and kingdoms."[5] And elsewhere, describing for his audience "the torments of hell," he identifies witchcraft as one of those four "universal sins" for which the damned will be most severely punished.[6] It was, in short, one of the enduring preoccupations of our friar's preaching career, a preoccupation that he tried to pass on to his audiences as well.

The European antiwitchcraft hysteria in its most virulent phase is usually dated from the late fifteenth to the late seventeenth century, with the period 1560–1660 representing the crest of this insidious wave. Before the sixteenth century and the outbreak of the great witch hunts, however, documentation illustrating the history of European witchcraft is lamentably scarce. Thus, Bernardino's sermons are of great interest and value to historians, cultural anthropologists, theologians, and other kinds of scholars, shedding, as they do, much light on this obscure realm of European daily experience.[7] For nearly forty years of his public career, motivated by an uncompromising spiritual zeal and some profound personal psychic drive, Bernardino waged a veritable one-man antiwitchcraft campaign. The spark of his campaign then went on to inflame some of his contemporaries, who joined in the endeavor to expose and eliminate these enemies of society.

The friar's public instruction represents an important contribution to a slow but steady process of transformation within the collective European imagination whereby an inchoate body of disparate beliefs and vague notions regarding superstition, simple sorcery (*maleficium*), pagan ritual, and demonology coalesced into what Jeffrey Burton Russell calls "the classic formulation of the Witch Phenomenon."[8] With the development of this "classic formulation," the witch came to be understood as a devil-worshiping, evil-working woman belonging to a massive, well-organized, international company of moral-social subversives who gather weekly at their sabbaths in remote parts of the countryside. Thus, what made the Great Witch Hunt possible, on the conceptual level, was the addition of the charges of diabolism—the idea of a pact with and worship of the Devil, evil sabbaths, and night flights—to the earlier, more benign view of the "witch" or "enchanter/enchantress" as merely a practitioner of simple, mechanical, superstitious sorcery who worked through the natural forces inherent in the material world.

Directly and indirectly, Bernardino helped, first, to crystallize and popularize this panic-raising image of the witch as evildoing, heretical, idolatrous "servant of Satan"; second, to convince society of the actual existence and peril of such a well-organized, self-conscious class of individuals (mostly women); and, third, to rouse people—popes, bishops, temporal powers, citizens of the towns, and peasants of the countryside—to take explicit, radical, systematic action to seek and destroy them.[9] In this chapter, we shall see how he accomplishes each of these tasks in his missions to the people of northern and central Italy during the early decades of the fifteenth century. In at least one noteworthy case—to which we now turn—news of the friar's doings in his homeland traveled far beyond the frontiers of Italy to sow fresh seeds in new territory.

1. Bernardino and the Witches of Rome, 1426

The most significant witch-related pages among Bernardino's collected works—most significant for what they reveal about fifteenth-century witch-related beliefs and about the decisive public influence of the preacher—occur within the same sermon that supplied the opening quotation of this chapter, number thirty-five of the forty-five preached to the people of Siena in the summer and autumn of 1427. The sermon, "Qui tratta delli tre peccati capitali," was delivered on Sunday, September 21, and focuses on the evils of pride, lust, and greed.[10] As background to this sermon, the reader should know that in the spring of (most probably) the previous year Bernardino himself had been summoned to Rome by Pope Martin V to stand trial before a massive phalanx of cardinals and masters of theology. The charge was heresy and centered on his new devotion to the Holy Name of Jesus, which involved the public display and reverencing of the "IHS" monogram tablet that he had designed. We shall discuss this trial later in this chapter (sec. 5), but for the moment, suffice it to say that, not only did Bernardino emerge victorious from the trial, but the pope also granted him the honor of preaching in St. Peter's Basilica before the very audience that had shortly before been ready to send him to the stake.

The dramatic trial of this already legendary "prophet" was not the only public spectacle that Bernardino's visit afforded the Eternal City. Afterward, the exonerated friar also preached to the populace at large and succeeded in persuading his audience to expose what he described as a vast number of witches and sorcerers, the most criminal of whom were brought to quick, fiery justice on the Capitoline Hill at the very heart of the city. As Carlo Ginzburg observes, the temporarily conquered "heretic" thus left Rome a conquering hero, a "hammer of heretics."[11] In due time, we shall ponder the significance of the juxtaposition of these two facts (Bernardino's own bitter heresy trial and his subsequent burst of witch-hunting fever); for the moment, let us simply note the "coincidence" and focus on the witch trial itself.

Though Bernardino's 1427 sermon is the primary focus of our attention in this section, it is not the only source of information about this episode of Roman history. In addition to Bernardino's brief mention of the trial again in a later sermon preached in Padua in 1443,[12] there are six other fifteenth-century sources—Italian, German, and Swiss—that mention the trial, thereby testifying to the notoriety of this episode in the early history of the European witch hunts. (Surprisingly, there is no mention of this trial in Bernardino's principal Latin treatise on witchcraft, *De idolatriae cultu*, composed several years later, in the period 1430–36, for the benefit of his fellow preachers.)[13] These six sources are:

a. The diary of Roman Senate scribe Stefano Infessura;[14]
b. The *Memoriale* of the fifteenth-century Roman chronicler Paolo di Benedetto di Cola dello Mastro del Rione di Ponte;[15]
c. The sermon "De sortilegiis" (before 1476) by Bernardino's Franciscan confrere and disciple, Giacomo della Marca;[16]
d. The *Dialogus de nobilitate et rusticitate* (1444–50) by ecclesiastical diplomat Felix Hemmerlin (Malleolus) of Zurich;[17]
e. The *Buch aller verbotenen Kunst, Unglaubens und der Zauberei* (1456) by Johann Hartlieb, personal physician to Duke Albrecht III of Bavaria;[18]
f. The *Continuatio* (after 1490) by Johann Chraft, "praedicatore Cambensi," of the *Chronica pontificum et imperatorum romanorum* of the Augustinian chronicler Andreas of Regensburg (Andrea Ratisbonensis, ca. 1380–ca. 1438).[19]

Although it is not demonstrable beyond doubt that Bernardino and all of these six authors are referring to the same trial, the evidence points in this direction, as we shall later see.

Before we proceed further, a word is in order about the date of the trial. Regrettably, despite the clamorous and fully public nature of this episode in the heart of a major city, we possess no definitive information about the exact year in which the trial occurred. In recounting the episode, the preacher gives no indication of chronology. Bernardino's principal account of the witch trial occurs in a sermon that he preached to the people of Siena on Sunday, September 21, 1427. The preacher simply introduces the narrative by saying, "Do you not know what was done in Rome while I preached there? . . . I want to tell you what was done in Rome,"[20] omitting his customary time-setting *exemplum* preamble ("a short while ago," "there was once," "eight years ago"). Likewise, the preacher's 1443 summary of the case contains no indication of its date. However, in Appendix 1, I explain that there is good reason to believe that the trial took place during the summer of 1426. Furthermore, lacking evidence to the contrary, scholars, myself included, assume that the witch trial in question occurred at the end of the same trip to Rome that began with Bernardino's own heresy trial.

We now turn to Bernardino's sermon, "Qui tratta delli tre peccati capitali," and the facts of the case. In this sermon on the capital sins, an account of the trial is given under the rubric of the sin of pride, for it is in this category that is classified belief in or practice of any of those benign or malicious magical, superstitious, person- or environment-manipulating, and future-predicting activities that can be termed witchcraft. It is pride, Bernardino explains, that drives us to want to do or see what is not ours, but rather God's, to do or see (R.1005). Technically, all these variously labeled activities and their respective practitioners (witches, sorcerers, soothsayers, conjurers, seers, magicians) had specific and distinct historic identities. However, in accordance with late medieval theology, Bernardino is either unaware of this fact or feels no need to make lexical distinctions, inasmuch as he acknowledges no real moral difference among the offenses that the various phenomena represent.[21] To him as to his ecclesiastical contemporaries, they were all varieties of condemnable *maleficium*, whose efficacy ultimately depended on the assistance of demons. Hence he feels free to use the various terms at all times quite indiscriminately and quite imprecisely.[22]

When he first broached the topic of witchcraft in his public preaching in Rome, Bernardino says, he received no response at all; people thought he was "dreaming" it all up.[23] However, a bit of spiritual coercion applied by the friar bestirred their consciences: "At one point it occurred to me to tell them that if anybody had information on any man or woman who practiced these things and did not report them to the authorities, he or she would be guilty of the same sin."[24] The results of his challenge were immediate: "And once I had finished preaching," the friar reports, "a multitude of witches and sorcerers were reported."[25] Bernardino was soon informed by his Franciscan superior that "[t]hey're going to burn the whole lot of them!" However, given the great number of accusations, "a consultation was held with the pope, and it was decided that only the worst of these women (*le maggiori*) would be arrested, that is, those women (*quelle*) who had committed the greatest crimes."[26]

Let us take brief note here of the details of the case thus far: the initial hesitation of the public to denounce the so-called criminals, the involvement of the pope, the number and gender of the culprits. First, why did Bernardino's Roman audience respond with such initial incredulity—or, better, with feigned ignorance? They thought he was "dreaming" it all up. As the friar confessed in Padua in 1423, other audiences had responded the same way to his sermons on witchcraft.[27] I am reluctant to believe that it was out of genuine ignorance of the phenomena in question. Was it instead due to fear of accusing their supposed "witch"-neighbors and thereby perhaps suffering retaliation from such powerful and often malicious practitioners of the occult? Or was it because they really did not share Bernardino's opinion that such activity—the practice of witchcraft in its various modes—was really so harmful, sinful, or diabolical? As we saw, it was only Bernardino's terror tactic (added to his already thoroughly demonized characterization of sorcery and superstitious practices) that moved them to action. What we have here may be the same phenomenon observed by scholars regarding the growth and development of the witch craze in other parts of Europe; that is, it was only with the intrusion by intellectual elites, with their learned notions of diabolical witchcraft, that certain practices of simple sorcery and certain practitioners—among them innocent folk healers—long tolerated as harmless and indeed necessary by the ordinary citizens of Europe came to be seen, respectively, as heinous acts of subversive evil and as malicious servants of Satan.[28] If correct, what this thesis means, in effect, is that the witch craze was to a large extent the creation of inquisitors, theologians, and preachers like Bernardino.[29] We shall return to this topic of audience response at the conclusion of this chapter, for it was by no means uniform in the case of Bernardino: as we shall see, in Siena in 1427, the friar's attempt at instigating a witch hunt appears to have been received with utter indifference, while in Todi, in 1428, his preaching did enjoy some degree of success.

Another small but noteworthy detail, repeated in the friar's 1443 account of the trial, is the consultation held with the pope on the matter. The pontiff in question was Martin V, the Roman nobleman Oddo Colonna. Martin's name does not usually figure in the documents and histories of late medieval witchcraft, apart from the brief mention of his 1418 reissuance at the Council of Constance of Alexander V's 1409 bull giving the Inquisitor of Avignon jurisdiction over cases involving witchcraft.[30] Bernardino's statement is here an indication that the witchcraft problem had once again reached the attention of the highest office of Christendom. Though Martin's involvement in the matter did not reach the same intensity as that of, for example, the earlier John XXII or the later Innocent VIII, he did consider the problem serious enough to order the burning of the worst of the culprits. As already mentioned, after his own IHS heresy trial, Bernardino preached in St. Peter's an extensive series of sermons at papal invitation; we wonder how influential Bernardino's own oratory was in sensitizing this pontiff (now a friend and ally of the friar) to the gravity of this crime.[31]

Finally, let us consider the number and gender of the accused. As far as quantity is concerned, although some of the accusations may have been false, and although we have no idea of the range of activity included in these denunciations, the picture here is that of widespread involvement in witchcraft-related practices, not in a remote mountain village or isolated agricultural community, but in the heart of one of the major cities of Europe, and, as Ginzburg points out, "in the very heart of Christianity."[32] At the same time, however, another impression here transmitted is one of relative leniency toward the phenomenon. The majority of the accused were never apprehended, and of those apprehended—if Bernardino is accurate—only two are mentioned as having been given the death sentence. Later, during the height of the witch craze, such leniency would again be the mark of Italy, where relatively few executions were carried out in comparison with the rest of Europe, even though the number of prosecutions was, nonetheless, substantial.[33]

Next, as far as gender is concerned, Bernardino first says in this sermon that "a great quantity of men *and* women were accused." Yet immediately thereafter in the preacher's account, the group that is rounded up consists simply of "those *women* who had committed the worst crimes," and later, only two executions are specifically mentioned, both of unnamed women. We see then that those involved in such activity were both men and women, but that only women ended up being implicated as the worst of the practitioners.[34] The preponderance of women among the suspects squares with what we read in the rest of Bernardino's preaching on the subject and confirms what we encounter in studies of the witch craze in the rest of Europe across the centuries; women seem to have made up the large majority of the cases involved. In his Siena 1427 account, as everywhere else in his denunciation of witchcraft, Bernardino uses both masculine and feminine references; yet it is the latter that dominate, leaving audiences with the distinct impression that witchcraft is, above all, the domain of women. The female was, indeed, thought to have a certain congenital affinity for the occult: As Bernardino explains, repeating familiar medieval lore, the female connection with witchcraft goes back all the way to the first woman, Eve. It is "because she wanted to be an enchantress," says the preacher, that our first mother fell to the temptation of the serpent.[35] Like mother, like daughter, medieval and early modern society concluded.

Not only was witchcraft most typically the realm of the female, it was, most especially, the realm of the *old* female, the *vetula* (or as Bernardino usually refers to her, "la vecchia rincagnata," the dog-faced old woman), a popular archetypal figure in Western literature from the days of antiquity.[36] Why old women—especially widows and spinsters—should be so implicated in the crime of witchcraft is no mystery: even if she had no connection to the profession of midwife or herbal healer, a physically decrepit, socially isolated, and perhaps eccentric or senile female was easy prey to such demonization. In this process, science as well played a role: According to the official medical teaching of Bernardino's day, all old women were thought, by their very biological nature, to be toxic, inasmuch as, with the cessation of menstruation, the poisons and infected humors naturally produced by the female body were no longer purged; hence a postmenstrual woman could bewitch or infect small babies with a mere glance.[37] Bernardino makes no reference to this piece of "scientific" information in his sermons but makes constant, demonizing reference to the old woman as witch and corrupter of innocent youth in general. Whatever scientific or theological explanation Bernardino might offer for this near fixation with the *vetula,* one can hardly keep from wondering what other, unconscious, factors were at work in the preacher's own psyche, compelling him to associate women—especially old ones—and witchcraft, and to wage such an impassioned campaign against them. What these were, we shall never know.[38]

Let us resume our examination of Bernardino's encounter with the witches of Rome. The preacher describes the case of one woman in particular:

> And among all of these women, there was one woman arrested who said and confessed without any torture that she had killed at least thirty young babies by sucking their blood; and she also said that she had freed sixty of them; and she said that every time she freed one of them, she had to offer a limb up to the Devil, and she would use the limb of some animal; and this is how she operated for a long time. And what's more, she confessed that she had killed her own son and had made a powder out of his body and used to give this powder to be eaten in her various activities.[39]

The above motifs—infanticide by bloodsucking and the preparation of magical powder from infant cadavers—are ancient elements in European folklore.[40] In his earlier preaching against witchcraft, Bernardino had already made references to bloodsucking, and, though magical powders made from the cadavers of the infant victims are not mentioned in these earlier sermons, I suspect that Bernardino was already aware of this element, which was to become a classic item of the witch's baggage.[41] The same can be said of another motif, here only implied—that of the formal pact between demon and witch: "She said that every time she freed one of them, she had to offer a limb up to the Devil." In his 1425 *exemplum*, the "Godmother of Lucca," Bernardino makes explicit the existence of the same type of tit-for-tat agreement—the Devil will reveal to the godmother-witch the location of her godson's lost gold florins on the condition that she create scandal by telling him that his wife is having an affair with the village priest. The Devil grants no favors free of charge, not even to members of his own sect![42]

The detail about "freeing the babies" calls for some comment. Freed from what, we might ask? The power of the Devil? The witch's own possession? Why so in some cases and not others? Bernardino never explains his remarks, taking for granted that his audience will understand the reference. As Carlo Delcorno, the latest editor of this Siena 1427 sermon cycle, rightly observes, the reference most likely means that the "witch" was actually a healer (and perhaps also a midwife) whose acts of "liberation" consisted in curing the child from its illness—the illness understood perhaps by both parent and witch as being the result of some act of *maleficium*, sorcery.[43] As we know from other trial records, many women accused of witchcraft were practicing folk medicine and were often referred to as *medica* or its equivalent, such as the woman of Brescia, "Maria la Medica," tried in 1480 for crimes similar to those of Bernardino's witch.[44] In a draft for another sermon against witchcraft, Bernardino makes ironic note of the competition between these unlicensed female practitioners (whom he stereotypes again as *vecchie rincagnate*) and the university-trained doctors: "O doctors, how much you have studied your grammar, logic, philosophy, medicine, amid much expense, peril, and labor, but it's the dog-faced old woman who gathers all the honor!"[45]

A further detail calls for comment. Both here and in his 1443 account of the trial, Bernardino specifically notes that the woman confessed to all of these deeds "without torture," thereby implying that her account was the spontaneous truth, and not the desperate invention of someone attempting to escape pain.[46] Yet this may not be the case at all. Commenting on the 1438 witch trial of the Frenchman Pierre Vallin of Dauphiné, whose trial record states that his confession was likewise made "voluntarily," Jeffrey Burton Russell explains that this "simply means that he was tortured, removed from the place of torture, and then given the choice of confessing voluntarily or of being returned to the torture chamber."[47] Hence, Bernardino's emphasis on the absence of torture in this Roman case is no reassurance of the truth of her confession.

The preacher's account continues, giving us more information about the modus operandi and paraphernalia of the so-called witch: "And she told of the way she used to go before daybreak to St. Peter's Square, and she would have with her certain little jars of ointments made out of plants that had been gathered on the feast of St. John the Baptist and on the Assumption."[48] All of Bernardino's sermons on witchcraft are rich depositories of detailed information on sorcery and other superstitious practices, and here the preacher reports yet another specific feature of popular belief, that of the special powers of plants harvested on certain auspicious days of the year, in this case June 24 (the feast of John the Baptist) and August 15 (the Assumption of Mary). The former date, June 24, figures widely in previous and ensuing accounts of witchcraft and related topics as a popular festival day for witches. Bernardino mentions it to both the Florentines and the Paduans in 1424, again as a propitious day for gathering magical herbs at dawn.[49] This traditional feast day for witches, June 24, coincides with the date of one of the ancient pagan seasonal festivals, that of Midsummer; on the eve of this day came the "climax of the fire and fertility rites celebrating the triumph of the sun and renewed vegetation."[50] The second date Bernardino mentions, August 15, is also fraught with significance: it is one of the great feasts of Mary, the virgin "Mother of God," whose stature in popular medieval Mariology was little less than that of a goddess. It is no wonder that the feast of the Assumption, celebrating her bodily entry into heaven—a distinction she shares only with Jesus Christ and no other mortal—would have been considered a particularly auspicious one by witches. Most witches appear to have been women, and their earliest identity as a distinct subculture within Christendom connected them to the so-called Society of Diana, another virgin divinity like Mary.[51] In ancient times, the festival of Diana (in Greek, Artemis) was celebrated on the Ides of August, that is, August 13, two days before the feast of Mary's Assumption.

Bernardino himself does not comment on the significance of these dates, but does explain the purpose of the ointments connected with them: "And they said that they would smear [these ointments] all over themselves and once they were covered, they believed that they were turned into cats, but that's not true. They only thought their bodies changed into something else, but it was all in their head."[52] The friar cites as his authority for this disclaimer the central ecclesiastical law text regarding witchcraft, the canon *Episcopi,* which, in truth, refers not to shapeshifting but to night flight on the backs of animals.[53] In a spirit of "rationality," this canon relegated the night-flight belief to the realm of mere diabolical illusion; nonetheless, it served at the same time to publicize more widely the existence and fear of witches and diabolical possession, a function that Bernardino's sermons fulfilled as well.[54] According to the canon and to Bernardino, witches may not really turn into cats or fly through the night, but that does not mean they are not under the spell of Satan (whom they can conjure up at will, like Bernardino's Godmother of Lucca),[55] nor that they are unable to be instruments of harm and death to their neighbors. Thus, as Franco Cardini points out, when Bernardino exhorts his audiences not to "believe" or "place their faith" in sorcerers, witches, and the like, what he means is: Do not seek the services of or become involved in any way with such people, not because their sorcery is bogus and impotent but because it is precisely the opposite—completely real and completely potent, thanks to their alliance with the Devil himself.[56]

The friar then explains to his audience that it is, in reality, the Devil, not the deluded, possessed witch, who visits the home of the innocent child victim and sucks the infant's blood. With a tone of scientific expertise, he then discourses on the power of the Devil to deceive these women and on the ready susceptibility of the human mind to optical illusion, using the example of a mirror, a popular tool in the working of the occult arts.[57] Bernardino further explains that when the Devil arrives at the homes of his victims, he does so in the guise of a cat:

> There are those who said they saw a female cat when he [the Devil] went to do these things; and some have even taken preventive action against it by throwing whatever they had in their hand at this cat, even managing to strike it. And there are some of these cats that, being struck, got their leg broken. And who do you think ended up with a broken leg? Not the Devil, but the possessed woman.[58]

Again, even though it is the woman who suffers the broken leg and not the cat-Devil, the only illusion is that it is the woman who does the deed; it is no illusion to believe that such frightful things as demonic possession and demonic infanticide do indeed occur.

This same detail of the infanticidal or otherwise malevolent cat also figures prominently in the three non-Italian contemporary sources describing this Roman witch case, that is, Felix Hemmerlin, Johann Hartlieb, and Johann Chraft. (The cat is missing in the three Italian sources, Stefano Infessura, Paolo dello Mastro, and Giacomo della Marca.) Hemmerlin's brief report explains that a clever *mulier strega* from Trastevere (a geographical detail unique to this account) used to transform herself into a cat in order to create a need for her services as healer (likewise, a unique detail). Once a cat, she used to "poison with evil spells children lying in their cribs; afterward, transforming herself back into human shape, she would cure them, collecting a fee [for her medical services]."[59]

Both Hartlieb's and Chraft's accounts agree with Bernardino's in the further detail of the wounding of the cat-witch by a quick-acting eyewitness.[60] Hartlieb's *Buch aller verbotenen Kunst, Unglaubens und der Zauberei* ("Book of All Forbidden Art, Superstition, and Magic"), written in a crude, archaic German, gives the following story, the most elaborate among the six accounts:

> A great sign of magic. Honorable prince, I will tell you something, which I and many people in Rome have seen and heard. It was in the sixth year of Pope Martin that an unbelievable thing happened in Rome, namely, that a certain woman and man turned themselves into cats, and killed very many children in Rome. One time, a cat came into the house of a citizen, and bit his child in the cradle. The child cried out, the father got up quickly and took a knife and stabbed the cat in the head as she tried to go out the window. The next morning very early, the woman sent for the holy sacrament [in order to put on a show of being a good Christian?]; her neighbors bewailed her illness, as is the custom there. The neighbor [the father of the child] also commiserated with her; she answered him: "If you were sorry for my sickness, you wouldn't have done that to me." On the third day, it happened that the woman developed a wound in her head. The neighbor remembered the cat and the woman's words as well; he brought the matter to the Senate. The woman was arrested and confessed; she said before the Capitol in a very loud voice that if she had her ointment [which would allow her to fly away and escape], she would be willing to leave. O how gladly would I and many a courtier have loved to have seen the ointment given to her! Then a doctor stood up and said that the ointment should not be given to her, since the Devil would like to cause great confusion with God's plan. The woman was burned at the stake, that I saw myself. Likewise many other people in Rome [saw it] as well.[61]

Note that Hartlieb initially specifies that both a man and a woman were responsible for the child murders, even though, as with Bernardino, the narration abruptly shifts to the feminine gender alone, with no further word of the male offender.

From Johann Chraft's continuation of Andreas of Regensburg's "chronicle of the Roman pontiffs and emperors," we have the following version of the story:

> In [Pope Martin V's] time [there was] a certain feline [*murilegus*] or cat in Rome [that] had been killing many babies lying in their cribs, seizing the opportunity when they were not being properly watched by their nurses. Finally, a certain wise old man, who was watching a little boy entrusted to him, pretending not to notice the cat entering the window in order to suffocate the boy, wounded this cat with a sword to the point of drawing blood. It was subsequently discovered, thanks to the traces of the blood and the presence of the wound, that this cat was an old woman living nearby who was being treated by a surgeon; whenever she wished, she would transform herself into a cat and suck the fresh blood from the children she had killed, in order to sustain her life.[62]

In Chraft, the one unique detail of note is the mention of the witch's need of "fresh blood" from the dead infant for the prolongation of her own life. In this account, furthermore, the mode of her discovery differs slightly from what we read in Hartlieb. Hemmerlin does not discuss the unmasking of the culprit. In substance, however, the account coincides with the other two non-Italian sources, again making it reasonable to conclude that the three authors are likely referring to the same episode in Roman history.

Some further word about our other three fifteenth-century sources—Stefano Infessura, Paolo di Benedetto di Cola dello Mastro, and Giacomo della Marca—is appropriate. Like the three non-Italian sources, neither Stefano nor Giacomo specifically links the execution of the Roman witch to the activity of Bernardino, whereas Paolo states Bernardino's involvement outright: "and he [Bernardino] had the sorcerer and witch Finiccola burned at the stake."[63] In Infessura, the link between Bernardino's preaching and the execution is made simply by juxtaposition: the news item about the execution of Finicella is given in a separate paragraph inserted between two other news items regarding Bernardino's activities in Rome.[64] In Giacomo's sermon, Bernardino's name is completely absent—strangely enough, since the two were close friends. Of all the sources, Paolo dello Mastro is the least helpful: all he reveals about the culprit in question is what I have just quoted, her name and profession, that is, "Finiccola," sorcerer and witch. Infessura is slightly more informative, but still rather sparing in his details regarding the witch and her modus operandi: he simply tells us that "Finicella" was burned at the stake because "she diabolically killed many children and put spells on many people." Giacomo, on the other hand, supplies a few more details: "Funicella" is specifically an old woman (as she is in only one other account, that of Chraft); she killed sixty-five children, including her own son, whose arm was used for the preparation of her diabolical brews (as in Bernardino's account, except for the detail of the arm); and she did all of this, it is implied, under the direction of the Devil, who convinced her with a bit of moral sophistry ("it was not a sin to kill the little ones, since they would be saved"). Giacomo also names as the source of this information the same Franciscan inquisitor, Nicholas of Rome, who had also been Bernardino's authority on the issue.[65] Neither of these three accounts relates any information about a wounded cat, the unmasking of the culprit, or the trial itself, beyond the fact of its having occurred and its outcome.

The similarity between the names of the witches—Finiccola, Finicella, Funicella—makes it reasonable to conclude that Stefano Infessura, Paolo dello Mastro, and Giacomo della Marca are speaking of the same person and the same episode.[66] We have already concluded that the three non-Italian sources are describing the same case. The question is now: Are our Italian sources referring to the same case as our non-Italian sources? In his annotated "Calendar of Witch Trials," Kieckhefer cautions against this identification, but I believe it is reasonable.[67] The agreement among the texts is substantial. Furthermore, as Kieckhefer's "Calendar" shows, until the late fifteenth century, witch trials, especially in Italy, were simply few and far between. It seems unlikely though not impossible that there was more than one such case even in Rome within the space of a few years. Infessura's *Roman Diary* and Paolo dello Mastro's *Memoriale,* whose entries cover the whole of Martin's pontificate, give notice of only this one trial.

We now return to Bernardino's text. The preacher concludes his account with a brief description of the fiery end of this woman, which, according to Infessura, "all of Rome went to see." She was "condemned to the stake and burned so that there was nothing left of her but ashes."[68] Another of her (female) colleagues in the profession, "who confessed to having done similar things," was also sent to the stake at the same time. The friar specifies, however, that this second woman was not strangled to death before being consigned to the flames, as was customary; she was still alive when they set her on fire, a gruesome specification, presumably meant to instill the fear of God in Bernardino's audience.[69]

Bernardino's account of the trial ends here. In conclusion, let us note that the friar's sermon contains nearly all of the classic components of the witch scenario that had been slowly coalescing in the collective imagination over the centuries as a mass of disparate folkloric beliefs metamorphosed into the complex drama of diabolical witchcraft. The culprits here are for the most part old women; they are in pacts with Satan and do his every bidding; this bidding frequently involves the kidnapping, bloodsucking, and murder of babies; and they have knowledge of secret herbal potions and creams that assist them in the working of their spells and various other acts of *maleficium* (sorcery or witchcraft).[70] These women furthermore believe that they can transform themselves into cats with the help of their magic ointments, but this is simply a diabolically induced delusion; it is the Devil who transforms himself into a cat in order to stalk his infant victims.

From other sources, we learn that these magic ointments "enable" the witches to fly through the air to arrive at the appointed time and place for their regularly scheduled secret nocturnal assemblies under the direction of Satan, their master. This notion of the assembly is yet another universal item in "the classic formulation of the Witch Phenomenon."[71] Like much else in the baggage of the European witch, it has its roots in pagan mythology, specifically in the un-Christian but nondiabolical "Society of Diana," an innocuous, festive ride and gathering of women under the tutelage of the pagan goddess of the moon and the hunt.[72] Turned into a demonized witch phenomenon by the theologians and canonists of Christian Europe, the assembly was by the end of the fifteenth century to be known (with tinges of anti-Semitism) as the witches' "sabbath."[73] With the passing years, it slowly acquired ever more heinous, orgiastic characteristics. During Bernardino's lifetime, the gathering was called by various names; the preacher himself, in one of his 1424 sermons to the Florentines, refers to it by the Italian term *tregenda:* "And others talk of the *tregenda* of Thursday night, which is all a dream and a diabolical illusion. Just make sure you are not in mortal sin, as I told you before, and you won't have to be afraid, for yourself or your kids, of witches, the *tregenda,* spells, or incantations!"[74]

As to what Bernardino imagined as occurring during the *tregenda,* we cannot be completely sure, since the notion of the "sabbath" was still in its developmental phase. The friar's 1424 sermon does not describe this convocation of witches. His later treatise on witchcraft and superstition, *De idolatriae cultu* (1430–36), contains a reference to the *tregenda,* though the word itself does not appear in the text. This Latin work nonetheless gives us some idea of his conception of the regular witches' assemblies, which eventually evolved into the "sabbath." Bernardino's text is, however, merely a repetition of the classic description supplied by the famous canon *Episcopi*. Making its first appearance in a tenth-century anthology of legal documents compiled by Regino of Prüm for the archbishop of Trier, *Episcopi* represents the Church's principal position statement with respect to the witch phenomenon. Most of Bernardino's own passage is copied verbatim from this canon:

> *Among these most impious wild brutes are* some most wicked women and even sometimes men who believe and openly profess that they go riding on certain beasts along with Diana *(or Iobiana*[75] *or Herodias)* and countless other women, traveling over great distances in the silence of the dead of night, obeying her commands as if she were their mistress, and are pressed into her service on certain nights, *such as Thursday and Sunday. They also claim that some children, especially small boys, can be changed by them into a lower or higher form* (in deterius vel in melius) *or transformed into some other appearance or likeness.*[76]

Note that in Bernardino's mind, the *tregenda* has not yet quite become the sabbath; he makes no explicit mention of the Devil's presence or of licentious behavior at these meetings of the society of Diana. Nonetheless, he may have assumed, and expected his audience to assume, that neither was really absent from the picture.

Although he had previously said that it was "just a diabolical illusion" (B.169–70), the *tregenda*, it would seem, is what Bernardino has in mind in a somewhat confused passage later in the same Siena 1427 sermon containing his report on the witches of Rome. In this passage, the friar tells the story of a cardinal's page who stumbled across a "wild" nocturnal assembly near Benevento in southwest Italy:

> Hey, do you know what these enchanters do, huh? Let's look at the facts. Once, in Rome, there was a page of one of the cardinals who, going to Benevento at night, saw a crowd of people—women and children and young people—dancing in an open field; the sight filled him with fear. Then after looking for a little while, he took courage and went, with a bit of fear, to the place where these people were dancing, and little by little he got closer to the spot and saw that they were all very young people. He actually got up the courage to join in the dancing. And so the whole gang went on dancing until the ringing of matins. As soon as the bells struck matins, all of these women [Bernardino switches to the feminine here, *tutte*] left in an instant except one

> girl, that is to say, the girl whom this guy was holding by the hand. She wanted to leave with the other women but this guy kept her back: she pulled and he pulled. He held onto her in this way for so long that daybreak soon arrived. Seeing how young she was, he brought her to his own house. And listen to what happened next: he kept her for three years with him and she never spoke a word. And it was discovered that this girl was from Slavonia. Just think about that, what a fine job that was, taking a little girl away from her father and mother in that way.[77]

This account is followed immediately by the friar's injunction to "exterminate" any "enchantress or sorceress, or enchanters or witches."[78] Yet taken by itself, this story—probably appropriated, as we shall see, from an older source—offers no grounds for seeing in it a description of the witches' sabbath. For one thing, the Devil, or his surrogate in the form of the usual female divinity, is completely absent. As it stands, all this scene really describes is a night of dancing by a group of young men and women; there is nothing explicitly supernatural, let alone diabolical, in what Bernardino describes. Of course, our seemingly verbatim *reportatio* may be at fault by failing to record all of the preacher's narration, or it could be that Bernardino, improvising his retelling of the tale, simply forgot in the heat of the moment to supply all the necessary facts to convey the true nature of this assembly.

If we pay close attention, however, there are certain details in this story of the cardinal's page that do at least insinuate the presence of evil, and that most likely would have raised the suspicions of contemporary audiences. To begin with, the mention of the town of Benevento in this passage is significant, the association of that area with magic and pagan rites having been long established. By the age of the Lombard domination of Italy, a special cult had developed around a certain ancient walnut tree, cut down in the seventh century by the bishop, Saint Barbato.[79] At least some of Bernardino's public is likely to have been attuned to this allusion and thus assumed that any nocturnal gathering in that vicinity could only imply the practice of witchcraft. The friar's second geographic specification is also an important detail in this regard. The alien land of "Slavonia" (in Italian, *Schiavonia,* that is, the Balkans) was thought to be home to the Bogomils, a notorious heretical sect of the earlier Middle Ages that strongly influenced and abetted the even more notorious Cathars of southern France, the Rhineland, and Lombardy.[80] Heretics—Bogomils, Cathars, Waldensians, Nicolaitans—were all still feared and believed to be living in northern Italy, as Bernardino himself teaches. For the preacher and his contemporaries, where there was heresy, there was also likely to be sorcery, diabolism, and allied aberrations, for the sins of the heretic and of the witch frequently overlapped.[81]

Finally, the predominant role played by women in this story would have been yet another cause for suspicion by Bernardino's audience. Though the passage is confusing on this point—as in his account of the witches of Rome, Bernardino here starts out using both masculine and feminine pronouns but then inexplicably switches to the feminine alone—the overall impression conveyed is that women formed the more conspicuous part of this nighttime assembly. In another unclear passage in a 1423 Paduan sermon, Bernardino makes passing but disapproving reference to the pagan "feast of Bacchus," where "beautiful young women are thrown into agitation," which may be what the preacher believes the cardinal's page to have stumbled across.[82] The gathering could also have been some agrarian or fertility rite, or possibly a St. Vitus' (or St. John's) dance, in which unmarried women participated in large numbers.[83] In any case, Bernardino's was a society in which women, married or unmarried, were usually restricted to the home, and hence "there were so very few gatherings to which an honest woman could go."[84] This was not one of them. As in the case of heretics, the misogynistic premises of the age assumed that where there were women, there was bound to be mischief, if not outright evil, such as that of witchcraft, the quintessentially female crime. However, the real crime in this story, let us note, is perpetrated by the male intruder, the cardinal's page, who ends up kidnapping the girl!

Bernardino relates this story as if it were a fact of fairly recent occurrence. But let us not be deceived in such cases by assurances of historical veracity on Bernardino's part. In our preacher's sermons, even the most fantastic accounts of the supernatural are introduced in the same realistic, "historical" fashion—stories that have been subsequently traced back to the usual collections of legends, fables, and *exempla* in widespread circulation in the Middle Ages, such as the *Gesta romanorum*, the *Thousand and One Nights*, and Peraldus's *Summa virtutum et vitiorum*.[85] As far as his tale of the cardinal's page, I suspect that Bernardino has, in fact, recast the story of "Eadric Wild, Lord of Lydbury North," included in Walter Map's *De nugis curialium* (ca. 1180), "one of the most famous collections of gossip, lore, and satire of the twelfth century."[86] In this tale, Eadric, returning home after a day of hunting with his page, loses his way late one night in a wild landscape. On the edge of a forest, he stumbles across a house in which he sees a large number of noble, comely ladies dancing and singing. Despite their noble appearance and outwardly innocent comportment, the ladies, we are told, are actually demonic spirits. Falling in love at first sight with one of them, Eadric enters the house to join the party and ends up, after a fierce struggle with her companions, running off with the nubile object of his desire. Three days and nights of total silence on her part ensue while Eadric has his way with her.

The story goes on from there, but what remains is irrelevant to our present concerns; what is sufficiently clear is the kinship between Map's tale and that of Bernardino. Both stories involve the figure of the page (though in different roles); a remote country setting; the nocturnal dance of "unusual" ladies; a protagonist who, after initial fear, draws courage and penetrates the group, then takes a fancy to one of the ladies, whom he seizes; a struggle between the two, resulting in his kidnapping of her; and a "three-unit" period of complete silence on her part (three years in Bernardino, three days in Map). Bernardino did not necessarily encounter this story directly in Map; he may have heard it from or read it in some other source or in some other version. The essential plot of "Eadric Wild" is, in fact, a traditional one in the folktale repertory, that of the "Swan Maiden," according to Thompson's classification.[87]

As in Bernardino's tale, in "Eadric Wild" nothing explicitly diabolical or immoral is perpetrated by the supposedly evil nocturnal dancers. (Again, it is the Christian male intruder who does evil by kidnapping and raping the young lady.) Nonetheless, the narrator's comments cast the story as a tale of an encounter with the diabolical. Map's introduction to the story makes reference to "Dictynna and the bands of Dryads and Lares," that is, the pagan goddess Diana and her "society" of wood nymphs and other mysterious companion spirits whom Christian Europe had long since demonized, amalgamating them into the witch phenomenon. Then, at the end of the tale, the narrator informs us that the story has been about "demons that are *incubi* and *succubi*, and . . . the dangers of union with them." Yet Eadric and the putative succubus go on to have a seemingly happy, normal marriage—indeed, producing a son who grows to become "a man of great holiness and wisdom"![88] As for Bernardino's own version of the legend, although it likewise offers very little by way of actual evil, that is how our preacher means it to be understood: as a tale of evil, diabolical women, "enchantresses," a label that in Bernardino's usage is synonymous with witches.

The "one hundred accusations" filed with the inquisitor after Bernardino's preaching in Rome demonstrate that the preacher's audience was indeed persuaded by his antiwitch oratory. Did he meet the same response elsewhere? Unfortunately we do not have a complete record of the preacher's successes and failures in the routing of witches and can cite only two other examples, contrary in their outcomes. Earlier in the same year (1426) Bernardino had preached on the same topic in the Umbrian hill town of Todi: though there was a delay of two years, concrete results of that preaching mission did indeed surface in 1428, when a certain Matteuccia Di Francesco was burned at the stake, as we shall see in the next section of this chapter. We shall later see other forms of positive results—for example, the destruction of a "magical" well in Arezzo, and the staging of "bonfires of vanities," which included witch-related paraphernalia, in Florence, Perugia, and elsewhere. Back in Siena in 1427, alluding to his successful solution to the witch problem in Rome, Bernardino encouraged his audience to "send up a little bit of incense to the Lord God here" as well—that is, send to the stake the witches, sorcerers, and other devotees of the black arts practicing in the city and surrounding territory. Yet, surprisingly and ironically, in his own hometown, according to the research of Bernadette Paton, Bernardino's oratory fell on deaf ears:

> Bernardino's denunciations of witches in 1427, like the earlier sermons of 1425 on the same subject, appear to have aroused little local response from either populace, authorities or clergy. The medieval inquisitorial and secular courts of Siena have attracted enough attention to enable us to trace their activities with some degree of accuracy, and the pattern of trials does not suggest an upsurge of interest in heresy or witchcraft in the fifteenth century. The case is, indeed, the reverse.[89]

We cannot be completely certain as to why the Sienese reacted with such indifference. One important reason is likely to have been what Paton calls the traditional "conservatism" of most Sienese theologians, catechists, and preachers with respect to witchcraft. That is, as a rule, they tended to dismiss the issue as having to do with harmless superstition and mere illusion, and were unwilling to ascribe to it either the epidemic proportions, the malevolent, heretical nature, or the demonic peril that the "radical" Bernardino preached in Siena. "Even among Bernardino's Franciscan Observant followers in Siena the subject of the witch or heretic appears to have aroused little interest or concern."[90]

We are left with the compelling question: Why, when most of his Sienese peers were only mildly concerned by the supposed phenomenon of witches, did Bernardino decide to wage such a fierce, relentless campaign against them? To begin with, given Bernardino's extensive traveling, Paton suggests that he had greater opportunity than his contemporaries at home to come into contact both with "witches" (as in Rome) and with the "novel demonological ideas" containing a more alarming, more demonized depiction of witches and their craft. Paton further sees Bernardino's antiwitch campaign as an extension of the general "purging mentality" of this tenacious—not to say fanatical—reformer of Church and society. Also present, she believes, is a degree of "personal paranoia" in Bernardino, who himself had suffered persecution as a heresiarch for his "idolatrous" cult of the Holy Name of Jesus.[91] Together, these reasons go a long way toward explaining the passion and fury of the friar's antiwitch campaign. Undoubtedly, however, there were further emotional drives within the deeper, and now inaccessible, recesses of Bernardino's psyche.[92]

2. The Witch of Todi, Matteuccia Di Francesco

The 1426 trial in Rome was not the only one connected with the name of Bernardino of Siena. On March 20, 1428, in the Umbrian hill town of Todi, a woman from the nearby castle of Ripabianca, Matteuccia Francisci, or Di Francesco, disciple of "the Enemy of Mankind," after being led through town "on a donkey with a paper hat on her head and her hands tied behind her back," was burned at the stake.[93] The charge: a series of crimes of witchcraft "documented" for the years 1426, 1427, and 1428, not by "malignant and suspicious people," but by "honest and truthful citizens," many of whom were former clients, willing beneficiaries of her assistance. The complete text of this trial, "one of the oldest of its kind for Italy,"[94] has survived and is filled with intimate detail as to the witch's activities, clients, recipes, incantations, and other components of her trade.

Bernardino is explicitly mentioned in the records of this trial: in two separate paragraphs, some of Matteuccia's crimes are dated specifically "before the coming of friar Bernardino."[95] At the request of the local bishop, the friar had delivered a course of sermons to the people of Todi in early 1426, arriving in that town in mid-January and remaining until early March.[96] His preaching apparently met with great popular success, for, according to one chronicler, at its termination the friar was escorted from the town by a procession of 1,800 citizens, "not counting women and children."[97] There is no explanation in the text itself why "the coming of friar Bernardino" is significant here, significant enough to warrant inclusion in the official record. At first glance, the inclusion might seem inappropriate or irrelevant. But given what we have just said about the zealous antiwitchcraft campaign of the itinerant preacher, we are probably safe in concluding that it was thanks to Bernardino's public harangues that such a servant of "the Enemy of Mankind"[98] was finally brought to "justice." It was most likely he who opened the town's eyes to the grave "evil" and "danger" this woman represented, a woman who apparently until that point had been peacefully tolerated, and, indeed, actively patronized by her neighbors and by clients from near and far.

What we do know for certain is that, as a concrete memorial of his preaching mission there, Bernardino made specific suggestions for a series of penal code reforms that were approved and adopted as official law by the government of Todi on March 10, 1426. These new *reformationes*, discovered and published for the first time in 1976, do not mention Bernardino's name; however, the minutes of a town council meeting held on January 27 of that same year (while Bernardino was still in Todi) speak explicitly of "some statutes, laws, and ordinances" that the friar had proposed to the government. Thus we can assume that these *reformationes*, which became law on the day of (or the day before) the friar's departure from the city, are the same as or somehow incorporate Bernardino's original proposals.[99] Among the ten items legislated by the Priors of Todi at this time is the brief, simply worded ordinance "De pena incantatorum et facturariorum," against "enchanters and spell-makers": "that no one must conjure up devils or carry out or cause to be carried out any spells or acts of witchcraft."[100] The same ordinance goes on to mandate death by fire as punishment for such criminals (*dictos incantatores, maliarios sive facturarios*), expressly allowing the use of torture "according to the nature of the crime and the condition of the persons involved." So, not only did Bernardino leave an imprint on the imaginations of the citizens of Todi, but he also left his enduring mark on the very law of the land, a law that two years later was used to bring Matteuccia to trial.

Not surprisingly, as Giovanni Bronzini observes, the specifics of the accusations against Matteuccia are just as we find them in Bernardino's sermons—the friar, in turn, having borrowed freely from past literature, such as William of Auvergne and the canon *Episcopi*. Bernardino's visit, Bronzini notes, is explicitly referred to in the trial records "as if to a panacea."[101] I would further conjecture that through the direct intervention of Bernardino, who supplied the "facts" of the witch's modus operandi, the inquisitors specified the nature of some of the crimes to which Matteuccia in the end confessed. That is to say, not only did Bernardino's preaching cause her to be brought to trial, but it may well have furnished some of the charges against her. What has been said of the Inquisition in general can likely be said here of Matteuccia's prosecutors, the Court of Malefactors of Todi: they "were taught what to look for, and they . . . found it, whether it existed or not."[102] In this case, the teacher in question was Bernardino of Siena.

Lending support to this conjecture is the research of another scholar, Richard Kieckhefer, who, independently of Bronzini and with no reference to Bernardino, has examined the Matteuccia records. Kieckhefer's key observation about the Matteuccia trial is to note at one point in the records an unusual shift in the types of crimes the woman began to confess. This is a phenomenon he has observed in other trials of the pre-1500 period and for which he offers a plausible explanation. In the first part of the trial, Matteuccia appears to be a simple sorcerer and herbal healer, engaged in many of the same harmless superstitious or "magical" practices and folk remedies that Bernardino describes in detail and condemns in so many sermons. She seems to have been regarded as a reliable professional by her compatriots, who made frequent recourse to her talents. The majority of her services were provided to people in physical pain and emotional anguish, who perhaps could not afford the fees of a professional doctor. As the trial record describes, Matteuccia's clients were "those who were suffering in their bodies, heads or other parts of their bodies," "persons affected by spirits," as well as "many lovers" to whom she gave "remedies" so that "they could obtain favors and turn their lovers' love towards themselves."[103] On one occasion she even supplied the concubine of a priest of the town of Castello della Pieve with "a remedy to prevent her from becoming pregnant." One of the rare prescriptions Matteuccia dispensed for malicious purposes was given to a woman who, "confessing that she loved a certain man, said that she would like to spread her hatred so that her man would abandon his wife." The prescription apparently worked.[104]

By far the largest category of Matteuccia's clients described in the text represented battered wives, who, given the prevailing attitudes of Church and society with respect to male prerogative and wifely duty, could expect little solace elsewhere. The first case of physical and emotional abuse concerned yet another sacerdotal concubine, that "of a certain priest of the castle of Prodo in the district of Orvieto [who] . . . did not look after her and have intercourse with her but rather beat her every day." This, according to the text, was another success story for Matteuccia. A second woman "went to Matteuccia complaining of her husband, saying that he treated her badly and begging her to give her a remedy for the many humiliations he caused her." Yet another housewife from Orvieto arrived on this "witch's" doorstep to find an escape from the daily beatings inflicted on her by a brutal husband. In fact, the text summarizes, "[f]urthermore, not content with these things and adding evil to evil, Matteuccia advised many women who were beaten by their husbands."[105] Some of the real evildoers of the situation—abusive husbands—seem to have escaped the attention of Matteuccia's prosecutors.

Such are the clients and services reported in the first eight and a half pages of testimony. The impression thus far made is, again, that of a folk healer–sorcerer who, though now and then making brief, undramatic reference in her incantations to the Devil and "the spirits," was working largely to relieve suffering. This is not to say that fear and suspicion of her on the part of her contemporaries would have been entirely unreasonable. If indeed all of the testimony is reliable, then the fact remains that, however rarely and nonconspiratorially, Matteuccia did invoke evil spirits, and she did aid and abet the doing of "evil," however petty and localized. Even in our more sophisticated scientific age, who would feel comfortable having such a "professional" as a next-door neighbor?

Yet discomfort with a superstitious, perhaps eccentric, woman—whose superstitious worldview was fully shared by her "good Christian neighbors"—is one thing; an impassioned crusade against a putative member of a so-called diabolical, subversive witch sect is another. The record of the trial suggests how the former was inflamed into the latter. At one point well into the trial record, the woman's "confession" takes a sudden, unexpected dramatic turn. Kieckhefer alerts us to this change:

> Towards the end, however, one can discern a clear caesura: the tone of the allegations shifts abruptly, and one finds Matteuccia confessing to all the crimes perpetrated by members of the devil's sect. The emphasis is still largely upon bewitchment, but the maleficent acts are different in kind from those in the earlier period of the trial, and from those in records of witnesses' depositions.[106]

The last three pages of testimony give us an astonishingly different picture of Matteuccia and her activities.[107] The modus operandi of the diabolical witch, made familiar to us by Bernardino's preaching, is here fully present in all its details—sabbath, unguents, animal transformation, bloodsucking, and infanticide. Even the locale of the witch conventions is the same: "In the company of other witches she often went to the walnut tree of Benevento and to other walnut trees anointing herself with an oil made from the fat of vultures, the blood of bats, the blood of babies, and other ingredients." The text further tells us that Matteuccia herself arrived at Benevento in the form of a fly, and that it was "the greater Lucifer" who presided at the meeting, attended by "many witches and enchanted spirits," and who ordered them "to go and destroy children and to do other wicked deeds." Five specific cases of infanticide by bloodsucking are detailed, including all the relevant names, places, and dates. Finally, after informing us as to the exact schedule of her airborne travels to Benevento (in April, May, August, September, March, and December, on Mondays, Saturdays, and Sundays), the text concludes with the assurance that all of the above was confessed "spontaneously" by the defendant "and saying she has no defence."[108] What are we to make of this sudden shift? Kieckhefer has concluded: "Though there is no mention in the record that the later admissions were made under judicial coercion, it is difficult to account for the abrupt change by any other hypothesis. Clearly in this trial the notions of diabolism were superimposed on earlier charges in the course of judicial interrogation."[109]

Although we cannot be sure how this one trial was conducted, and although there is no mention in the text of the presence of an official ecclesiastical inquisitor, the behavior of Matteuccia's prosecutors may not have been far from that typical of the Inquisition. For instance, as to inquisitorial procedure, we are told:

> The Inquisitors in particular habitually used set formularies of questions and answers that determined in advance much of what they would "discover." These formularies were in Latin and could be "translated" for the accused in such a way that he would understand whatever the Inquisitor chose. Having received the answer he wished, he had only to record it as a response to the Latin query, which might have a wholly different meaning from what the prisoner understood. If such devices failed, there was always torture, which was extensively, viciously, and persistently used and could break all but the most heroic spirits.[110]

If Kieckhefer's reading of the Todi evidence is correct, therefore, before the arrival of Bernardino, it could very well be that neither Matteuccia nor her *compaesini* saw her activities as manifestations of a pact with the Devil or as evidence of intentional, heretical, society-subverting malevolence. Before the arrival of Bernardino, she was, perhaps, in their eyes and her own, no devil-worshiper seeking the overthrow of the established order, but simply a freelance folk "doctor" responding to individual cases of need. This may explain why she was able to live peaceably among her neighbors for years, until 1428, by which time the lingering words of the "learned" friar had finally transformed her into a death-deserving "witch."

However, to agree here with Kieckhefer and conclude that it was a third party (namely, Bernardino) who made Todi see a demon-serving witch where there was none is not necessarily to subscribe to his larger thesis. This larger thesis concludes from such evidence that there existed a decided gap between the "learned notions" of the intellectual elite (particularly regarding the diabolical sabbath) and popular belief, and sees an ever-increasing "polluting" of the latter by the former (until their full merger by the year 1500 or so). The 1428 Todi trial is one in a series examined by Kieckhefer giving evidence of this "imposition of learned notions" upon those of the common masses: "Indeed, all valid and relevant evidence indicates that this pattern was typical."[111] Carlo Ginzburg contests this view, instead pointing to much data that suggest, in fact, that "the Sabbath (*diabolism*)" is "rooted in popular culture," and is not "an image elaborated exclusively or almost exclusively by the persecutors," as "the thesis, still commonly accepted," would have it.[112] Hence, if Ginzburg is right—evidence is still insufficient for deciding the matter—then the distinction between "learned" and "popular" with respect to notions of witchcraft must be less clearly drawn than hitherto theorized.[113] In any case, what is certain is that the arrival of friar Bernardino in Todi in 1426 radically changed the reputation and fate of a woman who had apparently until then lived unmolested by her neighbors and by the authorities of both Church and city hall.

3. The Godmother of Lucca

Other significant witch-related pages among the works of Bernardino are those in which he recounts the story of "the godmother (*comare*) of Lucca." The tale in question occurs within the 1425 Florentine sermon against witchcraft, "Come non dei dar fede a incantesimi e indovini" ("How one must not believe in incantations and divinations").[114] Occupying four of the twenty pages of this sermon text (C.209–12), "The Godmother of Lucca" represents one of the longest of all of Bernardino's surviving *exempla*, a further indication of the intensity of the friar's antiwitchcraft feeling and of the interest in such stories on the part of those who recorded the preacher's sermons. The tale proves to be yet another rich and vivid depository of witch folklore. Delivered with all of the narrative, dramatic skill for which Bernardino is famous, it is another highly effective way in which the preacher's audience came to be alerted to and instructed in the nature and ways of witches.

Bernardino begins his narrative by affirming that the tale he is about to relate is a true episode of a recent occurrence in nearby Lucca: "Essemplo palpabile e vero, e non sono ancora otto anni."[115] It involves an unfortunate young man who has just lost, somewhere, somehow, a large sum of money. Distraught by this loss, he decides to enlist the help of "an old godmother of his" who is said to have knowledge of "incantations," "these medicines," and the retrieval of stolen goods.[116] As with any typical old *comare* with lots of free time on her hands, he finds the woman at her doorstep watching the passersby, and pitifully describes his woes: "She was at her door and he said to her: 'My dear mother, I need from you a great favor because I am in great agony over the sixteen florins I have lost. . . . I know that you have the power of a seer. I beg you to help me get out of this trouble or else I will go to pieces over it.' "[117]

At first the godmother denies any such power—"My dear son, I don't know how to do any of these things you say"—but at the insistence of the distraught man, who appeals to their kinship, she yields and tells him to return the next morning. Tonight, she must "sleep over it": "io mi ci voglio su pensare stanotte." The young man takes his leave, but is suspicious: "Why couldn't she tell me what I want to know right away?" He decides to return to his *comare*'s house that very night to spy upon her activities. Later that evening, "hiding himself in a corner near her back door, and, having first asked for God's protection, he set himself to listening and paying attention to what she might do."

The scene that then unfolds before his eyes—the encounter between the Devil and the witch—is conjured up before us with a theatrical flourish: "Lo and behold: in the first hours of sleep, this woman opens the door to her vegetable garden and comes out completely naked and her hair all undone, and she begins to do and say her various signs and conjurations, and to shriek out and call the Devil."[118] Bernardino does not explain the significance of the *comare*'s startling state of undress, but his audience would probably have recognized it as a common feature of nocturnal invocation or worship of the Devil, implying sexual relations between witch and demon; for instance, we find it as well in the very early 1375 witch case of another old woman, Gabrina Albetti (or degli Albeti) of Emilia.[119] In the other (Siena 1425) version of "The Godmother of Lucca," the tale is condensed to just one brief page, but the woman's nakedness is one of the concrete details

It is likely that these same "good and prudent men" were also among those

> who were astounded that friar Bernardino would presume to say such things about someone [i.e., brand Amedeo as a heretic, declare him and all those who associated with him to be excommunicated, and call for his expulsion from the city] even before he was summoned and warned by the vicar of the Lord Archbishop or the Inquisitor of Heretical Depravity, since these are duties which pertain to them as vicar and inquisitor (who comes from the Order of Preachers), who customarily first of all summon and warn and interrogate such [suspect] persons; and if they confess or are otherwise proven [guilty] in the judicial forum, [their names] are published afterwards as heretics in the Church of Saint Eustorgius.[139]

Amedeo won his case against Bernardino. However, the victory was short-lived. After Bernardino's death in 1444, Amedeo and his supporters opposed the friar's canonization with the claim that Bernardino had died in mortal sin for not having made the necessary restitution to Amedeo mandated by the 1441 sentence. This we learn from Pope Nicholas's 1447 bull, *Universalis ecclesiae regimini,* which responded to Amedeo's protest by overturning Bernardino's 1441 "conviction." Even though the 1441 libel trial had been conducted by a person of great stature and professional credibility, the Milanese humanist *canonicus* Giuseppe Brivio,[140] the pontiff exonerated the deceased Bernardino of all charges of wrongdoing and ordered all official records of the affair to be destroyed, claiming that deceit had been used in securing permission for the trial and that the trial itself had not been held according to due form.[141]

Nonetheless, the above-described "astonishment" certain witnesses felt about the affair underscores the crux of the issue: Bernardino had no authority to declare individuals heretics and excommunicated, and from a public pulpit, no less. The friar's behavior in this case lends credence to the charges of arrogance and imprudence when faced by those who presumed to contradict him, for which another respected contemporary, Augustinian humanist theologian Andrea Biglia, repeatedly admonishes Bernardino.[142] Knowing the grave consequences—religious, social, psychological, and economic—that could plague a suspected heretic in that society, one wonders how Bernardino could so freely hand down from his pulpit personal sentences of heresy and excommunication. True, by the fifteenth century, thanks to repeated abuse of this disciplinary measure and the diminishing temporal power of the Church, excommunication itself was no longer taken as seriously as in previous ages; nonetheless, as we see in the experience of Amedeo de Landis, it had not lost all of its destructive potential.

Indeed, Amedeo's reputation and career were severely damaged. As instructed by the preacher, parents stopped sending their sons to the school of this supposed "immoral man" (*ribaldus*) and "follower of John Hus," and began to shun the entire family.[143] Moreover, one witness testified:

> . . . one of his infant children, I believe, died at that time because master Amedeo's wife who was nursing her son in the cradle suffered from so great a depression because she was being shunned by other people that she lost her milk and could not find any neighbor who was willing to give the child a little bit of milk or give any help to the wife of master Amedeo because brother Bernardino had warned that no help must be given to this person etc. and because of this the child starved to death.[144]

We can well understand why Amedeo would thus be little disposed to like Bernardino, and why this feeling endured beyond the friar's death.

What, finally, were these "heretical" notions with which master Amedeo was corrupting his students? These we know only from the depositions of witnesses in favor of Amedeo, but it would seem that he was advising young people not to make impulsive decisions about entering religious life, that is, without having first tested whether their vocation was truly from the Holy Spirit and whether they had the physical and mental capacity to endure the austerities of that discipline. Amedeo also stated in public his opinion that a good Catholic who loved God and neighbor and gave alms did not have to spend so much time visiting churches as was then the custom. Furthermore, he had been bold enough to claim that it was his duty as a Christian to openly protest all clerical abuse, that is, as Amedeo himself put it, to "shout out" whenever he saw "sheep being eaten by wolves."[145]

The preceding description does not exhaust the facts of the Amedeo de Landis case in its convoluted entirety, but the remaining facts are irrelevant to our present concerns. What is above all important is the vivid illustration it provides of both the great degree of inflammable hysteria attached to the label of "heretic" and our preacher's efficacious role in igniting such emotion—and a brutal, concrete response from the masses of his listeners.[146]

The reaction of fear and rage by Amedeo's less reflective contemporaries toward their resident arithmetic teacher was inevitable, given the catechesis they had received from preachers as to the nature and modus operandi of the heretic. Indeed, when we examine Bernardino's portrait of heretics and their behavior, we find some of very same fantastic elements—in particular, secret gatherings, sexual promiscuity, and ritualistic infanticide—already encountered in his account of witches. "These charges are all ancient," Russell points out, commenting on the persecution of the Cathars and Waldensians of Southern France: "The Syrians brought them against the Jews, the Romans against the Christians, and the Christians against the Gnostics. Now they were being brought against the medieval heretics."[147] Bernardino, too, made his active and substantial contribution to what Norman Cohn has called "the demonization of medieval heretics."[148] As heretics were demonized, they became increasingly the object of fear and persecution. And, in a case of guilt by association—or, perhaps better, in a kind of *communicatio idiomatum*—the witch grew ever more terrifying and dangerous in the eyes of Christian Europe.

According to Bernardino, the same fundamental motivation drove both heretic and witch to their evil "professions": pride, the first great sin of the once fair Lucifer. "All of the instigators of heresies," he declares, "are full of pride and are hard of heart; out of pride in their own 'knowledge' and 'wisdom,' they organize their own sects in order to appear to know and put on a show of knowing more than the approved doctors of the Holy Church."[149] Since heretics often believe themselves the recipients of new, special "inspirations" from the Spirit, Bernardino goes to great lengths to teach his audiences how to distinguish good "inspirations" from bad, providing twelve specific, easy-to-apply rules. The friar's rules for what is technically known as the "discernment of spirits" are contained in both a Latin treatise, *De inspirationibus*, and, in abridged form, in two of his vernacular sermons preached to the Sienese in 1427.[150] In these two latter sermons, we also find disquieting portraits of the "demonized" heretic:

> There's a sect of these people in a certain place who still conduct an accursed ritual that I will tell you about. Deep in the night they all get together, men and women all in the same room, and they stir up quite a broth among themselves. And they have this lamp, and when the time seems right to extinguish it, they extinguish the lamp and from then on, it's a free-for-all, people jumping on whoever happens to be next to them. . . . Ooo, ooo, ooo! Just listen to the curse that has taken hold of them![151]

Bernardino goes on to describe more specifically a certain group in northwest Italy, most probably the Waldensians, who had fled to the Alpine regions to escape persecution. Regrettably, most of the knowledge we have of such secret nocturnal activities is what preachers like Bernardino say of them and what tortured suspects eventually confessed to their inquisitors. From the friar we have the following report:

> And there are some of these people there in Piedmont and five inquisitors have already gone to exterminate this curse; all of them were killed by these wicked people.[152] Not only that, there's no inquisitor who's willing to go there to deal with this business. And do you know what the name of this group is? They're called "the people of the keg [*barilotto*]." They have this name because once a year they take a small child and toss it among themselves back and forth, until it dies. Once it's dead, they make a powder of its body and put the powder in a wine keg and each one drinks from this keg. They do this, they say, so that they will go unseen in what they do. We have a friar in our order who used to be one of them and it was he who told me all of these things—that they carry on in what I think are the most depraved ways imaginable.[153]

Predictably, Bernardino's report of the "sect of the keg" spread to other parts of Italy. In Rome—thanks, it would seem, to Bernardino—this same infanticidal practice involving a wooden keg (the *barilotto*) was ascribed to another heretical group, the "Fraticelli de opinione," radical Franciscan dissidents tried by papal inquisitors (Bernardino's friend John of Capistrano among them) in the Castel Sant'Angelo in 1466. The report was to receive even greater circulation when humanist-historian Biondo Flavio included it in his *Italia illustrata* (1448–53). Not surprisingly, the "keg" motif began to show up in Italian witch trials: in one Piedmontese trial, for example, held in 1470 in the town of Biella, near Vercelli, the accused Giovanna Monduro was asked "whether she had drunk of the keg."[154] Bernardino's voice had, at times, a long and far-reaching echo.

Another antinomian heretical group of recent memory, which Bernardino discusses at length, is that of Fra Dolcino, the illegitimate son of a priest, and his "bellissima femmina," Margherita Boninsegna, who operated in Piedmont until the group was besieged in their mountain refuge between Novara and Vercelli and finally, after much effort, was destroyed.[155] Dolcino's sect and the other varieties of sexually promiscuous heretical groups, Bernardino explains, are all descendants of the "Nicolaitans" of the Book of Revelation (2:6). The "Nicolaitans" were a group organized by Nicolaus of Antioch of Acts 6:5, or so says the friar, deriving his information (or, rather, misinformation) from the *Expositio in Apocalypsim* by Matthew of Sweden, confessor of Saint Brigit: "This Nicolaus was a deacon and received the Holy Spirit along with the other apostles; and once he had received the Holy Spirit, he was given the care of widows. This man had a wife and she was extremely beautiful and he was crazy in love with her and thought of no other god except his wife."[156] Bernardino goes on to describe in detail the behavior of the Nicolaitans, their principal group activity being sexual—specifically, wife-swapping. Sexual license, the dissolution of the marriage bond, and the fomenting of wifely insurrection are also characteristics, Bernardino elsewhere claims (in "Della resia e altre belle cose," C.224–41), of another contemporary group, the band of penitential Third Order Dominicans organized and herded from town to town by the charismatic apocalyptic Dominican preacher Manfredi da Vercelli.[157] Sexual impropriety (in the form of public nudity) also characterizes the behavior of another heretical apocalyptic group, which I call "the Naked Band of Fermo," ridiculed from the pulpit by Bernardino:

> Listen to this one. About twelve years ago, there was one [of these false prophets] near Fermo who came out from the woods teaching his novelties and craziness. He drew a huge crowd of people to himself, telling them that one day they would go to the Holy Sepulcher on foot. And on the appointed day, he had them all strip naked, men and women, and they set off, going toward the town of Fermo. When the brigade of that town saw these people approaching they began to ask: "Oh, what's the meaning of this? What new fad is this? Why are you going around this way?" He answered: "We want to go to the sea, and when we get there, the sea will open up for us and we will enter into it and will reach Jerusalem without getting our feet wet." When the news [of this band] reached the ears of sir Louis, the lord of Fermo, he had them all locked up.[158]

Likewise from the friar, we have this further description of "depraved" heretical behavior:

> Oh, and another one of these [heretics] was going around begging with one of his sisters and painting angels. They were saying that she was pregnant with the Holy Spirit and were distributing her milk—he used to squeeze the milk from her, putting his hands all over her breasts! What outrageous depravity! Do you think that's a rational thing to do, going around squeezing the milk from a woman? I don't care who's doing it, I say these things are not pleasing to God.[159]

Bernardino the Heresiarch, Rome 1426 and Basel 1438

Such reports supplied further grist for the ever-intensifying antiheretic and antiwitch mill. As the portrait of the heretic grew in fearsome demonic repulsion, so too did that of the witch. The great irony in this case is the fact that Bernardino himself was the victim of this same process of demonization of the heretic. As already mentioned, he had to face much violent public opposition and vitriolic vituperation as demagogue and heresiarch, especially from the learned elites of both Church and humanist society. The cause of this hostility was his promotion of the cult of the Holy Name of Jesus, represented by his blue and gold IHS sunburst monogram. At the conclusion of his rousing sermons on the Name of Jesus, Bernardino would raise up his large IHS tablet for veneration by the audience, who, already emotionally stirred by two or three hours of the preacher's oratory, soon burst out into fits of loud, copious weeping and violent, uncontrolled shrieking.

This histrionic public spectacle repeated itself in one town after another. Before long, theologians were rushing to their desks to prepare treatises against Bernardino, charging him with a whole string of capital offenses: encouragement of idolatry, magic, and the Hussite heresy; destruction of reverence for the Eucharist and the Cross; intolerant self-righteousness; and "iudaica pravitate," the latter being a reference to the Hebrew Tetragrammaton ("YHWH"), frequently used in magic spells.[160] Offering his tablet to the crowds "as if he were Moses on Mount Sinai," Bernardino was even accused of being the "beast of the Apocalypse" and the Antichrist himself.[161] The anti-Bernardino clamor grew, and the inevitable soon came: a summons from Rome to face trial as a heretic before the papal court.

At the time of the summons (most probably in early 1426), Bernardino was preaching in Viterbo; taking leave of the Viterbesi, the preacher somberly described his plight: "I am going to Rome to be cremated by fire and you, enjoying peace and tranquillity, will remain behind. They are calling me a heretic and the word circulating in Rome is that I must be burned at the stake."[162] Indeed, arriving in the city, he found, "chi mi voleva fritto e chi arostito," "some wanted me roasted, others wanted me fried" (R.183). Given the enormity of the crimes imputed to him, Bernardino was interrogated by an assembly of fifty-two theologians and a host of cardinals and other curial prelates. However, with the help of the by then highly regarded John of Capistrano, Bernardino succeeded in winning formal acquittal. But this did not silence the suspicion and the rumors. Charges were renewed against Bernardino with the change of popes in 1431; Martin's successor, Eugene IV, eventually responded on January 8, 1432, with the bull *Sedis Apostolicae*, exonerating Bernardino once and for all of all charges of heterodoxy and praising him as, among other things, "a most acute and rigorous eradicator of heresy . . . and a most famous preacher and a most righteous teacher of the Catholic faith in almost all of Italy and beyond, approved and noted among the other famous heralds of the Word of God of the present age."[163]

Despite the publication of Eugene's bull, Bernardino could not rest tranquilly. Enough suspicion lingered in the minds of certain prelates that, at the March 15, 1438, session of the Council of Basel, an inquiry was once more held regarding Bernardino the "heresiarch." This time, however, the charges led nowhere.[164] Indeed, in Rome, in that same year, Bernardino was promoted to Vicar General of all the Franciscan Observants in Italy (he had, since, 1421, been Observant vicar for Tuscany and Umbria). Nonetheless, as Origo points out, it is noteworthy that no mention of the cult of the Holy Name was made in any of the thirty-three articles presented as cause for Bernardino's canonization, and that the feast of the Holy Name of Jesus had to wait until 1530 for formal inclusion in the liturgical calendar of the Church.[165]

5. The Power and Omnipresence of the Devil

At the same time that the demonization of both heretics and witches was occurring, another dark, ominous figure was gaining ever greater prominence in the catechesis of the Church and the collective imagination of Christian society: the Devil. This increasingly fearful awareness of Satan and his works in the everyday life and world of ordinary men and women has been identified as yet another crucial contribution to the eventual outbreak of the witchcraft conflagration in Europe, and is of prime relevance to our discussion of Bernardino's campaign against witchcraft.[166]

Between the time of the Church Fathers and the Middle Ages, a major change of heart had taken place in Christianity at large toward Satan and his role in the world. Although prudently mindful of the power and presence of Satan, Christianity at the time of the early Fathers was robustly self-confident in the face of demonic attempts to bring the Church of Jesus of Nazareth to defeat. The early Christian Church knew that its faith was more powerful than Satan and any of his works. In marked contrast, among medieval and later Reformation Christians, a fearful, doubting pessimism dominates. For early Christians, Satan and his henchmen were "mere external enemies, doomed to be defeated again and again, and finally cast down for ever, by the bearers of a militant faith."[167] This was not the case for late medieval and Reformation Christians. By the late Middle Ages, as Norman Cohn explains, the once external enemy had come to take up residence within the very confines of their own minds: "No longer imagined as causing drought or bad harvests or epidemic, demons have come to represent desires which individual Christians have, but which they dare not acknowledge as belonging to themselves. People feel themselves victims of forces which they are quite unable to master."[168] Given, therefore, what Cohn has described as the "morbid fascination"[169] with the Devil and his powers that took full hold of the Christian imagination, the transformation of isolated cases of simple sorcerers into a vast network of organized devil-worshipers appears more readily understandable, if not, indeed, inevitable.

Did friar Bernardino contribute to the creation of such an atmosphere of fear and paranoia? Once again, the answer is a decided yes. To begin with, Bernardino explicitly confirms, although in slightly different terms, Cohn's description of the dramatic shift in Christian self-confidence with respect to the Devil. Consider the warning Bernardino gives to the Florentines on the dangers of spiritual isolation:

> Someone might ask: "But, the holy fathers who lived in the desert and in their hermitages all by themselves, how did they manage?" I will tell you. In those days, the blood of our Lord Jesus Christ was [still] very hot; in the early Church [Christians] were of great perseverance, and the Devil did not have as much malice as he does today after [accumulating] so much experience—every day he learns more from experience than what he knew before; and our faith has grown cool because of our sins, and therefore we are much more in danger.[170]

Confirmation of Bernardino's acute awareness of and near obsession with this powerful demonic force, Satan, can be found in theologian Andrea Biglia, the preacher's Augustinian censor, whom we have already had occasion to cite. Concerned about the scenes of mass emotion that Bernardino staged in his preaching campaigns, Biglia wrote a treatise against Bernardino, "De institutis, discipulis et doctrina fratris Bernardini Ordinis Minorum," accusing him, in respectfully moderate, measured terms, of encouraging idolatry, social unrest, and perhaps even heresy—the same charges, ironically, that Bernardino then projected onto "witches." One further specific criticism Biglia brings against Bernardino is his excessive preoccupation with Satan:

> [S]ome people might perhaps reproach you for the insurmountable audacity of your speech; as for me, there is one thing you are wont to do that I confess I

> do not like at all: that, as seems to be clear, one hears coming from your mouth in your sermons the name of the Devil no less than that of Jesus. Now, there is no one who does not know that this name is to be execrated and, as it were, spat at, I might even say, by all the faithful. Why therefore is it necessary for you to have this name on your tongue so frequently when we believe that it should be abhorred by every pious person? And, unless I am mistaken, you yourself remember that when in Bologna you kept repeating, among other things, that accursed name, a little housewife had spat on the ground, as it happens, in a gesture of rustic simplicity. I refrain from describing how harshly you scolded the trembling woman, shouting at her that she was the one whose body contained thousands of devils—those were your words.[171]

What kind of example are we giving to the impressionable laity? Biglia further asks, reminding Bernardino: "How easily the masses take their example from us! As when [for instance] a certain widowed mother attempted to reprimand her daughter for having that same despicable name so often on her lips, the daughter immediately answered her back, saying why should she not be able to do the same thing at home that you [Bernardino] do so frequently in your sermons?"[172]

Another of Bernardino's contemporaries, Enea Silvio Piccolomini (Pope Pius II), a great admirer, not critic, of the preacher's, tells us of this "trick" involving the Devil, which Bernardino played on his Perugian audience in 1425:

> While preaching among them, [Bernardino] one day promised to show the Devil to them, and held the people in suspense for many days with this promise. And so everyone came to his sermon to see the Devil. After many days, he said, "I will keep my promise, and, although I promised to show you one Devil, I will in fact show you many devils: turn and look at each other and then you will see the Devil, for you who do the work of the Devil are yourselves devils."[173]

Reading Bernardino's sermons—several of them devoted completely to the figure of the Devil—one is obliged to agree with Andrea Biglia: Satan and his activity seem never to have been far from the friar's mind and concern.[174] Indeed, Bronzini has spoken of the way in which the friar's sermons have thoroughly "quotidianized" (*quotidianizzato*) the presence and activity of the Devil, at work in all sizes and shapes.[175] "How many devils," Bernardino asks his audience in the basilica of Santa Croce, "are there here right now among us?" His answer: "The whole church is filled with them, at least one for every person. . . . He's in our presence and knows what we do or say or speak without our seeing or hearing him."[176] Every so often, Bernardino will even apostrophize the Devil, as, for example, when he scolds him for having sent the rainstorm that forced the friar to cut short the previous day's sermon.[177] Moreover, Bernardino's sermons are filled with what he presents as "true stories" of the Devil, his demons, and their intimate involvement in the daily lives of men and women. This involvement is so intimate as to reach the point, as we have seen, of engaging in sexual intercourse with them and producing children through such monstrous unions.

The Devil has such great desire for our destruction, proclaims the friar, that it is "beyond all understanding" (B.159). "His principal activity is that of sowing error in the Church of God and extinguishing the light of faith in humankind; he's just like the crow who rushes to pluck out the eye of a cadaver."[178] The human soul is constantly under siege by the Devil; in fact, the more committed to God the soul, the greater is the "battle" waged by Satan for its downfall (C.204). He "proves" this with the following story of one of the "holy fathers":

> They say a certain holy father was once led by an angel to a monastery of saintly monks, and showed him the entire church. The church was filled with flies. The holy father asked: "What's the meaning of all these flies here?" The angel said: "They're not flies, they're demons to deceive the monks." The holy father said: "If these monks are as holy as you say, then they [the demons] are wasting their time." The angel said: "They conspire to poison the monks in whatever area they can and therefore they're always on the alert." Then the angel led him to the market square of the city and the holy father saw but one demon sitting atop the city gate in reverie and leisure. He said to the angel: "Now this is something: here where so many sins are committed, there's only one demon, and he's up there so leisurely sitting, while over there in the monastery there were so many of them." The angel replied: "Here there's no need for the Devil to exert himself much—the people commit so many sins on their own that he's satisfied enough; with evil souls he doesn't have to work hard; but with good souls, he has to be always on his toes and ready to strike at any given moment."[179]

The Devil, however, does not limit his personal visits to just monasteries and convents. Demonic forces can also visit and occupy the private homes of men and women as well. They sometimes even take on the appearance of a deceased person (OOQ.V.299) or some other human form, as in the case of a man from a small town near Mantua who complained to

Bernardino of a most troublesome spirit (*uno spirito*) who had taken up residence in his house. This spirit chatted with the family, ate and drank with them, and even sang, danced, and slept in the same bed with his daughter! The gregarious ghostly houseguest, needless to say, quickly wore out his welcome and was finally exorcized through recourse to confession, holy water, and Bernardino's favorite remedy, the Holy Name of Jesus.[180]

Borrowing heavily from the *Centiloquium*, a work then thought to be by Bonaventure, but now attributed to Marchesinus de Regio, Bernardino devotes entire sermons to spelling out the formal distinctions between true "miracles," acts that defy the laws of nature and that only God can perform, and the mere "marvels" wrought by the Devil. The Devil, we learn, is obliged to work within the constraints of nature's laws, but, nonetheless, has a knowledge of those laws far surpassing that of ordinary mortals.[181] On many other occasions, the preacher so accentuates the powers of Satan that his theology at times seems to approach dualism, in which dominion of the world appears nearly equally shared by the principle of Good and the principle of Evil. In one place we even find the friar stating baldly: "There are two captains (*capitani*) of this world; one is God, the other is the Devil" (R. 673). Elsewhere, quoting John 12:31 (perhaps his inspiration for the previous statement as well), Bernardino refers to Satan with the title "prince of this world" (B.173). True, in the preceding remarks the preacher does reassure his listeners that, as the Gospel promises, "this prince" will be overthrown, that Jesus will utterly triumph, and later (B.178), that all those who call on the name of Jesus in the state of grace and with deep faith will overcome all demons, dangers, and poisons, as promised in Mark 16:17. But the indeterminate future tense of those first two statements as well as the difficulties of those obligatory preconditions (the state of grace and a deep faith), together with the friar's many hyperbolic descriptions of satanic power, probably left many listeners feeling rather pessimistic as to who was going to win the battle for their soul, God or Satan. First of all, consider the intelligence of Satan:

> He was created in the beginning with the greatest of knowledge, and he still possesses that knowledge, except that now he is not in the grace of God, as are the good angels. . . . He knows all the states and conditions of men; he knows all the powers of plants and precious stones. One demon knows more than all the knowledge of all men gathered together. Therefore, with so much knowledge and with so sharp an intellect, do you know what he does? He approaches a man and carefully sizes up his condition and wherever he finds in him a weak, easily tempted spot, he goes in and tempts him, and, unless

> there is really great resistance, rarely does he lose the battle, nor does he have to exert much energy.[182]

Among his many other special qualities and talents is his ability to travel everywhere he wishes and penetrate anything, even the human body:

> . . . he is by nature so porous (*sottile*) that he could pass right through a wall or a stone as if it were an open window; he can enter into the bodies of men and women, though not into their souls. . . . [H]e goes everywhere you do and hears and listens to all of your conversations and thoughts and sees everything you do. . . . In the blink of an eye he can travel from east to west from one end of the earth to the other. . . . Everything he does, he does invisibly . . . there is nothing that we don't do in secret that either the good angel or the bad doesn't see.[183]

It is consoling to know, as Bernardino points out in the above passage, that at least one's soul is impermeable to demonic forces. But this one limitation is well compensated: because Satan has been around since the creation of time, he has at his disposal millennia of firsthand experience of the world and of humankind, and does not hesitate to employ this knowledge in his siege against that tiny bastion of the human soul (B.161). However, we at least have the small consolation of knowing that the Devil will win no beauty contests. Once extremely beautiful, the Devil is now unspeakably ugly: "Even though you may not believe that the Devil is black as he is shown in paintings, his appearance is so frightening that I believe that if a thousand men, all of a sudden, were to see the demon as horrible as he really is, they would all die of fright right on the spot."[184]

Bernardino's list of the powers and qualities of the Devil goes on for several more paragraphs. Certainly what we have heard is sufficient to appreciate the extent of the friar's estimation of the forces of evil in the world. To add to this disheartening picture, the preacher reminds us that it is God who permits the Devil to have free rein (or nearly free rein) in this world, either to test and prove our faith or to punish us because of our lack thereof (B.168–71). What about the case of a poor "pure little kid" who is suffering from the evil doings of some witch? Bernardino asks, answering, "God allows it because of your sin, O father and mother, and permits [the child] to be tormented in his body but not in his soul . . . in order to torment you through him."[185]

As far as the Devil's modus operandi is concerned, it is in the realm of magic, superstition, fortune-telling, and witchcraft that Satan busies himself in an especially alacritous way. In fact, the very first evil deed wrought by the Devil on earth involved this "art" (*arte*), for, as Bernardino explains, when he said "Lady Eve, eat this fruit and you will know good and evil, you [and your husband] will be like gods," he was dealing in divination.[186] The friar condemns those who involve themselves in witchcraft, magic, and superstition as "angels of the Devil" and "deniers of God and the saints" (C. 208). Citing Deuteronomy 13, Bernardino points out again that all such activity is idolatry and that to believe in any of it is to "adore the Devil" (B.168). Many of the so-called prodigies produced through this "art" are simply "delusions of the Devil" (B.177). "There are many who say: 'I have captured the Devil in this little jar.' It's not true: you're the one who's been captured by him."[187] However, Bernardino admits that, given his knowledge, long experience, speed of travel, and other talents and resources, the Devil can work "marvels," often doing so through the agency of his servant, the witch. Thus, given the intimate association between witch and Devil, as the latter came to be accorded an ever greater and ever more efficacious hand in the daily life and fortunes of the Christian, so too did fear and persecution of the former grow inexorably.

6. Bernardino's Guide to Sorcery, Superstition, and Folk Medicine

Lest his audiences labor under any doubt about exactly which demon-inspired, "idolatrous" practices he is referring to, Bernardino supplies detailed lists of the simple sorcery, common superstitions, and folk remedies practiced in his day. Indeed, he seems to take pleasure in delivering such minutiae-filled descriptions of these remedies and other superstitious practices, further indication of his great fascination with the topic. In reality, he was simply contributing to an already ancient genre of ecclesiastical literature, the *indiculi superstitionum*, "the inventory of superstitions," whereby, since at least the sixth century, the Church taught its clergy to recognize these sinful activities.[188] Let us take a look at a few samples from this abundant store of medieval folklore, "all of it," Bernardino points out, "heretical and forbidden by the Holy Church" (B.188).[189]

As far as magical "medical" cures are concerned, Bernardino complains that "for every infirmity from the sole of one's feet to the top of one's head, people seek to be healed with the help of the demons" (OOQ.III.321). For such healing and for protection against disease and misfortune in general, many varieties of amulets, talismans, and other magical charms bearing written magical inscriptions (in Bernardino's Italian, *brevi* or *brievi*) were worn or placed at strategic locations in the home. The friar spends much time discussing these objects—he has examined some of them carefully for himself, he says—condemning their use, while teaching his listeners how to distinguish demonic "brevi" from Christian ones, such as that of the Gospel of St. John.[190] As for more specific cures, we learn from Bernardino that a temporary cure for epilepsy and jaundice was to dance wildly in church on the feast of the Assumption or of St. Bartholomew (OOQ.I.114; B.164). The preacher debunks this "miracle," this "opera diabolica," by pointing out that in all of that jumping around, "the body humors are dissolved" for a brief period—hence the temporary cessation of symptoms (B.164). To heal a cut, bruise, or other bodily wound, you must recite the chant of the "Three Good Friars."[191] Curing lumbago is a more complicated affair: you must first lie on the floor, then have a woman who has given birth to twins and who is holding a distaff in each hand kick you in the lumbar region and walk over you three times (OOQ.I.115). In the case of toothache, you must touch the ailing tooth with the tooth of a hanged man or with the bone of some other dead person (ibid.). Alternatively, if your toothache happens to occur at the right time of the liturgical year, you can place a sword between your teeth while the bells are ringing on Holy Saturday (ibid.).

Many superstitious remedies and recipes involved the sacraments and sacramentals of the Church, including and especially the consecrated host:

> Oh, what shall I say about the horrendous abuse of the holy sacraments, the most holy chrism and the most holy Body of Christ? Oh, what abomination! Oh, what wickedness! Oh, what horrendous crime! Oh, what a tremendous judgment is prepared for these most wicked men and women, about whom I can neither speak nor keep silent![192]

Accordingly, the preacher issues a special warning to parish priests to keep the consecrated host locked up and out of the hands of those "damned old sorcerer women" (G.227). Yet elsewhere he acknowledges that it is the priests themselves who use the host and the sacred chrism for the confection of magic charms and spells, or else dispense them to others for use in such preparations (OOQ.VII.416–17). Bernardino was not fabricating this last, surprising charge: We know from other sources that clerical involvement in witchcraft and related offenses was far from rare in the friar's age. Indeed, in 1422, during the height of Bernardino's public preaching campaign, a group of friars from the preacher's own Franciscan order were put on trial in Venice for allegedly sacrificing to demons.[193]

Returning to Bernardino's inventory of superstitions, we are told that in order to protect yourself against fire as tradition advises, you must drink a raw egg on Ascension Day (B.182). If you wish to grow in wealth, eat boiled fava beans on the calends of January (B.188). To chase away a storm that might threaten your crops, you must bare your bottom to the approaching clouds. This "prescription," however, has its drawbacks, the friar explains: "There was a certain woman in Genoa who, seeing the bad weather coming and wanting to chase it away with a spell, raised up her skirts from behind and pointed [her rear end] toward the bad weather. Just at that moment, lightning struck and killed her, because she had faith in such foolishness."[194] On the subject of thunder, Bernardino elsewhere informs his reader in passing that "today there exist in the Barbary States (*Barbaria*) some northern peoples (*de gentibus Aquilonis*) who worship the thunder as their god" (OOQ.I.110). What the preacher does not say, however, is that he is passing on information that is at least two hundred years old, taken verbatim from William of Auvergne, who died in 1249 and whose *De legibus* supplies much of the information we find in Bernardino's principal treatise on witchcraft, *De idolatriae cultu*. It may also be that William, in turn, was citing an older source. Thus did the medieval imagination continue to meld past with present and fact with fiction, transmitted from one unquestioned *auctoritas* to another.

Although he debunks some of the medical remedies here under his condemnation, Bernardino openly acknowledges the fact that many "magical" remedies really do work. This is thanks to the assistance of the Devil, but it occurs also with the permission of God, who in this way tests the faith of Christians, seeing if they are strong enough to resist this form of demonic temptation. Thus, the preacher warns, sinful, superstitious practices and witchcraft may heal the body but endanger the soul, leading it to "final perdition."[195]

Included in Bernardino's sweeping condemnation of superstition is astrology, "l'arte della scienza estrologia" (B.180). He treats the topic most extensively in his second sermon to the Sienese in 1427, on "the marvelous care that God has over human nature and how God protects us with his angels" (R.116–40). Bernardino admits that astrology is a science "permitted by the Church" (B.180), since everyone in his day, in both Church and society, believed that the heavenly bodies exercised an unquestionable influence on all bodies under the lunar sphere, including human ones. This belief was founded on the scientific teaching that everything in the universe, including humankind, was all of a piece, inasmuch as all its parts were made of the same four elements—earth, air, water, and fire—and possessed the same four qualities, heat, cold, dryness, and humidity.[196] Accordingly, the study of astrology was included in the medical school curriculum. Indeed, "[b]etween astrology and medicine . . . strong ties existed. . . . [T]he good physician was supposed always to tal astral influences—on the patient at conception and at crises of life and ol health or illness, on medications, and on parts of the body—into account."[197] Bernardino himself acknowledges this, referring approvingly to the doctor who will not administer medicine under certain astrological conditions lest it be useless or harmful (R.120).

In view of this universally accepted "scientific" teaching, the preacher opens his 1427 Sienese sermon on astrology with a brief lesson in cosmology, listing the names of the planets and the signs of the zodiac. There are, he specifies, "seventy-two constellations, which are in continual movement in their orbits and have governance over our bodies" (R.119). Proof of this influence, he says, is the movement of the tides ("Who's been to Venice? Has anyone been there? Those who have know whether this is true or not") and the fact that trees that are not cut down under a full moon produce bad timber (R.119). Bernardino hastens to add that these influences are exercised only over our bodies, not our souls (R.119). Yet elsewhere he somewhat contradictorily admits that "certain human impulses toward this or that object are at times due to the disposition or condition of the celestial planets."[198] As for our bodies, all it takes is a small antidote to overcome any astral influence, Bernardino reassures his listeners: "Doctors who know the planets and signs and constellations from which we have our governance, having to give a medicine to a sick person, give it in such a way, with some other small ingredient—be it herbs or certain waters or other drugs—that it takes away from the planet in question whatever power it may have."[199] As for our souls, Bernardino tells us, they are under the guidance of heavenly ministers sent by God:

> But [watching] over our souls are the angels. These angels lead us and coax us and illuminate us in all those things that we must do. These angels have brought you to listen [to this sermon] in this square, and this whole square is filled with angels who are making you stay attentive to the words that are spoken by me to the praise of God—and you are so attentive that if even old St. Paul were preaching, I don't think you could be more attentive. And where does this come from? Not from me certainly, but from the angels.[200]

Bernardino rejects any kind of astrological determinism—"There are those who say 'I was born in such-and-such a constellation, therefore I can't help being the way I am by nature' "—on the theological principle that our God-given free will is never nullified by any external force (R.118). If it were, then we could never speak of moral responsibility, nor, hence, of reward or punishment. Quoting "the saying of the pagans" (in this case, Ptolemy), Bernardino reminds his listeners that the "the wise man will know how to subjugate the stars" (R.125; see also OOQ.III.136). More important, we must keep in mind that God created all things, including the planets, for the benefit of humankind, not its detriment. To say that the planets make one do evil is thereby to impute evil to God, their maker (R.118, 122, 123–24).

As far as using astrology to predict the future, Bernardino concedes that this too is possible, but "if [astrologers] make the tiniest mistake [in their calculations], they haven't accomplished a thing" (B.180). Furthermore, "the stars enable them to predict things only in a general way, for instance: 'There's going to be plague or war or famine or peace or abundance or health in Florence.' Do you understand? Only in a general way, but they can't see anything more specific, for instance, 'This man is going to die, that one will live, etc.' "[201] To illustrate the absurdity of giving credence to astrological predictions, the friar recounts the following *exemplum*, taken perhaps from Jacques de Vitry:

> One day, a certain lord who had an astrologer in whom he placed great faith, saw his astrologer in great melancholy. He asked him what was wrong with him, but the astrologer refused to answer, and that just made the lord's desire to find out the reason grow stronger and stronger. Finally, the astrologer asked pardon of his lord and explained that through his art he had learned that the lord was to die that very year. With great wailing and many tears, he threw his arms around his lord and kissed him in order to console him. The lord, believing him, dropped to the floor in a dead faint and was carried to bed. A fever took hold of him in his grief and wailing, and he could find no peace.
>
> One of his barons, a magnanimous man, hearing that his lord was ill, went to him and with great tenderness asked him about his illness and told him to command of him whatever could be of help to him in any way. And thus the baron tried to comfort his lord. The lord told him, "My problem is this: My astrologer has told me that he has seen in his books and cards that I must die this year. This has grieved me so much that a fever has taken hold of me." The baron then comforted him, saying: "Have no fear. I shall find out how this astrologer knows this."
>
> And so he went off to the astrologer and asked him how he came to learn that the lord was to die that year. The astrologer, amid many tears, told him: "For such-and-such a reason and conjunction of such-and-such a star in

> such-and-such a constellation." And he added many reasons for which the matter had to unfold as he said. The baron then asked him: "Say, tell me, by the way, have you seen how much time *you* still have to live?" The astrologer answered: "Oh, I've known that for a long while. I can count on living for about another twenty years." At that point, the baron drew his knife and said: "You want to bet?" And he struck him so many times with the knife that he killed him. "You're sure not going to live twenty more years now!" And he had a laugh over him and his craft.
>
> The baron returned to his lord, laughing, and said: "The astrologer told me so-and-so and such-and-such and that he still had twenty years to live. But I killed him and he couldn't see that coming, just as he can't see what's coming in your life." The lord burst out laughing, got out of bed completely cured, and lived for many years thereafter.[202]

The friar's ultimate moral judgment on belief in such astrological determinism and fortune-telling is that "this is all openly and clearly heresy and sin" (R.118). He warns that the Devil frequently uses astrology in order to lead humans into eternal perdition (OOQ.III.136).

7. The Destruction of the Pagan Well, "Fontetecta"

Bernardino's sermons on the "idolatry" of superstition in its various forms represent at times the preacher at his most outspoken and colorful rhetorical best. Yet we know from his earliest biographers that he was likewise no less bold in putting words into action. The destruction of "Fontetecta" ("Covered Spring"), just outside the Tuscan city of Arezzo, is a case in point. This episode is mentioned by more than one of Bernardino's earliest biographers and can be seen depicted by artist Neri di Bicci in a panel painting now in the Pinacoteca of Arezzo.[203] The most complete account of the Fontetecta affair is to be found in the *vita* written by an anonymous contemporary Franciscan confrere of Bernardino's—hence its informal name of *Vita anonima*—who concludes his narration of the episode by assuring us, "I heard these few things about his life from older members of our Order and from citizens of Siena, and some things I heard from him himself. And I know am not lying."[204] What follows is a summary of the episode as described by our anonymous friar. Not only does it illustrate another facet of Bernardino's antiwitchcraft activity, the episode also represents further documentation of the survival of pagan practice in Christian Europe well into the fifteenth century—in this case, not in the isolated recesses of the countryside, but at the very doorstep of a major urban center.[205] Equally important, it attests to the power of Bernardino's oratory to sway the masses to do his bidding.

The Fontetecta was an old Roman well in the middle of the woods one mile from the city that had become, or, rather, had remained, popular in the Aretine territory as a center of miraculous healing. Its waters, endowed with "supernatural power," attracted all sorts of "witches and enchanters, both men and women, from all parts." In addition, mothers of sick infants would make pilgrimage to the spring to immerse their children in its "exceedingly frigid" waters. Most of these children died from the cold, but "these pestilent women" simply attributed this to the will of God and not to "their perversity and the frigidity of the waters."[206] During a course of sermons preached to the people of Arezzo, most likely in 1425, Bernardino railed against this place of pagan superstition and sin. He was met with great opposition, however. As our anonymous biographer explains:

> Since this well was a profitable commodity for certain people, these people rose up against this man of God, claiming—especially certain fellow religious—that he was acting in that way out of hatred and jealousy toward them, under the cloak of the zeal of piety, and so they incited the leaders and governors of the city against him, saying that friar Bernardino was a Sienese and a Ghibelline and against the ruling party of the city.[207]

Accordingly, the preacher and his entire entourage were expelled from the city, not without "great shame and humiliation on [Bernardino's] part," and warned never to return.

Yet return he did some years later, most probably in 1428, when he was invited to preach an entire Lenten cycle by Arezzo's new, more favorable, ruling party.[208] This time, we are told, Bernardino made no explicit mention of the well in his preaching. Instead, at the conclusion of one particularly successful sermon ("extremely beautiful, extremely consoling and extremely pleasing to the entire people and clergy") on the Sunday after Easter, the preacher suddenly announced to the congregation: "Anyone who is a true Christian and friend of God, follow me!" A crowd of people heeded the call and followed him behind a large wooden cross specially prepared for the occasion. The friar and his colleagues led the band straight to Fontetecta, where, under his supervision, they proceeded to destroy the well, filling it with rocks, stones, and earth. In its place, Bernardino had a chapel built in honor of the Virgin, where many miracles soon began to occur. A more splendid and still extant church, Santa Maria delle Grazie, decorated by Aretine painter Parri Spinelli upon

Bernardino's commission,[209] was eventually built on the spot, "innumerable and stupendous miracles continuing to occur" there. Thus did the friar turn his "great shame and humiliation" into yet another personal triumph, as he had done in Rome in 1426.

Thus also, at Fontetecta, superstitious practices—the "marvels" of the Devil—were replaced, through the friar's intervention, by miracles of the Virgin. In one of his antiwitchcraft sermons, delivered to the people of Florence just before his unsuccessful 1425 mission to Arezzo, Bernardino had, in fact, instructed his audience to do just that, namely, turn away from pagan superstition and turn instead to the Virgin Mary: "Beg her to save you from the many dangers we face, since we are besieged by the Devil, the world, and the flesh. . . . One prayer to Mary is worth more than to all the other saints put together."[210] Unfortunately, medieval Marian devotion produced a further crop of Christian superstition, abuse, and outright fraud. Bernardino's own Mariology frequently reaches the point of becoming sheer Mariolatry. As Hilda Graef has pointed out, the friar's unbridled enthusiasm for singing Mary's praises carries him to "astonishing lengths" and "pious absurdities."[211] For instance, as Graef points out, in his sermon on "the superadmirable grace and glory of the Mother of God" (OOQ.II.370–97), Bernardino "attempts to prove nothing less than that the blessed Virgin is in some respects superior to God Himself."[212] Indeed, in that sermon, Bernardino illustrates this claim about Mary's *potestas:* "The blessed Virgin could do more concerning God than God could do concerning himself."[213]

Yet even while committing frequent excesses of his own, Bernardino is not unaware of the excesses of others in the realm of Marian devotion:

> And, oh, oh, by the way, the milk of the Virgin Mary! Ladies, where are your heads? And you, fine sirs, have you seen any of it? You know, they're passing it off as a relic. It's all over the place. Don't you believe in it for a moment. It's not real. Don't you believe in it! Do you think that the Virgin Mary was a cow, that she would give away her milk in this way—just like an animal that lets itself be milked?[214]

However, the preacher's suspicion of relics was not all-encompassing.[215] With not a trace of skepticism, for instance, Bernardino tells the Sienese in one of his 1425 sermons of the great treasure from Bethlehem preserved in the city of Rome: "And therefore the Book of Ecclesiastes says that the ox and the ass that were in Bethlehem at the time of the birth of our Saviour Jesus Christ did not touch the straw upon which Christ lay out of reverence for him, and that straw is still preserved, it's in Rome."[216] On the subject of relics, here as elsewhere, Bernardino proves to be a man of contradiction.

8. Popular Piety and Christian "White Magic"

Even though Bernardino did not seem to acknowledge the fact, there was at times an extremely fine line between the condemnable "black" magic of the sorcerers and the healers and the acceptable "white" magic of these ecclesiastically sanctioned relics, the devotions of popular piety, and the formal sacraments and sacramentals of the Christian religion itself. Frequently, what separated the former from the latter was simply the intention of the practitioner, if not the distinctions made by Church law, and if not the actual mechanics and instruments of the practice. In condemning certain practices as pagan superstition while approving others as laudable acts of piety, Bernardino never clearly enunciates the criteria used to make such distinctions, beyond that of intentionality: "Carrying a little bit of olive branch out of reverence is good; likewise with other things, [such as] the Gospels or prayers; but not with a bad intention, for you would then be going against God."[217] In the end, some of his judgments seem inexplicable and, indeed, arbitrary. For example, carrying an arrow around on the feast of St. Sebastian or a little cross made out of an olive branch blessed on Passion Sunday—the latter today a widely diffused and orthodox Christian practice—takes you out of the realm of reverence and into that of "devilry" (B.176).

Be that as it may, let us hear what else the friar offers his audiences as acceptable, Church-sanctioned substitutes for the remedies, charms, and amulets of black magic and superstition. As he explains in his sermon "Del dimonio scacciato" ("On the Devil driven away"), holy water offers "a thousand remedies against demons and temptations and plague and sickness and every diabolical affliction and against every danger" (B.177). Scripture, he tells the Paduans in 1423, is likewise a secure resource for the Christian: to protect yourself against witchcraft, you can, for example, recite the prologue to the Gospel of St. John (OOH.III.176; see also B.79), in addition to carrying portions of that text around with you in the form of a "breve" or amulet. The same Gospel of St. John, we might add (as Bernardino does not), was also used by sorcerers in their spells, exorcisms, and charms.[218] To achieve and maintain the good health, good fortune, and safety of body and soul, what the friar recommends as the most efficacious remedy of all is the Holy Name of Jesus. Following two 1424 sermons to the Florentines on the Devil and his ways, Bernardino delivered another two on the power of Jesus' name, in which he assures his audience, among other things, that

> at the name of Jesus, the demons flee and have no power. God left and granted the name of Jesus first to the Apostles and then to us to use over the demons. . . . In the last chapter of St. Mark, as I told you so many times in these days, Jesus said: "In my name you will cast out demons." . . . So holy and terrible is the name of Jesus. Holy for the saints and good people, terrible for demons and evil people and those in the clutches of the Devil. . . . Serpents flee at the odor of the flowers of certain fragrant vines. So, too, the demons at the fragrance of the name of Jesus.[219]

For those who have real faith in its power, the Holy Name will keep away not only the demons, but also "brigands and highway robbers," the plague, all poisons, shipwreck, the perils of warfare, and, indeed, all the tribulations of life (B.200, 202, 205). According to an eyewitness to Bernardino's preaching on the Holy Name in Siena in 1425, several demon-possessed women and men were immediately freed of their "unclean spirits" once the friar had held up for public display his IHS tablet.[220]

Accordingly, Bernardino persuaded most of northern and central Italy to place his IHS sunburst monogram on the walls and façades of its churches, public buildings, and homes, where they remain today. But the monogram was not meant merely for decoration. As we saw, the friar's impassioned sermons on the Holy Name were frequently followed by its public veneration, such as in the case of the just-quoted 1424 Florentine sermon. The emotional preparation for that veneration was in this case a dramatic retelling of the martyrdom of St. Paul, taken from legendary accounts of that event:

> So, he stretched out his neck for the executioner. The executioner raised his sword and cut his head off. "Jesus, my love," he cried out. He then lifted his head from the ground. "Jesus, my love," he said again and fell down once more. He lifted himself three times repeating the name of Jesus as if to say, "I preached your name while alive, now I preach it dead. Now, now, Jesus, my love, Jesus, my love!" And in this way did he expire and find himself with his Jesus in blessed paradise.[221]

The anonymous scribe who witnessed Bernardino's delivery of this sermon in Florence, and passed on to future generations a vivid *reportatio,* tells us that at this point a much-inflamed Bernardino uncovered his large, brightly painted IHS tablet and displayed it to the kneeling crowd, who, caught up in the emotion of the moment, "all began to cry aloud out of love for Jesus" (B.214).[222]

Such scenes of devotional response convinced the friar he had indeed done his work well. But to many of his contemporaries, as already noted, they were a disturbing spectacle of disorder, both civil and spiritual. More specifically, there were those who saw little difference between this new devotion and the practice of magic: "Why else do we reprove and condemn wizards, soothsayers, and magicians," asked Andrea Biglia, "if not for the fact that they elicit the response and aid of demons through the use of certain letters to which they have attached their faith. And all of this is a form of sacrilege, to confuse the symbols with the things they represent."[223] The suspicion of Bernardino's contemporaries toward veneration of the IHS monogram is all the more understandable when we remember that "the most powerful and terrible magic spells in the Judaeo-Christian tradition used the Tetragrammaton (YHWH, the four Hebrew letters of the Name of God)."[224] Curiously enough, Bernardino shows no awareness of this association, and was completely taken by surprise, it would seem, by the hostile reaction of the theologians. Yet "word magic has always been a powerful element in both high and low magic; the belief that power over a thing's name is power over the thing itself is world-wide."[225] Enough people shared Biglia's concern that the matter eventually led to the heresy trial described earlier in this chapter, an ordeal from which Bernardino escaped sadder but wiser.

9. Seek and Destroy: The Response to Bernardino

Bernardino's last word on witches and witchcraft is an unconditional statement and an imperious command: All witch-related practices are "mortalissimo peccato" (R.1299). Witches must, therefore, be sought out and destroyed at the stake.[226] After all, was not the command of God recorded in the Book of Exodus clear and unconditional on this matter? "You shall not permit a sorceress to live" (Exodus 22:18). Did not Jesus say, "Anyone who does not remain in me will be thrown out like a branch and wither; people will gather them and throw them into a fire and they will be burned" (John 15:6)? We recall the tone of self-satisfaction with which Bernardino reported to the Sienese the results of his witch hunt in Rome, exclaiming, "If I could only make the same thing happen here in Siena! Oh, let's send up to the Lord God a little bit of the same incense right here in Siena!" (R.1007). After describing in gruesome detail the fiery end of Finicella and one of her colleagues, the preacher orders his listeners to "immediately accuse before the inquisitor" anyone involved in these activities. "Do as I tell you," the friar warns; otherwise, "you will have to answer for it on the day of judgment" (R.1011). It is not just negligent individuals, he further warns, but entire communities who will pay for allowing such practices to go on in their midst. This is an offence for which "God frequently sends his scourge down upon cities" (R.1004): "[S]ee to it that all of them are exterminated in such a way that their seed is lost; for I promise you that if you don't offer a little bit of this sacrifice to God, you will see his even greater vengeance descend upon your houses and upon your cities. . . . Oh! do as I say: give a bit of this fragrance to the Lord God; don't wait for his vengeance."[227] If these mortal sinners are allowed to live, Bernardino incessantly warns, God will be unsparing in his punishment:

> Do as I say, so that you will not be held to account on the Judgment Day for not preventing so much evil by denouncing it. And I tell you as well, that once a man or a woman is accused [of witchcraft], if anybody goes to give them help, then the curse of God will come upon their house, and they will see its effects in both their body and their possessions, and then, even in their soul. . . .
>
> Therefore if you don't give some display [of resolve to punish these people], what the prophet Micah says in chapter five will happen to you: "I will demolish the cities of your land and tear down all your fortresses; and I will cut off sorceries from your hand, and you shall have no more soothsayers." These things are meant for you, Siena.[228]

However, Bernardino failed to rouse his compatriots to action in Siena, and there is no evidence of his having done so in Florence either, these being the two towns in which he preached most of the sermons quoted in this chapter. Nonetheless, he succeeded in Rome, Todi, and Arezzo, where, as we saw, his words were translated into concrete law and visible public action. Yet even in Florence and Siena, the friar did succeed, at least in a metaphorical way, in sending up "a little bit of incense" and "fragrance" to the Lord God. This took the dramatic form of the popular, elaborately produced "bonfires of vanities," public spectacles that he staged in those and other communities he visited. With a large portion of local citizenry and leadership in attendance, these "bonfires" involved the burning, in major civic arenas, of not only cosmetics, wigs, and clothes, as well as playing cards, dice, and other gambling items, but also magical books, amulets, and other instruments of magic, sorcery, and superstition. At his canonization trial, these bonfires were to be officially cited as an example of Bernardino's outstanding achievements in "destroying demons and their works to the praise and glory of the almighty God," and thus proof of his canonizable sanctity.[229] The unnamed scribe responsible for preserving Bernardino's 1424 Florentine sermon cycle has left us an animated, almost breathless account of one such psychologically charged collective ritual:

> The commotion is great. The people are restless. Santa Croce, both the church and the square, was filled with people from town and countryside, men and women, in the thousands. The clamor of the boys and young men was so great that brother Bernardino was obliged to end his sermon, come out of the church onto the square with many friars, and have the bonfire ignited. . . . [Y]ou never saw more beautiful flames, going way up into the air to the spite of the enemy of God, the Devil, and to the glory and praise and honor and reverence of our Lord Jesus Christ supreme God. Who lives and reigns *in secula seculorum*. Amen. The shouting, I can't begin to describe, it seemed like thunder, and the tears shed out of piety, what great devotion. Amen.[230]

Through the staging of these spectacles, through the more concrete legal successes of Rome, Todi, and Arezzo, and through his preaching in general, what Bernardino succeeded in doing was not only to send to the stake for the crime of diabolical witchcraft women who may very well have been guilty of simple sorcery and what we would today consider harmless superstition; more important, he also succeeded in provoking or intensifying the general climate of fear and suspicion about witches that hung over the cities and towns of Italy and beyond. Indeed, as Cardini has argued, popular preachers like Bernardino (often serving as or belonging to the same religious orders as the Inquisitors themselves) are at the very origins of the Great Witch Hunt.[231] As it turns out, during the height of the European witch-hunt era (1560–1660), the number of executions for witchcraft in Italy (along with Spain and Portugal) was rather low in comparison with the rest of Europe. Nonetheless, a substantial number of prosecutions took place, an indication of the amount of fear attached to the figure of the witch. Indeed, Italy represents the site of some of the earliest prosecutions, beginning in the late fourteenth and early fifteenth centuries.[232]

By any standard, Bernardino was one of the most influential popular preachers of medieval and early Renaissance Italy. He and his band of preaching disciples combed the Italian peninsula for most of the fifteenth century, and where they did not arrive personally, their written word did, diffused over the vast international Franciscan network. It will therefore come as no surprise to learn that historians charting the growth and development of the European witch craze all point to a dramatic rise in antiwitch literature and prosecution beginning in the second quarter of the fifteenth century—that is to say, precisely in those years in which Bernardino, at the height of his career, was preaching sermons such as the one we have examined here.[233] Bernardino's preaching in turn found its place within the larger, impassioned campaign for reform of the Church "in head and members" provoked by the crisis of the Great Western Schism (1378–1417) and intensified by the reform Council of Constance (1414–18). Inasmuch as one can single out causes in the large, complicated picture of human affairs, Kieckhefer sees this reform drive as the "spark" igniting the intensification of witchcraft prosecution in the mid–fifteenth century, with the zealous Bernardino contributing a note of fanaticism to what was otherwise a much-needed and long-overdue attempt to purge and restore the ecclesiastical and social order.[234]

The contribution of our friar to this crescendo is unquestionable. Reports of the 1426 witch trial instigated by Bernardino, which "all of Rome went to see," reached Germany and Switzerland and—it is reasonable to conjecture—all those lands where the eyewitnesses may have had their home, as well as where Bernardino and his disciples were to bring their preaching campaigns. "Witch trials inspired more witch trials, because the report of action in one place would stimulate passions elsewhere. Oral report alone might have sufficed for this effect, but it was supplemented by inflammatory written accounts."[235] Included among such accounts were the writings and reported sermons of Bernardino disseminated after his death throughout Europe and beyond. By the close of the fifteenth century, the fear inspired by preachers such as Bernardino would become paranoia, and the suspicion, aggressive intolerance. The eventual result was the great witch mania that was to plague Western Christianity for the next two centuries. Back in the early fifteenth century, however, another mania was being prepared in Italy, this one against the "unmentionable vice" of sodomy. Here, too, Bernardino played a leading role, as we shall see in the next chapter.

PLATE 1 Agostino di Duccio (1418–81). Scene from Portal Architrave: The Devil is expelled through Bernardino's Bonfire of Vanities. Chiesa dei SS. Andrea e Bernardino, Arezzo. Photograph courtesy Alinari/Art Resource, New York.

> *"You never saw more beautiful flames, going way up into the air to the spite of the enemy of God, the Devil, and to the glory and praise and honor and reverence of our Lord Jesus Christ supreme God. The shouting, I can't begin to describe, it seemed like thunder, and the tears shed out of piety, what great devotion."*
>
> Eyewitness to Bernardino's bonfire, Florence, April 9, 1424.

PLATE 2 Luca Signorelli (ca. 1450–1523). *The Damned in Hell.* San Brizio Chapel, Duomo, Orvieto. Photograph courtesy Alinari/Art Resource, New York.

"There are two captains of this world; one is God, the other is the Devil."
Bernardino of Siena, Siena 1427, Sermon 23.

PLATE 3 Neri di Bicci (ca. 1418–ca. 1492). Predella of the *Madonna of the Misericordia;* Saint Bernardino of Siena: *The Destruction of Fontetecta*. Pinacoteca, Arezzo. Photograph courtesy Alinari/Art Resource, New York.

PLATE 4 Fiorenzo di Lorenzo. *Saint Bernardino Restores to Life a Young Man Killed by a Fall* (1473). Galleria Nazionale dell'Umbria, Perugia. Photograph courtesy Alinari/Art Resource, New York.

> *"If each and every miracle [performed by the blessed Bernardino] were to be catalogued, enormous volumes would not suffice to contain them all."*
>
> Pope Nicholas V, Bull of canonization, "Misericordias Domini," May 24, 1450.

CHAPTER THREE

"Even the Devil Flees in Horror at the Sight of This Sin"

SODOMY AND SODOMITES

"Bernardino marks an epoch in the history of moral theology in Tuscany. No preacher or writer before him so explicitly treats sexual practices, both inside and outside marriage." So remark David Herlihy and Christiane Klapisch-Zuber in their monumental study of early-fifteenth-century Italian family life, *Tuscans and Their Families: A Study of the Florentine Catasto of 1427*.[1] And of all the various sexual practices indulged in by his audience, both inside and outside of marriage, the one about which Bernardino has the most to say is sodomy. Although the sin of sodomy was traditionally referred to as "the unmentionable vice," this is decidedly not the case with Bernardino. Mention it he does, and with such frequency and such analysis of detail that Bernardino's discourses have been described as "perhaps the most extensive and vivid commentary on sodomy in late medieval Italy . . . by a single contemporary."[2] Furthermore, this commentary comes from one of the individuals bearing great responsibility for instilling and exacerbating in his contemporaries what Romano Canosa has called *la grande paura*, "the great fear," of Quattrocento Italy, that of sodomy, resulting in what Michael Rocke claims to be "the first wide-scale persecution of homosexual behavior in European history, carried out by Florence and other Italian cities."[3] Just as with anti-Semitism and the antiwitch anxiety, Bernardino's age also saw a marked rise in awareness and intolerance of homogenital activity, well documented in the literature and legislation of both ecclesiastical and civil origin, as the studies of Canosa, Rocke, and Ruggiero have shown.[4] This crescendo of "sodomophobia" in Quattrocento Italy is part of an older and larger phenomenon across Europe of growing intolerance, documented by Boswell and Greenberg, resulting in ever more stringent, if not always enforced, legislation against it.[5]

The number of sermons among the preacher's extant works devoted to the topic of what he calls "l'abominabile peccato della maladetta sodomia" ("the abominable sin of accursed sodomy") causes it to be ranked among the friar's most frequently addressed themes of his entire repertoire. Bernardino places sodomy alongside witchcraft on his "Top Twelve" list of major evils that especially provoke the wrath of God on states and kingdoms.[6] Furthermore, together with witchcraft, political factionalism, and usury, it is one of the four "universal sins" that will merit particularly gruesome punishments in hell for their perpetrators (OOQ.III.367–68). Sodomy has the distinction (shared with few other issues) of being represented, as the subject of one or more complete sermons, in each of Bernardino's extant cycles and in his collection of Latin treatises. We find six sermons on this topic among the four published vernacular sermon cycles (Florence 1424 and 1425; Siena 1425 and 1427), three among the sermons delivered in the vernacular but recorded in Latin (Padua 1423, Assisi 1425, Perugia 1425), and, finally, in the critical edition of the friar's Latin *opera omnia*, one complete, lengthy treatise, plus an early draft of a sermon.[7] Sodomy makes frequent parenthetical appearances in other sermons as well, such as and most notably in sermon 47 of the Florence 1425 cycle, "On Youth and the Vice of Lust," and in his 1427 Siena sermon on the "three capital sins," which we examined in the previous chapter for his remarks about witchcraft and the trial of "Finicella" (R.1021–23). The question obviously represented an object of the gravest concern and the deepest repulsion for the preacher.

Sodomy is a sin Bernardino sees everywhere, as he tells his Sienese audience: "And as we are preaching here now in this Campo [the town's public square], so too we must preach in every corner of Siena, in every house, in every shop, in every stable, because I don't think there's a single place that's not contaminated and corrupted [by this sin]."[8] Sodomy, furthermore, is "that beast [of Revelation 13] . . . which holds reign over the earth."[9] Indeed, some towns are "so infected by this wickedness (O abominable wickedness) that in a certain sense you could say that certain cities have publicly established horrendous gymnasia where one can train oneself in the abomination of this disgrace so that the best young men might be available in brothels of sodomy."[10] Hence Bernardino's determination to preach openly about such a distasteful topic, despite the great moral conflict within himself over addressing such scatological material in public (G.98).

Yet, as Bernardino discreetly boasts, he has received divine confirmation of this decision in the form of a miraculous sign from heaven, which took place before a crowd of a thousand marveling witnesses: after one of his public sermons on the "fire" of sodomy (Bernardino gives neither place nor date), a flame or ball of fire appeared in the air above him (R.1158).

1. Definitions and Distinctions

Such were the dimensions of the problem in Quattrocento Italy, at least according to the friar's reckoning. However, before we proceed any further in our exposition and analysis of his remarks on the subject, a clarification of terminology is in order. Precisely what sin was Bernardino preaching against in all of these sermons? What did the friar and his audiences understand by the term *sodomy*?

The avoidance of the terms *homosexuality* and *homosexuals* in the title of this chapter and in our discussion thus far has been deliberate. The focus of Bernardino's moral instruction is the sin that he and all of his contemporaries call "sodomy," not "homosexuality," an act committed by persons labeled "sodomites," not "homosexuals." Although in many minds today the terms may seem interchangeable, in fact they are not. Neither Bernardino nor his contemporaries used the latter two terms, for they did not yet exist, being products of the late nineteenth century. Bernardino speaks of the *sodomita* (the same word in both Italian and Latin) or the *gomorrhaeus* or *gomorrhaeanus* (from the biblical town, Gomorrah). Absent from the Bible,[11] the terms *homosexual* and *homosexuality* were also absent from the vocabulary of medieval and Renaissance Christian Europe, because the understanding of the phenomenon nowadays implied by those terms was by and large absent from the scientific, legal, and theological knowledge of the day. Although in speaking of the phenomenon, late medieval–early modern figures often give us the distinct impression that their term *sodomy* encompassed something more than the sum of the specific behaviors it outlaws, in their formal written legal and moral codes, they refer simply to a list of acts, not an orientation. That is to say, there was no understanding of homosexuality as an involuntary, psychologically constituted, perhaps genetically determined orientation of a person's fundamental identity and erotic attraction. As in Scripture and as it was to remain until recently, Christian doctrine and law of Bernardino's age—at least in their formal definitions and descriptions—described sodomy as an act, not an orientation, one specific manifestation of that universal, postlapsarian infection of concupiscence engaged in by persons whom we would call today "heterosexuals."

Bernardino will at times speak of sodomy becoming a defining and chronic *habitus* of the repeat offender. However, scholastic theology said the same about any and every habitual vice (or virtue); thus, statements to this effect should not be understood as implying a modern awareness of the profound psychosexual dimensions of the homosexual orientation.[12] This is not to say that there were not isolated Christian intellectuals, such as Marsilio Ficino, who speculated that the propensity to same-sex attraction might be a congenital condition determined, for example, by one's astrological profile.[13] Nor is it to deny that a certain few members of the humanist literary elite may indeed have had some understanding of same-sex attraction as a distinct orientation, which they called "masculine love."[14] However, these views do not seem to have had any influence on the thinking of Bernardino and the legal-theological mainstream that we are specifically examining in this chapter.

It was Michel Foucault who, in the introductory volume to his *History of Sexuality*, first made this landmark distinction between the "sodomite" of the "ancient civil or canonical codes" and the "homosexual person," the latter category coming into existence for the first time in 1870 in the literature of forensic medicine.[15] Foucault's claim has provoked much debate, extending to wider and deeper issues of sexuality, epistemology, ontology, and the relation between language and reality.[16] The details of the controversy need not detain us here, but let me point out that Foucault limits his statement specifically to the "ancient civil or canonical *codes*," and does not claim that all sectors, texts, and persons of Greek, Roman, and Christian society understood the behavior in question in the same way.[17]

The sermons and treatises of the very "mainstream" Bernardino of Siena confirm the Foucault thesis.[18] Bernardino's premodern understanding of the phenomenon is clear in many statements he makes in the sermons in question. For example, in one sermon Bernardino condemns the sodomite for lustfully "scoping out" (*vagheggiare*) in church both *il garzone e la garzona*, "the young boy and the young girl" (R.1161). Elsewhere, he states that males will inevitably turn to sodomy in the absence of a sexual outlet in the form of a wife: "Woe to him who doesn't take a wife when he arrives at the proper age and has just cause to do so! Because by not taking a wife, men become sodomites."[19] In these examples, the friar implies that the passage from one kind of sexual object to another is casual and presumably reversible, the lust of the male settling rather easily for its release on another male when a certain female is unavailable or undesirable.[20] That this belief was not unique to Bernardino, but was the accepted understanding of his age, is evident in the rationalization on the part of both Church and state that sanctioned the maintenance of public brothels as a preventive against male sodomy. This appears also to have been the understanding of the author of the Book of Genesis, who has Lot attempting to stave off the gang of townsmen threatening to sodomize his male guests by offering them instead his virgin daughters upon whom to vent their lustful rage.[21]

"Sodomy" and the "Sin against Nature"

Having made this distinction, we return to our original question: to what was Bernardino referring when he spoke of the sin of "sodomy"? Strangely enough, in all of the hundreds of pages of sermon texts devoted to this paradoxically omnipresent yet nonetheless "unnatural" sin, the preacher never stops to give a careful definition of the term. In fact, the medieval theological concept of "sodomy" was "that utterly confused category,"[22] which by Bernardino's time had come to refer to a wide variety of disparate sexual behaviors, all theoretically connected, as we shall presently see, by the common trait of somehow being "against nature," as the medieval mind understood that phrase. In reality, as Mark Jordan has most recently and most ably documented in his book *The Invention of Sodomy in Christian Theology*, "the category 'Sodomy' [had] been vitiated from its invention by fundamental confusions and contradictions," the product of "unstable terms," "unfaithful descriptions," and "inconsistent arguments."[23] The confusion and ambiguity—in terminology and "real-life" referent—begins with Scripture itself and the indeterminacy of its sexual vocabulary, particularly in the Pauline letters.[24] Bernardino was not aware of these deeper historical and theoretical "confusions and contradictions" and uses the term confidently, without explanation or qualification, taking it for granted that his audience will understand what behavior(s) he has in mind.

However, although Bernardino never defines the term *sodomy*, he does give us, in two of his sermons on marriage, a definition of the expression "against nature." In his 1424 sermon on the "marriage debt," Bernardino warns couples that they must never go "against nature" in marriage. He then asks, "What does 'against nature' mean? Every time you go against the natural use, that is, in such a way that conception and pregnancy cannot take place."[25] Quoting Augustine by way of the *Decretum*, Bernardino then lists, not the specific acts "against nature," but instead the various categories of what he calls "carnal sins," one of which is the "sin against nature." This, he says, is "sodomy and other acts against nature in women and men."[26] (The other carnal sins are simple fornication, adultery, incest, and *stuprum*, which he defines as sexual activity involving nuns, priests, friars, and other religious.) In his 1427 sermon on the same topic of marriage, the friar lists the various *freni*, "brakes" or "restraints" on sexual expression in marriage. The second one is: "Do not go against nature; that is, do not go beyond the form of marriage. Every time you go beyond the rational way, you are acting against nature. . . . Hear me: every time [husband and wife] join together in such a way that children cannot be conceived, it is a mortal sin, every time."[27]

However, in all but one sermon on the subject of the "unmentionable vice," Bernardino uses the one term *sodomy*, not "sin against nature," to name the behavior he is condemning. The one exception is the friar's Latin treatise *De horrendo peccato contra naturam* ("Concerning the horrendous sin against nature"), his most extensive treatment of the question, meant for an audience of fellow preachers and clerics (OOQ.III.267–84). Yet the content of this discussion of the "sin against nature" is the same as that of all the vernacular sermons on "sodomy." Hence, the two terms would appear to be interchangeable in Bernardino's vocabulary, sodomy and the "sin against nature" both covering all forms of sexual activity not leading to procreation. However, this was not always the case historically, even among the friar's contemporaries. In his *Summa theologica* (1440–54), for example, Antonino of Florence lists sodomy as one of the four subcategories of the overall category of the *vitium contra naturam* (the others are masturbation, *innaturalitas*—presumably, heterosexual anal intercourse and oral sex—and bestiality). However, in the remainder of the chapter in question, the Dominican gives the distinct impression that he has in mind only sodomitic acts between two men, even when using the term *vitium contra naturam*.[28] On the other hand, Bernardino's disciple Giacomo della Marca uses the one word *sodomy* to describe both the larger category of these four varieties of sin against nature and its specific male homogenital form.[29] By contrast, the great Franciscan *Summa theologica* of Alexander of Hales, one of Bernardino's most frequently cited reference works for all matters of moral theology, uses only the term "sin against nature," which he describes as

> defilement sometimes performed against oneself, and this is called masturbation [*mollities*] and sometimes with another man or woman, and this occurs

> in multiple ways, that is to say, between a male and a female in the vessel not allowed for such an act, or between a woman and her husband in a disordinate way; next, between one male and another male or a female with another female; lastly, it is done with an irrational thing [i.e., an animal].[30]

In reality, Alexander's *Summa* never really defines the sin; that is, it never offers us an abstract statement about its essential nature. Instead, it merely lists the behaviors that fall under that rubric. The word *sodomy* appears nowhere in the *Summa*'s discussion of the topic; the term makes an appearance only in a much later and separate section of the *Summa* listing crimes that merit the death penalty.[31]

As in Antonino's *Summa* and Bernardino's preaching, in most people's minds and imaginations in fifteenth-century Italy, the term *sodomy* seems to have referred to, above all, anal intercourse (or its interfemoral simulation) and oral sex between two male parties. This is demonstrated by the fact that in the Middle Ages and Renaissance, "most sodomy legislation referred specifically to sexual contacts between men."[32] Among this legislation was Florence's law of April 17, 1432, instituting its "Office of the Night," the text of which "implied that it was intended only to police male homosexual activity."[33] When we take a census of the concrete examples Bernardino gives of this sin in his preaching, we find that the overwhelming majority refer specifically to male homogenital behavior, although he never explicitly mentions or even alludes to the fact of oral sex or anal penetration, actual or simulated. It behooves us to keep in mind, nonetheless, that by Bernardino's time, the term *sodomy*, as well as the "sin against nature," theoretically embraced a large spectrum of sinful activity involving women, beasts, or no partner at all (i.e., masturbation), all of which activities at one point or another we encounter in the friar's sermons on the topic. As a result, in certain moments we cannot be completely sure which of these behaviors the friar is specifically referring to.[34] In the pages that follow, due note of these other forms of "sodomy" will be taken; however, our principal concern in this chapter is, as it was in Bernardino's preaching, male homogenital activity.

Sodomy, Pedophilia, and Ephebophilia

A further element must be introduced into our description of Bernardino's understanding of sodomy. Although never making the claim explicit, the preacher simply takes for granted that all adult male sodomites are either pedophiles or ephebophiles, that is, attracted either to boys or to teenagers.

This automatic identification between sodomy and pedo- or ephebophilia is the assumption behind many of Bernardino's remarks, an assumption presumably shared by his audience, for the preacher never pauses to defend or explain the fact.[35] For example, the preacher quotes a long passage in Latin from what he describes as "the most beautiful authority I've ever seen on the subject," Jerome's *Adversus Iovinianum,* beginning, "Amor forme rationis oblivio est et insanie proximus" ("Love of physical appearance is forgetfulness of reason and is close to insanity," R.1143). In translating the Latin into Italian for his audience, as was his custom, Bernardino automatically and without explanation inserts the phrase "of the handsome boy," thus transforming Jerome's generic warning about the irrationality of love into a statement about pedophilia.[36] Elsewhere, in his Latin sermon on the "horrendous sin against nature," the friar likens what he calls the "Gomorrahn" to the supposedly deaf Egyptian asp (of Psalm 58:4–5) and asks: what makes the sodomite deaf? His answer: "id est carnis adolescentum et epheborum luxuriosus amor," "namely, the lustful love of the boys' and young men's flesh" (OOQ.III.280). Still elsewhere, he denounces the sodomites as idolaters, the object of their idolatry being the young boys whom they adore with "their mental and corporal eyes" (B.59). And to cite a final example, one of the portraits Bernardino paints for the Sienese in 1427 begins, "There was once a famous sodomite in a certain land, not quite a year ago, who one night was in his bed with a boy . . ."[37]

Given what we know from other sources, it would seem that Bernardino is accurate in his characterization of the typical sodomitic relationship of the period. "Regarding the traditional societies of medieval and early modern Europe, the most persuasive view now holds that homosexual behavior usually occurred between an 'active' adult and a 'passive' adolescent."[38] At the same time, Bernardino leaves us with the impression that this gross disparity in age is yet another offending feature of the sodomitic relationship, although he never states this outright. Yet in Quattrocento Italy, in this respect—the markedly differing ages of the partners—same-sex liaisons were little different from heterosexual marriages. Demographic statistics of the early fifteenth century show an enormous gap in age (at the time of first marriage) between the typical Tuscan husband and his usually adolescent wife.[39] Hence, the word *pederasty* was by and large missing from the contemporary vocabulary,[40] even though Bernardino condemns in sodomitic relationships what he tranquilly but contradictorily accepts in heterosexual marriages.

Bestiality, Female Sodomy, Heterosexual Sodomy

Before we go on to see what the friar has to say about male homogenital behavior, a word is in order about his references to the other legally defined forms of "sodomy": bestiality; the "unnatural vice" in its female variety; and sodomy involving a man and a woman, which included both oral sex and anal intercourse (the latter "presumably an effective form of birth control" in an age of limited contraceptive options).[41]

Bernardino takes little note of bestiality, the topic coming up only once in his preaching. In *De horrendo peccato contra naturam*, he explains that the unspecified "worst crime" [*pessimo crimine*] of which Joseph accused his brothers before their father Jacob in Genesis 37:2 was sodomy, namely, "this wicked vice that is done with beasts or with others" (OOQ.III.279). The friar most likely took his reading of the biblical text from either Alexander's *Summa* or the *Glossa ordinaria*, both of which identify the crime of Joseph's brothers as bestiality.[42] Presumably, Bernardino did not believe this crime was widespread among his (largely urban) listeners; hence the meager reference to it. It was, nonetheless, a crime that would have inspired great horror in Bernardino and his contemporaries, not only because it was unnatural, but because it could—or so they believed—result in monstrous half-human, half-animal births. In his sermon on sodomy, Giacomo della Marca reports that one of his confreres told of seeing such a creature, half-pig and half-human, born of a sow in the Salerno region; likewise, Giacomo further reports, there have been sightings of a "cow-man," a man with the head of a beaver, a boy with canine mouth and teeth and donkeylike ears, and many other similar grotesque products of intercourse between man and beast.[43]

Female homogenital activity makes only three brief appearances in all of Bernardino's preaching.[44] It appears in the Latin treatise we have just quoted, in which Bernardino glosses Romans 1:26–27:

> Sinners of this type, because of their ignorance and blindness, are said to be perverted "*a vulva*"[45] because, as the Apostle testifies in Romans 1:26–27, *God led them to their ignominious passions*—that is to say, it was by divine permission—*for their women changed the natural usage into that which is against nature,* that is, against the instinct, ordinance, and determination of natural law, so that women polluted women; which is against the nature of the individual because this is how one becomes defiled; and against the nature of the species because in this way it will be exterminated; and, moreover, against the nature of the genus, since no other animal of the female genus behaves in this way.[46]

Another acknowledgment by the friar of the existence of the "unnatural vice" among women and of its categorization as a form of sodomy can be found in his 1425 Florentine sermon "Of the Ignorance of the City of the Demon and of Its Ruin." The friar therein deciphers the prophet Ezekiel's thrice-repeated exclamation of "Iniquity! Iniquity! Iniquity!" as a condemnation of the three forms of sodomy: "How is [this sin] committed? Either male with female, or male with male, or female with female."[47] However, curiously enough, having thus specified the extent of the sin, the preacher has nothing further to say about the last item on this list of three, "female with female" sexuality.

A final and equally fleeting allusion to female homoeroticism occurs in a 1427 sermon to the Sienese on loving one's neighbor. To illustrate his claim, "How many things we begin to desire simply by the sight of them!" Bernardino uses the following example: "If one of you women here were to strip stark naked and stand right here . . . how many men and *how many women* do you think would fall into temptation? I say many and many just by seeing her."[48] Thus, Bernardino seems to accept female same-sex attraction casually, without shock or surprise, and expects his audience to do the same. However, beyond these three brief allusions, our preacher simply ignores this phenomenon of female sexual activity in all of his discussions and diatribes. This is somewhat surprising, since his sermons were delivered before audiences in which the women apparently formed the single largest category of listeners.[49]

Bernardino was not alone in this virtual disregard of female homoeroticism. Although the existence of female sodomy was generally acknowledged in the Middle Ages and Renaissance by both the theological and the medical doctors, it receives very little attention in the documents of these centuries, ecclesiastical or secular.[50] It is absent, for example, in that otherwise conscientious encyclopedia of sin and virtue, Dante's *Divine Comedy.* Yet in Dante's Florence of the early fourteenth century, the incidence of female homogenital activity was sufficient to strike the notice of a visiting Spanish doctor, Arnaldo di Villanova, who, in 1309 (twelve years before the death of Dante), reported it as especially common among widows and the wives of overseas merchants. Sexual activity between women, he added, was widespread in all of Tuscany.[51] In general, however, legal documentation of such activity is scarce, with relatively few cases reaching the courts. Why was this so? Despite Arnaldo's report of Florence, this "crime" may indeed have been rarer than its male counterpart, or may simply have gone unreported in many cases, being harder to prove medically or legally. Another reason may be that female sodomy was considered less offensive and less threatening than male homogenital behavior, inasmuch as the latter behavior not only involved "wasting of the seed," but also shamefully degraded the privileged status of the male to that of the inferior female, as McNeill and others have argued, noting the connection between misogyny and what can be called "sodomophobia." However, when and where it did reach the courts, this female "crime" was treated with equal severity.[52]

Heterosexual sodomy, by contrast, receives much attention and vituperation in Bernardino's survey of contemporary sexual mores. Although he never specifies the category any further, heterosexual sodomy then included both anal intercourse—actual or interfemorally simulated—and oral sex. In one sermon, the friar strikes an analogy between the three types of swine (the wild boar, the domestic pig, and the porcupine) and the three types of sodomites, identifying the second group as "those devil-possessed husbands [who do it] with their own wives. Behavior [wicked enough] to darken the sun!"[53] Elsewhere, he states:

> Not only is this wickedness waged against males but also against females, and especially within holy, ratified matrimony. Wherefore in [the *Decretum*], XXXII, quest. 7, canon *Adulterii*, Augustine says, "The evil of adultery surpasses that of fornication, but is surpassed by incest; however, it is worse to lie with one's mother than with the wife of another; but worst of all is that which is done against nature, as when the man wishes to use that member of his wife which is not permitted him." He continues: "This [use] which is against nature is indeed abominable when done with a prostitute but even more abominable when with one's own wife."[54]

Accepting these premises, Bernardino draws the following logical conclusion: "From these words of Augustine, it is evident that it is more horrible to abuse one's wife against nature, than to engage in adultery or to fornicate with one's own mother."[55] Indeed, matrimonial sodomy is at the focus of one particularly wrathful moment in the friar's preaching, though the precise nature of the behavior—anal intercourse? oral sex?—is nowhere specified:

> Oooo! Have I heard stories! . . . Aooo! Once I was in a certain place where some man had taken as his wife a beautiful young woman. They lived together for six years, and she was still a virgin. That is, she had been with him in all those years in a state of most grave sin against nature. Oh, what disorder, oh, what grievous shame! Ooo, ooo, ooo! Do you know what this poor little thing

> was reduced to? She was all wasted, pale, pasty, sallow. She begged me for the love of God to help her if I could in any way. She said she had been to the bishop about this matter and even to the mayor; but they answered her that they needed proof of what she was charging. O what ignorance is this to need proof and witnesses for these kinds of things! I'll tell you what is needed: a bonfire, a bonfire. . . . If it were up to me, I would . . . [the friar breaks off his sentence]. Uuuh! "*Zelus domus tue comedit me.*" Zeal for your house has consumed me: just thinking about it, I feel myself all consumed.[56]

Accordingly, Bernardino even advises priests who have heard the confession of a wife sodomized by her husband to report the case to the bishop so that she may be able to separate from that husband with the blessing of the Church.[57] Somewhat surprisingly, however, when Bernardino raises the topic of sodomy (along with masturbation) as grounds for separation in the later Latin treatise *De horrendo peccato contra naturam* (meant for clerical eyes only), he is more circumspect and, indeed, inconclusive on the question:

> *Quaestio.* But can a wife dismiss her husband because of this crime?—The *Gloss* responds, XXXII, quest. 7, in the canon *Omnes* on the word "sodomite," saying: "It seems that a husband can be dismissed because of sodomitic activity; XXXII, quest. 7, *Adulterii;* there it is said that that crime is greater than adultery.—Likewise: What do you say, if he pollutes his own wife outside of the cloister of shame, or if he pollutes himself with his own hand? Can he be dismissed because of this? It seems so because the word 'adultery' refers to all illicit intercourse and all illicit use of the members, as per XXXII, quest. 4, *Meretrices,* and the following canon; this Laurentius [Hispanus] concedes. I hardly believe that a husband can be dismissed because of any of these [crimes], as per XXXV, quest. 3, *Ordinaria.*" End of quotation from the *Gloss.* The first opinion is held by Huguccio and Raymundus in his *Summa,* under the article concerning the number of witnesses. Innocentius is opposed, Extra, *De divortiis,* chap. 1.[58]

In true scholastic manner, the Gloss on canon law begins by appearing to accept (*Videtur quod,* "it would seem that") the thesis, which, however, in the end, it rejects (*Vix credo,*" "I hardly believe"). Following the Gloss is Bernardino's summary statement about the lack of agreement among the "doctors" with respect to the issue, and on that note Bernardino's *quaestio* comes to its inconclusive end. Bernardino has dutifully reported the opinions of the authorities, pro and con, but is curiously ambiguous as to what his own final judgment is on the question. Antonino of Florence, on the contrary, unambiguously allows for *divortium* (that is, separation) in this case.[59] Bernardino certainly suggests separation as a possibility, and that mere suggestion is sufficient to impress upon his readers the enormity of this "crime" in his and the Church's eyes. So evil is the crime that even that most sacred and most inviolable of unions, the sacramental marriage between two Christians, can sometimes be dissolved because of it.

2. Sodomy as the "Worst Crime"

According to the criteria of medieval moral theology, sodomy was sinful because it was "unnatural." It was unnatural because, as the Genesis Sodom and Gomorrah story and other scriptural passages—according to the medieval reading of those texts—make clear, the Creator intended that genital activity be restricted exclusively to that between a man and a woman and be conducted in such a way that it was always open to procreation. Hence, there could be no sex outside the "proper vessel," no coitus interruptus, nor any other form of birth control beyond abstinence. Above all, there was to be no genital activity between members of the same sex, especially males, the experience of Sodom and Gomorrah serving in the medieval mind as an ominous and vivid warning. Thus, the point of departure was both Scripture and natural law, understood primarily in a physicalist (anatomical) sense based on the teleology (ultimate objective) of the reproductive organs and on supposed observation of nature. Bernardino does not enter into the teleological argument with his audiences, but it would have been present in his thoughts when he delivered his remarks on procreation, as we will later see. The argument based on nature is explicit in Bernardino, who points out that nowhere among the animals do you find this "abominable" vice of sodomy. Every other vice can be found among the animals, "lust in the donkey, dog, and pig; cruelty in the lion, avarice in the wolf," but never this one (OOQ.IX.429; see also B.32). Yet, as Bullough has pointed out, for Bernardino and for his contemporaries, "what constituted natural was selectively chosen. . . . In effect, the appeal to nature was a teaching device used to reinforce theoretical assumptions. It was not really based upon observations of what took place in nature since anything contrary to the preconceived notions was ignored."[60]

In Bernardino's eyes, sodomy is not only an act against nature; it is a direct affront against God. In its essence, this sin, like witchcraft, is but another form of idolatry, and hence an infraction of the First Commandment. The friar explains how this is so, citing the prophet

Jeremiah (7:18) as his authority: "[W]hat crimes are perpetrated by such Gomorrahns is declared by Jeremiah when he adds '*et libent*,' that is, they gladly offer sacrifice '*diis alienis*' [to strange gods], that is, to the demons of the underworld. . . . [T]he Gomorrahns sacrifice as many boys to the demons as they deliver over to this wickedness."[61] He repeats this teaching to the Florentines in his allegorical gloss on Revelation 14:9–10, "Those who worship the beast and its image . . . will also drink the wine of God's wrath," asking them: "Who is it that worships this beast? The sodomites. And as Scripture says, their belly is their god. Whenever you love anything more than you love God, that thing becomes your God. And [Scripture] says: 'Those who adore the beast or its image.' What is its image? The appearance of the cute little boy before the mental and corporal eyes of the sodomites."[62] Yet again, this time to the Paduans, he states outright, "God gave the commandment, 'Non coli plures Deos. *Deus tuus unus est*'; but the sodomites make for themselves many gods, because they are in love with many boys."[63]

We have already heard Bernardino cite Augustine's authority in claiming that, among the various forms of "carnal sin," the "sin against nature" is the worst, even worse than incest between parent and child.[64] Yet the moral gravity of this "crime" goes even further, the friar claims. Sodomy has the distinction of being the absolute "worst sin" of all on the hierarchical tree of universal moral evil. On at least three separate occasions, he declares unconditionally: "The doctors say that God hates nothing as much as He does the sin against nature. . . . [In hell] those who have lived in this vice suffer more pain than any other, for this is the worst sin that exists. . . . Job [31:11] also tells us that this wickedness is the greatest iniquity."[65]

However, we should not take at face value the friar's pronouncements of sodomy as the "worst crime"; contradicting himself, he elsewhere confers pride of place as "worst offense" upon, instead, the sin of blasphemy. As he explains in *De horrendo peccato blasphemiae et de impietatibus eius*, "blasphemy embraces within itself and surpasses all other evils" and "offends God more directly that all other sins," so much so that one could say that "in blaspheming, the tongue of the blasphemer becomes just like a sword penetrating and tearing asunder the heart of God."[66] Still elsewhere, both homicide and failure to make restitution in cases of usury are called the worst crimes (A.289; OOH.III.225a). In another sermon, Bernardino bestows a primacy of sorts on the crime of witchcraft, inasmuch as he claims that when God's wrath finally strikes earth, it will first fall upon those involved in witchcraft (R.1006). In short, on this as on other points of moral evaluation, Bernardino proves self-contradictory; what we observed about the friar in chapter 1 here bears repeating: not always a man of careful, measured, sober speech, Bernardino will at times make sweeping superlative statements, above all for the heightened rhetorical effect and direct emotional impact they afford, unmindful of the logical—or rather, illogical—ramifications of his utterances.

Bernardino also seems completely unaware that some of the best and most widely cited minds of medieval theology disagreed with his assessment. In the *Summa theologiae,* Aquinas, for example, tells us (1^a, 2^{ae}, q. 73, art. 5) that, although there is more shame attached to "carnal sins"—of which "the sin against nature" is a variety (2^a, 2^{ae}, q. 154)—they incur less guilt, and hence are of less moral gravity, than spiritual sins. Dante Alighieri, another medieval author of genius and enormous moral status much studied by Bernardino and recommended by him to his audiences as edifying spiritual reading, likewise accords sodomy a far lower degree of moral gravity. In the *Divine Comedy,* one of the most influential popular "catechisms" of late medieval and Renaissance Italy, Dante places sodomy only at Hell's midpoint, in the circle of the Violent.[67] The worst sin for the Florentine poet, a meticulous student of theology and philosophy, is instead "treachery to lords and benefactors," punished in the last circle of the Fraudulent, where we find the betrayer of Jesus, Judas Iscariot, together with Brutus and Cassius, the assassins of Julius Caesar.

What makes Bernardino so confident in his judgment of sodomites as these "accursed enemies of God" (R.1142)? It is his reading of Scripture. According to Bernardino, Scripture demonstrates that "God has always poured down His wrath upon this sin more than any other."[68] There is no other sin punished as fiercely as sodomy: witness the fate of Sodom and Gomorrah "and those other cities. . . . God so hates this sin that He eradicated so many cities on account of this single sin."[69] Indeed, it was because of sodomy, the friar claims, that God unleashed the Flood upon the whole earth—a claim with absolutely no basis in Scripture, which Bernardino probably copied from the *Historia scholastica* of Peter Comestor, who in turn had borrowed it from St. Methodius of Olympus.[70] However, humankind did not learn its lesson from the Flood, and soon returned to its sodomitic ways. Indeed, at the preordained time of the Incarnation, "as some doctors say," since "God so abominates this sin, it was only after some difficulty on His part that He permitted His Son to be incarnated in that flesh which He saw so foully contaminated."[71] The friar repeats this curious and little-known "fact" of salvation history twice elsewhere (OOQ.III.276 and D.279), identifying Augustine as his source.[72]

Since sodomy is the very worst sin, when faced with the moral dilemma of having to choose between it and another evil, one must choose that other evil. For example, Bernardino tells menstruating wives that they may licitly consent to intercourse with their husbands in order to keep them from turning to sodomy, even though, as he elsewhere teaches, children conceived during menstruation are certain to be born "monstrous or leprous" or otherwise malformed, for "a child conceived in such a time is never born without some great, conspicuous defect."[73] Even death is a lesser calamity to the wife than being sodomized:

> And therefore, O woman, learn this lesson today and tie a string around your finger to remember it: if your husband asks you to sin against nature, never consent to it. . . . Even if you are pressured to do so, even if you are threatened, accept death before ever consenting to that sin. If he were to kill you because you refused, know and be assured that your soul will go immediately into the glory of eternal life. Do you understand what I've said?[74]

Returning to the "better death than sodomy" motif, Bernardino apostrophizes the souls of those Sienese children who perished in the "Black Death" of 1400: "O you blessed tiny little children who departed this life because of the plague: at least you were not contaminated by such a sin! You now stand in the presence of God and, together with Him, are singing that song that can only be sung by virgins."[75] Then to the mothers in his audience, the friar offers this moral counsel:

> O ladies, make sure you don't send your sons around [where there are sodomites]; send instead your daughters, because there's no danger for them if you send them among such people. They will not be contaminated by anything; and even if they were seized and violated, at least there wouldn't be as much danger and as much sin as there would be [if yours sons were violated]. If there is no other way, I permit it as the lesser evil.[76]

In giving such advice, Bernardino would say that he was simply being faithful to the teaching of Scripture and following the example of Lot, whose story he had recounted for his listeners, step by step, earlier in the same sermon. In Genesis 19:8, Lot responds to the invading gang of men (and boys!) who wish to have intimacies with his male guests in these words: "I beg you, brothers, not to do this wicked thing. I have two daughters who have never had intercourse with men. Let me bring them out to you, and you may do to them as you please. But don't do anything to these men, for you know they have come under the shelter of my roof."[77] Bernardino includes this moment in his re-creation of the episode, specifying that the guests were "two very handsome young men." However, he omits one detail, Lot's protest against violation of the hospitality code ("they have come under my roof"), since he and his generation, it would seem, did not understand its relevance to the episode: "At that point, seeing this worst of all intentions that they had and in order that they not commit that sin, Lot said: 'I have here at home my two daughters: I want to give them to you, and you can have your way with them. Just let alone these two young servants of God.' "[78]

It was this same medieval hierarchy of sin—whereby female sexual violation, even the gang rape of one's own adolescent daughters, was deemed a lesser moral evil than male sodomy—that permitted, if not encouraged, the civil governments of Bernardino's age to maintain public houses of prostitution; here the dangerous force of frustrated male carnality could be safely diffused, and unmarried men could vent their lust into the "natural vessel," rather than through the "unnatural act."[79] This "safety valve" was also predicated on the already mentioned belief on the part of Bernardino and his contemporaries that libidinous males, even sodomites, could readily switch from one sex to the other in their search for sexual gratification. McCall summarizes the Christian moral tradition on the subject of legalized prostitution:

> It was St. Augustine himself, in a more practical mood, who had said that if prostitution were to be suppressed, capricious lusts would then overthrow society; and this sentiment was reiterated in the later period by Aquinas, who wrote in his *Summa Theologica* [II-II, x, ii], apropos of prostitution, that if you were to take away the sewer, the whole palace would soon be filled with corruption.[80]

This no doubt explains Bernardino's virtual silence on the topic of prostitution. Knowing that our preacher normally slams down a heavy hand on any form of "aberrant" sexual activity, one would have expected otherwise. Instead, not a single sermon nor substantial part of a sermon on this topic has come down to us from Bernardino's prolific production, despite the huge investment of human and material resources that this commerce entailed and the many evils therein involved: not only fornication, but presumably also adultery, contraception, abortion, child abandonment, and heterosexual sodomy. As for Bernardino's moral evaluation of that "profession," all we find in the sermons are a couple of brief though firm contradictions of those who claim that "fornication and going to prostitutes" are not mortal sins (R.589, OOH.III.255b), with a reminder that prostitution is tolerated only in order to prevent greater evil (D.374–75).[81] In one of his Mary Magdalene sermons, Bernardino digresses to advise women on how to avoid falling into a life of prostitution; his basic advice is to simply avoid pimps and *vetulae,* those "evil old women" in collusion with pimps, and to learn how to recognize the usual traps—duly described—that men set out for women.[82] Bernardino is well aware of the existence of the officially sanctioned "place of the prostitutes" in Siena (right behind City Hall, where he was preaching), for he mentions it at least three times in the 1427 sermon cycle delivered in his hometown (R.842, 876, 1063) and several times uses the comparison with prostitutes to ridicule and shame extravagantly dressed and cosmeticized women (R.1059, 1071, 1088, 1091). Furthermore, as the canonization trial depositions inform us, Bernardino devoted some of his apostolic efforts to the conversion of these "wayward women," obtaining, we are told, great success in these endeavors.[83] In short, while Bernardino did not approve of prostitution, he largely kept silent on the question, since the Church had already given its seal of approval to this "lesser evil" for the greater good of society.

3. Scripture, Science, and Reason against Sodomy

Although today's theological debate surrounding homosexuality has called into radical question the scriptural and natural law premises upon which the Catholic Church's condemnation of such behavior is grounded, this was not the case in the doctrinally self-confident age in which the friar was teaching. Thus, it may come as no surprise to discover that the friar spends little time explaining and proving exactly why sodomy was a sin in the eyes of God and the Church. For the friar and, presumably, for the majority of his contemporaries, this was simply self-evident: all of the usually cited sources of moral doctrine—Scripture, natural law, and the Church's "constant tradition"—were resoundingly clear, unambiguous, and unanimous in their condemnation of that vice.

As far as the Bible is concerned, of the six classic passages upon which the Church has traditionally rested its scriptural case against homogenital behavior, Bernardino cites only two, Genesis 19 (the story of Sodom and Gomorrah) and Romans 1:26–27 ("Therefore God handed them over to degrading passions. Their females exchanged natural relations for unnatural, and the males likewise gave up natural relations with females and burned with lust for one another").[84] We have already quoted and commented on the vivid retelling of the Sodom and Gomorrah story that the friar delivers in his Siena 1427 sermon, assuring his audience that "everyone was involved in that sin, boys, youths, and adults," all of whom quickly came to know that "Lot had in his house two very beautiful young men" and so besieged the house (R.1147–48).

As for the New Testament, Bernardino was apparently aware of the fact that Jesus of Nazareth, the founder of Christianity, made no pronouncements at all on the subject of sodomy, a curious and inconvenient detail given the supposed enormity of this "worst crime" of humanity. Unable to ignore this conspicuous lacuna in Jesus' teaching, Bernardino raises the subject by imagining a logical objection from his audience: "Why didn't Christ condemn [sodomy] in all the time that he was in the flesh, as he did hypocrisy?" The friar responds with the by then conventional explanation that Jesus was completely silent on the subject for the simple reason that nowhere on the face of the earth was sodomy being practiced during Jesus' lifetime: "Listen to this, the night of his birth, according to what that devout doctor saint Jerome says, all sodomites in the entire universe, in fact, died on that night. The light dispersed the darkness . . . they were all exterminated and killed and [by Jesus' adulthood] they still hadn't returned to that evil practice because the terror of punishment was still fresh then."[85] This was true throughout the period of the early Church, according to Bernardino, because "the heat of the blood of Christ was still boiling in the minds of his people" (D.279). "One of the proofs of this," he asserts, is that "although the demons, as we read, tempted people in every other crime, even through visible apparitions, no one, according to what is written in the *Lives of the Fathers,* was ever tempted by the vice against nature."[86]

The astounding occurrence of the universal sodomite massacre occasioned by Jesus' nativity that Bernardino so self-assuredly quotes from St. Jerome is only one of the many references to the doctors of the Church that the friar uses to impress upon his listeners the gravity of this sin. In Bernardino's mind, if a "doctor" has said it, it is an unquestionable truth, the pronouncements of the "doctors" representing an *auctoritas* seemingly equal in importance to Scripture itself. "There is no sin that is greater," he states outright, the consensus of the "doctors" being "that nothing displeases God as much as the sin against nature" (R.1164, B.64–65). Another doctoral *auctoritas,* Augustine, even contributes a bit of "scientific" information—"one doctor says that in whatever spot sodomy has taken place, the morning dew does not fall"—thereby demonstrating that even the physical world is in some way disfigured by "so horrible a vice."[87] This last statement about the morning dew is typical of the medieval *forma mentis,* which saw nature as a *speculum Dei,* a vast allegorical spectacle imparting moral messages, large and small, about God and God's will for humanity. Thus, the phenomenology of the morning dew teaches us something about sodomy, as do the supposedly gruesome present-day conditions of the Dead Sea, a "mirror" of the monstrous abnormality of the sins of Sodom and Gomorrah that lie buried beneath it.[88] The animal kingdom is an especially important source of moral education for the Christian; we have already taken note of Bernardino's remark about the absence of such a vice among this realm of God's creation. Elsewhere the preacher reminds his audience that "there is no animal that sins against nature except horses and donkeys, who are almost of the same nature."[89] Still again, he states: "Take the example of the animals. You see the lion involves himself with the lioness, the male bear with the female bear, the male donkey with the female, etc., and you see *quod omne simile appetit suum simile* ["like always seeks like"]. Except the accursed sodomite, who doesn't put himself in accord with those intentions as do the rational and irrational animals."[90]

With these references to the world of natural science, Bernardino brings us to the other foundation on which the Church's antisodomy case stands, the natural law/teleological argument. This argument reasons that God created two complementary sexes, male and female, and, furnishing them with suitable, complementary genitalia, gave them the command to "be fruitful and multiply and fill the earth" (Genesis 1:28). Because it violates the complementarity of the sexes and because it uses the genitalia in a way for which they were not intended (namely, nonprocreatively), sodomy is therefore "unnatural" and an act of direct disobedience to God, nature's author:

> Don't you see that you are showing yourself to be against God, who said to the man and the woman, our first mother and father: "*Crescite et multiplicamini, et replete terram*? Increase and multiply, and fill the earth?" O sodomite of the Devil, what are you doing? It's as if you're saying to God: "I want to spite you; I don't want anyone to be born."[91]

In one of his 1427 sermons on matrimony, Bernardino explains to the Sienese that matrimony was, in fact, the very first sacrament instituted by God in heaven: "prima fu ordinato questo sacramento che niun altro" (R.549). "Why did God first institute matrimony in heaven?" he then asks. "In order to fill the earth and, afterward, the seats in Paradise [left vacant by the fallen angels]."[92] Bernardino elsewhere repeats the same teaching on the purpose of the creation of the human species—"God made man to fill up the seats of the angels" (R.1149)—and, in doing so, was simply handing on completely orthodox, time-honored tradition to be found, for example, in Augustine's *Enchiridion ad Laurentium* (R.549, n. 76).

But sodomy is not only an act of disobedience. It is, according to Augustine, nothing less than murder, "not by the sword, but by the deed itself." And not only are sodomites murderers, they are—"even more horrible to think"—*filicidae,* killers of their own children (OOQ.III.274–75).[93] However, their victims, "the babies who were never born," are not silent; they scream up to God: "Revenge, revenge, revenge" (R.1154). Turning from pathos to logic, Bernardino exclaims: "O frenzied one of the Devil, don't you see you are not behaving according to reason? What can a person living in the world have that is more precious than children? A good, God-fearing child is worth more than the rest of the world."[94] Furthermore, he asks, "what would become of the human species, if everyone did as you did [namely, engage in sodomy]?" (R.1156; see also OOQ.III.275).

Bernardino's last question was not an idle one inserted for rhetorical effect. It represented a very real concern for the preacher and his contemporaries, who, traumatized by repeated and dreadful visitations of uncontrollable plague, were living in the midst of a demographic crisis of massive proportions. As David Herlihy points out, "from the middle fourteenth to the middle fifteenth century, the dominant factor in Tuscan social history was a radical decline in the size of population."[95] Since the first outbreak of the "Black Death" in 1348, Tuscany, together with all of Italy and the rest of Europe, had suffered disastrous population losses, references to which come up several times in Bernardino's antisodomy sermons (e.g., B.22, B.47, G.103, G.107). The plague, of course, was not the only recurrent form of mortality in those years; there were as well the demographic ravages of everpresent famine and warfare. In all of these disasters, Bernardino is quick to implicate the sodomites. Not only are they not working to produce more babies to replenish the communities, it is their sin that enrages God, who responds with just punishment through the means of pestilence and "exterminations."

The friar is adamantly consistent in his claim that war, famine, and pestilence are God's ways of chastising humanity for its sins, especially sodomy. The theme is recurrent throughout Bernardino's preaching: "[W]hen God holds in abomination a town, he blows it away like dust in the wind. . . . The Angel of the Abyss will force you [to amend your ways] with wars; he is God's Exterminating Angel, as the Book of Revelation says."[96] Mothers who encourage the vice of sodomy in their sons by dressing them up in enticing, effeminate fashions are given this warning:

> And what do you say? "Oh, it's completely harmless, no one's going to get hurt, he's just a boy, after all." If he were a girl, perhaps you wouldn't be doing this, because she could get herself pregnant this way. And since he can't get pregnant, you're happy and offer up your "flatcake" to the "queen of heaven."[97] And you just keep on doing such things so much that you are provoking the wrath of God; and God, seeing this and all the other vices, is threatening you and says: "My wrath will come down over your head." Do you know what he will do? He will send you wars, plagues, and famines in order to punish the sodomites, so much so that you won't be left with either livestock, or farms or gardens or money or even your very population. In all of these ways, God will show his wrath, saying: "Upon each and every thing shall my wrath descend."[98]

To the young sodomites themselves, the friar addresses these words of threat and irony: "O my lads, if you want to exterminate your city and motherland, I tell you, keep on being sodomites; I tell you, if you want her to be exterminated, then don't give up your sodomizing."[99]

4. The Causes of the Sodomitic Vice

In the course of preaching against this "worst crime" and on related topics, Bernardino identifies for his audiences the root causes of this vice, as well as those circumstances that represent the near occasions of sodomitic sin. Again, underlying all of these descriptions of cause is the friar's fundamental premise that sodomy is simply a further manifestation of the generic sin of *luxuria*, concupiscence, by which all human beings are tempted and that all willfully choose. However, unlike all other sin, the sodomitic desire is unique in its etiology: the primary source of this form of temptation, the friar specifies, is not the Devil, but instead represents the direct "invention of the hearts of the impious."[100] Nonetheless, this vice has more specific, external causes as well; in fact, at one point or another, the preacher identifies so many different causes that we are left with the impression that, despite its status as an "unnatural" condition, there is a rather long list of common environmental or social situations and behavioral practices that will cause it to come readily forward.

One major category of causes centers on women. We have already heard Bernardino claim at the beginning of this chapter that the lack of the sexual outlet of a wife is guaranteed to drive a man to sodomy: "Woe to him who doesn't take a wife when he arrives at the proper age and having just cause to do so! Because by not taking a wife, men become sodomites" (A.416). But what about women without the sexual outlet of a husband? They seem not to have been considered in great danger of falling into the female varieties of sodomy, since the preacher never addresses the issue. Be that as it may, another cause having to do with women is their vanity, more specifically, their stomach-turning cosmetics, as the preacher says in one of his many sermons on this ancient motif of ecclesiastical oratory:

> And you, you foolish women, don't you know that it's because of all of your painting and smearing that your husbands are sodomites? And I tell you that you at times are the reason, you, because of your cosmetics. Don't you see that you're ruining yourselves and making yourselves hated by the men? This one's mouth smells from so much painting and smearing, this other one stinks of sulphur, this other one daubs herself with this and that. You send off such a stench to your husbands that you make them become sodomites.[101]

A further way in which women caused men to turn to sodomy was the great expense they represented as prospective brides; many men, Bernardino complains, are discouraged from marrying at all because of the enormous cost of taking a bride, and so turn to the money-saving alternative of sodomy instead (G.95, R.1090). Our preacher, we might note, was not alone in blaming women for turning men into sodomites. One of Dante's warrior-sodomites in *Inferno* 16, Jacopo Rusticucci, claims that it was his shrewish wife who drove him to this vice, a claim that medieval commentators of *The Divine Comedy* had no trouble accepting as valid justification for his behavior and that we find in other Italian sources.[102]

Another cause of sodomy is wealth, along with the self-indulgence and sloth it brings. In his 1424 sermon to the Florentines on sodomy, Bernardino makes a direct connection between the sybaritic lifestyle of that economically prosperous city and the outbreak of this sin:

> Water that remains stagnant, what happens to it? It becomes smelly, and starts producing frogs, lizards, serpents, and other filthy things. If Florence remains immobile in its abundance of food, corpulence, in great profit, and no wars,

> no pestilence, what a stink of sin there is! How many serpents and scorpions of ill will, how much lust, how much pride, how much sodomy! The stink will reach the heavens themselves.[103]

Further on, he states as a general rule that there are "three things [that] make the fire of sodomy grow, the first of these being the abundant fuel of eating, drinking, gorging, and stuffing oneself."[104] Second on the friar's list is lack of gainful employment (and here Bernardino is clearly referring to the rich upper classes): all dressed up in their attention-getting finery but with nothing to do, young people will inevitably fall into sodomitic debauchery. Hence Bernardino's imperative: "Those who don't work must be thrown out of the city" (B.46). The third cause is simply the company of older sodomites. The friar warns parents to keep their young sons far away from sodomites lest they be turned into sodomites by the "contagion," even merely verbal, of the older men: "Mind you that if you associate with a leper, immediately you will get stricken with [that disease]. . . . One contaminated person is sufficient to contaminate in one shop a hundred or more people. All it takes is one rotten apple . . . if you go to the coal-seller's shop, you can expect to come away blackened."[105]

Under the same rubric of the corrupting influence of adults, Bernardino singles out another cause of the sodomitic vice among boys: it is the bad parenting of their own mothers and fathers.[106] The preacher has, indeed, much to say about the role of parents in the formation of sodomites. Boys become sodomites, he asserts, "all because of the coldness of paternal love" (B.41). What the friar means by this is that, once children reach adolescence, if not earlier, parents pay no further attention to their discipline, spiritual training, and psychological nurturing and simply abandon them to their own whims and evil devices. By the time they reach the age of eighteen, they have become "unbridled horses, with no fear of God or of the saints or of mothers or of parents in them" (B.41). This is guaranteed to happen when parents spoil their child, "sparing the rod" and neglecting their Christian duty, especially that of bringing the child to confession, communion, and public sermons (B.39–42, E.42, R.1144).

But in some cases the situation is even worse, the sin of certain parents being not one of simple omission, but rather, *horribile dictu,* one of outright commission. Mothers and fathers, Bernardino declares, mincing no words, "you are the pimps of your own sons!"[107] Why is this so? Because it is they who willingly consent to or even instigate and encourage sodomitic relationships between their boys and older men of wealth and power in exchange for money or some other personal advantage or favors.[108] One way in which parents attract the attention of these potential "benefactors," the friar suggests, is to dress up their sons in stylish, enticing clothing, for example, "a short doublet [and] stockings with a tiny patch in front and another in the back, so that they show a lot of flesh for the sodomites."[109] They "send them out wearing see-through shirts, with little doublets that don't cover half their bodies, with flamboyant clothes and stockings slit up the legs, with braids in their hair."[110] The results of all this are boys "who have become girls . . . all dolled up like young maidens."[111] Such parents will know the punishment of God, the friar guarantees his audience in a not uncharacteristic moment of fire-and-brimstone rhetoric: "woe to you and to you! . . . Woe, woe to you! I'm warning you here and now: you will soon be experiencing it from every side" (R.1145). One form of this divine punishment, Bernardino adds, is a personal visit from the Devil himself, who will show up at their doorstep to seize the sinful child from his father's side and "carry him off in flesh and blood to hell" (E.40).

The Emasculating Mother as Culprit

Although Bernardino brings these charges against both parents, it is the mothers whom he especially singles out as culprits in this emasculation of their sons:

> Oh, you women, it is you too who turn your sons into sodomites! When you send them outdoors, make sure you polish them up good! . . . To the house of the Devil, all of you—you are the cause of much evil. *Oimmé, oimmé!* Don't you see that you are acting like their pimps? . . . Oh, silly, foolish woman, it appears you make your son look like yourself, so that to you he's quite becoming: "Oh, isn't he the handsome lad!" And even: "Isn't he the pretty girl!" *Oimmé, oimmé, Oimméeee!*[112]

What Bernardino here insinuates is that certain mothers actually take sinful pleasure in seeing themselves somehow mirrored in their emasculated sons. He of course does not enter into a psychosexual analysis of how and why this is so, nor can we do so here. Is the gratification merely that of seeing perpetuations of themselves (albeit in androgynous form), or is it that of seeing masculine identity and power reduced to feminine status? Or is it the pleasure of seeing their own child the object of sexual attraction to rich, powerful sodomite patrons, as we heard him previously charge? Unfortunately, nowhere else does the preacher repeat the accusation. He does, however, continue to single out mothers as prime agents in the production of sodomite sons. In a 1425 sermon to the Sienese, he informs us that mothers encourage the emasculation and hence "sodomitization" of their sons "out of pleasure" (*per diliziosità*), pleasure in seeing them dressed in the latest and most revealing fashions (G.102). Again, however, having made the charge, he goes no further in explaining the nature of the evil pleasure he imputes to mothers.

A further element is introduced in a 1425 sermon to the Florentines. There the preacher again condemns mothers for effeminizing their sons, but this time adds an oblique allusion to the presence of an unholy sexual dynamic, not between boy and adult sodomite, but between parent and child:

> If they were to come to me to confess, if I were to hear their confession, I'd sooner give absolution to the Devil before I would give it to any of these women, if they didn't amend their ways. I am referring to the mothers who send out their sons dressed up so wickedly. O what a wicked world! The evil things that go on between one relative and another, between brother and sister, between mother and son! They skimp on the cloth to feast on the flesh. But let's say not much more about this, though you yourselves know much more! I would have dropped dead if I hadn't mentioned it, my conscience would have given me no peace.[113]

The only concrete example that Bernardino gives of these "evil things" that happen in families is the case of a certain brother whose sexually alluring clothes so inflamed his sister with lust that it drove her to an act of fornication—with another (unspecified) male, not with her brother—resulting in her pregnancy (E.43). No mother-son *exempla* are offered, but Bernardino was clearly warning his audiences about the dangers of incest. Is he saying, therefore, that an erotic, incestuous love is also at work in these mothers, who, in clothing their sons with the latest effeminate fashions, "skimp on the cloth to feast on the flesh"? But why then would they, the mothers, be sexually attracted to what is in effect a little girl, unless they were themselves "sodomites"? Here as elsewhere, trying to pursue the logic of Bernardino's disparate statements on the same subject leaves us lost in a labyrinth of contradictions and questions without answers.

In his Latin treatise *De horrendo peccato contra naturam*, we find Bernardino again focusing on the role of parents in the formation of young sodomites, although this time with equal emphasis on both mothers and fathers. As is the friar's wont, the topic is introduced by means of a scriptural verse allegorically containing the moral lesson he is trying to impart. The verse in question is Jeremiah 7:18, "The children gather wood, the fathers kindle fire, and the women knead dough to make flatcakes for the queen of heaven."[114] The prophet Jeremiah is here denouncing the Israelites for their worship of foreign idols ("the queen of heaven" is Ishtar, the Babylonian-Assyrian goddess associated with the planet Venus), but Bernardino extracts a different message from this verse. For the preacher, the verse is really about the creation of young sodomites and the role that each party—father, mother, son—plays in that creation. The "wood" collected by the sons represents all those persons, places, and events that are occasions of this sin; the fathers' "fire" is their own bad example and the unspecified "other ways" by which they incite the child to sodomy. The mothers' "dough-kneading" occurs "when they effeminize their sons, raising them in the midst of limitless pleasures; and thus do they produce 'flatcakes,' that is, sons exceedingly pleasing for the purposes of such crimes, for 'the queen of heaven,' that is, the iniquity of the Gomorrahns."[115] The effeminizing activity for which Bernardino inculpates mothers is here only vaguely described: "raising [their sons] in the midst of limitless pleasures." However, it is made more specific in another sermon containing the same image from Jeremiah: "mothers prepare the dough," says the friar to the Florentines in 1425, "by dressing up their sons in too fine a fashion. How do [the sons] become flatcakes? When they submit to the act of sodomy."[116]

Thus, to repeat by way of summary, boys become sodomites through the agency of both parents, but it is the mother who, according to Bernardino, plays a larger role in this process of corruption. The mother effeminizes her son by the way she dresses him, and this effeminization leads to his becoming a sodomite. The last step in the process—from effeminization to "sodomitization"—is unclear in Bernardino's text (and in his mind as well, I suspect). Does the effeminized boy turn sodomite because he then automatically begins to desire other males? Or is it because, in his effeminate, sexually enticing attire, he is more likely to fall victim to an adult sodomite and thus by contamination acquire that same habit himself? The friar may see both as possible scenarios.

That mothers resort to clothing their sons in such fashions would have come as little or no surprise to Bernardino's audience, for Christian audiences were quite accustomed to listening to clerical harangues about the supposedly endemic female vice of vanity of dress. This was a time-honored, well-publicized topos of Christian antifeminist literature, extending in a direct line all the way back to Tertullian (ca. 160–ca. 225).[117] Little wonder then that, so possessed by this vice, women would indulge in it even in attiring their children. Bernardino does not explicitly state this logical conclusion, but hints in this direction in his Latin treatise *De christiana modestia*, "On Christian Modesty." Inveighing (yet again) against males who wear flamboyant, revealing clothes, the preacher suddenly turns to address the women of their household—"O you mothers and sisters and maids and sisters-in-law"—and scolds them for tolerating such clothing. These fashions, he declares, are "signs and tokens of your own great senselessness, foolishness, or, indeed, shamelessness."[118] That is to say, the same foolish, sinful dress that women indulge in, they willingly allow, and perhaps even encourage, in their males. In so doing, they create the circumstances wherein men turn to or are made to turn to sodomy.

It likewise comes as no surprise that in his remarks on the parental causes of sodomy Bernardino focuses more attention on the mother, rather than the father. As Herlihy and Klapisch-Zuber point out in their study of the early-fifteenth-century Tuscan population, despite what one reads in contemporary father-centered humanist treatises on child pedagogy, it was the mother who had the larger role in the rearing of the children, in both physical nurturing and moral-affective formation.[119] This was true even in those households where a father was young, healthy, and present. However, in Bernardino's age, the presence of such a father or any father in the home could not be taken for granted, especially in well-to-do mercantile or patrician families: Paternal absenteeism was indeed a conspicuous social feature of fifteenth-century Tuscan society. This was due, in the first place, to the constant demands of overseas or out-of-town employment. Mortality was another factor: Death took many husbands from their young wives, leaving Quattrocento Tuscany with a considerable population of fatherless children. Summarizing the results of his and Klapisch-Zuber's analysis of the *catasto* records, Herlihy describes the typical demographic situation as follows:

> At Florence in 1427, the average age of first marriage for girls was 17 years, and they married grooms some 13 years older than themselves. In spite of the risks of child-bearing, the young brides had a good chance of surviving their much older husbands. . . . Many young widows would not remarry. . . . [A]bout 25 per cent of women in their 40's were living as widows, and they constituted an absolute majority of the female population from about the middle 50's.[120]

Fathers, therefore, were frequently a remote or short-lived reality for many Tuscan boys, who, in generational terms, overlapped with their own very young (often adolescent) mothers. Thus, even their proximity in age brought mothers and sons into a more intimate—perhaps inappropriately intimate—relationship.[121] This is not simply late-twentieth-century conjecture: The phenomenon was sufficiently widespread to provoke public concern even at the time. According to Herlihy and Klapisch-Zuber, there is evidence of a widespread anxiety in late medieval–early Renaissance Tuscany about what was perceived as a disturbing feminization of society, with potentially dangerous results for young masculine identity. The two authors quote a number of contemporary voices to this effect, Bernardino among them, although they end by admitting that the "complexity of Tuscan values and behavior in the fourteenth and fifteenth centuries prevents us from making too simplistic a judgment" on the question: "Did the world of the Tuscan towns really belong to the women, as Boccaccio claims?"[122] Whatever the domestic reality was, the concern was voiced. The research of Richard Trexler confirms this contemporary perception of an emasculation of males by "too much exposure to their mothers"—and, he adds, too much solicitation by adult sodomites. Trexler remarks that "there can be little doubt" that the increased popularity and importance of adolescent male confraternities in the period was "meant in part to be an answer to this threat."[123] Conclusions such as these must be tentative; yet, as we saw in chapter 1, Bernardino's own experience confirms the stereotype of Tuscan childhood we have just described: the friar's earliest and most formative years, like those of many of his contemporaries (if the statistics are to be believed), were utterly dominated by female presence.[124] Was this presence, we wonder, an emasculating one for Bernardino? And are we hearing echoes of it, perhaps only unconscious on his part, in his sermonizing on child pedagogy and maternal behavior?

5. Adolescent Sexuality and Sodomy

Bernardino devotes much of his time to sodomitic activity involving adolescents and preadolescents, hoping to nip this "abominable vice" in the bud by giving parents what amounts to a complete lesson on its early phenomenology. Centuries before Freud, Bernardino understood that sexuality with its imperious drives was awakened in a person very early in life—indeed, in childhood. Furthermore, along with all of Christianity until only recently, the friar was a thorough Augustinian in his conviction of the youthful propensity to grave sin, especially in the realm of sexuality. Once children reach the age of reason, Bernardino reminds mothers and fathers, they are capable of committing mortal sin and thus risking eternal damnation (E.40–41).[125]

Sodomy is no exception to this general rule. For many youth, the friar declares, perdition through the crimes of sodomy and other forms of sexuality came very early in life: "I've heard it from a most worthy man, who told me that he believed that more [boys] are lost [to sin and corruption] between the years of eight and fifteen than at any other period of life."[126] The friar never gives the identity of this "most worthy man," but elsewhere remarks,

> When your little children die at seven or ten years or younger, you don't have to grieve them; in fact, you can celebrate, because they have gone to increase the number of the blessed souls in eternal life and are now before God praying for you. When your young sons die at ten years or older, then indeed cry for them, because God had given you them as males and the Devil made them females through the accursed vice of sodomy.[127]

And still elsewhere:

> They aren't even dry behind the ears and they're already contaminated and sodomites! Just look at them, fathers and mothers, it's astounding: At such a tender age and they're already contaminated by sodomy![128]

Not all such contamination, of course, came voluntarily to these young people. As Bernardino laments and as court records attest, sodomitic rape of youth was no rare occurrence in Quattrocento Italy.[129] Yet for some, the experience of sodomy was not a one-time episode, but developed, voluntarily or involuntarily, into a long-term relationship. Bernardino warns that, once initiated, even voluntary sodomitic relationships could be extremely difficult to break, and, as an *exemplum* of this, recounts the "true story" of *uno garzonetto* (a young lad) of Verona who in 1423 was knifed to death by his soldier-lover. The murder occurred in a fit of insane rage because the soldier's adolescent partner had decided to terminate the relationship, persuaded to do so by Bernardino's own preaching. The boy, says the preacher, was a "real martyr for Christ," whereas the soldier, after a long chase, was captured, tortured, and drawn and quartered, "and a piece of his body was hung at every gate of the city" (E.27).

Bernardino was well aware that in adolescence—for him, between the ages of fourteen and twenty-five—lust had the greatest power over the human body and soul: "It consumes or blinds the light of the intellect and of reason" as no other vice does (E.44). Yet the promptings of the sexual drive can make themselves felt even earlier in life. To shake parents from their illusions about youthful behavior—"But they're only kids, you say" (E.44)—he reports the following string of startling and "true" cases: "Hostiensis and other doctors tell of a nine-year-old boy who impregnated his babysitter. In Venice a seven-year-old girl became pregnant, and not being able to deliver, she dropped dead and died, and in her memory they had a tomb made that openly described the affair in writing. King Solomon, son of David, we read, already had children at the age of eleven."[130]

Whatever the age of the boy, that which the Devil does not accomplish through the promptings of lust, he accomplishes, the friar suggests, through the glitter of gold, that is, through the youth's pursuit of money:

> I've heard about those [boys] who paint themselves up and go around bragging about their sodomizers and make it into a profession for profit and incite others to do likewise. . . . [A]t night, after bedtime, when [your son is] asleep, take his money pouch and put it to your ear, wait and listen for what the coins inside will tell you; if there are any and you don't know where he got them, listen to the coins; they will scream: "Fire! Fire! Fire!"[131]

The temptation to this sin is so great and so omnipresent that "the young boys who do not allow themselves to be contaminated [by sodomy] ought to be canonized as saints."[132] If he had sons of his own, Bernardino declares, he would ship them out of Italy as soon as they reached the age of three and not let them return until they were forty years old, since this abominable vice is so pervasive throughout the country (R.1147). It is not without reason that all of Italy, the preacher informs his listeners with shame in his voice, is notorious throughout the world as a haven for sodomites (G.104–5, R.1148–49); this was a common European perception of the time, as we know from other sources as well.[133] And on the whole peninsula, among the worst offenders are the Florentines: "What devil-possessed people! What things have been reported to me by people worthy of trust! Sons of good fathers seized from their sides and taken from their homes so much so that Sodom and Gomorrah didn't do half of what is done in Florence with nothing to put a stop to it."[134] Yet Siena was in no better shape:

> As for me, I don't want to die in this city, if I can help it . . . because you are all entangled in this sin [of sodomy]. . . . I don't believe there's a single spot in the city that is not contaminated and corrupted. . . . *Oimmè,* what you

> have been reduced to, O city of Siena! In what darkness you are, that a small boy can't be sent out on the street without being seized and corrupted.[135]

The reputation of all of Tuscany is so bad that Genoa, Bernardino points out, even has an ordinance prohibiting Tuscans from serving as schoolmasters within the city (G.103, B.35).

In making such assertions about the prevalence of sodomy among his contemporaries, Bernardino was not guilty of his usual rhetorical excess; what the preacher claims in his sermons, we find corroborated in the court records of the period. These show that in fifteenth-century Italy, a surprisingly high percentage of males did not reach adulthood without having had some direct, personal exposure to homogenital activity, transient or long-term, active or passive. The best available statistics come from the city of Florence. Summarizing his analysis of the seventy-year activity of the city's special antisodomy magistracy, the Office of the Night (1432–1502), Michael Rocke reports:

> In this small city of around only 40,000 inhabitants, every year during roughly the last four decades of the fifteenth-century an average of some 400 people were implicated and 55 to 60 condemned for homosexual relations. Throughout the entire period corresponding to the duration of the Office of the Night, it can be estimated that as many as 17,000 individuals or more were incriminated at least once for sodomy, with close to 3,000 convicted.[136]

Indeed, Rocke concludes, sodomy "was part of the whole fabric of Florentine society, attracting males of all ages, matrimonial status, and social rank."[137] The picture is the same in Venice, as Ruggiero reports in his study of sexual activity in that city based on court records of the late medieval–early Renaissance period: "At the lower levels of society at least, homogenital encounters were a fairly regular part of late boyhood and adolescence, facilitated by the crowded conditions of life and the sharing of beds."[138]

In view of these statistics and the preacher's near obsession with the "unmentionable vice," one cannot help but wonder whether Bernardino had not had some "sodomitic" experiences of his own in youth. If so, these may not necessarily have been voluntary. We recall his angry statement about the daily peril to the young from sodomites in his hometown, Siena: "a little boy can't be sent into the streets without being taken by force and corrupted" (R.1155). Was Bernardino speaking from direct personal experience? Had he been the victim of sodomitic assault? Our sources speak of no such assault, although this could indeed have befallen Bernardino, without a trace being left on the historical record—except, perhaps, in the indirect form of his own vociferous campaign against sodomites.

Yet our sources do speak of attempted conquests of the young Bernardino by adult sodomites. The friar's boyhood companion Leonardo Benvoglienti tells us that the teenage Bernardino, a handsome lad and of exceedingly pleasing, refined personality ("cum formosus esset et natura delicatus valde"), was approached on two occasions by older men making sodomitic propositions. On the first occasion Benvoglienti recounts, Bernardino's would-be seducer was "a certain citizen, not of the lower classes," and we are told the boy responded with a resounding punch on the man's chin, creating an echo that "filled nearly the entire square."[139] In Benvoglienti's second episode, since the admirer in question had been insistent in his importunities, Bernardino put into action a more studied response:

> It also happened at that time [of adolescence], that after another malicious and evil man—not a citizen [of Siena] however—had many times expressed with impure words and signs a filthy and unspeakable desire toward Bernardino, Bernardino, that mirror of purity, asked some of his close friends and companions—like him, young men of good reputation—to help him be freed of this annoyance. And having consulted with them, he told each of them to arm themselves with stones. Once they had done so, they sought the evil man. Finding him near the gate of the Magnificent Lord Priors of the city, Bernardino said: "We mustn't cause a scene here near the town hall; let's draw him away from the square and then we'll chase after him with the stones." Immediately thereafter, that man, blinded by evil lust, gazing intently at Bernardino, held out to him a handful of florins, and made signs as if to say: "All of these are yours if you say yes to me." The clever lad nodded to him, signaling him to leave the square. As soon as they had left the square and were on the road of Porta Salaria, Bernardino shouted out to that man: "O wicked, immoral man, you deserve to be burned at the stake! Everyone, get him! Get him! Get him!" And, shouting aloud, he began to pelt the man with stones. His friends as well responded in unison with shouts and stones and filled the air with their noise. The wicked man fled.[140]

Another contemporary Franciscan preaching confrere of Bernardino's, the Blessed Michele Carcano (†1485), also thought this episode significant enough to include in one of his panegyrics on Bernardino, in a sermon delivered in L'Aquila on the occasion of the solemn "translation" of the body of the by then canonized preacher to its new home in the splendid Renaissance church built in his honor. Carcano confirms the fact that the boy Bernardino was "refined indeed and noble" (*quippe iuvenis delicatus et nobilis*) and was "a most handsome youth" (*pulcherrrimus iuvenis*), while specifying that Bernardino's propositioner was "a certain Florentine legate [*legatum*]."[141] Maffeo Vegio likewise makes reference to the episode: speaking of the head-turning handsomeness and charm of the boy Bernardino—"delicatam adolescentis naturam . . . elegantiam formae et pulchritudinem"—Vegio tells us that they were of such a quality as to draw the attention of "shameless men" ("nec caruit insidiis impudicorum aliquorum hominum").[142]

Neither Benvoglienti nor Carcano makes any further comment about these episodes beyond the illustrations they give of Bernardino's inviolate chastity and abhorrence of evil.[143] Bernardino never mentions these episodes in his sermons, but in view of the notoriety of the friar's later antisodomy campaigns, his biographers deemed them significant enough to be among the few specific details included about Bernardino's boyhood when compiling their *vitae* decades later. These episodes obviously lingered in their memories, as they did in Bernardino's, fueling the fury of his antisodomy campaign.

6. Bernardino and Vincenzo, a Particular Friendship

Another explanation in psychological terms for the vehemence of Bernardino's campaign against this "worst sin" is that it represented, not anger over the memory of an assault, as we have just suggested, but rather conflict over his own repressed homoerotic feelings. At least one scholar who has studied the life and utterances of the friar has come to the conclusion that behind the cloak of zealous moral reformer was a self-hating, repressed "homosexual."[144] Though unprovable, the thesis is nonetheless suggestive and merits serious consideration. Certainly, given his obsession with the topic of sodomy, Bernardino has called down on his own head such speculation.

Whether we are conscious of it or not, our sexuality pervades much of who we are and what we do in our lives. This is even more the case when our sexuality is in a state of conflict within ourselves and with society at large. Our unresolved sexual conflicts have a deep influence on the manner in which we experience, interpret, and respond to the world in all spheres of life, including the spiritual and the religious. In his study of Renaissance artist Michelangelo, psychiatrist Robert Liebert goes so far as to claim that "All behavior, whether it is personally adaptive and socially fulfilling or personally and socially maladaptive, represents the expression of intrapsychic conflict."[145] And what greater realm of conflict in the human heart than that of emotional intimacy and sexuality?

If Bernardino were erotically attracted to other males and were in conflict over this—as inevitably he would have been—then our understanding of the motivation behind his campaign against sodomy must necessarily change. To the list of motivating factors explicitly acknowledged by the friar—Scripture, theology, science—we must add two others, two psychological forces unknown to him. These are called, in the language of psychoanalysis, "projection" and "reaction formation." As Greenberg explains in his discussion of the sudden rise in hostility toward same-sex behavior in the High Middle Ages and the Gregorian reform:

> When a conflict . . . cannot be eliminated or recognized, it does not disappear but is driven underground and lives in the unconscious. Psychological defense mechanisms develop to prevent knowledge of the conflict from reaching the level of awareness. Projecting one's own unacceptable desires onto someone else is one such mechanism; reaction formation, in which one reassures oneself against the suspicion of having forbidden desire by an exaggerated repudiation and hostility, is another. Knowledge that someone else has the tabooed desire and acts on it places the repression from consciousness of one's own desire in jeopardy, and thus evokes the punitive reaction. It is fueled by the energy of the repressed impulse.[146]

Was Bernardino's own fiery public campaign against sodomy a reflection of the fiery war of repression within his own psyche? Given the current state of evidence surrounding the life of the friar, we cannot know, though the suspicion remains a thoroughly reasonable one. What we do know is that the deepest, most intimate emotional attachment of Bernardino's adult life was, in fact, to another male, friar Vincenzo of Siena, his constant companion for over twenty-two years. Vincenzo has the distinction of being the only figure from Bernardino's personal life for whom the preacher publicly divulges his feelings—apart from very fleeting references to Zia Bartolommea and a couple of his disciples—in all of the thousands of pages of sermons and treatises.

Vincenzo's death preceded Bernardino's by two years, an event that was, for the preacher, "a sword of pain through my heart," as he confesses in his "Pia deploratio," a poignant, grieving tribute to his beloved friend inserted in his commentary on the Beatitude, "Blessed are those who mourn" (OOQ.VI.385–90). This highly emotional account of a long and intimate bonding—again, not unusual in Bernardino's clerical "world without women"[147]—employs the kind of language that later ages or other cultures would permit only between members of the opposite sex. What David exclaimed of Jonathan (2 Samuel 1:26), Bernardino would have said of Vincent, "your love to me was wonderful, passing the love of women":

> How is it that you were torn from me, my Vincent? How is it that you were seized from my hands, O man of one mind with me, man according to my heart? We have loved each other in life, how is it that we have been separated in death? . . .
>
> My soul had adhered to him, and love had made one of our two. Since, therefore, we were one heart and one soul, the sword which pierced his soul likewise pierced mine, and rending it placed one half in heaven, leaving the other half in the mud. I, I am this miserable one half lying in the mire, cut off from my better half, and it is said to me: "Do you weep?" . . .
>
> I shudder at death, both at my own and at that of my dear ones; and Vincent was dear to me, wholly so. Or was he not dear to me, he who was my son by profession, my father by solicitude, my companion in travelling, my teacher by office of master, my mother by love, having an equal share in my soul, intimate with me by affection. . . .
>
> In fine I weep, my Vincent, though not over you, yet on your account. Hence I am affected entirely, gravely, because I love exceedingly.[148]

In themselves, this friendship and this document do not prove anything about Bernardino's sexual orientation. Let us note that Bernardino's lamentation relies heavily on at times verbatim borrowings from a similar elegy written by Bernard of Clairvaux at the death of a family member, his brother. Bernard, in turn, is likely to have been inspired by Augustine, who, in *Confessions* 4.4, mourns with the vocabulary of a lover the death of his friend Nebredius. The tradition of passionate, yet non-erotic, male friendship goes back even farther than Augustine, of course; "in Greek and Roman military societies . . . male relationships were imagined to involve a distillation of the best elements of male character into a lofty mutual love."[149] In the Christian world, a tradition of idealized, male, "spiritual"—though nonetheless passionate—friendship also flourished. This was especially true in the homosocial world of monastic and male religious life in general, in which, as we heard said with respect to Bernardino's early moral training, women were avoided like "deadly serpents." The medieval Christian ideal of "spiritual" male friendship perhaps finds its most celebratory expression in the writings of Saint Aelred of Rievaulx, who pointed to the relationship—described by him as a "heavenly marriage"—of Jesus Christ and John his "beloved disciple" as a model for intimate monastic friendships.[150]

We must keep in mind that the expressions of affection and grief in Bernardino's "Pia deploratio" spring from a culture that possessed different rules for putting emotion into words and had not sexualized all expressions of male-to-male affection, as Thomas Stehling's anthology of "medieval poems of male love and friendship" illustrates.[151] However, just as there are no grounds for supposing a homoerotic bonding when reading such deeply charged displays of affection as Bernardino's lamentation for his lost Vincenzo, there are likewise no grounds for excluding it. Mirroring the conclusions of Stehling, Greenberg's remarks about medieval expressions of friendship are here relevant:

> It bears emphasizing that powerful feelings of love and intimacy do not necessarily imply awareness of sexual interest or attraction. . . . Nevertheless, even if strong feelings of love and intimacy are sometimes free from any sexual element, often they are not. Just as it would be wrong to read a sexual meaning into every expression of love, it would be a mistake to dismiss the possibility of sexual interest in the entire body of homophile poetry and letters of passionate friendship and love written by eleventh- and twelfth-century monks and priests.[152]

Indeed, as John Boswell points out with some degree of irony, "the single source of writing about romantic love during the first millennium of the Christian tradition is monastic literature. Monks fell in love with each other—often."[153] Certainly, monks, followed by the friars, did not cease to fall in love with each other after the first millennium, any more than the rest of the literate population, who expressed that love in prose and verse much like Bernardino's "Pia deploratio." As Boswell has shown in his *Same-Sex Unions in Premodern Europe,* same-sex lovers even ritualized the public declaration of their love in liturgical ceremonies bearing an uncanny resemblance to the heterosexual marriage rite, which cannot all be explained away as "mere" nonromantic, non-erotic friendship rituals (*pace* Shaw, Johansson, Percy, et al.).[154] Again, some of this prose and verse, seemingly homoerotic to us in the late twentieth century, did not spring from homoerotic desire and can be explained in terms of social context and rhetorical conventions. However, the law of averages forces us to admit that not all of this considerable body of literature can be read in this "heteronormative" fashion. Despite its spiritualized form and vocabulary, Bernardino's "Pia deploratio" may be a case in point. As Allen Frantzen reminds us, one is often obliged to "read between the lines" in order to find the vestiges of homosexual identity, sentiment, and culture in history, vestiges that until very recently have been nearly universally interpreted according to the reigning heteronormative biases of conventional scholarship.[155] Our expanded consciousness about the reality of homosexuality no longer allows such an automatic reading of history, including Bernardino's relationship with Vincenzo.

7. Bernardino's Portrait of the Adult Sodomite

After this digressionary peek into the mysteries of Bernardino's psychosexual private life, we return to his antisodomy sermons to resume our exposition and analysis of their contents.

Knowing that there were parents who might want to excuse juvenile same-sex activity with a "boys will be boys" attitude (E.42), the preacher is at pains to convince them to take seriously any signs of sodomitic activity or tendencies in their adolescents: "And especially take note if he starts to disobey you, know that he has become effeminate; you'll be sorry later if you neglect the situation now."[156] If these early propensities and indications are not extinguished, the boy is destined to become a full-fledged, incorrigible sodomite. With the passing of the years and as with all forms of vice, sodomitic lust becomes more entrenched in his heart: "An old habit is never corrected because it is never abandoned" (D.117). If he passed his thirty-third year without amending his ways, the sodomite could give up hope of any recovery and eternal salvation. He has mostly likely gone beyond the point of no return:

> Why? Because the Devil has by then put a whole legion of demons [into these sinners] and makes them so hardened that they lack any desire to correct themselves. . . .
>
> The Devil has so blinded [the sodomite], that if he passes his thirty-third birthday [still in this sin], it is almost impossible for him to save himself. It's still possible but it will be very difficult to rid himself of it. . . . [I]t is almost impossible.
>
> Go and read the *Decretum*, Distinction 7, chapter *Sicut*, and you will find [that it says] that anyone who passes his thirty-third year still entangled in that sin mustn't hope to be acceptable to God.[157]

The reason Bernardino specifies thirty-three as the crossing of the Rubicon for the sodomite most likely has little to do with empirical evidence. That number appears to have been chosen merely because it represents the mortal lifespan of Jesus Christ.[158] However, Rocke conjectures that "Bernardino's insistence on the critical age of thirty-two or thirty-three might also have been related to a basic event in the life course of local men, who typically married at around this age."[159] Furthermore, although Bernardino does not mention the fact in his sermons, his audiences most likely would have understood that the passage from youthful sodomy to its adult version usually entailed the passage from a passive to an active role, this role-switching in effect representing the crossing over from "effeminate" adolescence into masculine adulthood. That this was the experience of Bernardino's contemporaries is again shown by the court evidence examined by Rocke and Ruggiero, sodomy cases being then adjudicated according to age and the passive/active factor.[160]

To prevent this passage from occurring, and indeed to exterminate the sin even after it has occurred, Bernardino floods the imagination of his audience with visions of the supposedly frightful life of the adult sodomite. That life, says the preacher, is one of constant frenzy, obsession, slavery, and insanity, for sodomy destroys all faculties and all good ordering of the mind (OOQ.III.269, R.1143, D.272). To begin with, what Bernardino says of the lustful in general applies most especially to sodomites:

> What is the desire [of the lustful man]? To engage in lust. What does he need? Those things with which he can continue to live out his lust: to be healthy, young, rich, and powerful. He loves all of these things so much because they are the means for fulfilling his desire. It seems a great evil to him to be sick, or become poor, or, even more, to grow old—if you were to tell him that he's getting grey hair, he would spit in your face.[161]

The sodomite's unceasing thought is that of satisfying his appetite, respecting neither time nor place nor person. Even at Sunday Mass he is in pursuit of his prey (R.1161), whom he allures with promises of sweets and other rewards.[162] Of this sodomitic erotomania, the friar warns especially the women in his audience:

> . . . these types are never satisfied. Oh, woman, take note, if he's trapped in this vice, you'll never be able to satisfy him! He always complains about everything you do, always. When he comes home, he comes in turmoil, with a head full of frenzy, and nothing does he care for the judgment of God or

> honor in this world. He's always cranky and agitated, he's afraid—he's afraid of falling out of favor with his wicked little boy. . . . He obeys the boy like a servant and does everything he can to grant his wishes.[163]

The lust never exhausts itself, not even with age; the insanity lasts one's entire lifetime: "O crazy old men, crazier in old age than you were in youth!" (B.50). And how does such a life end? In desperation and perdition. Unrepentant sodomites, says the friar, are the "sons of diffidence" of whom Paul speaks in Ephesians 5:6 and on whom the wrath of God will descend (OOQ.III.283). The warning Bernardino gave to sodomites approaching their thirty-third year applies all the more to those in advanced old age: although "as long as there's life, there's hope," in reality, the souls of such criminals have little chance of being saved. "This crime, once it has become habit, seizes the unfortunate soul and holds and controls it with such violence, and leads it to desperation so that its eternal life and salvation are doubtful."[164] If they die unrepentant, their destiny is hell, and there "all sodomites will be such burning charcoals that the smoke will reach all the way to the blessed in heaven, who will rejoice over it."[165]

Sodomy, Sin of the "Elites"

Among those burning souls looked down upon by the rejoicing blessed in heaven will be many personages from the upper echelons of society, for, according to a popular conception amply expressed in contemporary literature, sodomy was a vice especially associated with the aristocracy, the clergy, and the world of the university and lower schools.[166] In reality, as the court records examined by Rocke and Ruggiero show, sodomy was a feature of all ranks and classes of society, with neither nobility nor clergy nor teachers (nor artists) accounting for anything but average percentages of the total caseload.[167] Bernardino, however, was unaware of these statistics, for his sermons simply reinforce the traditional stereotype of sodomy as, above all, the vice of the social elites. One example is Bernardino's allegorical interpretation of Revelation 8:7, "When the first [angel] blew his trumpet, there came hail and fire mixed with blood, which was hurled down to the earth. A third of the land was burned up, along with a third of the trees and all green grass." The incinerated "third" of trees supposedly represents those sodomites who reach old age never having repented of their sin; counted among them, the friar specifies, are persons "learned in worldly knowledge, teachers or men of higher rank, be it secular or spiritual." He then goes on to complain in the same paragraph, "[T]his sin is excused away by saying, after all, all the respectable men of society are of this art."[168] Returning to the same scriptural verse a year later, the friar reiterates: "A third part of the trees burned—that is, doctors, prelates, learned men [*dottori, prelati, savi uomini*], trees that were meant to produce fruit but instead produce only smoke" (G.109).

In view of the actual forensic statistics, which paint a more "egalitarian" picture, we wonder how the normally sharp-eyed Bernardino could make such an assertion about the sociology of sodomy. Ignoring empirical observation in favor of literary authority, our preacher may be remembering his study of the *Divine Comedy.* In his pilgrimage through hell, Dante the Florentine encounters on the burning, smoking plain of the sodomites his own teacher, Brunetto Latini, and many other "respectable men of society": "In brief, let me tell you, all here were clerics and respected men of letters of great fame."[169] In the next canto, the pilgrim meets another elite group, the warrior-sodomites, among them Jacopo Rusticucci, who blamed his shrewish wife for driving him to this sin. Whether or not Dante was his source, Bernardino was not the only ecclesiastical teacher to spread this misconception about the socioeconomic profile of sodomy. The list of sodomites given by Antonino of Florence in his *Summa theologica* includes only figures of the highest rank: Jove the supreme god, Virgil the supreme poet, and two supreme commanders of ancient Rome, Julius Caesar and Octavian.[170]

As we see by his inclusion of the category of "prelates" in the aforementioned lists of "incinerated" sodomites, Bernardino does not hesitate to publicize the fact that, yes, even members of his own spiritual elite, the clergy, are guilty of this crime. In his Latin treatise against sodomy, the friar again refers openly and casually to this fact when he states that "if the preacher himself is infected with this sin, the sodomite [listening to his sermon] will be less disposed to accept reproach" (OOQ.III.280). Another, though more oblique, example is the second of the two successive sermons against the "unmentionable vice" preached to the Paduans in 1423, "De amore condemnante." That morning the Gospel reading from Matthew included the verse "Do and observe all things whatsoever [the Scribes and Pharisees] tell you, but do not follow their example" (Matthew 23:3), and Bernardino begins: "In this gospel Christ is talking about none other than priests and religious; and although the material of this gospel reading is most outstanding, regarding the behavior of priests of this age, it is better to keep silent rather than speak."[171] So, "instead," the preacher goes on to deliver his previously planned sermon on sodomy (with no further reference to the clergy), to conclude his treatment of the topic begun on the day before. Yet knowing that "the behavior of priests and religious of this age" frequently included sodomy, could Bernardino possibly have been unaware of the statement he was implicitly making and of the irony of his dismissive opening remark?[172]

8. The Cure: Terror, Shame, and Destruction

Bernardino makes use of the chilling apocalyptic image of blood, hail, and fire incinerating the "sodomitic third" of the earth's population not simply to deliver a statistical prediction about demographic devastation in the future. His concern was more immediate: to terrorize sodomites out of their sinful behavior, right then and there. In attempting to eradicate "so abominable a vice," the friar devotes his energy above all to this "pastoral" technique of terror, rather than to a cold, logical exposition of Scripture, ecclesiastical tradition, or natural law teleology. In Bernardino's eyes, the most efficacious remedy for the evil of sodomy is a hard-hitting emotional appeal to fear, horror, disgust, shame, and guilt. The remedy is, furthermore, applied with a vigor, drama, and wrath equaling that of any "fire and brimstone" popular preacher before or after him.

Bernardino's antisodomy preaching is an attack on the senses, both morally and literally: in calculated fashion he fills the eyes, ears, and noses of his listeners with constant, threatening evocations of fire, smoke, and sulphur, ready to be unleashed by a wrathful, vengeful God. Of all the sense organs, Bernardino makes a particular appeal to the nose, opening *De horrendo peccato contra naturam* with the disdainful confession that "[s]tench and horror, indeed a horrible stench fills my soul at the mere thought [of this sin]" (OOQ.III.267). The lying, seductive words of the sodomite, Bernardino elsewhere declares, "stink" like sulphur; in fact, "the whole body of the sodomite is nothing but stench."[173] Therefore, Bernardino instructs his listeners to spit in disgust when they encounter any sodomite: "Spit hard! Maybe the water of your spit will put out their fire. Everybody spit hard, like this!" Apparently the whole audience did as he bid them, for the scribe reports that "it sounded like thunder."[174] Another salubrious, olfactory tactic of shame and guilt, advises the friar, is to shout to the sodomites when in their company, " 'Oh boy, do you stink!' If they ask you, 'Oh, really, of what?,' tell them: 'Of sulphur.' "[175] So repulsive is sodomy to sight, smell, and moral sensibility that even the Devil himself, being of a most "refined" and "natural" temperament, flees in horror from this hideous "unnatural" vice.[176]

But it is, above all, fire that represents the dominant imagery of Bernardino's antisodomy sermons, as it does in this account of a "real life" experience of the friar's recounted to the Sienese in 1427:

> I don't know if any man or any woman heard those screams a few nights ago. The screams were incredibly loud, but sometimes we're so distracted with our own affairs that we don't hear certain things. Let me tell you what happened to me.
>
> A few nights ago, I woke up to recite Matins and thought I heard someone screaming: "To the fire, to the fire, to the fire!" I said to myself: "Something must be burning." And putting my hands to my ears like this [Bernardino must have cupped his ears at this point] to see if I couldn't hear more screams, I heard coming from another neighborhood: "To the fire, to the fire, to the fire!" I stood there by myself, trying to figure out what was going on, but couldn't see anything. I then heard another confused, dull scream as if it were coming from a cave: "To the fff . . . , to the fi . . . , to the fire!" [the preacher is here imitating the only partially audible words of the screams]. "O dear Lord, whatever does this mean?" And in that state of mind, I heard yet another scream, and this time it seemed as if it were coming from within the shops: "To the fire, to the fi . . . , to the fff . . . !" I was becoming really scared at this point, but I stayed there to listen. I heard screams coming from the whole city, even from people's beds themselves: "To the fi . . . , to the fire, to the ffff . . . !" The same thing seemed to be coming from the stables: "To the fire, to the fire, to the fire!" From every corner came the scream: "To the fire, to the fire, to the fire!" From every corner: "To the fi . . . , to the fi . . . , to the fire!" Standing there, I soon heard the whole city full of voices all screaming: "To the fi . . . to the fff . . . , to the fire!"[177]

Bernardino says nothing further about this strange but supposedly true nocturnal experience; no one in the audience seems to have jumped up, in answer to the preacher's question, to corroborate the report—at least not according to what our diligent scribe Benedetto has recorded. Whether they believed it literally true or not, Bernardino's audience most likely understood the story's moral intent. The incessant summons "to the fire" was a threatening reminder, not only of the raging, dangerous lust of the sodomites, but also of their eventual punishment as well, both temporal and eternal: Being burned alive at the stake was a widespread form of punishment provided by medieval law for convicted sodomites, while, of course, the fires of hell represented the eternal destiny of such unrepentant criminals.[178]

Switching imagery, elsewhere Bernardino depicts sodomy as a cancerous limb that must be excised from the body politic; this he tells "princes and other rulers" in the Latin treatise addressed to them, *De regimine principium et quorumcumque regentium*, which immediately follows *De horrendo peccato contra naturam*.[179] Those responsible for the public good must also ostracize from the community all men who refuse to work and to take wives, for these, as the friar already told us, are sure signs that they are sodomites (B.46–47). Exhorting legislators and citizens to respect justice by applying the law to its fullest severity, Bernardino approvingly recalls the example of Genoa:

> O Genoa, may God preserve you always! If Siena were to do what they do there, everyone would be burned at the stake, because everyone, young and old, is entangled [in this sin]. If this seems cruel to you, then at least try it in part as an example to the rest, because one can't leave Tuscany without having it thrown up to you twelve times a day that here justice is not being done as far as this vice is concerned. Whoever is responsible for this will have to render account one day. Remember [the proverb]: "the pitying doctor makes the wound fester."[180]

Likewise the friar praises Venice for its unflinching commitment to "justice" in punishing and torturing sodomites with the three elements most appropriate to their crime: pitch, sulphur, and fire.[181] Bernardino even gives a detailed account (allegorized in good medieval fashion) of one death by fire that he had witnessed personally in the "Serenissima" Republic:

> I saw three things happening together. I saw [the sodomite] placed at the stake, and tied all the way up. [I saw] a keg of pitch, brushwood, and fire, and an executioner who set him on fire, and a lot of people, all around, watching. The sodomite felt the smoke and the fire, and he burned to death; the executioner felt only the smoke, and whoever was standing around watching saw nothing but smoke and fire. What this stands for is that: in hell the sodomites will burn with smoke and fire [while] their torturers down there will get the smoke. . . . Those who stand watching [represent] the blessed spirits in paradise who see the punishment of the sodomites and rejoice over it because they see the justice of God shining forth from it.[182]

In his sermon notes, known as the *Itinerarium anni*, Bernardino makes a point of recording the example of Cardinal Gabriel Condulmier (the future

Pope Eugene IV), who, as papal legate in Bologna, had three sodomites burned at the stake, and ordered as well that their house be destroyed, never to be rebuilt *in aeternum* (OOQ.VIII.298; see also F.229). To the Sienese in 1427, Bernardino relates how another city, Paris, was cleansed of its sodomites by one anonymous but enterprising individual:

> There was once a king in Paris—I don't know if it was Saint Louis—and since this vice was rampant [in that town], a man approached him and said: "If you want, I will get rid of this vice in such a way that in the end there won't be any of it left. If you give me permission [to do as I see fit], I will clean up this whole city of yours." The king said: "What are you going to do, burn the whole place down?" The other guy said no, he had a better way. Asked what this better way was, he answered: "The first thing I want from you is full authority to do things my way; the matter will be taken care of with method and mercy." Receiving the man's word that he would do as he promised, the king gave him permission and said: "Go and do what needs to be done." The guy then asked for a certain number of armed men to be under his command, men who would do exactly as he ordered. The king had them given to him.
>
> Granted this permission, the guy went around the whole city, and at every intersection had a bonfire of brooms built. When the city was filled with these bonfires, he then combed the city, and whenever he received notice of some public sodomite, he had him immediately seized and thrown into the nearest bonfire at hand and had him burned immediately. Having burned that one, he resumed his tour of the city, and, when he got word of another, he immediately had him thrown into the bonfire.
>
> And so on in this way for several days, so that the entire city was purified in very little time, and from that day till now, that sin is not committed in that town.[183]

Undisturbed that such a "remedy" entailed rampant vigilante terrorism and the suspension of what today we call civil rights and due process of law—these legal protections did exist in that age, albeit in different forms—Bernardino recommends it in all sincerity to his audience. With equal sincerity and equanimity does he also claim the entire city of Paris to be free of sodomy! Undoubtedly the traveling salesmen in his audience could tell him otherwise.

To the Florentines the friar tells another version of the story, this time extending his death-by-fire list to include all accomplices as well: Bernardino wants consigned to the bonfire "everyone who is to blame for this sin, fathers, mothers, and friends."[184] As still another version of the *exemplum* illustrates, the sword can prove as effective as fire:

> There was a king who had a great hatred for this vice and wanted to rid his country of it, but not seeing how he could do this, he was all depressed. A valorous citizen who hated this sin as well told him to give him free rein and he would do the job. So it was granted and the man armed himself fully with a brigade of soldiers. Covering the territory, he encountered one of [these sodomites] whom he knew well and said to his men: "Give it to him good." "Now to this one." "Now to this next one." So in this way he had them all cut to pieces, without any other formalities.[185]

Although not quite in the same terms as in the *exempla* just recounted, Bernardino did succeed in having his wish for more severe antisodomy legislation granted in several of the towns he visited, as we shall see in the next section.

In addition to Bernardino's incessant preaching and campaigning for new legislation, another grand public gesture of antisodomy consciousness-raising that he staged was the public burning of the *Hermaphroditus*, a book that he considered a most dangerous fomenter of sodomy. The *Hermaphroditus* was a notorious collection of classically elegant but obscene Latin poetry—dedicated to Cosimo de' Medici—containing explicit (though mostly satiric) references to sodomy and sodomites; its author, Antonio Beccadelli ("Il Panormita"), composed the work in Siena in the very same years (mid-1420s) when Bernardino was conducting his public missions there and in other Tuscan cities. Bernardino never mentions the volume or its author in any of his sermons—it is Lorenzo Valla who tells us of the public burnings.[186] However, Beccadelli's work is surely among those Bernardino has in mind when in *De horrendo peccato contra naturam* he generically condemns "those books written in our days which encourage this crime [of sodomy] by inspiring hatred for holy matrimony."[187]

Another such work was undoubtedly Boccaccio's curious antifeminist diatribe, the *Corbaccio*. Unlike Beccadelli's *Hermaphroditus*, the *Corbaccio* is explicitly condemned by Bernardino in more than one sermon, along with Ovid's *Art of Love*. The preacher claims that the *Corbaccio* has been responsible for turning many men into sodomites, although he never explains precisely how the book wrought such an effect. (It was, presumably, by turning men away from women and matrimony by the extremely dismal portrait of the two contained therein.) In one of the unpublished Perugian sermons of 1425, Bernardino encourages the women of his audience to round up materials for the next bonfire of vanities, telling them: "O ladies, have you seen the *Corbaccio*, the *Book of a Hundred Tales* [i.e., *The Decameron*] and those vanities of Petrarch? Know that because of that book, the *Corbaccio,* millions of men have become sodomites. Likewise Ovid's *De arte amandi* and *Criseida* [i.e., Boccaccio's *Teseida*?], etc. Bring them all to me so that we can sacrifice them up to God."[188] In his Florence 1425 sermon on studies, he likewise warns his audience to "keep away from the study of immoral books like the *Corbaccio* and other books written by messer Giovanni Boccaccio, who, with all due respect, wrote many of them. It would have been better had he kept quiet; he was a man of worth, if only he hadn't done or written those stupidities; perhaps in his old age he repented of them."[189] Bernardino does not mention sodomy on that occasion, but, as always, it could not have been far from his mind.

9. The Response of the Towns

In the adulatory account of the friar's career included in his famous *Lives of Illustrious Men,* Florentine bookseller-biographer Vespasiano da Bisticci boasts of Bernardino's success in eliminating the "sin against nature" from one unnamed capital of sodomitic vice:

> There was a certain city of Italy in which every vice had multiplied and had risen sky-high, and especially the accursed and abominable and detestable sin of sodomy. The people were so entrenched in this blindness that the almighty God would have had to make sulphur and fire rain down again from the heavens, just as he did in Sodom and Gomorrah. Seeing this so great excess, Saint Bernardino began with his sermons to denounce and curse the perpetrators of such iniquity, and with the maledictions and terrible outcries in his sermons, he succeeded in extinguishing the vice entirely in that city and made the people come to hold that accursed and abominable sin in horror and detestation.

Moreover, Bernardino's success, according to Vespasiano, did not stop there: "and his words had such great power that he purged not only that town, but all of Italy from all the iniquity with which it was filled."[190] The bookseller-biographer does not reveal the name of the Italian city in question, but it is highly unlikely that what he boasts of in typical bombastic humanist style about Bernardino's success is anything but wishful thinking. From what we know of fifteenth-century Italy, Bernardino certainly did not rid the peninsula of "all the iniquity with which it was filled." Nonetheless, the eloquent and respected friar's ominous warnings about sodomy did not go unheeded, even if they never reached the same level of success as Vespasiano claims. Several towns in northern and central Italy—Bernardino's principal preaching territory—remobilized their legislative power in the course of the fifteenth century in an attempt to eradicate the "sin against nature" through the passing of stricter laws and harsher punishments, as called for by our preaching friar. Of these, the legislation of four in particular can be directly linked to Bernardino: Perugia, Siena, Todi, and Massa Marittima.

Perhaps the most impressive examples of Bernardino's influence on contemporary legislation are the sweeping penal reforms instituted in 1425 by Perugia, which came in the wake of the friar's preaching missions there and which we shall see again in greater detail in the next chapter with respect to the Jews. Promulgated on November 4, 1425, "in conformity to the teaching of the same venerable servant of Jesus Christ," Perugia's *Statuta Sancti Bernardini* outlawed a whole list of sinful activities "because of which the wrath of God justly descends upon the Christian people and earthquakes, plagues, famines, wars, schisms, and infinite scandals increase among the Christian people."[191] Sodomy, not surprisingly, was one of these vices. Indeed, the Bernardino-inspired Perugian provisions against sodomy are long and detailed, specifying fines and punishments for a wide spectrum of possible sinful scenarios and partner configurations.[192] The law, however, we might point out, never specifies which acts are to be considered "sodomy," thus perpetuating the state of ambiguity we have already underscored in the literature of the age. Be that as it may, for a first offense, the law exacts a fine of two hundred "pounds of *denarii*"; a second offense orders the offender to be burned at the stake "in such a way and so that he is completely killed." Most of the rest of the law concerns young boys and teenagers (*pueri* and *iuvenes*), either as unwilling victims of sodomitic advances or attacks or as willing participants. Here the penalty was either two hundred pounds of *denarii* or death at the stake for, respectively, attempted abduction or attempted rape and the consummated attack. Anyone seeking to coerce a boy or youth (even indirectly, as through a relative, a teacher, or a patron) with verbal or physical force or violence was subject to fines ranging from fifteen pounds to the death sentence, depending on the type of coercion used and the harm done (for example, fifty pounds for striking a person without drawing blood, one hundred for drawing blood).

As for consenting youth caught in the act of sodomy, their punishment was to be a prison sentence of three months if they were between the ages of twelve and fifteen, while those older were to pay a fine of fifty pounds. Furthermore, "since many are the devices of evil men who attempt to engage in lust against nature with which they seduce and draw boys and youths into committing the aforementioned sin of sodomy," the law strictly prohibits adult males from visiting schools "where grammar and the abacus are taught."[193] In Perugia, it seems, other locales much favored by sodomites for the perpetration of their crimes were the *pigliatoria*, presumably hut-like constructions used to trap pigeons. These and similar structures were henceforth banned from the city and its suburbs. Article 14 of the *Statuta* also abolishes, as encouragements to sodomy and causes of bankruptcy, the Perugian *societates tripudiantium*, sumptuously organized parties on the feast of St. Herculanus. In conclusion, after stipulating that cases might be brought to court and adjudicated according to any of the traditional judicial procedures (*per inquisitionem, accusationem vel denunciationem*) the law forbids any form of assistance or mercy to those guilty of the aforementioned crimes.

In formulating its new code in 1425, the government of Perugia had consulted a similar series of reform legislation promulgated earlier that same year by the Sienese, once again directly pursuant to a preaching mission in the city by Bernardino.[194] Bearing the name of the person who inspired them, the new Sienese statutes were called the *Riformagioni* (or *Riformazioni*) *di San Bernardino*.[195] However, when we examine the text of these *Riformagioni*, we find only one brief line about sodomy: "in the future anyone who is reputed to be a sodomite," it states laconically, is to be barred from public office.[196] The brevity of this antisodomy provision leads one to assume that Siena had already had a sufficiently extensive and stringent (albeit unenforced) law on this topic, unlike, perhaps, Perugia, which was obliged to draw up new, long, detailed legislation. William Bowsky's description of Siena in the previous centuries confirms this assumption. In his study "Police Power and Public Safety in Siena, 1287–1355," Bowsky assures us that the "medieval Sienese was most horrified of and angered by sodomy, fearing the unleashing of divine wrath against the community that permitted it. The sodomite, or procurer for a sodomite, who did not pay three hundred lire within a month of sentencing was, reads a statute, 'to be hanged by his virile members in the principal market place, and there remain hanging . . . for an entire day.' "[197] Presumably some such penalty remained in effect in the early fifteenth century; hence the brevity of the city fathers on the subject in drawing up the new 1425 Bernardinian reforms.

The town of Todi, just fifty kilometers from Perugia, and Bernardino's next stop during his 1426 preaching campaign through Tuscany and Umbria, emulated the reforming spirit of Perugia and Siena. In our discussion of the trial of Matteuccia Di Francesco, the woman of Todi burned at the stake for crimes of witchcraft, we had occasion to mention the Bernardino-inspired reform laws passed in that town just as the friar concluded a preaching mission there.[198] In addition to their new ordinance against witchcraft, the town fathers also ratified an amendment to existing law making sodomites the target of even more severe persecution and penalties. The Todi antisodomite reform is far briefer than its Perugian counterpart and deals only with cases involving adult males twenty-five years old or older. (Presumably the punishment of younger criminals remained as it was in the existing law being hereby amended.) The punishments described in the Todi reform are of comparable severity to those of Perugia of the previous year, except, however, for the added stipulation that convicted criminals are to be led through the streets with the hands and genitals tied while being whipped. Torture, the new law states, may also be used in the course of the trials, if necessary.

Eighteen years later, Bernardino's influence was undiminished, and we find his name associated with yet another set of new laws passed by the preacher's birthplace, Massa Marittima, near the Tuscan coast, where in that same year (1444) he had preached a Lenten series.[199] Having already gathered on March 29 to discuss "how abominable are the sins of blasphemy and sodomy," the town magistrates convened again on April 7 to hold deliberations regarding "the amendment of the Statutes on blasphemy, sodomy, and the observance of holy days" and to elect four officials who "would decide what provisions needed to be taken regarding the aforementioned subjects and *who would confirm their decisions with the venerable father Friar Bernardino*."[200] Among the several provisions eventually made into law on September 8 by the "praiseworthy office of Magnificent Lord Priors" of Massa with respect to "certain matters that Friar Bernardino had preached about," we find the following: "That all those men who are twenty-five years of age and have not taken a wife are to be punished."[201] Although the words *sodomy* and *sodomites* are not found in this new statute, we can be sure that the legislation was an antisodomy measure, since, as we have learned through Bernardino's own preaching, it was commonly assumed that unmarried males were likely to turn to sodomy in order to satisfy their lust. Hence, such men were to be held in great suspicion and monitored carefully; indeed, in Massa Marittima, they were to be, in some unspecified form, punished outright.

These are the only towns for which concrete evidence exists documenting Bernardino's direct influence in the enactment of new antisodomy legislation. Surveying the other parts of Italy in this same period, however, we do find the same heightened awareness of the crime of sodomy, and a more severe penal response to it. And in one case, that of Florence, it is not unreasonable to suspect that the hand (or voice) of Bernardino, a frequent visitor to the town, was involved.

During his two successive and lengthy preaching missions to Florence in 1424 and 1425, Bernardino publicly complained that there already existed on the city books "good ordinances concerning the correction and punishment of sodomites made by good men, but there are so many more evil men that these laws are not enforced."[202] The friar suggests that one reason for this is that those responsible for enforcement of the law seek, not the well-being of the republic, but rather, their own self-interest; they reason: "maybe I'll get into similar trouble one day and will also need help from someone [to escape punishment]."[203] And so the friar came and went, without the city taking any action against sodomy. Several years later, however, in 1432, Florence finally granted the friar's wish with the creation of a special magistracy, the "Office of the Night" (*Ufficiali di notte*), whose sole function was to police and prosecute the crime of sodomy.

Thanks to Michael Rocke's excellent new study of the records of the Office of the Night, we now know more about the nature and policing of sodomy in Florence than perhaps any other city in Italy at the time (1432–1502). Rocke's study confirms Bernardino's claim about Florence's relative indifference to the enforcement of the antisodomy laws, an indifference that changed dramatically with the creation of the prodigiously busy Office of the Night.[204] Though no mention is made of Bernardino, the law that promulgated this new magistracy specifically cites Scripture in its opening sentence—"[The government] wishes to root out of its city the abominable vice of sodomy, called in the holy scriptures the most evil sin"[205]—thereby testifying to the effectiveness of the catechetical lessons taught to them by Bernardino and his preaching confreres. In the long run, however, even this new "tough" measure, with its thousands of prosecutions, ended in failure. Sodomites continued to engage in their activity in Florence as in other parts of Italy. Later in the century, another fanatical preacher of reform, Girolamo Savonarola, would rise again in Florence and renew the attempt to eradicate the "sin against nature," but in the end it was he, not the sin of sodomy, that disappeared in the flames of the stake. The exclamation of one of the Florentine magistrates upon the news of the death of Savonarola in 1498 has become famous: "Praised be God, we can now go sodomize!"[206]

Not many years thereafter, in 1502, the long reign of the Office of the Night came to an end.

To return to the early fifteenth century, in 1448, the town of Lucca also established a special magistracy for the policing and prosecution of the crime of sodomy, called the "Officers of Decency."[207] In his study of Bernardino's activity in the Lucchese territory, Eugenio Lazzareschi claims that the "numerous decrees" against sodomy, blasphemy, and "excessive luxury" passed by Lucca in the mid–fifteenth century by its lord, Paolo Guinigi, were the "fruit of the Saint's ardent preaching."[208] Lazzareschi offers no concrete evidence for this conclusion, other than that the new laws postdate Bernardino's visit to the city. Bernardino may indeed be ultimately responsible for this legislation; however, to date, the only documented preaching mission undertaken in Lucca by our friar took place in 1424, more than two decades before Guinigi's reforms.[209] Bernardino is likely to have made other trips to Lucca, a Tuscan city not too remote from his home base in Siena; in any case, his word, no doubt, remained.

In Venice, another city near and dear to Bernardino's heart, sodomy also increasingly became a public concern during the friar's lifetime. Yet in contrast to that of the other towns we have just examined, Venice's rigorous new antisodomy legislation of the fifteenth century preceded Bernardino's arrival, a fact that reminds us that there were other preachers and other forces waging war against the "sin against nature." There is no record of Bernardino's having been to Venice before 1422, the year in which he preached a Lenten series that succeeded in capturing once and for all the attention and hearts of the populace.[210] Subsequent visits (most likely in 1429 and 1442) drew equal enthusiasm from the Venetians, who later in the century bestowed on him the title of co-patron of their renowned republic.[211] Despite Bernardino's relatively late appearance on the Venetian scene, a rapid look at its legislative response to the "crime against nature"—the subject recently of significant new research by Guido Ruggiero—is here appropriate, supplying as it does some further background to the larger object of our concern, sodomy in Quattrocento Italy.

Since the previous century (extant records begin with 1348), Venice had had its "Lords of the Night" (*Signori di Notte*), who handled sodomy cases along with other sex crimes. However, tellingly, at one point, in response to what was perceived as the growing threat of the "unmentionable vice," prosecution of such cases was reorganized and made more severe: in 1406, the republic transferred responsibility for the handling of sodomy cases to the higher *Consiglio dei Dieci*, the "Council of the Ten," "one of the most important councils of state," composed of representatives of "the most important families of the city," with "virtually unlimited power to take up, and deal internally with any matter they deemed a threat to the security of Venice." This transfer of power resulted in "a dramatic rise in prosecution."[212]

Again, the 1406 judicial reorganization came before Bernardino's first visit in Venice, but we can be sure the friar's subsequent visits served to exacerbate the climate of antisodomitic fear and hostility hovering over the city. Although Venice passed no new legislation during or immediately after Bernardino's mission there, the text of a 1458 antisodomitic law contains echoes of the friar's oratory, with its oft-repeated apocalyptic warnings about the wrath of God:

> As it is clear from Divine Scripture that our omnipotent God, detesting the sin of sodomy and wishing to demonstrate that fact, brought down his wrath upon the cities of Sodom and Gomorrah and soon thereafter flooded and destroyed the whole world for such horrible sins, our most wise ancestors sought with all their laws and efforts to liberate our city from such a dangerous divine judgement.[213]

It was a fear that after Bernardino's lifetime became paranoia. As Ruggiero tells us, "[a] paranoia that seems at times to have shared certain affinities with the witch scares that were to sweep Europe shortly appears to have gripped Venetian authorities in the mid decades of the fifteenth century."[214] The "paranoia" was so great, we might here add, that it caused even traditional pious practices involving male nakedness to come to the disapproving attention of the Council of Ten. A noteworthy example is the case of the four Franciscan friars arrested for infraction of the antisodomy law in 1420.[215] What had the friars done to call down such a charge upon themselves? In what I assume was emulation of their founder and his literal enactment of Jerome's famous ascetic adage "Naked to follow the naked Christ" (*nudus nudum Christum sequi*), they had marched naked through the streets of the city, carrying a large cross and followed by a large crowd. After due judicial inquiry into the matter, the friars were eventually exonerated; however, to the superiors of these friars a stern warning was issued by the Council, which was "greatly displeased" by this naked procession: the unclothed gang of four, though acquitted, was nonetheless to be given some form of in-house punishment as an object lesson to them and their fellow Franciscans.

The young nobles of the penitential confraternity of Santa Maria di Valverde were not as lucky. These men too were arrested in Venice in 1438 for violation of the sodomy laws. What had been their actual "crime"? The young men had appeared naked at the Church of Santa Maria Zobenigo and "were whipped by their confraternal brothers as a sign of repentance."[216] This—naked flagellation—was by no means an unknown practice in Christian confraternities (despite a 1296 papal bull issued by Boniface VIII against a certain group of fervent souls who prayed *au naturel*).[217] However, in the changed climate of mid-fifteenth-century Venice—changed, ironically, thanks to the preaching campaigns of Bernardino and his confreres—it was enough to earn four of the young nobles in question convictions for sodomy-related activity.[218]

This brings us to the end of our survey of the antisodomy response of the Italian towns most intimately associated with the preaching of Bernardino of Siena. It also brings us to the end of our examination of Bernardino's campaign against the "abominable sin against nature." We have explored the nature, contents, and goals of that campaign; we have also looked at its origins in Scripture, natural law, ecclesiastical tradition, "science," and Bernardino's own psyche. By way of conclusion, it is appropriate to return to the issue of origins. In an attempt to fathom the intensity of the antisodomy emotion that charged the social-spiritual climate of Renaissance Venice, Guido Ruggiero has raised the question: Were there any other motivating forces, beyond the certainly influential example of Sodom and Gomorrah, at play here? Was it only fear of divine retribution that fueled the sodomophobic passions of the late Middle Ages and early Renaissance? The historian believes there was, indeed, a further, psychosocial factor:

> Sodomy threatened to undermine the basic organizational units of society—family, male-female bonding, reproduction—which struck at the heart of social self-perception. Fornication with nuns certainly hurt God, but sodomy destroyed society with or without his wrath. Sodomy must have been seen as such an upset of the natural social order.[219]

Yet in the perennially family-centered, "heteronormative" Christian Europe, sodomy had always represented a potential "upset of the natural order." Why then, in early Quattrocento Italy, did it begin to assume such a menacing face in the eyes of society? The "unmentionable vice" had been a constant feature of European civilization; did it suddenly become more prevalent and hence more persecuted? This is a question to which there can be no secure answer: what appears to be the greater visibility of sodomy in Quattrocento Italy may merely be a function of more historical documents having survived from that time and place than from previous times and other places.

What we do know, instead, is that in the Italy of Bernardino's lifetime, sodomy was not the only menace that threatened to dissolve the bonds holding society together. That society was already besieged by natural disasters (plague and famine), ecclesiastical chaos (the Great Western Schism and its enduring fallout), enemies both within (heretics) and without (Islam and the Turks), and incessant, destructive wars on the international, national, and local level. In the less chaotic past, sodomy—though in theory always a condemnable evil—could be more easily overlooked. Not so in the troubled fifteenth century: as preachers like Bernardino reminded them, Christian society no longer had the luxury of allowing sinners and other nonconformists to ply their trade as freely as they may have done in the past; they had to be eliminated or securely contained, lest greater disaster strike from above. At the same time, the sodomites performed the socially useful function of scapegoats: how much easier and gratifying it was for people to blame sodomites for the present woes and tribulations, rather than God, the mysterious forces of nature, or themselves. How much easier and gratifying it was to blame as well the witches and the category of people we now turn to examine—the Jews.

CHAPTER FOUR

"All Jews Are the Chief Enemies of All Christians. . . . If You See a Jew in Need, You Must Help Him with an Authentic, Just, Holy, and Active Love"

REAPPRAISING BERNARDINO'S ANTI-SEMITISM

Outside of Italy, it is only in recent years that Bernardino of Siena's name has begun to appear in the scholarly literature on witchcraft and sodomy. Even in the most thorough works on these topics, the friar's significance has been largely overlooked. Quite opposite is the case when we turn to the history of Jews in Italy. Here we find that Bernardino has long since been identified by both Jewish and Christian chroniclers of "the longest hatred of human history"[1] as a major protagonist in the history of Christian anti-Semitism. Like the antiwitchcraft and antisodomy sentiment already examined, anti-Semitism also intensified in late medieval and early modern Italy, owing, in part, to the expanded activity of Jewish moneylenders, and culminating in the creation of the Jewish ghettos in the sixteenth century.[2] And Bernardino's leading hand in this crescendo of anti-Jewish feeling has been consistently featured in one history book after another, since at least the nineteenth century. There is, however, a universal flaw in this literature: All previous scholarship assessing Bernardino's role in the history of European anti-Semitism is marred by a serious want of close, thorough, and well-documented examination of the life and works of the friar, and has instead been constructed on a narrow, shallow plain of evidence.

As early as 1965, in his *Jewish Bankers and the Holy See,* Léon Poliakov, elder historian of anti-Semitism, had underscored this inadequacy of scholarly research into the anti-Jewish activity of the Dominican and Franciscan friars:

> The classics of Jewish history mention the systematic hostility shown by the mendicant orders towards the Jews. There is nothing surprising about the fact that institutions created to combat heresies and strengthen the Christian

faith should have adopted such an attitude. Unfortunately, apart from general statements occasionally supported by a few examples, there is an absence of serious works devoted to these questions.[3]

The scholarly situation as Poliakov described it decades ago still applies to Bernardino in the 1990s: many generalities, few concrete examples, no thorough documentation or well-informed overall assessment of the friar's anti-Jewish activity. Scholars have too frequently contented themselves with repeating the terse judgments of those early and influential "classics of Jewish history," whose authors had apparently formulated their judgments without a thorough command of the extant historical records or the extensive Bernardinian corpus of sermons, treatises, notes, and other contemporary documents. As for direct evidence from Bernardino, we find the same two or three quotations repeated over and over, as the sole basis of these scholars' reconstructions of the friar's thinking and feeling on the Jews. Since Poliakov wrote the words quoted above, much new scholarship has been published in various languages on European anti-Semitism, but it fails to focus on Bernardino of Siena in any specific or substantial fashion.

One example is Diane Hughes's otherwise fine article "Distinguishing Signs: Ear-rings, Jews and Franciscan Rhetoric in the Italian Renaissance City."[4] Although Hughes specifically focuses on the Observant Franciscans of fifteenth-century Italy and brings to our attention much new information about their contribution to the rise of anti-Semitism in the first half of that century, her work is parsimonious as far as Bernardino is concerned. A single quotation from Bernardino is used to support the author's depiction of the friar's anti-Semitism, a depiction fundamentally in agreement with the much older histories (Milano's and Roth's) to which the author refers us.[5] Another even more recent work is Robert Bonfil's survey *Jewish Life in Renaissance Italy;* the treatment of Bernardino therein likewise displays the traits of the older scholarship that Poliakov described.[6]

Before we begin our investigation of the complex question of Bernardino and the Jews, it will be useful to review the characterization of the friar we find in those older, much-quoted "authorities" responsible for establishing his modern reputation on the subject. To begin with, all are in agreement that Bernardino looms large in any account of Quattrocento anti-Semitism. Moritz Güdemann states in his still often cited 1884 work, *Geschichte des Erziehungswesens und der Cultur der Juden in Italien während des Mittelalters,* that the friar was "[o]ne of the most powerful and at the same time most anti-Semitic preachers" whose "anti-Semitism was for later preachers a normative example and an inexhaustible resource."[7] Yet in the "classics of Jewish history" of our own century, there is disagreement among them as to the precise scope, intensity, and efficacy of Bernardino's preaching against Jews and Judaism. On the one hand, Cecil Roth declares, "[John of Capistrano's] own zeal was rivalled, if not outdone, by that of his former master, Bernardino of Sienna. . . . The latter's saintly qualities were wholly submerged when Jews were concerned, they and personal cleanliness being among his greatest abhorrences."[8] On the other hand, according to Poliakov's own "general statement," the Sienese friar had a much more subdued temperament and passive role: "[Capistrano's] master and friend [Bernardino of Siena] was more kindly a character, content to call for the isolation of the Jews and observance of the canonical legislation. This did not prevent his audience from drawing conclusions of summary brutality from his sermons when the opportunity arose."[9]

In his *Storia degli ebrei in Italia,* Attilio Milano instead speaks of Bernardino's anti-Semitism essentially as a consequence of his humanitarian concern for the dire plight of the poor, whose poverty, as he and his followers believed, had been created or at least maintained by their usurious creditors. Summarizing what he calls the early-fifteenth-century "anti-Jewish crusade of the Friars Minor," Milano claims that "[i]ts principal argument was not religious, that of the Jew who was to be considered inferior inasmuch as he had rejected the Messiah and his teachings, but one that was strictly social: the Jew was to be eliminated inasmuch as he was a supporter of a system of economic oppression that plagued the poor."[10] As for Bernardino and his role in the fifteenth-century crescendo of Mendicant anti-Semitism, the friar, Milano further states, was simply the first to define the "struggle" in these economic terms.[11] True, Bernardino's preaching "left a legacy of bitter feelings that resulted in heavy trials for Italian Jews," says Milano, but "[t]he exceptional merit [*eccezionale merito*] of this friar was that of having brought to the forefront of public awareness the problem of the poverty of the masses, as well as that of having insisted on the necessity of new forms of help for the benefit of these masses."[12] In Milano's eyes, the greater enemy was Bernardino's younger contemporary and friend, John of Capistrano, "scourge of the Jews," who, the historian asserts (without citing his source), in 1447 had even "offered to the pope a small fleet on which to load all the Jews of the papal states in order to ship them to some faraway land."[13]

Yet another, far more irenic and idiosyncratic, impression of Bernardino's rapport with his Jewish contemporaries is suggested by a fourth historian, Moses Shulvass, who prefers to minimize the extent and impact of this "crusade of the Friars Minor." In *The Jews in the World of the Renaissance*, Shulvass twice underscores the fact that when Bernardino "came to L'Aquila in Southern Italy in 1438 and preached before the king and large crowds, many Jews also came to hear him speak."[14] The implication here is that, in the absence of legislation mandating Jewish attendance at "missionary sermons" aimed at their conversion, as Shulvass assumes was the case in L'Aquila in 1438, the presence of Jews at the friar's sermons was evidence of "the mutual theoretical interest of both religions in each other, accompanied by mutual respect." According to Shulvass, whatever anti-Jewish preaching there was in Renaissance Italy was of a kind that "only slightly and very briefly disturbed this harmony [between Jews and their Gentile neighbors]."[15]

Thus, in describing and evaluating Bernardino's anti-Semitism, the historians who have been the most widely heeded authorities on the question fail to agree about its precise nature and contours. However, lack of unanimity on the topic is not the only problem with this past scholarship. What is also lacking is a direct, intimate, and thorough acquaintance with the friar's works. Rarely does a scholar of Italian Jewish history quote Bernardino directly, and nowhere does one quote him extensively. A thorough examination and reappraisal of the evidence is very much in order.

1. Jews and Judaism in Bernardino's *Opera Omnia*

For the sake of convenience, we may divide references to the Jews in Bernardino's sermons and treatises into two categories. The first category contains that body of material pertaining to the Jews of the friar's own day. Within this category, a further distinction can be made between what Bernardino says about contemporary Jewish faith in general theological and social terms, and what he says about moneylenders and moneylending. These latter sermons, treatises, and scattered remarks on moneylending (then referred to as "usury") need to be examined separately, since only on the rarest of occasions do they actually mention the Jews by name. It is true that moneylending was in that age the Jewish trade par excellence, but numerous Christians were also engaged in the same "evil," and to these Christians Bernardino makes abundant explicit reference. For this reason, it is theoretically impossible to prove that the friar intended these discourses as primarily anti-Semitic attacks, as many critics have unquestioningly assumed. The qualification *primarily* is important here in that we are attempting to go beyond the impressionistic generalities of past evaluations and gauge with greater precision the depth and extent of Bernardino's own personal anti-Semitism. Consequently, the question of whether or not, or to what extent, we can include this enormous body of usury material is significant and will be taken up later in this chapter. Nonetheless, even if we grant that the usury sermons are not primarily anti-Jewish statements, the reality is that some Jews were moneylenders, and thus fell under the friar's condemnation of that profession as well. Furthermore, even if the friar was not using these anti-usury discourses as a convenient means to assail the Jews, in several cases the practical consequence of these sermons was an assault on the Jews in the form of legal measures having an adverse effect on their moneylending livelihood.

Our second principal category is that of the ancient Jews. Here we shall consider Bernardino's remarks about the Jews and Judaism of the Bible, which come principally, but not exclusively, in his Good Friday retellings of the passion and crucifixion of Jesus. This genre of sermon, the Good Friday Passion story, represented perhaps the very peak and centerpiece of Bernardino's and all Franciscan popular oratory. The Franciscan friars' most intense and best-attended preaching took place during the forty days of Lent and culminated on Easter Sunday, to which Good Friday was a dramatic and, some might argue, an even more engaging prelude. Lenten preaching's explicit purpose was moving the people to repentance and confession of their sins, the latter sacrament being an annual obligation imposed on all the faithful, under pain of mortal sin, by the Fourth Lateran Council (1215). Given the abundant dramatic potential of the subject matter, the naturally theatrical Bernardino delivered some of his most highly charged sermons on Good Friday, and thus, on such occasions, anything he had to say about the Jews is likely to have found ready reception in the hearts and minds of his attentive and emotionally stirred audience.

With respect to these separate categories, let us note, the friar never uses the terms *ancient* and *contemporary* in speaking of the Jews. The distinction is mine, not Bernardino's. In Bernardino's vocabulary, the Jews of both groups are all simply *iudaei,* and not, as is customary in other literature of the period, *hebraei* for the ancient people and *iudaei* for the modern. The friar gives no indication of recognizing any significant difference between the Jews of old and the Jews of his own day (for example, he appears completely unaware of the thirteenth-century debate over the difference between biblical Judaism and Talmudic, postbiblical Judaism.)[16] This assumed identity between ancient and contemporary takes on special significance in discussions of the Jews' anti-Christian behavior, as manifested specifically in their treatment of Jesus during the last days of his life. Like forefathers, like sons, the implied message seems to have been, although we have no incontrovertible proof that this identification was Bernardino's conscious intent.[17] Nonetheless, it behooves us to pay careful attention to what the friar has to say about the Jews and Judaism in these moments of narrative reconstruction or theological exegesis of Scripture.

Before we begin to examine the material in question, a great paradox must be noted, one that has gone unnoticed in all of the previous literature on the subject. Despite Bernardino's long-standing and widespread reputation as persistent persecutor of the Jews, the fact is that the friar devotes little time to the specific topic of the Jews per se in his preaching and in his writing. In the entire extant Bernardinian corpus (comprising thousands of pages of printed text filling at least twenty volumes, plus several more codices of unpublished sermons), there is not a single sermon, treatise, or any other writing of any genre dedicated solely or principally to Jews or Judaism. As we shall see, with just three exceptions, the relatively few explicit references to the Jews in Bernardino's work are typically brief, casual, and incidental, consisting of no more than two or three sentences. This is in significant contrast with the amount of space devoted to the other classes of people whom Bernardino singles out as grave threats to the social-moral order, namely, witches, sodomites, political factions, and vain women who are bankrupting their husbands and the commonwealth with their extravagant expenditures on clothing. I will later speculate as to why this is so; for now let us simply note the paradox.

2. Padua 1423: Repromulgating Canon Law

We begin with Bernardino and contemporary Jews, this material falling under two rubrics. The first can now be labeled "The Canon Laws of Segregation," and the second "The Campaign against Usury." The essential message in both cases is that the Jews are a threat to Christian society and must be stringently isolated. This is even more the case for Jews engaged in usury, because usury (then defined as the lending of money at any rate of interest whatsoever) is a mortal sin, and Christians who interact with or even passively tolerate such sinners will provoke the wrath of God upon themselves and their towns. Bernardino spells out this message in no uncertain terms on two occasions during a long cycle of sermons delivered in Padua on the main square in 1423 before an audience that included the city's principal political powers (the *rettori*), university professors and students, the clergy, and an ample crowd of ordinary citizens.[18]

Among all of the friar's explicitly anti-Jewish remarks, the two Paduan passages in question are the most extensive. Recorded for posterity in condensed Latin form by the jurist Daniele de Purziliis, these declarations represent momentary digressions coming—somewhat ironically—in the midst of two sermons entitled "On the acquisition of divine love" ("De emenda charitate divina") and "On conversion to Jesus" ("De conversione ad Jesum"). As for the first of these sermons, "De emenda charitate divina," its anti-Jewish remarks appear in the "second principal part" of the friar's discourse, entitled "Questions and answers regarding divine love" (OOH.III.331b). At one point, the preacher says that there are three things that one must always keep in mind: first, that God is the creator and must be beseeched with prayer and tears so that one might be spared his judgment; second, that human beings are "dust of the most vile kind"; and third, that one's neighbor is to be loved (OOH.III.333b). But what about the Jews? How do they fall under this command to love one's neighbor? Bernardino begins his answer: "Regarding them, since I hear that in this city of Padua there are many Jews, I want to tell you some things about associating with them and other truths concerning them." Bernardino's "truths" turn out to be a list of prohibitions that the friar has extracted from ecclesiastical law, duly citing the specific canons as his *auctoritates*.[19] In paraphrase, the prohibitions are:

¶. It is a mortal sin to eat or drink with Jews.

¶. It is a mortal sin to seek help from a Jewish doctor.

¶. Christians are not allowed to bathe in the company of Jews.

¶. Jews may not construct new synagogues, nor enlarge old ones.

¶. Jews must be under curfew during Holy Week "lest they murmur about the Passion of Christ."

¶. Jews must wear some sign or badge identifying them as Jews.

¶. It is a mortal sin for Christians to socialize with Jews in their homes.

¶. It is a mortal sin for Christians to act as wet nurses or otherwise help to raise the children of the Jews or serve as midwives for them, even to wash the newborn child.

¶. Money, in any case, must not be accepted from usurious Jews for such obstetric services, because this money in reality belongs to another [i.e, to the lender's clients].[20]

As we note, the underlying goal here is, above all, to keep Jews physically and emotionally separate from Christians. Though unspoken by the preacher, one reason for this social isolation was fear of Jewish proselytizing. As Thomas Chobham's popular *Summa confessorum* warns, "the Jews are experts in the law according to its letter; therefore they can more easily corrupt simple Christians than can the pagans."[21] As we will later hear, Bernardino also feared for the physical safety of the Christians.

The friar interrupts the enumeration of these laws to pose, in scholastic fashion, a series of casuistic "queries" relating to the last issue raised, that is, the question of how to deal with money received from Jews for legitimate services, as a gift, or in the case of a Jew who converts to Christianity (OOH.III.334a–b). Aquinas is the authority cited to resolve the issue, the important distinction being between Jews who are moneylenders and those who are not.[22] Responsibility toward creditors is also considered a part of this overall "query." These issues having been clarified—their solutions are not relevant to our present concerns—the friar resumes his catalog of "truths":

¶. It is a mortal sin to accept a gift of unleavened bread from Jews.

¶. It is a mortal sin to rent houses to Jews (or Christians) to be used for moneylending.

¶. Priests may indeed exact tithes from Jews living in their parish.[23]

And a final question: "I ask whether one is ever permitted to do good to Jews or to love them. I respond that, in so far as general love is concerned, yes, it is permitted to love them, but where special love is concerned, no, it is not; you must avoid loving them with a special love."[24]

In this same 1423 Paduan cycle, Bernardino returns to the subject of loving Jews with a "general love" in two other sermons, "De amore lato per charitatem" (OOH.III.160–63, on Jesus' command "Love your enemy," Matthew 5:43), and "De amore irato," on the theme of "hate the sin, but love the sinner" (OOH.III.225–28). The substance of what the friar preaches regarding the Jews in these Paduan sermons is repeated in his Latin treatise *De proximorum dilectione* (OOQ.III.120–33), as well as in his 1424 sermon to the Florentines on restitution ("Che cosa si ì obbligati a rendere," A.328–42) and his 1425 sermon to the Sienese on charity ("Questa è la predica de la carità," G.215–24). In surprising contrast to what we heard in "De emenda charitate divina," Bernardino's message in all of these five other sermons about loving Jews with a general love is not at all grudging and cautious. It is quite positive, even exhortatory. To begin with, there is no doubt that Jews are to be embraced by the general love of the Christian. As Bernardino observes at the opening of "De amore lato": "The first form of love is called general, and includes friends, enemies, pagans, Jews, Christians, father, mother, children, and neighbors, and everyone else."[25] Likewise he says to the Sienese in 1425: "The first form of love is called general and contains what you must do; that is to say, you must love your son, your brother, your relative, the Jew, the pagan."[26]

The friar then goes on to explain in "De amore lato" that this general love must be "authentic, just, holy, and active" (*verus, justus, sanctus, operosus*), stating that "We must seek the good of our neighbor just as we seek our own good."[27] He then concludes: "These are the characteristics of general love with which we must assist both our friends and enemies. . . . Therefore, if you see a Jew in need, you must help him and everyone else [in need], with an authentic and just, holy and active love; if you neglect to do so, hell awaits you."[28] Bernardino repeats the essence of this message to the same Paduan audience in "De amore irato," based on the Gospel story of Jesus' angry cleansing of the Temple (John 2:13–17):

> Christ behaved in this way to make us understand that we must get angry at our sins and the sins of others; not at the person himself, but at his sin; for we must love others in such a way that their errors may not be loved, because all men have been created by God. . . . I tell you that unless you treat him [the enemy whom you have pardoned] in the same way that you treat your other neighbors and friends, in the spirit of love and general charity, with deeds and signs, greeting him when you meet him on the street; and if he greets you and you do [not] answer him, then you commit a sin, and similarly in the case of the Jew or any other pagan, unless expressly forbidden by the Church, because we must not hate the sinner, just the sin.[29]

Not only is the friar's counsel to love the Jew in these five sermons more emphatic and more positive, it is also without restriction. Whereas in "De emenda charitate divina," Bernardino explicitly excludes the Jew as object of the "special love" of the Christian, in both "De amore lato" and "De proximorum dilectione," the preacher makes no such exclusion, nor does he even raise the distinction in the remaining two sermons. Indeed, no friend or enemy, it would seem, is to be excluded even from "special love," also called "spiritualis" (OOH.III.162a) and "operalis" (OOQ.III.126). Bernardino uses the rubric of "special love" to remind his audience that they must respond in a direct, concrete fashion to a neighbor in need, whether such need be spiritual, corporal, or material. In other words, the general/special distinction appears in the end simply a means the preacher uses to divide the sermon material, rather than corresponding to ontologically or phenomenologically different forms of love, as he suggests in "De emenda charitate divina."

In any case, we are left with the considerable problem of how to resolve the apparent gross contradiction in Bernardino's teaching about the Jews. On the one hand, as the preacher exhorts, good Christians are to sincerely love their Jewish neighbors with an "authentic, just, holy, and active" love, greeting them in friendly fashion when passing on the street and assisting them in their moments of need; while on the other, they are to minimize all contact with them, restrict their freedoms, and (as we will later hear Bernardino say) hold them suspect as "members of the Devil" and "the chief enemies of Christendom." Having repeated the mandate to love the Jews on several different occasions, Bernardino, we are to suppose, truly meant what he said and was not simply guilty of a thoughtless, momentary slip of the tongue. Assuming he was not forgetful of what he said about the Jews from one moment to the next, we must conclude that Bernardino himself saw no contradiction in what he was advising. Yet carrying out both sets of advice would seem to be, on both the spiritual and the psychological level, simply impossible, requiring an almost schizophrenic rapport with another human being.

Leaving the contradiction unresolved, we return to "De emenda charitate divina." The friar ends his anti-Jewish digression in the sermon with a reference to "the multitude of Jews who reign [*qui regnant*] in this city" (OOQ.III.334b). Bernardino knew that there was an unusually large population of Jews in Padua, an important university town renowned across Europe. However, he believes that the local authorities have been excessively indulgent toward them and neglectful of the "truths" he has just called to their attention. This sentiment, I suspect, lies behind that verb *regnant* in the finale to his speech. As we know from other contemporary records, the Paduan Jewish community was indeed noteworthy for its size, and under the Carrara family had enjoyed remarkable freedom and well-being. But this relatively happy state of affairs had been eroding considerably since 1405, the year in which Venice annexed the city, ending the Carrara rule and depriving the Jews of their citizenship and their right to own real estate.[30] Evidently, by 1423 the "privileged" Jewish situation had not eroded sufficiently to please the friar. Bernardino takes the opportunity to scold his Paduan audience—which included, as already noted, many civil and ecclesiastical authorities—for violating Christian law by allowing Jews to build or enlarge their synagogues or to go about the streets unmarked by the mandatory badge identifying them as Jews.[31] This infraction of the badge ordinance by Paduan Christians especially vexes Bernardino. It drives him to the point of questioning the authority of the pope to allow such a contravention of canon law. In view of Bernardino's usual reluctance to criticize the papacy or any of the Church's leadership in public, this is a significant utterance indeed:

> I am amazed as to why they are not wearing their badges here, and in Vicenza and Verona, so that they might be recognized. And asking why this was so, I was told that they have an exemption from the Pope. There are those who say that the Pope does not have the power to concede this [privilege] against [the decrees of] four councils; but I don't want to act against the decision of the Pope.[32]

The well-informed and well-traveled Bernardino must have been aware that the papacy not only granted many such badge exemptions, but had routinely granted other privileges and protection to the Jews. Martin V's personal physician was the renowned professor of medicine Elia Sabbati (di Sabbato), who, by papal decree, had been given Roman citizenship for himself and his descendants, exemption from the badge, the right to bear arms, and "full freedom to travel by land or sea with his personal effects and books."[33] Popes had, in fact, been granting Roman citizenship to Jews since at least the thirteenth century.[34] With respect to the Jews, the Franciscans, including Bernardino, and the papacy were in opposing camps, and this opposition resulted, as we shall later see, in more than one papal bull against the Mendicant anti-Jewish preaching.

As far as the badge is concerned, the friar explains to the Paduans the justification behind this public identification of the Jews (OOH.III.334a): it is a means to prevent fornication between Jewish men and Christian women (as could happen easily in a house of prostitution).[35] As Hughes reminds us, "By the middle of the fifteenth century, it had become extremely difficult to distinguish Jews from Christians. They spoke the same language, lived in similar houses, and dressed with an eye to the same fashions."[36] Despite having just claimed that he does not want to contradict a papal decision, the friar then proceeds to order the Paduans to do just that: "but the citizens [of these towns] must see to it that something is done about this [laxity] and some law is passed regarding the badge: the reason for it is, if they don't wear a badge, they will mix themselves with Christian women; and this is against the canon *Nonnulli*, concerning the Jews."[37] Bernardino adds the sarcastic taunt, "if the Jews themselves believe that their faith is superior, they should wear the badges so that they can be recognized and shouldn't be ashamed to be known as Jews."[38] We must acknowledge that the anxiety expressed over Jewish-Christian sexual coupling is not the friar's alone. It is the same concern expressed by canon 68, *In nonnullis provinciis*, of the Fourth Lateran Council (1215), which Bernardino invokes. Pointing out that Mosaic law itself legislates the wearing of special articles of clothing as the basis of differentiation from the rest of the population, the canon states:

> A difference of dress distinguishes Jews or Saracens from Christians in some provinces, but in others a certain confusion has developed so that they are indistinguishable. Whence it sometimes happens that by mistake Christians join with Jewish or Saracen women; and Jews or Saracens with Christian women. In order that the offence of such a damned mixing may not spread further, under the excuse of a mistake of this kind, we decree that such persons of either sex, in every Christian province and at all times, are to be distinguished in public from other people by the character of their dress—seeing moreover that this was enjoined upon them by Moses himself, as we read.[39]

This same canon mandates a curfew for Jews during Holy Week, another restriction of rights for which Bernardino demands reinforcement in this same Paduan sermon. The justification he gives is that of the Council Fathers. The curfew is to be reinforced, as we read here in the second half of Canon 68, out of reverence for "the Redeemer":

> They shall not appear in public at all on the days of lamentation and on Passion Sunday; because some of them on such days, as we have heard, do not blush to parade in very ornate dress and are not afraid to mock Christians who are presenting a memorial of the most sacred passion and are displaying signs of grief. What we most strictly forbid, however, is that they dare in any way break out in derision of the Redeemer. We order secular princes to restrain with condign punishment those who do so presume, lest they dare to blaspheme in any way him who was crucified for us since we ought not to ignore insults against him who blotted out our wrongdoings.[40]

Conversion to the Redeemer Jesus Christ is the topic of the second Paduan sermon of 1423, containing another set of explicit anti-Jewish exhortations by Bernardino. The last of those delivered in the city that year, the sermon in question, "De conversione ad Jesum," is followed by a long footnote of the reporter De Purziliis describing the tearful, tumultuous departure of the friar from Padua—an indication, it would seem, of the great success of his mission there (OOH.III.362a). Furthermore, it is revelatory of the depth of the preacher's concern about the Jewish question in Padua that he should return to the subject at the very close of his preaching mission.

True conversion and authentic Christian living, the friar teaches in this sermon, entail a host of specific behaviors and renunciations, among them the abandonment of idolatrous or superstitious beliefs and practices. It is immediately after the mention of idolatry and superstition that Bernardino delivers his second list of prohibitions concerning the Jews. This juxtaposition of idolatry, superstition, and Judaism may seem strange, but the friar was simply reflecting the standard classification of medieval theology, which saw these phenomena as varieties of the same generic sin, that is, "sin committed directly against God." For example, in the *Summa theologica* of Alexander of Hales, one of Bernardino's principal theological sources, discussion of the Jews occurs in the *Tractatus Octavus* (*De peccatis in Deum, in proximum, in se ipsum,* "Concerning sins against God, one's neighbor, one's self"), *Sectio* I (*De peccatis in Deum,* "Concerning sins against God"), *Quaestio* I (*De peccatis quibus dehonoratur omnipotentia divina,* "Concerning sins by which divine omnipotence is dishonored"), and *Titulus* II (*De iudeais et paganis,* "Concerning the Jews and the pagans"). Titles I and III of that same *sectio* are, respectively, *De idolatria* ("Concerning idolatry") and *De haeresi* ("Concerning heresy"), while the next *quaestio* bears the title *De peccatis quibus dehonoratur divina sapientia seu de divinatione* ("Concerning sins by which divine wisdom is dishonored, that is, concerning divination").[41] Thus, not only did medieval theology look upon all Jews as sinners, it saw little moral difference between the most pious adherent of the ancient faith of Abraham, Isaac, and Jacob and the most newly hatched, antinomian, self-proclaimed prophet to come out of the woods, or the most simple-minded, superstitious, or crazed "witch" and "magician."

The first of the friar's new set of caveats in "De conversione ad Jesum" is as startling as it is blunt: "Beware of accepting cups or pots from the Jews, since I can't help believing that their women urinate into them in order to mock Christians."[42] To this the friar adds, "But what should I say of those who pawn sacramental vessels and chalices to the Jews? I believe that they urinate in [them as well], and do every kind of shameful act [upon them] in order to mock the Christian faith."[43] The graphic bluntness of Bernardino's statement is by no means uncharacteristic of the saint, of his age, or of traditional Christian writings against the Jews. "Medieval Franciscan literature is not prudish in its language. . . . What Giotto was not ashamed to paint in the Last Judgement of the Scrovegni Chapel, the friars openly preached."[44] Some may still suspect that De Purziliis, our Paduan "reporter," has perhaps put words into the preacher's mouth, but perusal of the whole corpus of the Bernardinian vernacular sermons—the work of several independent transcribers—will uncover much vocabulary of the same odor and flavor. For example, we have Bernardino's candid remark to himself upon seeing the coat of arms of a political faction hanging above a crucifix: "O Lord God, oh, you have the Devil right above you, and it can be said that he is pissing on your head!"[45] At another point in his preaching, the friar likens the thief and the sodomite to human excrement: "If someone decided to clean out his bowels and let loose in the trash pile of a room, he would stink up the whole house with his excrement. Likewise, the thief, represented by the excrement, and the sodomite, who is represented by the urine."[46]

In any case, urinating into Christian vessels is but one way the Jews deride Christians, according to Bernardino, who seems to believe that the Jews will lose no opportunity to make fools of Christians. Hence he gives his second warning, that of not renting church buildings to them, adding, "what is worse, I have heard that Jews [have been allowed to] mock Christ himself in the presence of Christians."[47] In view of this, he exhorts the citizens of Padua "to reconsider the exemptions of the Jews and to pass laws requiring that they wear the badge."[48] Jews must not be allowed to go unrecognized, nor must Christians "patronize Jewish shopkeepers on Sundays and holy days" (ibid.). Bernardino then returns to the topic of renting to the Jews, specifying that

> anyone who rents houses to Jewish usurers, and likewise to Christian usurers, commits mortal sin by keeping that money and is obliged to make restitution to those from whom the usury was exacted. . . . And take note that if a prelate rents houses to Jewish usurers, he is *ipso facto* suspended. Similarly, religious who rent houses to Jewish usurers are *ipso facto* excommunicated; if any guild [*collegium*] or corporation [*universitas*] rents houses to either Christian or Jewish usurers, it is *ipso iure* placed under interdict.[49]

The next warning is already familiar to us from the previous sermon, and therefore is left unfinished in the text: "Likewise in the case of a Christian wet nurse who nurses the children of the Jews, as I have said elsewhere: She is prohibited from accepting money for that service, etc."[50] The audience hears again the law forbidding the construction of new synagogues and is informed of the prohibition against the use of Jewish brokers or intermediaries in conducting business or contracting marriage. The intimate degree of daily social interaction and mutual personal familiarity and trust implied by these remarks—Italian Jews were even helping Christians to find wives and husbands—that rendered such a warning necessary was not a figment of Bernardino's excited imagination, as the historical evidence from fifteenth-century Italy attests.[51]

Finally, Bernardino raises the subject of Jewish doctors. His advice to the Paduans is to "beware of turning to Jews for medical help and of accepting medicines from them." Why this advice? "For in Avignon there was once a Jewish doctor who at the point of death boasted that he had killed off many Christians with his medicines."[52] Given that these words were coming from a respected and generally well-informed man of God whom many already revered as a saint, we wonder how many Paduan listeners and subsequent readers of this *reportatio* accepted the friar's words as a statement of truth. As for the source of this chilling piece of information, Bernardino is silent. It is, of course, possible for there to have been such a doctor, but more likely, we have here yet another piece of fantastic anti-Semitic libel. True or not, Bernardino's claim would have fueled and perpetuated the already old, widespread Christian fear about the secret homicidal conspiracy of the Jews. This same anxiety had led Christians of the previous century to allege that Jews had caused the Black Death of 1348 by poisoning public wells, thereby provoking a series of mass lynchings and burnings.[53] In reality, however, despite the accusations spread about him by people like Bernardino, "society was not ready to reject the Jewish doctor," neither in the fourteenth century nor in Bernardino's century.[54] As we shall later hear, Bernardino will have more to say about Jewish doctors and Christian patronage of them.

A further association that the mention of the Avignon doctor is likely to have conjured up in the minds of Bernardino's audience, although the friar makes no direct allusion to it, is that of ritual child murder, a widespread variation on the broader theme of the Jew as murderer. According to this medieval notion, Jews habitually kidnapped and, as part of their Passover ritual, tortured and killed Christian children, whose blood they mixed into their matzoh (which could possibly be the rationale for Bernardino's warning to his audience not to eat this bread). The myth persisted among Christians, even though expressly condemned by papal bulls.[55] The most infamous case of ritual child murder in Italian history was to occur thirty years after Bernardino's death and involved "little Simon" (Simonino) of Trent. Simon's mutilated cadaver was found on Easter Sunday morning in 1475 in a creek near the home of the town's three Jewish families. All of the Jews in Trent (approximately thirty) were immediately charged with the murder, tried without defense, and either imprisoned or burned at the stake. "Little Simon" was soon beatified by popular acclaim, and his cult remained alive in Trent for four hundred years. In October 1965, the cult of "beato Simonino" was finally abolished with papal approval, the complete lack of evidence and scandalous legal irregularities of the trial having by then been amply exposed.[56]

We might also note that Bernardino's report about the Jewish doctor-assassin of Avignon did not die with the friar. Sixty years later it was repeated to a large public audience by a fellow Observant, the "blessed" Bernardino Tomitano of Feltre. A popular preacher with great devotion to and of the same zealous reforming stamp as his namesake, Tomitano was, however, a far more pertinacious anti-Semite who had been barred from preaching in more than one Italian town for fear that he would provoke riots among the citizenry with his inflammatory anti-Jewish oratory. He was also the driving force behind the establishment of the *monti di pietà*, that is, publicly sponsored pawn shops designed to give the poor an alternative source of "sin-free," low-cost, non-Jewish credit.[57] Addressing the Sienese in 1486, Bernardino the younger gave the same warning about patronizing Jewish doctors, adding that "St. Bernardino reports that one of their own kind confessed to him that a Jewish doctor of Avignon said on his deathbed that he was not so unhappy to die, since he had already killed many thousands of Christians with his deadly prescriptions."[58] In repeating the story, let us observe, Bernardino the younger embellishes it—the criminal becomes an unrepentant, arrogant boaster, his victims now numbering "many thousands of Christians"—attaching the *auctoritas* of his by then canonized spiritual father to his own exaggerations. Undoubtedly, it was a story that Tomitano repeated on more than one occasion; in doing so, he not only disseminated further this piece of anti-Jewish libel, but magnified as well the anti-Semitic reputation of Bernardino of Siena.

3. The So-called *Testamento di San Bernardino*

The anti-Jewish remarks uttered by Bernardino of Siena in Padua in 1423 were to have an even longer echo. Two hundred years later they were extracted and disseminated in a rabidly anti-Semitic pamphlet called the *Copia del Testamento di San Bernardino di Siena*, which merits a brief digression into the topic of the posthumous destiny of Bernardino's anti-Jewish sermons. Despite its title, the pamphlet is in reality a collection of miscellaneous anti-Semitic items, only the first of which—the first five pages of sermon extracts—has any direct connection to Bernardino. Composed by an anonymous but, as the title page declares, "devout religious . . . with permission of his superiors," for the benefit "of all the faithful," the pamphlet most likely comes from the pen of a Franciscan: the author dates it, "Padua, the feast of St. Francis, 1670," and, in addition to Bernardino of Siena, quotes extensively the other Franciscan Bernardino, Bernardino of Feltre.[59]

The title of the pamphlet derives from our Bernardino's declaration from the Paduan sermon, "De conversione ad Jesum," with which the body of the pamphlet text begins, "Since I am about to depart from you, my children, I now want to do the duty of the good father. This will be my last testament."[60] The anonymous author introduces this quotation with the solemn announcement: "Saint Bernardino of Siena speaks to your hearts, O faithful, with supreme attention, serenity, and devotion; and here are his holy words."[61] Following that are extracts in Italian from the two sermons that have just been examined, Bernardino's "De emenda charitate divina" and "De conversione ad Jesum." After repeating the friar's long exhortation on the Holy Name of Jesus (which makes no mention of Jews or Judaism), the "devout religious" then lists ten of the anti-Jewish prohibitions enumerated by Bernardino in the two Paduan sermons.

Bernardino did not write any of the remaining thirty-one pages, nor is he even mentioned therein. The content and language of those pages are at times of an anti-Semitic intensity and vehement paranoia that even in his frankest moments our preacher never permitted himself to express in public. Accordingly, the Venetian government banned the work in 1685, but it still managed to circulate and be reprinted.[62] Again, most of this pamphlet has nothing to do with the life and activity of Bernardino of Siena. However, since the work bears in its title Bernardino's name, and hence his spiritual authority, the friar became, in effect, guilty by association, and thus continued to grow in anti-Semitic stature even long after he had departed this world.

For their length and passionate explicitness, the two Paduan 1423 lists examined above and extracted in the *Testamento* are unique among all the anti-Jewish utterances contained in the friar's sermons, Latin or vernacular, with one exception, to which we shall shortly come. Nowhere else do we find Bernardino dictating in the same crude, unequivocal, and emphatic way the systematic segregation and otherwise methodical repression of the Jews, which in reality had already been mandated by the Church's own canon law. In contrast, the sermons on usury, fiery and intransigent though they are, rarely use the word *Jew* or any of its related forms and synonyms, except for one notable paragraph (to be examined in the next section). Similarly, Bernardino's histrionic retellings of the Passion story, for all of their hyperbolic denunciation of the malice of the Jews of fourteen hundred years ago, never go on to counsel active retaliation toward the present-day descendants of Jesus' persecutors. Outside of these two Paduan sermons, we encounter no analogous anti-Jewish moment in Bernardino's oratory, with, again, the one exception already mentioned.

This exception is found in the twenty-first sermon of the 1425 Florentine Lenten cycle, on the topic of "keeping good company." The friar's message here is simple: In order to preserve one's faith and virtue, one must stay away from evil people. He then offers a list of examples of people to avoid, placing Jews in the same category as rapists of nuns, sodomites, heretics, and "evil women" (witches? prostitutes? procuresses?):

> O blind world! You and your crazy idea of freedom! You don't even punish any of these devil-possessed men who go and defile the monasteries! Don't associate with any sodomite or else he'll stick to you; likewise, don't associate with any heretic lest he contaminate you; likewise, don't associate with any Jew, because it is prohibited in the Decretal. You have given them [the Jews] so much arrogance in your territory,[63] and nowadays you're becoming just like them. You are going against the orders of the holy Church. Any evil woman in your neighborhood, don't let her come close to your house. . . . [E]vil is always the enemy of the good. The basilisk poisons a man with its sight; one glance of the evil eye kills the soul.[64]

Interestingly enough, in the later Latin treatise on the same subject, *Quantae efficaciae sit in bonum et in malum societas bona vel mala*, Bernardino excludes any explicit mention of the Jews, even when he discusses the necessity of segregating evil people (OOQ.VII.158). However, returning to the "reported" vernacular sermons, in the midst of a diatribe against political factions, we find the friar slipping into his remarks this parenthetically brief, albeit sarcastic, call for the enforcement of the Jewish badge law:

> I told you that whoever wore the insignia of a faction, whether Guelf or Ghibelline, in any shape or form, was nothing but a devil-worshiper. The

> reasons, the authorities and examples, you already heard two days ago, but I didn't tell you what I will tell you today. Oh! Are there any Jews here? I can't tell, because I can't recognize them. If they had an "O" on their chest, I would recognize them.[65]

Having thus reminded his audience of the badge law, the preacher drops the subject and resumes his discourse on the evils of political factionalism.

4. The Campaign against Usury

Another important repository of Jewish-related remarks in Bernardino's *opera omnia* are his sermons and treatises on usury. Moneylending was then commonly associated with the Jews, although they were far from possessing a monopoly on it. Progressively barred by Christian law from most other livelihoods, many Jews turned to the unloved but accessible profession of moneylending—without which, however much it was condemned by the Church, society could not function. Although, like prostitution, moneylending enjoyed little social or moral esteem and was tolerated as a necessary evil, it was for the Jews both a sufficiently profitable and an easily transportable profession.[66] These were important considerations, since European Jews were the constant victims of exorbitant forced loans and taxes, as well as capricious expulsions and exiles. Even papal protection came at enormous financial cost to the Jewish community.

Before we examine Bernardino's sermons and treatises on this question, a general word of introduction to the moral issue of usury will be helpful in contextualizing the friar's remarks. Unlike today, "usury" in the Middle Ages and Renaissance meant the asking or receiving of any sum of money (or substitutes therefor) in a loan, above and beyond the principal. As such, in those centuries of burgeoning capitalism, usury was one of the most passionately debated moral issues of society. In discussing usury, one was, in effect, discussing the cost of credit (be it to investors, merchants, or private citizens), one of the central cogs that enabled the wheels of society's economic machinery to move forward. Even in Bernardino's lifetime, his own Franciscan order found itself at times obliged to make recourse to moneylenders, including Jewish ones.[67] Bernardino, nonetheless, considered the lending of money at interest to be a scandalous affront against charity. Assistance to another human being in need should be entirely gratis, "for are we not all brothers and sisters? All from the same temporal father and spiritual father, God . . . ?"[68] Against this widespread "evil"

Bernardino waged steady and implacable warfare. As a quick parenthesis or an extensively analyzed theme, usury makes numerous appearances in the friar's sermons and treatises. Indeed, according to John Noonan, Bernardino's works (together with those of his contemporary Antonino of Florence) represent the most complete treatment of that moral issue in the first fifteen centuries of Church tradition.[69]

We cannot summarize here the friar's entire discourse on usury, nor the many facets of this complex moral-economic-social issue, examined in magisterial and complementary fashion by John Noonan's *Scholastic Analysis of Usury* and Léon Poliakov's *Jewish Bankers and the Holy See.*[70] Suffice it to say that Bernardino's handling of the question is representative of his approach to every moral issue. For all of his subtle and seemingly technically adept analysis, the friar's treatment of the problem is fraught with contradictions and inconsistencies, while his ultimate moral judgment is one of unwavering intransigence, painted in black and white.[71] Usury is an evil per se and *in se,* and he resolutely sweeps away the various legal fictions used to circumvent the law:[72] "Alexander of Hales says that . . . not even if Saint Peter the Apostle himself were to return to earth could he make usury licit, even at only 1 percent interest. . . . Therefore, it's impossible for God ever to permit usury to be licit. It's either one of two things. Either it's of its own nature evil, or it's of its own nature good."[73]

Although Church tradition was long and clear in its stance against the taking of interest, there had, nonetheless, been "no agreement on the natural-law reasons why usury [was] a sin. Every juristic reason offered [had] been criticized by at least one prominent writer."[74] The Church failed in its attempt to offer a thoroughly coherent, convincing argument against usury as a violation of supposed "natural law" and therefore an "intrinsic evil," independent of any consideration of intention, circumstance, consequence, and the other elements constitutive of the moral act. Thus the picture was not as simple and cut-and-dried as Bernardino would have his audiences believe. It was to take a few more centuries, but eventually economic realities and the fundamental flaws in the Church's logical analysis caused the usury prohibition to come tumbling down, after its centuries-long reign.[75]

With this larger picture in mind, we can now turn to the specifically anti-Jewish content of Bernardino's usury sermons and treatises. The principal question is: Where, how, and to what effect does Bernardino expressly cite or allude to the Jews or Judaism in all of this large body of material covering several hundred pages of printed text? To begin with, one rarely comes across the words *Jew*, *Jewish*, or *Judaism* in these Latin treatises and vernacular sermons on moneylending.[76] Indeed, in all of the published vernacular sermons on this or related economic themes, I have found only one instance of such a reference (D.375–76). In the Latin treatises, although more references are found, they are still by no means numerous, and certainly far from what one would expect from a man widely reputed to be the leader of the so-called fifteenth-century Franciscan anti-Semitic brigade. One conspicuous concentration of these references is contained in those chapters in the *Tractatus de contractibus et usuris* in which Bernardino, with neither rancor nor disdain, refutes the Jewish pro-interest argumentation.[77] Furthermore, there is in all of the three hundred pages of this treatise only one page of openly hostile anti-Semitism.

The "Usury-Jew Synonym Theory"

One might object that the relative paucity of direct reference to the Jews makes little effective difference. As Bonfil claims in his recent *Jewish Life in Renaissance Italy*, in order to attack the Jews and stir up anti-Semitic feelings, all one had to do was to attack the usurer, which, for Bernardino's audiences, would have automatically and universally been understood as a synonym for "Jew."[78] In other words, the usury discourse supposedly served as a convenient smokescreen for the friar's anti-Semitism. True, several of the towns he visited subsequently passed anti-usury legislation that directly affected the Jews, but, let us note, not only the Jews. Likewise, Mendicant preaching frequently provoked violence against the Jews, but such violence, we are told, typically occurred during Lent, especially after Good Friday Passion sermons, and not after sermons on usury, which occurred throughout the year.[79] "Every year we live in fear of this day," wrote Rabbi Joseph Cohen about Good Friday in the decade 1470–80, a remark that appears applicable to earlier decades as well.[80] There is, however, no documented or even alleged instance of anti-Jewish violence after a sermon (on any topic) by Bernardino.

It is necessary to question seriously whether in his own mind the friar made what Bonfil claims to be an automatic and exclusive identification between Jew and usurer, thus intending the Jews as the principal if not sole target of his anti-usury polemic. The question is of prime importance if we are to arrive at a more accurate measurement of the dimensions of Bernardino's own anti-Semitism, as distinct from that of Bernardino da Feltre, John of Capistrano, and the other Franciscan Observants, and if we are to advance beyond the unquestioned generalizations and undocumented assumptions of the past.

We have already pointed out that what Bernardino has to say about usury and the usurers reflected upon and affected the Jews, inasmuch as they were so intimately associated with the moneylending profession. Yet, as Bernardino well knew, in fifteenth-century Italy, the overwhelming majority of usurers were Christian; it hardly seems likely that in his preaching against this vice, he would simply ignore this majority and focus only on the few Jewish practitioners, as Bonfil would have us believe. Furthermore, the moral issue of usury was relevant not merely to the specific kind of moneylending or pawnbroking for small consumer loans by which Jews typically earned their living; it involved as well many different, not necessarily Jewish-related, varieties of banking procedures, business investments, contracts, and other financial interactions, including, most notably, the *monti*, the investment institutions established by the governments of Florence, Venice, and Genoa to finance their public debt.[81] Another such public investment institution was the dowry fund, the *monte delle doti*, established by Florentine fathers to raise the exorbitant sums necessary to marry off their daughters. These, according to bookseller-biographer Vespasiano, Bernardino declared an "extremely illicit" form of usury and "a worse kind of contract than that of the Jew who lends money with the little red cloth"—a remark significant for the explicit distinction it makes between Jewish and non-Jewish usury.[82]

This wide spectrum of financial transaction is fully embraced by Bernardino's principal discussion of the moral-economic issue of usury, a very lengthy and repeatedly republished treatise entitled *Tractatus de contractibus et usuris* (OOQ.IV.117–416). Reading such a treatise and listening to Bernardino's sermons against usury, the friar's Christian audiences understood them to be directed at themselves, and not simply as an anti-Semitic smokescreen. Again, we are told by Vespasiano, Bernardino preached one morning in the Cathedral of Florence against usury, focusing on "contracts and restitutions." After the sermon, humanist Giannozzo Manetti complained to the preacher of the rigor of his anti-usury teaching, exclaiming, "You have sent us all to damnation." Thereupon followed a debate in which Bernardino made the just-quoted remark about the *monti*. What is important here is the response of Bernardino's Christian listeners; they did not dismiss the friar's remarks as applying merely or principally to the Jews, but saw them as aimed directly at themselves.[83]

A careful reading of the sermons and treatises in question makes it clear that in preaching against usury, Bernardino has in mind as his target all usurers, Christians and Jews alike. As we saw, the 1423 Paduan sermons make explicit acknowledgment of the existence of Christian usurers (OOH.III.361a), and there as elsewhere Bernardino has no more regard for them than for their Jewish counterparts. (Let us note, by the way, that the preacher delivers those Paduan lists of anti-Jewish prohibitions in sermons on love and conversion, and not in those on usury or other economic themes, another strong indication that Bernardino made a distinction between the Jew qua Jew and the Jew qua moneylender.) Moreover, in most sermons large segments of the friar's condemnation are directed to the Christian usurer alone; a recurrent example is Bernardino's important and widely discussed subtopic of restitution, a moral question of concern only to Christians who sought reconciliation with the Church and complete absolution from the sin of usury. Jews, simply by virtue of being Jews, were thought to be automatically damned, and hence, as far as the Christian preacher was concerned, the issue of restitution was irrelevant to their life and eternal destiny.

The largely, if not exclusively, Christian focus of Bernardino's message is also true of the friar's many *exempla*. Not one of the usurers in any of Bernardino's anti-usury *exempla* is identified as Jewish. Most are explicitly and unmistakably Christian, as when Bernardino repeatedly speaks of the usurer denied burial in holy (that is, Christian) ground (R.375), and when he ridicules the hypocritical usurer "always in attendance at the first Mass of the day, kissing the feet of the saints and burning their noses [with votive candles]. He's on time for Mass because he doesn't sleep at night because of his avaricious desires and dreams."[84] Most of the "real life" examples of the tormented lives and demon-attended deaths of usurers that Bernardino relates, one after another in a long series, to the Sienese in 1425 explicitly involve Christian, and only Christian, usurers, as the pointed references to the sacraments of confession and communion, as well as to priests, friars, and monasteries, indicate (G.123–28). Perhaps the best known of these Christian-usurer *exempla* is that of the "Miracle of the Miser's Heart," involving St. Anthony of Padua, which was later depicted in bronze by Donatello on his celebrated 1447–48 altarpiece for the Basilica del Santo in Padua.[85]

Contemporary Italian texts outside the Bernardinian corpus also provide further explicit and abundant recognition of the usurer as Christian. One of the early fifteenth-century biographies of Bernardino, known as the *Vita anonima*, concludes its account of the friar's miracles and other marvelous deeds by describing in vivid detail the clamorous conversions of two notorious usurers, one in Vicenza, the other in Alexandria: both men were Christians.[86] During Bernardino's lifetime, the most notorious and wealthiest usurer in Milan was, again, a Christian, Tommaso Grassi, who is remembered both for his posthumous benefactions to the city and for his alleged attempt to use Bernardino's anti-usury preaching to drive out his competitors, an episode memorialized in the *Novelle* of Matteo Bandello.[87] Another case in point is Bernardino's older contemporary, "the merchant of Prato," Francesco di Marco Datini (ca. 1335–1410). As a Christian operating a bank for three years, and hence a member of the *Arte del cambio,* Datini would have "necessarily [drawn] upon himself the stigma of 'usurer,' " as his biographer, Iris Origo, explains, for in the early fifteenth century little distinction was made between the banker and the pawnbroker.[88] And Christian bankers in Bernardino's Italy were legion.

The further evidence afforded by the most popular contemporary fiction—such as Dante's *Divine Comedy,* Boccaccio's *Decameron,* and the many other widely read collections of tales and legends—also does not support what can be called "the usurer-Jew synonym theory." Whether they are portrayed as good or evil, friend or foe, in a positive, negative, or neutral light, the Jews in the most enduringly popular literature of medieval and Renaissance Italy are by no means all usurers, nor are all the usurers therein Jews. In Dante's *Divine Comedy* (*Inferno* 17), a work of enormous and immediate influence in establishing in the Italian popular imagination the historical archetypes of the various categories of sinners, the usurers are all of prominent Christian families, including the Scrovegni of Padua, the later patrons of the Arena Chapel adorned with the celebrated frescoes of Giotto. In Boccaccio's well-known tale of Abraham the Jew (*Decameron* 1: 2), the Jewish protagonist is not identified as a usurer; he is, instead, "a merchant and an extremely upright and honest man," a noteworthily positive characterization inasmuch as the *Decameron* was produced right after the Black Death, which is said to have occasioned a rise in anti-Semitism.[89] Another well-known Tuscan collection of tales of abiding popularity, dating from Bernardino's childhood, is Franco Sacchetti's *Trecentonovelle,* containing "by far the greatest number [of contemporary Jewish figures] found in any one collection of tales," according to David Salgarolo's "The Figure of the Jew in Italian Medieval and Renaissance Narrative."[90] As Salgarolo reports, "Sacchetti has not depicted his Jewish figures as usurers, not even the negative ones. He appears to have been much more concerned with the negative effects of Christian usury and condemns it severely in other novelle."[91] Sacchetti, let us note, was no stranger to Jewish moneylenders, nor they to him. While composing most of his *Trecentonovelle,* Sacchetti was serving as *podestà* of San Miniato, a small town within the Florentine territory, precisely during the period in which Jewish moneylenders were first allowed into the town (1393).

In the well-known collection entitled *Gli Assempri*, compiled by Bernardino's older contemporary and fellow Sienese Filippo degli Agazzari of Lecceto (†1422), we find several usurer-villains (in eleven of the sixty-one stories): not one of them is Jewish, and many, if not all, are explicitly Christian. As Bernadette Paton concludes in her wide survey of the literary production of the Sienese clergy, *Preaching Friars and the Civic Ethos: Siena, 1380–1480*, "Neither Filippo nor his contemporaries characterise usurers as Jews."[92] Thus, it is imprudent to assume that for Bernardino and his audience, the unqualified noun *usurer* always meant only or even primarily the Jew.[93] We might also add here that the verb *judaizare*, which, beginning in the mid–twelfth century with Bernard of Clairvaux, was frequently used to mean "to engage in moneylending," in Bernardino is used only once and only in its older patristic sense of "to engage in or advocate Jewish practices," being applied in criticism against those Christians who keep the sabbath on Saturday, like the Jews, as well as Sunday.[94] Hence, the "usurer-Jew synonym theory" finds little substantiation in the works of Bernardino of Siena; furthermore, given the aforementioned evidence in the other literature of the period, I suspect that for as many people as made that identification, there were equal numbers who did not.

Returning to the friar's Latin treatises on the subject of usury, as mentioned earlier, there is one only viciously anti-Semitic page among the hundreds in this body of sermon material. Although alone in its genre within the nine volumes of works coming directly from Bernardino's hand, it is an incriminating one for the friar as far as his anti-Semitism is concerned. Yet at the same time, it too calls into question the usury-as-smokescreen theory, inasmuch as, if indeed Bernardino were self-protectively using the usury discourse to mask an anti-Semitic intent, why would he then unmask himself so flagrantly and so needlessly by denouncing the Jews in such explicit, "smoke-free" terms? Be that as it may, the denunciation in question occurs in "sermon" 43 of the treatise entitled "How much usury is in opposition to God and renders the usurer an idolater. And how grave a blasphemy of God and his faith it is to allow moneylending."[95] In chapter 3 of that work, the friar lists all the many evils—temporal, spiritual, and corporal—that inexorably descend upon those towns and their citizens who permit the practice of usury. Evil number four of the *mala temporalia* is the concentration of all of the public and private wealth into the hands of a few persons; this, the friar explains, becomes an even greater evil when those few persons happen to be Jews:

> The fourth evil result is the concentration of money and wealth into one place. It is usually the case that when wealth and money are concentrated into fewer and fewer hands and purses, it is a sign of the deteriorating state of the city and the land. This is similar to when the natural warmth of the body abandons the extremities and concentrates only in the heart and the internal organs; this is seen as the clearest indication that life is slipping away and that the person is soon to die. And if this concentration of wealth in the hands of the few is dangerous to the health of the city, it is even more dangerous when this wealth and money is concentrated and gathered into the hands of the Jews. For in that case, the natural warmth of the city—for that is what its wealth represents—is not flowing back to the heart to give it assistance but instead rushes to an abscess in a deadly hemorrhage, since all Jews, especially those who are moneylenders, are the chief enemies of all Christians.[96]

Bernardino's warning about Jewish draining of Christian wealth through usury was already a popular, well-seasoned anti-Semitic topos, introduced by his fellow Franciscan Nicholas of Lyra (†1340).[97] With its image of blood and death, it evokes the familiar association of Jews with bloodsucking, and, by extension, with ritual murder, of which we have already spoken.[98] However, it is important to note, Jewish usurers are here evoked as only a smaller, albeit more dangerous, subset of the larger category of usurers; again, the two terms *usurer* and *Jew* are not, for Bernardino, coextensive. Furthermore, to call Christians and Jews "enemies" is simply to point out what had been the case, to greater or lesser degrees, since the earliest Jewish Christians were expelled from the Temple in Jerusalem and persecuted by the likes of Saul of Tarsus. This is what the New Testament, the unquestionable, unerring "word of God," taught—at least as understood by Bernardino and his age.

In the succeeding paragraphs, Bernardino digresses briefly on the topic of Jewish "malice" toward Christians:

> I am not a little astonished and I neither can nor want to cease being astonished over how so great an insanity reigns among Christians; so great a folly and so great an ignorance rules them; or better, a blindness so overshadows them that they are unaware of the consummate, devious malice that the Jews employ when they interact with Christians. All Christians are kings in the blood of him who is "the first-born of the dead and the prince of the kings of the earth" (Rev. 1:5); as true kings, they have possession of wealth that the

> Jews, in the just judgment of God, lost because of their lack of faith and the stubbornness of their hearts. Christians, indeed, have three types of wealth: temporal, corporal, and spiritual. And since the Jews are not able to take this wealth away from them by violence, they strive to seize it by malice and work to at least diminish it by various kinds of subterfuge.[99]

Through usury, medicine, and insidious conversation, Bernardino continues, the Jews steal the worldly, bodily, and spiritual possessions of the Christians:

> The Jews extort the temporal wealth of the Christians by public usury, as is clear to all; they attempt to take away their corporal wealth, that is, their health and life, when, against all ecclesiastical law, they seek by all means to be physicians of the body. Even the most ignorant and most rustic of [these physicians] are patronized by many incredibly senseless Christians, who completely entrust their health and life to them, rather than to the most learned and experienced Christian doctors. How many Christians they have killed either through ignorance or malice, God only knows. As for [the Christians'] spiritual wealth, that is to say, their faith and their obedience to ecclesiastical precepts, together with the other spiritual treasures of true Christians, this the Jews do not cease to seize, scatter, consume, devour, and dissipate through their poisonous flatteries, false friendships, noxious gifts, counterfeit camaraderie, devious betrayals, acquired privileges, and favors, dragging down the unfortunate souls of Christians to hell along with themselves.[100]

This fear of the putative, not-so-secret intention of the Jews to destroy the Christians and their religion was not original with Bernardino. It was nearly as old as Christianity itself, reiterated with constant and equal vitriol throughout the centuries. It was a fear that Bernardino shared with Thomas Aquinas, one of the most "reasonable" minds of the Middle Ages, who, "like almost all Christians of his era, believed Jews were profoundly dangerous and that contact with them should be avoided whenever possible. In his writings on Jews, evidence of this fear manifests itself everywhere. . . . Aquinas was firmly convinced that . . . Christian society was obligated to take elaborate precautions to guard against them."[101]

In one of the friar's vernacular sermons on usury, what is abstract and generic in this Latin passage is made specific and concrete: "In Bassano, in the territory of Lombardy," Bernardino explains to the Florentines, "there was a Jew who lived there for forty-two years, lending money, lending money at interest; he cleaned out that place so thoroughly that there isn't a cent to be found in either the town or its countryside."[102] This specific leitmotif about the Jews "cleaning out" or exhausting Christian wealth with their moneylending is yet another traditional note of anti-Jewish literature; we find it expressed, for instance, in decree 67 (*De usuris Iudaeorum*) of the Fourth Lateran Council, and we find it, closer in time and space to Bernardino, in the deliberations of the Sienese government, which, on December 21, 1393—well before the beginning of Bernardino's anti-usury campaign—allowed more Christian moneylenders to set up shop in town, so that "the Jews will not consume this city, as they already have, having made it a wasteland."[103]

This brief and almost parenthetical news item from Bassano is the sole direct reference to contemporary Jews in the numerous vernacular usury sermons, just as the three paragraphs quoted above from the Latin sermon 43 represent the sum of anti-Jewish diatribe in Bernardino's Latin works. In the same vernacular sermon in which he tells of the Jew of Bassano, the friar speaks of the Old Testament Jews, but this is merely to explain why they were allowed to charge interest in certain circumstances (D.373–75), as he does in the Latin treatises. The Old Testament is a sacred text in Bernardino's eyes, and he is unwilling to ridicule or condemn its contents, especially on points of moral law.

5. The Passion Sermons

The season of Lent was an important time for itinerant preachers like Bernardino. Preachers could count on an exceptionally large and regular attendance at their daily sermons, this attendance being part of the conventional penitential rituals of society. At the same time, in those days of limited opportunities for free social entertainment and for the hearing of news and novelties from other towns and lands, it was not only piety that motivated people to listen to three or four hours of oratory. Indeed, as we saw in chapter 1, the Lenten series of public sermons was so much an expected and desirable feature of fifteenth-century Italian public life that it was often the secular authorities who assumed responsibility for arranging and paying for the annual Lenten visit of the preaching friar.

The climax of the season may have been Easter Sunday for the theologians, but for the people, I suspect, it was Good Friday. The liturgical year knew no greater opportunity for moving the hearts of sinners to repentance than the Good Friday sermon. In Bernardino, as in many other Franciscans, this entailed a scene-by-scene, lachrymose dramatization of the

Passion of Christ, from the initial events in the Garden of Gethsemane to the final entombment, with an uninterrupted appeal to raw emotion: sorrow, anger, fear. The principal object of this one-man *sacra rappresentazione* (sacred drama) was to instill in the listener a love of Jesus and a hatred of sin. In reality, the hatred it instilled may well have included hatred of the Jews, for throughout the retelling the friar does not fail to identify and emphasize the culpability of the Jews in the execution of Jesus.[104] However, Bernardino was not taking unwarranted liberties with the scriptural text, the "revealed word of God," which indeed gives an unflattering portrait of the Jews as persecutors of the nascent Christian sect. To be sure, neither the New Testament nor Bernardino ever counsels the faithful to go forth and avenge the murder of their savior, but there was, without a doubt, a connection between such sermonizing and the recurrent outbreak of violence against the Jews at this time of the year all across Christian Europe, albeit none of it directly linked to our preacher.

We have no way of knowing how many times Bernardino actually preached such a "narrative reenactment" Passion sermon, in which the Jews would be normally be prominent among the dramatis personae. Only five of his Good Friday texts are extant; they vary much in content, and in only one are the Jews mentioned extensively. Two of the five come directly from Bernardino's own hand, the long *Tractatus de passione Domini Nostri Iesu Christi* (OOQ.II.188–293) and another Latin treatise, *De sacratissima passione et mysteriis crucis* (OOQ.V.68–170). The remaining three texts are *reportationes* of sermons, recorded as the friar was delivering them to the people: "De amore dolente" (OOH.III.296–304), "Della passione del nostro signore Gesù Cristo" (B.282–311), and "Della passione di Gesù Cristo" (E.344–84). Of these five compositions, two (*De sacratissima passione* and "De amore dolente") are not narrative accounts of the Good Friday drama, but are instead prosaic expositions of the theological fruits of Jesus' suffering and death, with hardly a mention of the Jews. Among the remaining three narrative reenactment compositions, only the *Tractatus de passione* (a Latin treatise destined for an audience of fellow preachers) is noteworthy for the explicit attention to Jewish responsibility for the death of Jesus.

This is not the case in the two vernacular *reportationes* of his Passion sermons. Actually preached to an audience, these contain far fewer and always more neutral references to the Jews, although the traditional expression "perfidious Jews," used in the Catholic Good Friday prayers until the Second Vatican Council (1962–65), makes an appearance in them as well.[105] In the vernacular sermons, Bernardino substitutes the generic term *il popolo* for *the Jews.* The reason for this difference is open to speculation. Did the vernacular sermons actually contain the same kind of direct anti-Jewish accusations, but for some reason—lack of time or attention, or censorship—were omitted by the scribes? Or did Bernardino himself omit such remarks for fear of rousing the crowd to violence and incurring censure? We cannot answer these questions with any certainty; but, as we shall later see, Bernardino indeed had reason to fear censure from the papacy, which was taking steps in these years to restrain the anti-Jewish preaching of the Mendicants.

In the *Tractatus de passione,* Bernardino's anti-Jewish utterances, though more frequent than in his other discussions of the Passion, are still only sporadic and parenthetical. They typically take the form of impassioned, melodramatic, but brief apostrophes that interrupt the narrative in order to highlight some particular facet of the *culpa Iudaeorum,* Jewish guilt. Several of these apostrophes are lifted by Bernardino verbatim from previous authors. A good example is the friar's, or more accurately, Bonaventure's comment on the delivery of Jesus into the hands of Pontius Pilate: "First, Christ is denounced by the Jews before Pilate the governor. 'O horrible impiety of the Jews, which could not be satiated by such insults but went further and, raging with the madness of wild beasts, exposed the life of the Just One to an impious judge as if to be devoured by a mad dog!' "[106] In another verbatim appropriation, this time from Simone da Cascia's *De gestis Domini Salvatoris,* Bernardino comments on the Jews' reluctance to enter the Roman praetorium for fear of ritual defilement (John 18:28):

> But the chief Priests and the whole council of the Jews *did not enter Pilate's headquarters lest they contaminate themselves and not be able to eat the Passover,* which they were celebrating at that time. Indeed the Jews, paying such diligent attention to more vile ceremonies, always fell into the pit of great evils. O accursed blindness and perverse character of the Jews! They feared they would defile the Passover if against their traditions, they entered the headquarters of the governor, but they did not fear leading to an unjust death the just and innocent Lord Jesus Christ.[107]

In his exposition of Jesus' "seven last words," Bernardino underscores in his usual poetic but hyperbolic fashion Jesus' great act of love in uttering the words of pardon, "Forgive them, Father, for they know not what they do" (Luke 23:34): "Consider, my soul, 'how copiously flowed the sweet love of our Lord Jesus upon his impious enemies when with all of his heart he became not only their pardoner, but also most effective intercessor and most pious defender.' "[108] This love and plea for forgiveness of those involved in Jesus' crucifixion, Bernardino explains, extends even to the Jews, but only to the *iudaeos ignorantes,* that is, those who did not know that Jesus was the Son of God. It does not extend to those who did:

> [I]t can be understood from the great benevolence of Christ that only those Jews who were completely ignorant of Christ were included in this prayer for forgiveness; if those who knew him were meant to be included in this prayer, there would have been no point in the Savior's having specified the cause of the pardon: *since they know not what they are doing;* for the word *since* [*quia*] is always an indication of cause. How could those who knew what was being done and what they were doing or consented to the killing of the Son of God be included in this prayer, when the word *since* is specified as an indication of cause only in cases of ignorance? Also, how could the Gentiles or the unknowing Jews have been excluded, since he prayed for sinners and wanted *all men to be saved*?[109]

Yet elsewhere, Bernardino does not spare even the *iudaeos ignorantes.* In another Latin work on "the multiple forms of ignorance," he seems to contradict what he stated in the *Tractatus de passione* by claiming that the ignorance of the Jews did (and does) not exculpate any of them for killing the Messiah. Quoting Alexander of Hales's *Summa theologiae,* the friar explains that in certain matters of faith and morals, it is the responsibility of every person to seek and know the truth. In such cases—and knowing the identity of the Messiah is one of them—ignorance cannot be given as an excuse. To support his claim, Bernardino then cites canon law, saying "it is stated [there] that ignorance of the fact does not excuse the Jews who did not believe that Christ had come. The reason for this is that such ignorance is crass and negligent. They could have known that Christ had come on the basis of Christ's own works, of those of his disciples, and of the entire array of scriptural testimony."[110]

The preacher's teachings on the moral culpability of the Jews for the death of Jesus are marked by further contradiction. Bernardino categorically states on at least five separate occasions that "[i]ntention judges all human actions," repeating the common Latin proverb "Quidquid agant homines, intentio iudicat omnes" (OOQ.I.382, 433; IV.270, 343, 433). As a corollary to this, the friar even states that if you engage in an act that you firmly though erroneously believe to be a mortal sin, then it becomes a mortal sin in your case (F.19). In one of the Siena 1425 sermons, Bernardino admits that the Jews crucified Jesus in good faith, that is, "believing themselves to do good, and sentencing him to death, saying . . . 'It is better that one person die for the people, than for so many people to perish.' And they believed that they were doing good."[111] Yet in the case of the Jews, their "good" intention of avoiding a greater evil by allowing a smaller one does not excuse them morally. That is because, the friar says, their judgment was so impaired, because they were already "so filled with and darkened by sin and iniquity" (F.41).

A major figure of the Passion story especially "darkened by sin and iniquity" was Judas Iscariot. In Christian literature, sacred and profane, Judas was often seen as the exemplification par excellence of Jewish evil and perfidy.[112] This, however, is not the case in Bernardino's sermons. The Passion sermons do dutifully include a description of the betrayal of Christ by Judas, and a mention of his subsequent suicide, but Bernardino does not dwell on either scene. Moreover, and more important for the present discussion, in the two dozen or so times the friar mentions Judas in his sermons and treatises, nowhere does he speak, directly or indirectly, of him as representative of the Jewish people as a whole. Bernardino acknowledges that Judas betrayed Jesus because he was "most avaricious," but adds no comment on that vice as a stereotypically Jewish trait (OOQ.III.101). The name of Judas—with no mention of his avarice—comes up twice in the usury sermons, but only as a point of comparison; that is to say, Bernardino warns that usurers who do not repent will die in a state of greater despair than that of Judas. Indeed, Bernardino sheds a slightly kinder light on Judas by pointing out on three occasions that the fallen apostle showed genuine contrition for his sin, confessed it publicly, and made restitution by returning the thirty silver pieces (these being the essential components of the sacrament of confession); unfortunately, however, he despaired of God's mercy, his suicide being a greater sin than his betrayal of Christ.[113]

Jesus may have forgiven the "unknowing" Jews, but his followers never did. Bernardino fails to see the irony in the contrast between Christian treatment of the Jews and the meekness, mercy, and love, which he has just invoked, of the founder of their faith. Notwithstanding Jesus' plea, the lot of all the Jews since their slaughter of "God" has been one of unceasing punishment. Such are the mysterious ways of cosmic justice, says the friar in another verbatim borrowing from Simone da Cascia. Bernardino reiterates the classic Christian theory of the perpetual guilt of the "deicidal" Jews, originally formulated by Augustine and re-elaborated throughout the centuries. He never mentions, however, the other commonly accepted Augustinian teaching, that of the need to preserve the Jewish remnant as testimony to the truth of Christianity.[114] As the preacher explains, the children of the Jews will be made to pay for the sins of their parents for as long as time shall last:

> But *the entire people in response said: Let his blood be upon us and our children* [Matthew 27:24–25]. How terrible indeed is the judgment upon the Jews that into that condemnation in which the parents had placed themselves they also led their own children, so that it became the personal responsibility not only of those already alive, but also those who were to be born. "But I know not by what so hidden demerit this responsibility followed them, or what was the justice so hidden that, with God's permission, parents were able to make liable to punishment for so great a crime their children not yet born, so that this condemnation fell upon not only those about to be born, but also all those who would be born up until the present day."[115]

It was, of course, inflammatory preaching such as Bernardino's that ensured that, generation after generation, the sons and daughters of the "God-killing" Jews would continue to pay for the one (and forgiven) sin of their "knowing" and "unknowing" mothers and fathers.

6. Miscellaneous Teachings on Judaism

Nowhere else may one find in Bernardino as many references to the Jews as in the Passion sermons. As for the remainder of the extant Bernardinian corpus, we find only brief moments of sermons devoted exclusively to the Jews or Jewish faith per se. However, the sum of these widely dispersed, often parenthetical teachings, though meager and fragmentary, gives us a sufficient idea of Bernardino's view of the Jewish religion. At the same time, all of Bernardino's teachings on the Jews—unflattering and unsympathetic as they might be—derive from the common, orthodox patrimony of the Christian tradition; nothing is of his own creation. Although Bernardino is not the origin of this tradition, by transmitting it, he did contribute his share to the continued "demonization" of the Jews that occurred in the course of the Christian centuries.

As for that demonization, the specific traditional theme of the Jews as supposedly worshipers and accomplices of the Devil comes up in Bernardino's preaching only once and only parenthetically. In his sermon "The Fallen and Ruined World," Bernardino raises and answers the question, "Why did Jesus allow himself to be taken up to the mountaintop and be tempted by Satan?" (Matthew 4), borrowing his explanation from one of his oft-quoted *dottori:* "Saint Augustine responds: If Christ let himself be beaten and crucified by the Jews, members of the Devil [*membra del dimonio*], how much more did he not have to let their leader do so to him? In this way he wanted to give us an example of [how to] oppose and combat [the Devil]."[116] In referring to the Jews in this fashion, Bernardino could claim to have found his justification not only in Augustine, but in Christian Scripture itself. To the Jews who rejected him, the Gospel of John has Jesus saying, "You belong to your father the devil and you willingly carry out your father's desire" (John 8:44). Other passages in Scripture, notably in the letters of Paul (1 Corinthians 10:20), teach, explicitly or implicitly, that all those who do not serve the Christian God are servants of Satan, Jews included. The Book of Revelation twice condemns the Jews as members of "the synagogue of Satan" (2:9 and 3:9), a term destined to have a long popularity among Christian writers, beginning in the fourth century with Church Father John Chrysostom and his *Discourses against Judaizing Christians,* and here echoed in the Bernardino passage just cited.[117] In his Latin treatise *On the Torments of Hell,* Bernardino uses the expression "synagogue of sinners" (*synagoga peccantium*), but does so referring to all sinners in general, with no mention of the Jews at all in the entire work (OOQ.III.369).

On the positive side, the friar acknowledges that the Jews and Christians are actually in agreement on many (unspecified) issues (OOQ.I.6); that we have them, the Jews, to thank for preserving Scripture (OOQ.I.9); and that their condition was once one of "purity" and great "nobility" (OOQ.II.372–73). On at least two occasions he recounts the traditional *exemplum* included in Etienne de Bourbon's *Tractatus de diversis materiis praedicabilis* of the God-fearing Jew who flees in horror at the blasphemies of his Christian companion.[118] In the latter *exemplum,* however, the two men were gambling at the time. Although Jews and the vice of gambling were closely associated in the popular imagination,[119] Bernardino never refers to this association, aside from this *exemplum.* Instead, he does mention, at least three times, another sin closely associated with the Jews: avarice. Indeed, in his view it is their avarice that drives the Jews to interpret the scriptural prohibition against usury in a self-serving way ("so that they understand what they want, not what they should") and that keeps them from converting to Christianity, which would mean "losing their wealth and honors."[120]

Their misinterpretation of the biblical usury text is just one of many ways in which the Jews fail to properly understand Scripture, according to Bernardino. The people of Moses were, and presumably still are, spiritual infants, as Bernardino explains in his gloss on Paul's letter to the Galatians 4:1–7:

> Note as well that the Jews were children under the law in four ways: in their speech, since they discoursed only of petty, that is, present, goods and not of eternal ones; in their understanding, since they paid attention only to the external meaning of words and not to their interior sense, just as children do in studying their schoolbooks; in the quality of their love, since they were enticed by the promise of temporal things, just as children are enticed by an apple; by their subjection to fear, since they were terrified by the scourge of present events, just as children are terrified by the rod.[121]

Elsewhere, quoting the *Arbor vitae* of Ubertino of Casale, who in turn quotes Bernard of Clairvaux's *Sermons on the Canticle of Canticles*, Bernardino observes that the Jews boast of other great men in their history bearing the name Jesus. However, unlike the name of the Christian Jesus, the names of those Jews "neither give light nor nourish nor heal; and thus, darkness envelopes the synagogue to this very day, toiling in hunger and infirmity; and it will not be healed nor satisfied until it acknowledges that Jesus is the lord of Jacob and of the ends of the earth."[122] The incomprehension of "the synagogue" is yet another conventional *locus communis* of the Christian polemical tradition against the Jewish faith. An unflattering etymology of the word *synagogue* had long since been popularized by Isidore of Seville, who drew it from the teachings of Augustine. As we read in a late-fourteenth-century treatise on the Church written in Siena by an otherwise unidentified Dominican bishop—to cite one example close to Bernardino in time and space—the word *synagogue* ultimately means "a gathering of the herd," that is, "of irrational animals who, although they have sense, they lack intellect; and while they attend to the literal meaning [of Scripture], they do not admit its allegorical-mystical meaning."[123]

Another traditional leitmotif of Christian doctrine was that of the necessary servitude of the Jews. As Bernardino explains, clinging like slaves onto Moses' law of fear, rather than like children onto Christ's law of love, "[the Jews] must be, willingly or unwillingly, the servants of the Christians," a clear echo of Thomas Aquinas's statement, "it is true . . . that Jews, in consequence of their sin, are or were subject to perpetual slavery."[124] As Bernardino further emphasizes, the coming of Jesus was their ruin (OOQ.VI.154 and IX.65). Then, contradicting what he preached in his Passion sermons, he states that the Jews' failure to believe in the true Messiah was not due to ignorance, but out of "hardness of heart" (OOQ.IX.73). But it was also their very Law that kept their eyes veiled and "prevented them from coming to grace."[125] Lacking in faith in Jesus the Savior, the Jews were already damned to hell, along with a whole list of unbelievers, as Bernardino points out more than once: "but if you see a Saracen, a Jew, a Patarino [a Lombard heretic], an excommunicate who dies with no sign of the sacrament, you must not pray for them; you would be sinning [if you were to do so], because you can be sure they are going to hell and they must not be prayed for."[126] The latter mandate against prayers for the Jews includes, it would seem, even those offered for their conversion; nowhere does Bernardino even suggest to his listeners that they make Jewish conversion the intention of their prayers.

In the very first treatise of his Latin *opera omnia*, *De fidei firmitate*, Bernardino explains that the tragic history of the Jews since the crucifixion of Jesus is one of the proofs of the veracity of the Christian faith. In chapter 3 of this treatise, "Christiana fides ex Iudaeorum captivitate ostenditur esse vera," the friar describes in detail the tribulations of the Jewish people, punished by God for rejecting the Messiah as no other nation before or since:

> As long as they adhered to the true faith, God exalted them above all the races of humanity, as is clear in the land that He gave them and in the Law and the kingdom and the temple and the victories and the miracles and the kings and the Prophets and the cult and the other favors. But after they denied the Son of God and rejected his faith, no race has been so crushed and humiliated by the oppression of tyrants, thieves, and assassins, by schisms and pogroms, by internal dissension and sieges, by plagues, by disasters, by the sword, by famine, by captivity, by violent death, by slaughter, by servitude, by scorn, by enslavement, and by despair. All of these curses have befallen them, as we find written in books.[127]

Now, the friar repeats, a nation "most abject, most wretched, weak and meretricious beyond all other nations," they wait "in vain" for their messiah.[128] However, they will convert to the true faith at the end of the world, Bernardino assures his audience several times (OOQ.III.198–99; VII.97; IX.290–91), alluding to the by then old and commonly accepted belief that the conversion of all Jews would be one of the imminent signs of the apocalypse.[129] In the meantime, the Jews—an ungrateful, hypocritical people who killed the son of the same God who, throughout history, had showered them with favors, miracles, and protection (OOQ.V.87–88; VI.432)—were not to be trusted, even those who had been baptized:

> There are certainly many who are full of error and heresy but who seem, in their external appearance, to be just. If these people were to show on the outside what they held in their heart, they would be burned at the stake. Among such people are to be numbered those who have lapsed into the wicked heresy of the Freedom of the Spirit [i.e., of the Free Spirit]. . . . To this number can be added many other heretics and schismatics and very many baptized Jews, and the sect of the heretical friar Dolcino, all of whom, though maintaining the external appearance of a morally upright life, are inside full of error. . . . All of the aforementioned individuals, and many like them, outwardly conform to the tenets of Catholic behavior, and claim to be thus with their words and their deeds. They are just like children in school, however: when the teacher is present, they sit up straight and are well-behaved merely out of fear; but when the teacher is absent, they turn completely to uproar and foolishness.[130]

Despite baptism, "once a Jew, always a Jew," the friar seems to intimate.

7. The Effect of Bernardino's Preaching Campaigns

Bernardino's anti-Semitic and anti-usury exhortations did not fall on deaf ears.[131] They had a concrete, if at times only temporary, effect in at least some of the towns visited by the preacher. Indeed, Italy during Bernardino's lifetime witnessed a dramatic rise in anti-Jewish legislation, which either outlawed (their and all) moneylending, imposed the yellow badge, or painfully restricted other aspects of their daily life, such as their purchase of meat and wine and their commerce with Christians in general. In only a few cases (Siena, Perugia, Amelia, Orvieto, Vicenza) do we have documentation directly connecting Bernardino's name with such legislation. However, his influence was undoubtedly a determining factor in other towns as well, and where his influence was lacking, there were many other zealous Observant Franciscan confreres who combed Italy with their anti-usury and anti-Jewish preaching in this century. What Diane Hughes observes about the fifteenth-century badge laws is likely true of Italian anti-Jewish legislation of this period in general: "Even when a direct connection cannot be found, Franciscan sermons had usually prepared the ground."[132] Nonetheless, since we are trying in this chapter to identify as precisely as possible Bernardino's specific contribution to fifteenth-century anti-Semitism, and not that of the Observant Franciscans in general, the discussion that follows is restricted to those cases in which Bernardino's influence on the local legislature is explicitly documented or reasonably and strongly suspected.

From the previous chapter, we recall that on June 8, 1425, Bernardino's hometown, Siena, approved its *Riformagioni di frate Bernardino,* which included an anti-usury provision, just as the friar was concluding a fifty-sermon preaching mission to his hometown begun on April 20.[133] (Just five years earlier, spurred by unnamed "valenti maestri di teologia," Siena had passed legislation dated June 7, 1420, against Jewish moneylending, but evidently to no effect.)[134] According to Felix Alessio, these new Bernardino-inspired 1425 laws were designed "to strike against the Jews and the usurers."[135] However, the text of the anti-usury article as reproduced by Alessio speaks, in generic and laconic terms, only of prohibition of "illicit and usurious contracts" and of the exclusion of the makers of such contracts ("usurarij, bistractieri e comperatori di grano ad novello") from public office and honors. It makes no mention of the Jews by name, even though Jewish moneylenders would necessarily have suffered the effect of the law.[136]

In any case, Bernardino's legal victory against Sienese usury was short-lived, for just two years later, in the summer of 1427, we find the preacher referring three times (albeit only in passing) to the presence of Jewish moneylenders in the city (R.981, 983, 984). At one point Bernardino even scolds—in a rare tone of defensiveness—those voters who permitted the exercise of their profession in the city: "And I want to add something else: I don't say it either out of hatred or in any way to wish evil on anyone and I mention no names; I say only this: if you were in some way responsible for the Jew being able to lend at interest here in Siena, you who agreed to it with your vote, you have incurred this greater excommunication. Have you understood me?"[137] Bernardino then reminds the Sienese of the consequences of "keeping the Jew in your house"—that is, it will bring about "the ruin of your city and the excommunication of the pope, which means you can't save your soul."[138] Bernardino refers in the above passage to those who had already voted to allow the Jewish moneylenders back into Siena; yet, according to Alessio, notwithstanding the threat of ruin and excommunication, the formal abrogation of Siena's anti-Jewish laws did not come until two years later, on February 29, 1429, at which time the city granted its Jews a certain degree of freedom of worship.[139]

Ten years later, in 1439, Siena did pass a Jewish badge law. Bernardino's name is not attached to the law, but it would finally have satisfied the friar's loudly communicated desire for the public marking of Jews. However, just nine days after its passing, moneylenders were granted an exemption to the new rule.[140] Indeed, from the fourth decade of the fifteenth century onward, the records of the Sienese government show a consistent and growing endorsement of and dependence upon its Jewish moneylenders, even as it exploited them, for example, in the form of forced loans. This crescendo culminates in the *Capitoli* of 1457, with their generous provisions for Jewish moneylending, including citizenship. The Jewish position of relative privilege confirmed by these *capitoli* was "not even put into crisis by institution of the Monte Pio" (the secular Sienese version of the Franciscan-inspired loan institution, the *monte di pietà*) in 1492.[141] According to Sofia Boesch Gajano, such a favorable attitude had earlier been characteristic of the Sienese government for the entire second half of the fourteenth century, lasting until 1412, at which time there commenced a twenty-seven-year interval of intolerance and denunciation of moneylending, Jewish or otherwise.[142] Yet, as we have just heard, according to Bernardino's preaching in the summer of 1427, the Sienese were not intolerant enough.

The experience of Siena was similar to that of other towns of Italy. They expelled the Jews or severely curtailed their moneylending in transitory fits of religious zeal and economic anger, only to be obliged to recall them and restore their privileges within a short period of time because their credit services and tax contributions had proved necessary for the conduct of public life in the town. For instance, to secure papal permission for its pro-moneylending *Capitoli* of 1457, Siena sent an embassy to Rome, declaring that "because of the wars that it has had to wage for many years, the city of Siena could not continue to be governed without the moneylender."[143]

Florence is another case we must examine, since it was a city in which Bernardino spent much time, preaching many of the sermons cited in this book. By the time Bernardino arrived in Florence in 1424 for his first major Lenten mission, there were no Jewish moneylenders in the city. Describing them as "enemies of the Cross, of our Lord Jesus Christ and of all Christians," Florence had already expelled all Jewish moneylenders from within its city limits with a law of January 24, 1406 (and repeated in its Statutes of 1415), well before the friar's arrival.[144] The January 1406 law had originally intended its prohibition to take effect in all of the towns, villages, and castles under Florentine dominion by September 1 that same year, but protests from the Jews and from the *comuni* of these outlying areas succeeded in blocking this extension. An international trade and banking center, Florence itself could get along without Jewish moneylenders thanks to their numerous Christian counterparts, who either ignored or circumvented the usury prohibition in place since 1394. Nonetheless, on June 12, 1430, "in order to prevent the poor of Florence from being ruined, especially in this time of plague by so heavy a burden of usury" exacted by the local Christian lenders, the *Signoria* passed a law to allow Jewish lenders into the city.[145] The law, however, was never acted upon. It was only with the coming to power of Cosimo de' Medici in 1434 that opposition to Jewish lending began to crumble, and with a law of October 17, 1437, the first Jewish moneylenders were allowed into the city.[146] Bernardino's preventive preaching to the Florentines had come to naught.

Elsewhere in Tuscany, in Lucca, Bernardino is said by one sixteenth-century chronicler to have occasioned the expulsion of the Jews from the city in 1443, but this news item is erroneous; Bernardino was nowhere near Lucca in the early 1440s nor until his death in 1444.[147] Erroneous, too, is the notice of an anti-Jewish uprising of the people of Viterbo supposedly provoked by Bernardino of Siena in 1429, as one chronicler of the city, Bussi, reports. The Franciscan preacher in question was, rather, a certain Guglielmo da Venosa.[148] Also mistaken is the statement made by Ugo Cassuto and repeated by Cecil Roth that in L'Aquila, in the Kingdom of Naples, Bernardino delivered twelve anti-Jewish sermons in the presence of King Renato in 1438, implying that Bernardino succeeded there too in inculcating his anti-Semitism in another powerful political leader. In truth, what the original fifteenth-century sources of this information (John of Capistrano and Bernardino of Aquila) tell us is simply that one summer around the feast of the Assumption (August 15) Bernardino preached for twelve days in the presence of Renato (reg. 1435–42), and that also present were "innumerable throngs of the faithful, as well as Jews."[149] No mention is made of the specific themes of those sermons. On this same occasion, by the way, the famous "miracle of Collemaggio" is supposed to have occurred in L'Aquila. A star, we are told, hovered over the head of Bernardino as he preached before the crowd on the feast of the Assumption, as a sign of favor and appreciation from the Virgin Mary for the preacher's eloquent words of homage.

As we saw in the previous chapter, following the example of Siena, the city of Perugia drafted in 1425 a new set of legislative reforms bearing the name of our preacher, the *Statuta Sancti Bernardini*, promulgated on November 4 of that year. Bernardino had been the guest of the Perugians in

1425 from September 19 through late October or mid-November, preaching on his usual repertoire of assorted themes—angels, suffering, detraction, confession, matrimony, the Holy Name of Jesus, purgatory, and heaven—and several sermons on restitution and trade.[150] Acting "in conformity to the teaching of the same venerable servant of Jesus Christ," Perugia was determined through these new ordinances to purge itself of all those sinful activities "because of which the wrath of God justly descends upon the Christian people and earthquakes, plagues, famines, wars, schisms, and infinite scandals increase among the Christian people."[151] The longest and most detailed of these new laws is the one devoted "to the extirpation of the depravity of usury, which leads souls to Gehenna and dries up the well of charity."[152] In its seven pages of description, this 1425 Perugian statute abolishes any previous legislation allowing financial transactions that entailed the loan of money at interest. Regarding the Jews, we find this single article:

> Moreover, we rule that, for the complete extirpation of the malice and perfidy of the said usurers, from this day forward, no Jew, either on a loan or on a deposit or contracted by any other title, is to receive money from any Christian in the form of interest; and any Jew who disobeys this law, *ipso facto,* is to be personally punished, if he can be caught, by the amputation of his right foot, and must *de facto* let this amputation be done to him by the incumbent Lord Mayor of the city of Perugia; if he cannot be caught, then let a ban be announced regarding the mandatory amputation of his leg, so that if he were to return within the walls of the town of Perugia he must have his right leg amputated; and in any case, his entire family is to be expelled from the city, territory, and district of Perugia.[153]

Let us note that the new Perugian statute in its entirety makes it clear that usury was a multidimensional issue, extending beyond the limited sphere of Jewish moneylending, discussion of the latter being restricted to one article of the larger law. The legislation as a whole cannot be seen simply as an attack on the Jews alone; they were but one component of a considerably greater issue.[154] Furthermore, the law does not expel those Jews who were not engaged in moneylending. In any case, by 1428, if not sooner, the anti-usury articles of the *Statuta Sancti Bernardini* were simply being ignored, for in that year we find the Perugian government contracting loans with both Jewish and Christian lenders to finance yet another military campaign.[155]

In later years, Perugia was to intensify its legislation against all Jews, at least on paper. In 1432 it imposed the badge law, while in 1439 it decreed a whole list of anti-Jewish restrictions concerning, among other things, the employment of wet-nurses and foster mothers and the buying and selling of wine and food. (Perugian Jews, the law specifies, were not to touch fruit at market unless they had already purchased it.) Bernardino's name is nowhere attached to these laws, but given the return visits of the friar to the city (in February 1427 and September 1438) it is not unreasonable to hypothesize his influence on their creation.[156] They are certainly well in keeping with his mind on the matter. However, as Toaff points out, the badge law in Perugia as elsewhere met with the same fate as the *Statuta Sancti Bernardini* and proved to be a "relatively obvious failure," while with respect to the 1439 provisions, there is reason to believe that "not all of these norms, and perhaps none of them, were applied in Perugia with the same zeal with which they had been formulated."[157]

In the autumn of 1426, Bernardino visited another smaller Umbrian town, Amelia. The precise date of his arrival there is unknown, but he apparently remained until the very end of December, at which time he proceeded to Orvieto. Fragmentary *reportationes* of five of his Amelian sermons have come down to us. Although none of them has usury or other economic issues as its theme, Bernardino is certain to have spoken of these matters, given what occurred at the same time in Amelia's City Hall: according to Shlomo Simonsohn, it was Bernardino who persuaded the town to cancel its *condotta* with its one Jewish moneylender, Magister Angelo, son of Aleuccio of Perugia. Having canceled his *condotta*, the General Council of the People then voted Magister Angelo's expulsion on December 30, but the expulsion never took place. By November 7, 1427, the moneylender and the government of Amelia had signed a new agreement for the continuation of his residence and business in Amelia.[158] Thus we can reckon another failure for Bernardino.

Leaving Amelia, Bernardino continued his mission through Umbria, and some time in early January of 1427 arrived in Orvieto, where, from January 12 to February 16, he preached to the populace.[159] Although none of his Orvietan preaching has survived, Bernardino would again have preached from his large but nonetheless limited repertoire of stock sermons. His visit again resulted in the promulgation of new legal *riformanze* by the town government. Dated February 16, 1427 (the date of Bernardino's last sermon there), these reforms explicitly acknowledge in their preface the role of the preacher in their promulgation.[160] The prologue to the new law informs us that, among other things, Bernardino "preached and admonished the people of Orvieto that for the salvation of their souls" they were all to "refrain most of all from associating with the Jews, and that any immunities and exemptions that had been granted to the Jews by the government of Orvieto and any agreements contracted with the Jews and signed, especially those allowing them to lend money at interest, be declared null and void."[161] After this preamble, the text goes on to describe the enactment of the new law by Lord Crescimbene of Orvieto, who

> after due consultation upon the question of the Jews, having invoked the name of the Most High, rose to his feet and proceeded to the podium and advised that in order to avoid the punishment of excommunication, which the said venerable friar Bernardino in his preaching had pronounced upon all those having illicit commerce with the said Jews and giving them assistance, advice, or support, especially in the lending of money at interest, that by the authority of the present General Council, all immunities, exemptions, agreements, and contracts given and granted by the government of the said City to one or another of the same Jews and initiated and signed with them either in the present or the past be declared null and void.[162]

In the Veneto, the town of Vicenza also passed anti-Jewish legislation, likewise linked to Bernardino, in this same period. This we know through the testimony of Bernardino's younger contemporary, the well-known canonist Alessandro de Nevo (†1486). In his frequently republished *Consilia contra judaeos foenerantes,* de Nevo tells us that the Jews were expelled from Vicenza immediately following a preaching visit from Bernardino. The friar is said to have read aloud from the pulpit, canon law text in hand, the ecclesiastical decrees against the Jews, and condemned as blasphemers those who claimed that moneylenders were a necessary assistance to the poor, thus denying the providence of God.[163] De Nevo's *consilia* were formal legal opinion papers that "became the principal arsenal from which the Italian Franciscans drew their theoretical anti-Jewish arguments" in the half-century after Bernardino's death.[164] Elsewhere, they invoke the preaching of the friar to bolster de Nevo's own case against Jewish moneylenders. In *consilium* number four, after referring approvingly to the expulsion of the Jews from Padua and Vicenza just a few years prior to his writing, the canonist paraphrases the same infamous paragraph from Bernardino's sermon on usury (quoted above) concerning the danger that Jewish moneylenders represent to the health of a town.[165] Thus did the preaching of the friar endure in its influence even after his death. However, as Meneghin points out, in Vicenza as elsewhere, "the absence of Jewish moneylenders did not last long."[166]

There may have been other towns and cities in this same period whose expulsions of the Jews or severe curtailment of their activity could be traced to Bernardino and his preaching campaign, but we thus far possess no explicit documentary evidence. The city of Padua is a case in point, where Bernardino preached twice early in his career (1413 and 1416) and at least twice again at the height of his fame (1423 and 1443).[167] As already mentioned, the condition of the Jews in Padua began to deteriorate shortly after the city came under the rule of Venice in 1405. The Venetians who "had shown themselves rather severe toward the Jews"[168] since at least the end of the fourteenth century (before, that is, Bernardino's own arrival there) had passed a Jewish badge law as early as August 27, 1394, although it had to be repromulgated in more explicit terms on November 3, 1426, along with other anti-Jewish measures.[169] On May 30, 1430, the Consiglio Cittadino of Padua asked the Venetian Senate to enforce the same badge law in Padua, since "it is a shameful thing and ignominious to the Christian name that the Jews are not distinguishable from the Christians."[170]

Seven years earlier, with a law of September 26, 1423, Padua had deprived the Jews of their right to private property (note that Bernardino had been in the city just several months before, from mid-February through April 19).[171] On September 6, 1431, a further law was passed, this one expelling Jewish moneylenders from Padua unless they accepted certain further restrictions on their activity.[172] Finally, in June 1455, eleven years after Bernardino's death, the moneylenders were all expelled from Padua, although some remained to continue their lending clandestinely or else moved to the immediate outskirts of the city.[173] The motivation behind these legal actions on the part of the Paduans was, according to Ciscato, "religious terror," fear of divine retribution, such as that expressed in their 1488 refusal of a Jewish *condotta* request: if they were to let the Jews back into the city, the city fathers stated, "in addition to the other evil and harm which would thereby happen, we greatly fear, and it is almost certain, that the plague would immediately break out in the city."[174]

Back in Umbria, the town of Todi also passed two new laws in 1436 against the Jews, one (March 29) prohibiting the ritual slaughter of meat and preparation of wine by the Jews, and the other (June 19), the badge law.[175] Bernardino's name is not attached to these provisions, but we know that his influence had been strongly felt in the town. Similar is the case of the duchy of Milan, where Bernardino, much favored by citizens and duke Filippo Maria Visconti, preached on repeated occasions. On September 20, 1443, Visconti abruptly canceled all the *condotte* he had granted to moneylenders in his territory, Christians and Jews alike, citing the injunctions of divine and canon law.[176] The same abolition of licenses was extended to Mantua as well within a few years, but shortly thereafter we find the Jewish moneylenders receiving new *condotte,* as if nothing had changed in the interim.[177]

8. Assessing the Evidence

Having completed our review of the evidence, we can now offer some general conclusions about the nature and extent of Bernardino's anti-Semitism. First of all, the total of explicit anti-Jewish remarks scattered among the friar's works represents the equivalent of no more than nine or ten pages of printed text among the several thousand pages of his published collected works. This is in marked contrast with the scores of pages (representing entire sermons and treatises) that the friar devotes to the witch, the sodomite, the political faction member, the vain woman, and the gambler. This tally includes the anti-usury sermons and related economic discourse. As in the rest of his works, in these treatises and sermons, both Latin and vernacular, one rarely comes across the words *Jew, Jewish,* or *Judaism.* While there is no doubt that Bernardino's anti-usury preaching added fuel to the anti-Semitic sentiment of his audiences, for the reasons described above, it is inaccurate to claim that the Jews were either the primary or the exclusive target of this moral-economic discourse.

Second, although it did great harm to the Jews, the highly charged rhetoric of Bernardino's invective against the Jews was characteristic of his invective against all those classes of people whom he considered a grave danger to Christian society. In this sense, Bernardino was as anti-Semitic as he was antisodomite, antiwitch, antiblasphemer, anti–anybody who dissented from divine law and therefore endangered Christian society. Regrettable as it may have been in its effect, Bernardino's hyperbolic anti-Jewish vituperation is little different from that which he directed against these other groups. Indeed, in comparison with the latter body of invective, his remarks on the Jews end up appearing somewhat restrained. To those examples we have seen in the previous chapters of this book, let me add one further, Bernardino's solution for the problem of feminine fashions, which are bankrupting the fathers and husbands of Tuscany: "Do you know what needs to be done? First of all, we should burn at the stake the woman who dresses [in this way], then her mother who allows her to do so, and then afterward, the dressmaker who provides her with the clothes."[178]

Bernardino was a popular preacher of distinctively and characteristically Franciscan and Mediterranean stamp. Accordingly, one of the primary tools of his oratorical trade—having its precise counterpart in the devotional art of the Franciscan churches—was the direct appeal to crude, heightened emotion. More than by logical argumentation or by a long recitation of scriptural, doctoral, and canonical *auctoritates* (the other standard tools of the medieval preacher's trade), Bernardino frequently attempts to win the audience over to the Church's point of view by taking aim directly at their hearts. Whatever the subject, this often entailed a heavy dose of impassioned oratory in the form of the hyperbolic description, exclamation, threat, and fulmination. Inevitably the Jews fell victim to this rhetoric, along with a wide host of others.

Third, in the specific legal, theological, or biblical content of Bernardino's sermons, regarding the Jews, their religion, or their place in Christian society, there is simply nothing new. Without exception, all of what Bernardino communicated about the Jews was already an established part of Catholic tradition. This was transmitted to him either in Sacred Scripture, canon law, the Church Fathers (Augustine, Jerome, Chrysostom), the medieval *magistri* like Aquinas and Hales, or the sermons and treatises of popular preachers and spiritual writers, such as the vehemently anti-Semitic fourteenth-century Dominican preacher Giordano da Rivalto, and Bernardino's older contemporary Vincent Ferrer, "scourge of the Jews."[179]

As already mentioned, with little interest in personal speculation, together with much fear of disturbing the orthodox order by creating theological "novelties," Bernardino saw his own official task primarily as that of communicating to the people in clear and simple terms what we might call today the "official catechism" of the Church, as formulated by its duly authorized "doctors." "The doctors teach us [preachers] and we make a bouquet of them and pass it on to you," he reminds his audience.[180] Respecting the medieval rhetorical convention of teaching and persuasion by "ratio, auctoritas, exemplum," Bernardino was well aware of the crucial importance of the "doctors" to his preaching. As we heard him tell the people of Siena in 1427: "Do you know why [I had so much success in Lombardy]? Because I was constantly armed with the sayings of the doctors" (R.325). In this sense, although at times radical in its adherence to the letter of the law and intense in its emotional register, Bernardino's catechism is fundamentally conservative.

Fourth, although the message Bernardino imparts to his Christian audiences about their Jewish neighbors is overwhelmingly negative, it is not completely nor unrelievedly so. I am referring to the friar's repeated message that Christians should always nurture for and demonstrate toward the Jews some form of "love" and should always be ready to come to their assistance in time of need. True, such counsels, however often reiterated, pose grave difficulties of interpretation and logical coherence within the larger, complete context of Bernardino's teachings about the Jews, and are overshadowed by his other remarks counseling a different attitude. But the fact remains that Bernardino did make such irenic statements about the Jews, presumably with sincerity. These statements, however, have been overlooked by every previous discussion of Bernardino's attitude toward the Jews.

Fifth, Bernardino's anti-Semitism is not John of Capistrano's anti-Semitism; neither is it Giacomo della Marca's nor Alberto da Sarteano's, nor Bernardino da Feltre's. However much overlap there may have been in the style and doctrine of the fifteenth-century Observant preachers, they were autonomous agents with individual identities and distinct messages. We must allow them their individuality. This is too often forgotten by scholars, who tend to lump them all together in describing Franciscan anti-Semitism in this century. Some scholars have also assumed, if only implicitly, that all of what Bernardino's disciples or contemporary Franciscan confreres preached about the Jews can somehow be attributed to their *caposcuola*, Bernardino. Although in the long run the collective effect of Franciscan preaching on the life of the Jews might have been the same—that is, a deplorable decline in the quality of their existence—it behooves us to acknowledge and be mindful of the effective difference between what Bernardino himself preached and did during his own lifetime and what contemporaries and successors preached and did, using (or misusing) his name and his texts as their own *auctoritas*. The exaggerations of Bernardino of Feltre and the misattributions of the so-called *Testamento di San Bernardino* are two cases in point.[181]

How much is Bernardino responsible for the anti-Semitic trend during the fifteenth century? Did he actively encourage his disciples to "go and do likewise" with respect to the Jewish question? Or did they go out and do what they did, unbidden by him and to a degree he never intended? It is here important to note that as a rule, these specific men—Bernardino, Capistrano, Sarteano, Della Marca—traveled and worked separately, often at long distances from each other; as to what they talked about when they did come together, we have little concrete information. Until we complete the in-depth, *ad fontes* examination called for by Poliakov of the anti-Jewish activity of these friars and the nature of their personal interaction, collaboration, and ministerial coordination (or lack thereof), scholarly scrupulosity requires that the answers to these questions be postponed.

Although few, the anti-Jewish pages in Bernardino are hostile, and it is a hostility that, in the end, was not neutralized by his contradictory counsels to "love" the Jews and help them in need. The aim of this chapter is neither to exculpate Bernardino from the charges of anti-Semitism nor to deny that he had a notable share in exacerbating the climate of fear and intolerance of the Jews in fifteenth-century Italy. Whatever Bernardino's personal intent toward the Jews, the truth is that his "few" pages did great harm to both Jews and Christians. My goal in this chapter has been, instead, to undertake the first thorough, fully documented investigation of Bernardino's anti-Semitism in order to arrive at a more accurate picture of its specific extent, contours, and consequences. That picture now appears to be a little more nuanced and complicated than previous accounts would suggest.

In any case, given the hostility expressed in those "few pages," we wonder why there are not more of them. Why was the friar able to contain or why did he decide to contain his hostility within what amounts to mere brief minutes of sermon time? Only conjecture is possible. Bernardino undoubtedly did preach more on the subject of the Jews, but the sermons containing this material were never recorded or have not survived. I suspect, however, that what he had to say about the Jews in these unrecorded or lost sermons was fundamentally the same as what we have seen above in content, tone, and quantity. I do not believe the friar ever preached an entire sermon on the Jews, nor do we have any evidence indicating that he ever engaged in public or private debate with them. The principal topics of Bernardino's mature preaching career are remarkably uniform and were ultimately anthologized by the friar himself in the *quaresimali* and other sermon cycles and treatises of his Latin *opera omnia*.[182] These volumes have come down to us intact and contain just those few Jewish-related passages cited above. If Bernardino had felt the need for a whole sermon or separate treatise on the Jews qua Jews, he would have included such a text in his carefully composed *quaresimali* and formal Latin treatises.

But to return to our question, why do we not find more explicit anti-Jewish invective in Bernardino? The evidence affords at least two different and opposing interpretations.

The first possible answer is that the Jewish question (as distinct from the issue of usury), although a cause of great concern and hostility, was simply not a primary or constant preoccupation for the friar—that there were more dangerous enemies of society or more pressing social-moral problems that engaged his attention. To begin with, let us recall that the Jewish population of fifteenth-century Italy was relatively modest. Simonsohn tells us that "before 1500," the total number of Jews in central and northern Italy "varied between 8,000 and 12,000." These several thousands were, furthermore, distributed into isolated groups of "minuscule" dimensions scattered over a large territory.[183] Jews thus represented a less visible class of "enemy" than the others addressed by the friar. Of all the places in which Bernardino preached, Padua had one of the largest, most active Jewish populations; hence his perceived need to be more outspoken on the Jewish question. This was not the case in Florence and Siena, two other venues of extensive preaching by our friar. Neither of those two city-states had a Jewish presence of such noteworthy proportions as Padua; as already mentioned, in Florence, at the time of his preaching missions there (1424 and 1425), there was no Jewish community at all.[184]

However, a second explanation is possible for the hostile but few anti-Jewish pages in Bernardino. It could indeed be the case that the preacher wanted to preach more extensively against the Jews, but was prevented from doing so by direct or indirect external pressure. This pressure may have come from the towns that played host to Bernardino, which did not want outbreaks of violence against the Jews, civic life being then already sufficiently tumultuous. We recall, for instance, the rioting that broke out in Viterbo in 1429 against both the Jews and the local town officials protecting them after the preaching visit of Franciscan Guglielmo da Venosa. However, if town governments put restraints on Bernardino's preaching—such as Florence did in 1488 to Bernardino da Feltre[185]—the fact has gone unrecorded or as yet undiscovered.

The episcopacy and the papacy would have represented more certain sources of restraining pressure upon Bernardino. Unfortunately, no research has been conducted into the response of the bishops of Bernardino's time to the Jewish question and to the preaching of the friars. Yet, as Norman Roth reminds us, it was the bishops, and not the papacy, who had more direct, effective jurisdiction on the local level over the Jews.[186] There is little to report, however, on Bernardino's rapport with the bishops of his day.

We do know that Bernardino earned the enmity of many high-ranking, respected theologians, such as Andrea Biglia, who would have communicated their concerns about Bernardino to the local bishop. In addition to his criticism of the fundamental theology of Bernardino's cult of the Holy Name of Jesus, Biglia was worried that Bernardino might be using his great demagogic sway over the masses to rouse them into open defiance of legitimate Church authority.[187] One bishop made this accusation against Bernardino in 1426: "Christ did not enter Jerusalem on Palm Sunday with as much honor and clamor and racket as this beast [Bernardino] has received." The bishop in question was James of Spoleto, complaining about the friar's triumphal arrival at the Umbrian town, where the streets had been lined with people waving olive branches to greet him.[188] To this accusation Bernardino is reported to have responded with arrogance, "What is it to the bishop if these people, out of the devotion they have for me, want to receive me with olive branches?" In turn, Andrea da Cascia, the chronicler of this event, protests, "See how great is his pride that he desires to be honored by the people just as Christ was." Yet this is the only such story we have to report; the rancor of Bishop James notwithstanding, in the following year, Bernardino was offered the episcopal seat of Siena, followed by that of Ferrara in 1431 and that of Urbino in 1435, all of which he refused.

There is, instead, more to report with respect to the papacy. In the course of Bernardino's lifetime, petitioned by the Jews, the papacy issued more than one bull forbidding preachers to engage in anti-Jewish oratory because of the violence subsequently inflicted upon the Jews by Christians.[189] Martin V issued two stern warnings during Bernardino's preaching career, one dated February 20, 1422, and the other, far longer and more detailed, dated February 13, 1429. Martin's 1422 bull was a stringently elaborated reissue of Calixtus II's *Sicut Judeis*, which since the twelfth century had been considered the classic statement of general papal policy toward the Jews—in theory, at least, but not in the vicissitudes of actual, inconsistent practice.[190] Martin had also reissued *Sicut Judeis* earlier in his pontificate, on January 31, 1419, to reaffirm Jewish rights and protections, but the 1419 bull makes no mention of anti-Jewish preachers.[191]

In his 1422 bull, the pope again confirmed all the traditional privileges, exemptions, and protections of the Jews (no forced baptisms or service, no disturbance to their festivals nor harm to their persons), explaining that he was doing so in response to protests of the Jews over Christian preachers, specifically the Mendicants (the Franciscans and Dominicans), who were rousing the masses against the Jews with their calumnious anti-Jewish preaching. The bull flatly contradicts the attitudes and comportment that Bernardino, under the authority of canon law, attempts to impose upon his 1423 Paduan audience:

> [W]e have just received the complaint of certain Jews bringing to our attention the fact that some preachers of the word of God, Mendicants as well as those of other orders preaching to the people, among other things, are explicitly instructing Christians to flee from and avoid association with the Jews, and not to interact with them in any way, nor bake their bread for them, nor give them or receive from them fire or other things necessary for work, nor nurse or feed Jewish children. They have also preached that anyone who does any of the above things incurs *ipso facto* grave sentences of excommunication and ecclesiastical censures; because of this, conflict and scandals at times arise between them and the Christians, and cause is given to the Jews (who would perhaps convert to the Christian faith if they were treated kindly and humanely) for persevering in their unbelief.[192]

Martin's letter goes on to condemn the type of calumny disseminated about the Jewish people that we heard in Bernardino's story of the doctor of Avignon:

> [M]any Christians even assert on the basis of imaginary pretexts and false reports that the Jews in times of plague and other calamities, put poison into the wells and mixed human blood in their matzoh; thus unjustly charging the Jews with these evil crimes, they assert that such things were done in order to bring about the destruction of humanity. Because of these stories, the people are roused against the Jews and kill them, and subject them to and afflict them with various persecutions and molestations.

No one is mentioned by name in the bull: was Bernardino of Siena among those preachers whom the pope and the representatives of the Italian Jewish communities who secured the bull had specifically in mind?[193] We unfortunately have no way of knowing.

Strangely enough, the bull was revoked one year later on February 1, 1423, by the same pope, who now claimed that the 1422 "apostolic letter" had been "extorted from us through circumvention and importunity." Although the reasons for this papal about-face remain obscure, John of Capistrano's influence, on the one hand, and putative Jewish support of the Hussite rebellion, on the other, are both suspected.[194] Nonetheless, on February 13, 1429, Martin issued another, even lengthier, bull, *Quamquam Iudei,* reaffirming, albeit just for Italy, Jewish privileges and protections, and repeating in even more rigorous terms the 1422 warning to Christian preachers. The latter, in fact, were to now face excommunication if they violated the bull's prohibition. Martin's successor, Eugene IV, also confirmed Jewish rights and protections in his reissue of *Sicut Judeis* on

February 6, 1433, followed two years later (February 20, 1435) by a bull that again warned Christian preachers not to rouse the masses against the Jews with their sermons.[195] Hence Bernardino's hands or rather his tongue would have been tied by express papal command. Even though, beginning in 1426 with his Roman heresy trial victory, Bernardino was to become increasingly the object of the personal esteem and favor of the pontiffs (Martin V and Eugene IV), the preacher could not claim exemption from such papal bulls, nor could the pope have granted it to him, even had he been of a mind to do so.

Hence, to recapitulate, according to this second interpretation of the evidence, the "hostile but few" explicit anti-Jewish statements in Bernardino are to be explained, not by a lack of anti-Semitic desire on the preacher's part, but rather by papal restraint on the Mendicants. Such a conclusion is plausible, but not without a major difficulty: Knowing the uncompromising character of our preacher—who, after all, counseled the Paduans to disobey the papal exemption of the Jewish badge law—and the irrepressible nature of his most ardent convictions (he constantly risked death and personal harm rather than be silent on controversial topics), one would expect his true convictions and desires, frustrated in the preaching arena, to have found adequate expression outside that arena. That is, blocked by papal mandate from publicly preaching against the Jews, Bernardino might be expected to have disseminated his ideas, vented his emotions, and agitated against the Jews through other means and in other forms, written or otherwise. However, this is not the case. The above-described tally concerning the relative rarity of explicit Jewish reference in the Bernardino corpus includes the friar's personal notebooks, letters, scriptural glosses, and other works coming from his own hand, not destined for the public eye or ear, and spanning the long years 1417–43. In other words, even in his private writings, Bernardino spent little time on the Jews. Furthermore, there is as proportionately little explicit Jewish reference in all of the many contemporary biographies, chronicles, diaries, and other rich archival material documenting Bernardino's life, thought, and public enterprises as there is in the works coming from Bernardino himself. If Bernardino had been the rabid, obsessive anti-Semite that he is sometimes portrayed as, it seems unlikely that this fact would not have shown forth in at least some of this considerable documentation.

Hence, uncomfortable as it may be, we must conclude on a note of indecision. To summarize: Although the first of the two interpretations of the evidence described above seems far more compelling than the second, both readings, different and divergent, remain valid possibilities. That is to say, we find relatively scarce explicit Jewish reference in Bernardino either because the Jews qua Jews interested him only moderately as a moral concern, or because he was restrained by papal mandate.

Looking at the entire body of Bernardino's teachings on the Jews, we can distinguish two goals therein. Bernardino's first goal was to alert Christian society to and protect it from the threat of Jews, who might try to persuade Christians into apostasy or seek revenge on them by inflicting bodily harm. By way of protection, the preacher simply called for the effective enforcement of the Jewish isolation provisions already promulgated by canon law. Bernardino's second goal was to eliminate what he considered a gross offense against charity, universal brotherhood, and economic justice by eliminating the charging of interest on loans, especially those made to the poorer elements of society. This meant driving the usurer, both Christian and Jewish, out of business. Again, Bernardino does not call for anything not already mandated by Scripture or canon law. He never calls for violence against the Jews, although one wonders what the friar expected his audiences to do with the anti-Jewish anger he stirred in them with his preaching. Furthermore, and somewhat surprisingly, he never calls for nor ever participated in any methodical campaign of conversion of the Jews, such as the compulsory sermon attendance decreed by the Council of Basel, only one of several repressive anti-Jewish measures contained in its September 7, 1434, decree *De Iudaeis et neophytis.*[196] Bernardino's goal seems to have been, above all, isolation of the Jews, although he makes no explicit mention of segregating them in a separate area of the cities or towns, as the Council of Basel decreed, and as the bishop of Bologna, Niccolò Albergati, had decreed in 1417 for the Jews of that city.[197]

One fifteenth-century account of Bernardino's life, the so-called *Vita anonima,* and one Roman chronicle of the same century, Paolo dello Mastro's *Memoriale,* do make brief references to Bernardino's having converted Jews, but such conversions seem not to have been the result of a special, deliberate campaign on the friar's part, and may simply have been a secondary effect of the normal course of his preaching. Elsewhere it is pointed out (by the same *Vita anonima* and by John of Capistrano) that Jews were in attendance—voluntarily, the sources intimate—at the friar's sermons on various occasions along with the customary Christian crowds from all walks and stations of life.[198] Bernardino may have written such an apologetic treatise as *De christianae fidei firmitate* (OOQ.I.5–47) with an eye to the conversion of Jews. However, what the prologue to that treatise tells us is that the work was written to confirm Christians in their faith and to convince "omnes haereticos et paganos" of the truth of the Christian faith. There, as elsewhere, we find no explicit reference to a desire or need for the conversion of the Jews. The only time the topic of Jewish conversion comes up—in passing—is in the preacher's discussion of eschatological subjects, to confirm the traditional belief that Jews will be converted at the end of the world.

How successful was Bernardino in reaching his anti-Jewish goals? In the short run, his failures were at least as many as his successes, if indeed not of greater number. Few of the anti-Jewish measures passed by Italian towns during Bernardino's lifetime proved effective. Even in those cases in which these provisions were not legally overturned, there was "an enormous gap between the letter of the law and the reality of daily life."[199] In the long run, the story is different: Life became increasingly difficult for the Jews in Italy after Bernardino's death, with the institution of the *monti di pietà* in the last quarter of the fifteenth century and of Jewish ghettos in the sixteenth (beginning in Venice in 1516). In these and other tactics to isolate the Jews and restrict what we would call today their "human rights," the oratory of the Franciscan preachers played a role. Though neither institution—the *monte di pietà* and the ghetto—had ever been part of his explicitly articulated program, Bernardino, I believe, would have approved both measures and would have counted them as further successes for the Church and his order, and himself as part of that Church and that order.

"[O]ne would like to know what exactly it was that in the fifteenth century provoked the spread of such hatred for the Jews," asks Italian historian Corrado Vivanti.[200] A completely satisfying answer to this question, involving as it does so great and so long-lasting a collective sentiment as anti-Semitism, will probably always elude us. The same is true for the witch phobia and the "sodomophobia" we have examined in the previous chapters. Nonetheless, the various social, economic, political, ecclesiastical, demographic, and other crises and stresses already identified in the previous chapters assuredly played an important role: in fueling the anxiety of preachers like Bernardino about the plight of Christian society and its future survival, they fueled a search for relief of that anxiety through the quest for scapegoats. These were found, not only in the person of the witch and the sodomite, but also in the Jew.

As Bernardino describes them, the explicit, conscious grounds for his opposition to the Jews are both theological and economic. Theologically, Bernardino was convinced that the Jews had misunderstood divine revelation and their own history and were waiting in vain for a messiah who had already come. Furthermore, the Messiah's arrival had rendered the Jewish faith obsolete and futile. In the friar's eyes, the Jews were simply wallowing in ignorance and in stubborn opposition to "the one, true faith." From his study of the New Testament, he knew that the Jews had persecuted and sought to eliminate this "heretical" new sect, Christianity, and believed that this was still their intention in his own day. He further believed that their opposition also took the form of a not-so-secret, widespread conspiracy against Christianity and Christians, sometimes reaching the point of homicide.

On an economic level, the problem was lending at interest, the issue first assuming troublesome proportions some centuries before Bernardino, in the High Middle Ages, during Europe's shift from a precapitalist "gift economy" to the profit economy of the new world of international trade and commerce. As John Hood reminds us,

> Medieval Christians were deeply ambivalent about money and commercial change. After all, Saint Paul had declared that money was the root of all evil. Yet in the new market economy of twelfth- and thirteenth-century Europe, money and commercial exchange were increasingly important; more than ever, human relations seemed to be governed by cold calculation and economic self-interest rather than Christian love.[201]

As an Observant Franciscan devoted to poverty, Bernardino felt this ambivalence, even centuries after the onset of the economic shift. On an economic level, Bernardino sincerely believed that the lending of money at interest represented a grave offense against charity and one of the principal means whereby the poor became poorer and were trapped in their poverty. He also saw the accumulation of the wealth of a town in the hands of the few as a grave danger to the town's very survival. As moneylenders, Jews were guilty on both accounts, and thus earned the friar's hostility.

CONCLUSION

"I Heard the Sound of You in the Garden, and I Was Afraid"

Long neglected outside of his native land by scholars of the history, culture, and society of Western Europe, Bernardino of Siena is finally being recognized as a presence to be reckoned with. In our attempts to describe and understand the birth and development of many significant events and ideas of early-fifteenth-century Italy, this prodigiously active and influential preacher necessarily commands a place of special prominence. In the forty years of his public career, his preaching campaigns brought him to almost every corner of northern and central Italy, with excursions beyond, to the north and south. And where he himself did not reach, his written word or oral report of his word and activity did.

Our preacher had much to say to his contemporaries—from popes and emperors down to peasants and housewives—on almost every important topic involving the conduct of their daily lives, collective and individual, public and private, civic and religious. Among these many topics, there were three in particular in which Bernardino's teaching and influence especially claim our attention, witchcraft, sodomy, and Judaism, for these represented some of the most pressing, anxiety-raising social-moral issues of his generation—then, as we might add, as, mutatis mutandis, now. Indeed, Bernardino's lifetime coincided with a marked upsurge in the fearful demonization and persecution of all three of these categories of people. The witch, the sodomite, and the Jew challenged the social-moral sensibilities of early-fifteenth-century Italian society not only because they practiced sorcery or engaged in sexual behavior "against nature" or professed a faith other than Christianity—all of this, to be sure, was vexation enough—but also because they obliged their contemporaries to face other, larger, and most uncomfortable issues intimately and inescapably connected to who they were and what they did: the feminine and feminine power, the body and sexuality in all varieties, the unconquerable allure of paganism, and the failures and limitations of Christianity as a coherent, universally convincing response to the mystery of God and life.

On each of these three topics, Bernardino's sermons communicate to us something of exceptional, and at times unequaled, value. Regarding witchcraft and its related phenomena (superstition, magic, and folk healing), before the late sixteenth century and the onset of the Great Witch Hunt, documentation illuminating this wide realm of lived, daily experience is rare; hence the crucial importance of the preacher's testimony. Likewise, Bernardino represents one of the single most important sources of explicit information about and insight into the sexual issues, mores, and *mentalité* of his age; while this is true for sexuality in general, it is especially true for the specific and more elusive subcategory of sodomy.[1] Finally, along with his fellow Franciscan Observant preachers, Bernardino has long been cited as a major protagonist in the realm of Quattrocento anti-Semitism, though as we saw in the preceding pages, his own active engagement in this tragic phenomenon of European history has been less than previous scholarship has led us to believe.

Bernardino's sermons and treatises afford us an ample window onto what the Christian faithful in the pre–witch craze era believed, or rather were taught to believe, about the figure of the witch and her (or his) activities. This large body of popular instruction also represents one phase in that slow coalescence of disparate beliefs and shadowy notions concerning superstition, simple (that is, nondemonic) sorcery, pagan mythology, and practices into "the classic formulation of the Witch Phenomenon,"[2] which was to be a crucial part of the fundamental intellectual framework justifying and fueling the great witch craze of the succeeding centuries. Through his impassioned sermons publicizing an ever more demonized and subversive image of the witch and related practitioners, Bernardino helped create the general level of fearful, if not paranoid, awareness of these noncomformist elements within the bosom of Christian society. He even succeeded in bringing these "servants of Satan" to a fiery justice, as in the case of Finicella of Rome and Matteuccia of Todi. Furthermore, news of what happened in Rome in 1426 spread beyond the city and beyond Italy; and hence the preacher set in motion a domino effect: "Witch trials inspired more witch trials, because the report of action in one place would stimulate passions elsewhere. Oral report alone might have sufficed for this effect, but it was supplemented by inflammatory written accounts."[3] When it overtook Europe, the witch craze was to strike Italy with less virulence than in Northern Europe, but this was only in terms of numbers of final executions, not those of actual formal prosecutions, which were still high with respect to the peninsula's record of the previous centuries. Hence, it represents a phenomenon to be dealt with in writing the history of early modern Italy.

True, as he himself admits, Bernardino's antiwitch preaching was met with initial skepticism on the part of his audiences and, as the research of Bernadette Paton has shown, our friar was alone among, at least, his Sienese clerical contemporaries in taking the witchcraft threat so seriously. Yet, as the Finicella and Matteuccia trials and the new anti-witchcraft laws demonstrate, Bernardino ultimately succeeded in overcoming this skepticism in at least some quarters, most notably in Rome, which saw the pope involve himself directly in the Bernardino-inspired witch trial. Furthermore, given what was to happen in Italy and the rest of Europe later that century and in the following centuries in the form of witch hunts, prosecutions, and executions, it would seem that Bernardino did not long remain alone in his efforts to sensitize the populace to this threat.

Thanks, in part, to Bernardino, sodomy too became the "great fear" of Quattrocento Italy, as Romano Canosa has labeled it. Although in preceding centuries the Church had never considered homogenital behavior as anything but sinful and punishable, in fifteenth-century Italy, public awareness and prosecution of "the sin against nature" began to reach proportions never before seen. The creation, during Bernardino's lifetime, of Florence's "Office of the Night" and, in Venice, the transfer of jurisdiction over sodomy from the "Lords of the Night" to the higher "Council of the Ten" are symptomatic of this crescendo of fear and repression. Publicizing a thoroughly demonized portrait of the sodomite as deadly public menace, Bernardino disseminated as well the image of an angry, vengeful, destroyer God who will lay waste those towns and states that practice or allow this "worst crime," just as he did in the case of Sodom and Gomorrah. In the short run, Bernardino and his colleagues succeeded in this consciousness-raising campaign, as one town after another passed ever stricter laws against same-sex genital activity. In the long run, however, the friar met with utter failure, as people simply continued to *sodomitare* with the passive complicity of lawmakers and citizenry who allowed the antisodomy laws to be neglected or annulled. Bernardino believed that sodomitic activity was merely another form of postlapsarian animal lust that could be eliminated by religious and psychological terror tactics, legal punishment, and the avoidance of idleness. He and his ecclesiastical contemporaries did not know that they were dealing, not only with lust, but also with one of the most powerful forces known to humanity, love and the need to connect intimately with another human being.

Bernardino's teachings on the Jews bring us into more complicated terrain. What Poliakov called the "classics of Jewish history" have transmitted, by and large, the image of a rabidly anti-Semitic Bernardino. Thoroughly obsessed with the Jewish question, this Bernardino supposedly made Jews the constant, primary target of his personal vitriol and public campaign of social isolation, doing so, if not in always in explicit terms, then through the convenient and not-so-opaque smokescreen of his anti-usury oratory. We need to revise this image. To begin with, such sweeping, unsubstantiated claims as "*In every sermon* of Bernardino of Siena the subject of usury occupied the *central* position," or that, in Perugia in 1425, "the Jews constituted *the major target* of [Bernardino's] fiery sermons,"[4] collapse under the weight of abundant concrete evidence to the contrary. Whenever and wherever he rose to speak in public, Bernardino had much more than usury or the Jews on his mind. The Jews were not the exclusive or even the primary target of Bernardino's anti-usury sermons. The primary targets of those sermons were the usurers, of whom far more were Christian than Jewish; their primary concern was the plight of the poor, who, Bernardino sincerely believed, had been made or kept poor by their creditors.

The scarcity of direct, explicit reference to the Jews in all of Bernardino's works, both inside and outside his economic sermons and treatises, and in the large mass of contemporary documentation surrounding the friar (biographies, letters, diaries, etc.), is noteworthy. This relative silence may have been the result of external restraints on the preacher (such as from the papacy); while not excluding this possibility, I believe a more reasonable conclusion is that Bernardino was, in fact, only moderately interested in the question of the Jew qua Jew. Again, Jews were certainly not his primary target. It is unlikely that any class of "sinner" or "enemy" can lay claim to that title. Bernardino had many targets, all of whom he tried to shoot down in the most effective rhetorical manner, using the highly charged, hyperbolic language of a popular Mediterranean Franciscan preacher. This is the most important way in which traditional "form" (the genre of the medieval popular Franciscan sermon) determined "content." If one were to read, solely and exclusively, the excerpted body of Bernardino's remarks against the witch or the sodomite in the same fashion in which too many scholars in the past have excerpted and read the anti-usury sermons and anti-Jewish passages, one would likewise arrive at the same erroneous impression that the witch or the sodomite (or the vain woman, or the political faction member, or the blasphemer, or the gambler) was the principal target of Bernardino's venom and campaign. Evaluations about any one part of the friar's opus can only be made within the context of the entire body of Bernardino's oratory and the complete repertory of his public activity.

This is not to say that Bernardino had a high regard for the Jews or wanted Christian society to make easy accommodation for or with them. They were, after all, as he declares, "the chief enemies of all Christians," and he called explicitly for their isolation in accordance with duly promulgated canon law. Their conversion interested him less or not at all; there is no call for it in any of his sermons or treatises. Conversion of the Jews brought about by Bernardino's oratory is mentioned by a few of the early biographies and archival sources, but this may simply be a hagiographic topos. However, at the same time that Bernardino demonized the Jews, he also, contradictorily, preached some form of "love" for them: "If you see a Jew in need, you must help him with an authentic, just, holy, and active love," the friar mandates on more than one occasion. This is not to deny that, the mandate to "love" the Jew notwithstanding, the friar's preaching had an injurious, at times pernicious, effect on the lifestyle and destinies, individual or collective, of the Jews. However, this effect is difficult to pinpoint in specific terms or quantity, especially in its long-term traces and consequences. It would seem that most of the new anti-moneylending laws passed during Bernardino's lifetime in the towns he visited—the most concrete sign of his influence—were either abolished or ignored within a relatively short period of time. Even the *monti di pietà*, the Franciscan-sponsored credit institutions of the later century, by no means put the Jewish moneylenders out of business. Bernardino's preaching certainly served, in a general and diffused manner, to fuel a more intense anti-Jewish feeling in the Italian populace at large. But how does one document or measure this intangible emotional effect? For as many outbursts of anti-Jewish sentiment as are recorded in fifteenth-century Italy, one can cite at least as many examples of either a pro-Jewish or neutral disposition of the heart. One supposes, nonetheless, that had Bernardino and his fellow Franciscans not preached their anti-Semitic doctrines, Italian Christians in that century would have responded more hospitably to their Jewish neighbors than they did.

There is, finally, the question of Bernardino's own anti-Semitism, as distinct from that of his Observant contemporaries and that of his later followers. No one in the past has attempted to separate the one phenomenon from the other, assuming that fifteenth-century Observant anti-Semitism was simply all of a piece, with Bernardino as the all-controlling *caposcuola* or "cookie-cutter" role model for a long list of preachers. The jury is still out on this question, since no one has yet done the in-depth research into the thought and activity of this host of friars on the Jewish question, long called for by Léon Poliakov. Much closer, careful exploration and examination of the Jewish-related utterances and public deeds of these other men, individually and comparatively, remains to be done. (Given what we already know, however, the anti-Semitism of Bernardino of Siena appears clearly far more benign than that of his namesake, Bernardino of Feltre, with whom he is at times misidentified.) When all is said and done, it might prove impossible or meaningless in terms of ultimate social effect to fully distinguish the separate teachings of these individual Franciscans; nonetheless, scholarly integrity requires at least an honest attempt. Until the completion of further research into the careers and *opera omnia* of the remaining Observant preachers, the unsubstantiated generalizations and assumptions of the past can no longer be accepted.

Further research is needed as well to compare and contrast more thoroughly Bernardino's teachings about the witch, the sodomite, and the Jew with those of his peers, the other Italian popular preachers, Franciscan or otherwise, active in late medieval and early Renaissance Italy, both before, during, and after his lifetime. It would be illuminating to trace the *longue durée* of popular preaching attitudes about these members of the social underworld and to see more precisely where Bernardino stands on this doctrinal spectrum. Little can now be said on this topic, since we lack both serviceable editions of the primary texts and monographic studies of these individual preachers on which to base a reliable comparative analysis. The current interest in popular preaching as a focus of scholarly research is a relatively new phenomenon, dating only to the late 1970s, and hence this lack of texts and scholarship should not surprise us.[5]

A few further conclusions emerge about Bernardino and his sermons against the social underworld of his time. First, in all that he said about the witch, the sodomite, and the Jew, Bernardino invented nothing *ex nihilo*. He took all of his raw material from the orthodox tradition of the Catholic Church, even though the Church at times chose to overlook some of its own teachings. What was new was the gravity, the vehemence, the literalness, and the captivating persuasiveness with which he preached about these classes of people. Unpalatable and at times even horrifying, the principal "facts," images, mandates, and predictions encountered in Bernardino's oratory ultimately derive from Sacred Scripture, the authorized "doctors" (among them Ambrose, Augustine, Jerome, Chrysostom, and Gregory), and canon law. Although there were, over the years, many theological *magistri*, bishops, fellow religious, and others who did not like the style and some of the content of Bernardino's preaching, the only actionable cause of official concern on the part of the ecclesiastical authorities about the friar's preaching was his "novel" IHS monogram of the Holy Name of Jesus. This, too, eventually passed the test of orthodoxy. In everything else Bernardino was a faithful, if fanatical, son of the Church.

Second, as unsavory as it may now strike us, the response that Bernardino tried to evoke—both emotionally and in concrete political-social action—to the threat of the witch, the sodomite, and the Jew, was fundamentally logical, given the premises supplied by Scripture, the "doctors," and canon law, as then interpreted. In medieval and Renaissance Christian society, there was (theoretically) no place for the nonconformist and certain categories of unrepentant sinner. "Error has no rights," as the Church was fond of proclaiming in a later age. Again, apart from his "novel" additions to the cult of the Holy Name, no one accused Bernardino of falsifying Christian doctrine or canon law. For the witch, the sodomite, the Jew, and, indeed, all other members of the category of nonconforming "Other," Bernardino had inherited a considerable amount of already well-articulated "persecuting discourse" from his predecessors. By his preaching, Bernardino saw to it that this "inheritance" would be confirmed more deeply, disseminated more widely, and passed on more securely to another generation of European Christians.

Inasmuch as Bernardino was simply being faithful to the teachings of the Church and was respecting what he understood to be the inexorable logic of divine cause and effect (effect: plagues, wars, and other disasters; cause: divine punishment for tolerating sin and nonconformity), it may seem technically incorrect to label the friar a fanatic. He was only trying to be a "good Christian." However, in Bernardino's own time, even the papacy chose to ignore or overrule the duly promulgated teachings of the Church—fortunately so for many people, such as the Jews. Thus, in this sense Bernardino was indeed, paradoxically, a fanatic. Unlike most of his contemporaries, our friar would tolerate little difference between officially professed ideology and actual praxis; he would accept little compromise between what he and the whole Church (at least in theory) believed to be God-given mandate and what Machiavelli was later to call "the effectual reality of things." For better or worse—better in the case of the Jews, worse in the case of clerical mores—an abyss had always existed in Christianity between ideology and praxis, and would continue to exist, however much it would shrink in the reform era of the post-Tridentine Church. In the Middle Ages, the institutional Church had, at least implicitly, come to resign itself to the fact that some of the teachings of Jesus—radical poverty, for example—were impracticable in the real world, and that its dream of creating the perfect theocracy, a pure and all-embracing *societas christiana,* was illusory. Bernardino was less inclined to do so.

When we look at the specifics of Bernardino's theology and program of social reform, the label of fanatic seems appropriate indeed. In many areas of moral theology, such as the then burning and divisive issue of usury, there was a legitimate difference of "doctoral" opinion as to the options available to the Christian. In these situations Bernardino usually chose a position of intransigent absolutism, instead of a more reasonable and a more intellectually honest acknowledgment of the pluralism in the teaching magisterium of the Church and of what moral theologians today call the "integrity" of the specific moral case, fully and adequately considered. "You have sent us all to damnation," Giannozzo Manetti complained to Bernardino after one of his sermons on usury, a complaint repeated no doubt on other occasions by other listeners. Bernardino's fanaticism also drove him at times to disregard due process of law and individual civil rights as then provided for. This we saw in his treatment of the "heretic" Amadeo de Landis and in his injunction to summarily round up and consign to the stake all suspected sodomites, dispensing with any prior interrogation or formal trial. Bernardino's obsession with the Devil also raised eyebrows among his contemporaries, contributing further to the image of the friar as a person of theological and psychological intemperance. This stigma of fanaticism may in fact have been responsible for the waning of Bernardino's fame in the two or three generations following his death, though this is pure speculation on my part. However, favoring this hypothesis is the fact that the friar's popularity surged once again in the post-Tridentine Church, a time when the call for the same Bernardinian type of austere, exacting, uncompromising reform increased in volume among Catholics, lay and clerical alike.

Bernardino's fanaticism did not stand in the way of his gaining a wide hearing from the populations of his time nor of his imposing his will on them. The friar's experience confirms in a vivid way what other sources indicate, namely, that the relationship between popular preacher and civil society was intimate and privileged. A thoroughly accepted and integrated feature of the daily routine of fifteenth-century Italian life, preaching missions to the cities, towns, and villages were actively encouraged, programmed, and financed by local governments, as we know from the extant letters of formal invitation and financial receipts. Moreover, it would appear that, despite the fact that civil authorities were footing the bill for his preaching missions, Bernardino by and large seems to have had great freedom of speech in his sermonizing, as the blunt and bitter criticism of local policy and social order he habitually launched at his hosts would indicate. Commensurate with their oratorical charisma and intellectual prowess, fifteenth-century popular preachers wielded considerable socioeconomic and political power, enough to force towns and cities to rewrite their penal codes, as did Bernardino in Siena, Perugia, and Todi, and enough to bring an entire city to submission, as Savonarola was later to do in Florence. In the long run, however, even the personal charisma and political acumen of a Bernardino and a Savonarola proved incapable of withstanding the many disparate forces—political, economic, and emotional—militating against their vision of the perfect Christian theocracy.

Bernardino's experience also invites us to reflect on the relationship of the popular preacher not only to secular society, but also to the institutional Church, upon which he necessarily depended for his status as duly authorized teacher of the Christian faithful. Though the preacher-hierarchy relationship was technically one of subordination and submission of the former to the latter, the "charismatic" or "informal" power of a successful popular preacher like Bernardino rivaled at times that of the official ecclesiastical leadership, that is, the local bishops and the pope.[6] "It seems to me that you're not only our bishop, you're our pope and emperor as well," we heard one enthusiastic layman exclaim to Bernardino, who was protesting (with false modesty?) his lack of authority to intervene in local parish affairs.[7] Inasmuch as the canonical office of preacher did not endow him with any executive, legislative, or judicial authority, Bernardino's well-demonstrated powers in these realms were indeed both "informal" and "charismatic," derived from the force of his own personality. As for the episcopacy, we unfortunately do not know as much as we would like about Bernardino's relationship with the various bishops of his times. Despite evidence showing some antagonism between Bernardino and individual bishops, our preacher was able to enter and preach in numerous dioceses over several decades, seemingly unimpeded; this suggests a great deal of unopposed freedom on Bernardino's part and a great deal of support from the ranks of the Italian episcopacy. Furthermore, his own three-time nomination as bishop (of Siena, Ferrara, and Urbino) would also indicate that Bernardino was considered by the papacy, the local churches (who then, unlike now, had much to say in the selection of their own bishop), and at least some of the bishops themselves to be very much *persona grata*.

The papacy did put limits on the freedom of the preachers, as in the several bulls forbidding anti-Jewish Mendicant preaching. However, the degree of actual compliance with the dictates of those bulls is not clear. As mentioned, once the matter of the Holy Name of Jesus "heresy" was resolved, Bernardino enjoyed friendly, unantagonistic relations with the popes of his adulthood, Martin V and Eugene IV. Neither Martin nor Eugene seems to have resented or sought to restrict Bernardino's informal or charismatic power. This is due not only to Bernardino's apparent personal "conquest" of Martin and Eugene themselves, but also to his publicly professed pro-papal ideology and his careful avoidance of outright conflict with that office. With the exception of his one isolated call in Padua to overturn the papal Jewish exemptions, Bernardino's public statements about the papacy are all deferential and supportive of the papal status quo. In Bernardino's sermons, the pope is consistently and respectfully referred to as "our holy father," who "loves dearly" his flock and represents "our God on earth," hence commanding our utmost obedience.[8] Needless to say, none of the conciliarist notions of his age finds a place in the friar's ecclesiology.

In view of the great chaos inflicted upon the Church by the popes of his lifetime during the Great Schism and earlier, Bernardino's submissive, uncritical attitude toward the papacy is nearly astounding. Yet at the heart of this deferential attitude is Bernardino's sincere belief that, recent turmoil notwithstanding, the monarchical constitution of the Church represented the eternal will of God and functioned for the good of the Church, *ex opere operato,* despite the personal shortcomings, and indeed crimes, of the incumbents of the various Church offices, popes included. On a more pragmatic level, it was in Bernardino's self-interest to cultivate the good graces of the papacy by preaching a pro-papal ecclesiology, for, in the face of severe opposition from the larger Franciscan order, his much beleaguered Observant movement depended on the papacy for its survival. Thanks to Bernardino's diplomacy and personal reputation, papal support was indeed forthcoming, and the Observance fully triumphed by the end of Bernardino's lifetime. At the same time, let us note, the papacy, besieged by the still unconquered forces of conciliarism and numerous political enemies, domestic and foreign, also found it in its best self-interest to maintain the loyal support of such influential, power-wielding figures as Bernardino. It would not have escaped the attention of the papacy, for instance, that Bernardino counted among his friends and admirers one of the principal personalities and guarantors of the success of the Council of Constance, the emperor Sigismund, who asked the preacher to escort him to Rome for his imperial consecration in St. Peter's.[9]

A further word is in order about Bernardino as "persecutor" of the social underworld of his time. As David Nirenberg has pointed out, the "persecuting discourse" of a figure such as our preacher could triumph and acquire potency in a community only if the "agents" of that community chose to find it "meaningful and useful," if the conditions of local time and space allowed people to respond affirmatively to it.[10] The great popularity that Bernardino enjoyed—as evidenced by the palm-bearing masses who greeted his entrance into their towns (as in Spoleto) and who crowded the churches and squares to listen to his sermons—allows us to conclude that the response to Bernardino's message was, in general, enthusiastically positive. The more local, more specific, and more nuanced response (or responses) is more difficult to gauge, though not impossible: we have done so in the previous pages by examining, for example, the various new reform laws and the judicial trials Bernardino inspired. It can also be measured to some degree by citing, as we have, the occasional chronicle, private letter, or diary entry describing one individual's personal, eyewitness reaction to the friar.[11] However, we would like to know this response in more intimate detail, especially that of the average "middle class" member of his audience. What change did Bernardino's preaching really effect in his listeners? Once the friar left town, the festivities were over, and the burst of religious fervor had subsided, what real resonance did his message continue to have in the hearts of the housewives, shopkeepers, and craftsmen? How differently did they lead their lives and treat their neighbors? These are questions to which we have only limited answers.

That Bernardino did inspire religious fervor among the masses, however impermanently, is beyond doubt, as the evidence in the preceding chapters demonstrates. Hence we ask: What made massive numbers of people in Bernardino's time and place listen so respectfully and so eagerly to him and then respond, by and large, affirmatively, if only temporarily and imperfectly from his perspective, to his message of persecution? Much credit must of course be given to the captivating quality of the friar's oratory, his personal charisma, and his reputation for wonder-working sanctity. But there were inevitably other factors at work, outside and beyond Bernardino, favoring such a response to his message about the witch, the sodomite, and the Jew.

Undoubtedly relevant here are the by now familiar psychosocial theories about the need of a dominant culture for some marginalized and persecuted "Other" to use as a foil against which to confirm its own collective identity, unity, and order.[12] Battling a common enemy is, after all, a most effective way of strengthening the social bond of a community. Preachers like Bernardino played a major role in identifying these common enemies, in distinguishing "us" from "Other" and in determining what was socially acceptable and what was not. The Other also functions as a convenient receptacle for the psychological projection on the part of the Christian majority of their own religious doubts or unacceptable, hence repressed, drives and desires. What one cannot emotionally or morally accept and adequately express in one's own public behavior is instead projected onto and persecuted in another person or class of persons. Gavin Langmuir has spoken at length of this in his analysis of the medieval Christian response to the Jews. According to Langmuir, the Jews served as scapegoats through which Christians sought to resolve the conflict between what he calls their "religion" and their "religiosity," that is, between what the Church required Christians to believe and what they actually believed in their own hearts. One example is the accusation against the Jews of Eucharistic host desecration, seen as a projection of the Christians' own doubts about transubstantiation.[13] A similar psychological dynamic could well have been operative in Christian society's response to sodomites and witches, especially with respect to issues of sexuality and gender. From its earliest years, Christianity had great difficulty integrating within its theological system the messy complexities of both sexuality (and the body in general) and the feminine; no wonder then that the sexually potent and "gender-bending" figure of the sodomite and of the powerful, independent chthonic woman, the witch, would represent a threat to its order.

However, more important and more specific to Bernardino's time and place in history, what made the people respond affirmatively to the friar were the same factors that drove Bernardino himself to preach his message of persecution in the first place. I am referring to the multifaceted crisis of early-fifteenth-century Christendom, of which the Great Schism was but one element.[14] As for the schism, even granting that its impact on the general population was not as great as some scholars have described in the past, such a major disruption of ecclesiastical (and therefore political) order could not last for forty years without affecting in a profound if only unconscious way the collective psyche of the Christian faithful. To this social-political-ecclesiastical disorder we must add the chronic and endemic woes that premodern humanity faced daily in its struggle for survival in a frequently brutal natural and social habitat: plague; famine; drought; murder, rape, and pillage by omnipresent mercenaries and other marauders; exploitation, economic or otherwise, by unjust lords and sovereigns; war between nations, city-states, political factions, and clans; and the chaos of unstable town government. These were the all too familiar daily experiences of contemporary life, cited constantly and precisely as such—familiar and daily—in Bernardino's sermons.

Bernardino himself responded to the distress of his age with fear and anxiety; it is difficult to imagine his audience responding otherwise. To this list of emotions, we can add a further, perhaps unrecognized one, anger—anger born of the impotence and passivity with which Bernardino and his contemporaries by and large had to endure the afflictions brought upon them by mother nature and the at times equally uncontrollable forces of their fellow human beings. What did they do with all of this seething black emotional energy? One of the things they did was to transform it into religious indignation and expel it in easy, socially acceptable fashion upon a convenient scapegoat. A perennially convenient scapegoat was the alien, nonconforming Other in their midst. Then as now, the human psyche required the gratification of blaming someone else for its woes, of exacting punishment from him or her, and of gaining release, if only temporarily, from its own state of impotence by oppressing those even more impotent than itself. Bernardino played an important role in, if not always instigating, then assuredly intensifying, the collective emotional reactions of his audience, and in determining which specific scapegoats among the many possible were most "deserving" of this "sacrificial" honor. As we saw, he chose the witch, the sodomite, and, to a lesser extent, the Jew. We will of course never really know to what extent Bernardino created, rather than reflected, the emotions, convictions, and concrete choices of his audience. Given the conditions of contemporary life, the preacher's audiences were not likely to have come to his sermons as mere tabulae rasae, as far as fear, anxiety, anger, and the desire for a scapegoat are concerned. In any case, even if his sermons were not the cause of these emotions, they certainly quickened them, channeling their energies in directions and against targets suggested to the preacher by his own theology and his own psychic demons.

The cataclysmic events of recent history and current events were in themselves unsettling enough to Bernardino and his contemporaries; yet heightening the terror that they inspired was the confirmation they supplied—or were thought to supply—of the rapidly approaching end times of human history.[15] Along with many of his contemporaries, ecclesiastical and lay, Bernardino fervently believed that humankind had advanced well into the penultimate age of its long, woe-filled existence. Though he would not predict its arrival in exact chronological terms, Bernardino believed that the final age was imminent. Not far from the horizon were the even more cataclysmic events of the age of the Antichrist and the final cosmic struggles between God and Lucifer, the prelude to the Second Coming of Christ. Although more acute than that of some of his contemporaries, Bernardino's apocalypticism was part and parcel of that general, all-pervasive "apocalyptic imagination," as Emmerson and Herzman have called it, so utterly constitutive of the consciousness, the "mentality," of the medieval Christian well into the fifteenth century, if not beyond. The "apocalyptic imagination" supplied the hermeneutical key with which Christians made sense of the crowded past, interpreted the anxious present, and predicted the mysterious future, employing the same common language and symbols supplied them by that enigmatic last book of the New Testament, the Book of Revelation, to which they were constantly, inexorably, and sometimes fatally attracted.[16] The ordinary Christian did not doubt the Book of Revelation as divine truth with immediate relevance to his or her life—hence the popular allure of a Bernardino, a Manfredi da Vercelli, or a Savonarola, who seemed able to unlock the secrets of its mysterious prophecies and thereby explain the true meaning of the disquieting events of their time and place in history.

As for that time and place in history, they have traditionally been called the Italian Renaissance, the moment of joyous "rebirth," the ebullient "reflowering" of Western civilization. However, suffused as they are with apocalyptic anxiety, Bernardino's sermons contribute to the further dismantling of this already crumbling portrait of the Italian Renaissance as an optimistic period of intellectual-religious illumination and cultural-scientific progress, the dawn of the modern world, bursting forth after the long, dark winter of the superstitious Middle Ages. As Charles Stinger has remarked, "what now seems increasingly problematic is in what sense this persistently corporative, anxious and markedly penitential world of fifteenth-century Italian urban society can be described as Renaissance."[17] This is precisely the vision of contemporary society with which Bernardino presents us: corporative, penitential, and, above all, fearful. The evidence of Bernardino's sermons suggests that despite the glorious, forward-looking achievements of art and culture of his illustrious "Renaissance" contemporaries—Brunelleschi, Alberti, Masaccio, Ghiberti, Donatello, Leonardo Bruni, Guarino Veronese, Poggio Bracciolini, Lorenzo Valla—the everyday world, interior and exterior, of the masses of citizenry was conducted pretty much along lines that had been long drawn in the medieval past.

More than he feared the witch, the sodomite, and the Jew, Bernardino—and many of his contemporaries—feared God and his wrath. Bernardino's God, the *mysterium tremendum,* was a harsh, vengeful taskmaster, quick to punish disobedience with death and destruction in the form of plagues, marauding armies and highwaymen, famines, droughts, and other human-made and natural disasters. Yes, God was "merciful" as well; but the demands of relentless justice—rewarding the good, punishing the bad—always and inexorably took precedence over the appeals of mercy. "Where justice and charity collide, justice must always prevail," Catholic theology was later and axiomatically to declare. In accordance with Isaiah 58:1, the friar believed that his task of moving sinners to repentance was better accomplished by emphasizing their wickedness and God's "justice," rather than their goodness and his mercy. This is known, not surmised, from Bernardino's explicit word; as we saw, it was a conscious part of his professional and personal *forma mentis.* Bernardino was able to preach so vividly and persuasively this message of wrathful divine justice for the simple reason that he fully believed and felt it himself. The fear he preached came directly from his own heart, instilled there by his experience of life and by his fervent study of Scripture, especially the Book of Revelation, which told him that the world was about to commence the final chapter of its travailed existence.

That existence had had its primal roots in fear:

> They heard the sound of the Lord God walking in the garden at the time of the evening breeze, and the man and his wife hid themselves from the presence of the Lord God among the trees of the garden. But the Lord God called to the man, and said to him, "Where are you?" He said, "I heard the sound of you in the garden, and I was afraid, because I was naked; and I hid myself." [Genesis 3:8–10.]

Ever since Adam and Eve bit into the forbidden fruit, fear has been an indelible part of what Torquato Tasso has called *l'aspra tragedia dello stato umano,* "the bitter tragedy of the human condition."[18] Since the dawn of recorded history, and most likely even before, human action and reaction, even when masked by arrogance, bravado, and aggression, have in great part been determined by this one emotion, fear. Human history has too often been the sad spectacle of men and women, individually and collectively—the high and mighty no less than the humble and lowly—moving about and responding to their environment and other human beings out of undisguised animal fear. Fifteenth-century Italy, despite its many glorious and sublime accomplishments in art, architecture, and literature, with its exaltation of the "dignity and excellence" of the human person, enjoyed no exemption from this melancholy and perennial fact of the human condition.

APPENDIX ONE

The Date of the Roman Witch Trial and of Bernardino's Heresy Trial

❧❧❧❧ In recounting the facts of the Roman witch trial resulting in the execution of "Finicella," Bernardino gives no indication of the date of these events; he simply states that they occurred when he was in Rome ("quello che si fece a Roma mentre che io vi predicai," R.1006). The important question becomes: when was Bernardino in Rome? Unfortunately, given the present state of evidence, it is impossible to reconstruct the friar's itinerary with complete certainty.[1] We know that at one point in the late 1420s Bernardino had been summoned to Rome by Pope Martin V to stand trial for heresy, a charge deriving from his propagation of the "novel" cult of the Holy Name of Jesus with its public veneration of the "IHS" monogram. Bernardino was not only acquitted of the charge, but was also asked to remain in the city to deliver a series of sermons—114 of them—in St. Peter's and elsewhere.[2] Scholars have been divided between a 1426 and a 1427 date for this heresy trial and ensuing public preaching, most accepting Longpré's persuasive, well-documented chronology, which argues for the later of the two dates.[3] However, subsequent evidence from the extensive 1427 correspondence (March 11–August 13) between the Roman Curia and the government of Siena concerning Bernardino's nomination as bishop of that city and the 1445–48 canonization trial depositions all but establishes the year of the heresy trial as 1426.[4] Further evidence—a June 5, 1426, letter from Martin V granting to Bernardino four new convents for his Franciscan Observance—would indicate that the trial had already been completed by that date.[5]

As for the burning of Finicella and her companion, testimony from Bernardino's canonization trials places that event in the year 1426 as well.

Sienese diplomat Leonardo Benvoglienti, a childhood friend as well as a biographer of Bernardino, stated in his 1448 deposition that he had heard Bernardino preach in Rome in 1426, "adding that in Rome and also in Perugia . . . he [Bernardino] had several witches burned at the stake." Unfortunately, this assertion is followed by the troubling line: "Interrogated as to how he knew this, [Benvoglienti] answered that he had heard it said [*dixit audivisse*]." Thus, what we have is Benvoglienti, in 1448, trying to remember events of at least twenty years before, notice of which came to him at least in part by hearsay. Precisely what information Benvoglienti received by hearsay is unclear—the burning of the witches both in Rome and Perugia or just in Perugia (where by his own account he does not seem to have witnessed Bernardino's preaching)? It may indeed be the case that Benvoglienti heard Bernardino preach in Rome in 1426, as he declared to the papal canonization committee, but he may not have remained in the city long enough to be present at or to at least learn firsthand of the burning of the witches itself.[6]

As for the other fifteenth-century primary sources that speak of this witch trial, they are of little help to us in establishing the exact date of the event. Stefano Infessura tells us that the trial took place in 1424; however, the dates contained in Infessura's diary are highly unreliable, as with many early chronicles.[7] There is no other evidence indicating a 1424 visit to Rome by Bernardino; any scholar asserting such a visit does so only on the unsteady ground of the Infessura diary.[8] Another consideration that would tend to eliminate 1424 as a date for the Roman preaching and witch trial is the fact that Bernardino preached a whole sermon on the topic of witchcraft during his 1425 mission to Siena (April 20–June 1), and there is not the least mention of this trial in this or any of the sermons from this series. Thus, one is led to suspect that the "Finicella" episode had not yet occurred.

Johann Hartlieb, a supposed eyewitness to the trial, places the event "in the sixth year of Pope Martin," that is, 1423, whereas in Felix Hemmerlin, the assigned date is 1420.[9] Johann Chraft simply says the episode took place "during the reign of Pope Martin." Paolo dello Mastro gives 1442 as his date (an impossibility, since Bernardino recounts the episode in 1427), while Giacomo della Marca gives no indication of time at all. Thus, none of these six sources confirms the 1426 date for which the previously cited evidence argues. Yet at the same time, none of them is of such reliability with respect to its dating of events as to oblige us to alter our conclusions, namely, that after his own heresy trial in the spring of 1426, Bernardino went on to preach his 114 sermons in Rome, resulting (after his departure from the city?) in the trial and burning of Finicella and another anonymous witch, most likely sometime in the summer of that same year.[10]

It is possible that Leonardo Benvoglienti's memory was faulty—that is, the Bernardino-provoked witch burning did not take place in 1426. In that case, there is no evidence at all to support the traditional assumption that Bernardino's own heresy trial and the "Finicella" witch trial occurred during the same Roman trip. The latter could easily have taken place during another of the preacher's visits to the city, even though we cannot be certain precisely how many visits to Rome Bernardino made and what, if any, preaching he did on those occasions. We do know that, as of September 1427 (the date of the antiwitchcraft sermon examined above), Bernardino's most recent visit to the city had been earlier that same summer of 1427: On July 12, we can place him securely in Rome, refusing before Martin V his nomination as bishop of Siena. However, we do not know whether he did any public preaching while in Rome on this occasion; the precise dates of his arrival and departure are themselves unknown.[11] There is no evidence of any other Roman preaching mission by Bernardino beyond the one immediately following his heresy trial; thus, the traditional placement of the two trials in the same year remains a reasonable, though of course tentative, conclusion.

APPENDIX TWO

The Jewish Prohibition List, Padua 1423

("De emenda charitate divina" [OOH.III.333b–34b]; see chapter 4, section 2; paragraph divisions added.)

Secunda pars principalis: Constat interrogationibus et responsionibus novem questionum spectantium ad charitatem divinam.

. . . et tertia est cognitio proximi amando proximum, sicut te ipsum, et subvenire in necessitatibus suis. Sed quid dicam de Judaeis, an sunt Christi nostri, etc., circa quos quia audio quod in hac civitate Paduae sunt multi Judaei, aliqua de eorum conversatione, et aliquas vertitates de ipsis dicere volo.

Prima veritas est, quod quandoque tu bibis, et comedis cum Judaeis, tu semper peccas mortaliter, ut in cap. *Saepe,* de Judaeis, et 27, q. I, de Judaeis; nam sicut est prohibitum eis comedere nobiscum: ita est prohibitum nobis comedere cum illis.

Secunda veritas est, quod non licet alicui infirmo ad sanitatem recuperandam uti aliquo Judaeo; dico quia semper peccat mortaliter, ut in cap. nulli, et in cap. *Omnes,* cap. 27, q. I.

Tertia veritas, quod non licet intrare balneum cum Judaeis, ut in dictis juribus allegatis.

Quarta non licet Judaeis, ampliare, vel de novo facere Synagogas, sicut scio factum fore contrarium in hac civitate, ut Extra de Judaeis, cap. *Judae.*

Quinta veritas est, quod diebus quibus legitur Passio Domini, debent stare clausi, ne susurrent de Passione Christi, ibi.

Sexta veritas est, quod, in qualibet terra Judaei debent portare aliquod signum, per quod cognoscantur Judaei a Christianis; et miror, quare non portant hic, Vicentiae, et Veronae signa, ut cognoscantur; et volens informari, dictum est mihi quod habent privilegium a Papa; et sunt quidem dicentes quod Papa non potest id concedere contra quatuor concilia; sed de hoc nolo agere contra determinationem Papae. Sed cives deberent providere super hoc, et aliquid de signo statuere: ratio est quia si non habent signum, se immiscent mulieribus Christianis; et est contra cap. *Nonnulli,* de Judaeis; et ipsi Judaei si credunt suam fidem fore meliorem, deberent portare signa ut cognoscerentur, et non deberent vercundari cognosci pro Judaeis; sed nil aliud vult dicere, nisi quod conscientia remordet eos, spernendo fidem suam; et bene faceret communitas supplicare Papae, quod non obstante privilegio eis indulto, concedere velit, quod possint cogi gestare signa; ita incogniti possunt se immiscere cum foeminis Christianis, vel Christiana quoties stat domi cum Judaeis famulando eis, toties peccat mortaliter; quia est prohibitum, de Judaeis, cap. Judaei cum Judaeis, contra istas, quae nutriunt, et lactant filios Judaeorum similiter in illis, quae obstetricant, seu lavant pueros, et foetus Judaeorum, stando et comedendo in eorum domibus, peccant mortaliter: nec licet ipsis obstetricibus accipere pecunias a Judaeis eo quod elevaverint filios suos, si sunt usuraii; quia illae pecuniae sunt aliis obligatae.

Septimo quaero; numquid liceat tonsoribus, procuratoribus, obstetricibus, advocatis, medicis, et huiusmodi personis accipere salarium laborum a Judaeis usurariis, seu a Christianis usurariis, nihil habentes aliud quem de usura. Thomas dicit, quod sive tales Judaei, et Christiani habeant aliquid non acquisitum de usura, tamen si est obligatum aliis pro usuriis acceptis, quod non licet aliquid accipere a talibus, quia accipit illud, quod est alteri obligatum: multo ergo minus licet accipere aliquid ab eo qui omnia habet ex usuris; quia accipit quod est alterius, et alteri obligatum; tamen nutrix seu obstetrix potest elevare filios Judaeorum, et usurariorum sine aliquo praemio: sed non licet eis servire, vel secum comedere, nec stare domi, ut dixi. Similiter medicus potest mederi Judaeo, et usurario sine praemio, quia peccatum in talibus est recipere ab eis aliquid, quod sit alteri obligatum: unde nota duo genera servitiorum in talibus; quia si est tale servitium propter quod usurarius non efficitur impotens divitiis; quia tu das tuum pannum, et ipse dat tibi pretium: vel das illi alias res minori pretio, pro quo non efficitur impotens; quia habet a te rem aequivalentem pretio tibi dato, et tunc tu potes illud facere sine peccato, ut alio modo, quam effici impotens: sicut si notarius scribit illi, vel procurator, vel tonsor, sive medicus, et huiusmodi; quia recipiendo salarium, vel praemium ab eis, diminuitur eorum substantia aliis obligata; quia non recipiunt rem aliquam, quae recipiat fruitionem, seu aequipollentem, nec venit illis in bonis aliqua utilitas, et tunc est peccatum.

Octavo quaero, quid debet fieri de eo, quod tu recepisti a Judaeo et usurario? Respondeo quod tu debes illud restituire, ut alias tibi dixi. Sed ante debeo restituire utilitatem ipsi Judaeo, vel Christiano usurario? Respondeo, quod in Christiano facito sicut alias tibi dixi; sed quia Judaeus numquam est aptus restituire, nec tenetur licite. Thomas dicit, quod, tu non debes restituire Judaeis, sed illis qui fuerunt damnificati ab illis Judaeis per usurariam pravitatem; sed si aliquando recepisti damnum aliquod a Judaeis, tu potes de illo lucro tantum retinere quaesitum quantum fuisti damnificatus a Judaeis, et ab inde supra tu debes omnia restituere; et si nescis damnificatos, tunc debes reddere pauperibus Christi, vel vertere in pios usus.

Nona veritas, nunquid liceat recipere illud quod tibi donat Judaeus? Respondeo, si est usurarius non: idem in Christiano foeneratore: et si recipis, debes restituire damnificatis ab eis per usurariam pravitatem, vel ut supra dixi.

Decimo quaero, si Judaeus vult effici Christianus, et haberet multa bona, quid debet fieri de illis bonis? Et utrum possint illli dimitti illa bona? Respondeo, aut habuit de usuriis, et tunc plurimi dicunt restitui debere male ablata his a quibus extorta fuerunt per usuram: et si aliqua bona incerta supersunt, et tunc de illis incertis dominus Episcopus potest illi providere, dando illa amore Dei ei, si non reperiuntur cuius fuerint, sicut ipse Episcopus daret aliis Christianis pauperibus.

Sed quaero, nunquid recipientes azyma a Judaeis peccent; et dico quod peccant mortaliter.

Item quaero, nunquid locando domos Judaeis peccent. Et dico, si locas domos tuas Judaeis usurariis, et similiter Christianis ad usum usurarum, tu peccas mortaliter.

Tertiodecimo quaero, utrum sacerdos possit petere decimas a Judaeis, sub cuius parochia stant; et respondeo quod sic, ut in cap. sup. cit.

Quartodecimo quaero nunquid liceat benefacere Judaeis, et amare eos? Respondeo, quod in iis, quae concernunt amorem generalem, licet eos amare; sed in his, quae concernunt amorem specialem, non; sed fuge amare ipsos speciale amore; et ideo si concedis ad pensionem domum, vel stationem Judaeis, ut foenerentur, tu teneris ad restitutionem, et peccas mortaliter.

Unde cavete vobis a praedictis, quae ideo hic tetigi propter multitudinem Judaeorum, qui regnant in hac civitate, ut sitis spaientes a conversatione eorum.

NOTES

CHAPTER ONE

1. Bernardino degli Albizzeschi was born in Massa Marittima, a mining town then under Sienese domination some thirty miles southwest of Siena. Iris Origo's *The World of San Bernardino* (New York: Harcourt, Brace & World, 1962) remains the best biography of Bernardino available in English, followed by A. G. Ferrers Howell's much earlier but still useful *S. Bernardino of Siena* (London: Methuen, 1913). Among the biographies in Italian, Vittorino Facchinetti's *San Bernardino da Siena mistico sole del 400* (Milan: Casa Editrice Santa Lega Eucaristica, 1933) is the most exhaustive and cites extensive original sources, but is frequently far from impartial in its descriptions and evaluations. Raoul Manselli's entry on Bernardino in the *Dizionario biografico degli italiani* (9:215–26) is a succinct, reliable summary of the friar's life and works.

2. Johannis Bandini de Bartholomaeis, *Historia Senensis,* continued by Franciscus Thomasius, in *Rerum Italicarum Scriptores,* 25 vols., ed. Ludovico Muratori (Milan: Palatin, 1723–51), 20: col. 25A. This attendance figure refers to Bernardino's 1425 visit to Siena; however, in 1427, the numbers in attendance, if anything, would have been higher, Bernardino's fame having increased in the interim. The *Historia Senensis* also makes note of the fact that in attendance were not only the residents of Siena proper, but also crowds of country folk ("sed confluentium etiam Rusticorum").

3. The description of Bernardino's voice comes from his contemporary and early biographer, humanist Maffeo Vegio: "quippe cui ita vox lenis, clara, sonora, distincta, explicata, solida, penetrans, plena, redundans, elevata, atque efficax erat," *Vita sancti Bernardini senensis,* in *AASS* (Maii tomus V, die vigesima), 3:18.122F. I use the translation of Eugene Policelli, *Humanism in the Life and Vernacular Sermons of Bernardino of Siena* (Ph.D. thesis, University of Connecticut, 1973), 142–43. It is Bernardino himself who tells us how long a sermon could last: "Venite a udire el predicatore, due o tre ore che vi diletta!" ("Come and listen to the preacher for he will delight you for two or three hours," A.451)

4. The first quotation is from the most recent editor of Bernardino's vernacular sermons, Carlo Delcorno, R.9; it is Enea Silvio Piccolomini (the future Pope Pius II) who tells us that people flocked to hear Bernardino "tamquam propheta" ("De Bernardino Senensi," in *De viris illustribus,* ed. Adrian van Heck [Vatican City: Biblioteca Apostolica Vaticana, 1991], 37; also excerpted in OOH.I.xliv).

5. Quoted by Lester K. Little, *Religious Poverty and the Profit Economy in Medieval Europe* (Ithaca: Cornell University Press, 1978), 219.

6. Iris Origo, *The Merchant of Prato: Francesco di Marco Datini* (London: Jonathan Cape, 1957), 311–12.

7. "Usa a le chiese spesso e a' predicari, ché molti buoni assempri e costumi v'imparerai; e diviene l'uomo molto savio e avveduto e usante e parlante," Paolo da Certaldo, *Libro di buoni costumi*, ed. A. Schiaffini (Florence: Le Monnier, 1945), 100.

8. Ferdinand Schevill, *Siena: The History of a Medieval Commune* (1909; New York: Harper & Row, 1964), 394.

9. "Oh! quanti saranno stamane che diranno: 'Io non sapevo quello che io mi facevo; io mi credevo far bene, e io facevo male.' E ricordandosi di questa predica, dirà in sé: 'Oh! io so' ora dichiarato di quello che io debbo fare.' . . . E quando tu andarai a fare uno contratto, tu vi pensarai prima dicendo: 'Che disse frate Bernardino? Elli mi disse così e così: questo è male, non si convien fare: questo è bene, questo vo' fare.' E questo t'averrà solo per la parola che tu odi nella predica. Ma ditemi: che sarebbe elli el mondo, cioè la fede cristiana, se elli non si predicasse? In poco tempo la fede nostra sarebbe venuta meno, ché non credaremo a nulla di quello che noi crediamo. E per questo ha ordinato la santa Chiesa che ogni domenica si predichi, o poco o assai, pure che si predichi" (R.149).

10. "E se di queste due cose tu non potesse fare altro che l'una, o udire la messa o udire la predica, tu debbi più tosto lassare la messa che la predica; imperò che la ragione ci è spressa, che non è tanto pericolo dell'anima tua a non udire la messa, quanto è a non udire la predica. . . . Ma dimmi: che credaresti tu del Santo Sacramento dell'altare, se non fusse stato la santa predicazione che tu hai udita? Tu avaresti la fede della messa solo per la predicazione. Più: che sapresti tu che cosa fusse peccato, se non per mezzo della predicazione? Che sapresti tu d'inferno, se non fusse la predica? Che sapresti tu di niuna buona operazione, come tu la debbi fare, se non per mezzo della predica?" (R.149). See also OOH.III.168b–169b, where Bernardino gives the same advice about choosing the sermon over Mass, adding, however, that one must not skip Mass on Sundays or other holy days of oligation. Bernardino's authority here is "Archdeacon" Guido de Baisio (da Baiso), *Rosarium*, p. 2, C. 1, q. 1, c. 94 (see OOQ.III.291, n. 2). On the relative importance of preaching, especially with respect to the Eucharist, see also OOQ.III.190, 291 ("per praedicationem dimittuntur peccata mortalia" ["through preaching mortal sins are forgiven"]), 382; and OOQ.VI.287, where, citing 1 Corinthians 1:17, Bernardino states that preaching is a "greater" and "more useful" office than baptizing. A meticulous exposition and enthusiastic celebration of the importance of preaching to the Church is contained in the earlier and influential *Treatise on the Formation of Preachers*, by thirteenth-century Dominican Master General Humbert of Romans, in *Early Dominicans: Selected Writings*, ed. Simon Tugwell (New York: Paulist Press, 1982), passim, but see esp. 258–59 (IV.XXI.269), where Humbert points out that Jesus celebrated Mass only once (on Holy Thursday night), but "devoted his whole life to preaching, even more than to prayer." See also St. Paul, Romans 10:14.

11. John O'Malley, *Praise and Blame in Renaissance Rome: Rhetoric, Doctrine and Reform in the Sacred Orators of the Papal Court, ca. 1450–1520* (Durham: Duke University Press, 1979), 4.

12. Denys Hay, *The Church in Italy in the Fifteenth Century* (Cambridge: Cambridge University Press, 1977), 67. I have corrected Hay, who mistakenly says "Dominican Observants."

13. Jacob Burckhardt, *The Civilization of the Renaissance in Italy* (1860; New York: Modern Library, 1954), 350–51. Burckhardt's statement about "a scornful humanism," however, needs to be qualified. As we now know, not all humanists scorned the Mendicants (much less Bernardino), just as not all Mendicants scorned humanism. The anticlerical humanist Poggio Bracciolini and

the antihumanist cleric Giovanni Dominici did not speak for the entirety of their respective professions.

14. Daniel Bornstein, *The Bianchi of 1399: Popular Devotion in Late Medieval Italy* (Ithaca: Cornell University Press, 1993), 19. For some recent studies of preaching in medieval and early modern Italy, see Carlo Delcorno, *Giordano da Pisa e l'antica predicazione volgare* (Florence: Olschki, 1975); Peter F. Howard, *Beyond the Written Word: Preaching and Theology in the Florence of Archbishop Antoninus, 1427–1459* (Florence: Olschki, 1995); Roberto Rusconi, *Predicazione e vita religiosa nella società italiana da Carlo Magno alla Controriforma* (Turin: Loescher, 1981); and Daniel R. Lesnick, *Preaching in Medieval Florence: The Social World of Franciscan and Dominican Spirituality* (Athens: University of Georgia Press, 1989).

15. The three quotations are, respectively, from St. Catherine of Bologna, "The Admirable Instructions of Saint Catherine of Bologna which she gave unto her Sacred Virgins, composed by herself . . . ," in *The Rule of the Holy Virgin S. Clare. Together with the Admirable Life of S. Catherine of Bologna,* ed. D. M. Rogers, English Recusant Literature: 1558–1640, vol. 274 (London: Scholars Press, 1975), 212; *The Oxford Dictionary of the Christian Church,* 2d rev. ed., ed. F. L. Cross and E. A. Livingstone (New York: Oxford University Press, 1984), 163; Ernest H. Wilkins, *A History of Italian Literature,* revised by Thomas G. Bergin (Cambridge: Harvard University Press, 1974), 133.

16. Lazaro Iriarte, *Franciscan History: The Three Orders of St. Francis of Assisi* (Chicago: Franciscan Herald Press, 1983), 127.

17. "Qui ne dum eius conventum senensem obsiderent aut portas clauderent civitatis ne discederet; sed nihil aliud excogitari posset quod non agerent." The entire letter (Archivio di Stato di Siena, Concistoro, Copialettere, 1625) is reproduced by Enrico Bulletti, "Predicazione senese dell'anno 1425," *BSB* 4 (1938): 236–40.

18. Cesare Sgariglia, "Due documenti relativi a S. Bernardino," *MF* 3 (1888): 160. For legislation on the part of the town of Gubbio preparing for a visit by Bernardino, see Giuseppe Mazzatinti, "S. Bernardino da Siena a Gubbio," *MF* 4 (1889): 150–51.

19. Dionisio Pacetti, "La predicazione di S. Bernardino da Siena a Perugia e ad Assisi nel 1425," *CF* 10 (1940): 6.

20. Cannarozzi has reproduced the letter in its entirety in the introduction to the first volume of the Florence 1424 cycle; see A.xxxix–xl. The letter is undated; Cannarozzi (A.xxxviii–xxxix) believed it to be in reference to Bernardino's Florentine mission of 1425, but this cannot be, since Bruni was not chancellor in those years. Bruni served as chancellor for the first time in 1410–11 and then again uninterruptedly from 1427 to his death in 1444. For the official request from the town of Grosseto, see Enrico Bulletti, "Frate Bernardino è pregato di una breve predicazione a Grosseto," *BSB* 4 (1938): 242. For Bruni's letter seeking the services of Antonino, see Howard, *Beyond the Written Word,* 138–39; and 87–89 for the competition among Italian towns for preachers.

21. Celestino Piana, "I processi di canonizzazione su la vita di San Bernardino da Siena," *AFH* 44 (1951): 419, n. 2, and 420–21, for the incidents at Padua, Vicenza, and Viterbo and the Siena sodomite episode; the "many traps" quotation comes from Paolo Sevesi, "Un sermone inedito del B. Michele Carcano su S. Bernardino da Siena," *SF* terza serie, 28 (1931): 89, which mentions the Padua and Vicenza plots; for the L'Aquila pulpit episode, see Paolo Sevesi, "Tre sermoni inediti su S. Bernardino," *BSB* 1 (1935): 236.

22. A. G. Little, "Nota Fr. Francisci Ariminensis O.M. Conv. de relatione S. Bernardini Senensis ad Fratres Observantes," *AFH* 2 (1909): 164–65.

23. Piana, "I processi di canonizzazione," 417–26.

24. For the history of the Franciscan Observance, see Martino Bertagna, "L'Osservanza e S. Bernardino," in *Atti-Vicenza,* 207–12; Mariano D'Alatri, "A proposito degli inizi dell'Osservanza," in *Atti-Vicenza,* 203–12; Kaspar Elm, "Riforme e osservanze nel XIV e XV secolo," in *Atti-Assisi,* 149–67, as well as his "L'osservanza francescana come riforma culturale," *Le Venezie francescane,* nuova serie 6 (1989): 15–30; the two essays by Mario Fois, "Il fenomeno dell'Osservanza negli ordini religiosi tra il 1300 e il 1400. Alcune particolarità dell'Osservanza francescana," in *Lettura delle fonti francescane attraverso i secoli: il 1400,* ed. Gerardo Cardaropoli and Martino Conti (Rome: Ed. Antonianum, 1981), 53–105, and "I papi e l'Osservanza minoritica," in *Atti-Assisi,* 29–105; Raoul Manselli, "L'osservanza francescana. Dinamica della sua formazione e fenomenologia," in *Reformbemühungen und Observanzbestrebungen im spätmittelalterlichen Ordenswesen,* ed. Kaspar Elm (Berlin: Duncker & Humblot, 1989), 173–87; John Moorman, *History of the Franciscan Order from Its Origins to the Year 1517* (Oxford: Clarendon Press, 1968), 441–500, 569–85; Duncan Nimmo, "The Genesis of the Observance," in *Atti-Assisi,* 109–47, now incorporated in his *Reform and Division in the Franciscan Order (1226–1538)* (Rome: Capuchin Historical Institute, 1987); Dionisio Pacetti, "S. Bernardino da Siena Vicario Generale dell'Osservanza (1438–1442) con documenti inediti," *SF* 42 (1945): 7–69; Mario Sensi, *Dal movimento eremitico alla regolare osservanza francescana. L'opera di fra Paoluccio Trinci* (Assisi: Edizioni Porziuncula, 1992); and André Vauchez, "Alcune riflessioni sul movimento dell'Osservanza in Italia nel secolo XV," in *Ordini mendicanti e società italiana XIII@-XV secolo* (Milan: Mondadori/Il Saggiatore, 1990), 306–10.

25. Casimiro Centi, Introduzione, *Enciclopedia bernardiniana,* 4 vols., ed. Enrico D'Angelo et al. (L'Aquila: Centro Promotore Generale delle Celebrazioni del VI Centenario della Nascita di San Bernardino da Siena, 1980–85), 1:v. In truth, Bernardino should more properly be labeled its third founder, St. Bonaventure (ca. 1218–74), "the Seraphic Doctor," having just claim to second place, after St. Francis himself.

26. Moorman, *History of the Franciscan Order,* 467. The original line is "sancti Bernardini, michi alterius patris, quia ipse praelatus meus, alterius filii, quia ego doctor suus" (quoted in Johannes Hofer, *Johannes Kapistran: Ein Leben im Kampf um die Reform der Kirche,* 2d ed. [Heidelberg: F. H. Kerle Verlag; Rome: Editiones Franciscanae, 1964], 100). Capistrano's superior status did not stop him from attending and recording extensive personal notes on at least two full sermon cycles delivered by Bernardino in Assisi and Perugia in 1425; see Dionisio Pacetti, "La predicazione di San Bernardino da Siena a Perugia e ad Assisi nel 1425," 9:512–14.

27. For the sources, form, and content of Bernardino's oratory, see my "Vernacular Sermons of San Bernardino da Siena, O.F.M. (1380–1444): A Literary Analysis" (Ph.D. thesis, Harvard University, 1983), as well as Gustavo Cantini, "San Bernardino da Siena perfetto predicatore popolare," in *SBSSR,* 203–45; Carlo Delcorno, "L'*ars praedicandi* di Bernardino da Siena," in *Atti-Siena,* 419–49; and Zelina Zafarana, "Bernardino nella storia della predicazione popolare," in *Atti-Todi,* 41–70. See also Delcorno's useful bibliographic survey, "Rassegna di studi sulla predicazione medievale e umanistica (1970–1980)," *Lettere italiane* 33 (1981): 235–76.

28. Sermon #3, "Nella quale tratta delle parti vuole avere il predicatore e l'uditore," R.141–73.

29. Quoted by Etienne Gilson, "Michel Menot et la technique du sermon médiéval," in *Les idées et les lettres,* 2d ed. (Paris: Librairie Philosophique J. Vrin, 1955), 101, n. 1.

30. However, in the Florentine and Sienese sermons of 1424 and 1425, we find Bernardino often and somewhat abruptly tacking onto the end of his sermon a quick, literal summary of and "spiritual" commentary upon the day's Gospel, distinct in tone and content from the long scholastic moral-doctrinal analysis that he has just completed; see, e.g., sermon 19, Florence

1424, on restitution, A.287–307; the transition to the new exposition occurs, unannounced, on 303; for more explicit transitions, see A.106 ("per venire al santo evangelio") and C.18–19 ("ma per avere parte nella lettera e breve sposizione dico"). In the latter type of exposition, Bernardino seems to be briefly reverting to the older patristic "modo istoriale" of homiletics, which the *artes praedicandi* recommended for preaching "pro rusticis," but which Bernardino ended up rejecting completely, as we see in the later Siena 1427 sermons; see Zafarana, "Bernardino nella storia," 53–57.

31. Augustine, *On Christian Doctrine,* trans. D. W. Robertson, Jr. (New York: Library of Liberal Arts, 1959), 136. Augustine's "certain eloquent man" is Cicero.

32. On the origins of the thematic sermon, see David D'Avray, *The Preaching of the Friars: Sermons Diffused from Paris before 1300* (Oxford: Clarendon Press, 1985), 163–76, and James J. Murphy, *Rhetoric in the Middle Ages: A History of Rhetorical Theory from St. Augustine to the Renaissance* (Berkeley: University of California Press, 1974), 325–26. For medieval rhetorical theory in general, see Richard McKeon, "Rhetoric in the Middle Ages," in *Rhetoric: Essays in Invention and Discovery,* ed. Mark Backman (Woodbridge, Conn.: Ox Bow Press, 1987), 121–66.

33. Gilson, "Michel Menot," 108.

34. James J. Murphy, ed., *Three Medieval Rhetorical Arts* (Berkeley: University of California Press, 1971), 112. For the 1200 years of silence, see Murphy, *Rhetoric in the Middle Ages,* 300: "[T]he Church did not produce during its first dozen centuries any coherent body of precepts that might be called a rhetoric of preaching."

35. Gilson, "Michel Menot," 95–96. In addition to serving the purposes of logical analysis, the division of the text into carefully enumerated parts was also a mnemonic device.

36. Anscar Zawart, *The History of Franciscan Preaching and of Franciscan Preachers (1209–1927): A Bio-bibliographical Study* (New York: Wagner, 1928), 280.

37. Cynthia L. Polecritti, "Preaching Peace in Renaissance Italy: San Bernardino of Siena and His Audience" (Ph.D. thesis, University of California, Berkeley, 1988), 11.

38. Facchinetti, *S. Bernardino da Siena,* 22. This fact is noted in Guarino's *Epistolario* (ed. R. Sabbadini [Venice: R. Deputazione Veneta di Storia Patria, 1915–19], 1:376, letter 239); in a marginal note by Guarino's son, Battista (reproduced by Facchinetti, *S. Bernardino da Siena,* 22, n. 2); and in Ludovico Carbone's oration at the death of Guarino (*Prosatori latini del 400,* ed. Eugenio Garin [Milan: Ricciardi, 1952], 401).

39. "E qui vedi come questo calore è vivificante, che fa vivare l'anima e anco il corpo. E sappi che altra dottrina e altra scienzia è questa, che non è la rettorica di Tulio. Questa rettorica della parola di Dio è migliore. Che dice? Dice: '*Qui sitit, veniat ad me et bibat.* Chi ha sete, venga a me e beia.' E perché questa parola sia detta a' popoli, acciò che la dottrina sia predicata, inde Isaia al capitolo LVIII così dice a noi: 'Clama, ne cesses, quasi tuba exalta vocem tuam, et annuntia populo meo scelera eorum. Chiama e grida, e non ti ristare colla tua voce; come una tromba . . . , così grida tu alto e basso, e annunzia al mio popolo le loro scelleranze e le loro peccata' " (R.161–62).

40. "E questi giovani che studiano el Ciciarone, fanno bene per sapere favellare, ma io non odo che ce ne sieno molti, che è grandissima vergogna a questa città a non esserci una brigata di giovani valenti che sappino dire quattro parole se fusse di bisogno" (F.53–54).

41. See John W. O'Malley, "Form, Content and Influence of Works about Preaching before Trent: The Franciscan Contribution," in *I frati minori fra '400 e '500,* ed. R. Rusconi (Assisi: Università di Perugia, Centro di studi francescani, 1986), 27–50.

42. "[N]on dice la dichiarazione di Platone, né di Galieno né d'Ipocrasso, né di molti altri filosafi, che non la biasimo, no; però non la voglio lodare come quest'altra si de' lodare lei.

Imperò che come una medesima acqua si può conduciare per uno canale di pietra lavorato e pulito, e un altro la può conduciare per una forma di terra, che sarà uno loto al pari di quella; così, dico, è altra dottrina quella che parla della salute dell'anima, che non è quella che parla della salute del corpo. L'uno parla de' naturali; l'altro delli spirituali beni; e qui vedi quanto è meglio '*eloquia Domini*,' che niuno altro parlare" (R.153–54).

43. Murphy, *Rhetoric in the Middle Ages*, 276.

44. "Quarta et ultima christianae fidei firmitas est divinae providentiae aequitas et pietas. Si Dominus Iesus Christus fuisset erroneus, tunc, quantum ad omnia supradicta, providentia Dei fuisset impia et iniqua, quia per testimonia sua summam occasionem dedisset et dari permisisset omnino errandi. Praeterea, nullatenus enim credibile est quod Deus nullam rectam viam salutis generi humano providerit" (OOQ.I.19).

45. James F. Keenan, "The Function of the Principle of Double Effect," *Theological Studies* 54 (1993): 298.

46. "La vita apostolica abbiamo presa sotto el serafico Francesco che ci comanda nella sua Regola fra l'altre cose: predicate a' popoli de' vizi e delle virtù e della pena e della grolia; e io ò promessa d'osservarla" (B.1).

47. A.134 ("Tutta la nostra vita è una tela di ragno di peccati fatta per dimonio"); OOQ.I.178, 206.

48. Jean Delumeau, *Sin and Fear: The Emergence of a Western Guilt Culture, 13th–18th Centuries*, trans. Eric Nicholson (New York: St. Martin's Press, 1990).

49. Ibid., 4–5.

50. See, for example, Coloman Viola's critique, "Jugements de Dieu et jugement dernier: Saint Augustin et la scolastique naissante (Fin XIe–milieu XIIIe siècles)," in *The Use and Abuse of Eschatology in the Middle Ages*, ed. Werner Verbeke, Daniel Verhelst, and Andries Welkenhuysen (Leuven: Leuven University Press, 1988), 246–47, n. 6. Delumeau has since published another monumental volume on the "reassuring" aspects of Christian doctrine and the "feeling of security" in Western Christianity: *Rassurer et protéger. Le sentiment de sécurité dans l'Occident d'autrefois* (Paris: Fayard, 1989). However, these feelings of "security" and "reassurance" would appear to be more characteristic of early modern European society and Christianity, as most of the texts cited therein are of the seventeenth century and later.

51. For further discussion of the topic, see my study, "What Happens to Us When We Die?: Bernardino of Siena on 'The Four Last Things,'" in *Death and Dying in the Middle Ages*, ed. Edelgard E. DuBruck and Barbara I. Gusick (New York: Peter Lang, forthcoming).

52. See the friar's Latin treatise entitled "Apertis rationibus demonstratur quod extra unicam et catholicam fidem nemo salvari potest; et quare tanta erit multitudo damnatorum et tanta paucitas salvandorum" ("With manifest reasons it is demonstrated that no one can be saved outside the one Catholic faith; and why there will be so great a multitude of the damned and so small a number of the saved," OOQ.III.380–91); see also OOH.III.172a. This was a traditional orthodox belief, that of the "massa damnata," of Augustinian origin. However, Bernardino tells us not to take the number 144,000 of the Book of Revelation literally (OOH.III.321a).

53. Evelyn Underhill, *Jacopone da Todi* (London: Dent, 1919), 220.

54. John V. Fleming, *An Introduction to the Franciscan Literature of the Middle Ages* (Chicago: Franciscan Herald Press, 1977), 186–87.

55. "Una re maxime excellit, in persuadendo ac excitando affectibus flectit populum, et quo vult deducet, movens ad lacrimas et, cum res patitur, ad risum." *De avaritia*, in *Opera omnia* (Turin: Bottega d'Erasmo, 1964), 1:2.

56. See Carlo Delcorno, "L'*exemplum* nella predicazione di San Bernardino," in *Atti-Todi*, 76–77.

57. "Dodici conclusioni toccaremo stamane del fatto di queste parti, e ad ogni conclusione vedremo la ragione, l'autorità e l'essemplo" (R.463).

58. "Ma dimmi: io ti voglio fare questo argomento, e che tu mi risponda a ragione. Credi tu che Idio sia buono? Dici di sì: oltre! O mi di': credi tu che queste costellazioni abino più forza che il tuo arbitrio? Se tu consenti e fai quello che esse ti fanno fare, e tu dici che se' sforzato e non puoi fare altro, oltre, rispondemi: chi è peggiore? o tu che fai questo male, o il pianeto che ti costregne a farlo? Risponde tu, se elli è più gattivo lui che ti costregne; e io ti dico, e Idio è peggiore che non se' né tu, né il pianeto imperò che elli ha fatto il pianeto che ti sforza a far male. Sì che Idio essendo la prima cagione, elli è peggio di tutti; sì che vede a ordine: se tu fai il male, tu se' gattivo; se tu dici: 'Io so' costretto a farlo,' quello che ti costregne è anco più gattivo, e chi fece quello, die essare più che niuno, cioè die essare pessimo" (R.123–24).

59. "Chi credi tu che possa più, o Idio o l'angiolo?—Più Idio.—Chi più, o l'angiolo o l'anima?—Più l'angiolo.—Chi più, o l'anima o le costellazioni?—Più l'anima.—Chi più, o le costellazioni o 'l corpo?—Più il corpo.—Chi più, o la ragione o la sensualità?—Più la ragione.—Chi più, o la santa Chiesa co' dottori o la tua opinione?—Più la santa Chiesa.—E però a quello che dice e crede e tiene la santa Chiesa t'atacca, e lassa quello che la openione tua ha tenuto" (R.125).

60. For examples, see my " 'To Persuade Is a Victory': Rhetoric and Moral Reasoning in the Sermons of Bernardino of Siena," in *The Context of Casuistry*, ed. James F. Keenan and Thomas A. Shannon (Washington, D.C.: Georgetown University Press, 1995), 78–80.

61. "I dottori c'insegnano e noi pigliamo i fioretti e diciagli a voi" (D.296).

62. The entire passage reads: "In sexta tuba, scilicet, in isto nostro tempore regnant superbi, pestiferi, et seminatores zizaniarum, et seditionum, bellorum; ideo dicit [Revelation 9:14] in isto sexto tempore: *Solve*, quod incoepit forte a quinquaginta annis citra; quia incipiendo a diabolo luxuriae, et a diabolo haereses, et a diabolo avaritiae, discurrendo per opera diaboli superbiae, videbis in universo orbe totum ordinem justistiae, bonarum operationum, ac morum honestorum, et pacis, et quietis fore perversum. In omni genere luxuriae, avaritiae, et haeresum in Ecclesia Dei: vide schismata Paparum, considera errores Enclif in Anglia quantum regnent; Usones in Boemia quam pullulaverint, et iam dispersi sunt in mentibus plurimorum in Italia, et utinam mentiar, quod hinc ad tempus modicum Italia, et mundus totus non repleatur illis haereticis pravitatibus; revolve bella, quae fuerunt a quinquaginta annis citra, et quot civitates, regna, et aedificia sunt deleta, quot partialitates, quot incendia, homicidia, et proditiones fuerint, et hodie regnent in universo, tam in Italia, quam in Francia, et Anglia, et in aliis mundi partibus; et videbis, quod sunt soluti supradicti spiritus infernales. Ideo bene venit tempus, ut dicatur, *Solve*, etc., quae omnia praeparant vestro Antichristo cito venturo" (OOH.III.353b). We shall hear Bernardino speak more about the omnipresent threat of heresy in chap. 2, sec. 4.

63. It was at the Council of Basel that Bernardino was accused of being a "heresiarch"; see "Tagebuchaufzeichnungen zur Geschichte des Basler Konzils 1431–1435 und 1438," in *Concilium Basiliense: Studien und Quellen zur Geschichte des Concils von Basel*, 8 vols., ed. Gustav Beckman et al. (1904; reprint, Nendeln, Liechtenstein: Kraus, 1971), 5:149.

64. "L'arte de' dicitori si è le cose alte de' cieli e delle stelle e della sacra teologia e astrologia farle toccare con mano, cioè dirle in sifatto stile e sì chiare a' nostri intelletti che quasi te le faccino toccare e palpare" (C.263).

65. "[E] però non sono da biasimare i dicitori e predicatori che, per mostrarti le cose alte di sopra a noi, il faccino con essempli grossi e palpabili, che quella è l'arte del dire ben chiaro. Gesù, fontana d'eloquenzia, usava sempre in parabole e cose palpabili per dare a 'ntendere ir regno del cielo; viene a dire per queste cose umane, si vengono ad intendere chiaramente le cose divine" (C.263–64).

66. "Questi esempri grossi si tengono meglio a mente che le ragioni e l'altre cose. Gesù Cristo parlava per similitudini d'esempri. . . . Poi che ci sono venute assai genti darò essempri tanto chiari, ch'io sarò inteso, e 'l mio parlare sarà utile a tutti voi" (A.371, G.327).

67. Bernardino's Italy is one of the most intensely studied times and places in all history, especially Tuscany, where the friar was born and raised and spent much of his preaching career; in this section, I am interested above all in the institutional-spiritual crisis of fifteenth-century Italy, and hence cite here only those works most directly relevant to this topic; the list, of course, could be expanded ad infinitum: Giuseppe Alberigo, "La problematica ecclesiologica tra XIV e XV secolo," in *Ambrogio Traversari nel VI centenario della nascita*, ed. Gian Carlo Garfagnani (Florence: Olschki, 1988), 3–25; Margaret Aston, *The Fifteenth Century: The Prospect of Europe* (New York: Norton, 1968), 117–73; Bornstein, *The Bianchi of 1399*, chap. 1, "The Religious Culture of Late Medieval Italy"; E. Delaruelle, E. R. Labande, and P. Ourliac, *L'Eglise au temps du Grand Schisme et de la crise conciliaire (1378–1449)*, vol. 14 of *Histoire de l'Eglise*, ed. A. Fliche and V. Martin (Tournai: Bloud & Gay, 1962); Hay, *The Church in Italy in the Fifteenth Century;* Denys Hay and John Law, *Italy in the Age of the Renaissance, 1380–1530* (London: Longman, 1989), 124–45; Francis Oakley, *The Western Church in the Later Middle Ages* (Ithaca: Cornell University Press, 1979); R. N. Swanson, *Religion and Devotion in Europe, c. 1215–c. 1515* (Cambridge: Cambridge University Press, 1995); Roberto Rusconi, *L'attesa della fine. Crisi della società, profezia ed Apocalisse in Italia al tempo del grande scisma d'Occidente (1378–1417)* (Rome: Istituto Storico Italiano per il Medio Evo, 1979).

68. *Oxford Dictionary of the Christian Church*, 163.

69. See OOH.III.351–56, especially 353b and 355b (the latter passage is spoken by Satan). Men of letters had also long been pointing to the same social, natural, ecclesiastical, and political disorders as manifestations of "a world grown old"; see James M. Dean, *The World Grown Old in Later Medieval Literature* (Cambridge: Medieval Academy of America, 1997).

70. See my article "Signs of the Apocalypse in Late Medieval Italy: The Popular Preaching of Bernardino of Siena," in *Medievalia et Humanistica: Studies in Medieval and Renaissance Culture* 24, ed. Paul M. Clogan (Lanham, Md.: Rowman & Littlefield, 1997), 95–122.

71. We cannot know, of course, the extent to which Bernardino caused, rather than merely reflected, the emotions and beliefs of his audience on any given subject.

72. Origo, *The World of San Bernardino*, 135.

73. For the condition of the Papal States both during and after the schism, see Peter Partner, *The Papal State under Martin V: The Administration and Government of the Temporal Power in the Early Fifteenth Century* (London: British School at Rome, 1958), passim; for Bologna, 86–93; and by the same author, *The Lands of St. Peter: The Papal State in the Middle Ages and the Early Renaissance* (London: Eyre Methuen, 1972), 366–446.

74. "De papatu deceptos plures novi. Et licet quidam eorum ex miris revelationibus hoc habuisse assererent, tamen semper illos, sicut exstiterunt, deceptos et illusos existimavi. Quod quanti periculi sit, nunc nostris temporibus experitur ipsa infelix Christianitas, in Infelice infelix [Bernardino is engaging in a wordplay on antipope Felix's first name], dum per hanc illusionem, ut manifesta indicia clamant, delusus antipapa tam horribile et scandalosum monstrum in Ecclesia parturivit; quod 'est iniquitas maxima, et negatio contra Deum altissimum' " (OOQ.VI.268; the quoted phrase comes from Job 31:28). See also the censure of Felix by the Council of Florence in *Decrees of the Ecumenical Councils*, ed. Norman Tanner (London and Washington, D.C.: Sheed & Ward and Georgetown University Press), 1:559–66.

75. See the Latin sermon "De veneratione sacrorum" (OOQ.I.238–55, esp. 251–55), as well as the vernacular *reportationes* "Del sacrilegio" (A.210–26, esp. 219–24) and "Questa è la predica che tratta del sacrilegio" (G.225–42, esp. 235).

76. "In omni genere luxuriae, avaritiae et haeresum in Ecclesia Dei: vide schismata Paparum" (OOH.III.353b).

77. "Se ci cacciassino tutti e cattivi [preti], pochi rimarrebbono e buoni, [ma] egli è meno male avergli non buoni che non avere niuno" (A.219). Elsewhere, the ignorance of parish priests who cannot even recite the Latin formula of Eucharistic consecration is the topic of one of Bernardino's most oft-cited *exempla* (R.579).

78. "Alcuni ci sono che dicono: 'Quando ci manderà Iddio un papa santo che lievi via questi [preti] cattivi'! Per tuo avviso, se tu avessi un papa sancto come tu vorresti, non leverà però via e prelati e i preti cattivi. Quale si converrà sostenere per amicizia dello imperatore e quale per amicizia di re o di baroni o d'altri signori temporali, e quali per amicizia dei cardinali o d'altri signori e prelati di santa chiesa. E pure se ne lieva alcuno, non è possibile che un papa viva tanto tempo che tutti e benefici abbia a rinnovare o mettere di nuovo, sicchè non farebbe nulla o poco di quello ti pensi. E signori vorranno e vescovi a loro modo, e al papa converrà loro condiscendere per bene di santa chiesa. E' impossibile a riformare santa chiesa, se prima el capo non s'accorda colle membra. In prima che 'l capo sia buono e tutte le membra sieno buone, che sono tutti e popoli e signori cristiani. Non dico per dare favore a' cattivi, ma per dare favore a' buoni e contradico a' cattivi. Non si fe' mai riformazione di chiesa generale, ma sì particulare. Bene à del nuovo chi crede che altrimenti si riformi. Aumenta e da' favore a' buoni e basta" (A.220–21).

79. Walter Brandmüller, "L'ecclesiologia di San Bernardino da Siena," in *Atti-Siena*, 405.

80. The Book of Revelation remained throughout Bernardino's life the most frequently cited and glossed scriptural text in all of his sermons. See Mormando, "Signs of the Apocalypse in Late Medieval Italy," 95–96.

81. Bornstein, *The Bianchi of 1399*, 200–201.

82. Aston, *The Fifteenth Century*, 10; Hay and Law, *Italy in the Age of the Renaissance*, 152. Hay and Law's description refers specifically to "the general European scene in the decades around 1400."

83. Gene Brucker, *Renaissance Florence* (Berkeley: University of California Press, 1969), 49.

84. Oakley, *The Western Church in the Later Middle Ages*, 115. While confirming the admittedly disquieting (at least to our modern sensibilities) conditions of popular religion in the "waning of the Middle Ages," Oakley argues that such forms of piety were in fact "signs of a deepening piety," rather than signs of the degeneration of the faith traditionally pictured by historians (120). See Roberto Rusconi's description of the apocalyptic unrest and other signs of the disturbed collective Italian psyche during Bernardino's lifetime in his *L'attesa della fine* (see n. 67 above).

85. *Paradiso*, XI, 79–83, in which Dante describes the initial growth of the Franciscan order.

86. These are the figures given by another "pillar of the Observance" and close friend, John of Capistrano, in his life of Bernardino, "Sancti Bernardini Senensis Ordinis Seraphici Minorum Vita," OOH.III.xxxix.a.

87. "A me mi pare che voi siate vescovo e papa e 'mperadore" (R.804).

88. "illud insuper aliquando joco attestans, fieri scilicet sibi injuriam, rogando ut alicujus privatae civitatis Praesulatum assequeretur, cum quamcumque introiret civitatem, non alia cum veneratione quam Praesul susciperetur, frequentaretur, coleretur; longeque satius sibi consultum videri, ut omnium Italiae civitatum, quam unius solius Antistes haberetur. . . . Cui simile est quod alii etiam roganti eum, cur Episcopatum Senarum recusaverat, respondit: Non recte sibi consuli, qui Papa jam esset, Episcopum dimissa longe excellentiore dignitate se fieri; illud certe quod supra diximus signficans, se, quamcumque introiret civitatem, non alia veneratione quam Praesulem suscipi, frequentari ac coli." Vegio, *Vita sancti Bernardini senensis*, 4:28, 125F–126A.

Cf. R.543: "Doh! Io non so' né papa, né imperadore, benché mi paia essare" ("Hey! I'm neither pope nor emperor, although it seems so to me"). Bernardino was formally offered and refused the episcopal sees of Siena (1427), Ferrara (1431), and Urbino (1435); this is the significance of the three bishop's miters one frequently sees at the saint's feet in his portraits.

89. "Quid episcopo, si iste populus ex devotione quam in me habet cum palmis olivarum volebat me recipere?"; Longpré, "S. Bernardin de Sienne et le nom de Jésus," *AFH* 39 (1936): 451–52.

90. A thorough critical study of these many biographical sources is very much in order. For a description thereof, see Pacetti, *De sancti Bernardini Senensis operibus ratio editionis critica* (Quaracchi: Collegio San Bonaventura, 1947), 210–16; Facchinetti, *S. Bernardino da Siena,* x–xvii; and Marina Montesano, "La memoria dell'esperienza di Bernardino da Siena nell'agiografia del XV secolo," *Hagiographica* 1 (1994): 271–86, whence the above quotation (272). Diana M. Webb discusses Bernardino at length in "Eloquence and Education: A Humanist Approach to Hagiography," *Journal of Ecclesiastical History* 31 (1980): 19–39, as does Remo L. Guidi, "Colombini, Bernardino da Siena, Savonarola: uomini e simulacri," *Benedictina* 35 (1988): 373–427; 36 (1989): 105–63, 349–439 (for Bernardino, see 36:105–63). As Montesano points out ("La memoria," 271, n. 1), although more exhaustive in its inventory of all biographical sources than any of the above, Bernhard Stasiewski's *Der Heilige Bernardin von Siena: untersuchungen über die quellen seiner biographen* (Munster: Aschendorffschen Verlagsbuchhandlung, 1931) must be used with caution, as it contains many errors. For a good discussion of the genre of hagiography, with further bibliography, see Thomas J. Heffernan, *Sacred Biography: Saints and Their Biographers in the Middle Ages* (New York: Oxford University Press, 1988); and, with exclusive reference to fifteenth-century Italy, Remo L. Guidi, "Questioni di storiografia agiografica nel Quattrocento," *Benedictina* 34 (1987): 166–252.

91. Bernardino's schoolmate, Leonardo Benvoglienti (dates of birth and death unknown), furnishes the most complete account of the first two decades of the friar's life. The *vita* of Maffeo Vegio, another contemporary (1407–58?), is also useful for this period of Bernardino's life. Capistrano's life of Bernardino also covers his childhood, but most of his information is taken from Benvoglienti. For the latter, see Giulio Prunai, s.v. "Benvoglienti, Leonardo," *Dizionario biografico degli italiani*, 8:703–5; and Franciscus van Ortroy's introduction to his edition of Benvoglienti's *vita,* "Vie de S. Bernardin de Sienne par Léonard Benvoglienti," *AB* 21 (1902): 53–58. For Vegio, see Webb, "Eloquence and Education," 28–38, and Remo L. Guidi, "Maffeo Vegio agiografo di S. Bernardino da Siena," in his *Aspetti religiosi nella letteratura del 400*, 3 vols. (Vicenza: L.I.E.F., 1974), 2:63–96.

92. Piana, "I processi di canonizzazione," 138.

93. Saint Antonino tells us in his brief sketch of Bernardino's life that Bernardino's mother died as a result of giving birth to her first and only child, Bernardino: "ex vehementi partus eius dolore" (*Opera historiale,* also known as the *Chronicon* [Nuremburg, 1484], par. III, tit. 24, cap. V, fol. 234, recto.) If by this Antonino means that she died in the act of giving birth or shortly thereafter, he is inaccurate; we know that Nera died in 1383, three years after Bernardino's birth. Yet there may be some truth to Antonino's claim. Nera may not have died in childbirth or soon after, but, never having produced another child, she may have been permanently debilitated by or developed some illness from the pregnancy or delivery whose effects caused her death three years later. It is also possible that Nera had been in poor health before her pregnancy and that childbirth exacerbated a preexisting illness. Though not infallible in his reporting, Antonino (1389–1459) was a contemporary of Bernardino's and a long-term resident—and later archbishop—of Florence, a city that Bernardino and his closest friends visited regularly. He was also a pious man of intelligence and of scholarly repute, not likely to repeat gossip. Hence, what he says is

not so easily dismissed. Where did Antonino obtain this information? Was it only rumor? If so, had the young Bernardino himself known of and believed this "fact" about his mother's death? If he did, what was his reaction, we wonder, to the discovery of his being, in effect, a matricide?

94. For the ages of Nera and Tollo at their marriage, see Capistrano's sermon on Bernardino, Ferdinand Doelle, "Sermo S. Iohannis de Capistrano de S. Bernardini Senensis," *AFH* 6 (1913): 85. Benvoglienti confirms Nera's age as well in his *Vita Sancti Bernardini Senensis,* 60, s. 2. See also Enrico Bulletti, "I genitori di S. Bernardino da Siena," *SF,* serie terza 21 (1949): 131–33.

95. The only family member he mentions—twice, in passing—is his aunt Bartolommea, whom we shall meet below (R.1329, 1375).

96. "Hanc igitur ipse non aliter ac matrem venerabatur, visitabatque saepius, fruebaturque frequenti ejus colloquio." Vegio, *Vita Sancti Bernardini Senensis,* 1:6, 118F; see also Benvoglienti, *Vita Sancti Bernardini Senensis,* 63–64, s. 8. The same two sources tell us that such was the emotional-spiritual bond between Bernardino and Tobia that years later, when Bernardino was preaching in Milano, he abruptly suspended his sermon, rendered speechless by the sight of Tobia's soul rising to the heavens. It was later verified that cousin Tobia had indeed died at the very day and hour of Bernardino's vision.

97. "Felix enimvero Bernardinus, tot feminarum necessitudine et obsequiis, tamque egregie instituta earum vita tantaque virtute!" Vegio, *Vita Sancti Bernardini Senensis,* 1:7, 119B. For Bernardino's "petticoat government," Origo, *The World of San Bernardino,* 15.

98. "Ad tantamque sanctitatis excellentiam pervenerat, ut audito nomine Jesu, inenarrabili exultans laetitia, neque ulla vi vocem valens comprimere, identidem illum crebro singultu vocans prosiliret; et cum prudentissima omnium judicio esset, tanto tamen saepe rapiebatur fervore spiritus, ut cui ignota fuisset ejus sapientia et sanctitas, insanire procul dubio, dum illum nominari audiret, crederetur." Vegio, *Vita Sancti Bernardini Senensis,* 1:7, 119A.

99. "Jam vero earum exemplo et exhortatione, majora quam solitus est aggrediebatur: nam viliores jam et pauciores sumere cibos, augere jejunia, vigilias, visitationem ecclesiarum, studia sacrae lectionis, orare frequentius incipiebat. Jam duris in stratis, ac in iis quidem vestem semper indutus, somnos capiebat: jam cilicio saepe utebatur, jam disciplinis etiam multoties corpus castigabat, operiens cum Propheta in jejunio animam suam, et ponens vestimentum suum cilicium. Atque haec in privato quodam domi loco secreta habere, cognoverunt aliquando quidam socii ejus, cum parvo etiam altari ac superposita figura Salvatoris crucifixi, ardentique ante eum lampade. Quin et urticis se verberasse aliquando deprehensus est." Vegio, *Vita Sancti Bernardini Senensis,* 1:8, 119C–D.

100. Since the middle- and upper-class infant was usually sent away to a wet nurse, contact with either mother or father was minimal for the first year or so. Moreover, it is unlikely that Tollo's job—like most male employment—left him much time to devote to building a deep relationship with his son.

101. Piana, "I processi di canonizzazione," 133–34, and Benvoglienti, *Vita Sancti Bernardini Senensis,* 61, s. 4.

102. See the synopsis in *Medieval Sermon Studies* 33 (Spring 1994): 42–43, of Rosemary Hale's paper, "Late Medieval Sermons and the Paradigm of Saint Joseph: The Social Construction of Masculinity," delivered at the Twenty-eighth International Congress on Medieval Studies, Kalamazoo, Michigan (May 1993). See also David Herlihy, *Medieval Households* (Cambridge: Harvard University Press, 1985), 127–29. As for emasculated boys, others among Bernardino's Italian contemporaries shared the same anxiety; see below, chap. 3, sec. 4, "The Causes of the Sodomitic Vice."

103. "El più allegro vecchio che fusse mai nel mondo. . . . E gli sciocchi dipintori el dipingono vecchio maninconoso e colla mano alla gota, come s'elli avessi dolore o maninconia"

(A.278–79). For Bernardino's Latin treatise on Joseph, *De sancto Ioseph sponso beatae Virginis*, see OOQ.VII.16–30.

104. Origo, *The World of San Bernardino*, 44.

105. Ibid., 72; the "great defender" remark comes from Luigi Russo, "Caterina Benincasa e Bernardino da Siena," *Belfagor* 12 (1957): 131.

106. Ida Magli, "L'etica familiare e la donna in S. Bernardino," in *Atti-Aquila*, 116. Elsewhere Magli calls Bernardino an "implacable enemy of women" (*Gli uomini della penitenza. Lineamenti antropologici del Medioevo italiano* [Milan: Garzanti, 1977], 150, n. 46).

107. See my "Bernardino of Siena, 'Great Defender' or 'Merciless Betrayer' of Women?" *Italica* 75 (1998): 22–40.

108. The description of Onofrio in the previous sentence and that of Giovanni da Spoleto as representive of high culture are from Piero Bargellini, *San Bernardino da Siena*, 6th ed. (Brescia: Morcelliana, 1980), 19, 21; the remaining two quotations are from Leonardo Benvoglienti, *Vita Sancti Bernardini Senensis*, 61, s. 4. For Giovanni, author as well of a treatise on the Great Schism, see Federico Cesare Goffis, "Giovanni di ser Buccio da Spoleto," *Enciclopedia dantesca*, 6 vols., ed. Umberto Bosco (Rome: Istituto della Enciclopedia Italiana, 1970–78), 3:192–93; Jacques Monfrin, "Il dialogo di Giovanni da Spoleto a Jacopo Altoviti vescovo di Fiesole," *Rivista di Storia della Chiesa in Italia* 3 (1949): 9–44; Paolo Nardi, "Appunti sui maestri e gli studi giovanili di San Bernardino da Siena," *Annuario dell'Istituto Storico Diocesano di Siena* 1 (1992–93): 201–22; Pietro Rossi, "La 'Lectura Dantis' nello Studio senese: Giovanni da Spoleto maestro di rettorica e lettore della Divina Commedia (1396–1445)," in *Studi giuridici dedicati e offerti a F. S. Schupfer* (Turin: Fratelli Bocca, 1898), 153–74.

109. Benvoglienti, *Vita Sancti Bernardini Senensis*, 61, s. 4.

110. William W. Meissner, *Ignatius of Loyola: The Psychology of a Saint* (New Haven: Yale University Press, 1992), 10.

111. Vegio, *Vita Sancti Bernardini Senensis*, 2:13, 121C; the account of the dream follows in 2:14. In his sermon on Bernardino, Capistrano tells us that in this same period of life, just before entering the Franciscans, Bernardino "suffered great distress . . . for all of his friends had been sent into exile" ("Nam magnas angustias passus fuit, dum omnes amici sui . . . essent exilio proscripti," Doelle, "Sermo Sancti Iohanni de Capistrano," 88).

112. For Bernardino and the plague of 1400, only one of several return visits of that scourge between 1348 and the friar's death and "almost as severe as the first outbreak half a century before," see Origo, *The World of San Bernardino*, 18, and Bernardino's own remarks at R.1152. In his 1427 sermons to the Sienese, Bernardino continually refers to plagues as instruments of divine castigation; see, for example, R.168, 171, 202, 204, 214, 358, 393, 401, 410, 437, 440, 975, 998–99, 1000, 1023, 1065, 1086, and 1373. The warning about the Destroyer is from R.1065, where Bernardino expands upon Jesus's statement in Luke 13:5 ("[U]nless you repent, you will all perish just as they did") with a reference to Revelation 9:11; the original Italian reads: "Se voi non ritornarete a penitenzia del peccato vostro, voi sarete tutti martoriati dal maladetto Sterminatore, e verranno sopra a voi i guai radoppiati."

113. "Non vedi tu, quando hai il fanciullo che latta, che elli è già grande, e elli è avezzo a quello latte, e tu madre per farlo divezzare e tu poni l'amaro col dolce, che tu vi poni suso talvolta un poco d'assenzio? E come il fanciullo vuole suggiare, e elli sente l'amaro; e come il sente subito torce il viso dalla poccia, e fa 'tpu, tpu, tpu!' e sputa fuore, perché il truova amaro; e piccolo piccolo comincia a sentire dell'amaro del mondo. E come tu odi del fanciullo, così è di tutti noi; avendo delle cose dolci, elli ci è dimolto amaro con esse. Vedi quanti pericoli ci so' in queste delizie; quanti scandali! E quali si può dire che sieno i morsi del mondo. E quando tu il

considerrai, e tu dirai: 'O mondo traditore, io non ti credo più,' avendo tu veduto costui grande e alto, ora essere piccolo e basso; colui era ricco, ora è povaro, e così non ci è niuna cosa stabile. Doh! crede come in ogni cosa il mondo t'inganna" (R.284–85).

114. Vegio, *Vita Sancti Bernardini Senensis,* 2:13, 121C.

115. "Vidit se in quodam esse magno agro inculto, in quo excelsa turris, atque in turri fenestra, per quam flamma ingens exibat, in medioque flammae femina quaedam, resolutis crinibus pansisque manibus, sublata alte et ter repetita voce Franciscam inclamabat." Ibid., 2:14, 121D.

116. There is a second, markedly different, version of the dream reported by the slightly later anonymous account of the friar's life known as the Rouge Cloître *Vita,* produced between the years 1453 and 1457, most likely by a younger Franciscan contemporary of the friar's and named after the Belgian monastery that houses the original manuscript. (For the text of the Rouge Cloître *Vita,* see Baudouin de Gaiffier, "La Vie de S. Bernardin du manuscript de Rouge-Cloître," *AB* 71 [1953]: 282–322.) The Rouge Cloître account is iconographically much less puzzling and idiosyncratic, and much more Franciscan and hagiographically conventional: the wild, uncultivated field of Vegio's report is eliminated, while a more reassuring fountain is added; the phallic tower is replaced by a patrician building with many windows, located near a specifically Franciscan convent, and the frenzied woman in such a disturbing state of dishevelment becomes, instead, a far less startling, male, celibate figure, a Franciscan friar. Not surprisingly perhaps, this "Franciscanized" account is the version of the dream usually reported by modern biographers, their ultimate source being, not the long-unknown Rouge Cloître *Vita* (only published in 1953), but the life of Bernardino first published in 1572 by the German Carthusian hagiographer Laurentius Surius in his *De probatis Sanctorum historiis.* (The Surius *Vita* is an anonymous account written in the last decades of the fifteenth century—after 1481—by a contemporary of Bernardino's, perhaps a certain Antonio Neri of Arezzo; I have used the 1875–80 edition of Surius, *Historiae seu vitae sanctorum,* 13 vols. [Turin: Marietti], 5:618–55. For Surius, see Facchinetti, *San Bernardino da Siena,* xv.) I believe the earlier, Vegio version to be more authentic: Unlike the author of the Rouge Cloître life, Vegio could boast of a long-standing personal relationship with Bernardino, quoting from time to time bits of firsthand conversation with the preacher (e.g., "id quod et memini ab eo mihi dictum fuisse," *Vita Sancti Bernardini Senensis,* 4:28, 125F).

117. "Quorum significationem, dum ea aliquando narraret, talem etiam afferebat; ut ager, mundus; turris, Deus; ignis, Spiritus sanctus; femina, Religio seu Ecclesia intelligeretur. Dicebat quoque eam tam recenti memoria tenere, ac si tunc contigisset." Vegio, *Vita Sancti Bernardini Senensis,* 2:14, 121D.

118. "Adeo vero studiose in ea incumbebat opera quae mundo humilia et despicabilia videntur, seipsum plane contemnens, et generis sui nobilitatem pro nihilo ducens, ut homines plebei, qui ante eum noverant, non alio quam insani et stulti loco eum haberent." Surius, *Vita Sancti Bernardini Senensis,* 5:631, s. 23.

119. In this passage Bernardino is describing the travails of earning one's living by begging: "Sai come molte fanno? El povaro o 'l frate chiede la limosina; e ella dice: 'Oh, aspettate.' E egli aspettarà talvolta una mezz'ora; e infine quando l'ha fatto stentare, e ella gli gitta uno pane da la finestra, e daragli talvolta intro 'l capo. Questo pur posso io dire di prova, che quando andavo acattando, gittandomi una il pane a quel modo, egli mi gionse in sul dito, e dolsemi molto bene" (R.1194–95).

120. Vegio, *Vita Sancti Bernardini Senensis,* 2:15, 121F.

121. "Cum enim quadam die pergeret ad domum nutricis sue, ut eam visitaret, [ad] adhuc novitius existens, quidam illic affuit de affinibus eius, qui assumptum ab eo religionis habitum

moleste tulit; et obiurgans eum multis contumeliosis verbis, inter alia sic ait: 'Putabamus sperantes te in seculo honorabiliter vivere, uxorem ducere fecundam, prolem gignere letabundam ut domus tua sobole propagata opibus extolli, genusque tuum famosius potuisset augeri. Denique quid est frater nisi porcus, utpote qui iugiter otiosus et cum inertia vivens, aliorum labores edit, et semper pabulo intendit ut bene pinguescat?' " Rouge Cloître *Vita,* 304, chap. 12. The Surius *Vita* tells the same story in much the same terms, 5:631, s. 23, as does Antonino, *Opera historiale,* par. III, tit. 24, cap. V, fol. 234, recto. Giacomo della Marca mentions as well the impassioned oppposition of Bernardino's family to his entrance into religious life—although presumably not his entire family, since, for example, his cousin and surrogate mother, Tobia, was herself a member of the Third Order of St. Francis (Carlo Delcorno, "Due prediche volgari di Jacopo della Marca recitate a Padova nel 1460," *Atti dell'Istituto Veneto di Scienze, Lettere ed Arti* 128 [1969–70]: 199).

122. Roberto Rusconi, "Apocalittica ed escatologia nella predicazione di Bernardino da Siena," *Studi medievali* 22 (terza serie, 1981): 85–86.

123. See the source-identifying footnotes to the various OOQ volumes; Rusconi, "Apocalittica ed escatologia," 86–92; and Pacetti, "Gli scritti di San Bernardino da Siena," in *SBSSR,* 109–30. For Ubertino and Bernardino, see also the two studies of E. Blondeel d'Isegem, "L'influence d'Ubertin de Casale sur les écrits di Saint Bernardin de Sienne," *CF* 5 (1935): 5–44, and "Encore sur l'influence d'Ubertin de Casale sur les écrits de S. Bernardin de Sienne," *CF* 6 (1936): 57–76. Bernardino had ready access to Olivi's works in the Franciscan library at Santa Croce, Florence: see Raoul Manselli's two studies, "Due biblioteche di 'Studia' Minoritici. Santa Croce di Firenze e il Santo di Padova," in *Le scuole degli ordini mendicanti, secoli XIII–XIV* (Todi: Centro di Studi sulla Spiritualità Medievale, 1978), 353–72, and "Firenze nel Trecento: Santa Croce e la cultura francescana," *Clio* 9 (1973): 325–42. Bernardino's letter to friar Giacomo della Biada at Santa Croce asking him to send him Olivi's *Expositio super Matthaeum* is extant; see OOQ.VIII.321.

124. Another Franciscan author of a similar passionate, ascetic stamp who spoke to Bernardino's heart and who is often quoted in his sermons was the thirteenth-century poet Jacopone of Todi, the "troubadour" of God's love and of Lady Poverty. See Underhill, *Jacopone da Todi,* and Fleming, *An Introduction to the Franciscan Literature,* 108–9.

125. Dionisio Pacetti, "La libreria di San Bernardino da Siena e le sue vicende attraverso cinque secolo," *SF* 62 (1965): 3–43.

126. Bernardino's relationship with the humanist movement that was rapidly diffusing through Italy during his lifetime was cordial but superficial; he maintained long-term relations with several of the leading humanists of his day, showing no hostility toward the burgeoning new study of the "pagan" classics. Although traces of what could be called a humanist temperament can be found in certain of Bernardino's utterances, our preacher was, by and large, not interested in the literary-cultural world of the humanist scholars. See Mormando, "The Humanists, the Pagan Classics and S. Bernardino da Siena," *Laurentianum* 27 (1986): 72–97, as well as Joseph F. Bernard, Jr., "San Bernardino of Siena: His Relation to the Humanist World of the Early Italian Renaissance" (Ph.D. thesis, Yale University, 1973), and Policelli, *Humanism in the Life and Vernacular Sermons of Bernardino of Siena.*

127. See Ernesto Bellone, "S. Bernardino come 'auctoritas' nelle opere del Beato Angelo da Chiavasso (1410 c.–1495)," in *Atti-Siena,* 333–57. The sermons of Giacomo della Marca, John of Capistrano, Roberto Caracciolo, Michele Carcano, and Bernardino da Feltre cite Bernardino as *auctoritas* many times. For the sermons of Bernardino as a source for contemporary painting, see Carl B. Strehlke, "La *Madonna dell'Umiltà* di Domenico di Bartolo e San Bernardino, " *Arte cristiana* 705 (1984): 381–90.

128. John of Capistrano, *Vita sancti Bernardini senensis,* OOH.I.xxxviii.b. See also Moorman, *A History of the Franciscan Order,* chap. 39, "Great Was the Company of the Preachers."

129. "Conati sunt imitari modum et regulam et stilum ipsius sancti Bernardini," "Sermo de sancto Bernardino predicatorum nostri temporis principe," in *Sermones de laudibus sanctorum* (Reutlingen: Michael Greyyff, ca. 1495). The pages of this edition are unnumbered; the Bernardino sermon is the final one of the collection. The list in question appears in the first column of the penultimate page.

130. One figure given by an anonymous contemporary biographer is 4,000, citing as his authority the papal bull of canonization; Sevesi, "Tre sermoni inediti su S. Bernardino," 171. As for Bernardino's miracles, the papal bull "Misericordias Domini," issued by Nicholas V on May 24, 1450, merely states that "if each and every miracle were to be catalogued, enormous volumes would not suffice to contain them all," *Bullarium franciscanum,* vol. 1 (1431–55), ed. U. Hüntemann (Quaracchi: Collegio San Bonaventura, 1929), 701, doc. 1364. See also Origo, *World of San Bernardino,* 241–49, and Piana, "I processi di canonizzazione," 87–90.

131. Ferrers Howell, *S. Bernardino of Siena,* 211–13; Edward Hutton, *The Franciscans in England, 1224–1538* (London: Constable, 1926), 228–29.

132. Enea Silvio Piccolomini, *De viris illustribus,* 39.

133. *Bullarium franciscanum,* 1:701, doc. 1364.

134. Delcorno, "Due prediche volgari di Jacopo della Marca," 201.

135. For the information and quotations given in this and the previous sentences, see Origo, *World of San Bernardino,* 247. See also Daniel Arasse, "Fervebat pietate populus: art, dévotion et société autour de la glorification de saint Bernardin de Sienne," *Mélanges de l'École Française de Rome (Moyen-Age et Temps Modernes)* 89 (1977): 189–263; and Diana Webb, *Patrons and Defenders: The Saints in the Italian City States* (London: Tauris Academic Studies, 1996), 300–305.

136. Bernardino's lifetime coincided with the blossoming not only of art in general but of full-fledged, realistic portraiture as a distinct genre. This may explain why Bernardino, it seems, has the distinction of being the first saint in Church history for whom we have an indisputably authentic portrait in art. Many of the earliest portraits were presumably based on his death mask or on other portraits that had made use of the mask. Some of these same early depictions of the saint were also by artists—like fellow Sienese Sano di Pietro—who had seen and interacted with Bernardino in life. See Daniel Arasse, "Saint Bernardin ressemblant: la figure sous le portrait," in *Atti-Siena,* 311–32; Julia Cartwright, "S. Bernardino in Art," in Ferrers Howell, *S. Bernardino of Siena,* 326–49; Keith Christiansen et al., *Painting in Renaissance Siena, 1420–1500* (New York: Metropolitan Museum of Art; Harry Abrams, 1988), 11, 138, 153–54, 164–66, 169, 268–69; Michael Mallory and Gaudenz Freuller, "Sano di Pietro's Bernardino Altar-piece for the Compagnia della Vergine in Siena," *Burlington Magazine* 133 (1991): 186–92; Origo, *World of San Bernardino,* 3–4. Also on an iconographical note, according to a census of Italian images of saints painted in the period 1420–1539, Bernardino ranks number nine in order of frequency (the number eight niche is occupied by Peter the Apostle, while Bernard of Clairvaux and Michael the Archangel compete for tenth place). See Peter Burke, *The Italian Renaissance: Culture and Society in Italy,* rev. ed. (Princeton: Princeton University Press, 1987), 162–64.

137. Personal communication from Anne T. Thayer, April 1997.

138. Priscilla S. Albright, "Pintoricchio's Frescoes in the San Bernardino Chapel in Santa Maria in Aracoeli, Rome" (Ph.D. thesis, University of California, Berkeley, 1980).

139. *Titian, Prince of Painters. Exhibition at the National Gallery of Art, Washington, D.C., October 28, 1990–January 27, 1991* (Venice: Marsilio Editori, 1990), 170. For Bernardino's long-enduring reputation in Venice, see Rona Goffen, *Piety and Patronage in Renaissance Venice:*

Bellini, Titian and the Franciscans (New Haven: Yale University Press, 1986), Appendix 1, 157–58, and passim.

140. Émile Mâle, *L'art religieux de la fin du XVIe siècle, du XVIIe siècle et du XVIIIe siècle. Étude sur l'iconographie après le Concile de Trente*, 2d ed. (Paris: Colin, 1951), 484–86; and Vincenzo Pacelli, "L'iconografia di San Bernardino da Siena dopo il Concilio di Trento," in *Atti-Siena*, 665–76. For Cornelius a Lapide's comment on and use of Bernardino's sermons, see Felice Alessio, *Storia di San Bernardino e del suo tempo* (Mondovì: Graziano, 1899), 51, n. 2, and 317; and Serafino (Paolo) M. Gozzo, *S. Bernardino da Siena "esegeta"* (L'Aquila: Del Romano, 1982), xxi.

141. Martino Bertagna, "La Commissione Bernardiniana (1940–1966)," *AFH* 70 (1977): 546.

142. We are fortunate in possessing nearly twenty volumes of Bernardino's works in the form of sermons, treatises, sermon drafts and notes, outlines, and letters, covering thousands of pages. A census and description of all surviving works bearing Bernardino's name can be found in the 1947 summary volume prepared by Dionisio Pacetti and the Quaracchi critical-edition commission, *De sancti Bernardini Senensis operibus ratio editionis critica*, supplemented by the introductory essays to the various Quaracchi volumes themselves.

143. Twenty-one of these letters are reproduced in OOQ.VIII.311–32; the last one is appended to the Introduction to the successive volume, OOQ.IX.34*–35*. Some letters, to be precise, were written on behalf of Bernardino, rather than by him. Included among them is the clarification of the Franciscan rule (mostly the work of Nicholas of Osimo) disseminated by Bernardino while vicar general of the Observants (OOQ.VIII.317–20). The most interesting one is perhaps that written to Suor Nicolina, abbess of the Monastery of Santa Marta in Siena, on how to pray (OOQ.VIII.321–23). In letter 3, Bernardino writes to Caterina Colonna, countess of Montefeltro and Urbino and niece of Pope Martin V, declining her invitation to come to preach in her domains (OOQ.VIII.312–13).

144. Delcorno's edition is based on the 1880–86 Banchi edition (Bernardino of Siena, *Le prediche volgari di S. Bernardino da Siena . . .*, 3 vols., ed. Luciano Banchi [Siena: Tipografia editrice All'insegna di S. Bernardino]), reprinted in 3 vols. by Piero Bargellini (Milan: Rizzoli, 1936). Incorporating manuscripts not utilized by their predecessors, two other scholars have published portions of the same sermon cycles: Dionisio Pacetti, ed., *Bernardino da Siena. Le prediche volgari inedite (Firenze 1424, 1425; Siena 1425)* (Siena: Cantagalli, 1935), and Giacomo V. Sabatelli, ed., *Bernardino da Siena. La fonte della vita: prediche volgari scelte e annotate* (Firenze: Libreria Editrice Fiorentina, 1964).

145. See Pacetti, "La predicazione di San Bernardino da Siena a Perugia e ad Assisi nel 1425"; for the Padua 1443 sermons, see also Pacetti, *De sancti Bernardini Senensis operibus*, 143, 170–74. For Daniele de Purzillis, or more properly, da Porcìa, see Donato Gallo, "Predicatori francescani nella cattedrale di Padova durante il '400," *Le Venezie francescane*, nuova serie 6 (1989): 175, n. 86.

146. Carlo Delcorno, *Prediche volgari sul Campo di Siena, 1427*, 2 vols. (Milan: Rusconi, 1989); see 67–69 for his manuscript list.

147. On the issue of multiple *reportationes*, see Salvatore Tosti, "Di alcuni codici delle prediche di S. Bernardino da Siena con un saggio di quelle inedite," *AFH* 12 (1919): 187–263; and, more recently, Delcorno, "Note sulla tradizione manoscritta delle prediche volgari di San Bernardino da Siena," *AFH* 73 (1980): 90–123, and the same author's "La diffrazione del testo omeletico. Osservazioni sulle doppie reportationes delle prediche bernardiniane," *Lettere italiane* 38 (1986): 457–77. For one sermon in the Padua 1423 cycle preserved in a

different version, see Pacetti, "Una predica sul SS. Nome di Gesù tenuta a Padova nel 1423 da S. Bernardino da Siena e raccolta da un suo anonimo ascoltatore," *MF* 42 (1942): 257–76. Alda Rossebastiano Bart has discovered several Florentine sermons in a new *reportatio*, which she publishes in "Frammenti dei quaresimali fiorentini di S. Bernardino da Siena," *SF* 78 (1981): 251–305. For the still unresolved question of the "Osservanza 28" codex, see Pacetti, "Le prediche bernardiniane di un codice senese in una recente pubblicazione," *AFH* 34 (1941): 133–85, and Benvenuto Bughetti, "Il codice bernardiniano contenente gli schemi del Santo in volgare per la Quaresima di Firenze 1425," *AFH* 34 (1914): 261–83. Cannarozzi quotes and discusses the same manuscript at length in the introduction to his edition of the 1425 Florentine sermons (C.xxv–lxxv); for further excerpts, see also his notes to the individual sermons.

148. "E però esso magno e grande Iddio ispirò uno che si chiamò Benedetto di maestro Bartolomeo cittadino di Siena, e era cimatore di panni; il quale avendo donna e più figliuoli, e avendo poca robba e assai virtù, lassando stare per quello tempo il lavorare, ricolse e scrisse le presenti prediche *de verbo ad verbum*, non lassando nissuna parola che non scrivesse, come lui predicava. . . . E per notare le virtù e grazie di detto Benedetto cimatore, stando alla predica, scriveva in tavole di cera collo stile, e, detta la predica, tornava alla sua buttiga e scriveva in foglio tutto quello che avevo scritto nelle predette tavole di cera; per modo che lo giorno medesimo, innanzi che si ponesse a lavorare, aveva scritta due volte la predica. La qual cosa chi bene notarà, trovarrà essere così miracolosa come umana, che in sì brevissimo tempo scrivesse tante cose due volte, non lassando una minima paroluzza di quelle che uscivano di quella santa bocca, che lui non scrivesse; come per lo presente libro si manifesta" (R.82–84).

149. The merchant who several years later copied for his own use Bartolommeo's *reportatio* records for posterity this account of his labors: "Questo libro è di Ghoro di Michelangiolo ligrittiere [i.e., fabric merchant]. El quale à scritto di sua propria mano. Cominciolo a dì primo di maggio MCCCCLXVI. E scrisselo i dì di feste. E alchuna volta a veglia. E finito a dì 25 di genaio la mattina della conversione di sam Paolo anno detto. Pregho chi l'à in presta che'l debbi riguardare da ogni suo contrario imperò che io ci durai una grande fadiga e patij dimolti disagi. E ogni cosa feci per amore di Dio e di santo Bernardino. E loro el sanno, siché chi legge preghi per me" (Sabatelli, *Bernardino da Siena. La fonte della vita*, 483–84).

150. "O da la fonte, che state a fare il mercato, andatelo a fare altrove! Non odite, o voi da la fonte? . . . Attende tu che scrivi, e scrivele bene, acciò che tu non pigli errore" (R.710–11 and 772–73).

151. The date of birth of this "new history" is difficult to pinpoint; "[f]or many people, the new history is associated with Lucien Febvre and Marc Bloch, who founded the journal *Annales* in 1929," Peter Burke, "Overture; the New History, Its Past and Its Future," in *New Perspectives on Historical Writing*, ed. P. Burke (University Park: Pennsylvania State University Press, 1991), 7.

152. Bronislaw Geremek, *The Margins of Society in Late Medieval Paris* (Cambridge: Cambridge University Press, 1987).

153. For instance, the fairly recent, thirteen-volume *Dictionary of the Middle Ages*, ed. Joseph R. Strayer (New York: Scribners, 1982–89), contains no entry on, and hardly a mention of, sodomy or sodomites.

154. The development of this pattern of persecution and the common plight of these oppressed minorities of Christian Europe have in recent years been described in such general surveys as R. I. Moore's *The Formation of a Persecuting Society: Power and Deviance in Western Europe, 950–1250* (Oxford: Blackwell, 1987), and, in a slightly more popular though still informative fashion, by Andrew McCall's *The Medieval Underworld* (New York: Barnes &

Noble, 1993, orig. pub. 1979) and Jeffrey Richards's *Sex, Dissidence and Damnation: Minority Groups in the Middle Ages* (London: Routledge, 1991). See also Joan Young Gregg's introductory material in her anthology of sermon *exempla, Devils, Women, and Jews: Reflections of the Other in Medieval Sermon Stories* (Albany: State University of New York Press, 1997).

155. It is displayed most prominently on the façades of the city halls of Siena and Florence. In the sixteenth century, the same monogram was adopted, with some modification, by Ignatius of Loyola as the emblem of the Society of Jesus.

156. Eugenio Garin, *L'umanesimo italiano*, 6th ed. (Bari: Laterza, 1975), 48, and Maria Sticco, *Poesia e pensiero in San Bernardino da Siena*, 2d ed. (Milan: Società Editrice "Vita e Pensiero," 1945), 34.

157. Origo, *World of San Bernardino*, 91, 93, 228.

158. In his now classic study of the rise and development of the demonization and persecution of minority groups in Christian Europe, R. I. Moore sees "a period of major growth" in this process occurring "between the middle of the fifteenth and the middle of the seventeenth century" (*Formation of a Persecuting Society: Power and Deviance in Western Europe, 950–1250* [Oxford: Blackwell, 1987], 99). I will supply further references on the historical destinies of these three groups in the respective chapters that follow. I will also explain, in chap. 3, sec. 1, the avoidance of the term *homosexuals* in my discussion of Bernardino's campaign against sodomy.

159. Studies describing this crescendo for the three groups studied in this book will be cited in the respective chapters devoted to them.

160. Indeed, in his brief of October 19, 1956, Pope Pius XII proclaimed Bernardino official patron saint of all advertisers and publicity agents. Bertagna, "La commissione bernardiniana," 545.

161. See also the various essays in Scott L. Waugh and Peter D. Diehl, ed., *Christendom and Its Discontents: Exclusion, Persecution, and Rebellion, 1000–1500* (Cambridge: Cambridge University Press, 1996).

162. Innocent III (Lothario dei Segni), *On the Misery of the Human Condition (De miseria humanae conditionis)*, trans. Margaret M. Dietz (Indianapolis: Library of Liberal Arts/Bobbs-Merrill, 1969), 14–15.

CHAPTER TWO

1. "Non vi so meglio dire: al fuoco, al fuoco, al fuoco! Oimmè! O non sapete voi quello che si fece a Roma mentre che io vi predicai? O non potrei io fare che così facesse anco qui? Doh, facciamo un poco d'oncenso a Domenedio qui a Siena!" (R.1006–7).

2. This is how Bernardino and the other members of what can be called the "learned elite" viewed these practices. What the putative practitioners were actually doing and how they and the general population viewed what they were doing is another question, beyond the scope of this work. We will take up later the distinction between the notions of the learned elite and those of popular tradition. For the moment, let us hear the conclusion of Joseph Klaits: "If delusions lay behind the witch hunts, they appear in most cases to have originated in the minds of the prosecutors, not the accused. After a century of witchcraft scholarship, it is at last becoming apparent that there is no reliable evidence of the existence of devil-worshipping witch cults and that the relatively few individuals who sincerely believed themselves to be devotees of Satan typically acquired such beliefs by suggestions from preachers or prosecutors." *Servants of Satan: The Age of the Witch Hunts* (Bloomington: Indiana University Press, 1985), 12.

3. "Non est civitas, non castrum, non patria quae pythonibus et pythonissis, incantoribus et incantricibus, divinatoribus et streghis atque stregonibus non sint plenae" (OOQ.III.321; see also OOQ.V.237).

4. According to Bernadette Paton, who has done extensive studies of the theological, moral, and pastoral literature produced in late-fourteenth- and fifteenth-century Siena (including Bernardino's sermons), "superstition" was a "catch-all label" for Bernardino and his contemporaries, defined broadly as "the failure of any individual to confine his belief in or use of the sacred to those doctrines and activities sanctioned by the church." One anonymous Dominican author defined it as "a belief in the power of any words or writings 'that are not those of God himself,' or the use of symbols and images that belong to God, such as the sign of the cross, for illicit purposes." Most commonly, however, the term referred to the "ignorant belief in the miraculous properties of objects and words not sanctified by the church, or the attribution of supernatural powers to a sacred object where such properties were not accorded it in orthodox theology." For the preceding definitions, see Bernadette Paton, " 'To the fire, to the fire! Let us burn a little incense to God': Bernardino, Preaching Friars and *Maleficio* in Late Medieval Siena," in *No Gods Except Me: Orthodoxy and Religious Practice in Europe, 1200–1600*, ed. Charles Zika (Melbourne: History Department, University of Melbourne, 1991), 15–16; see also her *Preaching Friars and the Civic Ethos: Siena, 1380–1480* (London: Centre for Medieval Studies, Queen Mary and Westfield College, University of London, 1992), 272–81.

5. "De duodecim sceleribus propter quae Deus patrias et regna saepe iudicat et flagellat" (OOQ.III.319–29).

6. The others are sodomy, political factionalism, and usury, OOQ.III.367–68.

7. The bibliography on witchcraft is now too vast to summarize in one note. For specifically pre-sixteenth-century witchcraft history, especially in Italy, see Giuseppe Bonomo, *Caccia alle streghe. La credenza nelle streghe dal secolo XIII al XIX con particolare riferimento all'Italia* (reprint, Palermo: Palumbo, 1971); Gene A. Brucker, "Sorcery in Early Renaissance Florence," *Studies in the Renaissance* 10 (1963): 7–24; the three works by Franco Cardini, "Magia e stregoneria nella Toscana del Trecento," *Quaderni medievali* 5 (1978): 121–55, *Magia, stregoneria, superstizioni nell'Occidente medievale* (Florence: La Nuova Italia, 1979), and "La predicazione popolare alle origini della caccia alle streghe," in *La strega, il teologo, lo scienziato: Atti del convegno "Magia, stregoneria e superstizioni in Europa e nella zona alpina." Borgosesia, 1983*, ed. Maurizio Cuccu and Paola Aldo Rossi (Genoa: E.C.I.G., 1986): 277–93; Norman Cohn, *Europe's Inner Demons: An Enquiry Inspired by the Great Witch-Hunt* (New York: Basic Books, 1975); Carlo Ginzburg, *Ecstasies: Deciphering the Witches' Sabbath* (New York: Pantheon, 1991); Richard Kieckhefer, *European Witch Trials: Their Foundations in Popular and Learned Culture, 1300–1500* (Berkeley: University of California Press, 1976), and his *Magic in the Middle Ages* (Cambridge: Cambridge University Press, 1989); Henry Charles Lea, *Materials toward a History of Witchcraft*, ed. Arthur C. Howland (Philadelphia: University of Pennsylvania Press, 1939); Raoul Manselli, "Le premesse medioevali della caccia alle streghe," in *La stregoneria in Europa (1450–1650)*, ed. Marina Romanello (Bologna: Il Mulino, 1975), 39–62; Edward Peters, *The Magician, the Witch, and the Law* (Philadelphia: University of Pennsylvania Press, 1978); Jeffrey Burton Russell, *Witchcraft in the Middle Ages* (Ithaca: Cornell University Press, 1972). On witchcraft in general, two useful works are Russell's *A History of Witchcraft: Sorcerers, Heretics, and Pagans* (London: Thames & Hudson, 1980), and, especially, Brian P. Levack, *The Witch-Hunt in Early Modern Europe*, 2d ed. (London: Longman, 1995).

8. Russell, *Witchcraft in the Middle Ages*, 227. Russell's work (a most thorough study of the earlier history of witchcraft to which the present chapter is greatly indebted) traces this

transformation, as does Norman Cohn's *Europe's Inner Demons*. See also Russell's *A History of Witchcraft*, 37–89. For the distinction between sorcery and witchcraft, see ibid., 18–26. "The simplest sorcery is the mechanical performance of one physical action in order to produce another: tying a knot in a cord and placing it under a bed to cause impotence. . . . More complex sorcery goes beyond mechanical means and invokes the aid of spirits" (ibid., 18).

9. Although charges of collective worship of the Devil will be rare in Italy at the height of the great witch hunts, it is nonetheless there that one finds not only a large number of the earliest witch trials but also the earliest clear prosecutions specifically for diabolism in the late medieval period (Levack, *The Witch-Hunt in Early Modern Europe*, 222–23; Kieckhefer, *European Witch Trials*, 21).

10. The witch trial here discussed is at R.1006–13. There has been no thorough study of Bernardino's account of this case; brief discussions of it can be found in Bonomo, *Caccia alle streghe*, 118–20, 262–63; Ginzburg, *Ecstasies*, 297–300; Kieckhefer, *Magic in the Middle Ages*, 194–95. The trial (but not Bernardino) is also mentioned in Russell, *Witchcraft in the Middle Ages*, 217. In addition, Carlo Delcorno's copious notes to his 1989 edition of the Siena 1427 sermon here in question (R.1006–13) have been most valuable to me in this study. On Bernardino and his witchcraft-related ideas in general, see also Giovanni Battista Bronzini, "Le prediche di Bernardino e le tradizioni popolari del suo tempo," in *Atti-Todi*, 121–34, and Cleto Corrain and Pierluigi Zampini, "Spunti etnografici nelle opere di S. Bernardino da Siena," *La palestra del clero* 44 (1965): 882–905.

11. Carlo Ginzburg, *Ecstasies: Deciphering the Witches' Sabbath* (New York: Pantheon, 1991), 298.

12. The 1443 Padua sermon cycle is yet unpublished; the passage in question has been excerpted by Delcorno, R.1006–7, n. 123. As far as one can judge from the extracts Delcorno provides, Bernardino's 1443 account agrees in substance and detail with his 1427 version of the episode, with some slight variation, which will be pointed out as we proceed in our analysis:

"Unde me predicante Rome de istis feci conscientiam omnibus scientibus strigones et dyabolicas strigatrices quod irent ad inquisitorem. . . . Unde accidit quod post illam admonicionem quam feci Rome, prout retulit nostri ordinis inquisitor, inde ad paucos dies venerant bene centum accusatores. Unde consilium quatenus diceret papa Martino, qui ordinavit ipsas capi et sic capte fuerunt multe strige, inter quas fuerunt tres pessime capte, quorum una confessa fuit sponte quod interfecerat triginta infantulos et liberasse sexaginta." ("Wherefore while I was preaching in Rome about these people, I aroused the consciences of all those knowing male witches [*strigones*] or diabolical female witches [*strigatrices*], that they were to go [report them] to the inquisitor. . . . Wherefore it happened that after this admonition which I gave in Rome, according to what the inquisitor of our order relates, a few days later no fewer than one hundred accusers came forward. Wherefore a consultation was held with Pope Martin, who ordered these women to be arrested, and many witches were thus arrested, among whom there were three women who were the worst cases, one of whom confessed of her own accord that she had killed thirty little babies and had set sixty free.")

I avoid translating Bernardino's masculine noun, *strigones,* with the later English term *warlocks,* on the basis of Russell's observation that the word *warlock* "always applied to female as well as male witches, and there is no justification for using 'warlock' as the male equivalent of female 'witch.' 'Witch' is applied to both sexes" (*History of Witchcraft*, 12). Note, further, that in reproducing Bernardino's Paduan sermon quote from an unpublished *reportatio,* Delcorno (R.1006, n. 123) mistakenly refers to its source as the "Seraphim" cycle. In fact, its source, the 1443 Padua cycle, is distinct from the "Seraphim" Lenten cycle that Bernardino preached (also in Padua) in 1423, as Delcorno himself points out (R.55 and R.59). The "Seraphim" cycle can be found in the 1745 edition of Bernardino's *Opera omnia*, ed. Johannis De la Haye (i.e., OOH).

13. The treatise is at OOQ.I.105–18. For the date of that treatise, see Pacetti, *De sancti Bernardini Senensis operibus*, 3–4.

14. *Diario della città di Roma*, ed. Oreste Tommassini (Rome: Istituto Storico Italiano, 1890), 25.

15. Published as an appendix to Paolo di Lello Petrone, *La mesticanza*, Rerum Italicarum Scriptores, 2d ed., 24/2 (Città di Castello: Casa Editrice S. Lapi, 1912), 81–102. Paolo's diary was also published in the last century: *Cronache romane inedite del Medio Evo: Memoriale di Paolo di Benedetto di Cola dello Mastro dello Rione de Ponte*, ed. Achille de Antonis (Rome, 1875). The entry in question on Bernardino and the Roman witch trial can also be found excerpted in Casimiro Romano, *Memorie istoriche della chiesa e convento di S. Maria in Araceli di Roma* (Rome: Rocco Bernabò, 1736), 418.

16. In Iacobus De Marchia, *Sermones dominicales*, ed. Renato Lioi (Falconara Marittima: Biblioteca Francescana, 1978), 1:424.

17. Excerpted in Joseph Hansen, *Quellen und Untersuchungen zur Geschichte des Hexenwahns und der Hexenverfolgung im Mittelalter* (Bonn: Carl Georgi, 1901), 109–10.

18. Excerpted in ibid., 130–31. For Hartlieb, see Richard Kieckhefer, *Forbidden Rites: A Necromancer's Manual of the Fifteenth Century* (University Park: Pennsylvania State University Press, 1997), 32–33.

19. Andreas's *Chronica* ends at 1422 (see the 1903 edition by Georg Leidinger in Andreas von Regensburg, *Sämtliche Werke* [Munich: M. Rieger'sche Universitäts-Buchhandlung]), but was subsequently "interpolatum et usque ad annum 1490 continuatum" by Chraft (whom I have been unable to identify; "Cambensis" most likely refers to Cham, in eastern Bavaria). I quote the 1723 edition published by Eccardus (Johann Georg Eckhart) in his *Corpus Historicum Medii Aevii*, 2 vols. (Leipzig: apud Jo. Frid. Gleditschii), 1:2159. Henry Charles Lea paraphrases this report (naming its source somewhat inaccurately as Andreas) in his *Materials toward a History of Witchcraft*, 3:1071.

20. "O non sapete voi quello che si fece a Roma mentre che io vi predicai. . . . Io vi voglio dire quello che a Roma si fece" (R.1007).

21. The lack of lexical discrimination is characteristic of witch-related literature in general, both medieval and modern, as Kieckhefer points out (*European Witch Trials*, 7–8). For witch-related terminology and lexical distinctions, see Russell, *Witchcraft in the Middle Ages*, 3–18; Levack, *The Witch-Hunt in Early Modern Europe*, 4–11; Kieckhefer, *Magic in the Middle Ages*, 8–16.

22. Russell, *Witchcraft in the Middle Ages*, 13. Bernardino variously and indiscriminately calls the practitioners of evil *strega*, *maliarda*, or *incantatrice* and their masculine equivalents. Other terms to be found in Italian sources are *masca*, *fara*, *malefica*, *sortilega*, *lamia*, *pythonissa*, *stria*, *herbaria*, *fascinaria*, *zobiana*, and *arlia*. See Cardini, *Magia, stregoneria, superstizioni*, 202.

23. "Avendo io predicato di questi incantamenti e di streghe e di malie, el mio dire era a loro come se io sognasse" (R.1007).

24. "Infine elli mi venne detto [i.e, mi capitò a dire] che qualunque persona sapesse niuno o niuna che sapesse fare tal cosa, che, non accusandola, elli sarebbe nel medesimo peccato" (R.1007 and Delcorno's accompanying note 126).

25. In his 1443 version of the story, he specifies that "one hundred accusers came forward," adding that his information about what occurred after his preaching came to him through the Franciscan Inquisitor: "Unde accidit quod post illam admonicionem quam feci Rome, prout

retulit nostri ordinis inquisitor, inde ad paucos dies venerant bene centum accusatores" (R.1006, n. 123).

26. "E come io ebbi predicato, furono acusate una moltitudine di streghe e di incantatori. E per la tanta quantità de li acusati, elli venne a me el guardiano [i.e., the superior of the Franciscan friary of Aracoeli, where Bernardino was most likely residing], e dissemi:—Voi non sapete? Elli va a fuoco ciò che ci è!—Io domando:—Come? che ci è? che è?—Elli sono stati acusati una grande quantità d'uomini e di femine.—Infine, veduto come la cosa passava, elli ne fu fatto consiglio col papa, e diterminossi che fusse prese le maggiori, cioè quelle che peggio avessero fatto" (R.1007).

27. In his "Seraphim" Lenten sermon on witchcraft (Padua 1423), using a similar expression, Bernardino admits: "Nonnulli credunt quod ego somniem iste, et quod dicam de capite meo" ("Some believe that I am dreaming up these things and that I make them up in my own head"; OOH.III.179b). At the beginning of another witchcraft-related Paduan sermon on the pseudo-miracles of the Devil, Bernardino says he anticipates derision from some of his listeners for preaching of such matters: "Sed non cogitantes facta animae deridebunt me, et ego deridebo eos" (OOH.III.176). Carlo Ginzburg characterizes the Roman audience's response as "astonishment," whereas I see it as indifference or feigned puzzlement, for, as Ginzburg himself admits, what, after all, would have astonished the audience? They had already heard all these traditional stories about both witches and heretics (*Ecstasies*, 298–99).

28. Theoretically, what separated the witch from both the magician and the simple sorcerer was that the witch not only invoked but also worshiped the Devil.

29. See Kieckhefer, *European Witch Trials*, passim, but esp. 75.

30. Russell, *Witchcraft in the Middle Ages*, 205.

31. We might ask the same question with respect to Martin's successor, Eugene IV, another pontiff on familiar terms with Bernardino, who published two letters on the subject of witchcraft during his reign. For English translations of his 1434 letter to the Inquisitor Pontus Fougeyron and his 1437 letter to "All Inquisitors of Heretical Depravity," see A. C. Kors and E. Peters, eds., *Witchcraft in Europe 1100–1700: A Documentary History* (Philadelphia: University of Pennsylvania Press, 1972), 98–101; see also Russell, *Witchcraft in the Middle Ages*, 220, 229, and Ginzburg, *Ecstasies*, 297. For Martin's letter, see Hansen, *Quellen und Untersuchungen*, 17. For the rapport between Bernardino and the two popes, see Massimo Miglio, "Il pontificato e S. Bernardino," in *Atti-Aquila*, 237–49.

32. Ginzburg, *Ecstasies*, 23. Ginzburg labels what Bernardino uncovered in Rome "a sect," even though Bernardino himself does not place any special emphasis here or elsewhere on the organized nature of the practitioners of witchcraft. As we shall later see, he does makes reference in the same sermon to a formal nocturnal gathering of "these enchanters" (*questi incantatori*). What he describes turns out to be a nighttime dance in a field of mostly women and young people, encountered by the servant of a cardinal near Benevento. But that is as explicit as he gets in suggesting the existence of an organizational structure. In his Latin treatise on witchcraft, Bernardino will also quote the famous canon *Episcopi*, which refers to the Society of Diana, another indication of formal organization and regularly scheduled interaction among these so-called witches.

33. Levack, *The Witch-Hunt in Early Modern Europe*, 91 and 223.

34. "Una grande quantità d'uomini e di femine . . . diterminossi che fusse prese le maggiori, cioè quelle che peggio avessero fatto" (R.1007). In his 1443 version of this episode, Bernardino mentions that among these "worst cases" were three women, not two. See n. 12 above.

35. "Perché ella desiderasse d'essere incantatrice" (R.227). See also B.184: "El dimonio la prima arte ch'elli facessi mai fu quella dello indovinare . . . così nel mondo [disse] a Madonna

Eva: 'Mangia di questo frutto e saprai el bene e 'l male, sarete iddii.' " ("The first art that the demon ever created was that of divination . . . thus he said on earth to lady Eve: eat of this fruit and you will know good and evil and will be gods.") In explaining why the sin of sorcery occurs more among women than men, Alexander of Hales claims that this "doctrina" was first taught to woman (i.e., Eve) by the Devil himself, "seeing that she had lesser powers of discernment of spirits" ("quia ipse diabolus primo transfundit eam in mulierem, utpote quae minus habebat discretionem spiritus," *Summa theologica* [Quaracchi: Collegio San Bonaventura, 1930], 3:778, art. 6). Peraldus and Antonino of Florence speak in similar fashion: see Jole Agrimi and Chiara Crisciani, "Immagini e ruoli della *vetula* tra sapere medico e antropologia religiosa (secoli XIII–XV)," in *Poteri carismatici e informali. Chiesa e società medioevali,* ed. Agostino Paravicini Bagliani and André Vauchez (Palermo: Sellerio, 1992), 248. Jacopo Passavanti says that this was rather the sin of both Adam and Eve ("questo fu il primo peccato de' nostri primi parenti"), *Specchio di vera penitenza,* "Trattato della Scienza," reprinted in Sergio Abbiati et al., *La stregoneria. Diavoli, streghe, inquisitori dal Trecento al Settecento* (Milan: Mondadori, 1984), 36.

36. On the *vetula,* see, e.g., R.552 (and n. 93); OOH.III.176b, 345a, 368; G.57, 60, 197; OOQ.IX.387, 388. *Rincagnato* is a favorite among Bernardino's colloquial adjectives. Its most common literal meaning today is "pug-nosed," a much too mild rendering in the present case. The word is, in fact, susceptible to a variety of disparate translations according to context; see Emilio Pasquini, "Costanti tematiche e varianti testuali nelle prediche bernardiniane," in *Atti-Siena,* 704, n. 60. The dark folklore surrounding the *vetula,* the old woman or crone, is ancient: see Agrimi-Crisciani, "Immagini e ruoli della *vetula,*" 224–61. See also Barbara G. Walker, *The Crone: Woman of Age, Wisdom and Power* (San Francisco: Harper, 1985). Two important *auctoritates* in the medieval career of the figure of the *vetula* were Ovid (for his portrait of the witch-procuress, Dipsas, in his *Amores*) and Pseudo-Ovid, author of the popular short work in verse, *De vetula;* see Cardini, *Magia, stregoneria, superstizioni,* 37, and Cohn, *Europe's Inner Demons,* 207.

37. Agrimi-Crisciani, "Immagini e ruoli della *vetula,*" 246–47; see also Shulamith Shahar, *Growing Old in the Middle Ages* (London: Routledge, 1997), 44. Even St. Anne, mother of the Virgin Mary, did not escape suspicion of sorcery (Agrimi-Crisciani, "Immagini e ruoli della *vetula,*" 243, n. 64). In the Roman case here under examination, Bernardino does not describe the culprit as an old woman, and of our other six sources, only two, Giacomo della Marca and Chraft, do so.

38. One cannot attribute it simply to his own misogyny, for as discussed in chap. 1, sec. 4, Bernardino's attitude toward women was more complicated than that. Nonetheless, there are those who claim that all males, by the mere fact of having been born of women, live in fear, and therefore hatred, of them at some deep subconscious level, for just as women are creators of life, they can also be its destroyers. We recall from chap. 1 Bernardino's childhood "petticoat government," i.e., the four pious matrons who raised the orphaned child, rigorously repressing all traces of his "shadow" side (especially sexuality and aggression) to create the future saint. Despite what the hagiographers say about these women, their pious intentions, and Bernardino's apparently loving response to them, such repression at their hands may possibly have left in Bernardino a lingering deposit of anger,which, unacknowledgeable and inexpressible in direct terms, was instead projected against the witch, that archetypal figure of the dark, mysterious, punitive woman. But here we leave scholarship for pure speculation. For male fear of women, see Walker, *The Crone,* 17–22; Russell, *Witchcraft in the Middle Ages,* 283 (279–85 for witchcraft and women in general); Shulamith Shahar, *The Fourth Estate: A History of Women in the Middle Ages* (London and New York: Methuen, 1983), 277 (and on witches in general, 268–80); Levack, *The Witch-Hunt in Early Modern Europe,* 143–44, and more generally on women, 133–41.

39. "E fune presa una fra l'altre, la quale disse e confessò senza niuno martorio, che aveva uccisi da XXX fanciulli col succhiare il sangue loro; e anco disse che n'aveva liberati LX; e disse che ogni volta che ella ne liberava niuno, ogni volta si conveniva dare uno membro al diavolo per sagrificio, e davane uno membro di bestia; e a questo modo facendo, continuò gran tempo. E più anco confessò, che ella aveva morto el suo propio figliulo [*sic*], e avevane fatto polvare, de la quale dava mangiare per tali faccende" (R.1007–8). The same numbers, thirty and sixty, for respectively the murdered and the spared infants, are given in the friar's 1443 account of this case (see n. 12 above). Hesitant to give credence to the woman's confession, the inquisitor obtained independent confirmation of the sudden deaths of these infants from the fathers of the victims, Bernardino assures us in the same paragraph.

40. See, for example, the index to Russell's *Witchcraft in the Middle Ages* under "Bloodsucking" and "Children." Bernardino makes a brief reference to the demons' love of blood at OOQ.IX.386, and elsewhere (G.279) states that it is because of the sins of the father that the Devil sucks the blood of a child. As many scholars in the past have suspected, the infant deaths imputed to witches may in fact have been the result of the parents' or nurses' own neglect, premeditated murder, or inexplicable illness and trauma, such as what is today called "Sudden Infant Death Syndrome."

41. See B.168 (Florence 1424) and G.279 (Siena 1425). Bloodsucking is also mentioned in one of the later Latin treatises, "De mandato divinae dilectionis," contained in the Lenten series, *De christiana religione* (1430–36); see OOQ.II.43. (For date of the treatise, see Pacetti, *De sancti Bernardini Senensis operibus*, 3–4.) As we will see below in sec. 4, "The Demonization of the Heretic," in an earlier sermon in this same Siena 1427 cycle in which he tells of the Roman trial, Bernardino describes the gruesome preparation of a concoction made of the powdered remains of ritually murdered children—made not by witches, but by the Piedmontese heretical sect of the "*barilotto*," i.e., "the keg," from which they drink the potion (R.793–94).

42. C.209–12. A greatly reduced version of the tale is found at G.196–97. This *exemplum* is discussed later in this chapter. In the Padua 1443 account of the Roman witch trial, Bernardino reproduces the dialogue between the Devil and the "witch" in direct discourse: see R.1008, n. 133. As Jacopo Passavanti explains, the pact could be either explicit or implicit (*Specchio di vera penitenza*, in Abbiati, et al., *La Stregoneria*, 34). For the scriptural source of the idea of the pact with the worship-hungry Devil, see Matthew 4:8–9, the temptation of Christ in the desert ("All these I will give you, if you will fall down and worship me"). Also included in the Devil-witch pact were sexual relations between the two parties, but here in 1427 Bernardino is silent on this detail, whereas in the "Godmother of Lucca" *exemplum*, he hints at it indirectly: the godmother-witch conjures up the Devil in a state of complete nudity and with her hair unbound (C.210).

43. R.1008, n. 132. Delcorno makes his observation about Finicella's "true" profession as if it were a confirmed fact, whereas it is, in reality, only conjecture; no documents identify Finicella's occupation as healer or midwife. We might also note here that nowhere does it even occur to Bernardino to recognize the existence and legitimacy of that separate though "unlicensed" class of benign society-serving women, the midwife-doctors and practitioners of folk medicine, in order to distinguish them from the category of malevolent sorceresses. For midwives and herbal healers, see Kieckhefer, *European Witch Trials*, 55–56, and Nancy G. Siraisi, *Medieval and Early Renaissance Medicine: An Introduction to Knowledge and Practice* (Chicago: University of Chicago Press, 1990), 27, 38, 44–46.

44. Russell, *Witchcraft in the Middle Ages*, 260–61.

45. "O medici, studuistis in gramatica, logica, philosophia, medicina, cum multis spensis, periculis et laboribus; e la vechi[a] rinchagnata n'à l'onore!" (OOQ.IX.369).

46. Note, however, that, along with all churchmen of his time, Bernardino accepted the employment of torture in criminal cases as necessary and useful for the execution of justice; see his remarks, e.g., at B.67. See also Peters, *The Magician, the Witch and the Law,* Appendix 1, "*Res fragilis:* Torture in Early European Law," 183–95.

47. *Witchcraft in the Middle Ages,* 257.

48. "E disse del modo come ella andava innanzi dì in su la piazza di Santo Pietro, e ine aveva certi bossogli d'onguenti fatti d'erbe che erano colte nel dì d santo Giovanni e nel dì de la Asunzione" (R.1008–9). Corrain and Zampini, "Spunti etnografici nelle opere di S. Bernardino da Siena," provide a lengthy list of popular superstitions mentioned in the works of Bernardino; for the St. John's Day plant-gathering, see 898–99.

49. B.186, OOH.III.179b, OOQ.IX.385. See also Russell, *Witchcraft in the Middle Ages,* 51, 61, and 201, and Cardini, *Magia, stregoneria, superstizioni,* 220. Like Bernardino's Roman witch, fourteenth-century French healer-sorcerers also gathered their herbs on Saint John's eve, to cite an example outside of Italy; see Pierrette Paravy, "Streghe e stregoni nella società del Delfinato nel XV secolo," in Bagliani and Vauchez, eds., *Poteri carismatici e informali,* 85–86.

50. Russell, *Witchcraft in the Middle Ages,* 51.

51. See Hilda Graef, *Mary: A History of Doctrine and Devotion* (London: Sheed & Ward, 1985), and Marina Warner, *Alone of All Her Sex: The Myth and the Cult of the Virgin Mary* (New York: Knopf, 1976). It is no coincidence that the cult of Mary and the cult of Diana (Artemis) both have as their historic center the ancient city of Ephesus. The Artemisium, great temple of Artemis (the Greek counterpart to the Italic Diana) in Ephesus, was one of the seven wonders of the ancient world. (For St. Paul's troubles with the statue merchants of the Artemisium, see Acts 19:23–40.) It was in Ephesus that Mary supposedly lived her final years and that popular devotion to Mary as *theotokos,* the "God-bearer" (in Latin, *Dei genitrix*), first developed. Amid great controversy, the ecumenical Council of Ephesus ratified the orthodoxy of that title in 731.

52. "E dicevano che con essi s'ognevano, e così come erano onte, lo' pareva essare gatte, e non era vero; però che il corpo loro non si rimutava in altra forma, ma ben lo' pareva a loro" (R.1009; see also G.278–79). Female shapeshifting and night flight are ancient motifs as well, harking back to, among other things, the Roman *strix* or *striga* (whence the Italian *strega,* witch), "originally a screech-owl, then a night-spirit and vampire, finally a witch" (Russell, *Witchcraft in the Middle Ages,* 15). In a famous scene from *The Golden Ass* (3:21, 24)—to cite just one well-known example from antiquity—the young Lucius Apuleius spies on the sorcerer Pamphilë one evening as she rubs an ointment onto her naked body and is transformed into an owl. Using the same ointment, Lucius is himself transformed into a jackass. A similar story of shapeshifting comes to us from one of Bernardino's own contemporaries, the Sienese humanist Mariano Sozzini the Elder. In a 1462 letter to Antonio Tridentone of Parma, Sozzini relates the story of "the witch of Asciano" told to him as a boy in 1420 by an old peasant, Nanni Ciancadiddio (or Cianchadeus), who swore vociferously that it was a true episode from his own childhood. Like Lucius in *The Golden Ass,* Nanni as a boy one night spied on a *vetula,* a nurse to whom he had been entrusted, as she smeared her naked body with magical ointment, turning into a goat in order to attend the witches' gathering at Benevento. Again, like Lucius, using the same ointment, Nanni is transformed into an ass and is transported from the countryside to the Piazza del Campo in the center of Siena. See Francesco Novati, "Una lettera ed un sonetto di Mariano Sozzini il vecchio," *Bullettino senese di storia patria* 2 (1895): 89–100. On Sozzini, see also Bonomo, *Caccia alle streghe,* 263–66. Sozzini's treatise, "De sortilegiis" (also called "De sortibus"), provides us with much detailed information about fifteenth-century folklore and witch-related beliefs. For a summary of its contents, see Ludovico Zdekauer, "Sullo scritto 'De sortilegiis' di M. Sozzini il Vecchio," *Archivio per lo studio delle tradizioni popolari* 15 (1896): 131–

37. Corrain and Zampini suggest that Sozzini may have taken some of his information directly from Bernardino, since in several cases the language is identical ("Spunti etnografici nelle opere di S. Bernardino da Siena," 883).

53. The canon *Episcopi* is reproduced in English in Kors and Peters, *Witchcraft in Europe*, 29–30.

54. See Cardini, "La predicazione popolare alle origini della caccia alle streghe."

55. C.210.

56. Cardini, "Magia e stregoneria nella Toscana del Trecento," 147. In a 1425 Sienese sermon on purgatory, Bernardino parenthetically asks the question, "Do bewitchments really happen?" ("Puossi fare malie?"). His answer is a decided yes, although, he qualifies, spells do not always work the way the spell-makers think they do (G.278–79).

57. R.1010; see also OOH.III.178a for further discussion by Bernardino of the same topic.

58. "Elli so' stati già di quelli che hanno veduta la gatta quando va a fare queste cose; e tali so' stati tanto preveduti, che hanno auto qualche cosa in mano e arandellato a quella gatta, e talvolta l'hanno gionta. E di quelle so' state, che hanno riceuta tal percossa, che hanno rotta la gamba. E a chi credi che sia rimasa la percossa? Pure a la femina indiavolata, none al diavolo" (R.1010; see also OOH.III.178a and the just cited G.278–79. Bernardino does not specify the color of the cat). This is, again, a traditional motif, that of the wound of the demonic animal, which, after the crime, is found on the body of the witch herself; see Russell, *Witchcraft in the Middle Ages*, 53.

59. The entire passage reads: "Et constat, quod tempore Martini pape de anno 1420 quedam mulier strega residens trans Tiberim se transformaverat in cattum et actus humano ritui raros immo impossibiles et solis cattis applicabiles et pure cattivos exercuit. Et inter cetera pueros in cunabulis iacentes maleficiis infecit, quos ex post sanando, dum converteretur in hominem, mercedem usurpavit. Et hoc eius finale lucrum sibi coaptando reputavit, et de his et aliis publice confessa iudicialiter igne concremata vitam finivit."

60. In Bernardino, this witness is unidentified; in Hartlieb it is the father of the child; in Chraft, simply "a wise old man."

61. "Ain groß zaichen von zaubrey. Erenreicher fürst, ich sag dir ain sach, die ich und manig man zu Rom gesehen und gehört habn. Es was in dem sechsten jar als bapst Martin gesetzt was, da stund uf zu Rom ain ungelaub, das etliche weib und man sich verwandelten in katzen und totten gar vil kinder zu Rom. Zu ainer zeit kam ain katz in ains burgers hus und paiß sein kind in der wiegen. Das kind schray, der vatter hub sich pald uff und nam ain messer und schlug die katzen, als sy zu ainem venster uß wolt, durch das haubt. Des morgens gar fru tett sich die fraw berichten mit den hailigen sacramenten; die nachpawrn clagten ir kranckhait, als da sitt ist. Der nachpawr clagt si auch; sy antwurt im: wär dir laid mein krankhait, du hettest mir das nit getan. An dem dritten tag erschall, das die frawe ain wunden in dem haubt het. Der nachpawr gedacht an die katzen, auch an ir wort; er pracht das an den senat. Die fraw ward gefangen und verjach; sy sprach vor dem Capitoln überlaut, hett sy ir salb, sy wölt hinfarn. O wie gern hett ich und maniger curtisan gesehen, das man ir die salb geben hett. Da stund uff ain doctor und sprach, das ir die salb nit solt geben werden, wan der tüffel möcht mit gotz verhenknuss groß irrung machen. Die fraw ward verprennt, das hab ich gesehen. Item zu Rom was sag, das der leut gar vil." (My thanks to Professors David Gill, S.J., and Michael Resler for their assistance with this translation.)

62. "Hujus temporibus murilegus sive cattus quidam Romae multos infantes in cunis jacentes, dum a nutricibus non bene custodiebantur, nacta oportunitate interficiebat. Tandem quidam vir senex sapiens, custodiens puerulum sibi comissum, simulans se cattum per fenestram ingredientem non videre, dum accessisset ad puerum suffocandum, ipse eundem cattum cum

gladio usque ad effusionem sanguinis vulneravit. Ex tunc per vestigia sanguinis, et vulnus illatum, compertum fuit, illum cattum esse unam vetulam, de prope commorantem, quae a Cirologo in cura habebatur, et quando voluit in cattum mutabatur, sicque de interfectis parvulis, ut se diutius conservaret, recentem sanguinem sugebat."

63. In Infessura, she is "Finicella," whereas Giacomo della Marca calls her "Funicella." The relevant passage in Paolo dello Mastro's chronicle reads:

"[I]n nelli 1442 dello mese di maio venne in Roma uno predicatore che ssi chiamava frate Bernardino, lo quale predicao in nella piazza dello Aracielo alla guglia: et piena la piazza e li mieroli di Campituoglio de gente, che fu stimato che a quelle prediche ce fossero X mila persone, e mise de molte paci in Roma, e fece battezzare parecchi iudii e fece abrusciare Finiccola che era una granne fattucchiera e strega." ("[I]n the year 1442 in the month of May a preacher by the name of Friar Bernardino came and preached in Piazza [Santa Maria in] Aracoeli at its summit, and the piazza [was] filled with people, as were the walls of the Campidoglio; it was estimated that there were 10,000 people at those sermons, and he caused many peace pacts to be made in Rome, and had many Jews baptized; he also had Finiccola, who was a big sorcerer and witch, burned at the stake on the Campidoglio.")

64. The entry reads:

"In quell'anno [1424] frate Bernardino fece ardere tavolieri, canti, brevi, sorti, capelli che fucavano le donne, et fu fatto uno talamo di legname in Campituoglio, et tutte queste cose ce foro appiccate et arse, et fu a 21 di iuglio [or July 11 or 25, or June 21 or 25, according to other MSS]. / Et dopo fu arsa Finicella strega, a dì 8 del ditto mese di iuglio [or June or July 28, according to other MSS] perchè essa diabolicamente occise de molte criature et affattucchiava di molte persone, et tutta Roma ce andò a vedere. / Et fece frate Bernardino in Roma de molte paci, et de molti abbracciamenti, et benchè ce fusse stato homocidio." ("In that year friar Bernardino had burned gameboards, song sheets, talismans, fortune-telling paraphernalia, and women's wigs, and a wooden chamber [?] was built on the Capitoline Hill and all of these things were placed in it and set fire, and this was on July 21. / And later the witch Finicella was burned, on the 8th day of the same month, because she had diabolically killed many children and had put spells on many people, and all of Rome went to see the sight. / And friar Bernardino brought about much peace and reconciliation even between parties where there had been a murder.")

65. "Item, quedam vetula Rome, nominata Funicella, interfecit 65 pueros et coxit brachium filii sui mortui pro incantionibus. Et dicebat sibi diabolus sic, quod non erat peccatum interficere innocentes, quia salvabantur. Et hoc dixit mihi magister Nicolaus de Roma, ordinis nostri, tum inquisitor, et conbusta est." ("Likewise, one old woman of Rome, named Funicella, killed 65 children and cooked the arm of her dead son for use in her spells. And it was the Devil who told her [to do] so, that it was not a sin to kill the little ones, since they would be saved. And this was told to me by master Nicholas of Rome of our order, who was then inquisitor, and the woman was burned at the stake.")

66. Casimiro Romano, who reproduces Paolo's entry on Bernardino taken from an unidentified source differing noticeably from Isoldi's 1912 critical edition, gives the name as "Maria Fenicella," *Memorie istoriche della chiesa e convento di S. Maria in Araceli di Roma*, 418.

67. Kieckhefer, *European Witch Trials*, 121.

68. "Infine costei fu condennata al fuoco, e fu arsa, che non vi rimase di lei se non che la polvare" (R.1011).

69. "Anco ne fu presa un'altra che confessò d'aver fatte simili cose, e fu condennata pure al fuoco, e morì per altro modo costei; che quando si misse nel capanello, non fu strozzata; anco vi fu messo il fuoco mentre che era viva, che non si vide di lei altro che cennere" (R.1011).

70. For a complete list of the classic components of the witch scenario, see Russell, *Witchcraft in the Middle Ages,* 23–24.

71. Ibid., 227.

72. See Bonomo, *Caccia alle streghe,* 16–37; Russell, *Witchcraft in the Middle Ages,* 46–49 and passim; and Ginzburg, *Ecstasies,* passim. In place of Diana as the mistress of the assembly, Christians sometimes put Herodias, the murderous wife of Herod, responsible for the execution of John the Baptist.

73. A variant of this same widely disseminated item of folklore forms the nucleus of one of the stories in Boccaccio's *Decameron,* Day 8, Novella 9. Boccaccio refers to the event as "andare in corso" (to go on the ride); in the *Decameron* it entails nocturnal gatherings in a secret place of sensual delights afforded to the members of a club of twenty-five men, under the direction of two disciples of the famous magician, Michael Scot (Michele Scoto). (For Michael Scot, see Kieckhefer, *Magic in the Middle Ages,* 123, 144, 165.) The men supposedly travel to the feasting place on the back of an obliging black horned beast—which must not, however, hear the mention of the name of God and the saints.

74. "E altri dice della tregenda el giovedì notte, che sono tutti sogni e lusioni diaboliche. Fa' di none stare in peccato mortale, come di sopra ò detto, e non avere paura per te né pe' tuoi figliuoli di streghe, o di tregenda, o di malie, o d'incanto!" (B.169–70). *Tregenda* seems not to have been a common term among Bernardino's contemporaries or predecessors. The only medieval document, aside from Bernardino's sermon, in which I have thus far encountered it is Passavanti's *Specchio di vera penitenza* (in Abbiati, et al., *La Stregoneria,* 40–41). The term does not appear in Ginzburg's *Ecstasies,* the longest treatment of the sabbath to date, nor in Russell's encyclopedic *Witchcraft in the Middle Ages.* As for Bernardino's use of the term in the sermon just cited (B.169–70), textual similarities lead me to suspect that Bernardino himself is either quoting, paraphrasing, or unconsciously remembering Passavanti's *Specchio.*

75. On the basis of Matthew 4:5 and 6, medieval Christians believed that the Devil was also able to transport people from place to place in supernatural fashion. I have been unable to identify "Iobiana" or the source from which Bernardino might have taken the name. Bernardino mentions "Zobiana" at OOH.III.178a, adding that "Herodiana and Zobiana are the same person" and that Zobiana is believed to return to the Jordan River each year in order to be baptized but finds the river dry. See also OOQ.IX.385 (Iobiana) and 386 (Giobiana). "Zobianae" as a synonym for witches occurs in a medical treatise on witchcraft written in Pavia by Antonio Guaineri (fl. 1410–40), though there is no evidence that Bernardino had consulted Guaineri or his work; see Agrimi-Crisciani, "Immagini e ruoli della *vetula,*" 254, n. 114. Discussing Guaineri, Russell says "the term [*zobianae*] . . . is unique here" (*Witchcraft in the Middle Ages,* 332; see also 206–7). Cardini simply lists it as a synonym for witch (*Magia, stregoneria, superstizioni,* 202). "Zobiana"—"a new name," according to Lea (*Materials,* 1:192)—is coupled with "Herodiana" (an amalgamation of Diana and Herodias) in the 1574 revised edition of the *Summa pacifica,* a confessors' handbook by friar Pacifico da Novara (d. ca. 1470), according to Lea (loc. cit.).

76. "*Inter has impiissimas feras sunt* quaedam crudelissimae mulieres et etiam quandoque viri, credentes et profitentes cum Diana *seu Iobiana vel Herodiade* et innumera multitudine mulierum equitare super quasdam bestias et multa terrarum spatia intempestae noctis silentio pertransire eiusque iussionibus obedire velut dominae et certis noctibus sicut nocte Iovis et nocte post dominicam diem, ad eius servitium evocari. *Asserunt etiam ab illis aliquas creaturas, maxime parvulos pueros, posse in deterius vel in melius permutare, aut in aliam speciem et similitudinem transformare*" (OOQ.I.117; the italicized sections represent Bernardino's additions to or modifications of the canon text). See also OOH.III.355b ("quod vetulae rugosae dicent

se ire ad cursum in Heroida [*sic*] in nocte Epiphaniae"). One of Bernardino's sermon outlines specifies that the canon *Episcopi* is referring to "streghis," witches (OOQ.IX.385). For the canon, see Russell, *Witchcraft in the Middle Ages*, 75–80, 291–93, and passim. See also n. 113 below for the Milanese cases of Sibillia and Pierina, who confessed to having participated in the weekly "game" (*ludum*) of "Madonna Oriente," a nocturnal assembly clearly ressembling that of Diana.

77. "Doh, sai che intervenne di questi incantatori, eh? Intriamo in practica. Elli fu a Roma uno famiglio d'uno cardinale, el quale andando a Benivento [*sic*] di notte, vidde in su una aia ballare molta gente, donne e fanciulli e giovani; e così mirando elli ebbe grande paura. Pure essendo stato un poco a vedere, elli s'asicurò e andò dove costoro ballavano, pure con paura, e a poco a poco s'acostò a costoro, che elli vidde che erano giovanissimi; così stando a vedere, elli s'asicurò tanto, che elli si pose a ballare con loro. E ballando tutta questa brigata, elli venne a sonare mattino. Come mattino toccò, tutte costoro in un subito si partiro, salvo che una, cioè quella che costui teneva per mano lui, che ella volendosi partire coll'altre, costui la teneva; ella tirava, e elli tirava. Elli la tenne tanto a questo modo, che elli si fece dì chiaro. Vedendola costui sì giovana, elli se ne la menò a casa sua. E odi quello che intervenne, che elli la tenne tre anni seco, che mai non parlò una parola. E fu trovato che costei era di Schiavonia. Pensa ora tu come questo sia ben fatto, che elli sia tolta una fanciulla al padre e a la madre in quel modo" (R.1012–13). Bernardino's final reproach is confusing: presumably its target is the band of "enchanters," who, the friar intimates, had kidnapped the girl from her home in "Slavonia"; yet the cardinal's page is also guilty here—in effect, of kidnapping the girl a second time.

78. R.1013. Bernardino's original Italian terms are *incantatrice*, *maliarda*, *incantatori*, and *streghe*. Although the list embraces both male and female, in his next utterance the friar uses only feminine forms: "fate che tutte sieno messe in esterminio" ("see to it that all of these women are exterminated"). Again, these and the other various witch-related labels, although technically referring to separate categories of practitioners, are used indiscriminately and interchangeably by the friar.

79. See R.1012, n. 172; Bonomo, *Caccia alle streghe*, 309; and Filippo Ermini, "Il culto degli alberi presso i Longobardi e il noce di Benevento," in his *Medio Evo latino. Studi e ricerche* (Modena: Società Tipografica Modenese, 1938), 115–19. As we shall see, Matteuccia of Todi, the "witch" brought to justice thanks to Bernardino's preaching, confessed to attending regular witch assemblies at the "walnut tree of Benevento." Sozzini's witch of Asciano was also headed for the same destination and, applying the magic ointment to her body, recited a formula very similar to that used by Matteuccia: "Sopra acqua et sopra vento menami a la noce di Benevento" ("Above water and above wind, lead me to the walnut tree of Benevento"); see Novati, "Una lettera," 97.

80. For the association of "Slavonia" (in Italian, *Schiavonia*), that is, the Balkans, with the Bogomils, see Ginzburg, *Ecstasies*, 76–77. For the Bogomils, see Russell, *Witchcraft in the Middle Ages*, 120–22, and Malcolm D. Lambert, *Medieval Heresy: Popular Movements from the Gregorian Reform to the Reformation*, 2d ed. (Oxford: Blackwell, 1992), 55–61. "Slavonia" was also the home of many of the slaves employed in Italian households. These resident aliens were easy targets in the popular mind as suspected witches; see Cardini, "Magia e stregoneria nella Toscana del Trecento," 128, and Iris Origo, "The Domestic Enemy: Eastern Slaves in Tuscany in the Fourteenth and Fifteenth Centuries," *Speculum* 30 (1955): 321–66.

81. See Vern L. Bullough, "Postscript: Heresy, Witchcraft and Sexuality," in *Sexual Practices and the Medieval Church*, ed. Vern L. Bullough and James Brundage (Buffalo: Prometheus Books, 1982), 206–17. We shall have more to say about this in sec. 4 below, "The Demonization of the Heretic."

82. "Festum Bacchi et ibi agitantur pulchrae iuvenes" (OOH.III.177b).

83. Russell, *Witchcraft in the Middle Ages*, 201.

84. The quotation is from Origo, *The World of San Bernardino*, 44. Freedom is a dangerous thing in and for a woman, Bernardino says; too much freedom, for example, led Mary Magdalene to her ruination, as it will any woman (B.145 and E.183). On the other hand, the Virgin Mary was preserved in her virginity and moral respectability (as, again, will be any woman) because she was ever accompanied by twelve "mystical" (i.e., allegorical) handmaidens, the foremost of whom was Madonna Clausura, "Lady Cloister" (OOQ.IV.473–75 and R.861–62).

85. See Delcorno, "L'*exemplum* nella predicazione di San Bernardino," in *Atti-Todi*, 71–107.

86. Russell, *Witchcraft in the Middle Ages*, 116. I cite the 1983 bilingual edition, Walter Map, *De nugis curialium, Courtiers' Trifles*, ed. and trans. M. R. James, revised by C. N. L. Brooke and R. A. B. Mynors (Oxford: Clarendon Press, 1983), 155–57, Dist. ii, c. 12, "Again of Such [Illusory] Apparitions."

87. The similarity is pointed out by the editors of *De nugis*, 149, n. 3. For the Swan Maiden, see Stith Thompson, *Motif-Index of Folk-literature: A Classification of Narrative Elements in Folk-tales, Ballads, Myths, Fables*, rev. ed. (Bloomington: Indiana University Press, 1989), D.361.1 (see also B.652.1), and Barbara Fass Leavy, *In Search of the Swan Maiden: A Narrative on Folklore and Gender* (New York: New York University Press, 1994).

88. *De nugis*, 159. In condemning men who use witchcraft to get women into bed with them, Bernardino acknowledges the fact of copulation between demons and human beings, but makes no mention of offspring (OOH.III.178a). The scriptural basis of the medieval Christian belief in incubi and succubi was Genesis 6:1, which tells of the "sons of heaven" who took the "daughters of man" for their wives (Kieckhefer, *Magic in the Middle Ages*, 197).

89. Paton, "To the fire," 9. See also chap. 7, "The Supernatural World," of her *Preaching Friars and the Civic Ethos*.

90. Paton, "To the fire," 26; see also 23–27, and her *Preaching Friars*, 295–303.

91. "To the fire," 28–29, and *Preaching Friars*, 302–5.

92. See n. 38 above.

93. Domenico Mammoli, *The Record of the Trial and Condemnation of a Witch, Matteuccia di Francesco at Todi, 20 March 1428* (Res Tudertinae 14. Rome: N.p., 1972), 39.

94. Candida Peruzzi, "Un processo di stregoneria a Todi nel '400," *Lares* 21 (1955): 2. Peruzzi gives the original Latin text of the trial record, whereas Mammoli provides an English translation as well (see previous note). For further discussion of the trial, see Claudio Bondì, *Strix. Medichesse, streghe e fattucchiere nell'Italia del Rinascimento* (Rome: Lucarini, 1989), 25–42; and, in more summary fashion, Bonomo, *Caccia alle streghe*, 119–20, Kieckhefer, *Magic in the Middle Ages*, 59–60, and *European Witch Trials*, 73; and Ginzburg, *Ecstasies*, 299.

95. Mammoli, *Record of the Trial*, 31.

96. Marino Bigaroni, "S. Bernardino a Todi," *SF* 73 (1976): 110–17. On the basis of new, compelling evidence, Bigaroni corrects the chronology of the friar's activities for the year 1426 previously established by Pacetti in his "La predicazione di S. Bernardino in Toscana," *AFH* 33 (1940): 317, and "Cronologia bernardiniana," in *SBSSR*, 452.

97. Bigaroni, "S. Bernardino a Todi," 117.

98. Mammoli, *Record of the Trial*, 29.

99. Bigaroni, "S. Bernardino a Todi," 116–17.

100. "Item decreverunt . . . quod nullus debeat incantare demones seu facere aut fieri facere aliquas facturas seu malias." Ibid., 123.

101. Giovanni Battista Bronzini, "La predicazione di Bernardino da Siena fra scrittura e oralità," in *Atti-Maiori*, 141.

102. Russell, *Witchcraft in the Middle Ages*, 159. They found what they were looking for especially if torture or the mere threat thereof were involved: "tortures could include having one's feet roasted until the bones fell from their sockets" (Cohn, *Europe's Hidden Demons*, 90).

103. Mammoli, *Record of the Trial*, 29, 31.

104. For the married man's would-be lover and the priest's concubine, see ibid., 35 and 36 respectively. The record describes the prescription in the later case: "Matteuccia told the woman to wash her hands and feet facing backwards and with her knees bent and when she had done so to take the water and throw it where the man and woman were going to pass."

105. For these battered wife cases, see Mammoli, *Record of the Trial*, 32–34. Abused wives also appear frequently among the clients of another "witch," Gabrina degli Albeti, brought to trial in 1375 in Reggio Emilia (Bonomo, *Caccia alle streghe*, 136).

106. Kieckhefer, *European Witch Trials*, 73.

107. Mammoli, *Record of the Trial*, 36–38.

108. Ibid., 38.

109. Kieckhefer, *European Witch Trials*, 73.

110. Russell, *Witchcraft in the Middle Ages*, 42–43.

111. Kieckhefer, *European Witch Trials*, 75.

112. Ginzburg, *Ecstasies*, 6, 7. Joseph Klaits reminds us that "the cultural distance between elites and populace was not at all fixed. . . . [H]igher and lower cultures should be regarded not as separate compartments but as overlapping categories with many points of contact. Witch hunting was one of the most dramatic areas of overlap" (*Servants of Satan*, 50–51).

113. What appears inaccurate in Ginzburg's criticism is his unqualified equation of "diabolism" with the sabbath. The sabbath was but one of diabolism's components, and had an ancient, benign (or at least nondemonic) preexistence as the Society of Diana. Independently of the impositions of the learned, the popular imagination may well have come on its own to believe in nocturnal gatherings convoked by some central, variously identified, non-Christian figure of leadership, such as in the late-fourteenth-century cases of two Milanese women, Sibillia and Pierina, who attended the weekly assembly (*ludus*, game) of "Signora Oriente." The two women were sent to the stake in 1390 as relapsed heretics (they are nowhere in the trial described as witches); previously in 1384 they had been tried and found guilty of heresy, but given light sentences of public penance. We have the summary texts of these four sentences, published (in both Latin and Italian) by Luisa Muraro, *La Signora del gioco. Episodi della caccia alle streghe* (Milan: Feltrinelli, 1976), 147–55 (discussion of the case and Italian trans.), 240–45 (Latin text). It is noteworthy that, just as in the Matteuccia trial record, mention of the Devil and of demonic activity occurs only and abruptly in the later (1390) trial of just one of the women, Pierina. This leads us to suspect that again, it was the Inquisitor who injected his "learned notions" of demonic witchcraft into what, according to the earlier 1384 testimony of Pierina and the consistent testimony of Sibillia in both 1384 and 1390, was "simply" a nondiabolical, albeit non-Christian, "game" or gathering of women. Pierina's confession of demonic activity may likewise have come about through torture or the threat thereof. For these cases, see also Kieckhefer, *European Witch Trials*, 20–21; Russell, *Witchcraft in the Middle Ages*, 211–12; Ginzburg, *Ecstasies*, 91–93; Bonomo, *Caccia alle streghe*, 16–17; and Cohn, *Europe's Inner Demons*, 217–18.

114. The same tale was told to the Sienese in 1425; a greatly condensed version can be found at G.196–97, while a longer one (taken from a different *reportatio* of the same Siena 1425 cycle) was published by Pacetti, in Bernardino da Siena, *Le prediche volgari inedite (Firenze 1424, 1425. Siena 1425)* (Siena: Cantagalli, 1935), 540–42. Bernardino also used the *exemplum* in Assisi that same year (1425), but the sermon in question has not been published; see Pacetti, "La predicazione di San Bernardino da Siena a Perugia e ad Assisi nel 1425," *CF* 10 (1940): 24.

115. Professor Christine Meeks of Trinity College, Dublin, has searched through the records of Lucca's Capitano del Popolo, Podestà, and the Sentenze e Bandi for the early decades of the fifteenth century, but has thus far found no trace of this case (personal correspondence, May 22 and December 16, 1996). Despite Bernardino's assurance that his story represents a "real life" occurrence, its origins may nonetheless be in the rich store of medieval narrative surrounding the partnership between the Devil and the sorceress or *vetula*. I have thus far not been able to find an exact counterpart to Bernardino's "Comare di Lucca" tale in earlier literature; however, Tubach's inventory lists several *exempla* of similar plot in which a sorceress or old woman assists the Devil in sowing discord between a happily married, virtuous couple (Frederic C. Tubach, *Index Exemplorum: A Handbook of Medieval Religious Tales* [Helsinki: Suomalainen Tiedeakatemia/Academia Scientiarum Fennica, 1969], nn. 4511 and 5361).

116. "Andò a una sua comare vecchia che sapeva, o diceasi che sapea questi incantamenti, e fare queste medicine, e ritrovare i furti" (C.209).

117. "Ella stava presso alla porta, e andato a lei le disse: 'Mona massaiuola, io vorrei da voi un grande servigio, perchè i' sono in una gran battaglia per fiorini sedici ch'io ò perduti; priegovi che vi piaccia di dirmi ove sono o chi me gli à tolti' " (C.209–10).

118. "Eccoti in sul primo sonno costei apre l'uscio dell'orto, ed esce fuori ingnudanata e tutta scapigliata, e comincia a fare suoi segni e suoi iscongiuri, e a gridare, e a chiamare i[l] diavolo" (C.210). For the formulas the *comare* may have used to conjure the Devil, see Kieckhefer, *Forbidden Rites,* 126–53.

119. Russell, *Witchcraft in the Middle Ages,* 209–10. Her case is discussed more extensively in Bondì, *Strix,* 5–22.

120. Mammoli, *The Record of the Trial,* 4.

121. "E il diavolo che è sempre presto e presente, subito venne a lei e dice: Che vuoi! che vuoi! che vuoi! che tanto m'ài chiamato?" (C.210).

122. "Il tuo compare, avendo la borsa de' danari in seno, e andando a dare mangiare al porco, i danari gli caddono nel porcile e non se n'avide; il porco prese la borsa in bocca, e stracciolla, e àssene inghiottiti dieci, e gli altri sono nel porcile" (C.211).

123. Witches apparently like to make trouble for priests: after this *exemplum,* Bernardino recounts another "true" story (G.197) that occurred in the Marches involving a jealous husband who sought information about the behavior of his wife from an "enchantress" (*incantatrice*). The enchantress lies to him, telling him his wife is in love with a priest; enraged, the man kills his wife and is in turn killed by her brothers.

124. "Disse il compare: 'Femina del diavolo e di mala ragione, tu ne menti per la gola, ch'io udi' stanotte quello [che] promettesti al diavolo. Io ò ritrovati i miei danari e tu se' degna d'essere arsa.' La voce si sparse per Lucca, e se non ch'ella si fuggì in sul contado di Pisa, ella era arsa meritamente e col bullettino vostro [i.e., the Florentine writ of extradition] fu sicura. Questo fu il propio vero miracolo ed essemplo a tutti gli uomini che l'odono" (C.212).

125. See OOH.III.178a. In this Padua 1423 sermon, "De amore miracoloso" ("Seraphim" cycle, no. 8), Bernardino condemns men who use sorcery in an attempt to force women to have sex with them. What happens instead, the friar explains, is that the Devil assumes the form of that supposedly spellbound woman and thus her would-be lover unknowingly engages in intercourse with the Devil. In the meantime, the woman alone remains in her own bed, dreaming of a scene of intercourse with her mere mortal seducer.

126. Kors and Peters, *Witchcraft in Europe,* 144–45.

127. "Some of the elite minds responsible for the witch image were morbidly obsessed with sex and as a consequence the image has been seen primarily as a manifestation of the

sexual anxieties, guilt and frustrations of celibate clergy. Repressed sexuality sought vicarious expression and in the subconscious of the ascetic cleric the death of a witch became a temporary symbol of victory against intolerable lust." G. R. Quaife, *Godly Zeal and Furious Rage: The Witch in Early Modern Europe* (New York: St. Martin's Press, 1987), 7 and 104. Yet Quaife himself does not subscribe to this explanation, cautioning: "Although some individuals might react in such a way to sexual anxieties there is no evidence that it was the norm" (104).

128. To the Paduans in 1423, Bernardino tells a similar tale; the text as it has come down to us is highly compressed: "Unde dum semel una juvenis vellet diligi a marito, ivit ad vetulam, quae in nocte expoliavit se nudam, et illa juvenis remanserat ibi cum una socia, et voluerunt videre quid facere ista anus, et illa incantatrix fecit venire unum daemonem qui minxit in uno urceo, et dixit, da bibere de hoc illi iuveni, et maritus diliget eam; et illa juvenis videns hoc, horrore percussa, noluit bibere." ("One time there was a young woman who wanted to gain her husband's love, so she sought help from an old lady, who at night stripped naked, and that young woman remained there with one of her girlfriends, both of them wanting to see what that old woman would do, and that enchantress conjured up a demon who pissed into a pitcher and said, 'Give this to the girl to drink and her husband will begin to love her,' and, seeing this, and struck with horror, that young woman refused to drink it.") OOH.III.179b. Bernardino makes brief reference to this tale in one of his sermon drafts; see OOQ.IX.386.

129. Indeed, the fifteenth-century French word often used for witchcraft or magic was *vauderie*, a term that originally referred to the heretical Waldensians. In a bull dated March 23, 1440, directed against the rebel council of Basel and antipope Felix V, Eugene IV also uses the word as a synonym for witchcraft. Bonomo, *Caccia alle streghe*, 52; Cohn, *Europe's Inner Demons*, 229; Russell, *Witchcraft in the Middle Ages*, 220.

130. Russell, *A History of Witchcraft*, 55. Edward Peters contests this claim by pointing out that, in fact, many witchcraft elements come directly from the civil and ecclesiastical literature against the *crimen magiae*, magic: "The witch of the late fifteenth, sixteenth, and seventeenth centuries derived from the magician more than from the heretic," *The Magician, the Witch and the Law*, 135.

131. "Ideo ab uno tempore citra multiplicati sunt in mundo, maxime in Italia, multi errores, quia spernuntur determinationes ecclesiae. Et licet navicula Petri conquassetur, et fluctuet hinc inde, sursum et deorsum, tamen semper durabit ecclesia donec sit mundus" (OOH.III.157b).

132. Hans Küng, *The Church* (New York: Sheed & Ward, 1967), 298; Cohn, *Europe's Inner Demons*, 23.

133. We will return to the question of chronology at the end of this chapter. For witchcraft and rebellion, see Levack, *The Witch-Hunt in Early Modern Europe*, 64–67 and 154–56.

134. For Manfred, see below in this same section.

135. "Cieco, sordo e mutolo è chi seguita questa resia; e simile chi crede o va drieto agl'incantamenti, o indovini, o all'altre diavolerie, che significano il dimonio meridiano" (C.235). Bernardino says he is referring to the "blind, deaf, and mute" possessed man of Luke 11:14, which in reality speaks only of a "mute demon." For the "noonday Devil," see Psalm 91:6.

136. "Or ti dico che se tu ti parti da questa fede, tu se' uno eretico" (R.1033). Bernardino on at least three occasions (OOH.III.158a, OOQ.III.109, R.825) specifically warns his audience against the heretical book *The Mirror of Simple Souls*, which we now know was written by Marguerete Porete, burned at the stake as a heretic in Paris in 1310. The *Mirror* was thought to be a work of the supposedly antinomian "heresy" of the "Free Spirit," as Bernardino points out ("sunt quidam qui lapsi sunt in damnatam heresiam de spiritu libertatis, quae doctrina ponitur in libro qui *De anima simplici* intitulari solet," OOQ.III.109). See Lambert, *Medieval Heresy*,

184–87, and Robert E. Lerner, *The Heresy of the Free Spirit in the Later Middle Ages* (reprint, Notre Dame: University of Notre Dame Press, 1991).

137. A note by Barbieri summarizes the little we know of Amedeo: born in Lodi, he was made a citizen of the Lombard capital in 1426 by the Duke of Milan, his protector. He was well known in the city as a man of great intellect and a skilled teacher of the abacus and geometry. Gino Barbieri, "L'usuraio Tomaso Grassi nel racconto bandelliano e nella documentazione storica," in *Studi in onore di Amintore Fanfani*, 6 vols., vol. 2, *Medioevo* (Milan: Giuffrè, 1962), 27, n. 12.

138. Celestino Piana, "Un processo svolto a Milano nel 1441 a favore del mag. Amedeo de Landis e contro frate Bernardino da Siena," in *Atti-Siena*, 778, and, for the quotations in the previous sentence, 781. The document that Piana has published represents the verbatim depositions of the witnesses against Bernardino; it was, by and large, unknown until its publication in 1982 and is the sole basis of our reconstruction of the facts of the case from the point of view of the alleged heretic, Amedeo. The two other fifteenth-century descriptions of the case both come from pro-Bernardino sources: Nicholas V's 1447 bull, *Universalis ecclesiae regimini* (*Annales Minorum*, ed. Lucas Wadding [Quaracchi: Collegio San Bonaventura, 1932], vol. 11, 316–21 [275.VIII]; also in *Bullarium franciscanum*, ed. Ulricus Hüntemann, vol. I [1431–1455] [Quaracchi: Collegio San Bonaventura, 1929], 530–33, n. 1056) and the preface to an anonymous *consilium iuridicum*, published by Piana in "Documenti intorno alla vita di S. Bernardino da Siena e codici delle opere," *BSB* 10 (1950): 159–62.

139. "Ex quibus dictis per fr. Bernardinum multi obstupuerunt de eo fr. Bernardino, qui praesumisset talia dicere de uno antequam requisitus et monitus foret per vicarium d. archiepiscopi, vel inquisitorem haereticae pravitatis, et quia talia pertinebant eidem vicario et inquisitori, qui est ordinis Praedicatorum, qui consueverunt primitus requirere et monere et interrogare tales; et si confitentur vel aliter probentur in foro iudiciali, publicantur postea pro haereticis in ecclesia S. Eustorgii," Piana, "Un processo," 781.

140. See Massimo Miglio, "Brivio (Brippius, Brippio), Giuseppe," *Dizionario biografico degli italiani*, 14:355–58.

141. *Universalis ecclesiae regimini*, in Wadding, 11:318. There is some uncertainty as to the precise facts of the case, since most of these derive from the one hearing conducted in 1441 before a papal legate, instigated by Amedeo himself against Bernardino in absentia. Even though witnesses included only Amedeo's friends, numbered among them, nonetheless, were a "doctor of both laws" and the rector of the Church of St. Protasius in Milan. There had been an earlier interrogation (in 1437, at the time of Bernardino's first denunciations of Amedeo) conducted by the archiepiscopal vicar and the local inquisitor. According to the text of the 1441 trial, Amedeo was found innocent of the charges at that time, whereas, according to the above-mentioned *consilium iuridicum*, he confessed (under torture or the threat thereof?) to heresy and disturbance of the public peace, but was released after promising to cease holding and professing his former opinions. (He was also given the punishment of weekly Friday fasting and Mass attendance on his knees for a period of one year.) Whatever the real outcome in 1437, it seems that by 1441 doubts about his orthodoxy were still in circulation and damaging his reputation, so much so that Amedeo asked for and received a new hearing from the pope. However, as the *consilium iuridicum* states, in his request to the pope, Amedeo had not mentioned Bernardino as the source of the calumny against him, only "someone from the Mendicant orders." The implication is, therefore, that had the pope known it was Bernardino who was the culprit in question, he would never have granted the new hearing. Indeed, Nicholas's bull (*Universalis ecclesiae regimini*, in Wadding, 11:318–19) states this explicitly. Yet one can understand Amedeo's reluctance to name Bernardino: by 1441, many of the preacher's contemporaries had already

unofficially canonized him a saint and—the pope included—were ill disposed to admit that the friar could be guilty of error or imprudence.

142. Andrea Biglia, "De institutis, discipulis et doctrina fratris Bernardini Ordinis Minorum," published by Baudouin de Gaiffier, "Le mémoire d'André Biglia sur la prédication de Saint Bernardin de Sienne," *AB* 53 (1935): 308–58; for the charges of arrogance, see 335:24; 342:10; 343:11. Later in life, Biglia repented of his opposition to Bernardino; according to a witness at Bernardino's canonization trial, the Augustinian confessed that he regretted writing the treatise and wanted to burn it. The letter that Biglia wrote to Bernardino seeking reconciliation is still extant, published, along with an English translation, by Joseph C. Schnaubelt, "Andrea Biglia (c. 1394–1435), His Life and Writings," *Augustiniana* 43 (1993): 147–48, 158–59. See also the entry "Biglia, Andrea," in *Dizionario biografico degli italiani,* 10:413–15; Rudolph Arbesmann, "Andrea Biglia, Augustinian Friar and Humanist," *Analecta Augustiniana* 28 (1965): 154–218; Anna Morisi, "Andrea Biglia e Bernardino da Siena," in *Atti-Todi,* 337–59; Katherine Walsh, "The Augustinian Observance in Siena in the Age of S. Caterina and S. Bernardino," in *Atti-Siena,* 939–50; and Diana M. Webb, "Andrea Biglia at Bologna, 1424–27: A Humanist Friar and the Troubles of the Church," *Bulletin of the Institute of Historical Research* 49 (1976): 41–59.

143. Piana, "Un processo," 770, 773.

144. "Et ulterius credo unum filium parvum mortuum fuisse dicta occasione, quia uxor mag. Amedei, quae lactabat filium suum in cunabulis, passa fuit tantam malanchoniam, quia evitabatur a personis aliis et perdidit lac et non potuit lactare filium suum et non reperit vicinam volentem eidem filio dare modicum lactis, nec auxilium aliquod uxori mag. Amedei ex eo quod fr. Bernardinus dixerat non debere dari eidem auxilium etc.; ex quo puer periit fame." Piana, "Un processo," 781.

145. Ibid., 766–67, 773, 774. In his Latin treatise *De octo beatitudinibus evangelicis,* Bernardino devotes a whole page to refuting "certain persons" who maintain that youths should not enter religious life until they have first proven they can sustain the rigors of that life (OOQ.VI.426–27). Amedeo, no doubt, is one of these "certain persons" to whom Bernardino refers.

146. This is the first examination of the case since the publication of the 1441 trial record by Piana in 1982. Previously, all discussions of the case simply took it for granted that Amedeo was indeed a demonic heretic and that Bernardino's behavior in this episode was completely unimpeachable. I am currently preparing a more thorough study of this case.

147. Russell, *History of Witchcraft,* 59.

148. Cohn, *Europe's Inner Demons,* chaps. 2 and 3.

149. "Tutti i motivi [i.e., *promotori*] delle eresie sono superbi e duri di cuore, che per superbia di loro scienzia e sapienzia cominiciano le sette per parere e mostrare di sapere più ch'e dottori approvati da santa chiesa" (C.236–37).

150. Sermons 37 ("Come si de' domandare a Dio . . .") and 38 ("Similmente che Idio c'insegni . . ."), R.761–820. *De inspirationibus* is to be found at OOQ.VI.223–311. Bernardino's treatise has the distinction of being the most methodical and practical treatment of the subject of "discernment of spirits," complete with twelve specific rules, before Ignatius of Loyola; see my study "An Early Renaissance Guide for the Perplexed: Bernardino of Siena's *De inspirationibus,*" in *Through a Glass Darkly: Essays in the Religious Imagination,* ed. John C. Hawley (New York: Fordham University Press, 1996), 24–49.

151. "Egli è anco in parte, che vi si tiene questo maladetto ordine ch'io vi dirò, che la sera di notte si ragunano tutti uomini e donne in uno luogo, e fanno uno brudetto di loro, e hanno uno lume, e quando lo' pare tempo di spegnarlo, lo spengono, e poi a chi s'abatte s'abatta, sia chi vuole. . . . Ou, ou, ou! Odi maladizione che l'è intrata adosso!" (R.793). Here Bernardino

alludes to a common charge raised against heretics, and less commonly against witches, that of homosexual behavior, or as it was called in those days, sodomy; see Russell, *Witchcraft in the Middle Ages,* 94–95, 180, 219.

152. Bernardino is here referring to an actual episode, i.e., the clash between Piedmontese heretics and inquisitors, even if some of the details he gives of their secret modus operandi are fictitious. See Delcorno's note 271 at R.793, citing Facchinetti, *San Bernardino da Siena,* 308; and Grado Merlo, *Eretici e inquisitori nella società del secolo XIV* (Turin: Claudiana, 1977), 80, 151.

153. "E sonne di queste tali genti qua in Piemonte, e so'vi andati già cinque inquisitori per levar via questa maladizione, e quali so' stati morti da queste male genti. E più, che non si truova inquisitore che vi voglia andare per mettarvi mano. E sai come si chiamano questi tali? Chiamansi quelli del barilotto. E questo nome si è perché eglino pigliaranno uno tempo dell'anno uno fanciullino, e tanto il gittaranno fra loro de mano in mano, che elli si muore. Poi che è morto, ne fanno polvare, e mettono la polvare in uno barilotto, e danno poi bere di questo barilotto a ognuno; e questo fanno perché dicono che poi non possono manifestare niuna cosa che ellino faccino. Noi aviamo uno frate del nostro Ordine, il quale fu di loro, e hamme dette ogni cosa, che tengono pure e più disonesti modi ch'io creda che si possino tenere" (R.793–94). Bernardino mentions this "secta Barilotti" in passing at OOH.III.158b, in the same breath with the sect of Fra Dolcino. (Elsewhere, he tells of a bishop of Ancona who one night saw in a meadow two demons tossing a child back and forth between themselves [D.409 and OOQ.IX.298].) The ultimate prototype of such secret nocturnal assemblies is the "Society of Diana," but "[h]ere the innocuously magical features of Diana's society have dissolved into the macabre and aggressive traits of the sect of the keg" (Ginzburg, *Ecstasies,* 299). Again, Bernardino's description of the group (which does not fail to include even the traditional motif of the extinguished lamp) also echoes the centuries-old calumnies traditionally used against dissident or other suspect minority groups, such as those raised by the second-century Justin Martyr against the Marcionites—sexual orgy, ritual infanticide, and sodomy. See Russell, *Witchcraft in the Middle Ages,* 86–95 (90 for Justin Martyr), and Cohn, *Europe's Inner Demons,* 1, 17, 19, 29–30. Similar scenes are described, to cite two further examples closer to Bernardino's time, in a well-known 1022 heresy trial of a group in Orléans (reports of which Bernardino may have come across) and in Guibert of Nogent's autobiography (*Self and Society in Medieval France: The Memoirs of Abbot Guibert of Nogent (1064?–c. 1125),* ed. John F. Benton [New York: Harper & Row, 1970], bk. 3, chap. 17). For the Orléans group, see Edward Peters, ed., *Heresy and Authority in Medieval Europe: Documents in Translation* (Philadelphia: University of Pennsylvania Press, 1980), 66–71.

154. "Se abbia bevuto dal bariletto [*sic*]," quoted in Bondì, *Strix,* 56. See Cohn's discussion of Bernardino's account of the "keg" in *Europe's Inner Demons,* 42–54. Cohn cites (49–50) this passage from Bernardino as the primary source of information about the origins of the *barilotto,* a recurrent heresy-related term and motif. He also conjectures (52) that it was Bernardino's friend, colleague, and "hammer of heretics," John of Capistrano, who ascribed the *barilotto* to the Fraticelli. Capistrano also passed on the information to Biondo Flavio, who mentions it in his *Italia illustrata* (Venice, 1510, 78, as Delcorno tells us [R.793, n. 269]).

155. C.118–19; see also OOH.III.158b. For Dolcino, see Lambert, *Medieval Heresy,* 202–3; and Giovanni Miccoli, "Note sulla fortuna di fra Dolcino," *Annali della Scuola Normale di Pisa,* 25 (1956): 245–49. As Bernardino points out (C.118), Dante discusses Dolcino in *Inferno* 28:55–60, but our preacher may also have read the medieval account of Dolcino, the *Historia fratris Dulcini.* According to Bernardino, when placed in the fire to be executed, Dulcino's "bellissima

femmina" was not harmed at all by the flames, until the demon inside her was exorcised by a priest using a consecrated host (C.119).

156. "Questo Nicolaio era diacano, e ricevé lo Spirito Santo cogli altri Apostoli; e poi che elli ebbe riceuto lo Spirito Santo, sì li fu data la cura delle vedove. Costui aveva moglie ed era bellissima, e elli n'era sì fortamente impazzato, che elli non pensava in altro iddio che la moglie" (R.792; see also C.117–18).

157. See Rusconi, *L'attesa della fine,* 236–46. For more on Bernardino and Manfredi, see also my study "Signs of the Apocalypse in Late Medieval Italy," 104–8.

158. "Odi. Già forse dodici anni fu a Fermo uno che uscì d'una selva, che dè a intendare sue novelle e sue pazzie, tirandosi assai gente dietro, dicendo che uno dì andarebbero al Sipolcro per terra. E quando gli parve, e elli gli fece spogliare tutti innudi, uomini e donne, e missorsi in via e andarono verso Fermo. Quando la brigata vidde questa gente, cominciarono a dire:—O che significa questo? Che novità è questa? Che andate voi facendo a questo modo—Elli rispondeva:—Noi voliamo andare al mare, e quando saremo gionti al mare, el mare s'aprirà, e noi entramo dentro e andaremo in Ierusalem senza bagnarci i piei in acqua.—Quando questa novella venne all'orecchie di misser Lodovico signore di Fermo, tutti li fece impregionare" (R.808–9).

Bernardino does not give the name of the Fermo leader, nor does he mention the group explicitly as an apocalyptic phenomenon, either here or in the other two places where we find brief allusion to the same group, OOQ.VI.256 and IX.418. The context of Bernardino's ridicule of the group is a general warning against irrational devotional practices and against placing belief in self-proclaimed prophets. It is Rusconi who alerts us to the apocalyptic character of the group and its activity: the journey to Jerusalem is their attempt at escaping the dangers of the end times. Bernardino's *exemplum* corresponds to an actual historical event, as we know from the contemporary *Cronaca fermana* of Antonio di Niccolò; the leader of this band (of approximately twenty men and women) was a "friar wearing the habit of those [fraticelli] *de paupera vita,*" of whom we know only his first name, Antonio. Their arrest took place on October 11, 1412. For this episode, see Rusconi, *L'attesa della fine,* 234–35.

159. "O, anco un altro il quale andava acattando con una sua suoro [*sic*], e dipengeva angioli, e andavano dicendo che ella era pregna di Spirito Santo, e andava daendo di quello latte; e colui il premeva e mettevale le mani in seno! O grande ribaldaria! Parti che questa sia cosa ragionevole, che uno vada premendo il latte a una donna? E sia chi si voglia, io dico che non piacciono a Dio queste tali cose" (R.809). Another eccentric "prophet" with whom Bernardino clashed in Genoa was Giovanni Votadeo (Vodadio), who wandered the cities of Liguria and Piedmont, dressed only in lambskin, and drawing the support of many devout if ingenuous souls. See OOH.III.158b and B.100; Origo, *The World of San Bernardino,* 28–29. According to Bernardino, Votadeo was connected in the popular imagination with the legendary figure of the "Wandering Jew" (OOH.III.158b; see also Corrain and Zampini, "Spunti etnografici," 890). Bernardino's ultimate advice to his audience regarding these Nicolaitan-type "prophets" is "to send them three eggs each and have them drink them because they need them since their real problem is only emptiness of the head, and for that there's no better medicine" ("Fate che voi li mandiate tre uova per una, e fate che egli le beia, però che li bisognano, perché il difetto loro è solo votamento di celabro, e non v'è miglior medicina di quella"), R.799.

160. We will have more to say about the cult of the Holy Name below in sec. 8. For the Tetragrammaton, see Kieckhefer, *Magic in the Middle Ages,* 4 and 21. For the history of the cult of the Holy Name, Bernardino's contribution to it, and its iconography, see Daniel Arasse, "Iconographie et évolution spirituelle: la tablette de saint Bernardin de Sienne," *Revue d'histoire*

de la spiritualité 50 (1974): 433–56; Peter R. Biasiotto, *History of the Development of Devotion to the Holy Name* (St. Bonaventure, N.Y.: St. Bonaventure College, 1943); Giuseppe Marchini, "Un'invenzione di S. Bernardino," in *Atti-Siena,* 639–55; Agostino Montanaro, *Il culto al SS. Nome di Gesù* (Naples: Istituto Grafico Editoriale Italiano, 1958); and Vincenzo Pacelli, "Il 'Monogramma' bernardiniano. Origine, diffusione e sviluppo," in *Atti-Maiori,* 253–59.

161. These are the principal charges contained in contemporary treatises written against Bernardino: the "Sermo contra imaginem nominis tabulellae, quae est imago et signum antichristi" by Augustinian theologian Andrea da Cascia; the "[Tractatus] contra novum characterem huius nominis Iesus" by Dominican magister Bartolommeo da Firenze; the anonymous "Tractatus . . . compositus contra nominis Iesu devotionem"; and the likewise anonymous "Articuli contra fratrem Bernardinum de Ordine Minorum, inventorem novi characteris nominis huius Iesus," all published by Ephrem Longpré, "S. Bernardin de Sienne et le nom de Jésus," *AFH* 28 (1935): 443–76; 29 (1936): 142–68, 443–77; 30 (1937): 170–92 (for the treatises, see 29:443–77 and 30:170–92. Longpré's article still remains the most thorough examination of the controversy surrounding Bernardino's cult of the Holy Name and the resultant heresy charges and trial. A good summary of the facts of the case is supplied by Origo, *The World of San Bernardino,* 117–30; see also, for a discussion of the anti-Bernardino treatises, Giovanni Gonnet, "S. Bernardino da Siena e la cosidetta 'eresia' del Nome di Gesù," in *Atti-Maiori,* 41–51. Yet Bernardino also had the support of the mob: Andrea da Cascia tells us that he was nearly lynched and that his brother was murdered for their opposition to Bernardino's IHS cult, the murder being proclaimed by the IHS devotees as "a miracle done in the name of the good Jesus" (Longpré, "S. Bernardin de Sienne et le nom de Jésus," *AFH* 29 [1936]: 460–61). Another treatise written against Bernardino, although in more restrained and polite terms, is Biglia's already cited "De institutis, discipulis et doctrina fratris Bernardini Ordinis Minorum" (see 333–34, s. 23, for the Moses reference).

162. "Ego vado Romam igne cremari, et vos pace et tranquillitate fruentes remanebitis. Aiunt enim me hereticum et fama viget in Urbe quod debeo comburi," *Vita anonima,* 319, s. 18.

163. "Acerrimus et rigorosus haeresum exstirpator . . . praeclarissimus fidei catholicae praedicator et instructor rectissimus in omni fere Italia et extra inter ceteros famosos evangelizatores verbi Dei praesentis aetatis probatus et notus," *Bullarium franciscanum,* 1: 272–78, doc. 40. Felice Alessio gives both the original Latin text of the bull (Appendix 1, 472–74) and an Italian translation (296–98) in his *Storia di San Bernardino e del suo tempo.*

164. Gustav Beckmann, ed., "Tagebuchaufzeichnungen zur Geschichte des Basler Konzils 1431–1435 und 1438," in *Concilium Basiliense: Studien und Quellen zur Geschichte des Concils von Basel,* ed. Gustav Beckman et al. (Nendeln, Liechtenstein: Kraus, 1976, reprint of 1904 Basel edition), 5:149; see also Joannis de Segovia, "Historia Gestorum Generalis Synodi Basiliensis," lib. 13, cap. 42, "Refragacio super cultu tabelle Ihesus laudesque fratris Bernardini promoventis," in *Monumenta Conciliorum Generalium Seculi Decimi Quinti,* ed. Caesareae Academiae Scientiarum Socii Delegati (Vienna: Holzhausen, 1886), 154–55. The *Vita anonima* (323–24, ss. 24–25) speaks extensively about Filippo Maria Visconti's defense of Bernardino during the Basel episode. For a summary of what we know of this episode of Bernardino's life, see Ferrers Howell, *S. Bernardino of Siena,* 181–86; and Gaudenzio Melani, "San Bernardino da Siena ed il nome di Gesù," in *SBSSR,* 286–87.

165. Origo, *The World of San Bernardino,* 129.

166. See, e.g., "Changing Views of the Devil and His Power," in Cohn's *Europe's Inner Demons* (60–74), which I here paraphrase. See also Jeffrey Burton Russell, *Lucifer: The Devil in the Middle Ages* (Ithaca: Cornell University Press, 1984), one of a series of volumes by Russell

on the figure of the Devil from antiquity to the twentieth century, and Elaine Pagels, *The Origin of Satan* (New York: Vintage, 1995). For the iconography of the Devil, see Luther Link, *The Devil: The Archfiend in Art from the Sixth to the Sixteenth Century* (New York: Abrams, 1995).

167. Cohn, *Europe's Inner Demons*, 73.

168. Ibid.

169. Ibid., 74.

170. "Dirà alcuno: 'O i santi padri che stettono soli nel diserto, ne' romitori come facevano?' Diroloti. Allora era il sangue del nostro Signore Gesù Cristo molto caldo; nella primitiva chiesa erano perseveranti e 'l dimonio non aveva tanta malizia quanto à oggi dalla sperienzia, chè ogni dì appara più per isperienzia che non faceva allora; e la fede è raffreddata pe' nostri peccati, però è maggiore pericolo" (D.8). I read *appara* as *impara*.

171. "Criminentur forte aliqui insuperabilem illam verborum audaciam; unum ferme agere soles quod michi ipsi nichil placere confiteor: non enim minus, ut fere in aperto est, diaboli quam Yhesu nomen ex ore in tuis praedicationibus auditur. At nemo nescit execrandum, ac paene ita et ego dicam, despuendum cunctis fidelibus hoc nomen esse. Quid enim opus est tam frequenter hoc in lingua versare quod cuique piissimo horrendum fore censemus? Atque ipse, ni fallor, meministi, cum Bononiae maledictum illud persaepe inter cetera revolveres, mulierculam, ut fit, rudi simplicitate in terram spuisse. Nec dicam quam acerrime trementem corripuisti, illam ipsam primam esse conclamans cuius corpore milia diabolorum, quippe hoc tuum vocabulam est, tenerentur inclusi." Biglia, "De institutis," 349.

172. "Ac quam facile ex nobis turbae exemplum accipiant! Cum vellet mulier vidua filiam corripere quod hoc ipsum execrandum nomen saepius in ore habebat, statim respondit illa, cur non idem liceret illi in domo quod ipse in tuis praedicationibus frequentares." Biglia, "De institutis," 349. The various names by which Bernardino refers to the Devil are diavolo, dimonio, Satanas ("Satan," also spelled Satanasso, Setenasso, Settenasso), Lucifero, Belzebub, and Cappelluccio. He explains to his audience that the many strange names one finds in magic amulets, such as "Astaroth," are also names of the Devil (OOH.III.177b). "Astaroth" (Ashtaroth), however, was, in reality, the name of a major demon, not the Devil himself. Bernardino does not always respect in his nomenclature the differences between the Devil and his major and minor demons. For this nomenclature, see Russell, *Witchcraft in the Middle Ages*, 18; Kieckhefer, *Forbidden Rites*, 154–69.

173. "Cum inter eos predicaret, obtulit se diabolum eis ostensurum pluribusque diebus populum hac spe suspendit. Itaque veniebant omnes ad sermonem visuri diabolum. Post plures dies 'Servabo,' inquit, 'quod promissum est; et cum unum promiserim diabolum ostendere, multos ostendam. Respice invicem alter alterum, et sic videbitis diabolos; nam vos ipsi diaboli estis, qui opera diaboli facitis,' " Piccolomini, "De Bernardino senensi," 39.

174. In addition to Bernardino's vernacular sermons quoted in this section, see as well the Latin treatise *De exercitu spirituum malignorum* (OOQ.VII.505–26) and the Paduan *reportatio* "De seminatione daemonii" (OOH.III.351–56).

175. Bronzini, "Le prediche di Bernardino e le tradizioni popolari," 124. Klaits speaks of the "folklorization" of the Devil in medieval European culture: "Extraordinary features of the landscapes, from giant boulders to the equally superhuman-seeming Roman roads, monuments, and bridges were attributed to satanic origin" (*Servants of Satan*, 62).

176. "Quanti dimoni sono ora qui presenti? Tutta la chiesa n'è piena, e almeno per tante persone ci sono tanti dimoni. . . . Adunqu'è in nostra presenza, e sa quante cose noi facciamo, o diciamo, o parliamo, sanza che noi lui veggiamo o udiamo" (B.160).

177. R.655; see also R.1284 and G.68, n. 49.

178. "Principale diaboli studium est 'in Ecclesia Dei seminare errores, et in homine extinguere fidei lumen; sicut corvus qui ad oculum caderis primo currit' " (OOQ.IX.368; the quoted section comes from Peraldus's *Summa virtutum ac vitiorum;* see also OOH.III.176a and 353a). Bernardino mistakenly gives the source as Gregory the Great's popular book of tales, the *Dialogues;* for Peraldus as source for Bernardino, see Delcorno, "L'*exemplum* nella predicazione di San Bernardino," 90–91, n. 2.

179. "Leggesi d'uno santo padre, che una volta fu menato dall'angelo ad uno monasterio di santi monaci, e mostrogli tutta la chiesa, e la chiesa era piena di mosche. Disse il santo padre: 'Che vogliono dire tante mosche.' Disse l'angelo: 'Non sono mosche ma sono dimoni per ingannare i monaci.' Disse il santo padre: 'Se sono così santi come tu di', invano ci stanno.' Disse l'angelo: 'Dove truovano niuna parte in loro s'ingegnano, quanto possono, d'avelenarli, e però istanno apparecchiati.' Poi il menò alla piazza dove si faceva il mercato nella città, e 'l santo padre vide uno dimonio solo istare sopra la porta pensoso e ozioso, e disse all'angelo: 'Questo è un gran fatto, che qui che si fanno tanti peccati, non c'è altro che uno dimonio solo, e quello si sta ozioso, e colà a quel monasterio n'era tanti.' Disse l'angelo: 'Qui non bisogna che il dimonio si dia troppo impaccio, che si fanno tanti peccati da loro che gli basta e non gli bisogna troppa fatica durare co' cattivi, ma coi buoni bisogna stare coll'arco teso.' " (C.215–16; see also OOH.163b.)

180. Bernardino tells the story more than once, the details changing from one version to the next. See B.199–200 and OOH.III.279b; for Capistrano's transcription of the story as told by Bernardino in Assisi in 1425, see Gustavo Cantini, "Una ignorata redazione latina di sermoni bernardiniani," *BSB* 2 (1936): 285–86 (where this "malignus spiritus" is described as being in human form [*in forma hominis*] and in love with [*philocaptum*] the daughter of the household). For another brief unpublished version (Padua 1443), see Delcorno, "Note sulla tradizione manoscritta delle prediche volgari di San Bernardino da Siena," *AFH* 73 (1980): 107, n. 2. In one sermon on Purgatory (G.277–78), Bernardino denies that souls of the dead can come back to "haunt" or otherwise vex the living, whereas elsewhere, quoting William of Auvergne's *De universo,* he seems to admit that they indeed can (OOQ.V.295–96).

181. "Dei miracoli di Dio e di quelli del dimonio," B.156–72; and "De amore miraculoso," OOH.III.176–78; see also OOQ.I.111–13, 118 and G.59–60.

182. "Fu creato al prencipio in grandissima sapienza, e in quella medesima sapienza s'è ora, salvo che non è in grazia di Dio, come sono gli angioli buoni. . . . Egli sa tutte le condizioni degli uomini; elli sa tutte le virtù dell'erbe e delle pietre preziose. Sa più uno dimonio solo che tutto el senno degli uomini raccozzato insieme. Sapiendo dunque tante cose, e avendo el sottile ingegno come elli à, sa' tu come farà? Andrassene a uno uomo, e considererà sottilmente la sua condizione, e ove el vedrà più debole e più inclinato, secondo natura, quivi entrerà a tentarlo e, rade volte, se non à una grande resistenza, perde la sua punga, e dura poca fatica" (B.157).

183. "Egli è di natura sottile; così passerebbe per uno muro o una pietra; come per una finestra aperta; può entrare ne' corpi degli uomini, ma non nell'anima . . . egli è in ogni luogo con teco, e ode e sente tutti e tuoi ragionamenti, e vede tutte l'operazioni che tu fai. . . . In poco spazio [di tempo], quanto è un battere d'occhio, sarà da levante al ponente, dall'uno capo del mondo all'altro. . . . Tutte le cose aopera invisibilmente. . . . Non facciamo noi cosa sì in segreto che dall'angiolo buono o reo noi non siamo veduti" (B.157–60).

184. "Non ostante che tu non creda el dimonio sia nero come si dipigne, è tanta la sua figura spaventevole che io credo che, se mille uomini, a un tratto, potessino vedere il dimonio nella sua propria figura orribile, che tutti di paura morrebbono a un tratto" (B.111–12).

185. "Fallo Iddio per lo tuo peccato, padre o madre, o e' permette che sia tormentato nel corpo, ma non nell'anima . . . per tormentare te in lui" (B.168; see also G.63).

186. "Così nel mondo a Madonna Eva: 'Mangia di questo frutto e saprai el bene e 'l male, sarete iddii' " (B.184; see also R.227).

187. "So' molti che dicono: 'Io ò inserrato el diavolo nella ampolla' e non è vero. Anco lui à inserrato te" (G.61). Conjurers would "trap" the demons in a bottle in order to force them to reveal secret information or lend needed assistance (Levack, *The Witch-Hunt in Early Modern Europe*, 36).

188. Peters, *The Magician, the Witch and the Law*, 14; see also 24, 58, 74, and 80; and Cardini, *Magia, stregoneria, superstizioni*, 197–98. For such *indiculi* in Bernardino, see, for example, OOQ.I.115–16, III.321, IX.384–88, and G.65. Several of Bernardino's superstitions also appear in the lists included in the important treatise on witchcraft and superstition, "De sortilegiis" (also known as "De sortibus"), by the preacher's Sienese contemporary, Mariano Sozzini, whom we have already had occasion to cite; see Zdekauer, "Sullo scritto 'De sortilegiis' di M. Sozzini il Vecchio," 131–37, and Russell, *Magic in the Middle Ages*, 207.

189. The reader is once again referred to Corrain and Zampini, "Spunti etnografici," for a convenient anthology of the ethnological information supplied by the friar.

190. See B.79 (St. John's Gospel), G.61–62, OOH.III.177b–78a, R.529–30 and R.1005, n. 111. For a discussion of these amulets, see Kieckhefer, *Magic in the Middle Ages*, 75–80; 77 for the SATOR-AREPO formula mentioned by Bernardino at G.62. See also Corrain and Zampini, "Spunti etnografici," 886. According to a seventeenth-century Florentine chronicler, Bernardino was responsible for popularizing in the city the use of IHS medals—in effect, Christian amulets—given to babies at the time of their baptism; see Enrico Bulletti, "Riflessi della devozione al Nome di Gesù," *BSB* 4 (1938): 134–35. For amulets given to babies, see also Christiane Klapisch-Zuber, "Blood Parents and Milk Parents: Wet Nursing in Florence, 1300–1530," in *Women, Family, and Ritual in Renaissance Italy* (Chicago: University of Chicago Press, 1985), 149–50.

191. OOH.III.176b, OOQ.IX.387, and B.163. This was a popular remedy; see Bronzini, "Le prediche di Bernardino e le tradizioni popolari," 146–47.

192. "Quid dicam de horrendis abusionibus sacramentorum sanctorum, sacratissimae unctionis et sacratissimi Corporis Iesu Christi? Proh nefas! O scelestum facinus! O horrendum scelus! O tremendum iudicium super huiuscemodi sceletissimos et scelestissimas praeparatum, de quibus fari nequeo et tacere non possum!" (OOQ.III.322).

193. Russell, *Witchcraft in the Middle Ages*, 210. For other examples of clerical involvement in witchcraft, see Kieckhefer, *Magic in the Middle Ages*, 56–58, 153–56.

194. "Fu a Genova una femmina che, vedendo el mal tempo, el volse incantare, e alzossi e panni dietro e vollesi verso el maltempo. Allora gionse uno tuono e amazzolla, perchè aveva la fede a tal pazzia" (G.64). On the subject of weather conjurers or *tempestarii*, see Manselli, "Le premesse medioevali della caccia alle streghe," 46, and Cardini, *Magia, Stregoneria, superstizioni*, 199–201.

195. OOQ.I.116–17. Bernardino addresses this issue many times: see, e.g., OOQ.IV.500, IX.388, B.170–71, C.207–8, and G.198–99.

196. Thérèse and Mendel Metzger, *Jewish Life in the Middle Ages: Illuminated Manuscripts of the Thirteenth to the Sixteenth Centuries* (New York: Alpine Fine Arts Collection, 1982), 181; see fig. 251 for a fifteenth-century Italian medical illustration of the human body that pairs the various zodiacal signs with the specific limbs and other body parts they govern.

197. Siraisi, *Medieval and Early Renaissance Medicine*, 67; see also Kieckhefer, *Magic in the Middle Ages*, 120–31.

198. "Quandoque insuper ex dispositione et habitudine caelestium planetarum fiunt in homine quidam impulsus ad hoc vel ad illud obiectum" (OOQ.VI.310).

199. "E medici li quali cognoscono i pianeti, e segni e le costellazioni, da' quali noi aviamo il governo nostro, avendo a dare una medicina allo infermo, la danno per modo con piccola cosa, o erbe o acque o altre speziarie, che quella piccola cosa fa tollare la forza alla pianeta che corre" (R.124).

200. "Ma sopra dell'anima sonno li angioli; li quali angioli c'inducano e sospingono e c'illuminano in tutte quelle cose che noi doviamo fare. E quali angioli v'hanno condotti qui ad udire in questo Campo, e tutto questo Campo è pieno d'angioli, i quali vi fanno stare attenti a udire le parole, le quali a lode di Dio vi so' dette da me; che state a udire tanto attenti, che a pena se fusse santo Pavolo che predicasse, non credo che steste più attenti. E questo donde viene? Non già da me, ma dalli angioli" (R.121).

201. "E nota che non possono vedere nulla per lo corso delle stelle, se none in generale, se non come dire: a Firenze sarà pistolenza, sarà guerra, sarà fame, sarà pace, sarà dovizia, sarà sanità. Intendi in generale, ma non possono vedere in particulare; cioè el tale morrà, el tale camperà eccetera" (B.180).

202. "Uno strologo d'uno signore, a cui el signore dava gran fede, veggendolo el signore un dì molto milinconoso, lo domandò quello ch'egli aveva, e non vogliendole dire, accendendosi in maggiore disiderio, quanto più el negava, tanto che gliele disse, e prima si fece perdonare, e poi gli disse che aveva veduto, per l'arte sua, che in quell'anno il signore doveva morire, e con molto pianto e lagrime l'abbracciò e baciò dicendoli si confortasse. El signore sel credette, e fessi morto, e vassene in sul letto, la febbre li comincia quivi, dolendosi e lamentandosi, e non trovava luogo. Uno de' suoi baroni che aveva l'animo magno, sente ch'el suo signore à male, vassene a lui e domandalo della sua infermità molto teneramente, e se può fare alcuna cosa comandi, e molto el conforta. Disse el signore: 'Il mio male è che 'l mio strolago m'à detto che à veduto ne' suoi libri e carte, ch'io debbo morire in questo anno, di che di questo io ò avuto tanto dolore che la febbre m'à sopraggiunto.' Allora el barone el confortò e disse: 'Non abbiate paura, che io voglio sapere come lo strolago el sa.' E vassene a lui, e domandalo a che modo egli à saputo che 'l signore abbia a morire in questo anno. Allora lo strolago, com molte lagrime, li disse: 'Per la tale e per la tale ragione e convinzione della tale stella nel tale segno.' E assegnò molte sue ragioni per le quali così doveva essere. Allora el barone gli disse: 'Or ditemi, avete voi veduto quanto tempo avete a vivere voi?' Disse lo strolago: 'Egli è buono pezzo el vidi, e ancora fate conto debbo vivere circa venti anni.' Allora el barone trasse fuora el coltello e disse: 'Ben lo voglio provare.' E dettegli tanti colpi col coltello che l'uccise. 'Or va' che non viverai venti anni,' e fessi beffe di lui e della sua arte. E andossene al signore ridendo e disse: 'Lo strolago mi disse così e così, e che aveva ancora a vivere venti anni, e io l'ò morto e non s'è opposto, e così non s'opporrà di voi.' El signore cominciò a ridere di gran voglia, e levossi suso sopra guarito, e visse molti anni" (B.180–81; recounted also in the Latin sermon "De divina protectione," OOQ.III.137–38; see also OOQ.IX.387). Found among the *exempla* of Jacques de Vitry in much the same form as narrated by Bernardino, the tale is ultimately of Persian origin; see Tubach, *Index Exemplorum,* n. 404, and Joseph Greven, ed., *Die exempla aus den Sermones feriales et communes des Jakob von Vitry* (Heidelberg: Carl Winter's Universitätsbuchhandlung, 1914), n. 20.

203. The episode is depicted in three scenes in the predella of a picture of the Madonna protecting the Magistrates of the Arezzo painted in 1456 (see plate 3).

204. *Vita anonima,* 304–38; the quotation is on 335, s. 38 ("Et hec pauca audivi a fratribus senioribus nostri ordinis et civibus Senensibus di vita sua et aliqua ab eo ego ipse audivi. Et scio quia non mentior"). This *Vita anonima* was also published in the same year by Ferdinand-Marie d'Araules (Delorme), *Vie de Saint Bernardin de Sienne. Texte latin inédit du XVe siècle* (Rome: N.p., 1906). In the van Ortroy edition (which I have used for this study), the Fontetecta episode

is found on 331–35; in d'Araules's, on 34–39. One of the witnesses in Bernardino's canonization trials alludes to the Fontetecta episode as an example of the preacher's great patience in enduring tribulation and opposition (Piana, "I processi di canonizzazione," 423–24).

205. Corrain and Zampini, "Spunti etnologici," 887.

206. Yet Bernardino at one point in his own sermonizing alludes, not unapprovingly, to the habit of Spanish mothers who do the same to babies in order to strengthen them (OOH.III.164b).

207. "Et quia locus iste magnum commodum prestabat aliquibus, surrexerunt illi contra virum Dei, et presertim religiosi quidam asserentes quod illud fiebat eis per odium et invidiam sub zelo pietatis, concitantes contra eum rectores civitatis et presidentes dicentes fratrem Bernardinum esse Senensem et gibellinum et contra partem civitatis" (*Vita anonima*, 332, s. 35).

208. There is some debate over the number of times and the precise years in which Bernardino preached in Arezzo. For a well-argued chronology and for Bernardino's visit to Arezzo in general, see Pacetti, "La predicazione di S. Bernardino in Toscana. Con documenti inediti estratti dagli Atti del Processo di Canonizzazione," *AFH* 34 (1941): 261–69. See also Giuseppe Rimbotti, "S. Bernardino da Siena ad Arezzo," *BSB* 9 (1943): 61–71, which, for reasons that are not clear, gives the dates 1440–41 for the destruction of Fontetecta (66).

209. This is what Giorgio Vasari tells us in the life of Parri Spinelli (1387–1452) (included in his *Lives of the Painters, Sculptors and Architects* [London: Dent, 1927], 1:257–63). Vasari recounts the Fontetecta episode, but says mistakenly that Bernardino had "a wood near a spring cut down" (259).

210. "A lei vi raccomandate che vi campi di tanti pericoli in quanti noi siamo insidiati dal dimonio, dal mondo e dalla carne. . . . Vale più una orazione alla vergine Maria che non vale a tutti gli altri santi insieme" (C.221).

211. Graef, *Mary: A History of Doctrine and Devotion*, 315–16.

212. Ibid., 316.

213. "Plus enim potuit Virgo facere de Deo, quam Deus de seipso" (OOQ.II.375, Graef trans.).

214. "O, o, del latte de la Vergine Maria; o donne, dove sete voi? E anco voi, valenti uomini, vedestene mai? Sapete che si va mostrando per reliquie; non v'aviate fede, ché elli non è vero: elli se ne truova in tanti luoghi! Tenete che non è vero. Forse che ella fu una vacca la Vergine Maria, che ella avesse lassato il latte suo, come si lassa de le bestie, che si lassano mugniare?" (R.809).

215. Bernardino's attitude toward relics and other exaggerations of medieval piety, together with his emphasis on the importance of rationality and solid learning in the exercise of the religious life (both clerical and lay), has caused some critics in the past to champion him as an enlightened exponent of the new *docta pietas* of the then burgeoning Renaissance, in opposition to the supposed *sancta rusticitas* of the moribund medieval *forma mentis* of the "Dark Ages." For a discussion and correction of this view, see my essay "The Humanists, the Pagan Classics and S. Bernardino da Siena," 72–97.

216. "E però dice l'Ecclesiastes che 'l bu' e l'asino che era in Betheleem quando nacque el nostro Salvatore Gesù Cristo, che non toccavano el fieno dove era Cristo, per riverenza rendarli, et è anco a Roma quello fieno" (G.227; in neither Ecclesiastes nor Ecclesiasticus [Sirach] can any such statement be found; see Cannarozzi's note 10 at G.240–41).

217. "A portare un poco d'ulivo, per reverenza, è buono; così dell'altre cose, o vangeli, o orazioni, ma non colla intenzione cattiva, che faresti contro a Dio" (B.176–77). For the overlapping domains of magic and religion, see Kieckhefer, *Magic in the Middle Ages*, 14–16, and Russell, *Witchcraft in the Middle Ages*, 10–11.

218. Kieckhefer, *Magic in the Middle Ages*, 74, 85; Russell, *Witchcraft in the Middle Ages*, 215.

219. "Le dimonia al nome di Gesù fuggono e non ànno possanza. Á lasciato e donato Iddio el nome di Gesù prima agli Apostoli e poi a noi sopra le dimonia. . . . Nell'ultimo capitolo di san Marco, come t'ò detto più volte in questi dì, disse Gesù: 'Nel nome mio caccerete e dimoni eccetera.' . . . Sicchè il nome di Gesù è santo e terribile. Santo à santi e alle buone persone, terribile a' dimoni e alle cattive persone e agli uomini indimoniati. . . . E serpenti fuggono all'o[dore] de' fiori delle viti odorifichi. Così fuggono e dimoni per l'odore del nome di Gesù" (B.197–99).

220. See the letter of Franciscus Mei of Siena to Matthaeus of Siena, abbot of St. Pancrazio in Florence, published by Salvatore Tosti, "De praedicatione S. Bernardini Senensis in patria civitate, anno 1425," *AFH* 8 (1915): 678–80 (680 for the cures).

221. "Così, quando distese el collo al carnefice, el carnefice alzò la spada e tagliogli la testa, Gesù, amor mio!, gridò. Alzossi la testa da terra, Gesù, amor mio!, disse, e ricadde; e innalzossi tre volte dicendo Gesù, quasi dica: 'Io t'ò predicato da vivo, ora ti predico da morto. Ora, Gesù, amor mio, Gesù, amor mio!,' e così spirò e trovossi col suo Gesù nel santo paradiso" (B.213).

222. I would disagree with Origo's statement, "Fra Bernardino, however, unlike many other preachers of his time, refused to make use, in his maturity, of emotional and dramatic appeals of this [histrionic] nature" (Origo, *The World of San Bernardino*, 264, n. 15).

223. "Aut unde magos, ariolos, praestigiatores reprehendimus et dampnamus nisi quod quibusdam caracteribus fide adhibita, demonum responsa atque auxilia eliciunt? Totumque hoc genus sacrilegi est, pro rebus figuras amplecti." Biglia, "De institutis," 318.

224. Russell, *Witchcraft in the Middle Ages*, 9.

225. Ibid.

226. Bernardino is again unique in this respect among his Sienese contemporaries and peers; as Paton points out: "In keeping with the tendency of the Sienese theologians to discourage popular belief in the power of streghe, there is no suggestion in their literature that people should actively seek out and destroy and denounce witches and sorcerers. Indeed, the opposite may be said to be true" ("To the fire, to the fire!" 25).

227. "[F]ate che tutte sieno messe in esterminio per tal modo, che se ne perdi il seme; ch'io vi prometto che se non se ne fa un poco di sagrificio a Dio, voi ne vedrete vendetta ancora grandissima sopra a le vostre case, e sopra a la vostra città. . . . Doh, fate quello ch'io vi dico: datene un poco d'odore a Dominedio; non aspettate la vendetta di Dio" (R.1013).

228. "Fa' quello ch'io ti dico, acciò che tu non abbi a rendere ragione al dì del giudicio, avendo tu potuto fare stroppiare dimolto male, che si sarebbe stroppiato avendola acusata. Anco vi dico un'altra cosa, che come niuno o niuna ne sarà acusata, se persona andarà per aitarla, a la sua casa sarà mandata la maladizione da Dio, e resentirassene sì ne la robba e sì nel corpo, e anco poi nell'anima. . . . Per la qual cagione, se voi no ne fate qualche dimostrazione, elli v'averrà quello che di voi dice Michea profeta al V capitolo: 'Perdam civitates terre tue, et destruam omnes munitiones tuas, et auferam maleficia de manu tua, et divinationes non erunt in te.' A te so' dette queste cose, Siena" (R.1011, 1013).

229. Piana, "I processi di canonizzazione," 383.

230. "El tumulto è grande, el popolo fremisce. Era la chiesa e la piazza di santa Croce tutta piena di cittadini e di contadini, di donne e d'uomini ch'erano parecchie migliaia. El grido de' fanciugli, garzoni era grande che convenne che frate Bernardino lasciasse la predica e venne di chiesa in sulla piazza con molti frati, e fece ardere el capannuccio. . . . [M]ai vedesti el più bel fuoco, che andava infino all'aria la fiamma in confusione del dimonio nimico di Dio, e groria e

onore e lalde e reverenza del nostro Signore Gesù Cristo altissimo Iddio. El quale vive e regna in secula seculorum. Amen. Le grida che v'erano non dico, che pareva che fossono tuoni; e i pianti per tenerezza ch'era una gran divozione. Amen" (B.87–88). Another bonfire of vanities is described at G.199.

231. See Cardini's already cited article, "La predicazione popolare alle origini della caccia alle streghe," passim.

232. Levack, *The Witch-Hunt in Early Modern Europe*, 222–23.

233. Momentum had been gaining since 1390. See Kieckhefer, *Magic in the Middle Ages*, 194–95, and his *European Witch Trials*, 10–26, esp. 21; Russell, *Witchcraft in the Middle Ages*, 200, 225–28; and Levack, *The Witch-Hunt in Early Modern Europe*, 185–86. Indeed, Russell singles out 1427 (the year in which Bernardino preached to the Sienese about his Roman witch-trial experiences) as a landmark year: "What did happen, beginning in 1427, was the publication of quantities of theoretical discourses devoted exclusively to witchcraft, and a vast increase in the number and scope of the witch trials" (*Witchcraft in the Middle Ages*, 200. Russell, however, does not mention Bernardino in his account of medieval witchcraft).

234. Kieckhefer, *Magic in the Middle Ages*, 199–200.

235. Ibid., 195.

CHAPTER THREE

1. David Herlihy and Christiane Klapisch-Zuber, *Tuscans and Their Families: A Study of the Florentine Catasto of 1427* (New Haven: Yale University Press, 1978, abridged trans. of original 1978 French ed.), 252. Even on matters of sexuality, Bernardino is quite willing to "call a spade a spade." An example is his blunt 1427 Siena sermon on marriage (R.573–605), for which one critic—writing in 1915—roundly scolded the friar, disapproving of his "lack of prudence" in preaching such a sermon before a crowd including "innocent young girls and boys": "I would not hesitate to call [the sermon] truly scandalous. . . . The Saint puts forth his best excuses, but to us they seem entirely insufficient." Cosimo Faggiano, "L'eloquenza volgare di San Bernardino da Siena, saggio critico," *Rassegna nazionale* (Firenze) 206 (1915): 185–86.

2. Michael J. Rocke, "Sodomites in Fifteenth-Century Tuscany: The Views of Bernardino of Siena," in *The Pursuit of Sodomy: Male Homosexuality in Renaissance and Enlightenment Europe*, ed. Kent Gerard and Gert Hekma (New York: Harrington Park Press, 1989), 8. Rocke's pages on Bernardino are now included in his excellent study of Florence's special antisodomy magistracy, the Office of the Night (1432–1502), *Forbidden Friendships: Homosexuality and Male Culture in Renaissance Florence* (New York: Oxford University Press, 1996), 36–44 and passim. I am greatly indebted to Rocke's work in evaluating and contextualizing many of Bernardino's claims and observations about sodomy. For Bernardino and sodomy, see also Romano Canosa, *Storia di una grande paura. La sodomia a Firenze e a Venezia nel Quattrocento* (Milan: Feltrinelli, 1991), 24–35.

3. Rocke, *Forbidden Friendships*, 7.

4. Guido Ruggiero, *The Boundaries of Eros: Sex Crimes and Sexuality in Renaissance Venice* (New York: Oxford University Press, 1985); see also Michael Goodich, *The Unmentionable Vice: Homosexuality in the Later Medieval Period* (Santa Barbara: ABC-Clio, 1979).

5. John Boswell, *Christianity, Social Tolerance, and Homosexuality: Gay People in Western Europe from the Beginning of the Christian Era to the Fourteenth Century* (Chicago: University of Chicago Press, 1980), 269–302; David F. Greenberg, *The Construction of Homosexuality* (Chicago: University of Chicago Press, 1986), 268–98.

6. See the Latin sermon "De duodecim sceleribus propter quae Deus patrias et regna saepe iudicat et flagellat," OOQ.III.319–29.

7. The texts in question are: *De horrendo peccato contra naturam*, OOQ.III.267–84; "Contra soddomiam," OOQ.IX.427–30; "De amore lamentanti" and "De amore condemnante," Padua 1423, OOH.III.190–94; "Del vizio dei sodomiti," "Della sodomia," and "Della dannazione dei sodomiti," Florence 1424, B.30–71; "Del peccato contra natura," Florence 1425, C.270–90; "Questa è la predica dello vizio della sodomia," Siena 1425, G.98–112; and "In questa reprende l'abominabile peccato della maladetta soddomia," Siena 1427, R.1139–68. The 1425 sermons preached in Perugia and Assisi have not been published; for a complete list and extracts, see Pacetti, "La predicazione di San Bernardino da Siena a Perugia e ad Assisi nel 1425," *CF* IX (1939): 494–520 and X (1940): 5–28, 161–88; for the sodomy sermons, IX: 506, X: 16, 166–69, 181, 187. A contemporary Perugian chronicler notes that Bernardino visited that city again on August 27, 1438, preaching against "ingratitude toward God" and sodomy (*Cronache della città di Perugia*, ed. Ariodante Fabretti [Turin: "Coi tipi privati dell'Editore," 1888], 21).

8. "E come noi predichiamo in questo Campo, così si vorrebbe predicare in ogni cortina di Siena, in ogni casa, in ogni buttiga, in ogni cantone, in ogni stalla; ché non credo che ci sia luogo che non sia contaminato e corrotto" (R.1152).

9. "Ista bestia est pessima sodomia quae regnat super terram" (OOH.III.188).

10. "Siquidem quaedam patriae in tantum hoc scelere sunt infectae . . . ut quodammodo publice in aliquibus civitatibus horrendum gymnasium constituerint, palaestram in illius flagitii abominatione exercentes, ita ut optimi epheborum in lupanari sodomiae ponantur" (OOQ.III.270).

11. It is an anachronism to say that the Bible condemns "homosexuality"; what it condemns is same-sex genital activity, although, expressing an exegetical opinion that is gaining currency among scholars, Daniel Helminiak maintains that "the Bible nowhere condemns same-sex acts in themselves" (*What the Bible* Really *Says About Homosexuality* [San Francisco: Alamo Square Press, 1994], 100). Hence the inaccuracy of the New American Bible's and New Jerusalem Bible's translation of 1 Timothy 10. One wonders why the NJB put the word *homosexual* in place of the phrase "those who are immoral . . . with boys or men," used in its first edition. "English translations of the lists of sinners at 1 Corinthians 6:9 and 1 Timothy 1:10 appear to the non-specialist to be precise and concrete renderings of specific Greek words, but in fact there is very considerable uncertainty about the meaning of many of the words involved," Boswell, *Christianity, Social Tolerance*, 337.

12. Greenberg reminds us that in Arabic and Greek medicine, medieval Christianity had found "non-voluntaristic," physiological explanations of the causes of "homosexuality," which, however, it chose to ignore, excising these passages from their translations: "When it came to homosexuality, few thinkers were able to overcome the ideological hegemony of the church" (*Construction*, 278–79).

13. See Ficino's *Commentary on Plato's Symposium*, *oratio* 6, chap. 14; and discussion by Giovanni Dall'Orto, "'Socratic Love' as a Disguise for Same-Sex Love in the Italian Renaissance," in *The Pursuit of Sodomy*, 33–65). In his 1992 study of Renaissance Italy, "La fenice di Sodoma. Essere omosessuale nell'Italia del Rinascimento" (in *History of Homosexuality in Europe and America*, ed. Wayne R. Dynes and Stephen Donaldson [New York: Garland, 1992], 61–83), Dall'Orto uses the terms *sodomite* and *homosexual* interchangeably, not accepting, one presumes, the crucial difference in understanding of human behavior and psychology implied by those terms. Yet this is a departure from the stance taken in his above-cited essay on Socratic love, in which he does acknowledge the distinction and suggests that we employ the less troublesome

and more inclusive term *homoeroticism* as a means to avoid the lexical-philosophical impasse (" 'Socratic Love,' " 34). The terms *sodomite* and *homosexual*, although overlapping, are by no means coextensive. In reality, the evidence Dall'Orto presents in his later essay, "La fenice di Sodoma," refers at most to a self-aware subculture of men who like to penetrate or be penetrated by other men, that is to say, sodomites; it does not describe necessarily homosexuals, that is to say, men who romantically love other males and want to commit themselves in enduring emotional relationships to men, penetration being a non-essential factor in their identity. For example, according to contemporary categories, Michelangelo was not a sodomite, inasmuch as he was never known to have engaged in sodomy as then defined. But he did love other males passionately and erotically, as his highly explicit love poetry indicates, and would thus today be considered a "homosexual."

14. See Joseph Cady, " 'Masculine Love,' Renaissance Writing, and the 'New Invention' of Homosexuality," *Journal of Homosexuality* 23 (1992): 9–40. For the Renaissance and homosexuality, see, for example, the two essays by Dall'Orto cited in the previous note; Jonathan Goldberg, *Sodometries: Renaissance Texts, Modern Sexualities* (Stanford: Stanford University Press, 1992); and James M. Saslow, "Homosexuality in the Renaissance: Behavior, Identity, and Artistic Expression," in *Hidden from History: Reclaiming the Gay and Lesbian Past*, ed. Martin B. Duberman, Martha Vicinus, and George Chauncey, Jr. (New York: New American Library, 1989), 90–105, with ample bibliography.

15. "As defined by the ancient civil or canonical codes, sodomy was a category of forbidden acts; their perpetrator was nothing more than the juridical subject of them. The nineteenth-century homosexual became a personage, a past, a case history, and a childhood, in addition to being a type of life, a life form, and a morphology. . . . Nothing that went into his total composition was unaffected by his sexuality. It was everywhere present in him. . . . It was consubstantial with him. . . . The sodomite had been a temporary aberration; the homosexual was now a species" (Foucault, *The History of Sexuality. Volume 1: An Introduction* [New York: Vintage, 1978], 43). On the same page, Foucault notes that the birth of the modern concept of the homosexual coincides with the publication of "Westphal's famous article of 1870 on 'contrary sexual sensations.' "

16. The debated questions are three: First, is it true that, before the nineteenth century and the advent of modern depth psychology and sociology, there was simply no analogous understanding of the homosexually oriented individual in the West, only that of the person who engaged in isolated acts of same-sex genitality? Second, in view of the fact that before the year 1870 the word *homosexual* or its equivalent was missing from the European vocabulary, is it true that the person himself or herself was also missing from the social scene? In other words, is it true that not even those persons engaging frequently and exclusively in same-gender sexual activity can be called "homosexual" because of the great difference in understanding (or self-understanding) implied by the two words *sodomite* and *homosexual*? Finally, is sexual orientation, homosexual or heterosexual, merely a historically relative product of culture and society, or is it a universal, involuntary, fixed, inherent quality of the human species? This last question finds the "social constructionist" theory pitted against the "essentialist theory," or, as John Boswell labels the two opposing sides, the "nominalists" versus the "realists" (Boswell, "Revolutions, Universals and Sexual Categories," in *Hidden from History*, 18–19). However, Boswell remarks: "I would no longer characterize the constructionist-essentialist controversy as a 'debate' in any strict sense: One of its ironies is that no one involved in it actually identifies him- or herself as an 'essentialist,' although constructionists (of whom there are many) sometimes so label other writers" (ibid., 34–35). Boswell's 1989 essay is an excellent summary discussion of

the theoretical question in all of its complexity (it can also be found in somewhat different form in *Salmagundi*, nos. 58–59 [Fall 1982–Winter 1983]: 89–113). For further elaboration, see also his 1990 essay "Concepts, Experience, and Sexuality," in which he concludes: "Primary ancient and medieval sexual constructs were unrelated to the modern differentiation between homosexual and heterosexual 'orientation,' 'identity,' or 'preference.' This does not mean that there was no awareness of specifically homosexual or heterosexual 'orientation' in earlier societies. Much evidence indicates that these were common and familiar concepts, which received little attention in the records of these cultures not because few people recognized them, but because they had little social or ethical impact" ("Concepts, Experience, and Sexuality," *Differences: A Journal of Feminist Cultural Studies* 2 [1990]: 81). However, with respect to medieval culture, Boswell makes an important exception: "most ancient and medieval writers *other than theologians* do in fact evince awareness of a basic dimorphism in sexual attraction . . . even theologians do *when writing about something other than theology*" (ibid., 77, emphasis added).

17. Though it now seems that ancient Greek and Roman society may well have had some notion of what we would today call the homosexually oriented person, representing a distinct psychological type and subculture, that "pagan" notion appears not to have passed into and is missing from the written codes of the Judeo-Christian moral-theological mainstream. See Amy Richlin, "Not Before Homosexuality: The Materiality of the *Cinaedus* and the Roman Law against Love between Men," *Journal of the History of Sexuality* 3, 4 (1993): 523–73. Yet the title of Richlin's article is misleading (she admits "the current title is provocative rather than exact" [574]). Although she entitles her work "Not Before Homosexuality," she cautions: "The firm starting point is that the modern term 'homosexuality' cannot be used of Greek or Roman sexual practice without a good deal of qualification" (525). Hence her discussion of Roman law is by no means a refutation of the Foucault thesis. Dall'Orto ("La fenice di Sodoma," 76–79) affirms the Foucault thesis about the official canonical-theological understanding of sodomy, but denies that "the people" (especially the sodomites themselves) ever subscribed to this official understanding of "the powers that be." It seems to me that Dall'Orto posits too large, too universal, and too clean a distinction between what the Church ("il Potere," "gli oppressori") taught and what the "people" ("gli oppressi") believed. Dall'Orto is also to be faulted for using Bernardino's utterances—in a subsection entitled "Autocoscienza ed autogiustificazione" (1992, 69–73)—as evidence for the interior state of the sodomite. For more on this epistemological debate, see David M. Halperin, "One Hundred Years of Homosexuality," in *One Hundred Years of Homosexuality and Other Essays on Greek Love* (New York and London: Routledge, 1990), 15–40; Arthur N. Gilbert, "Conceptions of Homosexuality and Sodomy in Western History," in *The Gay Past: A Collection of Historical Essays*, ed. Salvatore J. Licata and Robert P. Petersen (New York: Harrington Park Press, 1985), 57–68; Bruce R. Smith, *Homosexual Desire in Shakespeare's England: A Cultural Poetics* (Chicago: University of Chicago Press, 1991), 2–29; and Robert Padgug, "Sexual Matters: Rethinking Sexuality in History," in *Hidden from History*, 54–64.

18. The preacher's rapid canonization only six years after his death is testimony enough to his status among his contemporaries as an orthodox teacher. In contrast to Bernardino and the theological mainstream, Thomas Aquinas (who did not become the supreme theological arbiter of the Catholic Church until centuries after his death) followed Aristotle in believing that homoerotic desire was congenital. This did not prevent him, however, from condemning homoerotic behavior as abominably sinful. In reality, Thomas's discussion of sodomy or "the sins against nature" is riddled with contradiction, ambiguity, and incoherence, as Boswell demonstrates in *Christianity, Social Tolerance*, 318–30. See also Michael Crowe, "St. Thomas and Ulpian's Natural Law," in *St. Thomas Aquinas, 1274–1974, Commemorative Studies* (Toronto:

Pontifical Institute for Mediaeval Studies, 1974), 261–82; and Mark Jordan, *The Invention of Sodomy in Christian Theology* (Chicago: University of Chicago Press, 1997), 136–58.

19. "Guai a chi non toglie moglie avendo tempo e cagione legittima! chè non pigliandola doventano soddomiti" (A.416). As we saw in chap. 1, Bernardino had a paternal uncle, Angelo, who never married: we wonder what the young Bernardino's experience of this uncle was.

20. Yet at the same time, without realizing the implied contradictions of his remarks, Bernardino states that sodomites hate women and that this hatred is reciprocal (announced allegorically by Genesis 3:15). One of the places where he announces this is in Articulus II, Capitulum II ("Quod ex malitia serpentina gomorrhaei odiunt mulieres") of *De horrendo peccato contra naturam* (OOQ.III.276–79); see also D.276 and R.1158. The preacher tells the Paduans that the Devil has blinded the sodomites to the beauty of women: "so much so that even if they could have the most beautiful women in the world, they wouldn't touch them" ("Et vide ad quam caecitatem inducit diabolus istos; quia si possent habere pulchriores foeminas mundi non tangerent eas"; OOH.III.189a).

21. See Genesis 19:8; Bernardino, as we shall see, recounts and comments upon this biblical episode.

22. "That Utterly Confused Category" is the title of Jonathan Goldberg's introduction to his *Sodometries: Renaissance Texts, Modern Sexualities.* See also Vern L. Bullough, "The Sin against Nature and Homosexuality," in *Sexual Practices and the Medieval Church,* ed. Vern L. Bullough and James Brundage (Buffalo: Prometheus Books, 1982), 55–71; and Warren Johansson and William A. Percy, "Homosexuality," in *Handbook of Medieval Sexuality,* ed. Vern L. Bullough and James A. Brundage (New York: Garland, 1996), 155–89.

23. *Invention of Sodomy,* 160. Jordan's book is an excellent analysis of the birth and evolution of the theological concept of sodomy, focusing especially on Peter Damian, Alain of Lille, Albert the Great, and Thomas Aquinas.

24. See Helminiak, *What the Bible* Really *Says About Homosexuality,* passim; Robin Scroggs, *The New Testament and Homosexuality: Contextual Background for Contemporary Debate* (Philadelphia: Fortress Press, 1983), 99–122; Tom Horner, *Jonathan Loved David: Homosexuality in Biblical Times* (Philadelphia: Westminster Press, 1978), 93–99; Boswell, *Christianity, Social Tolerance,* 335–53; and James A. Brundage, *Law, Sex, and Christian Society in Medieval Europe* (Chicago: University of Chicago Press, 1987), 533–56.

25. "Che viene a dire contro a natura? Ogni volta che usi contro a naturale use, cioè in forma che non possa ingenerare e ingravidare" (A.388). For Bernardino and the marriage debt, see Dyan Elliott, "Bernardino of Siena versus the Marriage Debt," in *Desire and Discipline: Sex and Sexuality in the Premodern West,* ed. Jacqueline Murray and Konrad Eisenbichler (Toronto: University of Toronto Press, 1996), 168–200.

26. "Contro a natura è soddomia, e altri atti contro a natura in femmine e maschi" (A.389). The scribe may have left out parts of Bernardino's discussion of this topic, for this *reportatio* is filled with truncated sentences and other lacunae.

27. "Contro natura non operare. . . . Ogni volta che tu passi il modo ragionevole, tu fai contra natura. . . . ogni volta che usano insieme per modo che non si potrebbe ingenerare, ogni volta è peccato mortale" (R.588). Bernardino repeats the same "definition" at OOH.III.203b. Procreation, the continuation of the species, was a major factor in the condemnation of sodomy and other nonprocreative sexual activity (such as masturbation). This principle, in reality, involved the Church in considerable contradiction inasmuch as vowed religious life, that is, volontary celibacy, was taught to be the most virtuous form of Christian life; see Boswell, *Christianity, Social Tolerance,* 322.

28. *Summa theologica*, pars 2, titulus 5 ("De luxuria"), caput IV ("De vitio contra naturam") (Verona 1740; reprint, Graz 1959), 667–73. For the date of the *Summa*, see Howard, *Beyond the Written Word*, 30.

29. "[Q]uatuor sunt gradus istius bestiarum vitii: 1.—molliciei; 2.—immodalitatis; 3.—bestialitatis; 4.—sodomie." "De sodomia," in Iacobus de Marchia, *Sermones dominicales*, 1:450.

30. "Aliquando enim quis operatur turpitudinem in semetipso, et dicitur mollities; aliquando vero cum alio vel alia, et hoc contingit multipliciter, cum scilicet masculus cum femina in membro non ad hoc concesso, vel femina inordinate cum viro; deinde, cum masculus cum masculo vel femina cum femina; ultimo cum fit cum re irrationalis," *Summa theologica* (Quaracchi: Collegio San Bonaventura, 1930), 3:653.

31. Alexander of Hales, *Summa theologica*, vol. 4, part 2, 697.

32. Brundage, *Law, Sex, and Christian Society*, 533.

33. Rocke, *Forbidden Friendships*, 46.

34. This is true of all premodern sexual vocabulary in general, a confusion that "still bedevils many of our discussions of sexuality in the past: it is not always easy to know precisely which activities our sources are referring to," Nicholas Davidson, "Theology, Nature and the Law: Sexual Sin and Sexual Crime in Italy from the Fourteenth to the Seventeenth Century," in *Crime, Society and the Law in Renaissance Italy*, ed. Trevor Dean and K. J. P. Lowe (Cambridge: Cambridge University Press, 1994), 76.

35. As Rocke notes, "Virtually all of the contemporary novelle on homoerotic themes, from Boccaccio on, feature the love of mature youths or men for adolescents or young *garzoni*" (*Forbidden Friendships*, 95).

36. See also D.272: "Santo Geronimo: Amore della forma, cioè del garzone." Bernardino uses the same passage from Jerome in his Latin treatise on sodomy, making no additions to the original text. The friar, however, concludes: "Et licet de qualibet insania carnali intelligatur, de hoc tamen scelere tanto proprius intelligi habet, quanto prae ceteris aufert iudicium rationis" ("And although this passage is to be understood as referring to any form of carnal insanity, it is, however, so much more properly to be understood as referring to this wickedness [of sodomy] since it robs one of reason more than any other [form of lust]") (OOQ.III.269).

37. "Elli fu, non ha anco uno anno, uno famoso sodomitto in una terra, che si ritrovava la notte con uno fanciullo nel letto . . ." (R.1157). The target of Bernardino's story is hypocrisy: this "famous sodomite" protests against public preaching on such "dirty" matters in the presence of impressionable young people. See also R.1162 for another reference to the sodomite and his "garzone."

38. Rocke, *Forbidden Friendships*, 87–88; see also 12–13. However, as Rocke points out about fifteenth-century Florentine sexual vocabulary: "While [the term *sodomite*] included both a man who had sex with boys and a man who engaged in the same illicit sexual acts with women, it virtually never included their 'passive' partners of either sex" (ibid., 14).

39. Herlihy and Klapisch-Zuber, *Tuscans and Their Families*, 210–11; see also Christiane Klapisch-Zuber, "Childhood in Tuscany at the Beginning of the Fifteenth Century," in *Women, Family, and Ritual in Renaissance Italy* (Chicago: University of Chicago Press, 1985), 110.

40. Rocke, *Forbidden Friendships*, 12, 88.

41. Ruggiero, *Boundaries of Eros*, 118.

42. Alexander of Hales, *Summa theologica*, 3:654, quoting the *Glossa*. The Vulgate version of Genesis 37:2 quoted by Bernardino is "Ioseph accusavit fratres suos apud patrem crimine pessimo." Antonino of Florence also gives the same identification of this "crimine pessimo" of Joseph's brothers (*Summa theologica*, pars 2, titulus 5, caput 4, 673B). The New Revised

Standard Version renders the text as "Joseph brought a bad report of them to their father." Joseph, by the way, was obliged to confront the "sin against nature" again in the person of Potiphar, his Egyptian eunuch-master, who purchased him as a slave precisely with this "filthy use" in mind; so Antonino of Florence informs us (*Summa theologica*, 672D).

43. "Exemplum: quidam sotius meus dixit mihi se vidisse medium porcum et medium hominem, natum de suse, pendentem in Sessorio Salerni. Item, in Visso capud [*sic*] castroni, reliquum hominem. Item, in Sclavonia de vacca medium hominem et medium bovem. Item, quidam dixit mihi se vidisse in Camorano, conmitatus Anchone, puerum natum habentem os canis et dentes et residuum hominis et aures quasi asini." (Giacomo's list goes on.) "De sodomia," *Sermones dominicales*, 451–52.

44. I deliberately avoid the term *lesbianism* with reference to Bernardino's preaching for the same reasons I avoid the term *homosexuality;* it too bespeaks an understanding of human psychology and sexuality unavailable to the friar and his contemporaries.

45. This is a reference to the Vulgate, Psalm 57:4 (58:3 in the NRSV), "Alienati sunt peccatores a vulva," "the wicked go astray from the womb."

46. "Huiusmodi peccatores, exigente ignorantia et caecitate eorum, *a vulva* dicuntur . . . *nam feminae eorum immutaverunt naturalem usum in eum qui est contra naturam*, id est contra naturalis legis instinctum, ordinationem ac determinationem, ut scilicet feminae feminas pollueremt" (OOQ.III.268; the italicized portions represent direct quotations from Scripture).

47. The whole passage reads: "Perchè si chiamò giudicio di sodomia la iniquità? Perchè è contro all'equità della generazione delle umane creature, e contro al crescimento del cielo. Ezechiel profeta, al quinto capitolo, tre volte grida contro alla iniquità: 'Iniquità, iniquità, iniquità' per tre modi. Come si commette? O maschio con femina, o maschio con maschio, o femina con femina" (E.99). Bernardino says that the "Iniquity" exclamation comes from Ezekiel 5, but this is erroneous; what we do find in Ezekiel 21:27 (as Cannarozzi, the sermon's editor, points out [E.112]) is the cry: "A ruin, a ruin, a ruin."

48. "Se una donna di voi si spogliasse innuda, e fusse costà ritta . . . a quanti uomini *e donne* credi che venisse tentazione? Io ti dico, solo per vedere, a molti e molti" (R.478–79, emphasis added).

49. Origo, *The World of San Bernardino*, 44. Bernardino's sermons contain numerous direct addresses to women, who must have been present in conspicuously large numbers. As Origo points out, the public sermon was one of "the so few gatherings to which an honest woman could go" in those days, seeking escape from the cloistered labor of the home.

50. Albertus Magnus, Thomas Aquinas, and Bernardino's contemporary, Antonino of Florence, do take account of it. Greenberg, *Construction*, 274–75.

51. Canosa, *Grande Paura*, 24. Another documented reference to female homogenital activity is found in a mid-thirteenth-century penal code of Orleans that called for the amputation of a limb for the first two offenses and for burning at the stake for a third (ibid., 20). See also Jacqueline Murray, "Twice Marginal and Twice Invisible: Lesbians in the Middle Ages," in *Handbook of Medieval Sexuality*, 191–222, and Judith C. Brown, "Lesbian Sexuality in Medieval and Early Modern Europe," in *Hidden from History*, 67–75.

52. John J. McNeill, *The Church and the Homosexual*, 4th ed. (Boston: Beacon Press, 1993), 85–87; Canosa, *Grande Paura*, 163, which cites L. Crompton, "The Myth of Lesbian Impunity. Capital Laws from 1270 to 1791," *Journal of Homosexuality* 6 (1980–81). With respect to the link between "sodomophobia" and misogyny, Mark Jordan observes, "It is hard to find a single condemnation [of sodomy] in the theological tradition that does not rely on misogynistic logic" (*Invention of Sodomy*, 169). See also Beverly Wildung Harrison, "Misogyny and Homophobia:

The Unexplored Connections," in *Making the Connections: Essays in Feminist Social Ethics,* ed. Carol S. Robb (Boston: Beacon Press, 1985), 135–51.

53. "E porci domestici sono quegli che più a scoperta faccia, non curandosi nè d'onore nè di vergogna di mondo, con parenti e cor ogni materia; mariti indimoniati colle loro donne medesime. Cose da scurare el sole!" (B.33–34).

54. "Non solum autem in maribus, verum etiam in feminis, et maxime in sacro matrimonio constitutis, hoc scelus abominabile est. Unde XXXII, quaest. 7, in can. *Adulterii,* Augustinus ait: 'Adulterii malum vincit fornicationem, vincitur autem ab incestu; peius est enim cum matre quam cum aliena uxore concumbere; sed omnium horum pessimum est quod contra naturam fit, ut si et vir membro mulieris non ad hoc concesso uti voluerit.' Sequitur: 'Iste [usus] qui est contra naturam, exsecrabiliter quidem fit in meretrice, sed exsecrabilius in uxore' " (OOQ.III.275).

55. "Ex his verbis Augustini patet quod horribilius est abuti contra naturam uxore, quam adulterari vel fornicari cum propria matre" (OOQ.III.275–76). See also OOQ.I.209–10 and R.588–89.

56. "Oooh! Io ho saputo cose! . . . Aou! Una volta io mi trovai in luogo che uno avendo preso una bella giovana per moglie, ella era stata sei anni con lui, e anco era vergine: la quale era stata co' lui sempre in peccato gravissimo contra natura. O confusione, o vergogna grandissima! Ou, ou, ou! Sai come questa povaretta era fatta? Ell'era consumata, defunta, palida, smorta. Ella mi si racomandò per l'amore di Dio, dicendomi, s'io potessi per niuno modo, ch'io l'aitasse, dicendomi come ella era stata al vescovo per questa cagione, e anco al podestà; e quali dice che rispondevano a lei, che di ciò ch'ella diceva, bisognavano le pruove. O che ignoranzia è questa che e' bisogni le pruove, e' testimoni a queste cose! Un cappanello bisognarebbe, un cappanello! . . . che se io l'avesse a fare, io farei. . . . Uuuh! '*Zelus domus tue commedit me.*' El zelo della tua casa m'ha divorato, che pure a pensarlo, mi sento tutto consumare" (R.591). As Ruggiero notes with respect to fifteenth-century Venice's prosecution of sodomy: "Even when violence was involved, there was considerable hesitancy about being as strict with heterosexual acts labeled sodomy as with similar homosexual acts" (*Boundaries of Eros,* 120).

57. "Item tu sacerdos quum confitearis aliquam foeminam quae conqueratur quod eius maritus abutatur ea vitio sodomiae, vadas subito ad episcopum ut separet illum thorum" (OOH.III.203b).

58. "Quaestio. Sed numquid propter hoc scelus potest uxor dimittere virum suum?—Respondet *Glossa,* XXXII, quaest. 7, in can. *Omnes,* super verbo 'sodomita,' dicens: 'Videtur quod maritus possit dimitti propter sodomiticum opus; XXXII, quaest. 7, *Adulterii;* ibi dicitur quod illud crimen adulterio maius est.—Item. Quid dices, si propriam uxorem polluit extra claustrum pudoris, vel seipsum polluit propriis manibus? Numquid ob hoc dimitti potest? Videtur quod sic, quia nomine moechiae omnis illicitus concubitus et illicitus membrorum usus continetur, ut XXXII, quaest. 4, *Meretrices,* et canone sequenti; quod Laurentius [Hispanus] concedit. Vix credo quod propter aliquod istorum possit dimitti vir, ut XXXV, quaest. 3, *Ordinaria.*' Haec *Glossa.* Primum tenet Huguccio et Raymundus in *Summa* sua, rubrica de numero testium. Innocentius contra, Extra, *De divortiis,* cap. l" (OOQ.III.277; see the footnotes to that page for a complete identification of the legal texts here cited). Earlier Bernardino had also evoked the authority of Bonaventure on this issue, but deferred the question until the paragraph we have just quoted: "Proinde Bonaventura, in IV, dist. 38, super litteram, ait 'quod secundum quosdam propter hoc peccatum, scilicet contra naturam cum uxore, potest uxor dimittere et fugere virum'; sed de hoc infra dicetur" (OOQ.III.276).

59. *Summa Theologica,* pars 2, titulus 5, caput. 4, 672D. Giacomo della Marca announces the same permission in his sermon on sodomy ("De sodomia," in *Sermones dominicales,* 3 vols., ed. Renato Lioi [Falconara Marittima: Biblioteca Francescana, 1978], 1:462).

60. Bullough, "Sin against Nature," 56–57, paraphrasing John Noonan, Jr., *Contraception: A History of Its Treatment by the Catholic Theologians and Canonists* (Cambridge: Harvard University Press, 1966), 75. For the problems with Thomas Aquinas's definition and use of "natural law," see Boswell, *Christianity, Social Tolerance and Homosexuality,* 318–30; Crowe, "St. Thomas and Ulpian's Natural Law"; and more generally on the problems, logical and otherwise, with Aquinas's analysis of sodomy, Jordan, *Invention of Sodomy,* 136–58.

61. "Haec scelera perpetrentur a talibus gomorrhaeis Ieremias declarat, cum subdit: *et libent,* id est libenter sacrificent, *diis alienis,* id est daemonibus inferorum. . . . [G]omorrhaei tot filios daemonibus libant, quot saltem filios ex hoc scelere perdunt" (OOQ.III.269–70). St. Paul also associates the sexual "degradation" of the pagans with idolatry in Romans 1:25.

62. "Chi adora questa bestia? E sodomiti. E come dice la Scrittura, el ventre loro è il loro Iddio. Come tu ami più una cosa che Iddio, quella cosa è il tuo Iddio. E dice: Chi adora la bestia o la immagine sua. Quale è la immagine sua? L'apparenza della garzonaglia innanzi agli occhi de' sodomiti, mentali e corporali" (B.59).

63. "Unde Deus dedit praeceptum, Non coli plures Deos. *Deus enim tuus unus est;* sed sodomitae faciunt plures Deos, quia amant plures pueros" (OOH.III.189a). In the same passage, Bernardino describes how sodomy is a sin against several of the other Ten Commandments as well. The friar had probably covered the entire Decalogue in this sermon, but only seven were recorded by the scribe.

64. R.588–89, OOQ.I.209–10, III.275–76.

65. "Dicono e dottori che niuna cosa dispiace tanto a Dio quanto fa el peccato contro a natura [B.64–65]; Più pena sente [in inferno] uno che sia vissuto con questo vizio de la sodomia, che un altro; però che questo è maggior peccato che sia [R.1164]; Subdit etiam Iob quod tale scelus est iniquitas maxima" (OOQ.III.272). Antonino agrees with Bernardino on this point: "est superlativum mali, et peius dici non potest," *Summa theologica,* pars 2, titulus 5, caput 4, 669D.

66. "Blasphemia omnia mala in se comprehendit et superexcedit. . . . blasphemia immediatius quam cetera vitia offendi Deum. . . . illum blasphemando, lingua blasphemantis efficiatur quai gladius cor Dei penetrans et ensis Deum utique scindens" (OOQ.II.8–9; see also A.446–51 and F.148–49).

67. In several Italian cities of the late Middle Ages and Renaissance, the governing bodies paid scholars to deliver public readings from and lectures on the *Divine Comedy.* Boccaccio performed this service for Florence in the latter portion of his life, while in Siena, beginning in 1396, it was Bernardino's own teacher of the trivium, Giovanni di Buccio da Spoleto. See Rossi, "La 'Lectura Dantis' nello Studio senese," 153–74, and Nardi, "Appunti sui maestri e gli studi giovanili di San Bernardino da Siena," 201–22. For Bernardino's recommendation of Dante as most suitable spiritual reading for his audiences, see C.305; see also C.311–12 for more praise of Dante, and the discussion thereof in my own study, "The Vernacular Sermons of San Bernardino da Siena," 4–5.

68. "Iddio versò sempre sopra questo peccato l'ira sua più che sopra a niun altro" (D.277).

69. "O Sodoma, o Gomorra con quelle altre città, perché fusti tu somersa? . . . questo peccato tanto dispiacente a Dio, che per suo giudicio fece sonnabissare tante città per solo questo peccato" (R.1146).

70. D.277, OOQ.III.274 and accompanying n. 6.

71. "Immo aliqui doctores dicunt quod Deus adeo abominatur hoc vitium, quod cum difficultate permisit filium incarnari ea carne quam videbat adeo turpiter contaminari" (OOH.III.189b).

72. Antonino of Florence repeats the same information in his *Summa theologicae,* pars 2, titulus 5, caput 4, 670E, most likely taking it from the *Decretum* or some common medieval

reference work. Yet exactly where in Augustine (if he indeed is the correct source) is not known, as the Quaracchi editors note (OOQ.III.276, n. 3).

73. For the licitness of intercourse during menstruation as a prevention of sodomy, see A.387–88 and OOH.III.203a–b; for birth defects and menstruation, see R.592: "La cagione si è perché se si generasse in tal tempo, nascono poi figliuoli mostruosi o lebrosi, e mai la creatura che nasce generata in tal tempo non è senza grande e notabile difetto."

74. "E però, o donna, impara questo stamane, e legatelo al dito: se 'l tuo marito ti richiede di nulla che sia peccato contra natura, non li consentire mai. . . . E se pure fusse opressata, che elli ti minacciasse di volerti fare e dire, prima sostiene la morte, che tu facci tal peccato. E se elli t'uccidesse per quello, sappi e siene certa che l'anima tua andarà subito nella gloria di vita eterna. Avetemi inteso?" (R.590–91). Bernardino repeats this advice (better for the wife to die than to submit to sodomy) at A.388 and OOH.III.203b.

75. "O benedetti figliuoli piccoletti che ve n'andaste per la moria, che almeno non fuste voi contaminati di tal peccato! Voi state dinanzi a Dio, e cantate quello canto con lui insieme, che nol può cantare se non solo i vergini" (R.1142).

76. "O donne, fate che voi non mandiate più attorno i vostri figliuoli: mandate le vostre figliuole, ché non v'è pericolo niuno, se voi le mandate fra tali genti . . . e se pure elle fussero prese e disonestate, almeno non v'è elli tanto pericolo e tanto peccato, quanto è quello" (R.1155).

77. For a similar case, see also the Book of Judges 19:22–24, in which the unnamed host offers his own maiden daughter or a concubine to the men of Gibeah who want to rape his male guest.

78. "Allora vedendo Lot la loro pessima intenzione, e perché non facessero quello peccato, disse: 'Io ho qui in casa due mie figliuole: io ve le voglio dare, e fatene a vostro modo, e lassate stare questi due giovani servi di Dio' " (R.1147).

79. Richard C. Trexler, *Public Life in Renaissance Florence* (New York: Academic Press, 1980), 380. See also Greenberg, *Construction*, 283, n. 217: "The argument [for prostitution as a preventive of male sodomy] rests implicitly on the assumption that men would readily substitute one sex for another." However, as Deanna Shemek points out, "the Florentine effort to promote male heterosexual activity through legal prostitution backfired when women in the brothel found that their business improved if they themselves dressed up as men" ("Circular Definitions: Configuring Gender in Italian Renaissance Festival," *Renaissance Quarterly* 48 [1995]: 18). For more on prostitution in the period, see Brundage, *Law, Sex and Christian Society in Medieval Europe*, 521–30; Ruth Mazo Karras, *Common Women: Prostitution and Sexuality in Medieval England* (Oxford: Oxford University Press, 1996) and her summary article "Prostitution in Medieval Europe," in *Handbook of Medieval Sexuality*, 243–60; Maria Serena Mazzi, *Prostitute e lenoni nella Firenze del Quattrocento* (Milan: Mondadori/Il Saggiatore, 1991); and Jacques Rossiaud, *Medieval Prostitution*, trans. Lydia G. Cochrane (New York: Blackwell, 1988).

80. McCall, *The Medieval Underworld*, 180.

81. "[I]t was apparently a common belief among the laity that fornication was not really culpable, save when it was indulged in by monks, nuns, or married persons," James A. Brundage, "Adultery and Fornication: A Study in Legal Theology," in *Sexual Practices and the Medieval Church*, 131.

82. What was apparently Bernardino's stock sermon on Mary Magdalene has come down to us in several versions, each following the same outline: the Latin treatise, *De ardentissimo amore sanctissimae Magdalenae* (OOQ.IV.417–39), and *reportationes* of public sermons delivered in the vernacular on three separate occasions: Padua, 1423 (OOH.III.267–72, transcribed in Latin); Florence, 1424 (B.138–55), and Florence, 1425 (E.179–98). See OOH.III.269a–b for the list of

male traps. For an analysis of Bernardino's portrait of the Magdalene, see my study " 'Virtual Death' in the Middle Ages: The Apotheosis of Mary Magdalene in Popular Preaching," in *Death and Dying in the Middle Ages*, ed. Edelgard E. DuBruck and Barbara I. Gusick (New York: Peter Lang, forthcoming).

83. Piana, "I processi di canonizzazione," 383. The *Vita anonima* also mentions the friar's success in persuading prostitutes to reform their lives and marry (325, s. 26), as does Maffeo Vegio, *Vita sancti Bernardini*, 3.22.123F.

84. Romans 1:26–27 is only quickly noted in the friar's sermons (e.g., B.47–48, D.272, and OOQ.III.268), while Genesis 19 returns as a frequent reference. The other classic passages are Leviticus 18:22, Leviticus 20:13, 1 Corinthians 6:9–10, and 1 Timothy 1:8–10. For a critique of the traditional reading of these texts, see Helminiak, *What the Bible* Really *Says About Homosexuality*, passim; Scroggs, *The New Testament and Homosexuality*, passim; and Horner, *Jonathan Loved David: Homosexuality in Biblical Times*, 93–99; or, in more summary fashion, Vincent J. Genovesi, *In Pursuit of Love: Catholic Morality and Human Sexuality* (Wilmington: Glazier, 1987), 262–73, and McNeill, *The Church and the Homosexual*, chaps. 2 and 3. However, the principal scriptural passages out of which Bernardino weaves his sodomy sermons are John 5:8 ("Rise, take up your mat, and walk"), Psalm 14:1 ("They are corrupt, they do abominable deeds; there is no one who does good"), and Psalm 58:3 ("The wicked go astray from the womb"), all allegorically interpreted to accommodate the sermon's theme.

85. "Odi, la notte della sua natività, il devoto dottore santo Geronimmo dice, che tutti i soddomiti di tutto l'universo morirono di fatto in quella notte. La luce non istà con le tenebre. . . . erano stati tutti sterminati e morti e ancora non erano tornati al male uso di quello, che terrore v'era ancora fresco della punizione" (D.278–29); see also B.143 and OOQ.III.276, where he cites Jerome's gloss on Isaiah 9:1, "The people who walked in darkness have seen a great light," in his *Commentary on Isaiah*. However, Jerome's commentary on the verse (Bk. 3, s. 30) makes no mention of sodomites. Nonetheless, Bernardino was simply repeating a medieval *locus communis:* Antonino of Florence also mentions both this "fact" and the same source in his *Summa theologica*, pars 2, titulus 5, caput 4, 671a. It is also publicized in the *Legenda aurea*, according to Johansson and Percy, who do not specify where, however ("Homosexuality," 173). The poet Virgil, by the way, was thought to be counted among the sodomite casualties at the time of Jesus' birth (Pietro Agostino D'Avack, "L'omosessualità nel diritto canonico," *Ulisse* 7 [1953]: 686).

86. "In huius etiam signum, licet daemones de aliis criminibus legantur tentasse homines etiam visibiliter apparendo, nullum tamen in *Vitis patrum* legitur tentasse de vitio contra naturam" (OOQ. III.276; see also D.279).

87. "Dice uno dottore, che in qual luogo si ricorda el peccato de la sodomia, in quel luogo non vi cade il dì rugiada" (R.1151; the source is identified at G.101). This item was also part of common medieval lore; Hugh of St. Cher includes it in his biblical commentary (Johansson and Percy, "Homosexuality," 173).

88. For Bernardino's detailed description of the Dead Sea, see B.63, G.104, and OOQ.III.273.

89. "Niuno animale è che pecchi contro a natura se none e cavagli e gli asini che sono quasi d'una medesima natura" (B.32). Bernardino does not explain how horses and donkeys "sin against nature." Is it because they mate to produce the sterile mule? Nor does the friar explain how the moral category of "sin" can be applied to nonreasoning animals, even though he was not alone in doing so in that era. In the Middle Ages, there was indeed the custom of "excommunicating" animals and of bringing them to trial for crimes they had committed; see Jan M. Ziolkowski, *Talking Animals: Medieval Latin Beast Poetry, 750–1150* (Philadelphia:

University of Pennsylvania Press, 1993), 33, and the bibliographical references therein. For medieval notions of animal sexuality in general, see Joyce E. Salisbury, *The Beast Within: Animals in the Middle Ages* (New York: Routledge, 1995), chap. 3.

90. "Piglia essempio dagli animali. Vedi che leone s'impaccia co' la leonessa, l'orso coll'orsa, l'asino coll'asina etc., vedi *quod omne simile appetit suum simile.* Salvo che 'l maladetto sodomito, che non si congiogne con quelle intenzioni che fanno gli animali razionali e irrazionali" (G.107). The irony of Bernardino's Latin proverb "Like always seeks like" here escapes the friar: sodomites behave as they do precisely because they desire and seek their own kind.

91. "Non vedi tu che tu ti dimostri essere contra a Dio, el quale disse all'uomo e a la donna, primo nostro padre e madre: '*Crescite et multiplicamini, et replete terram?* Crescete e multiplicate, e riempite la terra?' O sodomito [*sic*] del diavolo, come fai tu? Elli pare che tu dica a Dio: 'Io voglio fare contra a te: io non voglio che e' nasca niuno' " (R.1153–54).

92. "Perchè lui ordinò il primo matrimonio in cielo? Perchè si riempisse la terra e poi le sediora di paradiso" (B.65; repeated at R.549).

93. The friar implies the same in the case of women who practice birth control (R.1156).

94. "O furioso del diavolo, non vedi tu che tu fai contra a ogni debito di ragione? Chi vive al mondo, che può avere più preziosa cosa, che avere figliuoli? Che vale più uno figliuolo buono sicondo Idio che tutto l'avanzo del mondo!" (R.1153).

95. David Herlihy, "Santa Caterina and San Bernardino: Their Teachings on the Family," in *Atti-Siena,* 919. The essay has been reprinted in D. Herlihy, *Women, Family and Society in Medieval Europe: Historical Essays, 1978–1991,* ed. Anthony Mohlo (Providence: Berghahn Books, 1995), 174–92.

96. "[Q]uando Iddio à in abominazione una patria, gli manda via come fa una polvere dinanzi al vento. . . . L'angelo dell'abisso vi costringe con le guerre; egli è lo sterminatore di Dio, come dice nell'Apocalis" (D.281–82).

97. Bernardino had previously quoted Jeremiah 7:18, which speaks of "flatcakes" being offered up to the "queen of the heaven," that is, Ishtar, the Assyro-Babylonian goddess of fertility. We will return to this verse in our next section, on the causes of sodomy.

98. "E sai che è? Che non v'è pericolo; non v'hai a mettare nulla; sai! Elli è maschio; se fusse femina, forse non faresti così, perché ingravidarebbe; e perché elli non ingravida, e tu ne se' contenta, e fai la schiacciata a la reina del cielo! E tanto farai così e così tu, che tu provocarai Idio a ira; e Idio vedendo questo e gli altri vizi, ti minaccia e dice: 'Egli verrà l'ira mia sopra di te.' Sai che farà? Elli ti mandarà guerra, pistolenzia e caristia per gastigare i sodomitti; che non vi rimarrà né bestiame, né pocissioni, né giardini, né denari, né eziandio persone: in ogni cosa dimostrarà l'ira sua, dicendo, 'Sopra d'ogni cosa discendarà l'ira mia' " (R.1023).

99. "O fanciulli, se voi volete sterminare la vostra città e la vostra patria, siate soddomitti; io dico se voi volete ch'ella sia sterminata, e non vi ristate mai di soddomittare" (R.405).

100. "Peccata nempe sceleris huius sunt proprie adinventiones cordium impiorum" (OOQ.III.271). Yet on other occasions Bernardino leaves the contradictory impression that it is indeed the Devil who leads men into this sin; e.g., he exclaims, "Tanta dimonieria è ne' soddomiti che lasciano lo 'ncrinamento naturale per lo incrinamento contro a natura. Ciechi, acceccati dal dimonio!" ("So much devilry is in the sodomites who abandon the natural inclination for the inclination against nature. Blind they are, blinded by the Devil"), A.414–15; see also E.33, OOQ.III.282, and OOH.III.189a.

101. "E voi, pazzarelle, vi credete per lo vostro lisciare che i vostri mariti non sieno sodomitti? E io vi dico che talvolta voi ne sete cagione voi, per lo vostro lisciarvi. Voi non v'avedete che voi guastate voi medesime, e fatevi odiare agli uomini. A chi puzza la bocca per

lo lisciare; chi s'insolfa; chi s'imbratta con una cosa e chi con un'altra; e date tanta puzza a' vostri mariti, che voi gli fate diventare sodomitti" (R.1089–90; see also OOQ.II.83). Yet at the same time, in his sermons on sodomy, Bernardino celebrates the beauty, superiority, and hence desirability of women, the purpose of such praise in these specific sermons, as Zafarana observes, appearing primarily as that of turning men away from thoughts of sodomy, rather than that of a genuine appreciation of women's attractiveness. (See, for example, R.560: "Che a la barba di tutti e soddomiti io voglio tenere co' le donne, e dico che la donna è più pulita e preziosa ne la carne sua, che non è l'uomo. . . ." ["To spite all the sodomites I want to side with the women and say that the flesh of a woman is more clean and more precious than that of a man. . . ."]) However, not all instances of praise of women in Bernardino are to be reduced to mere antisodomitic ploys, as Zelina Zafarana instead claims ("Bernardino nella storia della predicazione popolare," in *Atti-Todi,* 61–62, n. 3). For further discussion of this topic, see my essay "Bernardino of Siena, 'Great Defender' or 'Merciless Betrayer' of Women?" *Italica* 75 (1998), 22–40.

102. See Arnaldo d'Addario, "Rusticucci, Iacopo," *Enciclopedia dantesca,* 6 vols., ed. Umberto Bosco (Rome: Istituto della Enciclopedia Italiana, 1970–78), 4:1060–61, and Dall'Orto, "La fenice di Sodoma," 74.

103. "L'acqua che sta ferma, che fa? Diventa puzzolente, nascevi ranocchi, botte, serpenti e simili immondizie. Se Firenze starà ferma in abbondanza de' cibi, in grassezza, in guadagni grandi, e sanza guerra, e sanza pistolenza, quanta puzza di peccati ci sarà, quanti serpi e scorzoni di cattive volontà, quanta lussuria, quanta superbia, quanta sodomia!" (B.43).

104. "Tre cose fanno crescere il fuoco della sodomia: prima le molte legne del mangiare, del pappare, del bere e inzeppare" (B.45).

105. "Guarda se usi con uno lebroso subitamente te l'appicca; usa con uno cattivo subitamente ti contamina. Uno contaminato è sofficiente a contaminarne in una bottega cento o quanti ve ne saranno. Una mela fracida contamina tutte l'altre. E dalla cattiva conversazione vengono poi al parlare disonesto e ribaldo di sodomia. . . . Chi va là ove si fanno i carboni s'imbratta" (B.43–44; see also OOQ.IX.428).

106. The object of Bernardino's greatest concern in these sermons, let us note, is specifically the vulnerable class of adolescent males, who, in his eyes, were most in danger from the corruption of this sin.

107. "Sete ruffiani de' vostri figliuoli!" (B.41; see also R.1151).

108. B.40, R.1145, G.100. The fifteenth-century records of Florence's antisodomy magistracy, the Office of the Night, prove Bernardino right in his claims about the complicity, active or passive, of parents and other family members in what amounted to the prostituting of their sons; see Rocke, *Forbidden Friendships,* 175–82. The Dominican preacher Giordano of Rivalto, preaching in Florence in the previous century, made the same accusation of social-climbing parents (Harry J. Kuster and Raymond J. Cormier, "Old Views and New Trends: Observations on the Problem of Homosexuality in the Middle Ages," *Studi medievali* 24 [1984]: 605–6).

109. "Il farsetto a bellico, i panni a gamba con una pezza dinanzi e una di drieto, acciochè mostrino assai carne pe' soddomiti" (E.42–43; trans. Rocke, *Forbidden Friendships,* 38).

110. "Li mandano colle camice ben sottile, con farsettini a mezzo el corpo, con vestimenti frappati e calze a gamba fessa, con cercini in capo" (B.39, trans. Rocke, "Sodomites in Fifteenth-Century Tuscany," 12). We may here raise the same question Greenberg raises about John of Salisbury's similarly vivid description of the modus operandi of a courtly sodomite ("When the rich lascivious wanton is preparing to satisfy his passion he has his hair elaborately frizzled and curled; he puts to shame a courtesan's make-up, an actor's costume"): does the description suggest "fascination as well as aversion" on the part of Bernardino? (*Construction,* 293–94).

111. "Giovani figliuoli doventati fanciulle . . . allicchisati come donzelle" (B.35).

112. "O donne, e anco vo' gli fate sodomitti i vostri figliuoli! Quando voi gli mandate, pulitegli! . . . A casa del diavolo tutti quanti, che sete cagione di molto male. Oimmè, oimmè! O non ponete voi mente che voi vi fate loro ruffiani? . . . Doh, pazza, insensata, che pare che tu il miri tu; tanto te pare che stia bene: 'Oh, egli è il bel garzone!' Anco: egli è la bella femina! *Oimmé, oimmé, Oimméeee!*" (R.1151; I have used Rocke's translation, *Forbidden Friendships*, 38, for the grammatically perplexing second half of the quotation beginning, "O silly, foolish woman").

113. "Se si venissino a confessare da me, se io confessassi, tanto n'assolverei, io niuna quanto il diavolo, se non si amendassino. Dico delle madri che sì disonestamente mandano i loro figliuoli. Mondo lussurioso e brodoso, che vanno le cose sì male tra parente e parente; tra fratello e sorella, tra madre e figliuolo! Fa caro di panni per fare divizia di carne. Or non diciamo troppo, ma tu sai troppo! Sarei crepato s'io non l'avessi detto, che la coscienzia mi rimorderebbe" (E.43).

114. "Filii colligunt ligna, et patres succendunt ignem, et mulieres conspergunt adipem, ut faciant placentas reginae coeli et libent diis alienis et ad iracundiam me provocent" (OOQ.III.269; Bernardino also uses this image at G.103, R.1145, and D.275). I use the Revised Standard Version translation, slightly modified.

115. "Cum ipsos filios mares, in superfluis deliciis nutrientes, effeminatos efficiunt; et sic faciunt *placentas*, id est, filios ad talia scelera complacentes, *reginae caeli*, hoc est iniquitati gomorrhaeorum" (OOQ.III.269).

116. "La madre fa la pasta in acconciare i figliuoli troppo puliti. Quale è la schiacciata? Quando si sottomettono alla sodomia" (D.275).

117. For the problem of feminine vanity of dress and popular preaching against it in the period, see Thomas M. Izbicki, "Pyres of Vanities: Mendicant Preaching on the Vanity of Women and Its Lay Audience," in *De Ore Domini: Preachers and Word in the Middle Ages*, ed. Thomas L. Amos et al. (Kalamazoo, Mich.: Medieval Institute Publications, 1989), 211–34; Catherine Kovesi Killerby, "Practical Problems in the Enforcement of Italian Sumptuary Law, 1200–1500," in *Crime, Society and the Law in Renaissance Italy*, 99–120; Maria Giuseppina Muzzarelli, " 'Contra mundanas vanitates et pompas.' Aspetti della lotta contro i lussi nell'Italia del XV secolo," *Rivista di storia della Chiesa in Italia* 40 (1986): 371–90; and Ronald Rainey, "Dressing Down the Dressed-Up: Reproving Feminine Attire in Renaissance Florence," in *Renaissance Society and Culture: Essays in Honor of Eugene F. Rice, Jr.*, ed. John Monfasani and Ronald G. Musto (New York: Italica Press, 1991), 217–37.

118. "Absit etiam a christiana religione et debita honestate videre iuvenes nostri temporis, immo quod impudentius est, videre quandoque dementatos senes usque ad umbilicum palam curtos gerere farsectinos et ante et retro (ah pudet dicere!) tamquam impudici canes, omnia pudenda oculis cunctorum astantium ingerere impudenter. Sed verto me ad talia supportantes. Nonne, o vos matres atque sorores ceteraeque in domo domesticae et cognatae, amplius vos antiquae et senes, impudica talia quotidie aspicere et supportare, nonne, inquam, magnae vestrae insensibilitatis atque stultitiae seu potius impudentiae signa sunt ac indicia?" (OOQ.VI.18).

119. David Herlihy and Christiane Klapisch-Zuber, *Les toscans et leurs familles. Une étude du catasto de 1427* (Paris: École des hautes études en sciences sociales, 1978), 605 (not included in the abridged English translation).

120. Herlihy, "Santa Caterina and San Bernardino," 924.

121. Klapisch-Zuber, "State and Family in a Renaissance Society: The Florentine *Catasto* of 1427–30," in *Women, Family, and Ritual in Renaissance Italy*, 20.

122. Herlihy and Klapisch-Zuber, *Les toscans et leurs familles*, 605–6; the quotation is from 606.

123. Trexler, *Public Life in Renaissance Florence,* 379 and 382.

124. Herlihy, Klapisch-Zuber, and Trexler do not appear to have used the preacher's biography in their analyses; hence I am not arguing in circular fashion.

125. Yet Bernardino is unclear as to when one reaches this age of reason. At E.41, he says it is at "eight or ten years old," whereas on the previous page, he had told of "a boy of five years in the evil habit of swearing and never castigated" who was whisked away by the Devil, "with God's permission," and carried off "in flesh and blood" to hell. If this is not a case of scribal error, then either the friar is suggesting that even at five years old, certain children have already reached the age of reason and hence are morally responsible for their sins, or else Bernardino is guilty of a lapse in his own reasoning.

126. "Io udi' da valentissimo uomo, che disse che credeva si perdesse più dell'età da otto anni insino a' quindici anni, che di niun'altra età di cristiani" (E.42).

127. "Quando ti muoiono i fanciullini piccolini, da sette anni in giù o da dieci, non si vogliono piagnere, anzi farne festa, chè sono iti accrescere il numero de' beati in vita eterna, e orano dinanzi a Dio per voi. Quando i fanciulli muiono da dieci anni in su, piangerli pe' peccati, perchè Idio ve gli aveva dati maschi, e il diavolo ve gli fa femine per lo maladetto vizio della sodomia" (E.33).

128. "Non ànno asciutti gli occhi che sono contaminati e soddomiti! Guardategli, padri e madri, ch'è uno stupore, in quanta tenera età e sono già contaminati di soddomia!" (D.274).

129. See R.1155, B.31–32, and the index entry "rape, of males," in Rocke, *Forbidden Friendships.*

130. "Ostiensis e altri dottori dicono d'uno fanciullo di nove anni [che] ingravidò la balia sua. In Vinegia ingravidò una fanciulla di sette anni, e non potendo parturire, crepò e morì, e a memoria di ciò le fu fatto una sepultura patente co' lettere che la discrivono. Il re Salamone, figliuolo di Davit, si legge che in undici anni ebbe figliuoli" (E.39).

131. "Ó sentito di quegli che si lisciano e vannosi gloriando de' loro sodomitatori, e fannone arte per civanza, e vanno stimolando altri del brutto peccato. . . . [F]a' la sera, quando si va a letto, e lui dorme, ponti el suo borsello all'orechie, sta' a udire e denari quello che dicono; se ve n'è e tu non sappi donde gli abbi avuti, tu udirai e denari che gridaranno: 'Fuoco! Fuoco! Fuoco!' " (E.42; G.100). Some Florentine boys did indeed engage in sodomy for money; see Rocke, *Forbidden Friendships,* 165. Giacomo della Marca tells of one youth who reported earnings of 800 ducats through sodomy, while another earned 1,000 ("De sodomia," 1:452).

132. "I giovani garzoni che non si lasciano contaminare, si vorrebbono calonizzare per santi" (B.68).

133. Greenberg, *Construction,* 307–10.

134. "Gente indimoniata, delle cose che mi sono sute dette da persone degne di fede! E figliuoli de' buoni padri levati loro dal lato e tratti loro di casa a forza che Sodoma e Gamorra non fe' la metà di quello si fa in Firenze senza niuno freno" (B.31–32). For the European reputation of Florence as the city of sodomites, see Rocke, *Forbidden Friendships,* 3–4.

135. "Io vo' dire di me: io non morrò, s'io potrò, in questa patria . . . perché voi sete tutti invilupati in questo peccato . . . non credo che ci sia luogo che non sia contaminato e corrotto. . . . Oimmè, a che se' tu condotta, città di Seina! In che scurità se' tu, che e' non si può mandare uno fanciulletto per le strade, che elli non sia preso per forza e traviato" (R.1148, 1152, 1155). For such bold preaching in his hometown, by the way, our preacher narrowly missed being clubbed to death by four sodomites; so says friar Andrea Francisci of Siena in his deposition at Bernardino's canonization trial. See Piana, "I processi di canonizzazione," 420.

136. Rocke, *Forbidden Friendships,* 4. See Ruggiero, *Boundaries of Eros,* 137, for "the Florentine connection" with sodomy cases in Venice.

137. Rocke, *Forbidden Friendships,* 146.

138. Ruggiero, *Boundaries of Eros,* 136.

139. "Contingit his temporibus impubertatis, cum formosus esset et natura delicatus valde, quidam civis non de minoribus in campo seu magna platea civitatis iuxta fontem Bernardino turpe verbum dixisset. Ex quo malignitatem civis illius concepit floridus et honestissimus adolescens, statim auditis verbis, magno ictu pugno percussit civem illum infra mentum, credens percutere faciem, et tam magno sonitu, astantibus propinquis quamplurimis civibus, quod fere totam plateam replevit auditu." Benvoglienti, *Vita Sancti Bernardini Senensis,* 62, s. 5.

140. "Contigit etiam eisdem temporibus, cum quidam alius malignus et nequam, non civis tamen, pluries inhonestis verbis et nutibus ostenderet turpe desiderium et nefandum erga Bernardinum, idem Bernardinus speculum honestatis rogavit quosdam sibi coetaneos et bone opinionis adolescentes et sotios, ut eum adiuvarent a molestia illius. Et inter eos capto consilio, ordinavit quemlibet eorum implere sinus et cubitos lapidibus. Quo facto iniquum quesierunt. Eo reperto iuxta portam magnificorum Dominorum Priorum civitatis, ait Bernardinus: 'Non est hic faciendus rumor iuxta palatium, sed extrahamus eum de campo, deinde insequemur ipsum lapidus.' Evenit quod statim homo iniquitatis libidine excecatus, intuens Bernardinum, eidem plures florenos ostendit, tali nutu ac si diceret: 'Tui sunt omnes, si michi assenseris.' Tunc sapiens adolescens annuit illi, ut plateam exiret. Quam cum statim egrederetur per viam porte Salarie, illico Bernardinus exclamavit: 'Inique, reubalde, in igne cremande! ad eum! ad eum! ad eum!' Et cum voce lapidibus percutere cepit. Consotii vero vocibus et lapidibus una responderunt et insonuerunt. Iniquus ille fugiebat. Ille autem clamoribus et lapidibus currentes sequebantur usque fere ad Posterlam, ubi ab eorum oculis evanuit." Ibid., 62–63, s. 6.

141. Paolo Sevesi, "Un sermone inedito del B. Michele Carcano su S. Bernardino da Siena," *SF* terza serie 3 (1931): 83, 85. Sevesi has also published other sermons by Carcano on Bernardino; see his "Tre sermoni inediti su S. Bernardino," *BSB* 1 (1935): 205–36; 2 (1936): 58–65, 164–73.

142. Vegio, *Vita Sancti Bernardini Senensis,* 1.9.119F. The story is also repeated by Capistrano, who for the most part simply copies Benvoglienti (*S. Bernardini senensis . . . Vita,* OOH.I.xxxv, col. A); it was also included later in the century in the Surius *Vita* (620, ss. 4–5).

143. For example: "Haec duo signa publica evidentissme honestatis floridi adolescentis talem et tantam opinionem bonitatis et virtutis apud omnes generavit et auxit, ut, nedum aliquis amplius inhonestum aliquid ab eo tentasset, sed ab omnibus venerabatur, adeo ut coram eo etiam sui domestici nullum dedecus dicere presumpsissent" (Benvoglienti, *Vita Sancti Bernardini Senensis,* 63, s. 7).

144. This is the thesis of Ida Magli, Italian cultural anthropologist who has studied preachers of penance of the Middle Ages; see her "L'etica familiare e la donna in S. Bernardino," in *Atti-Aquila,* 124.

145. Robert Liebert, *Michelangelo: A Psychoanalytic Study of His Life and Images* (New Haven: Yale University Press, 1983), 3.

146. Greenberg, *The Construction of Homosexuality,* 288–89.

147. I borrow the phrase from the title of David F. Noble's book, *A World without Women: The Christian Clerical Culture of Western Science* (New York: Oxford University Press, 1992).

148. "Quomodo mihi avulsus es, Vincenti mi? Quomodo raptus e manibus, homo unanimis, homo secundum cor meum? Amavimus nos in vita; quomodo in morte separati sumus? . . . Adhaeserat anima mea animae illius et dilectio unam fecerat de duabus. Cum ergo essemus cor unum et anima una, hanc meam pariter et ipsius animam pertransivit gladius, et scindens, mediam partem locavit in caelo, atque aliam partem reliquit in coeno. Ego, ego illa portio misera

in luto iacens, truncata potiori parte; et dicitur mihi: Ne fleveris? . . . [M]ortem horreo meam et meorum. Meus Vincentius erat, meus plane. An non meus, cum fuerit professione filius, sollicitudine pater, peregrinatione socius, magisterio doctor, caritate mater, consors spiritu, intimus affectu. . . . Plango denique, mi Vincenti, et si non super te, propter te tamen. Hinc prorsus, hinc afficior graviter, quia vehementer amo." OOQ.VI.386, 389, 390, trans. Eric May, "The 'Pia deploratio' of St. Bernardine of Siena," *Franciscan Studies* 2 (1942): 245, 249. The sword image is to be found on OOQ.VI.385 (English trans., May, "The 'Pia deploratio,'" 244). Bernardino's contemporary, Franciscan preacher Michele Carcano, says Vincenzo was to Bernardino "in a certain way both his mother, taking care of his corporal needs, and his spiritual father, since he was his confessor" ("Vincentium, qui quodam modo et mater ei erat, curam eius corporalem gerendo, et pater ei spiritualis fuit, quia eidem confitebatur"), Paolo Sevesi, "Tre sermoni inediti su S. Bernardino," *BSB* 1 (1935): 206. For Vincenzo, see also Eric May, "The Friendships of St. Bernardine," *Franciscan Studies* 4 (1944): 257–61; and Martino Bertagna, "Fra Vincenzo da Siena," in *Enciclopedia bernardiniana*, 1:153–54.

149. Boswell, *Same-Sex Unions*, 65. As Boswell points out, "[c]ertainly the most controversial same-sex couple in the Christian tradition comprised Jesus and John, the 'beloved disciple.' The relationship between them was often depicted in subsequent art and literature as intimate, if not erotic" (138).

150. Boswell, *Christianity, Social Tolerance, and Homosexuality*, 226. For more on premodern concepts of friendship, see Brian McGuire, *Friendship and Community: The Monastic Experience, 350–1250* (Kalamazoo: Cistercian Publications, 1988); Reginald Hyatte, *The Arts of Friendship: The Idealization of Friendship in Medieval and Early Renaissance Literature* (Leiden: Brill, 1994); and Ulrich Langer, *Perfect Friendship: Studies in Literature and Moral Philosophy from Boccaccio to Corneille* (Geneva: Droz, 1994). Lucia Bertolini has published a critical edition of fifteenth-century Florentine texts on the subject, *De vera amicitia: I testi del primo Certame coronario* (Modena: Panini, 1993).

151. Thomas Stehling, *Medieval Latin Poems of Male Love and Friendship* (New York: Garland, 1984).

152. Greenberg, *The Construction of Homosexuality*, 285–86; see also Stehling, *Medieval Latin Poems of Male Love and Friendship*, xviii–xx.

153. John Boswell, *Rediscovering Gay History: Archetypes of Gay Love in Christian History.* The Fifth Michael Harding Memorial Address (London: Gay Christian Movement, 1982), 16. Even if not all members of medieval male religious communities were what we today call "homosexual," their environment certainly encouraged them in that direction, as David Noble points out: "the homosocial norms of the monastic community" fostered "a homoerotic ethos reminiscent of the academies of classical Greece" (*A World without Women*, 57; see also 154–55). What Noble says of the monasteries of the earlier Middle Ages, we might point out, was true for the Franciscan friaries of the Quattrocento as well.

154. Brent D. Shaw, "A Groom of One's Own?" (Review of John Boswell's *Same-Sex Unions in Premodern Europe*), *New Republic*, July 18 and 25, 1994, 33–41; Warren Johansson and William A. Percy, "Homosexuality," 178–79. A piece of evidence overlooked by Boswell, the Eastern Orthodox Church's Book of Canon Law, the *Pedalion*, acknowledges the frequently erotic nature of the relationships ritualized in the "brotherhood by adoption" or "wedbrotherhood" ceremony: In prohibiting the ceremony (in its chapter on marriage), the *Pedalion* states that wedbrotherhood "merely affords matter for some persons to fulfill their carnal desires and to enjoy sensual pleasures, as countless examples of actual experience have shown at various times and in various places," "Concise and Accurate Instructions Concerning

Marriages," chap. 10, "Brothership by Adoption," *The Rudder (Pedalion) of the Metaphorical Ship of the One Holy Catholic and Apostolic Church of the Orthodox Christians or All the Sacred and Divine Canons* . . . , trans. D. Cummings (Chicago: Orthodox Christian Educational Society, 1957), 997 (the ceremony is called "wedbrotherhood" in the index, 1033). At least eighty manuscripts containing this so-called wedbrotherhood ceremony are extant, the largest number being found in Italy (Boswell, *Same-Sex Unions,* 184, 258).

155. Allen J. Frantzen, "Between the Lines: Queer Theory, the History of Homosexuality, and Anglo-Saxon Penitentials," *Journal of Medieval and Early Modern Studies* 26 (1996): 255–96, 255 for the quotation in the previous sentence. An interesting case, recently uncovered, of homosexual verse that had been for centuries tranquilly interpreted in "heteronormative" fashion is that of thirteenth-century Italian poet Ser Pace. Ser Pace's amorous sonnets were dedicated to a secret lover whose name the poet encrypted in an ingenious code written into the sonnets. The brilliant investigative work of one scholar, Deborah Contrada, finally cracked the code, revealing the identity of Ser Pace's lover, another male, named Narducio. See Deborah L. Contrada, "The Resolution of Ser Pace's *nome secreto,*" *Italica* 66 (1989): 281–92.

156. "Et nota quod quando filius tuus non obedit tibi, scito quod ipse est effoeminatus, et de negligentia tua postea habebis dolorem" (OOH.III.189a).

157. "Perchè cagione? Perchè il diavolo v'à messi una legione di dimoni, e falli sì duri che non si vogliono corregere . . . [B.35]; Tanto el diavolo l'acieca, che se esso passa trentatre anni, quasi è impossibile che esso se ne rimanga. Pur può, ma è molto malagevole a levarsene. . . . E però è quasi impossibile [G.109–10]; Va', legge del Dicreto a la VII Distinzione, capitolo *Sicut,* e vedrai che non si debba sperare d'essere accetto a Dio colui che passa e' trentatré anni involto in quello peccato [R.1165]." See also OOH.III.189b, where, however, the age of thirty is given; this may be a scribal error, as also, perhaps, in the case of his statement at B.35, which specifies the age of thirty-two.

158. It is not the preacher who informs us of this, but rather one of his frequently quoted authorities, Hugh of Saint-Cher, in the *Postilla in epistolam ad Timotheum.* See Delcorno's note 203 at R.1165.

159. Rocke, *Forbidden Friendships,* 40.

160. Ibid., 51, 111; Ruggiero, *Boundaries of Eros,* 121–24.

161. "Che è il desiderio suo? Di potere lussuriare. Che è? Quello con che [pu]ò continuare; e prima l'essere sano, l'essere giovane, l'essere ricco e potente. Tutte ama queste tante cose che gli sono mezzo a empiere il suo desiderio, che troppo gli par male d'avere una infermità, o di diventare povero, e più d'invecchiare, che quando gli è detto ch'egli abbi un pel canuto, ti sputerebbe nel viso" (E.46).

162. Accordingly, candy sellers are condemned by the preacher as accomplices to the crime (B.45–46). The Florentine statutes of the "Capitano" (1322–25) "forbade innkeepers to serve a long list of delicacies and sweets, because they were said to attract 'many boys and men' who might fall into vice and 'perpetrate wicked sins that are abominable before God and men'" (Rocke, *Forbidden Friendships,* 21–22).

163. "E mai questi tali non si possono contentare. O donna, ponvi mente, che mai nol potrai contentare, se egli è involto in quello vizio! Di ciò che tu fai, sempre se ne lagna, sempre: quando egli torna a casa, torna turbato co la rabbia nel capo, e non si cura né del giudicio di Dio, né dell'onore del mondo. Egli sta sempre pieno di stizzo e di turbazione, e sempre teme e ha paura di non venire in disgrazia del fanciulletto tristo. . . . Servilmente ubidisce il fanciullo, e ciò che egli può fare, fa a petizione sua" (R.1144; see also B.31 and OOQ.III.268). Bernardino can leave us with the impression that all sodomitic relationships were unhappy, transient, clandestine affairs

involving little emotional reciprocity, whereas we know from other sources that "sodomites" of his day did commit to each other in what were, in effect, matrimonial states of enduring mutual affection. Alluding to this, Giacomo della Marca speaks of one "sodomite" who "took a youth for his wife" and another who "had wed a boy with a ring at the altar" ("De sodomia," 1:452, 460). For other examples, see Rocke, *Forbidden Friendships,* 122, 170, and, on 172, the case of Michele di Bruno da Prulli and Carlo di Berardo d'Antonio, who "swore over the holy stone on the holy gospels of God to remain faithful to Michele." On this whole historical phenomenon, see Boswell, *Same-Sex Unions,* passim.

164. "Tale scelus, cum in consuetudinem ductum est, ita infelicem animam rapit et tanta violentia tenet et ducit, quod in desperationem illam adducit, ita ut de aeterna vita ac de sua salute diffidat" (OOQ.III.283).

165. "Tutti e sottomiti, nello inferno, saranno carboni accesi che il fummo n'anderà a' beati in paradiso e goderannone" (B.67; for the source of this image, see the Book of Revelation 14:11).

166. Greenberg, *Construction,* 259, 305, 307; Rocke, *Forbidden Friendships,* 134–35.

167. Rocke, *Forbidden Friendships,* 134–35; Ruggiero, *Boundaries of Eros,* 109–45. Indeed, as we heard Ruggiero point out about Venice, "at the lower levels of society . . . homosexual encounters were a fairly regular part of late boyhood and adolescence" (*Boundaries of Eros,* 136). Similarly, we heard Rocke conclude for Florence, "[sodomy] was part of the whole fabric of Florentine society, attracting males of all ages, matrimonial condition, and social rank" (*Forbidden Friendships,* 146).

168. "E secondi, dico, sono uomini di mezzo tempo, intendenti in iscienza mondana, maestri o in maggiore grado, o secolare o spirituale. . . . [M]a scusano el peccato dicendo che tutti gli uomini da bene sono di quella arte" (B.50–51; see also OOQ.III.281, "quia in altis hominibus regnare solet").

169. *The Divine Comedy. Volume I: Inferno,* XV, 106–7, trans. Mark Musa (Harmondsworth: Penguin, 1984), 208. For an in-depth analysis of this canto offering an alternative reading, see Richard Kay, *Dante's Swift and Strong: Essays on Inferno XV* (Lawrence: Regents Press of Kansas, 1978).

170. Pars 2, titulus 5, caput 4, 668d–e.

171. "In hoc Evangelio Christus nihil tractat, nisi de sacerdotibus, et religiosis; et licet materia hujus evangelii sit singularissima; tamen pro meliori de factis sacerdotum praesentis temporis melius est silere, quam loqui" (OOH.III.190a).

172. On the topic of irony, one cannot help noting the fact that the renowned Renaissance artist responsible for one of the better portraits of Bernardino was none other than Giovanni Bazzi, better known as "Il Sodoma." This nickname was freely used by Bazzi himself, even in public documents (Greenberg, *Construction,* 308); he had earned it with just cause, if Giorgio Vasari is to be believed: see "Giovannantonio da Verzelli, called Sodoma, Painter (1477–1549)," in Vasari's *Lives of the Painters, Sculptors and Architects* (London: Dent, 1927), 3:285. The much-reproduced portrait by Sodoma of a somewhat sad and tired but gentle Bernardino is in the Museo dell'Opera del Duomo, Siena.

173. "Tutto el corpo del sodomitto non è altro che puzza" (R.1150).

174. "Sputate forte! L'acqua del vostro sputo, forse, ispegnerà el loro fuoco. E così ognuno isputi fortemente! *che parve un tuono*" (B.48).

175. "Quando tu ti ritrovi dove so' tali genti, o tu che se' netto, tu puoi dire:—Oh, ci pute!—Se t'è detto:—O di che?—Di':—Di solfo" (R.1150). The association of sin with bodily odor is recurrent in Bernardino. Earlier the preacher had told his audience that the excommunicated sinner is like a fart: "What is the filthiest sound that a man can make, do you know? It is the one

of the man who farts. He leaves the scene immediately and leaves his stink for everyone else. Likewise with the one who is excommunicated: he leaves his stink and goes off" ("Quale è il più sozzo suono che facci l'uomo, sa'lo? É quello che pute; che di subito va via, e lassa la puzza agli altri. Così è di colui che è scomunicato: lassa la puzza, e va via"), R.1031–32.

176. E.g., OOQ.III.271, B.65, D.274, R.1148–49. This was another medieval commonplace about sodomy. The English *Book of Vices and Virtues* says in similar vein, "The devil himself that purchaseth that sin is squeamish thereof when anyone does it," quoted by Vern Bullough, "The Sin against Nature and Homosexuality," 67. Likewise, Antonino of Florence says, "Sed in Compendio theologiae [i.e., the *Compendium theologicae veritatis,* once attributed to Albert the Great] dicitur, quod ipse diabolus tentans de hoc vitio, postquam inducit homines ad hoc, fugit abominans ex nobilitate suae naturae tantum scelus (*Summa theologica*, 671b). Giacomo della Marca also mentions the fact, citing the same source, the *Compendium* ("De sodomia," 1:459).

177. "Io non so se ci è niuno o niuna che abbi udite quelle grida che a queste notti so' state udite. Le grida so' state grandissime, ma talvolta altri non ode per cotali faccende che altri ha. Elli è intervenuto a me quello ch'io vi dico. Una di queste notti io mi levai a mattino; elli mi parve d'udire gridare: 'Al fuoco, al fuoco, al fuoco!' Io dissi in me medesimo: 'Qualche cosa debba ardere'; e così standomi attento s'io sentesse altro, ficcando così l'orecchie, e io odo gridare in un'altra contrada: 'Al fuoco, al fuoco, al fuoco!' E stando così da me medesimo, io pensavo e non vedevo nulla, e io sento un altro grido adentro adentro, come se una voce uscisse d'una caverna, una voce oscura: 'Al fu . . . al fuo . . . al fuoco!' 'O Signore Idio, che vorrà dire questo!' E stando in questo pensiero, e io sento poi l'altro grido e parmi che sia come dentro ne le buttighe: 'Al fuoco, al fuo . . . al fu . . . !' La paura e la temenzia mi cresce forte: io sto pure a udire, e io odo per tutta la città le grida insino ne le letta: 'Al fuo . . . al fuoco, al fu . . . !' Così mi pare sentire di dentro da le stalle: 'Al fuoco, al fuoco, al fuoco!' Ogni cantone v'è il grido: 'Al fu . . . al fu . . . al fuoco!' Così, stato poco poco, io sento tutta la città piena di voci, e gridano tutte: 'Al fuo . . . al fu . . . al fuoco!' " (R.1154–55).

178. Even the lesser penalties given to younger and passive sodomites were rather gruesome, as Ruggiero tells us, describing the case of the sixteen-year-old Venetian Carlo Bomben, who was subjected to severe mutilation of his genitals and his left arm (*Boundaries of Eros*, 124–25). See also Brundage (*Law, Sex and Christian Society*, 534–55) on the "grisly punishments mandated by medieval law for sodomy cases."

179. "Blasphemus enim incorrigibilis aut inemendabilis sodomita sic sunt in republic sicut morbidae oves in grege et sicut membrum cancrosum incurabiliter iugiterque serpens in humano corpore. Ergo idem de eo faciendum est pro reipublicae utilitate" (OOQ.III.302).

180. "O Genova, Idio ti mantenga sempre! Se si facesse a Siena quello che si fa là, tutti sarebbono arsi, che dal piccolo al grande ci è carimolato. E se ti paresse cosa crudele, fa' almeno che ne facci qualche poco, pure per essempro, chè non si può uscire di Toscana, che non ci sia gittato al volto dodici volte el dì, che qui non se ne fa giustizia di tal vizio. E chi è sopra di ciò, n'arà a rendare ragione, imperò che medico piatoso, fa la ferita puzzolente" (G.101). This sermon was preached to the Sienese in 1425; in a sermon preached to the Florentines that same year, in a somewhat confused passage, Bernardino says: "Move quickly to do justice with this sin [sodomy], so that the doctors [*medici*] don't run to treat the evildoers" ("Fa' tosto la giustizia di questo preccato, acciò che i medici non corrano a medicare i cattivi," D.118). Bernardino's editor, Cannarozzi (D.124, n. 41), Trexler (*Public Life in Florence*, 381), and Rocke (*Forbidden Friendships*, 42–43) all believe this remark to be an oblique but specific reference to the Medici family and its toleration of sodomy. But the thesis is not fully convincing. As we've just seen, Bernardino uses the same medical image in the same context when speaking to the Sienese that

same year, with no reference to the Medici family intended, since that family had no role in Sienese government. Elsewhere, speaking of the correction of sin on several different occasions, Bernardino likewise uses the image/proverb, striking an analogy between the confessor and the doctor (see R.324, 376, 377, 482, and OOQ.I.173, line 37). Finally, in 1425, when Bernardino made the remark in question, the Medici, although powerful, were not yet the sole or principal wielders of power in Florence (the Albizi were the leading political force in the city, and remained so until the early 1430s).

181. F.199. On the topic of the punishment of sodomy, Bernardino's theological handbook, the *Summa theologica* of Alexander of Hales (et al.), states "et non solum igne et gladio, sed omni genere tormentorum est istud flagitium exterminandum a saeculari poteste" ("this shameful crime is to be exterminated by the secular powers not only by fire and the sword, but by every form of torment," "De sententia iudiciali," 4:697).

182. "Io vidi concorrere tre cose. Vidi posto lui in su una colonna, alto legato; e una botte di pece, e stipa e fuoco, e uno manigoldo che faceva ardere, e molta gente vidi d'intorno che stavano a vedere. Il sodomita sentì fummo e fuoco, e fu arso; el manigoldo sentì solamente il fummo, e chi stava a vedere non vide altro che fummo e fuoco. A littera, in inferno e sodomiti arderanno di fuoco e di fummo; chi li tormenterà arà el fummo. . . . Quelli che stanno a vedere che sono intorno, sono e beati spiriti di paradiso, che veggono le pene de' sodomiti e sonne lieti e allegri veggendo in loro rilucere la giustizia di Dio" (B.66).

183. "Ché fu re in Parigi, e non so se fu santo Lodovico, che essendo il vizio grandissimo, uno gli disse:—Se voi volete, io farò stirpare questo vizio per sì fatto modo, che non se ne trovarà niuno. Se voi mi date l'albitrio, io vi nettarò tutta questa vostra città.—Disse colui:—O forse tu vorresti ardere tutta la città?—Elli rispose e disse di no, e che voleva tenere miglior modo. Domandando il modo, disse:—La prima cosa io voglio che voi mi diate pienamente l'albitrio, ch'io possa fare a mio modo,—e che farebbe con ragione e con misericordia. Promettendoli che così farebbe, li diè licenzia, e disse—Va' e fa' quello ch'è da fare.—Allora egli disse che voleva cotanti armati a suo comando, e che lui comandasse che l'ubidissero. Egli glil fece dare. Avuto la licenzia, elli andò per tutta la città, e a ogni incrociata fece fare uno cappanello di scope, e come ebbe piena tutta la città, e elli si misse ad andare per la città; e come gli veniva a notizia uno publico sodomitto, subito il faceva pigliare e mettare nel primo cappanello che elli trovava, e di subito vi faceva mettare fuoco. E così arso, andava pure per la città; e come aveva notizia d'un altro, subito il faceva mettare dentro. E così fece alcuni dì, intanto che tutta la città fu purificata in poco poco tempo; e da quello tempo in qua non si fa nulla di questo peccato in quello paese" (R.1159).

184. "Metterlivi dentro chi è cagione di questo [peccato], i padri, e le madri e compagni" (D.275).

185. "Uno re ch'avea molto in odio il vizio della soddomia e volealo stirpare dal suo paese, e non vedendo da qual canto cominciarsi, ne stava in grande malinconia. Un cittadino valente, a cui dispiaceva questo peccato, gli disse se gli desse balia che lo farebbe egli. E così fatto, armossi molto bene, con una brigata di provigionati; uscito per la terra, trovatone uno ch'egli conosceva disse: 'Date a costui,' e poi a un altro; e poi a quest'altro; e così gli fece tutti tagliare a pezzi, sanza altra condannagione" (D.117–18).

186. Valla mentions the burning of the *Hermaphroditus* by Bernardino in his *Antidoti in Pogium ad Nicolaum V libri IV*, in *Opera omnia* (Basel, 1543), 364, quoted by Celestino Piana, "S. Bernardino da Siena a Bologna," *SF* terza serie 17 (1945): 227–28. Beccadelli's work was published in late 1425–early 1426 (Antonio Beccadelli, *Hermaphroditus*, 2 vols., ed. Donatella Coppini [Rome: Bulzoni, 1990], Introduzione, 1: lxxiii). On Beccadelli, see also Canosa, *Grande*

paura, 82; and Greenberg, *Construction*, 308. Perhaps echoing in his title Dante's *Purgatorio*, 26:82 ("nostro peccato fu ermafrodito," i.e., male with female), Beccadelli's work deals with both heterosexual and same-sex love and lust; in fact, far more of the former than the latter. In his sermon on sodomy, Giacomo della Marca quotes *Purgatorio* 26:82, referring to sodomy as "illo innominabili vitio et sceleratissimo hermafrodite," but in doing so misunderstands Dante's use of the term (*De sodomia*, 1:449, 454).

187. "Quid dicam de quibusdam (proh nefandum scelus!) qui in fomentum huius sceleris condiderunt libros diebus nostris, in odium sacrum coniugium exponentes?" (OOQ.III.277).

188. "O domine, vidistis *Corbatium, librum de centu novelle* et alias vanitates Petrarche? Credatis quia ex illo libro *Corbatii* miliones sunt effecti sogdomitte, et Ovidio *De arte amandi* et *Criseida* etc. Omnes mictatis mihi, quia facemus sacrificuium Deo." Quoted by Carlo Delcorno, "L'*exemplum* nella predicazione di San Bernardino," in *Atti-Todi*, 85, n. 1; see also Salvatore Nigro, "Le brache di San Griffone. Novellistica e predicazione. Il *Novellino* di Masuccio Salernitano," in *Atti-Maiori*, 163–64.

189. "Che ti levi da studio de' libri disonesti, come il Corbaccio e altri libri fatti da messer Giovan Boccacci che, salva la sua reverenzia, ne fe' parecchi che fusse il meglio se ne fusse taciuto: valente uomo fu, se quelle bestialità non avesse fatte nè scritte; e forse in vecchiezza se ne pentè" (C.311–12). Earlier in the same sermon, Bernardino mentions again "the books of Ovid and other books of love" as unfit for the young scholar (C.311). Even though elsewhere he condemns the "vanities of Petrarch," in this sermon on studies, Bernardino praises him along with other Florentine literary luminaries, saying: "Il vostro poeta Dante, messer Francesco Petrarca, messer Coluccio [Salutati] notabilissime cose feciono e da commendargli grandissimamente" ("Your poet Dante, messer Francesco Petrarca and messer Coluccio wrote most outstanding things and are to be greatly commended," C.312). Bernardino again condemns the *Corbaccio* (along with Ovid's *Art of Love*) in one of his unfinished sermon drafts (OOQ.IX.406) and in one of the unpublished Paduan sermons of 1443, both quoted by Delcorno, "L'*exemplum* nella predicazione di San Bernardino," 85, n. 1.

190. *Vite di uomini illustri* (Florence: Rinascimento del Libro, 1938), 203.

191. "Ex quo ira Dei, et merito, venit in populo christiano, propter quam terremotus, pestilentie, fames, guerre, scismata, scandala infinita creverunt in populo christiano . . . inherendo doctrinis eiusdem venerabilis servi Iesu Christi." In A. Fantozzi, "Documenta perusina de S. Bernardino Senensi," *AFH* 15 (1922): 109. Fantozzi's article is followed by the complete text of the statutes, which are also dicussed in Claudia Cardinali, "Il santo e la norma. Bernardino da Siena e gli statuti perugini del 1425," in *Gioco e giustizia nell'Italia di Comune*, ed. Gherardo Ortalli (Treviso and Rome: Fondazione Benetton and Viella, 1993), 182–91. For Bernardino's Perugian visit, see Pacetti, "Cronologia," 452. The precise date of Bernardino's departure from Perugia is not known; it may have been anywhere from October 25 (Fantozzi, "Documenta perusina," 103, 107) to November 11 (Ottokar Bonmann, "Problemi critici riguardo ai cosiddetti Statuta Bernardiniana di Perugia [1425–1426]," *SF* 62 [1965]: 295).

192. The prologue to the Statuta reports that the original version of the new laws had to be mitigated due to its severity. Fantozzi published the one extant text of the *Statuta*, believing it to be the original, "austere" first edition. Bonmann ("Problemi critici," passim) has argued convincingly that Fantozzi's published statutes are in fact the second, tempered version; indeed, the long preamble to the Statuta makes reference to this ("rigorem illum curavimus mitigare," Fantozzi, "Documenta perusina," 110).

193. "Et quia cogitationes hominum sceleratorum, qui contra naturam luxuriari conantur, varie sunt ex quibus pueros et iuvenes subducunt et subthraunt [*sic*] ad praefatum peccatum

sodomie committendum; ideo statuimus et ordinamus quod nullus de cetero audeat seu presumat ire ad aliquas scholas, in quibus gramatica vel abacum docetur," ibid., 117.

194. For the Perugian government's letter to Siena requesting a copy of its new penal reforms, see Enrico Bulletti, "Nuovi documenti bernardiniani," *BSB* 9 (1943): 153.

195. Alessio, *Storia di San Bernardino e del suo tempo,* 211–13, has published what he calls "the most essential of these reforms"; we find them as well in Niccolò Piccolomini and Narciso Mengozzi, *Il Monte de' Paschi di Siena e le aziende in esso riunite,* 9 vols. (Siena: Lazzeri, 1891–1925), 1:111–12.

196. Alessio, *Storia di San Bernardino,* 212.

197. William M. Bowsky, "The Medieval Commune and Internal Violence: Police Power and Public Safety in Siena, 1287–1355," *American Historical Review* 78 (1967): 5.

198. See chap. 2, sec. 2. For the text of the new antisodomitic law, see Bigaroni, "S. Bernardino a Todi," 120–21.

199. Pacetti, "Cronologia," 462.

200. "Eligantur quatuor cives qui una sint cum d. Iudice d. Potestatis et debeant providere super predictis et *debeant se confirmare cum venerabili patre Fr. Bernardino . . . ,*" Benvenuto Bughetti, "Documenti bernardiniani di Massa Marittima," *BSB 9* (1943): 168, emphasis added.

201. "Quod omnes illi qui sunt etatis XXV annorum et non ceperint uxorem puniantur." Bughetti, "Documenti bernardiniani," 170.

202. "Sonci buoni ordini sopra la correzione e punizione de' sodomiti trovati pe' buoni uomini, ma e cattivi sono tanto più quantità che nulla s'osserva" (B.41–42).

203. "Forse a me toccherà a cadere in simile caso e arò bisogno d'essere aiutato" (C.229–30). For the possible role of political alliances and clientage in sodomy prosecution, see Rocke, *Forbidden Friendships,* 57.

204. Rocke, "Sodomites in Fifteenth-Century Tuscany," 8; see also his *Forbidden Friendships,* 19–36.

205. Rocke, *Forbidden Friendships,* 45.

206. "Lodato sia Iddio, ché si potrà soddomitare!" quoted by Roberto Ridolfi, *Vita del Savonarola,* 2 vols. (Roma: A. Belardetti, 1952), 2:27.

207. Rocke, *Forbidden Friendships,* 46.

208. Eugenio Lazzareschi, "San Bernardino of Siena sull'Amiata e nella Lucchesia," *Bullettino senese di storia patria* 20 (1913): 259.

209. Pacetti, "La predicazione di S. Bernardino in Toscana," *AFH* 33 (1940): 301–15.

210. For Bernardino in Venice, see Fernanda Sorelli, "Predicatori a Venezia (fine secolo XIV–metà secolo XV," *Le Venezie francescane (Predicazione francescana e società veneta nel Quattrocento: committenza, ascolto, ricezione. Atti del II Convegno internazionale di studi francescani. Padova, 26–27–28 marzo 1987),* n.s. 6 (1989): 142–48. Sorelli (144) makes mention of a possible 1405 visit of Bernardino to Venice, but given everything else we know of Bernardino's itinerary for that year and the next, it is doubtful that the young friar left Tuscany in those years; see Raoul Manselli, "Bernardino da Siena," *Dizionario biografico degli italiani,* 9:216–17.

211. Ruggiero, *Boundaries of Eros,* 110. See chap. 1, sec. 4 for Bernardino's enduring reputation in and co-patronage of Venice.

212. Ibid., 127; this is also the source of the other quotations in this paragraph.

213. Ibid., 109. This is, however, neither the first nor the only text of civil law, in truth, to contain such spiritual-apocalyptic language; we find it, for example, already in Justinian's *Corpus Juris Civilis* (*Novellae,* tit. 77, c. 1), quoted in part by Bernardino himself (OOQ.III.278); see also Bullough, "Sin against Nature," 58–59.

214. Ruggiero, *Boundaries of Eros,* 140.

215. Ibid., 141. Ruggiero's paragraph on this case appears to be the only published account of this episode. My retelling is a paraphrase of his own summary of court documents found in the Archivio di Stato di Venice (ibid., 196, n. 136).

216. Ibid., 141.

217. Lambert, *Medieval Heresy,* 183.

218. A further source of irony is that Bernardino in the devotional excesses of his early years as a Franciscan had staged such a bare-skinned public spectacle: he appeared in the Sienese village of Seggiano, "naked as the naked Christ" and bearing a crucifix in an attempt to convert the local populace. The episode is recounted in greatest detail in the authoritative early-sixteenth-century chronicle of friar Dionisio Pulinari da Firenze, *Cronache dei Frati Minori della Provincia di Toscana,* ed. S. Mencherini (Arezzo: Cooperativa Tipografica, 1913), 403–4; also excerpted in Piero Misciatelli, ed., *Le più belle pagine di Bernardino da Siena* (Milan: Treves, 1924), 281–82. I am preparing a longer study of this episode of Bernardino's life and its relationship to what I believe is an old (albeit well-circumscribed) traditional Franciscan practice of the literal enactment of Jerome's adage.

219. Ruggiero, *Boundaries of Eros,* 109–10; for a similar opinion, see Rocke, "Sodomites in Fifteenth-Century Tuscany," 15.

CHAPTER FOUR

1. Edward H. Flannery, *The Anguish of the Jews: Twenty-three Years of Antisemitism,* rev. ed. (Mahwah: Paulist, 1985), 2.

2. Giacomo Todeschini, "Teorie economiche francescane e presenza ebraica in Italia (1380–1462 c.)," in *Atti-Assisi,* 200–201. Gianfranco Fioravanti reports a striking increase in the number of anti-Jewish polemical writings in fifteenth-century Italy, especially beginning at midcentury in "Polemiche antigiudaiche nell'Italia del Quattrocento. Un tentativo di interpretazione globale," *Quaderni storici* 22, no. 64 (1987): 19–38. The first ghetto was that of Venice, 1516. For the history of the Jews in Italy, see, for example, the surveys of Attilio Milano, Cecil Roth, and Robert Bonfil cited in the pages and notes below—however, with the caution that I will be suggesting with respect to their treatment of Bernardino. Much new, more specialized research has been published in the past few decades on the Jews of Italy. For a survey and discussion of the *status quaestionis,* with abundant bibliography, see Shlomo Simonsohn, "Lo stato attuale della ricerca storica sugli ebrei in Italia," in *Italia judaica. Atti del I Convegno internazionale, Bari 18–22 maggio 1981* (Rome: Ministero per i Beni Culturali e Ambientali; Pubblicazioni degli Archivi di Stato, 1983), 29–37; Giacomo Todeschini, "Ebrei in Italia alla fine del Medioevo. Studi recenti," *Studi medievali* 30 (1989): 353–66; Corrado Vivanti, "The History of the Jews in Italy and the History of Italy," *Journal of Modern History* (1995): 309–57; and David B. Ruderman's introduction to *Essential Papers on Jewish Culture in Renaissance and Baroque Italy,* ed. David B. Ruderman (New York: New York University Press, 1992), 1–39.

3. Léon Poliakov, *Jewish Bankers and the Holy See from the Thirteenth to the Seventeenth Century* (London: Routledge & Kegan Paul, 1977), 139.

4. Diane Hughes, "Distinguishing Signs: Ear-rings, Jews and Franciscan Rhetoric in the Italian Renaissance City," *Past and Present* 112 (August 1986): 3–59. Another important work on the topic is Jeremy Cohen, *The Friars and the Jews: The Evolution of Medieval Anti-Judaism* (Ithaca: Cornell University Press, 1982). However, Cohen's book stops at the Black Death (1348) and must be used with caution; see Norman Roth's review in *Jewish Quarterly Review* 74 (1984): 321–25.

5. Hughes, "Distinguishing Signs," 19. Given the insufficiencies of these older histories, I would not share the confidence of Hughes's statement on the same page that the Observant friars' "role in creating a climate of hatred and fear of the Jew . . . does not need to be retold." As she herself admits, the most complete account thus far, Cecil Roth's *A History of the Jews of Italy* (Philadelphia: Jewish Publication Society of America, 1946), is "unfortunately unannotated" (nor does it have a bibliography). Attilio Milano's *Storia degli ebrei in Italia* (reprint, Turin: Einaudi Tascabili, 1992) also leaves much to be desired by way of annotated documentation of its facts, claims, and conclusions. Moreover, Robert Bonfil has called for new histories of Italian Jewish life in the Renaissance, for the older ones, he points out correctly, rely too heavily on an obsolete Burckhardtian vision of the period ("The Historian's Perception of the Jews in the Italian Renaissance: Towards a Reappraisal," *Revue des études juives* 143 [1984]: 59–82).

6. Robert Bonfil, *Jewish Life in Renaissance Italy* (Berkeley: University of California Press, 1994). See sec. 4 below, "The Campaign against Usury," for further discussion of Bonfil's treatment of Bernardino. Kenneth R. Stow, *Alienated Minority: The Jews of Medieval Latin Europe* (Cambridge: Harvard University Press, 1992), 208, 210, 212, 238, also takes brief note of Bernardino's anti-Jewish preaching.

7. Moritz Güdemann, *Geschichte des Erziehungswesens und der Cultur der Juden in Italien während des Mittelalters* (Volume II of *Geschichte des Erziehungswesens und der Cultur der Abendländischen Juden während des Mittelalters und der Neueren Zeit*) (Vienna: Hölder, 1884), 262.

8. Roth, *History of the Jews in Italy*, 162.

9. Poliakov, *Jewish Bankers*, 142. There is an error in Poliakov's next sentence. He speaks of "da Capistrano's vocation" but is clearly referring to Bernardino's vocation. The line should read: "Franciscan tradition holds that it was Vincenzo Ferrer, according to whom 'Christians should not kill Jews with a knife but with words,' who revealed Bernardino's vocation and appointed him his successor." There is, by the way, no historical evidence to substantiate the legendary interaction between Ferrer and Bernardino; see Manselli, "Bernardino da Siena," 217.

10. Milano, *Storia degli ebrei in Italia*, 162.

11. Ibid., 163. Milano's claim, by the way, that "[i]n every sermon of Bernardino of Siena the subject of usury occupied the central position," is simply not true, as the previous chapters of this book have demonstrated.

12. Ibid.

13. Ibid., 153, 157.

14. Moses Shulvass, *The Jews in the World of the Renaissance* (Leiden: Brill and the Spertus College of Judaica Press, 1973), 207; see also 344.

15. Ibid., 207. Not only is Shulvass's portrait of Renaissance Italy based upon an obsolete Burckhardtian interpretation of the period, but many of his individual claims are unpersuasive, especially in the absence of sufficient scholarly documentation (as in the works of Milano and Roth as well). Again, see Bonfil's critique of older Jewish histories (such as Shulvass's) built upon Burckhardtian foundations, "The Historian's Perception of the Jews in the Italian Renaissance." In his preface, Shulvass claims: "The new approach that opened society to the individual offered hitherto unimaginable opportunities to the Jew. . . . Affection for the Jew displaced hatred" (*Jews in the World of the Renaissance,* ix). As for Bernardino, Shulvass gives no indication in either his text or his critical apparatus of having read the friar's sermons or any of the material documenting his anti-Jewish impact on the towns he visited. Shulvass also states erroneously, "Missionary sermons which Jews were compelled to hear were only instituted late in the period as part of the open anti-Jewish policy of Pope Paul IV" (ibid., 207). This may be true as far as

universal papal mandate is concerned, but not for the various countries or smaller autonomous political entities of Europe, where secular powers had already mandated Jewish attendance at Christian preaching for the purposes of conversion (see Zawart, *History of Franciscan Preaching*, 247, and Richards, *Sex, Dissidence and Damnation*, 96). It is not clear whether L'Aquila in 1438 fell into this category (the city was then part of the Kingdom of Naples). Even if it did not, Shulvass does not consider the possibility that those Jews "voluntarily" listening to Bernardino were doing so for the purposes of being forewarned of and hence forearmed against new repressive sanctions or other unpleasant consequences that frequently followed upon the preaching of the friars.

16. For this debate, see, for example, Cohen, *The Friars and the Jews*, 51–76. The distinction between "anti-Judaism," that is, the religiously or theologically motivated hatred of Jews, and "anti-Semitism," the racially motivated hatred of Jews, is of course anachronistic with respect to Bernardino and his contemporaries. On this distinction, see John G. Gager, *The Origins of Anti-Semitism: Attitudes toward Judaism in Pagan and Christian Antiquity* (New York: Oxford University Press, 1983), 8–9, and Gavin Langmuir, *History, Religion, and Antisemitism* (Berkeley: University of California Press, 1990), 23–41, 275–305, 341–46, 366–68. As to the origins of anti-Semitism, Langmuir notes, "If antisemitism is defined as chimerical beliefs or fantasies about 'Jews,' as irrational beliefs that attribute to all those symbolized as 'Jews' menacing characteristics or conduct that no Jews have been observed to possess or engage in, then antisemitism first appeared in medieval Europe in the twelfth century" (ibid., 297).

17. We do find the message implied, however, in medieval art, as Bernhard Blumenkranz has pointed out: *Le juif médiéval au miroir de l'art chrétien* (Paris: Études Augustiniennes, 1966), 94. For the figure of the Jew in European art, see also Heinz Schreckenberg, *The Jews in Christian Art: An Illustrated History* (New York: Continuum, 1996), and Michael Camille, *The Gothic Idol: Ideology and Image-Making in Medieval Art* (Cambridge: Cambridge University Press, 1989), 165–94.

18. Facchinetti, *San Bernardino da Siena*, 337.

19. These Jewish-related canons may be found in English translation in Robert Chazan, *Church, State, and Jew in the Middle Ages* (West Orange, N.J.: Behrman House, 1980), 15–42. For further discussion of the topic, see Walter Pakter, *Medieval Canon Law and the Jews* (Ebelsbach am Main: Verlag Rolf Gremer, 1988); John A. Watt, "Jews and Christians in the Gregorian Decretals," in *Christianity and Judaism*, ed. Diana Wood (Oxford: Ecclesiastical History Society/Blackwell, 1992), 93–106; and Diego Quaglioni's two essays, "I giuristi medioevali e gli ebrei. Due 'consultationes' di G. F. Pavini (1478)," *Quaderni storici* no. 64 (an. XXII, 1987): 7–18 and " 'Inter Iudeos et Christianos commertia sunt permissa': 'Questione ebraica' e usura in Baldo degli Ubaldi (c. 1327–1400)," in *Aspetti e problemi della presenza ebraica nell'Italia centro-settentrionale, secoli XIV e XV*, ed. Sofia Boesch Gajano (Rome: Quaderni dell'Istituto di Scienze Storiche dell'Università di Roma, 1983), 273–306.

20. OOH.III.333b–34a. For the unabridged original Latin text, see Appendix 2.

21. "Quia iudei periti sunt in lege secundum literam, unde facilius possent corrumpere simplices christianos quam pagani," *Thomae de Chobham Summa confessorum*, ed. F. Broomfield (Louvain: Nauwelaerts, 1968), 252 ("De penitente suscipiendo," art. 6, dist. 1, q. 4a, cap. 9). Gregory X's letter of March 1274, "Turbato corde," addressed to Dominican and Franciscan inquisitors, expresses the same fear, quoted by John Y. B. Hood, *Aquinas and the Jews* (Philadelphia: University of Pennsylvania Press, 1995), 79. Hood's work is an excellent, succinct summary of the mainstream Christian doctrine on the Jews from the New Testament to Aquinas, to which I will be making frequent reference.

22. Note that here both Aquinas and Bernardino acknowledge the fact that not all Jews are usurers.

23. OOH.III.334b; see Appendix 2 for the original Latin text.

24. Ibid.

25. "Primus ergo amor est generalis, qui comprehendit amicos, inimicos, paganos, Judaeos, Christianos, patrem, matrem, filios, et proximos, et omnes alios" (OOH.III.160a).

26. "El primo amore è generale, e comprendevisi ciò che tu debbi fare; cioè debbi amare el tuo figliuolo, il fratello, el parente, el giudeo, el pagano" (G.216). Likewise to the Florentines in 1424, Bernardino states: "A ogni persona ch'è creatura ragionevole o cristiano, o saracino, o giudeo se' tenuto dimostrargli il segno di carità comuna" (A.329).

27. "Ideo debemus quaerere bonum proximi, sicut bonum nostrum" (OOH.III.161a).

28. "Istae sunt conditiones amoris generalis, quibus debemus et amicis et inimicis subvenire. . . . Unde si videris unum Judaeum in necessitate, tu debes ei subvenire, et omnibus aliis, cum vero et justo amore sancto et operoso; et nisi sic feceris, infernus te expectat" (OOH.III.161b). At the opening of the Latin treatise *De proximorum dilectione,* Bernardino does not explicitly mention the Jews, but it is clear they are included as fit recipients of Christian "general love": "Primus dicitur amor generalis, quo quilibet obligatur diligere amicos et inimicos, bonos et malos, fideles et infideles et quoslibet homines *ad imaginem Dei* factos" (OOQ.III.120). In Articulus II of the same treatise, on "amor specialis," he does mention the Jews by name: "[D]e necessitate teneatur homo ponere pro corporali necessitate proximi sui, etiam inimici et saraceni atque iudaei" (129).

29. "Ita facit Christus ad dandum intelligere, quod irasci debemus contra peccata nostra et aliena; non contra personam, sed contra culpam; quia sic sunt diligendi homines, ut errores eorum non diligantur, sed quia a Deo facti sunti. . . . Ego dico, quod nisi facias illi omnes actus quos facis aliis tuis proximis, et amicis, secundum amorem, et charitatem generalem cum actis et signis salutando eum quum ei obvias, et si te salutat, [non] respondendo ei, tu peccas, et similiter Judaeo et cuilibet alteri pagano, nisi foret prohibitum per Ecclesiam, quia non debemus habere odio peccatorem, nisi secundum peccatum" (OOH.III.225a, b). I have inserted the "non" left out by the scribe or editor, which is clearly indicated by the message Bernardino is imparting here and in the rest of the sermon. This passage finds its counterpart in the 1424 Florentine sermon on restitution: "A uno tuo nimico mortale se' tenuto di carità comuna aiutarlo, di sovvenirlo in caso stretto o di morte o di gran pericolo. E se' tenuto se ti saluta un tuo nimico di risponderli e di renderli il saluto. . . . Se mostri atti o segni di dispiacimento a qualunque persona si sia, o giudeo, o greco o saracino, o cristiano, sempre t'è peccato mortale" (A.329, 330).

30. See Antonio Ciscato, *Gli ebrei in Padova (1300–1800)* (1901; Bologna: Forni, 1967), 18–47; Philippe Braunstein, "Le prêt sur gages à Padoue et dans le Paduan au milieu du XVe siècle," in *Gli Ebrei e Venezia, secoli XIV–XVIII. Atti del Convegno internazionale organizzato dall'Istituto di storia della società e dello stato veneziano della Fondazione Giorgio Cini. Venezia, 5–10 giugno 1983,* ed. Gaetano Cozzi (Milan: Edizioni di Comunità, 1987), 651–70; and, in the same volume, Francesca Zen Benetti, "Prestatori ebraici e cristiani nel Padovano fra Trecento e Quattrocento," 629–50. Daniel Carpi has also written, in Hebrew, on the Jews of Padua, but his studies are untranslated and thus inaccessible to me.

31. Commonly known by its French name, *rouelle,* or *rotella* in Italian (from the Latin *rota,* "wheel"), the Jewish identification badge to which Bernardino refers was usually yellow, circular, and made of cloth. See "Badge, Jewish," *Encyclopaedia Judaica,* 4:64; Hughes, "Distinguishing Signs"; and Ariel Toaff, "The Jewish Badge in Italy during the 15th Century," in *Die Juden*

in ihrer mittelatlerlichen Umwelt, ed. Alfred Ebenbauer and Klaus Zatloukal (Vienna: Bohlau Verlag, 1991), 275–80.

32. "Et miror, quare non portant hic, Vicentiae, et Veronae signa, ut cognoscantur; et volens informari, dictum est mihi quod habent privilegium a Papa; et sunt quidem dicentes quod Papa non potest id concedere contra quatuor concilia; sed de hoc nolo agere contra determinationem Papae" (OOH.III.334a).

33. For the fifteenth-century popes and Jewish doctors, see Shlomo Simonsohn, *The Apostolic See and the Jews. History* (Toronto: Pontifical Institute of Mediaeval Studies, 1991), 172–74, and the pertinent papal decrees reproduced in Simonsohn's 1989 companion volume, *The Apostolic See and the Jews. Documents,* from which the quotation has been taken (624, doc. 563). For an extensive discussion of the figure of the Jewish doctor in the Middle Ages, see Joseph Shatzmiller, *Jews, Medicine, and Medieval Society* (Berkeley: University of California Press, 1994), passim, and for Elia, 68–70. A concise summary of and bibliography on doctor Elia's career may also be found in the *Encyclopaedia Judaica,* 6:649, under "Elijah ben Shabbetai Be'er." For Martin and the Jews, see Edward A. Synan, *The Popes and the Jews in the Middle Ages* (New York: Macmillan, 1965), 135–36; and the older but still informative Félix Vernet, "Le pape Martin V et les Juifs," *Revue des questions historiques* 51 (1892): 373–423. Chazan's *Church, State and Jew in the Middle Ages* also offers a useful anthology of significant medieval documents relating to or by the Jews of Europe, but does not cover Bernardino's lifetime. As to the social status of the fifteenth-century Roman Jews, Anna Esposito claims that they lived in a climate of "substantial acceptance," despite sporadic anti-Jewish outbursts coinciding with Franciscan sermons, Passion play performances, and the Carnival games; such outbursts, however, were "always circumscribed by the solicitations of the moment and were free of any real persecutory or discriminatory character" ("Gli ebrei a Roma nella seconda metà del '400 attraverso i protocolli del notaio Giovanni Angelo Armati," in *Aspetti e problemi della presenza ebraica,* 96).

34. Andrew Gow and Gordon Griffiths, "Pope Eugenius IV and Jewish Money-Lending in Florence: The Case of Salomone di Bonaventura during the Chancellorship of Leonardo Bruni," *Renaissance Quarterly* 42 (1994): 291.

35. For Jews, Christians, and prostitution, see Mazzi, *Prostitute e lenoni nella Firenze del Quattrocento,* 364–65.

36. Hughes, "Distinguishing Signs," 16.

37. "Sed cives deberent providere super hoc, et aliquid de signo statuere; ratio est quia si non habent signum, se immiscent mulieribus Christianis; et est contra cap. *Nonnulli,* de Judaeis" (OOH.III.334a).

38. "Et ipsi Judaei si credunt suam fidem fore meliorem, deberent portare signa ut cognoscerentur, et non deberent verecundari cognosci pro Judaeis" (OOH.III.334a).

39. *Decrees of the Ecumenical Councils,* 1:266. The canon's last line refers to the Mosaic law of *tzitzit* (fringes), that is, the wearing of a distinctive article of clothing as a reminder of their covenant with the Lord, as Hasidic Jews still do today (Solomon Grayzel, "The Papal Bull *Sicut Judeis,*" in *Essential Papers on Judaism and Christianity in Conflict: From Late Antiquity to the Reformation,* ed. Jeremy Cohen [New York: New York University Press, 1990], 248). Another article of clothing distinguishing Jew from Gentile in the Middle Ages was the pointed hat: "It would seem, however, that this distinction was instituted by the Jews themselves" ("Badge, Jewish," *Encyclopaedia Judaica,* 4:64).

40. *Decrees of the Ecumenical Councils,* 1:266.

41. Quaracchi: Collegio S. Bonaventura, 1930, 3:728. See also Camille, *Gothic Idol,* 165–94.

42. "Item caveatis accipere calices, vel urceos Judaeorum, quia non possum credere quin eorum mulieres intus mingant in vilipendium Christianorum" (OOH.III.361a).

43. "Sed quid dicam de illis, qui mutuant sacramenta, et calices Judaeis? Credo quod mingant intus, et faciant omne dedecus in vilipendium fidei Christianae" (OOH.III.361a). In Matthew Paris's *Chronica Majora*, we find the story of an English Jew who defecated on an image of the Virgin each time he used his latrine (cited by Little, *Religious Poverty and the Profit Economy*, 52–53; see also Camille, *Gothic Idol*, 186.)

44. Fleming, *Introduction to the Franciscan Literature*, 255.

45. "O Signore Idio, oh, tu hai il diavolo sopra di te, il quale si può dire che ti piscia in capo!" (R.475).

46. "Se uno si purga el corpo, et elli sgombrasse tra lo spazzo de la camara, apuzzarebbe tutta la casa co' lo sterco. Così el ladro, che s'intende per lo sterco, e 'l sodomito, che è l'urina" (G.209).

47. "Immo peius audivi, quod Judaei in praesentia Christianorum dicunt aliqua in vilipendium Christi" (OOH.III.361a).

48. "Item cives videant privilegia Judaeorum, et statuant statuta, ut ferant signum, ut cognoscantur ab aliis non exempti" (OOH.III.361a).

49. "Item quicunque locat domos Judaeis foenerantibus peccat mortaliter tenendo illos denarios, et similiter Christiano usurario. Et obligatur restituire illis, a quibus acceperat usuras. . . . Et nota quod si Praelatus locat domos Judaeis foenerantibus, est ipso facto suspensus. Similiter religiosi affictantes domos Judaeis foenerantibus sunt ipso facto excommunicati: si collegium, vel universitas locat domos Christianis usurariis, vel Judaeis foenerantibus, est ipso iure interdicta" (OOH.III.361a–b).

50. "Similiter in nutrice Christiana nutriente filios Judaeorum, ut alias dixi, prohibitum est illis capere denarios pro mercede, etc." (OOH.III.361b).

51. See, for example, Esposito, "Gli ebrei a Roma nella seconda metà del '400," 90–95.

52. "Item caveatis vobis mederi per Judaeos, et accipere medicinas Judaeorum. Nam Avenioni fuit unus Judaeus medicus, qui in puncto mortis gloriatus fuit, quod suis medicinis mori fecerat multos Christianorum" (OOH.III.361b).

53. There is no reference to Bernardino's homicidal Jewish doctor in Shatzmiller, *Jews, Medicine, and Medieval Society*, chap. 5, "Rejection: Apprehensions about Jewish Doctors." Yet interestingly enough, "[t]he best-developed legislation against Jewish doctors is to be found in the proceedings of the council of Avignon [the hometown of Bernardino's putative homicidal doctor] in 1337," which, however, was revoked four years later (ibid., 92, 93). In the Dauphiné in 1433 (ten years after Bernardino's Paduan sermon), the Inquisition made one Jewish doctor "confess" that "[Jews] have it as part of their customs that their doctors do not heal any [Christian] but rather kill as many of them as they can" (ibid., 86). For the Jews as poisoners, see also Joshua Trachtenberg, *The Devil and the Jews: The Medieval Conception of the Jew and Its Relation to Modern Antisemitism* (2d pbk. ed., reprint, Philadelphia: Jewish Publication Society of America, 1983), chap. 7, and Ginzburg, *Ecstasies*, 63–72.

54. Shatzmiller, *Jews, Medicine, and Medieval Society*, 94.

55. See, for example, Trachtenberg, *The Devil and the Jews*, chap. 10; Flannery, *The Anguish of the Jews*, 99–101; R. Po-chia Hsia, *The Myth of Ritual Murder: Jews and Magic in Reformation Germany* (New Haven: Yale University Press, 1988); and the various essays in Alan Dundes, ed., *The Blood Libel Legend: A Casebook in Anti-Semitic Folklore* (Madison: University of Wisconsin Press, 1991). For the papal condemnations, see Grayzel, "The Papal Bull *Sicut Judeis*," 239–40.

56. See R. Po-chia Hsia, *Trent 1475: Stories of a Ritual Murder Trial* (New Haven: Yale University Press, 1992), and the introductory essays by Anna Esposito and Diego Quaglioni in vol. 1 of their edition of the records of the trial, *Processi contro gli ebrei di Trento (1475–1478). Volume 1: I processi del 1475* (Padua: Casa Editrice Dott. Antonio Milani, 1990).

57. Carlo da Milano, "Panegirico inedito in onore di S. Bernardino tenuto a Firenze il 21 maggio 1493 dal B. Bernardino da Feltre," *BSB* 3 (1937): 102. On the *monti*, see, for example, Vittorino Meneghin, *Bernardino da Feltre e i Monti di Pietà* (Vicenza: L.I.E.F., 1974); Carol Bresnahan Menning, *Charity and State in Late Renaissance Italy: The Monte di Pietà of Florence* (Ithaca: Cornell University Press, 1993), with ample bibliography; and Maria Giuseppina Muzzarelli, "I francescani ed il problema dei Monti di Pietà," in *Atti-Aquila*, 83–95. Yet the *monti* did charge interest (albeit little) and therefore fell under moral attack, especially from the Dominicans. The ensuing long debate was never theoretically resolved; in the early sixteenth century, silence was simply imposed by Pope Leo X, who threatened excommunication upon anyone raising doubts about the canonical legitimacy of the institution (John T. Noonan, *The Scholastic Analysis of Usury* [Cambridge: Harvard University Press, 1957], 300).

58. "Retulit, S. Bernardinum, illorum concivem narrasse, medicum Hebraeum Avenione morientem dixisse, non adeo illibenter se mori, postquam praescripta dolosis pharmacis occidit multa milia Christianorum." "De Beato Bernardino Feltriensi . . . commentarius historicus," *AASS*, Septembris tomus VII, die vigesima octava, cap. XI, par. 266.

59. The edition available to me was that of Padua and Pesaro, 1733, "nella stamperia di Niccolò Gavelli." For the original date of publication, see *Copia del Testamento*, 31. The 1733 edition also includes a prayer (with no connection to the anti-Semitic theme) to another Franciscan, Anthony of Padua, but this section may possibly be an addition by a later hand (*Copia del Testamento*, 29).

60. "Ora voglio far l'ufficio di buon Padre mentre sono per separarmi da voi Figliuoli. Questo sarà l'ultimo mio testamento."

61. "S. Bernardino di Siena parla a' vostri cuori, o Fedeli, con somma attenzione, quiete, e divozione; ed eccone le sue sante parole."

62. Shlomo Simonsohn, *History of the Jews in the Duchy of Mantua* (Jerusalem: Kiryath Sepher, 1977), 86; and Meneghin, *Bernardino da Feltre*, 267, n. 17.

63. I have translated Bernardino's *terra* here as "territory" rather than "town," which it can also mean, as in the friar's remark, cited below, from D.375–76 concerning the Jew of Bassano. As we will see later in this chapter (sec. 7, "The Effect of Bernardino's Preaching Campaigns"), until October 1437, twelve years after Bernardino gave the sermon just quoted, when Cosimo de' Medici finally succeeded in getting legislation passed allowing Jewish moneylenders into Florence, there was no real Jewish community to speak of in the Tuscan capital. Before that year, the city's Jewish residents were rare and usually transient, in contrast to other towns under Florentine domination, such as Arezzo, where there had already been small but relatively stable and thriving Jewish communities for many years. The concern about Jewish arrogance is another traditional motif: In his *Etsi Judaeos* of 1205, Innnocent III reminded the faithful that "the perfidious Jews should in no way become insolent, but rather under the fear of slavery should always be made aware of their guilt and be forced to honor the Christian faith" (quoted by Hood, *Aquinas and the Jews*, 31).

64. "Mondo cieco! La vostra libertà pazza che non ne punite niuno di questi indiavolati che vanno a vituperare i monasteri! Non conversare con veruno soddomito, chè ti se n'appiccherà; simile non conversare con veruno eretico, chè non ti contamini; simile non conversare con veruno giudeo, chè nel Dicreto t'è proibito. E voi date loro tanta baldanza nella vostra terra;

quotation. Furthermore, the same bibliography cites the 1635 De la Haye edition of Bernardino's *opera omnia,* which gives the sermon a different name, "De impietatibus usurae." The 1635 version of the passage as cited by Poliakov differs slightly in its wording from that of the critical edition, although, in the end, the difference is not sufficient to change the passage's general sense. The English translation of Bonfil's book further compounds that inaccuracy by gratuitously substituting the word *Jews* for Bernardino's generic *usurers.* The quotation as it appears in the 1994 translation of Bonfil begins: "Money is the vital heat of a city. The Jews are leeches who ask for nothing better than the opportunity to devour an ailing member" (*Jewish Life in Renaissance Italy,* 24). The substitution does not occur in the original Italian version of the work (Florence, 1991), nor its Hebrew translation (Jerusalem, 1994). (My thanks to the anonymous member of the Judaica Division, Widener Library, Harvard University, for translating the Hebrew for me.) In fact, without the added word *Jews* in the opening line of the quotation, it is difficult to see how the passage could represent an "explicit occasion" in which "Bernardino was referring only to the Jews," as Bonfil claims.

99. "Miror nempe non parum, et ab admirationes cessare nescio nec volo, quomodo in christicolis tanta regnet insania, tanta vecordia dominetur ac tanta ignorantia, immo caecitas obtenebraverit eos, quod non advertunt consummatam ac excogitatam malitiam iudaeorum, qua utuntur cum conversantur inter christianos. Cum enim christicolae sint omnes reges in sanguine eius *qui est primogenitus mortuorum et princeps regum terrae,* Apoc. 1, 5, tamquam veri reges iusto dominio habent divitias suas, a quibus iudaei, iusto Dei iudicio, privati sunt propter incredulitatem et duritiam cordis sui. Habent, inquam, christiani divitias temporales, divitias corporales et divitias spirituales. Has quidem, quia non valent iudaei ab eis violentia auferre, subripere nituntur malitia, et varia cautela saltem diminuere moliuntur" (OOQ.IV.383–84).

100. "[D]ivitias temporales christicolarum publicis usuris extorquent, ut patet; divitias corporales, id est sanitatem et vitam, auferre conantur dum, contra omnia ecclesiastica instituta, corporum medicos omnino esse procurant, quibus etiam ignorantissimis et rusticanis mira insania potius multi christiani adhaerent atque de sanitate et vita sua in eis totam fiduciam ponunt, quam in peritissimis atque expertissimis medicis christianorum. Quot autem christicolas vel ignorantia vel malitia necent novit Deus. Divitias spirituales, id est fidem et ecclesiasticorum praeceptorum obedientiam cum ceteris spiritualibus thesauris verorum christicolarum, suis blanditiis venantis et amicitiis exquisitis et muneribus toxicatis et conversationibus simulatis et proditionibus excogitatis et libertatibus ac favoribus acquisitis rapere, dispergere, consumere, devorare, et dissipare non cessant, secum ad inferos christianorum insensatorum trahentes animas infelices" (OOQ.IV.384).

101. Hood, *Aquinas and the Jews,* 78, 84. Although affirming this, Hood remarks that Aquinas "harbored no special malice toward Jews" and indeed represented "the more tolerant tradition" with respect to Christian response to the Jewish question (111). Also within the "more tolerant tradition" is Alexander of Hales's *Summa theologica,* the theological textbook par excellence of the Franciscan order, and hence duly consulted by Bernardino on a variety of questions. Hales's brief, canon-law-based treatment of the Jews does little more than to affirm the "constants of Catholic social policy," i.e., Jews have a right to exist, to practice their faith without hindrance, and to be free from forced conversion, while nonetheless remaining in a position of subordination and segregation with respect to Christians (*Aquinas and the Jews,* 100–101; see also Stow, *Alienated Minority,* 259).

102. "A Bassano, terra di Lombardia, v'è stato a prestare uno giudeo quarantadue anni a prestare a usura, che à sì disfatto quella terra e 'l contado, che non vi si truova un danaio" (D.375–76). Bernardino was in Bassano in 1423 (Pacetti, "Cronologia," 451); the Jewish moneylender in Bassano at this time was Calimano del fu Caerson, whose condotta, once expired, was duly

renewed in 1426 and 1430; see Meneghin, *Bernardino da Feltre,* 424–25. Bonfil (*Jewish Life in Renaissance Italy,* 23) misattributes this quotation to Bernardino of Feltre; see Bonfil's cited source, Meneghin, *Bernardino da Feltre,* 424.

103. For the Lateran decree, see *Decrees of the Ecumenical Councils,* 1:265–66; for the 1393 Sienese law, see Zdekauer, "L'interno di un banco di pegno," 80, n. 1.

104. The Lenten cycle *De pugna spirituale,* containing the sermon "De malignitate Judaeorum qui fuerunt auctores passionis Christi" ("Concerning the malice of the Jews who were authors of the passion of Christ," OOH.III.115–16), was considered the work of Bernardino until the mid–twentieth century. As Pacetti convincingly argues ("Gli scritti di San Bernardino," in *SBSSR,* 64–66), this whole sermon cycle is instead to be attributed to an Augustinian preacher, most likely Michele da Massa (†1337). However, the centuries-old attribution to Bernardino may have contributed to the anti-Semitic reputation of the Franciscan.

105. Compare, for example, B.365 (from a vernacular *reportatio*) with OOQ.II.222 (from the Latin *Tractatus de passione*), both concerning Matthew 27:24–25 (the Jewish mob shouts to Pilate, "Let his blood be upon us and our children"). The vernacular scene does not even contain the word *Jew* and restricts its commentary to one terse line, "E bene portono [il suo sangue] loro poi in capo" ("And indeed do they bear [his blood] on their heads"). I quote the Latin treatise version above. For "perfidi giudei," see, e.g., B.282, OOH.III.301b.

106. "Primo quidem Christus accusatur, scilicet a Iudaeis coram praeside Pilato. O 'horrenda impietas Iudaeorum, quae tantis iniuriis satiari non potuit, quin potius, ferali rabie fremens, impio iudici, tamquam rabido cani, animam iusti deglutiendam exposuit!' " (OOQ.II.211). The quoted segment is lifted verbatim from Bonaventure's *The Tree of Life* (*Lignum vitae*), although Bernardino, in common medieval fashion, does not acknowledge his source. I use the translation by E. Cousins (Bonaventure, *The Soul's Journey into God, the Tree of Life and the Life of Francis* [New York: Paulist Press, 1978], 145).

107. "Sed principes Sacerdotum et omne Iudaeorum concilium *praetorium Pilati non intraverunt, ne contaminarentur, sed manducarent Pascha,* scilicet quod illo tempore celebrabant. Semper enim Iudaei, vilioribus caeremoniis studiosius intendentes, in magnorum malorum voraginem ceciderunt. O damnata caecitas et perversa conditio Iudaeorum! Verebantur contaminare Pascha, si contra traditiones suas praesidis intrarent praetorium, sed non verebantur ad mortem iniuste deducere iustum et innocentum Dominum Iesum Christum" (OOQ.II.212). For similar exclamations of sarcasm and condemnation in Bernardino, see OOQ.II.224, 225, 231–32, 260, and 263–64. Blessed Simone da Cascia (†1348) was an Augustinian hermit, close friend of the Franciscan "Spiritual" leader Angelo Clareno, and "one of the greatest spiritual writers of the fourteenth century" (Fleming, *Introduction to the Franciscan Literature,* 102; see also Pietro Bellini, "Simon Fidati de Cascia," *Dictionnaire de spiritualité* 14:873–76).

108. "Considera, anima mea, 'quam supereffluens fuit amor dulcis Domini nostri Iesu super impios hostes suos, quando non solum pleno corde fuit indultor, sed etiam efficacissimus intercessor et piissimus excusator' " (OOQ.II.234). Bernardino takes the quoted section verbatim from Ubertino da Casale's *Arbor vitae crucifixae Iesu.*

109. "Potest ex Christi magna benignitate comprehendi quod etiam ipsi Iudaei ad hanc intercessionem pro consequenda indulgentia pertinerent, illi dumtaxat qui Christum omnino ignoraverunt; si vero scientes in istam orationem venissent, frustra Salvator dimissionis causam innexisset: *quia nesciunt quid faciunt;* est siquidem 'quia' semper redditio causae. Quomodo ergo scientes quae fiebant et faciebant, aut consentiebant in nece Filii Dei, ad istam orationem potuissent pertinere, cum 'quia' tantum de ignorantia pro redditione causae proponatur? Quomodo etiam Gentiles seu Iudaei ignorantes potuissent excludi, cum pro

peccatoribus exoraret et velit *omnes homines salvos fieri*?" (OOQ.II.235). Again, Bernardino's (unacknowledged) source is Simone da Cascia's *De gestis Domini Salvatoris*. For the phrase "all men to be saved," see 1 Timothy 2:4. For the theme of Christ's forgiveness of the Jews in Aquinas and earlier theologians, see Hood, *Aquinas and the Jews*, 71–74.

110. "Dicitur quod ignorantia facti non excusat Iudaeos, qui non credunt venisse Christium. Ratio est, quia talis ignorantia crassa est et supina. Possent enim Christum venisse scire, tum ex operibus Christi, tum ex operibus discipulorum eius, tum ex collatione Scripturarum perhibitarum" (OOQ.III.362). For ignorance of the law, see also OOQ.I.178 and 206.

111. "Anco potranno pigliare essempio da' giuderi e quali crocifissero Gesù Cristo, nostro Salvatore, pensandosi di fare bene, e sentenziarlo a morte, e dicevano: *Melius est ut unus moriatur pro populo, quam tota gens pereat*. 'Egli è meglio che muoia uno per lo populo che perisca tanta gente.' E pensavano di fare bene" (F.41). See A.451–52, where Bernardino again states that the Jews crucified Jesus out of ignorance of his true identity, but still sinned in doing so: "Allora non sapevano quello che si dicevano e tu lo sai. Se avessino creduto [che] fusse stato el loro Iddio e il loro messia, non l'avrebbono crocifisso nè bestemmiato. Peccorono per ignoranza." Bernardino's analysis of the moral act is flawed by fundamental logical contradictions, especially with respect to the principle of intentionality; see my essay "To Persuade Is a Victory," 78–80.

112. Among the many studies of Judas Iscariot, see the recent work of William Klassen, *Judas, Betrayer or Friend of Jesus?* (Minneapolis: Fortress, 1996), as well as the many pages devoted to Judas in Raymond Brown's magisterial *The Death of the Messiah*, 2 vols. (New York: Doubleday, 1994), both studies supplying ample bibliography.

113. For Judas in the usury sermons, see OOH.III.224a and OOQ.IV.413–14; for Judas's confession, see OOH.III.224a, OOQ.III.101–2, and OOQ.IV.413–14; for his despair as the greater sin, OOQ.VIII.52. In addition to these passages and those listed in the indexes to the Quaracchi volumes, references to Judas in Bernardino can also be found at OOH.III.188a and 301b, OOQ.II.201–3, B.295–96, B.299, and E.354. For more on Judas in Bernardino and in Italian art, see my essay " 'Just as your lips approach the lips of your brother': Judas Iscariot and the Kiss of Betrayal," in *Saints and Sinners: Caravaggio and the Baroque Image*, ed. Franco Mormando, Exhibition Catalogue (Chestnut Hill, Mass.: McMullen Museum of Art at Boston College, 1999).

114. For a convenient summary of Augustine's teachings on the Jews, see Hood, *Aquinas and the Jews*, 10–15.

115. "*Respondens* autem *universus populus dixit: Sanguis eius super nos et super filios nostros*. Terribile quidem est iudicium Iudaeorum, quod in eadem damnatione qua erant ipsi patres, filios induxerunt, ut fieret obligatio personalis non tantum exsistentium, sed etiam futurorum. 'Sed nescio quo demerito tam occulto sit ista obligatio subsecuta, seu quae fuerit ista tam secreta iustitia, ut ad tantum scelus subeundae vindictae patres, Deo permettente, potuerint nondum natos filios obligare; ut nedum ad nascituros proximi temporis, sed usque in praesentiarum profluxerit damnatio ista, qua isti ut illi meruerint indurari, ac per hoc ut exceperunt sententiam, ita in vita ipsorum novimus obvenisse, etiam cum poena quae servatur aeterna' " (OOQ.II.222). The quoted passage comes from Simone da Cascia, *De gestis Domini Salvatoris*.

116. "Santo Agostino risponde: Se Cristo si lasciò da' Giudei, membra del dimonio, battere e crocifigere, quanto maggiormente dal capo loro dimonio se lo doveva lasciare fare? Volle così per darci esemplo di contrastare e combattere con lui" (A.76).

117. For Chrysostom, see Stow, *Alienated Minority*, 17; see also 25 and 234–35, as well as Trachtenberg, *Devil and the Jews*, chap. 1, "Devil Incarnal," and Cohn, *Europe's Inner Demons*,

64. For Paul, the Church Fathers, and the Jews, see Hood, *Aquinas and the Jews,* 9–18; see also Gager, *Origins of Anti-Semitism,* passim.

118. A.452 and F.150. The anecdote is also to be found in two unpublished *reportationes* of Bernardino's sermons from 1425, one from Siena and the other from Assisi; see Delcorno, "La diffrazione del testo omeletico," 468, and Pacetti, "La predicazione di San Bernardino da Siena a Perugia e ad Assisi nel 1425," *CF* 10 (1940): 20.

119. See Hughes, "Distinguishing Signs," 26–29.

120. OOH.III.159b ("sicut Judaei qui nolunt fieri Christiani ne perdant divitias et honores"), 221a ("Judaei ipsi non dicunt verum, quia cupiditas avaritiae facit eos intelligere quod volunt, sed non quod debent"); see also OOQ.VI.287, where Bernardino quotes Alexander of Hales's *Summa:* "Nam, cum essent avari, ne scilicet fierent fures aut usurarii in fratres suos, permissum est eis posse usuras exigere ab alienis."

121. "Nota etiam, quod Iudaei erant quadrupliciter parvuli sub lege, scilicet: locutione, quia de parvulis bonis scilicet de praesentibus, non de aeternis tractabant; cognitione, quia litterae tantum exteriori, non sensui interiori intendebant, sicut parvuli discentes quadernum; affectione amoris, quia promissione temporalium alliciebantur, ut parvuli pomo; timoris subiectione, quia timore flagellorum praesentium terrebantur, ut parvuli virga" (OOQ.IX.61).

122. "Illa enim nec lucent nec pascunt nec medentur; ideo synagoga in tenebris est usque adhuc, fame et infirmitate laborans, nec sanabitur nec satiabitur, donec sciat Iesum dominari Iacob et finium terrae" (OOQ.IV.489). See also OOQ.I.12 on the futility of the Jewish faith.

123. "Congregacio velut animalium irracionalium que, licet sensum habeant, intellectum tamen careant, dum litteram attendunt et allegoriam misticam non admittunt . . . ; hebreorum congregacio dicta fuit et dicitur proprie synagoga a forma quod est cum et gogos quod est gregacio, unde synagoga dicitur quasi gregum qui sunt peccorum concursio vel brutorum." The treatise is entitled "Liber dialogorum gerarchie subcelestis inter orthodoxum catholicum et cathecuminum Paucascium inquirentem de reformacione ecclesie militante." See Enzo Petrucci, "Gli ebrei in un inedito opuscolo anonimo sulla costituzione e riforma della Chiesa della fine del secolo XIV," in *Aspetti e problemi della presenza ebraica,* 319–20 for the passages quoted. Yet the treatise at the same time states that Jews must not be mistreated or forced to convert ("Gli ebrei in un inedito opuscolo anonimo," 319).

124. "Timor est servorum, sed amor est filiorum. Unde apparet etiam hodie de Judeis, qui volunt tenere legem timoris; quia opus est eis ut sint servi, velint nolint, Christianorum." The passage, from an unpublished sermon delivered by Bernardino in Perugia in 1426 and transcribed by John of Capistrano, is cited by Gustavo Cantini, "Una ignorata redazione latina di sermoni bernardiniani," *BSB* 2 (1936): 292–93. The quotation from Aquinas comes from his *De regimine judaeorum ad Ducissam Brabantiae,* in *Aquinas: Selected Political Writings,* ed. A. P. d'Entrèves (Oxford: Blackwell, 1954), 84.

125. OOQ.VI.159 and IX.192; cf. 2 Corinthians 3:12–16. As Hood observes, this insistence on the Jews' sinful "obstinacy," "veiled eyes," and other similar characterizations was one means by which religiously insecure Christians could explain away the disquieting fact that large numbers of Jesus' contemporary coreligionists had arrived at the conclusion that Jesus did not match the scriptural description of the Messiah; see Hood, *Aquinas and the Jews,* 8–9.

126. "Ma se vedi uno seracino, uno giudeo, uno paterino, uno scomunicato morire sanza niuno segno di sacramento, non debbi pregare per loro che peccheresti, perchè debbi essere certo che va in ninferno [*sic*], e per loro non si debbe orare" (D.224–25). See also D.50 (where he adds to the list "heretics, pagans, Barbarians, Slavs, Turks, [and] schismatics") and OOH.III.171b.

127. "Quamdiu enim steterunt in vera fide, exaltavit illos Deus super omne hominum genus, sicut patet in terra quam dedit eis et in Lege et regno et templo et victoriis et miraculis

et signis et Prophetis et cultu et beneficiis. Postquam autem Dei Filium negaverunt et eius fidem abiecerunt, nulla gens adeo fuit depressa et abiecta oppressionibus tyrannorum, latronum, sicariorum, schismatibus et depopulationibus, mutuis dissensionibus et obsidionibus, pestibus, cladibus, gladio, fame, captivitate, nece, strage, servitute, ludibriis, venditione et desperatione, sicut legitur super eos evenisse omnes has maledictiones" (OOQ.I.18). Cf. Aquinas, *Super Psalmos* 41.2: "If an infidel Jew asks a convert: Where is your God? The convert should give this witness to the faith: The presence of my God is manifest in your punishment—that is, the punishment of the Jews—which is that you are dispersed" (quoted by Hood, *Aquinas and the Jews,* 77).

128. "Quod gens iudaica, quae quondam pulcherrima fuit atque decora et nobilissima forma, modo manifeste apparet abiectissima, vilissima et turpissima, debilis et meretriculosa ultra omnes alias nationes . . . Iudaeos, qui sperant inaniter in suo venturo Messia" (OOQ.I.19; VII.453).

129. See Arsenio Frugoni's introduction to his edition of Joachim of Fiore's *Adversus Iudeos* (Rome: Istituto Storico Italiano per il Medio Evo, 1957), xxxii–xxxvii. The scriptural basis for this belief is Romans 11; see Hood, *Aquinas and the Jews,* 5–6, 77–78.

130. "Multi utique sunt erroribus et haeresibus pleni, extra tamen in apparentia iusti; qui, si extra ostenderent quod intus in corde credunt, iuste comburerentur. Inter quos numerandi sunt quidam qui lapsi sunt in damnatam haeresim de spiritu libertatis. . . . His quoque possunt etiam superaddi multi alii haeretici et schismatici et iudaei pluries baptizati, insuper et secta Dulcini haeretici; qui in apparentia tenentes honestam vitam, intus sunt erroribus pleni. . . . Omnes autem praedicti, et consimiles eis, catholicis operibus conformantur, verbis atque gestibus illud idem praetendunt, similes pueris cum sunt in scholis, qui, stande magistro, stant composti et modesti solummodo ex timore; sed, illo absente, tumultibus et stultitiis pleni sunt" (OOQ.III.109).

131. One would like to know the reaction of Bernardino's Jewish contemporaries to the friar's anti-Jewish preaching. Assuredly they did indeed react, but, unfortunately, I have come across no documentation in any form describing or even acknowledging the fact of Jewish reaction to our friar. As Marc Saperstein reports, as far as Jewish preaching is concerned, "[t]he record before the sixteenth century is almost entirely blank" ("Italian Jewish Preaching: An Overview," in *Essential Papers on Jewish Culture in Renaissance and Baroque Italy,* ed. David B. Ruderman [New York: New York University Press, 1992], 87).

132. "Distinguishing Signs," 20.

133. According to the chronology established by both Cannarozzi (F.xxiii) and Pacetti, "Cronologia," 452. Bernardino preached on the issue of usury in the thirtieth sermon of this Siena 1425 series (G.113–30). For the Jews of Siena, see Sofia Boesch Gajano, "Il Comune di Siena e il prestito ebraico nei secoli XIV e XV. Fonti e problemi," in *Aspetti e problemi della presenza ebraica,* 175–225; Nello Pavoncello, "Notizie storiche sulla Comunità ebraica di Siena e la sua Sinagoga," *La Rassegna Mensile di Israele* 36 (1970): 289–313; and Michele Cassandro, *Gli ebrei e il prestito ebraico a Siena nel Cinquecento* (Milan: Giuffrè, 1979).

134. Boesch Gajano, "Il Comune di Siena e il prestito ebraico," 200.

135. Alessio, *Storia di San Bernardino,* 211.

136. Ibid., 211–13. The text is also found in Piccolomini and Mengozzi, *Il Monte de' Paschi di Siena,* 1:111–12. There is no mention of the *Riformagioni di San Bernardino* in Sofia Boesch Gajano's long essay on Sienese regulation of Jewish moneylending. However, as she alerts us in her introduction, her "scrutiny of the archival sources has not been exhaustive [*sistematico*]" ("Il Comune di Siena e il prestito ebraico," 179).

137. "E anco ti voglio agiognere più; io non dico questo né per odio né per niuno modo di voler male a persona, e nol dico per nominare persona; dico solo il caso: se voi sete concorsi

in questo, che il giudeo per vostra cagione o per vostro aiuto presta a usura qui a Siena, colui che ha consentito col suo lupino, elli è corso in questa scomunicazione maggiore. Ha'mi inteso?" (R.1033). According to Alessio, the anti-Jewish provisions promulgated in 1425 were not officially annulled by law until February 29, 1429. Boesch Gajano makes no mention of the 1429 law in her "Il Comune di Siena e il prestito ebraico."

138. "Ora ti vo' mostrare quello che ne sequita a tenere il giudeo a casa vostra. . . . il guastamento de la vostra città, e . . . la scomunicazione del papa, che non ti puoi salvare con essa" (R.1033). Siena and other cities seeking to invite Jewish moneylenders into their territory requested and duly obtained papal exemptions from the canon law prohibition.

139. *Storia di San Bernardino,* 213. Either Alessio erred in his date or there had already been another repeal prior to the summer of 1427, as Bernardino suggests there was.

140. Boesch Gajano, "Il Comune di Siena e il prestito ebraico," 203.

141. Ibid., 202, 213, n. 100. Yet see the discussion of the ambiguities of such citizenship granted to Jews in Gow and Griffiths, "Pope Eugenius IV and Jewish Money-Lending in Florence," 290–92.

142. Boesch Gajano, "Il Comune di Siena e il prestito ebraico," 196–201.

143. Ibid., 206–7.

144. The law is quoted by Anthony Molho, "A Note on Jewish Moneylenders in Tuscany in the Late Trecento and Early Quattrocento," in *Renaissance Studies in Honor of Hans Baron,* ed. Anthony Molho and John A. Tedeschi (De Kalb: Northern Illinois University Press, 1971), 105, who offers further details of Florentine Jewish history. For more extensive coverage, see Gow and Griffith, "Pope Eugene IV and Jewish Money-Lending in Florence," esp. 285–93, and Umberto Cassuto, *Gli ebrei a Firenze nell'età del Rinascimento* (Florence: Galletti e Cocci, 1918), esp. 8–32 for the legislation and data discussed in the present paragraph. For Jews and Jewish lending in Arezzo, a town within Florentine dominion, see the Mohlo article just cited, as well as Roberto G. Salvadori and Giorgio Sacchetti, *Presenze ebraiche nell'Aretino dal XIV al XX secolo* (Florence: Olschki, 1990).

145. Cassuto, *Gli ebrei a Firenze,* 18.

146. Cassuto dates the effective beginnings of the organized Jewish community of Florence to this year. There were some Jews (doctors and merchants) in Florence previous to that date, but very few in number and often transient in nature. Nonetheless, because of Florence's convenient location, representatives of the Jewish communities of Italy held their 1428 congress there, resulting in the securing of the protective papal bull of 1429, which we shall discuss below (ibid., 20–21, 28–29).

147. Lazzareschi, "San Bernardino of Siena sull'Amiata e nella Lucchesia," 259. As mentioned in chap. 3, Bernardino's only documented trip to Lucca was in 1424; he could have made other, unrecorded, visits to the city, but this is not likely in the period here under question.

148. Bussi's *Storia di Viterbo* is quoted by Francesco Cristofori, "S. Bernardino da Siena in Viterbo," *MF* 4 (1889): 38, which also acknowledges the lack of agreement among chroniclers as to the identity of the preacher in question. Cesare Pinzi's well-documented *Storia della città di Viterbo* (Viterbo: Tipografia Sociale Agnesotti, 1899), 555–62, leaves no doubt that it was Guglielmo, and not Bernardino.

149. Capistrano, *S. Bernardini senensis . . . Vita,* OOH.I.xl, col. b. Capistrano also speaks of this L'Aquila mission in one of his sermons delivered in Vienna; see Gabriele Sartorelli, "San Bernardino da Siena ed il francescanesimo abruzzese del Quattrocento," *Bullettino della Deputazione abruzzese di storia patria* 70 (1980): 22. We know from other indications that the year was 1438 (Pacetti, "Cronologia," 457). The "miracle of Collemaggio" was also witnessed

and recorded by the Franciscan chronicler, Bernardino of Aquila; see *B. Bernardini Aquilani Chronica Fratrum Minorum Observantiae,* ed. Leonardus Lemens (Rome: Typis Sallustianis, 1902), 19, which tells us: "Hunc [Bernardinum] audivi Aquilae praedicare 12 praedicationes tempore quo erat Aquilae rex Renatus." For Bernardino's visits to and death in L'Aquila, see also Giacinto Marinangeli, "Eamus Aquilam! Ad Aquilam missus sum. Nota storico-critica," *Bullettino della Deputazione abruzzese di storia patria* 70 (1980): 164–65. Roth's statement is in his *History of the Jews of Italy,* 161, while Cassuto's is in his entry on Bernardino in the *Encyclopaedia Judaica,* 4:289.

150. Hence the claim that in Perugia in 1425 "the Jews constituted the major target of [Bernardino's] fiery sermons" is unsupported by the extant sermon evidence; Ariel Toaff, *Gli ebrei a Perugia* (Perugia: Deputazione di Storia Patria per l'Umbria, 1975), 60. Thirty-six of these sermons have come down to us in *reportatio* form, the work of John of Capistrano. They are as yet unpublished; for a list of titles and description of contents, see Pacetti, *De sancti Bernardini Senensis operibus,* 166–68, and "La predicazione di San Bernardino da Siena a Perugia e ad Assisi nel 1425," *CF* 9 (1939): 494–520; 10 (1940): 5–28, 161–88.

151. See above, chap. 3, sec. 7, "The Response of the Towns." For Jewish life in Perugia and in all of Umbria, see the three works by Ariel Toaff, *Gli ebrei a Perugia; The Jews in Umbria. Volume 1: 1245–1435* (Leiden: E. J. Brill, 1993); and *Love, Work, and Death: Jewish Life in Medieval Umbria* (London: Littman Library of Jewish Civilization, 1996).

152. Fantozzi, "Documenta perusina," 119–25.

153. "Insuper statuimus ad omnem dictorum usurariorum malitiam et perfidiam extirpandam, quod de cetero nullus hebreus mutuo vel in depositum vel alio titulo contractus pecuniam recipiat ab aliquo christiano sub usuris; et quicumque hebreus contrafecerit, ipso facto, si capi poterit, personaliter puniatur pena dextri pedis, qui sibi de facto debeat amputari per d[ominem] Potestatem civitatis Perusii qui pro tempore erit: et si capi non poterit, in banno dicti pedis sibi amputandi ponatur; ita quod quicunque venerit in fortiam comunis Perusii sibi debeat pes dexter amputari; et nichilominus tota sua familia a civitate, territorio et districtu perusino expellatur." Fantozzi, "Documenta perusina," 122.

154. Giacomo Todeschini is also of the opinion that the moneylending prohibitions in the Perugian statute were "not the fruit of a general antipathy [for the Jews], but the precise result of an economic and political plan," "Teorie economiche francescane e presenza ebraica in Italia," 216.

155. Toaff, *Gli ebrei a Perugia,* 62.

156. Pacetti, "Cronologia," 453, 457.

157. Toaff, "The Jewish Badge in Italy during the 15th Century," 278, and *Gli ebrei a Perugia,* 64. For copies of the laws, see Toaff's *The Jews in Umbria,* 1:434–37, doc. 840; 2:492–95, doc. 952.

158. For Bernardino's visit to Amelia and the titles of his five sermons there, see Pacetti, *De sancti Bernardini senensis operibus,* 168–69. For the case of Magister Angelo, see Toaff, *The Jews in Umbria,* 1:434–37, doc. 840; 408, doc. 790; 410, doc. 795; and 411, doc. 797.

159. Pacetti, "Cronologia," 453.

160. "Cum per ven. patrem Berardinum [*sic*] multis continuatis diebus proximus iam decursis in Civitate Urbevetana verbum dominicum fuerit predicatum." Sgariglia, "Due documenti relativi a S. Bernardino," 160.

161. "Predicavit et monuit Urbevetanum populum pro salute animarum ipsius . . . quod a conversatione hebreorum eo maxime singuli se abstineant, et quod immunitates et exemptiones eisdem hebreis concesse per Comunitatem Urbevetanam et pacta cum ipsis hebreis inita et

firmita, et presentim [*sic*] quod possint mutuari ab usuras, cassentur, tollantur, irritentur et annullentur." Sgariglia, "Due documenti relativi a S. Bernardino," 160.

162. "Surgens pedes et ad solitam arrengheriam vadens et Altissimi nomine invocato, consulendo super facto Iudeorum dixit et consuluit, quod ad evitandam excommunicationis penam quam dictus ven. frater Bernardinus predicando pronumptiavit [*sic*] omnibus habentibus commersium illicitum cum dictis hebreis et eis dantibus auxilium, consilium vel favorem et maxime in mutuando ad usuras, quod auctoritate presentis Generalis Consilii omnes immunitates, exemptiones, pacta et capitula eisdem Iudeis vel eorum alteri a Communitate dicte Civitatis concesse ac tribute et cum eis inita et firmata ex nunc in antea sint nulle." Sgariglia, "Due documenti relativi a S. Bernardino," 160.

163. *Consilia contra judaeos foenerantes*, in Nicolaus de Ausmo (of Osimo), *Supplementum Summae Pisanellae* (Venice: Leonardus Wild, 1489 [i.e., 1479]), 345r, col. b. The passage in question occurs in the unnumbered consilium placed between the second and third consilia and is entitled "Consilium domini Alexandro de Nevo. De Vincentia. Reprobatorium domini Angeli de Lastro super articulo: An iudei possunt conduci ad fenerandum cum dispensatione papae." Nievo calculates the year in question as 1441, but he was probably referring to Bernardino's mission there in 1443. For these *consilia*, see Quaglioni, "I giuristi medioevali e gli ebrei," 13, and Nelson, *Idea of Usury*, 21.

164. Poliakov, *Jewish Bankers*, 33–34.

165. Consilium domini Alexandro de Nevo, 352r, col. b.

166. Meneghin, *Bernardino da Feltre*, 385.

167. Pacetti, "Cronologia," 448, 449, 451, 461–62.

168. Ciscato, *Gli ebrei in Padova*, 155.

169. Ibid.

170. Ibid., 166.

171. Ibid., 39; Pacetti, "Cronologia," 451; and Pacetti, *De sancti Bernardini senensis operibus*, 133.

172. Ciscato, *Gli ebrei in Padova*, 240–41.

173. Ibid., 52.

174. Ibid., 50–51.

175. For the text of the laws, Toaff, *Jews in Umbria*, 2:466–68, doc. 903; and 2:470–72, doc. 910.

176. Shlomo Simonsohn, ed., *The Jews in the Duchy of Milan* (Jerusalem: Israel Academy of Sciences and Humanities, 1982), 1:32.

177. Simonsohn, *History of the Jews in the Duchy of Mantua*, 6–7.

178. "Sai che si vorrebbe fare? Egli si vorrebbe prima bruciare la donna che si veste, e poi la madre che 'l consente, e doppo loro el sarto che le fa" (R.1088).

179. Giordano (ca. 1260–1311), it would seem, was in favor of the expulsion of Jews and "did not even shy away from suggesting the extermination of Jews who exhibited hostility toward Christianity," Cohen, *Friars and the Jews*, 241. For Vincent Ferrer, see Flannery, *Anguish of the Jews*, 133–34.

180. "I dottori c'insegnano e noi pigliamo i fioretti e diciagli a voi" (D.296). See above, chap. 1, sec. 2.

181. Because of the similarities of name, among modern scholars the far more intense anti-Semitic activity of Bernardino of Feltre is at times mistakenly attributed to his older confrere, Bernardino of Siena. For instance, Cassuto corrects Graetz for such a mistake (*Gli ebrei a Firenze*, 182, n. 4). Toaff makes the same error in *Jews in Medieval Assisi*, 45, n. 147 (his source, Cristofani, in reality speaks of Bernardino of Feltre).

182. I am referring to the Quaracchi edition of Bernardino's *opera omnia.*

183. Simonsohn, "Lo stato attuale della ricerca storica sugli ebrei in Italia," 33–34.

184. In addition to the ancient community of Rome, Venice, Padua, and Verona were counted among the "principal centers" of Jewish life (Shulvass, *Jews in the World of the Renaissance,* 15). Michele Luzzati repeats Poliakov's estimation (based on unidentified statistical sources) that Jews on the Italian peninsula at the end of the Middle Ages and during the Renaissance numbered "quelques dizaines de milliers," rejecting Baron's figure of 120,000 as too high ("Per la storia dei rapporti fra ebrei e cristiani in Italia. Demografia e insediamenti ebraici nel Rinascimento," in *Ebraismo e antiebraismo. Immagine e pregiudizio,* ed. Cesare Luporini [Florence: Editrice La Giuntina, 1989], 185). Shulvass, in turn, tells us: "At the close of the Renaissance [late sixteenth century], there were about a thousand Jews in Venice. In Padua the Jews numbered about 600–700" (*Jews in the World of the Renaissance,* 16). Roberto Salvadori gives other estimates for the total Italian Jewish population: 50,000 for the year 1300; 120,000 for the year 1500 (*Breve storia degli ebrei toscani, IX–XX secolo* [Florence: Le Lettere, 1995], 120); Salvadori's figures are taken from Sergio Della Pergola, *Anatomia dell'ebraismo italiano* (Assisi-Roma: Carucci, 1976). As we saw, the total Jewish population of Trent in 1475 at the time of the murder of "little Simon" was approximately thirty persons. Most small towns, such as Arezzo, would play host to only one or two Jewish families, that number being sufficient to meet the moneylending needs of the community. This we know from the surviving legal contracts, called *condotte* (sing., *condotta*) between host town and Jewish family, granting, among other rights, the right to residence and the right to engage in moneylending. For a representative sample, see Mohlo, "A Note on Jewish Moneylenders in Tuscany."

185. See Meneghin, *Bernardino da Feltre,* 170–71, and Bonfil, *Jewish Life in Renaissance Italy,* 25.

186. Norman Roth, "Bishops and Jews in the Middle Ages," *Catholic Historical Review* 80 (1994): 1–2.

187. "De institutis, discipulis et doctrina fratris Bernardini," 323, sec. 11.

188. Quoted in the "Sermo contra imaginem nominis tabuellae, quae est imago et signum antichristi" by another critic of Bernardino's, Andrea da Cascia. Longpré has printed the entire sermon in "S. Bernardino de Sienne e le nom de Jésus," *AFH* 29 (1936): 443–61 (452 for the quotations above). The episode is also discussed by Edith Pasztor, "S. Bernardino da Siena e l'episcopato italiano del suo tempo," in *Atti-Siena,* 735–38.

189. See, for example, Simonsohn, *The Apostolic See/Documents,* 711, doc. 615, and 771–74, doc. 658, and the relevant pages in Simonsohn's companion volume, *The Apostolic See/History.* Even antipope Felix V (Amadeus VIII, duke of Savoy) issued a bull on March 10, 1444, at the request of the Piedmontese Jews, reprimanding Mendicants and preachers of other orders for inciting anti-Jewish sentiment among the populace; see Renata Segre, ed., *The Jews in Piedmont* (Jerusalem: Israel Academy of Sciences and Humanities and Tel Aviv University, 1986), 1:173–74, doc. 381. Shortly thereafter, "the bishop of Turin, Ludovico of Romagnano, [ordered] all the religious authorities in his diocese . . . to proclaim most solemnly during the mass that the Jews must not be harassed, must be allowed to enjoy their privileges and be provided with lodging and food" in accordance with their charters with Pope Felix and the Duke of Savoy (*Jews in Piedmont,* 175, doc. 382).

190. For the texts of Martin's two bulls, see Simonsohn, *The Apostolic See/Documents,* 711, doc. 615; and 771–74, doc. 658. For the history of *Sicut Judeis* and papal Jewish policy, see Grayzel, "The Papal Bull *Sicut Judeis,*" and Kenneth R. Stow, *Catholic Thought and Papal Jewry Policy 1555–1593* (New York: Jewish Theological Seminary of America, 1977). "Putatively, *Sicut*

iudaeis required no repetition at all, for it had been incorporated into Gregory IX's permanently binding Decretals" (Stow, *Alienated Minority,* 268).

191. Simonsohn, *The Apostolic See/Documents,* 679–80, doc. 596.

192. Ibid., 711, doc. 615.

193. Martin, by the way, has been described as "the pope who more than any of his predecessors gave voice to the principle of toleration, and in a language often infused with a spirit of humanity," but let us keep in mind that, as with all popes, his supposed toleration and spirit of humanity in the forms of official bulls had to be literally purchased by the Jews with large sums of money, and were not without their abrupt about-faces. The quoted description of Martin is from Gow and Griffiths, "Pope Eugenius IV and Jewish Money-Lending in Florence," 295. For the Jewish "purchase" of Martin's protection, see, e.g., Toaff, *Gli ebrei a Perugia,* 61; for more on Martin V, the Jews, and the Franciscans, see Simonsohn, "Divieto di trasportare ebrei in Palestina," in *Italia Judaica: "Gli ebrei in Italia fra Rinascimento ed Età Barocca." Atti del II Convegno Internazionale. Genova 10–15 giugno 1984* (Rome: Ministero per i Beni Culturali e Ambientali; Pubblicazioni degli Archivi di Stato, 1986), 39–53, esp. 42–49.

194. Simonsohn, *The Apostolic See/Documents,* 720, doc. 620. Simonsohn appends this note to the 1423 bull of revocation: "The reason given for the revocation does not shed light on the causes. Vernet, 'Martin V,' 381f., 415f., though attempting some explanation, resigns himself to '. . . le laconisme des explications déroute notre envie de savoir.' Simonsohn, *Kirchliche Judengesetzgebung,* pp. 28f., attributes the change of mind to anti-Jewish pressures exerted on the pope. Grayezel, *Sicut Judaeis,* p. 270, appears to accept this explanation. Hofer, *Johannes von Capestrano,* p. 110, attributes Martin's change of heart to Capistrano's influence." Indeed, with a bull dated June 7, 1427, Martin responded affirmatively to a petition by John of Capistrano "to approve the abrogation of all privileges granted to the Jews in violation of Church laws or of other laws in the dominions of Queen Johanna II of Naples" (Simonsohn, *The Apostolic See/Documents,* 753, doc. 646). It is Umberto Cassuto who suggests that putative Jewish support of the Hussites may have been a factor in the revocation of the bull. He offers as evidence the fact that the 1423 bull of revocation was "expressly sent to the legate of the Holy See in Bohemia and in certain parts of Germany" (Cassuto, *Gli ebrei a Firenze,* 27–28, n. 4).

195. Simonsohn, *The Apostolic See/Documents,* 815–16, doc. 694; and Gow and Griffiths, "Pope Eugenius IV and Jewish Money-Lending," 297. Eugene's 1435 bull is not included in Simonsohn's edition of the papal bulls.

196. *Decrees of the Ecumenical Councils,* 1:483–84. At the same time, the Council Fathers urge, "But the bishops and preachers should behave towards [the Jews and other infidels] with such charity as to gain them for Christ not only by the manifestation of the truth but also by other kindnesses."

197. Roth, *History of the Jews of Italy,* 160–61.

198. In the *Vita anonima,* the reference to the many Jewish conversions effected by Bernardino is on 325, s. 26; for Jewish attendance at his sermons, see the same *vita,* 313, s.10, as well as the already quoted passage from John of Capistrano about Bernardino's sermons at L'Aquila, *S. Bernardini senensis . . . Vita,* OOH.I.xl, col. b. Paolo di Benedetto di Cola dello Mastro's *Memoriale* (quoted in our discussion of the Finicella witch trial in Rome) tells us that, in addition to preaching to the masses and having "Finiccola" burned at the stake, Bernardino also "had many Jews baptized" (*Memoriale,* 90). Citing Ciaconius as his source, Wadding also includes this detail of the many Jewish conversions that took place during Bernardino's Roman visit (*Annales Minorum,* tom. 10, 1418–36, 80, num. 2). Stefano Infessura's *Diario romano* notes the preaching mission and the burning of Finicella, without any mention, however, of Jewish conversions (*Diario della città di Roma,* 25).

199. Vivanti, "History of the Jews in Italy," 330.

200. Ibid., 345.

201. Hood, *Aquinas and the Jews,* 24–25; see also Little, *Religious Poverty and the Profit Economy,* passim; for the Jews, see 42–57.

CONCLUSION

1. Herlihy and Klapisch-Zuber, *Tuscans and Their Families,* 252; and Rocke, "Sodomites in Fifteenth-Century Tuscany," 8.

2. Russell, *Witchcraft in the Middle Ages,* 227.

3. Kieckhefer, *Magic in the Middle Ages,* 195.

4. Milano, *Storia degli ebrei in Italia,* 163, emphasis added; and Toaff, *Gli ebrei a Perugia,* 60, emphasis added. Toaff's remark is, however, but a minor flaw in an otherwise excellent work among many other excellent works by the same author.

5. There are now several fine broad surveys of the form, content, and personalities of popular preaching in medieval and early modern Europe, such as Hervé Martin's *Le métier du prédicateur en France septentrionale à la fin du Moyen Age* (Paris: Cerf, 1988) and Larissa Taylor's *Soldiers of Christ* (New York: Oxford University Press, 1992); few, however, adequately address the topics of witchcraft, sodomy, and Judaism to be helpful in the task of contextualizing Bernardino within his *métier.* And those that do address these three topics, do so with a focus on times, places, and personalities so remote from Bernardino as to make comparative analysis with them, in my judgment, of little value.

6. For the concept of "informal" and "charismatic" power, see André Vauchez's introduction to the already cited *Poteri informali: chiesa e società medioevali,* 9–14.

7. See R.804 and above, chap. 1, sec. 3.

8. For the pope as "holy father," see, e.g., R.813 and R.873; for Bernardino's remark "Papa, qui dicitur 'amabilis pater,' " see OOQ.I.356. The statement about the pope's love for his flock ("E dommi a credare che il papa vi vogli bene") is at R.663, while the reference to the pope as God-on-earth can be found at R.1374 ("O non v'ho detto . . . che 'l papa è el nostro Iddio in terra?"). In a confused, perhaps improperly transcribed passage, Bernardino seems also to affirm papal infallibility; see B.94–95.

9. The imperial consecration took place in 1433. For Bernardino and Sigismund, see Benedetto Nesti, "San Bernardino e l'imperatore Sigismondo," *BSB* 7 (1941): 159–70.

10. David Nirenberg, *Communities of Violence: Persecution of Minorities in the Middle Ages* (Princeton: Princeton University Press, 1996), 5–7.

11. To the eyewitness accounts already cited, we might add that of Sandro di Marco dei Marcovaldi, citizen of Prato, who in a letter dated June 15, 1424, describes Bernardino's preaching mission to that Tuscan town. In this pious, enthusiastic account, Bernardino is praised as "a prophet and most strong captain . . . a most good and holy and just man endowed with all possible virtue," who seems "another Saint Paul for his doctrine and teachings" ("uno proffetta e chapittano forttissimo . . . bonissimo e santo e giusto uomo, chon ttute le virttù chessi possa dare in lui. E' pare uno San Pavolo per la sua dottrina e amaestramenti"). According to Sandro, as many as 8,000 people, from town and countryside, attended Bernardino's sermons on any given day, with many miracles (especially in the form of exorcisms) being performed by the friar. See Ridolfo Livi, "San Bernardino da Siena e le sue prediche secondo un suo ascoltatore pratese del 1424," *Bullettino senese di storia patria* 20 (1913): 460–63.

12. See Nirenberg, *Communities of Violence,* 241–43.

13. Gavin Langmuir, *History, Religion, and Anti-Semitism* (Berkeley: University of California Press, 1990). For "religion" and "religiosity," see 133–42; for host desecration, 249–51, 259–61, 300–301.

14. See chap. 1, sec. 3.

15. See again chap. 1, sec. 3.

16. Richard K. Emmerson and Ronald B. Herzman, *The Apocalyptic Imagination in Medieval Literature* (Philadelphia: University of Pennsylvania Press, 1992).

17. Charles Stinger, in his review of *Christianity and the Renaissance: Image and Religious Imagination in the Quattrocento,* ed. Timothy Verdon and John Henderson (Syracuse, N.Y.: Syracuse University Press, 1990), in *Renaissance Quarterly* 44 (1991): 826. For this reason, the very labels "medieval" and "Renaissance" are no longer as clear-cut and as mutually exclusive as they were once believed to be, especially for the period spanned by Bernardino's lifetime. Moreover, the term *early modern* is now increasingly replacing the term *Renaissance.*

18. Tasso, *La Gerusalemme liberata,* XX, 73.

APPENDIX ONE

1. The most recent and most scrupulous chronology is that assembled by Martino Bertagna, a member of the Quaracchi committee, which published the critical edition of Bernardino's *opera omnia* and prepared the Vatican documentation for the preacher's nomination as official "doctor" of the Roman Catholic Church. See his *Chronologia bernardiniana hucusque nota* (Rome: Tipografia Guerra e Belli, 1960), also published as part of the Vatican document *Sacra Rituum Congregatione Concessionis tituli doctoris in honorem S. Bernardini Senensis, confessoris ex ordine Fratrum Minorum . . .* (Città del Vaticano: N.p., 1966), 1–18. I have not been able to consult either one of these two editions of Bertagna's chronology. However, it was later reprinted in a revised version, which I cite in this study, in the *Enciclopedia bernardiniana,* "Cronologia di S. Bernardino da Siena," 4. xi–xxiii, shorn, unfortunately, of its scholarly apparatus. However, since the 1960 original on which this 1980 "perfected" version is based (according to Delcorno, R.61) was done with "scholarly rigor" and with "an abundance of documentation" (Teodosio Lombardi, *Presenza e culto di San Bernardino da Siena nel ducato Estense* [Ferrara: Centro Culturale Città di Ferrara, 1981]: 88–89), I have used it with confidence. For Bernardino's *curriculum vitae,* see also Manselli, "Bernardino da Siena," in *Dizionario biografico degli italiani,* 9:215–26, as well as the older but well-documented and still indispensable essays by Pacetti, "Cronologia," 445–63, and "La predicazione di S. Bernardino in Toscana," *AFH* 33 (1940): 268–318; 34 (1941): 261–83; and for the trial date, 33:299–301.

2. As Bernardino himself tells us; see R.850. See chap. 2, sec. 4 for Bernardino's trial.

3. Ephrem Longpré, "S. Bernardin de Sienne et le nom de Jésus," *AFH* 28 (1935): 457–65. Bertagna gives the trial date as 1426 ("Cronologia di S. Bernardino da Siena," xvii–xviii).

4. I accept Pacetti's and Bulletti's ultimate argument as the most plausible, namely, the trial had to be in the spring of 1426 because from March to August of the following year, Bernardino was the prime candidate for the episcopal see of Siena, and nowhere in the ample correspondence between the pope, various cardinals, and other members of the papal curia, on the one hand, and the "Magnifica Signoria" of Bernardino's hometown, on the other, throughout those many months of negotiation involving such an important appointment, do we find the least mention of the trial or the suspicion of heresy. See Pacetti, "La predicazione di S. Bernardino in Toscana," 300–301, n. 5, citing the research of Enrico Bulletti, "Per la nomina di S. Bernardino a Vescovo di Siena," *BSB* 5 (1939): 27–48. Celestino Piana also seems to favor the 1426 date, pointing to the Benvoglienti canonization testimony, which we shall examine shortly. He offers possible

confirmation of this date based on a 1427 remark of Bernardino's ("dissivi come essendo io a Roma, mi disse il papa che io venissi qua [i.e., Siena]; et anco il vostro vescovo, che è ora cardinale, anco mel disse," R.663) and on the itinerary of Antonio Casini, bishop of Siena, elevated to the cardinalate on May 24, 1426. See Piana, "I processi di canonizzazione," 420, n. 2.

5. Benvenuto Bughetti, "Documenta inedita de S. Bernardino Senensi, O.F.M. (1430–1445)," *AFH* 29 (1936): 485. Niccolò della Tuccia, a fifteenth-century chronicler of Viterbo, tells us that Bernardino preached in that city during Lent of 1426 (Niccolò was in the audience) and then proceeded to Rome. Niccolò does not say, however, that Bernardino went to Rome specifically to face trial, as Pinzi assumed (*Storia della città di Viterbo,* 3:553) and as Longpré denied ("S. Bernardin de Sienne et le nom de Jésus," *AFH* 29 [1936]: 460). Given Bulletti's evidence (see previous note), we can assume Bernardino was going to Rome because of a papal summons. However, it is surprising that Niccolò did not mention this detail, since, according to the *Vita anonima* of Bernardino (written by a contemporary confrere), the friar himself publicly announced the fact with great sorrow to the people of that town (see above, chap. 2, sec. 4).

6. Benvoglienti's testimony is found in Piana, "I processi di canonizzazione," 387. The original Latin reads: "Leonardus Bartholomei de Benvolientibus dixit et interfuisse Senis in anno praedicto [1425] ac etiam in anno Domini 1427 et Romae in anno Domini 1426, quibus temporibus beatus Bernardinus verbum Dei annuntiavit, addens quod Romae ac etiam Perusii in detestationem peccati sortilegi comburi fecit nonnullas sortilegas. Interrogatus quomodo scit, dixit audivisse."

7. This is due both to Infessura's faulty memory and disagreements among the manuscripts of the diary; see Tommasini's introduction to his edition of Infessura's *Diario romano.* Infessura makes no mention of Bernardino's own heresy trial. Furthermore, the connection between Finicella and Bernardino is made in the diary by mere juxtaposition of chronicle items. None of our other fifteenth-century sources (including, strangely enough, Bernardino's own friend and disciple Giacomo della Marca) mentions the friar's name in connection with the trial, except Paolo dello Mastro. A possible reason for this omission is that Bernardino's role in this affair seems to have been limited to his preaching on the topic, with no active, official part to play in the Inquisitional trial and execution themselves. Bernardino seems not even to have been present as a spectator at the trial and the execution (though he describes the latter in some detail), because in the 1443 version of the story he adds the phrase "according to what was recounted by the inquisitor of our order" ("prout retulit nostri ordinis inquisitor," R.1007, n. 123).

8. Carlo Ginzburg, the latest scholar to address this labyrinthine question of chronology, gives 1427 as the date of the witch trial, accepting Longpré's reconstruction of the sequence of events and assuming that this trial occurred during the same Roman sojourn in which Bernardino himself was put on trial for heresy (*Ecstasies,* 309). The latter assumption rests on the further assumption that by September 1427 Bernardino had preached publicly in Rome on only one occasion (see discussion below). The unannotated chronology that Delcorno offers in his edition of Bernardino's Siena 1427 sermons places both the heresy trial and the burning of Finicella under 1426, while omitting any mention of a trip to Rome in 1424 (R.55–56), and later in a footnote says, "There is some uncertainty as to the date [of the trial], but the episode seems to have occurred in the spring of 1426," citing Manselli, Origo, and Bertagna (R.183). Yet at R.1006, n. 123, he says "the facts [of the witch trial recounted here by Bernardino] date back to 1424," citing Infessura to that effect.

9. Hartlieb: "ich sag dir ain sach, die ich und manig man zu Rom gesehen und gehört habn. Es was in dem sechsten jar als bapst Martin gesetzt was" (Hansen, *Quellen und Untersuchungen,* 131); Hemmerlin: "Et constat, quod tempore Martini pape de anno 1420" (ibid., 110).

10. We do not know when Bernardino left Rome, but, according to Pacetti's chronology, he spent August and September of 1426 in Siena (Pacetti, "Cronologia," 453).

11. Bertagna, "Cronologia di S. Bernardino," xviii. On June 27, he was still in Urbino writing a letter to the pope about the episcopal nomination, while by August 15 he had arrived in Siena, beginning his famous course of sermons in the Piazza del Campo.

WORKS CITED

THE WORKS OF BERNARDINO OF SIENA: EDITIONS USED IN THIS STUDY

Le prediche volgari (Firenze 1424). Ed. Ciro Cannarozzi. 2 vols. Pistoia: Pacinotti, 1934.

Le prediche volgari (Firenze 1425). Ed. Ciro Cannarozzi. 3 vols. Florence: Libreria Editrice Fiorentina, 1940.

Le prediche volgari (Siena 1425). Ed. Ciro Cannarozzi. 2 vols. Florence: Rinaldi, 1958.

Opera omnia. Ed. Johannes De la Haye. Venice: Poletti, 1745.

Opera omnia. 9 vols. Quaracchi: Collegio San Bonaventura, 1950–65.

Prediche volgari sul Campo di Siena 1427. Ed. Carlo Delcorno. 2 vols. Milan: Rusconi, 1989.

OTHER EDITIONS, TRANSLATIONS, AND ANTHOLOGIES

Ecco il segno. Antologia dalle Prediche in italiano. Ed. Giacomo V. Sabatelli. Siena: Cantagalli, 1974.

Essempli grossi e palpabili. Rome: Edizioni Paoline, 1980.

Examples of San Bernardino. Ed. Ada Harrison. London: Howe, 1929.

La fonte della vita. Prediche volgari scelte e annotate. Ed. Giacomo Sabatelli. Florence: Libreria Editrice Fiorentina, 1964.

Le più belle pagine di Bernardino da Siena. Ed. Piero Misciatelli. Milan: Treves, 1924.

Le prediche volgari [Siena 1427 cycle]. 3 vols. Ed. Piero Bargellini. Milan: Rizzoli, 1936.

Le prediche volgari di S. Bernardino da Siena . . . [Siena 1427 cycle]. 3 vols. Ed. Luciano Banchi. Siena: Tipografia editrice All'insegna di S. Bernardino, 1880–81.

Le prediche volgari inedite (Firenze 1424, 1425; Siena 1425). Ed. Dionisio Pacetti. Siena: Cantagalli, 1935.

Sermons [Siena 1427 cycle]. Selected and edited by Nazareno Orlandi, translated by Helen J. Robins. Siena: Tipografia Sociale, 1920.

OTHER WORKS CITED

Abbiati, Sergio, Attilio Agnoletto, and Maria Rosario Lazzati. *La stregoneria. Diavoli, streghe, inquisitori dal Trecento al Settecento*. Milan: Mondadori, 1984.

Agrimi, Jole, and Chiara Crisciani. "Immagini e ruoli della *vetula* tra sapere medico e antropologia religiosa (secoli XIII–XV)." In *Poteri carismatici e informali: chiesa e società medioevali*, 224–61.

Alberigo, Giuseppe. "La problematica ecclesiologica tra XIV e XV secolo." In *Ambrogio Traversari nel VI centenario della nascita*, ed. Gian Carlo Garfagnani, 3–25. Florence: Olschki, 1988.

Albright, Priscilla S. "Pintoricchio's Frescoes in the San Bernardino Chapel in Santa Maria in Aracoeli, Rome." Ph.D. thesis, University of California, Berkeley, 1980.

Alessio, Felice. *Storia di San Bernardino e del suo tempo*. Mondovì: Graziano, 1899.

Alexander of Hales. *Summa theologica*. Quaracchi: Collegio San Bonaventura, 1930.

Andreas von Regensburg and Johann Chraft. "Chronica pontificum et imperatorum romanorum." In *Corpus Historicum Medii Aevii*, vol. 1, ed. Johann Georg Eckhart (Eccardus). Leipzig: Jo. Frid. Gleditschii, 1723.

Antonino of Florence. *Chronicon (Opera historiale)*. Nuremburg: N.p., 1484.

———. "De vitio contra naturam." In *Summa theologica*, 2:667–73. 4 vols. Reprint of Verona 1740 edition, Graz: Akademische Drucku. Verlagsanstalt, 1959.

Aquinas, Thomas. "De regimine judaeorum ad Ducissam Brabantiae." In *Aquinas: Selected Political Writings*, ed. A. P. d'Entrèves, 84–95. Oxford: Blackwell, 1954.

Arasse, Daniel. "Fervebat pietate populus: art, dévotion et société autour de la glorification de saint Bernardin de Sienne." *Mélanges de l'École Française de Rome (Moyen-Age et Temps Modernes)* 89 (1977): 189–263.

———. "Iconographie et évolution spirituelle: la tablette de saint Bernardin de Sienne." *Revue d'histoire de la spiritualité* 50 (1974): 433–56.

———. "Saint Bernardin ressemblant: la figure sous le portrait." In *Atti-Siena*, 311–32.

Arbesmann, Rudolph. "Andrea Biglia, Augustinian Friar and Humanist." *Analecta Augustiniana* 28 (1965): 154–218.

Aspetti e problemi della presenza ebraica nell'Italia centro-settentrionale (secoli XIV e XV). Ed. Sofia Boesch Gajano. Rome: Quaderni dell'Istituto di Scienze Storiche dell'Università di Roma, 1983.

Aston, Margaret. *The Fifteenth Century: The Prospect of Europe*. New York: Norton, 1968.

Augustine of Hippo. *On Christian Doctrine*. Trans. D. W. Robertson, Jr. New York: Library of Liberal Arts, 1959.

"Badge, Jewish." *Encyclopaedia Judaica* 4:64.

Bandello, Matteo. *Le novelle*. Ed. G. Brognoligo. Bari: Laterza, 1911.

Bandini de Bartholomaeis, Johannis. *Historia Senensis*. Continued by Franciscus Thomasius. In *Rerum Italicarum Scriptores*, 25 vols., ed. Ludovico Muratori. Vol. 20. Milan: Palatin, 1733.

Barbieri, Gino. "L'usuraio Tomaso Grassi nel racconto bandelliano e nella documentazione storica." In *Studi in onore di Amintore Fanfani*, vol. 2, *Medioevo*, 21–88. 6 vols. Milan: Giuffrè, 1962.

Bargellini, Piero. *San Bernardino da Siena*. 6th ed. Brescia: Morcelliana, 1980.

Barnabò da Siena. *Vita Sancti Bernardini Senensis. AASS*, Maii, Tomus V, die vigesima.

Bart, Alda R. "Frammenti dei quaresimali fiorentini di S. Bernardino da Siena." *SF* 78 (1981): 251–305.

Beccadelli, Antonio. *Hermaphroditus*. 2 vols. Ed. Donatella Coppini. Rome: Bulzoni, 1990.

Beckmann, Gustav, ed. "Tagebuchaufzeichnungen zur Geschichte des Basler Konzils 1431–1435 und 1438." In *Concilium Basiliense: Studien und Quellen zur Geschichte des Concils von Basel*, ed. Gustav Beckmann et al., 5:1–173. 1904. Reprint, Nendeln, Liechtenstein: Kraus, 1971.

Bellini, Pietro. "Simon Fidati de Cascia." *Dictionnaire de spiritualité* 14:873–76.

Bellone, Ernesto. "S. Bernardino come 'auctoritas' nelle opere del Beato Angelo da Chiavasso (1410 c.–1495)." In *Atti-Siena,* 333–57.

Benvoglienti, Leonardo. "Vie de S. Bernardin de Sienne par Léonard Benvoglienti," ed. Franciscus van Ortroy. *AB* 21 (1902): 53–80.

Bernard, Joseph F., Jr. "San Bernardino of Siena: His Relation to the Humanist World of the Early Italian Renaissance." Ph.D. thesis, Yale University, 1973.

Bernardino of Aquila: See Lemens.

Bertagna, Martino. "La Commissione Bernardiniana (1940–1966)." *AFH* 70 (1977): 527–55.

———. "Cronologia di S. Bernardino da Siena." In *Enciclopedia bernardiniana,* 4:xi–xxiii.

———. "Fra Vincenzo da Siena." In *Enciclopedia bernardiniana,* 1:153–54.

———. "L'Osservanza e S. Bernardino." In *Atti-Vicenza,* 207–12.

Bertolini, Lucia, ed. *De vera amicitia: I testi del primo Certame coronario.* Modena: Panini, 1993.

Biasiotto, Peter R. *History of the Development of Devotion to the Holy Name.* St. Bonaventure, N.Y.: St. Bonaventure College, 1943.

Bigaroni, Marino. "S. Bernardino a Todi." *SF* 73 (1976): 109–25.

Biglia, Andrea. "De institutis, discipulis et doctrina fratris Bernardini Ordinis Minorum": See de Gaiffier, Bauduoin.

"Biglia, Andrea." In *Dizionario biografico degli italiani,* 10:413–15.

Blondeel d'Isegem, Emmerich. "L'influence d'Ubertin de Casale sur les écrits di Saint Bernardin de Sienne." *CF* 5 (1935): 5–44.

———. "Encore sur l'influence d'Ubertin de Casale sur les écrits de S. Bernardin de Sienne." *CF* 6 (1936): 57–76.

Blumenkranz, Bernhard. *Le juif médiéval au miroir de l'art chrétien.* Paris: Études Augustiniennes, 1966.

Boccaccio, Giovanni. *The Decameron.* Trans. G. H. McWilliams. Harmondsworth: Penguin, 1972.

Boesch Gajano, Sofia. "Il Comune di Siena e il prestito ebraico nei secoli XIV e XV: fonti e problemi." In *Aspetti e problemi della presenza ebraica,* 175–225.

Bonaventure. *Opera omnia.* 10 vols. Quaracchi: Collegio San Bonaventura, 1882–1902.

———. *The Soul's Journey into God, the Tree of Life and the Life of Francis.* Trans. E. Cousins. New York: Paulist Press, 1978.

Bondì, Claudio. *Strix. Medichesse, streghe e fattucchiere nell'Italia del Rinascimento.* Rome: Lucarini, 1989.

Bonfil, Robert. "The Historian's Perception of the Jews in the Italian Renaissance: Towards a Reappraisal." *Revue des études juives* 143 (1984): 59–82.

———. *Jewish Life in Renaissance Italy.* Trans. Anthony Oldcorn. Berkeley: University of California Press, 1994.

Bonmann, Ottokar. "Problemi critici riguardo ai cosiddetti 'Statuta Bernardiniana' di Perugia (1425–1426)." *SF* 62 (1965): 278–302.

Bonomo, Giuseppe. *Caccia alle streghe. La credenza nelle streghe dal secolo XIII al XIX con particolare riferimento all'Italia.* Palermo: Palumbo, 1959.

Bornstein, Daniel E. *The Bianchi of 1399: Popular Devotion in Late Medieval Italy.* Ithaca: Cornell University Press, 1993.

Boswell, John. *Christianity, Social Tolerance, and Homosexuality: Gay People in Western Europe from the Beginning of the Christian Era to the Fourteenth Century.* Chicago: University of Chicago Press, 1980.

———. "Concepts, Experience, and Sexuality." *Differences: A Journal of Feminist Cultural Studies* 2 (1990): 67–87.

———. *Rediscovering Gay History: Archetypes of Gay Love in Christian History.* The Fifth Michael Harding Memorial Address. London: Gay Christian Movement, 1982.

———. "Revolutions, Universals and Sexual Categories." *Salmagundi* 58–59 (1982–83): 89–113. Revised version in *Hidden from History,* 17–36.

———. *Same-Sex Unions in Premodern Europe.* New York: Villard Books, 1994.

Bowsky, William M. "The Medieval Commune and Internal Violence: Police Power and Public Safety in Siena, 1287–1355." *American Historical Review* 78 (1967): 1–17.

———. *A Medieval Italian Commune: Siena under the Nine, 1287–1355.* Berkeley: University of California Press, 1981.

Bracciolini, Poggio. *De avaritia.* In *Opera omnia,* vol. 1. 4 vols. Photo-reprint of Basel 1538 edition, Turin: Bottega d'Erasmo, 1964.

Brandmüller, Walter. "L'ecclesiologia di San Bernardino da Siena." In *Atti-Siena,* 393–406.

Braunstein, Philippe. "Le prêt sur gages à Padoue et dans le Paduan au milieu du XVe siècle." In *Gli Ebrei e Venezia, secoli XIV–XVIII. Atti del Convegno internazionale organizzato dall'Istituto di storia della società e dello stato veneziano della Fondazione Giorgio Cini. Venezia, 5–10 giugno 1983,* ed. Gaetano Cozzi, 651–70. Milan: Edizioni di Comunità, 1987.

Bronzini, Giovanni Battista. "La predicazione di Bernardino da Siena fra scrittura e oralità." In *Atti-Maiori,* 129–49.

———. "Le prediche di Bernardino e le tradizioni popolari del suo tempo." In *Atti-Todi,* 111–52.

Brown, Judith C. "Lesbian Sexuality in Medieval and Early Modern Europe." In *Hidden from History,* 67–75.

Brown, Raymond E. *The Death of the Messiah: From Gethsemane to the Grave.* 2 vols. New York: Doubleday, 1994.

Brucker, Gene A. *Renaissance Florence.* Berkeley: University of California Press, 1969.

———. "Sorcery in Early Renaissance Florence." *Studies in the Renaissance* 10 (1963): 7–24.

Brundage, James A. "Adultery and Fornication: A Study in Legal Theology." In *Sexual Practices and the Medieval Church,* 129–34.

———. *Law, Sex, and Christian Society in Medieval Europe.* Chicago: University of Chicago Press, 1987.

———. "Usury." In *Dictionary of the Middle Ages,* ed. Joseph R. Strayer, 12:335–39. 13 vols. New York: Scribners, 1982–89.

Bughetti, Benvenuto. "Il codice bernardiniano contenente gli schemi del Santo in volgare per la Quaresima di Firenze 1425." *AFH* 34 (1914): 261–83.

———. "Documenti bernardiniani di Massa Marittima." *BSB* 9 (1943): 162–77.

———. "Documenta inedita de S. Bernardino Senensi, O.F.M. (1430–1445)." *AFH* 29 (1936): 478–500.

Bullarium franciscanum, ed. Ulricus Hüntemann. Vol. 1 (1431–55). 3 vols. Quaracchi: Collegio San Bonaventura, 1929–49.

Bulletti, Enrico. "Frate Bernardino è pregato di una breve predicazione a Grosseto." *BSB* 4 (1938): 242.

———. "I genitori di S. Bernardino da Siena." *SF,* terza serie, 21 (1949): 131–33.

———. "Nuovi documenti bernardiniani." *BSB* 9 (1943): 150–61.

———. "Per la nomina di S. Bernardino a vescovo di Siena (Carteggio ufficiale)." *BSB* 5 (1939): 28–48.

———. "Predicazione senese dell'anno 1425." *BSB* 4 (1938): 236–40.

———. "Riflessi della devozione al Nome di Gesù." *BSB* 4 (1938): 134–35.

Bullough, Vern L. "Postscript: Heresy, Witchcraft, and Sexuality." In *Sexual Practices and the Medieval Church*, 206–17.

———. "The Sin against Nature and Homosexuality." In *Sexual Practices and the Medieval Church*, 55–71.

Burckhardt, Jacob. *The Civilization of the Renaissance in Italy*. 1860. Reprint, New York: Modern Library, 1954.

Burke, Peter. *The Italian Renaissance: Culture and Society in Italy*. Rev. ed. Princeton: Princeton University Press, 1987.

———. "Overture: The New History, Its Past and Its Future." In *New Perspectives on Historical Writing*, ed. Peter Burke, 1–23. University Park: Pennsylvania State University Press, 1991.

Cady, Joseph. " 'Masculine Love,' Renaissance Writing, and the 'New Invention' of Homosexuality." *Journal of Homosexuality* 23 (1992): 9–40.

Camille, Michael. *The Gothic Idol: Ideology and Image-making in Medieval Art*. Cambridge: Cambridge University Press, 1989.

Canosa, Romano. *Storia di una grande paura. La sodomia a Firenze e a Venezia nel Quattrocento*. Milan: Feltrinelli, 1991.

Cantini, Gustavo. "Una ignorata redazione latina di sermoni bernardiniani." *BSB* 2 (1936): 284–300.

———. "San Bernardino da Siena perfetto predicatore popolare." In *SBSSR*, 203–45.

Capitani, Ovidio. "S. Bernardino e l'etica economica." In *Atti-Aquila*, 47–68.

———, ed. *Una economia politica nel Medioevo*. Bologna: Pàtron Editore, 1987.

Caracciolo, Roberto. "Sermo de sancto Bernardino predicatorum nostri temporis principe." In *Sermones de laudibus sanctorum*. Reutlingen: Michael Greyyff, ca. 1495.

Carbone, Ludovico. "Oratio habita in funere praestantissimi oratoris et poetae Guarini Veronensis." In *Prosatori latini del Quattrocento*, ed. Eugenio Garin, 383–417. Milan: Ricciardi, 1952.

Cardinali, Claudia. "Il santo e la norma. Bernardino da Siena e gli statuti perugini del 1425." In *Gioco e giustizia nell'Italia di Comune*, ed. Gherardo Ortalli, 182–91. Treviso: Fondazione Benetton; Rome: Viella, 1993.

Cardini, Franco. "Magia e stregoneria nella Toscana del Trecento." *Quaderni medievali* 5 (1978): 121–55.

———. *Magia, stregoneria, superstizioni nell'Occidente medievale*. Florence: La Nuova Italia, 1979.

———. "La predicazione popolare alle origini della caccia alle streghe." In *La strega, il teologo, lo scienziato. Atti del convegno "Magia, stregoneria e superstizioni in Europa e nella zona alpina." Borgosesia, 1983*, ed. Maurizio Cuccu and Paola Aldo Rossi, 277–93. Genoa: E.C.I.G., 1986.

Cartwright, Julia. "S. Bernardino in Art." In Ferrers Howell, *S. Bernardino of Siena*, 326–49.

Casimiro Romano (Casimiro da Roma). *Memorie istoriche della chiesa e convento di S. Maria in Araceli di Roma*. Rome: Rocco Bernabò, 1736.

Cassandro, Michele. *Gli ebrei e il prestito ebraico a Siena nel Cinquecento*. Milan: Giuffrè, 1979.

Cassuto, Umberto. "Bernardino of Siena." *Encyclopaedia Judaica* 4:289.

———. *Gli ebrei a Firenze nell'età del Rinascimento*. Florence: Galletti e Cocci, 1918.

Catherine of Bologna. "The Admirable Instructions of Saint Catharine of Bologna Which She Gave unto Her Sacred Virgins, Composed by Herself . . ." In *The Rule of the Holy Virgin*

S. Clare. Together with the Admirable Life of S. Catherine of Bologna, ed. D. M. Rogers. London: Scholars Press, 1975.

Chazan, Robert. *Church, State, and Jew in the Middle Ages.* West Orange, N.J.: Behrman House, 1980.

Chobham, Thomas. *Thomae de Chobham Summa Confessorum.* Ed. F. Broomfield. Louvain: Nauwelaerts, 1968.

Chraft, Johann: See Andreas von Regensburg.

Christiansen, Keith, Laurence B. Kanter, and Carl Brandon Strelhke. *Painting in Renaissance Siena, 1420–1500.* New York: Metropolitan Museum of Art and Harry Abrams, 1988.

Ciscato, Antonio. *Gli ebrei in Padova (1300–1800).* 1901. Reprint, Padua: Forni, 1967.

Cochrane, Eric, and Julius Kirshner, eds. *The Renaissance.* University of Chicago Readings in Western Civilization, 5. Chicago: University of Chicago Press, 1986.

Cohen, Jeremy. *The Friars and the Jews: The Evolution of Medieval Anti-Judaism.* Ithaca: Cornell University Press, 1982.

Cohn, Norman. *Europe's Inner Demons: An Enquiry Inspired by the Great Witch-Hunt.* New York: Basic Books, 1975.

Contrada, Deborah L. "The Resolution of Ser Pace's *nome secreto.*" *Italica* 66 (1989): 281–92.

Copia del Testamento di San Bernardino di Siena. Padua: Stamperia di Niccolò Gavelli, 1733.

Corrain, Cleto, and Pierluigi Zampini. "Spunti etnografici nelle opere di S. Bernardino da Siena." *La palestra del clero* 44 (1965): 882–905.

Cristofori, Francesco. "S. Bernardino da Siena in Viterbo." *MF* 4 (1889): 35–46.

Crowe, Michael. "St. Thomas and Ulpian's Natural Law." In *St. Thomas Aquinas, 1274–1974, Commemorative Studies,* 261–82. Toronto: Pontifical Institute for Mediaeval Studies, 1974.

d'Addario, Arnaldo. "Rusticucci, Iacopo." In *Enciclopedia dantesca,* ed. Umberto Bosco, 4:1060–61. 6 vols. Rome: Istituto della Enciclopedia Italiana, 1970–78.

D'Alatri, Mariano. "A proposito degli inizi dell'Osservanza." In *Atti-Vicenza,* 203–12.

Dall'Orto, Giovanni. "La fenice di Sodoma. Essere omosessuale nell'Italia del Rinascimento." In *History of Homosexuality in Europe and America,* ed. Wayne R. Dynes and Stephen Donaldson, 61–83. New York: Garland, 1992.

———. " 'Socratic Love' as a Disguise for Same-Sex Love in the Italian Renaissance." In *The Pursuit of Sodomy: Male Homosexuality in Renaissance and Enlightenment Europe,* ed. Kent Gerard and Gert Hekma, 33–65. New York: Harrington Park Press, 1989.

da Milano, Carlo. "Panegirico inedito in onore di S. Bernardino tenuto a Firenze il 21 maggio 1493 dal B. Bernardino da Feltre." *BSB* 3 (1937): 99–118.

Dante Alighieri. *The Divine Comedy.* Trans. Mark Musa. Harmondsworth: Penguin Books, 1984.

D'Araules, Ferdinand-Marie, ed. *Vie de Saint Bernardin de Sienne. Texte latin inédit du XVe siècle.* Rome: N.p., 1906.

D'Avack, Pietro Agostino. "L'omosessualità nel diritto canonico." *Ulisse* 7 (1953): 680–97.

Davidson, Nicholas. "Theology, Nature and the Law: Sexual Sin and Sexual Crime in Italy from the Fourteenth to the Seventeenth Century." In *Crime, Society and the Law in Renaissance Italy,* ed. Trevor Dean and K. J. P. Lowe, 74–98. Cambridge: Cambridge University Press, 1994.

D'Avray, David. *The Preaching of the Friars: Sermons Diffused from Paris before 1300.* Oxford: Clarendon Press, 1985.

Dean, James M. *The World Grown Old in Later Medieval Literature.* Cambridge: Medieval Academy of America, 1997.

De Beato Bernardino Feltrinensi . . . Commentarius Historicus. AASS. Septembris tomus VII, die vigesima ottava.

Decrees of the Ecumenical Councils. Ed. Norman Tanner. 2 vols. Washington, D.C.: Sheed & Ward and Georgetown University Press, 1990.

Delaruelle, E., E. R. Labande, and P. Ourliac. *L'Église au temps du Grand Schisme et de la crise conciliaire (1378–1449).* Histoire de l'Église, ed. A. Fliche et V. Martin, vol. 14. Tournai: Bloud & Gay, 1962.

Delcorno, Carlo. "L'*ars praedicandi* di Bernardino da Siena." In *Atti-Siena,* 419–49.

———. "La diffrazione del testo omeletico. Osservazioni sulle doppie reportationes delle prediche bernardiniane." *Lettere italiane* 38 (1986): 457–77.

———. "Due prediche volgari di Jacopo della Marca recitate a Padova nel 1460." *Atti dell'Istituto Veneto di Scienze, Lettere ed Arti* 128 (1969–70): 135–205.

———. "L'*exemplum* nella predicazione di San Bernardino." In *Atti-Todi,* 71–107.

———. *Giordano da Pisa e l'antica predicazione volgare.* Florence: Olschki, 1975.

———. "Note sulla tradizione manoscritta delle prediche volgari di San Bernardino da Siena." *AFH* 73 (1980): 90–123.

———. *La predicazione nell'età comunale.* Florence: Sansoni, 1974.

———. "Rassegna di studi sulla predicazione medievale e umanistica (1970–1980)." *Lettere italiane* 33 (1981): 235–76.

Dello Mastro, Paolo di Benedetto di Cola. "Memoriale." In appendix to Paolo di Lello Petrone, *La Mesticanza. Rerum Italicarum Scriptores,* 2d ed., v. 24, p. 2, ed. Francesco Isoldi, 81–100. Città di Castello: Casa Editrice S. Lapi, 1912.

Delorme, Ferdinand. "Une esquisse primitive de la vie de S. Bernardin." *BSB* 1 (1935): 1–23.

Delumeau, Jean. *Rassurer et protéger. Le sentiment de sécurité dans l'Occident d'autrefois.* Paris: Fayard, 1989.

———. *Sin and Fear: The Emergence of a Western Guilt Culture, 13th–18th Centuries.* Trans. Eric Nicholson. New York: St. Martin's Press, 1990.

de Nevo, Alexander. "Consilia contra judaeos foenerantes." In Nicholas of Osimo [Nicolaus de Ausmo], *Supplementum summae pisanellae.* Venice: Leonardus Wild, 1489 [1479].

De Roover, Raymond. *San Bernardino of Siena and Sant'Antonino of Florence: The Two Great Economic Thinkers of the Middle Ages.* Boston: Harvard Graduate School of Business Administration, 1967.

Doelle, Ferdinandus. "Sermo S. Iohannis de Capistrano de S. Bernardini Senensis." *AFH* 6 (1913): 76–90.

Dundes, Alan, ed. *The Blood Libel Legend: A Casebook in Anti-Semitic Folklore.* Madison: University of Wisconsin Press, 1991.

"Elijah ben Shabbetai Be'er." *Encyclopaedia Judaica* 6:649.

Elliott, Dyan. "Bernardino of Siena versus the Marriage Debt." In *Desire and Discipline: Sex and Sexuality in the Premodern West,* ed. Jacqueline Murray and Konrad Eisenbichler, 168–200. Toronto: University of Toronto Press, 1996.

Elm, Kaspar. "L'osservanza francescana come riforma culturale." *Le Venezie francescane (Predicazione francescana e società veneta nel Quattrocento: committenza, ascolto, ricezione. Atti del II Convegno internazionale di studi francescani. Padova, 26–27–28 marzo 1987)* nuova serie 6 (1989): 15–30.

———. "Riforme e osservanze nel XIV e XV secolo." In *Atti-Assisi,* 149–67.

Enciclopedia bernardiniana. 4 vols. (*Bibliografia; Iconografia; Vestigia; Biografia*). Ed. Enrico D'Angelo, et al. L'Aquila: Centro Promotore Generale delle Celebrazioni del VI Centenario della Nascita di San Bernardino da Siena, 1980–85.

Ermini, Filippo. "Il culto degli alberi presso i Longobardi e il noce di Benevento." In *Medio Evo latino. Studi e ricerche,* 115–19. Modena: Società Tipografica Modenese, 1938.

Esposito, Anna. "Gli ebrei a Roma nella seconda metà del '400 attraverso i protocolli del notaio Giovanni Angelo Armati." In *Aspetti e problemi della presenza ebraica*, 29–127.

Esposito, Anna, and Diego Quaglioni. *Processi contro gli ebrei di Trento (1475–1478)*. Volume 1: *I processi del 1475*. Padua: Casa Editrice Dott. Antonio Milani, 1990.

Fabretti, Ariodante, ed. "Cronaca detta diario del Graziani (dal 1309 al 1491)." *Archivio storico ialiano* 16 (1850): 53–750.

———. *Cronache della città di Perugia*. Turin: "Coi tipi privati dell'Editore," 1888.

Facchinetti, Vittorino. *San Bernardino da Siena mistico sole del 400*. Milan: Casa Editrice Santa Lega Eucaristica, 1933.

Faggiano, Cosimo. "L'eloquenza volgare di San Bernardino da Siena, saggio critico." *Rassegna nazionale* (Firenze) fasc. 37 (ottobre–dicembre 1915), vol. 205:261–81, 426–29; vol. 206:46–68, 166–89, 273–304.

Fantozzi, Antonio. "Documenta perusina de S. Bernardino Senensi." *AFH* 15 (1922): 103–54, 406–70.

Ferrers Howell, A. G. *S. Bernardino of Siena*. London: Methuen, 1913.

Fioravanti, Gianfranco. "Polemiche antigiudaiche nell'Italia del Quattrocento. Un tentativo di interpretazione globale." *Quaderni storici* n. 64, an. 22 (1987): 19–38.

Flannery, Edward H. *The Anguish of the Jews: Twenty-three Years of Antisemitism*. Rev. and updated ed. Mahwah: Paulist Press, 1985.

Fleming, John V. *An Introduction to the Franciscan Literature of the Middle Ages*. Chicago: Franciscan Herald Press, 1977.

Fois, Mario. "Il fenomeno dell'Osservanza negli ordini religiosi tra il 1300 e il 1400. Alcune particolarità dell'Osservanza francescana." In *Lettura delle fonti francescane attraverso i secoli: il 1400*, ed. Gerardo Cardaropoli and Martino Conti, 53–105. Rome: Antonianum, 1981.

———. "I papi e l'Osservanza minoritica." In *Atti-Assisi*, 29–105.

Foucault, Michel. *The History of Sexuality. Volume 1: An Introduction*. Trans. Robert Hurley. New York: Vintage, 1978.

Frantzen, Allen J. "Between the Lines: Queer Theory, the History of Homosexuality, and Anglo-Saxon Penitentials." *Journal of Medieval and Early Modern Studies* 26 (1996): 255–96.

Frugoni, Arsenio, ed. *"Adversus Iudeos" di Gioacchino da Fiore*. Rome: Istituto Storico Italiano per il Medio Evo, 1957.

Gager, John G. *The Origins of Anti-Semitism: Attitudes toward Judaism in Pagan and Christian Antiquity*. New York: Oxford University Press, 1983.

de Gaiffier, Baudouin. "Le mémoire d'André Biglia sur la prédication de Saint Bernardin de Sienne." *AB* 53 (1935): 308–58.

———. "La Vie de S. Bernardin du manuscript de Rouge-Cloître." *AB* 71 (1953): 282–322.

Gallo, Donato. "Predicatori francescani nella cattedrale di Padova durante il Quattrocento." *Le Venezie francescane (Predicazione francescana e società veneta nel Quattrocento: committenza, ascolto, ricezione. Atti del II Convegno internazionale di studi francescani. Padova, 26–27–28 marzo 1987)* nuova serie 6 (1989): 159–200.

Garin, Eugenio. *L'umanesimo italiano*. 6th ed. Bari: Laterza, 1975.

Genovesi, Vincent J. *In Pursuit of Love: Catholic Morality and Human Sexuality*. Wilmington: Glazier, 1987.

Geremek, Bronislaw. *The Margins of Society in Late Medieval Paris*. Trans. Jean Birrell. Cambridge: Cambridge University Press, 1987.

Giacomo della Marca: See Iacobus De Marchia.

Gilbert, Arthur N. "Conceptions of Homosexuality and Sodomy in Western History." In *The Gay Past: A Collection of Historical Essays*, ed. Salvatore J. Licata and Robert P. Petersen, 57–68. New York: Harrington Park Press, 1985.

Gilchrist, J. *Church and Economic Activity in the Middle Ages*. London: Macmillan, 1969.

Gilson, Etienne. "Michel Menot et la technique du sermon médiéval." In *Les idées et les lettres*. 2d ed. Paris: Librairie Philosophique J. Vrin, 1955.

Ginzburg, Carlo. *Ecstasies: Deciphering the Witches' Sabbath*. Trans. Raymond Rosenthal. New York: Pantheon, 1991.

Goffen, Rona. *Piety and Patronage in Renaissance Venice: Bellini, Titian and the Franciscans*. New Haven: Yale University Press, 1986.

Goffis, Cesare Federico. "Giovanni di ser Buccio da Spoleto." In *Enciclopedia dantesca*, ed. Umberto Bosco, 3:192–93. 6 vols. Rome: Istituto della Enciclopedia Italiana, 1970–78.

Goldberg, Jonathan. *Sodometries: Renaissance Texts, Modern Sexualities*. Stanford: Stanford University Press, 1992.

Gonnet, Giovanni. "S. Bernardino da Siena e la cosidetta 'eresia' del Nome di Gesù." In *Atti-Maiori*, 41–51.

Goodich, Michael. *The Unmentionable Vice: Homosexuality in the Later Medieval Period*. Santa Barbara: ABC-Clio, 1979.

Gow, Andrew, and Gordon Griffiths. "Pope Eugenius IV and Jewish Money-Lending in Florence: The Case of Salomone di Bonaventura during the Chancellorship of Leonardo Bruni." *Renaissance Quarterly* 42 (1994): 282–329.

Gozzo, Serafino (Paolo) M. *S. Bernardino da Siena "esegeta."* L'Aquila: Del Romano, 1982.

Graef, Hilda. *Mary: A History of Doctrine and Devotion*. London: Sheed & Ward, 1985.

Grayzel, Solomon. "The Papal Bull *Sicut Judeis*." In *Essential Papers on Judaism and Christianity in Conflict: From Late Antiquity to the Reformation*, ed. Jeremy Cohen, 231–59. New York: New York University Press, 1990.

Greenberg, David F. *The Construction of Homosexuality*. Chicago: University of Chicago Press, 1988.

Gregg, Joan Young. *Devils, Women, and Jews: Reflections of the Other in Medieval Sermon Stories*. Albany: State University of New York Press, 1997.

Greven, Joseph, ed. *Die exempla aus den Sermones feriales et communes des Jakob von Vitry*. Heidelberg: Carl Winter's Universitätsbuchhandlung, 1914.

Guarino Veronese. *Epistolario*. Venice: R. Deputazione Veneta di Storia Patria, 1915–19.

Güdemann, Moritz. *Geschichte des Erziehungswesens und der Cultur der Juden in Italien während des Mittelalters*. Volume II of *Geschichte des Erziehungswesens und der Cultur der Abendländischen Juden während des Mittelalters und der Neueren Zeit*. Vienna: Hölder, 1884.

Guibert of Nogent. *Self and Society in Medieval France: The Memoirs of Abbot Guibert of Nogent (1064?–c. 1125)*. Ed. John F. Benton. New York: Harper & Row, 1970.

Guidi, Remo L. "Colombini, Bernardino da Siena, Savonarola: uomini e simulacri." *Benedictina* 35 (1988): 373–427; 36 (1989): 105–63, 349–439.

———. "Maffeo Vegio agiografo di S. Bernardino da Siena." In *Aspetti religiosi nella letteratura del 400*, 2:63–96. 3 vols. Vicenza: L.I.E.F., 1974.

———. "Questioni di storiografia agiografica nel Quattrocento." *Benedictina* 34 (1987): 166–252.

Hale, Rosemary. "Late Medieval Sermons and the Paradigm of Saint Joseph: The Social Construction of Masculinity." Synopsis of a paper presented at the Twenty-eighth International

Congress on Medieval Studies, Kalamazoo, Michigan, May 1993. *Medieval Sermon Studies* 33 (Spring 1994): 42–43.

Halperin, David M. "One Hundred Years of Homosexuality." In *One Hundred Years of Homosexuality and Other Essays on Greek Love,* 15–40. New York and London: Routledge, 1990.

Handbook of Medieval Sexuality. Ed. Vern L. Bullough and James A. Brundage. New York: Garland, 1996.

Hansen, Joseph. *Quellen und Untersuchungen zur Geschichte des Hexenwahns und der Hexenverfolgung im Mittelalter.* Bonn: Carl Georgi, 1901.

Harrison, Beverly Wildung. "Misogyny and Homophobia: The Unexplored Connections." In *Making the Connections: Essays in Feminist Social Ethics,* ed. Carol S. Robb, 135–51, 289–90. Boston: Beacon Press, 1985.

Hay, Denys. *The Church in Italy in the Fifteenth Century.* Cambridge: Cambridge University Press, 1977.

Hay, Denys, and John Law. *Italy in the Age of the Renaissance 1380–1530.* London: Longman, 1989.

Heffernan, Thomas J. *Sacred Biography: Saints and Their Biographers in the Middle Ages.* New York: Oxford University Press, 1988.

Helminiak, Daniel A. *What the Bible* Really *Says About Homosexuality.* San Francisco: Alamo Square Press, 1994.

Herlihy, David. *Medieval Households.* Cambridge: Harvard University Press, 1985.

———. "Santa Caterina and San Bernardino: Their Teachings on the Family." In *Atti-Siena,* 917–34. Reprinted in *Women, Family and Society in Medieval Europe: Historical Essays, 1978–1991,* ed. Anthony Molho. Providence: Berghahn Books, 1995.

Herlihy, David, and Christiane Klapisch-Zuber. *Les toscans et leurs familles. Une étude du catasto de 1427.* Paris: École des hautes études en sciences sociales, 1978. Abridged English version: *Tuscans and Their Families: A Study of the Florentine Catasto of 1427.* New Haven: Yale University Press, 1978.

Hidden from History: Reclaiming the Gay and Lesbian Past. Ed. Martin B. Duberman, Martha Vicinus, and George Chauncey, Jr. New York: New American Library, 1989.

Hofer, Johannes. *Johannes Kapistran: Ein Leben im Kampf um die Reform der Kirche.* 2d ed. Heidelberg: F. H. Kerle Verlag; Rome: Editiones Franciscanae, 1964.

Hood, John Y. B. *Aquinas and the Jews.* Philadelphia: University of Pennsylvania Press, 1995.

Horner, Tom. *Jonathan Loved David: Homosexuality in Biblical Times.* Philadelphia: Westminster Press, 1978.

Howard, Peter F. *Beyond the Written Word: Preaching and Theology in the Florence of Archbishop Antoninus, 1427–1459.* Florence: Olschki, 1995.

Hsia, R. Po-chia. *The Myth of Ritual Murder: Jews and Magic in Reformation Germany.* New Haven: Yale University Press, 1988.

———. *Trent 1475: Stories of a Ritual Murder Trial.* New Haven: Yale University Press, 1992.

Huber, Raphael. *St. Anthony of Padua, Doctor of the Church Universal.* Milwaukee: Bruce Publishing Co., 1948.

Hughes, Diane Owen. "Distinguishing Signs: Ear-rings, Jews and Franciscan Rhetoric in the Italian Renaissance City." *Past and Present* 112 (August 1986): 3–59.

Humbert of Romans. *Treatise on the Formation of Preachers.* In *Early Dominicans: Selected Writings,* ed. Simon Tugwell. New York: Paulist Press, 1982.

Hutton, Edward. *The Franciscans in England, 1224–1538.* London: Constable, 1926.

Hyatte, Reginald. *The Arts of Friendship: The Idealization of Friendship in Medieval and Early Renaissance Literature.* Leiden: E. J. Brill, 1994.

Iacobus de Marchia. "De sortilegiis" and "De sodomia." In *Sermones dominicales.* 3 vols. Ed. Renato Lioi. 1:419–35, 449–62. Falconara Marittima: Biblioteca Francescana, 1978.

Infessura, Stefano. *Diario della città di Roma.* Ed. Oreste Tommasini. Rome: Istituto Storico Italiano, 1890.

Innocent III (Lothario dei Segni). *On the Misery of the Human Condition (De miseria humanae conditionis).* Trans. Margaret Mary Dietz. Ed. Donald R. Howard. Indianapolis: Library of Liberal Arts/Bobbs-Merrill, 1969.

Iriarte, Lazaro. *Franciscan History: The Three Orders of St. Francis of Assisi.* Trans. Patricia Ross. Chicago: Franciscan Herald Press, 1983.

Izbicki, Thomas M. "Pyres of Vanities: Mendicant Preaching on the Vanity of Women and Its Lay Audience." In *De Ore Domini: Preachers and Word in the Middle Ages,* ed. Thomas L. Amos et al., 211–34. Kalamazoo: Medieval Institute Publications, 1989.

Joannis de Segovia. "Historia Gestorum Generalis Synodi Basiliensis." In *Monumenta Conciliorum Generalium Seculi Decimi Quinti,* ed. Caesareae Academiae Scientiarum Socii Delegati. Vienna: Holzhausen, 1886.

Johansson, Warren, and William A. Percy. "Homosexuality." In *Handbook of Medieval Sexuality,* 155–89.

John of Capistrano. "S. Bernardini Senensis Ordinis Seraphici Minorum Vita." In *Sancti Bernardini Senensis Opera Omnia,* ed. Johannes de la Haye, 1: xxxiv–xliii. Venice: Poletti, 1745.

Jordan, Mark D. *The Invention of Sodomy in Christian Theology.* Chicago: University of Chicago Press, 1997.

Karras, Ruth Mazo. *Common Women: Prostitution and Sexuality in Medieval England.* Oxford: Oxford University Press, 1996.

———. "Prostitution in Medieval Europe." In *Handbook of Medieval Sexuality,* 243–60.

Kay, Richard. *Dante's Swift and Strong: Essays on Inferno XV.* Lawrence: Regents Press of Kansas, 1978.

Keenan, James F. "The Function of the Principle of Double Effect." *Theological Studies* 54 (1993): 294–315.

Kieckhefer, Richard. *European Witch Trials: Their Foundations in Popular and Learned Culture, 1300–1500.* Berkeley: University of California Press, 1976.

———. *Forbidden Rites: A Necromancer's Manual of the Fifteenth Century.* University Park: Pennsylvania State University Press, 1997.

———. *Magic in the Middle Ages.* Cambridge: Cambridge University Press, 1989.

Killerby, Catherine Kovesi. "Practical Problems in the Enforcement of Italian Sumptuary Law, 1200–1500." In *Crime, Society and the Law in Renaissance Italy,* ed. Trevor Dean and K. J. P. Lowe, 99–120. Cambridge: Cambridge University Press, 1994.

Kirshner, Julius. "Reading Bernardino's Sermon on the Public Debt." In *Atti-Siena,* 547–622.

Klaits, Joseph. *Servants of Satan: The Age of the Witch Hunts.* Bloomington: Indiana University Press, 1985.

Klapisch-Zuber, Christiane. "Blood Parents and Milk Parents: Wet Nursing in Florence, 1300–1530." In *Women, Family, and Ritual in Renaissance Italy,* 132–64. Chicago: University of Chicago Press, 1985.

———. "Childhood in Tuscany at the Beginning of the Fifteenth Century." In *Women, Family, and Ritual in Renaissance Italy,* 94–116.

———. "State and Family in a Renaissance Society: The Florentine *Catasto* of 1427–30." In *Women, Family, and Ritual in Renaissance Italy*, 1–22.

Klassen, William. *Judas, Betrayer or Friend of Jesus?* Minneapolis: Fortress, 1996.

Kors, Alan C., and Edward Peters, eds. *Witchcraft in Europe 1100–1700: A Documentary History.* Philadelphia: University of Pennsylvania Press, 1972.

Küng, Hans. *The Church.* New York: Sheed & Ward, 1967.

Kuster, Harry J., and Raymond J. Cormier. "Old Views and New Trends: Observations on the Problem of Homosexuality in the Middle Ages." *Studi medievali* 24 (1984): 587–610.

Lambert, Malcolm D. *Medieval Heresy: Popular Movements from the Gregorian Reform to the Reformation.* 2d ed. Oxford: Blackwell, 1992.

Langer, Ulrich. *Perfect Friendship: Studies in Literature and Moral Philosophy from Boccaccio to Corneille.* Geneva: Droz, 1994.

Langmuir, Gavin I. *History, Religion and Antisemitism.* Berkeley: University of California Press, 1990.

Lazzareschi, Eugenio. "San Bernardino of Siena sull'Amiata e nella Lucchesia." *Bullettino senese di storia patria* 20 (1913): 246–62.

Lea, Henry Charles. *Materials toward a History of Witchcraft.* Ed. Arthur C. Howland. Philadelphia: University of Pennsylvania Press, 1939.

Leavy, Barbara Fass. *In Search of the Swan Maiden: A Narrative on Folklore and Gender.* New York: New York University Press, 1994.

Lemens, Leonardus, ed. *B. Bernardini Aquilani Chronica Fratrum Minorum Observantiae.* Rome: Typis Sallustianis, 1902.

Lerner, Robert E. *The Heresy of the Free Spirit in the Later Middle Ages.* Reprint, Notre Dame: University of Notre Dame Press, 1991.

Lesnick, Daniel R. *Preaching in Medieval Florence: The Social World of Franciscan and Dominican Spirituality.* Athens: University of Georgia Press, 1989.

Levack, Brian P. *The Witch-Hunt in Early Modern Europe.* 2d ed. London: Longman, 1995.

Liebert, Robert S. *Michelangelo: A Psychoanalytic Study of His Life and Images.* New Haven: Yale University Press, 1983.

Link, Luther. *The Devil: The Archfiend in Art from the Sixth to the Sixteenth Century.* New York: Abrams, 1995.

Little, A. G. "Nota Fr. Francisci Ariminensis O. M. Conv. de relatione S. Bernardini Senensis ad Fratres Observantes." *AFH* 2 (1909): 164–65.

Little, Lester K. *Religious Poverty and the Profit Economy in Medieval Europe.* Ithaca: Cornell University Press, 1978.

Livi, Ridolfo. "San Bernardino da Siena e le sue prediche secondo un suo ascoltatore pratese del 1424." *Bullettino senese di storia patria* 20 (1913): 458–69.

Lombardi, Teodosio. *Presenza e culto di san Bernardino da Siena nel Ducato Estense.* Ferrara: Quaderni del Centro Culturale, Città di Ferrara, 1971.

Longpré, Ephrem. "S. Bernardin de Sienne et le nom de Jésus." *AFH* 28 (1935): 443–79; 29 (1936): 142–68, 443–77; 30 (1937): 170–92.

Lopez, Robert S. "Ebrei di passaggio nella letteratura medievale italiana." In *Italia judaica. Atti del I Convegno internazionale, Bari, maggio 18–22, 1981*, 455–66. Rome: Ministero per i Beni Culturali e Ambientali; Pubblicazioni degli Archivi di Stato, 1983.

Luzzati, Michele. "Per la storia dei rapporti fra ebrei e cristiani in Italia. Demografia e insediamenti ebraici nel Rinascimento." In *Ebraismo e antiebraismo: immagine e pregiudizio*, ed. Cesare Luporini, 185–91. Florence: Editrice La Giuntina, 1989.

Magli, Ida. *Gli uomini della penitenza. Lineamenti antropologici del medioevo italiano.* Milan: Garzanti, 1977.

———. "L'etica familiare e la donna in S. Bernardino." In *Atti-Aquila,* 111–25.

Mâle, Émile. *L'art religieux de la fin du XVIe siècle, du XVIIe siècle et du XVIIIe siècle. Étude sur l'iconographie après le Concile de Trente.* 2d ed. Paris: Colin, 1951.

Mallory, Michael, and Gaudenz Freuller. "Sano di Pietro's Bernardino Altar-piece for the Compagnia della Vergine in Siena." *Burlington Magazine* 133 (1991): 186–92.

Mammoli, Domenico. *The Record of the Trial and Condemnation of a Witch, Matteuccia di Francesco at Todi, 20 March 1428.* Res Tudertinae 14. Rome: N.p., 1972.

Manselli, Raoul. "Bernardino da Siena." In *Dizionario biografico degli italiani,* 9:215–26.

———. "Due biblioteche di 'Studia' Minoritici. Santa Croce di Firenze e il Santo di Padova." In *Le scuole degli ordini mendicanti, secoli XIII–XIV,* 353–72. Todi: Centro di Studi sulla Spiritualità Medievale, 1978.

———. "Firenze nel Trecento. Santa Croce e la cultura francescana." *Clio* 9 (1973): 325–42.

———. "L'osservanza francescana. Dinamica della sua formazione e fenomenologia." In *Reformbemühungen und Observanzbestrebungen im spätmittelalterlichen Ordenswesen,* ed. Kaspar Elm, 173–87. Berlin: Duncker & Humblot, 1989.

———. "Le premesse medioevali della caccia alle streghe." In *La stregoneria in Europa (1450–1650),* ed. Marina Romanello, 39–62. Bologna: Il Mulino, 1975.

Map, Walter. *De nugis curialium, Courtiers' Trifles.* Ed. and trans. M. R. James. Revised by C. N. L. Brooke and R. A. B. Mynors. Oxford: Clarendon Press, 1983.

Marchini, Giuseppe. "Un'invenzione di S. Bernardino." In *Atti-Siena,* 639–55.

Marinangeli, Giacinto. "Eamus Aquilam! Ad Aquilam missus sum. Nota storico-critica." *Bullettino della Deputazione abruzzese di storia patria* 70 (1980): 163–96.

May, Eric. "The Friendships of St. Bernardine." *Franciscan Studies* 4 (1944): 247–61.

———. "The *Pia Deploratio* of St. Bernardine of Siena." *Franciscan Studies* 2 (1942): 238–50.

Mazzatinti, Giuseppe. "S. Bernardino da Siena a Gubbio." *MF* 4 (1889), 150–51.

Mazzi, Maria Serena. *Prostitute e lenoni nella Firenze del Quattrocento.* Milan: Mondadori/Il Saggiatore, 1991.

McCall, Andrew. *The Medieval Underworld.* London: Hamish Hamilton, 1979.

McGuire, Brian. *Friendship and Community: The Monastic Experience, 350–1250.* Kalamazoo: Cistercian Publications, 1988.

McKeon, Richard. "Rhetoric in the Middle Ages." In *Rhetoric: Essays in Invention and Discovery,* 121–66. Ed. Mark Backman. Woodbridge, Conn.: Ox Bow Press, 1987.

McNeill, John J. *The Church and the Homosexual.* 4th ed. Boston: Beacon Press, 1993.

Meissner, William W. *Ignatius of Loyola: The Psychology of a Saint.* New Haven: Yale University Press, 1992.

Melani, Gaudenzio. "San Bernardino da Siena ed il nome di Gesù." In *SBSSR,* 247–300.

Melzi, Robert C. "The Perception of the Jews in Italian Renaissance Comedies." *Romance Languages Annual* 6 (1995): 294–305.

Meneghin, Vittorino. *Bernardino da Feltre e i Monti di Pietà.* Vicenza: L.I.E.F., 1974.

———. "S. Bernardino da Siena e un sermone in suo onore del B. Bernardino da Fossa." *BSB* 6 (1940): 203–33.

Menning, Carol Bresnahan. *Charity and State in Late Renaissance Italy: The Monte di Pietà of Florence.* Ithaca: Cornell University Press, 1993.

Merlo, Grado. *Eretici e inquisitori nella società del secolo XIV.* Turin: Claudiana, 1977.

Metzger, Thérèse, and Mendel Metzger. *Jewish Life in the Middle Ages: Illuminated Manuscripts of the Thirteenth to the Sixteenth Centuries.* New York: Alpine Fine Arts Collection, 1982.

Miccoli, Giovanni. "Note sulla fortuna di fra Dolcino." *Annali della Scuola Normale di Pisa* 2 (1956): 245–49.

Miglio, Massimo. "Brivio (Brippius, Brippio), Giuseppe." In *Dizionario biografico degli italiani,* 14:355–58.

———. "Il pontificato e S. Bernardino." In *Atti-Aquila,* 237–49.

Milano, Attilio. *Storia degli ebrei in Italia.* Reprint, Turin: Einaudi Tascabili, 1992.

Molho, Anthony. "A Note on Jewish Moneylenders in Tuscany in the Late Trecento and Early Quattrocento." In *Renaissance Studies in Honor of Hans Baron,* ed. Anthony Molho and John A. Tedeschi, 99–117. De Kalb: Northern Illinois University Press, 1971.

Monfrin, Jacques. "Il dialogo di Giovanni da Spoleto a Jacopo Altoviti vescovo di Fiesole." *Rivista di Storia della Chiesa in Italia* 3 (1949): 9–44.

Montanaro, Agostino. *Il culto al SS. Nome di Gesù.* Naples: Istituto Grafico Editoriale Italiano, 1958.

Montesano, Marina. "La memoria dell'esperienza di Bernardino da Siena nell'agiografia del XV secolo." *Hagiographica* 1 (1994): 271–86.

Moore, Robert I. *The Formation of a Persecuting Society: Power and Deviance in Western Europe, 950–1250.* Oxford: Blackwell, 1987.

Moorman, John. *History of the Franciscan Order from Its Origins to the Year 1517.* Oxford: Clarendon Press, 1968.

Morisi, Anna. "Andrea Biglia e Bernardino da Siena." In *Atti-Todi,* 337–59.

Mormando, Franco. "Bernardino of Siena, 'Great Defender' or 'Merciless Betrayer' of Women?" *Italica* 75 (1998): 22–40.

———. "An Early Renaissance Guide for the Perplexed: Bernardino of Siena's *De inspirationibus.*" In *Through a Glass Darkly: Essays in the Religious Imagination,* ed. John C. Hawley, 24–49. New York: Fordham University Press, 1996.

———. "The Humanists, the Pagan Classics and S. Bernardino da Siena." *Laurentianum* 27 (1986): 72–97.

———. " 'Just as your lips approach the lips of your brother': Judas Iscariot and the Kiss of Betrayal." In *Saints and Sinners: Caravaggio and the Baroque Image,* ed. Franco Mormando. Exhibition Catalogue. Chestnut Hill, Mass.: McMullen Museum of Art at Boston College, 1999.

———. "Signs of the Apocalypse in Late Medieval Italy: The Popular Preaching of Bernardino of Siena." In *Medievalia et Humanistica: Studies in Medieval and Renaissance Culture* 23, ed. Paul M. Clogan, 95–122. Lanham, Md.: Rowman & Littlefield, 1997.

———. " 'To Persuade Is a Victory:' Rhetoric and Moral Reasoning in the Sermons of Bernardino of Siena." In *The Context of Casuistry,* ed. James F. Keenan and Thomas A. Shannon, 55–84. Washington, D.C.: Georgetown University Press, 1995.

———. "The Vernacular Sermons of San Bernardino da Siena, O.F.M. (1380–1444): A Literary Analysis." Ph.D. thesis, Harvard University, 1983.

———. " 'Virtual Death' in the Middle Ages: The Apotheosis of Mary Magdalene in Popular Preaching." In *Death and Dying in the Middle Ages,* ed. Edelgard E. DuBruck and Barbara I. Gusick. New York: Peter Lang, forthcoming.

Muraro, Luisa. *La Signora del gioco. Episodi della caccia alle streghe.* Milan: Feltrinelli, 1976.

Murphy, James J. *Rhetoric in the Middle Ages: A History of Rhetorical Theory from St. Augustine to the Renaissance.* Berkeley: University of California Press, 1974.

———, ed. *Three Medieval Rhetorical Arts.* Berkeley: University of California Press, 1971.

Murray, Jacqueline. "Twice Marginal and Twice Invisible: Lesbians in the Middle Ages." In *Handbook of Medieval Sexuality,* 191–222.

Muzzarelli, Maria Giuseppina. " 'Contra mundanas vanitates et pompas.' Aspetti della lotta contro i lussi nell'Italia del XV secolo." *Rivista di storia della Chiesa in Italia* 40 (1986): 371–90.

———. "I francescani ed il problema dei Monti di Pietà." In *Atti-Aquila,* 83–95.

Nardi, Paolo. "Appunti sui maestri e gli studi giovanili di San Bernardino da Siena." *Annuario dell'Istituto Storico Diocesano di Siena* 1 (1992–93): 201–22.

Nelson, Benjamin. *The Idea of Usury: From Tribal Brotherhood to Universal Otherhood.* 2d enlarged ed. Chicago: University of Chicago Press, 1969.

Nigro, Salvatore S. "Le brache di San Griffone. Novellistica e predicazione. Il *Novellino* di Masuccio Salernitano." In *Atti-Maiori,* 151–80.

Nimmo, Duncan. "The Genesis of the Observance." In *Atti-Assisi,* 109–47.

———. *Reform and Division in the Franciscan Order (1226–1538).* Rome: Capuchin Historical Institute, 1987.

Nirenberg, David. *Communities of Violence: Persecution of Minorities in the Middle Ages.* Princeton: Princeton University Press, 1996.

Noonan, John T. *The Scholastic Analysis of Usury.* Cambridge: Harvard University Press, 1957.

Novati, Francesco. "Una lettera ed un sonetto di Mariano Sozzini il vecchio." *Bullettino senese di storia patria* 2 (1895): 89–100.

Oakley, Francis. *The Western Church in the Later Middle Ages.* Ithaca: Cornell University Press, 1979.

O'Malley, John W. "Form, Content and Influence of Works about Preaching before Trent: The Franciscan Contribution." In *I frati minori fra '400 e '500,* ed. R. Rusconi, 27–50. Assisi: Università di Perugia, Centro di studi francescani, 1986.

———. *Praise and Blame in Renaissance Rome: Rhetoric, Doctrine and Reform in the Sacred Orators of the Papal Court, ca. 1450–1520.* Durham: Duke University Press, 1979.

Origo, Iris. "The Domestic Enemy: Eastern Slaves in Tuscany in the Fourteenth and Fifteenth Centuries." *Speculum* 30 (1955): 321–66.

———. *The Merchant of Prato: Francesco di Marco Datini.* London: Jonathan Cape, 1957.

———. *The World of San Bernardino.* New York: Harcourt, Brace, 1962.

The Oxford Dictionary of the Christian Church. 2d rev. ed. Ed. F. L. Cross and E. A. Livingstone. New York: Oxford University Press, 1984.

Pacelli, Vincenzo. "L'iconografia di San Bernardino da Siena dopo il Concilio di Trento." In *Atti-Siena,* 665–76.

———. "Il 'Monogramma' bernardiniano. Origine, diffusione e sviluppo." In *Atti-Maiori,* 253–59.

Pacetti, Dionisio. "Cronologia bernardiniana." In *SBSSR,* 445–64.

———. *De sancti Bernardini Senensis operibus ratio editionis critica.* Quaracchi: Collegio San Bonaventura, 1947.

———. "La libreria di San Bernardino da Siena e le sue vicende attraverso cinque secoli." *SF* 62 (1965): 3–43.

———. "Una predica sul SS. Nome di Gesù tenuta a Padova nel 1423 da S. Bernardino da Siena e raccolta da un suo anonimo ascoltatore." *MF* 42 (1942): 257–76.

———. "La predicazione di San Bernardino da Siena a Perugia e ad Assisi nel 1425." *CF* 9 (1939): 494–520; 10 (1940): 5–28, 161–88.

———. "La predicazione di S. Bernardino in Toscana. Con documenti inediti estratti dagli Atti del Processo di Canonizzazione." *AFH* 33 (1940): 268–318; 34 (1941): 261–83.

———. "Le prediche bernardiniane di un codice senese in una recente pubblicazione." *AFH* 34 (1941): 133–85.

———. "S. Bernardino da Siena Vicario Generale dell'Osservanza (1438–1442) con documenti inediti." *SF* 42 (1945): 7–69.

———. "Gli scritti di San Bernardino da Siena." In *SBSSR,* 25–138.

Padgug, Robert. "Sexual Matters: Rethinking Sexuality in History." In *Hidden from History,* 54–64.

Pagels, Elaine. *The Origin of Satan.* New York: Vintage, 1995.

Pakter, Walter. *Medieval Canon Law and the Jews.* Ebelsbach am Main: Verlag Rolf Gremer, 1988.

Paolo da Certaldo. *Libro di buoni costumi.* Ed. A. Schiaffini. Florence: Le Monnier, 1945.

Paravy, Pierrette. "Streghe e stregoni nella società del Delfinato nel XV secolo." In *Poteri carismatici e informali. Chiesa e società medioevali,* 78–96.

Partner, Peter. *The Lands of St. Peter: The Papal State in the Middle Ages and the Early Renaissance.* London: Eyre Methuen, 1972.

———. *The Papal State under Martin V: The Administration and Government of the Temporal Power in the Early Fifteenth Century.* London: British School at Rome, 1958.

Pasquini, Emilio. "Costanti tematiche e varianti testuali nelle prediche bernardiniane." In *Atti-Siena,* 677–713.

Pasztor, Edith. "S. Bernardino da Siena e l'episcopato italiano del suo tempo." In *Atti-Siena,* 715–39.

Paton, Bernadette. *Preaching Friars and the Civic Ethos: Siena, 1380–1480.* London: Centre for Medieval Studies, Queen Mary and Westfield College, University of London, 1992.

———. " 'To the fire, to the fire! Let us burn a little incense to God': Bernardino, Preaching Friars and *Maleficio* in Late Medieval Siena." In *No Gods Except Me: Orthodoxy and Religious Practice in Europe, 1200–1600,* ed. Charles Zika, 7–36. Melbourne: History Department, University of Melbourne, 1991.

Pavoncello, Nello. "Notizie storiche sulla Comunità ebraica di Siena e la sua Sinagoga." *La Rassegna Mensile di Israele* 36 (1970): 289–313.

The *Pedalion:* See *The Rudder.*

Peruzzi, Candida. "Un processo di stregoneria a Todi nel '400." *Lares* 21 (1955): 1–17.

Peters, Edward. *Heresy and Authority in Medieval Europe: Documents in Translation.* Philadelphia: University of Pennsylvania Press, 1980.

———. *The Magician, the Witch and the Law.* Philadelphia: University of Pennsylvania Press, 1978.

Petrocchi, Giorgio. "Gli Ebrei, Dante e Boccaccio." In *Aspetti e problemi della presenza ebraica,* 343–59.

Petrucci, Enzo. "Gli ebrei in un inedito opuscolo anonimo sulla costituzione e riforma della Chiesa della fine del secolo XIV." In *Aspetti e problemi della presenza ebraica,* 307–42.

Piana, Celestino. "Documenti intorno alla vita di S. Bernardino da Siena e codici delle opere." *BSB* 10 (1950): 159–74.

———. "I processi di canonizzazione su la vita di San Bernardino da Siena." *AFH* 44 (1951): 87–160, 383–435.

———. "Un processo svolto a Milano nel 1441 a favore del mag. Amedeo de Landi e contro frate Bernardino da Siena." In *Atti-Siena,* 753–92.

———. "S. Bernardino da Siena a Bologna." *SF* terza serie 17 (1945): 213–61.

———. "San Bernardino da Siena teologo." In *SBSSR,* 139–201.

Piccolomini, Enea Silvio. "De Bernardino Senensi." In *De viris illustribus,* ed. Adrian van Heck, 37–41. Vatican City: Biblioteca Apostolica Vaticana, 1991.

Piccolomini, Niccolò, and Narciso Mengozzi. *Il Monte dei Paschi di Siena e le aziende in esso riunite.* 9 vols. Siena: Lazzeri, 1891–1925.

Pinzi, Cesare. *Storia della città di Viterbo.* Viterbo: Tipografia Sociale Agnesotti, 1899.

Polecritti, Cynthia Louise. "Preaching Peace in Renaissance Italy: San Bernardino of Siena and His Audience." Ph.D. thesis, University of California, Berkeley, 1988.

Poliakov, Léon. *Jewish Bankers and the Holy See from the Thirteenth to the Seventeenth Century.* London: Routledge & Kegan Paul, 1977. Originally published as *Les banchieri juifs et le Saint-Siège du XIII*e *au XVII*e *siècle.* Paris: S.E.V.P.E.N., 1965.

Policelli, Eugene F. "Humanism in the Life and Vernacular Sermons of Bernardino of Siena." Ph.D. thesis, University of Connecticut, 1973.

Pope-Hennessy, John. *Donatello Sculptor.* New York: Abbeville, 1993.

Poteri carismatici e informali: chiesa e società medioevali. Ed. Agostino Paravicini Bagliani and André Vauchez. Palermo: Sellerio, 1992.

Prunai, Giulio. "Benvoglienti, Leonardo." In *Dizionario biografico degli italiani,* 8:703–5.

Pulinari da Firenze, Dionisio. *Cronache dei Frati Minori della Provincia di Toscana.* Ed. S. Mencherini. Arezzo: Cooperativa Tipografica, 1913.

Quaglioni, Diego. "I giuristi medioevali e gli ebrei. Due 'consultationes' di G. F. Pavini (1478)." *Quaderni storici* n. 64, an. 22 (1987): 7–18.

———. " 'Inter Iudeos et Christianos commertia sunt permissa:' 'Questione ebraica' e usura in Baldo degli Ubaldi (c. 1327–1400)." In *Aspetti e problemi della presenza ebraica,* 273–306.

Quaife, G. R. *Godly Zeal and Furious Rage: The Witch in Early Modern Europe.* New York: St. Martin's Press, 1987.

Rainey, Ronald. "Dressing Down the Dressed-Up: Reproving Feminine Attire in Renaissance Florence." In *Renaissance Society and Culture: Essays in Honor of Eugene F. Rice, Jr.,* ed. John Monfasani and Ronald G. Musto, 217–37. New York: Italica Press, 1991.

Richards, Jeffrey. *Sex, Dissidence and Damnation: Minority Groups in the Middle Ages.* London: Routledge, 1991.

Richlin, Amy. "Not Before Homosexuality: The Materiality of the *Cinaedus* and the Roman Law against Love between Men." *Journal of the History of Sexuality* 3 (1993): 523–73.

Ridolfi, Roberto. *Vita del Savonarola.* 2 vols. Rome: A. Belardetti, 1952.

Rimbotti, Giuseppe. "S. Bernardino da Siena ad Arezzo." *BSB* 9 (1943): 61–71.

Rocke, Michael. *Forbidden Friendships: Homosexuality and Male Culture in Renaissance Florence.* New York: Oxford University Press, 1996.

———. "Sodomites in Fifteenth-Century Tuscany: The Views of Bernardino of Siena." In *The Pursuit of Sodomy: Male Homosexuality in Renaissance and Enlightenment Europe,* ed. Kent Gerard and Gert Hekma, 7–31. New York: Harrington Park Press, 1989.

Romano, Casimiro: See Casimiro Romano.

Rossi, Pietro. "La 'Lectura Dantis' nello Studio senese: Giovanni da Spoleto maestro di rettorica e lettore della *Divina Commedia* (1396–1445)." In *Studi giuridici dedicati e offerti a F. S. Schupfer,* 153–74. Turin: Fratelli Bocca, 1898.

Rossiaud, Jacques. *Medieval Prostitution.* Trans. Lydia G. Cochrane. New York: Blackwell, 1988.

Roth, Cecil. *A History of the Jews in Italy.* Philadelphia: Jewish Publication Society of America, 1946.

Roth, Norman. "Bishops and Jews in the Middle Ages." *Catholic Historical Review* 80 (1994): 1–17.

———. Review of Jeremy Cohen, *The Friars and the Jews. Jewish Quarterly Review* 74 (1984): 321–25.

The Rudder (Pedalion) of the Metaphorical Ship of the One Holy Catholic and Apostolic Church of the Orthodox Christians or All the Sacred and Divine Canons . . . Trans. D. Cummings. Chicago: Orthodox Christian Educational Society, 1957.

Ruderman, David B. "Champion of Jewish Economic Interests." In *Essential Papers on Judaism and Christianity in Crisis,* ed. Jeremy Cohen, 514–35. New York: New York University Press, 1990.

———. *The World of a Renaissance Jew: The Life and Thought of Abraham ben Mordecai Farissol.* Cincinnati: Hebrew Union College Press, 1981.

———, ed. *Essential Papers on Jewish Culture in Renaissance and Baroque Italy.* New York: New York University Press, 1992.

Ruggiero, Guido. *The Boundaries of Eros: Sex Crimes and Sexuality in Renaissance Venice.* New York: Oxford University Press, 1985.

Rusconi, Roberto. "Apocalittica ed escatologia nella predicazione di Bernardino da Siena." *Studi medievali* terza serie 22 (1981): 85–128.

———. *L'attesa della fine. Crisi della società, profezia ed Apocalisse in Italia al tempo del grande scisma d'Occidente (1378–1417).* Rome: Istituto Storico Italiano per il Medio Evo, 1979.

———. *Predicazione e vita religiosa nella società italiana da Carlo Magno alla Controriforma.* Turin: Loescher, 1981.

———. "S. Bernardino, la donna e la 'roba.'" In *Atti-Aquila,* 97–110.

Russell, Jeffrey Burton. *A History of Witchcraft: Sorcerers, Heretics, and Pagans.* London: Thames & Hudson, 1980.

———. *Lucifer: The Devil in the Middle Ages.* Ithaca: Cornell University Press, 1984.

———. *Witchcraft in the Middle Ages.* Ithaca: Cornell University Press, 1972.

Russo, Luigi. "Caterina Benincasa e Bernardino da Siena." *Belfagor* 12 (1957): 121–32.

Salgarolo, David. "The Figure of the Jew in Italian Medieval and Renaissance Narrative." Ph.D. thesis, Brown University, 1989.

Salisbury, Joyce E. *The Beast Within: Animals in the Middle Ages.* New York and London: Routledge, 1994.

Salvadori, Roberto G. *Breve storia degli ebrei toscani, IX–XX secolo.* Florence: Le Lettere, 1995.

Salvadori, Roberto G., and Giorgio Sacchetti. *Presenze ebraiche nell'Aretino dal XIV al XX secolo.* Florence: Olschki, 1990.

Saperstein, Marc. "Italian Jewish Preaching: An Overview." In *Essential Papers on Jewish Culture in Renaissance and Baroque Italy,* ed. David B. Ruderman, 85–104. New York: New York University Press, 1992.

Sartorelli, Gabriele. "San Bernardino da Siena ed il francescanesimo abruzzese del Quattrocento." *Bullettino della Deputazione abruzzese di storia patria* 70 (1980): 5–34.

Saslow, James M. "Homosexuality in the Renaissance: Behavior, Identity, and Artistic Expression." In *Hidden from History,* 90–105.

Schevill, Ferdinand. *Siena: The History of a Medieval Commune.* 1909. New York: Harper & Row, 1964.

Schnaubelt, Joseph C. "Andrea Biglia (c. 1394–1435), His Life and Writings." *Augustiniana* 43 (1993): 103–59.

Schreckenberg, Heinz. *The Jews in Christian Art: An Illustrated History.* New York: Continuum, 1996.

Scroggs, Robin. *The New Testament and Homosexuality: Contextual Background for Contemporary Debate*. Philadelphia: Fortress Press, 1983.

Segre, Renata, ed. *The Jews in Piedmont. Vol. I (1297–1582)*. Jerusalem: Israel Academy of Sciences and Humanities and Tel Aviv University, 1986.

Sensi, Mario. *Dal movimento eremitico alla regolare osservanza francescana. L'opera di fra Paoluccio Trinci*. Assisi: Edizioni Porziuncula, 1992.

Sevesi, Paolo. "Un sermone inedito del B. Michele Carcano su S. Bernardino da Siena." *SF* terza serie 3 (1931): 69–92.

———. "Tre sermoni inediti su S. Bernardino." *BSB* 1 (1935): 205–36; 2 (1936): 58–65, 164–73.

Sexual Practices and the Medieval Church. Ed. Vern L. Bullough and James Brundage. Buffalo: Prometheus Books, 1982.

Sgariglia, Cesare. "Due documenti relativi a S. Bernardino." *MF* 3 (1888): 160.

Shahar, Shulamith. *The Fourth Estate: A History of Women in the Middle Ages*. London and New York: Methuen, 1983.

———. *Growing Old in the Middle Ages*. London: Routledge, 1997.

Shatzmiller, Joseph. *Jews, Medicine, and Medieval Society*. Berkeley: University of California Press, 1994.

———. *Shylock Reconsidered: Jews, Moneylending and Medieval Society*. Berkeley: University of California Press, 1990.

Shaw, Brent D. "A Groom of One's Own?" (Review of John Boswell's *Same-Sex Unions in Premodern Europe*). *New Republic*, July 18 and 25, 1994, 33–41.

Shemek, Deanna. "Circular Definitions: Configuring Gender in Italian Renaissance Festival." *Renaissance Quarterly* 48 (1995): 1–40.

Shulvass, Moses A. *The Jews in the World of the Renaissance*. Trans. Elvin I. Kore. Leiden: E. J. Brill and the Spertus College of Judaica Press, 1973.

Simonsohn, Shlomo. *The Apostolic See and the Jews. Documents: 1394–1464*. Toronto: Pontifical Institute of Mediaeval Studies, 1989.

———. *The Apostolic See and the Jews. History*. Toronto: Pontifical Institute of Mediaeval Studies, 1991.

———. "Divieto di trasportare ebrei in Palestina." In *Italia Judaica: "Gli ebrei in Italia fra Rinascimento ed Età Barocca." Atti del II Convegno Internazionale. Genova 10–15 giugno 1984*, 39–53. Rome: Ministero per i Beni Culturali e Ambientali: Pubblicazioni degli Archivi di Stato, 1986.

———. *History of the Jews in the Duchy of Mantua*. Jerusalem: Kiryath Sepher, 1977.

———. "Lo stato attuale della ricerca storica sugli ebrei in Italia." In *Italia judaica. Atti del I Convegno internazionale, Bari 18–22 maggio 1981*, 29–37. Rome: Ministero per i Beni Culturali e Ambientali; Pubblicazioni degli Archivi di Stato, 1983.

———, ed. *The Jews in the Duchy of Milan*. Jerusalem: Israel Academy of Sciences and Humanities, 1982.

Siraisi, Nancy G. *Medieval and Early Renaissance Medicine: An Introduction to Knowledge and Practice*. Chicago: University of Chicago Press, 1990.

Smith, Bruce R. *Homosexual Desire in Shakespeare's England: A Cultural Poetics*. Chicago: University of Chicago Press, 1991.

Sorelli, Fernanda. "Predicatori a Venezia (fine secolo XIV–metà secolo XV)." *Le Venezie francescane (Predicazione francescana e società veneta nel Quattrocento: committenza, ascolto, ricezione. Atti del II Convegno internazionale di studi francescani. Padova, 26–27–28 marzo 1987)* nuova serie 6 (1989): 131–58.

Spicciani, Amleto. "La povertà 'involontaria' e le sue cause economiche nel pensiero e nella predicazione di Bernardino da Siena." In *Atti-Siena,* 811–34.

———. "Sant'Antonino, San Bernardino e Pier di Giovanni Olivi nel pensiero economico medievale." In *Una economia politica nel Medioevo,* ed. Ovidio Capitani, 93–120. Bologna: Pàtron Editore, 1987.

Stasiewski, Bernhard. *Der Heilige Bernardin von Siena: Untersuchungen über die quellen einer biographen.* Munster: Aschendorffschen Verlagsbuchhandlung, 1931.

Stehling, Thomas, trans. and ed. *Medieval Latin Poems of Male Love and Friendship.* New York: Garland, 1984.

Sticco, Maria. *Poesia e pensiero in San Bernardino da Siena.* 2d ed. Milan: Vita e Pensiero, 1945.

Stinger, Charles. Review of *Christianity and the Renaissance: Image and Religious Imagination in the Quattrocento,* ed. Timothy Verdon and John Henderson (Syracuse University Press, 1990), in *Renaissance Quarterly* 44 (1991): 824–26.

Stow, Kenneth R. *Alienated Minority: The Jews of Medieval Latin Europe.* Cambridge: Harvard University Press, 1992.

———. *Catholic Thought and Papal Jewry Policy 1555–1593.* New York: Jewish Theological Seminary of America, 1977.

Strehlke, Carl B. "La *Madonna dell'Umiltà* di Domenico di Bartolo e San Bernardino." *Arte cristiana,* n. 705 (1984): 381–90.

Surius, Laurentius, ed. "Vita S. Bernardini Senensis." In *Historiae Seu Vitae Sanctorum,* 5:618–59. 13 vols. Turin: Marietti, 1875–80.

Swanson, R. N. *Religion and Devotion in Europe, c. 1215–c. 1515.* Cambridge: Cambridge University Press, 1995.

Synan, Edward A. *The Popes and the Jews in the Middle Ages.* New York: Macmillan, 1965.

Taylor, Larissa. *Soldiers of Christ: Preaching in Late Medieval and Reformation France.* New York: Oxford University Press, 1992.

Thompson, Stith. *Motif-Index of Folk-literature: A Classification of Narrative Elements in Folk-tales, Ballads, Myths, Fables.* Rev. enlarged ed. Bloomington: Indiana University Press, 1989.

Thureau-Dangin, Paul. *The Life of S. Bernardino of Siena.* Rev. ed. Trans. G. von Hügel. London: Philip Lee Warner, 1911.

Titian, Prince of Painters. Exhibition at the National Gallery of Art, Washington, D.C., October 18, 1990–January 27, 1991. Venice: Marsilio Editori, 1990.

Toaff, Ariel. *Gli ebrei a Perugia.* Perugia: Deputazione di Storia Patria per l'Umbria, 1975.

———. "The Jewish Badge in Italy during the 15th Century." In *Die Juden in ihrer mittelatlerlichen Umwelt,* ed. Alfred Ebenbauer and Klaus Zatloukal, 275–80. Vienna: Bohlau Verlag, 1991.

———. *The Jews in Medieval Assisi, 1305–1487: A Social and Economic History of a Small Jewish Community in Italy.* Florence: Olschki, 1979.

———. *The Jews in Umbria. Volume I: 1245–1435.* Leiden: E. J. Brill, 1993.

———. *Love, Work, and Death: Jewish Life in Medieval Umbria.* London: Littman Library of Jewish Civilization, 1996.

Todeschini, Giacomo. "Ebrei in Italia alla fine del Medioevo. Studi recenti." *Studi medievali* 30 (1989): 353–66.

———. "Il problema economico in Bernardino." In *Atti-Todi,* 285–309.

———. "Teorie economiche francescane e presenza ebraica in Italia (1380–1462 c.)," in *Atti-Assisi,* 193–227.

Tosti, Salvatore. "De praedicatione S. Bernardini Senensis in patria civitate, anno 1425." *AFH* 8 (1915): 678–80.

———. "Di alcuni codici delle prediche di S. Bernardino da Siena con un saggio di quelle inedite." *AFH* 12 (1919): 187–263.

Trachtenberg, Joshua. *The Devil and the Jews: The Medieval Conception of the Jew and Its Relation to Modern Antisemitism.* 2d pbk. ed. Foreword by Marc Saperstein. Reprint, Philadelphia: Jewish Publication Society of America, 1983.

Trexler, Richard C. *Public Life in Renaissance Florence.* New York: Academic Press, 1980; Ithaca: Cornell University Press, 1991.

Tubach, Frederic C. *Index Exemplorum: A Handbook of Medieval Religious Tales.* Helsinki: Suomalainen Tiedeakatemia (Academia Scientiarum Fennica), 1969.

Underhill, Evelyn. *Jacopone da Todi.* London: Dent, 1919.

van Ortroy, Franciscus. "Vie inédite de S. Bernardin de Sienne par un frère mineur, son contemporain." *AB* 25 (1906): 304–38.

Vasari, Giorgio. *The Lives of the Painters, Sculptors and Architects.* London: Dent, 1927.

Vauchez, André. "Alcune riflessioni sul movimento dell'Osservanza in Italia nel secolo XV." In *Ordini mendicanti e società italiana XIII–XV secolo,* 306–10. Milan: Mondadori/Il Saggiatore, 1990.

Vegio, Maffeo. "Vita sancti Bernardini senensis." *AASS.* Maii tomus V, die vigesima.

Vernet, Félix. "Le pape Martin V et les Juifs." *Revue des questions historiques* 51 (1892): 373–423.

Vespasiano da Bisticci. *Vite di uomini ilustri.* Florence: Rinascimento del Libro, 1938.

Viola, Coloman. "Jugements de Dieu et jugement dernier: Saint Augustin et la scolastique naissante (fin XIe–milieu XIIIe siècles)." In *The Use and Abuse of Eschatology in the Middle Ages,* ed. Werner Verbeke, Daniel Verhelst, and Andries Welkenhuysen, 242–98. Leuven: Leuven University Press, 1988.

Vita anonima: See van Ortroy.

Vivanti, Corrado. "The History of the Jews in Italy and the History of Italy." *Journal of Modern History* (1995): 309–57.

Wadding, Lucas. *Annales Minorum.* 3d ed. Quaracchi: Collegio San Bonaventura, 1931–41.

Walker, Barbara G. *The Crone: Woman of Age, Wisdom, and Power.* San Francisco: Harper, 1985.

Walsh, Katherine. "The Augustinian Observance in Siena in the Age of S. Caterina and S. Bernardino." In *Atti-Siena,* 939–50.

Warner, Marina. *Alone of All Her Sex: The Myth and the Cult of the Virgin Mary.* New York: Vintage, 1983.

Watt, John A. "Jews and Christians in the Gregorian Decretals." In *Christianity and Judaism,* ed. Diana Wood, 93–106. Oxford: Ecclesiastical History Society and Blackwell, 1992.

Waugh, Scott L., and Peter D. Diehl, eds. *Christendom and Its Discontents: Exclusion, Persecution, and Rebellion, 1000–1500.* Cambridge: Cambridge University Press, 1996.

Webb, Diana M. "Andrea Biglia at Bologna, 1424–27: A Humanist Friar and the Troubles of the Church." *Bulletin of the Institute of Historical Research* 49 (1976): 41–59.

———. "Eloquence and Education: A Humanist Approach to Hagiography." *Journal of Ecclesiastical History* 31 (1980): 19–39.

———. *Patrons and Defenders: The Saints in the Italian City States.* London: Tauris Academic Studies, 1996.

Weinstein, Donald, and Rudolph M. Bell. *Saints and Society: The Two Worlds of Western Christendom, 1000–1700.* Chicago: University of Chicago Press, 1982.

White, T. H., trans. *The Bestiary.* New York: Putnam/Capricorn, 1960.

Wilkins, Ernest H. *A History of Italian Literature*. Revised by Thomas G. Bergin. Cambridge: Harvard University Press, 1974.

Zafarana, Zelina. "Bernardino nella storia della predicazione popolare." In *Atti-Todi*, 39–70.

Zawart, Anscar. *The History of Franciscan Preaching and of Franciscan Preachers (1209–1927): A Bio-bibliographical Study*. New York: Wagner, 1928.

Zdekauer, Lodovico. "L'interno di un banco di pegno nel 1417." *Archivio storico italiano* 17, ser. 5 (fasc. 1, 1896): 63–105.

———. "Sullo scritto 'De sortilegiis' di M. Sozzini il Vecchio." *Archivio per lo studio delle tradizioni popolari* 15 (1896): 131–37.

Zen Benetti, Francesca. "Prestatori ebraici e cristiani nel Padovano fra Trecento e Quattrocento." In *Gli Ebrei e Venezia, secoli XIV–XVIII. Atti del Convegno internazionale organizzato dall'Istituto di storia della società e dello stato veneziano della Fondazione Giorgio Cini. Venezia, 5–10 giugno 1983*, ed. Gaetano Cozzi, 629–50. Milan: Edizioni di Comunità, 1987.

Zimdars-Swartz, Sandra L. "Joachite Themes in the Sermons of St. Bernardino: Assessing the Stigmata of St. Francis." In *Il profetismo gioachimita tra Quattrocento e Cinquecento. Atti del III Congresso Internazionale di Studi Gioachimiti. S. Giovanni in Fiore, 17–21 settembre 1988*, ed. Gian Luca Potestà, 47–60. Genoa: Marietti, 1991.

Ziolkowski, Jan M. *Talking Animals: Medieval Latin Beast Poetry, 750–1150*. Philadelphia: University of Pennsylvania Press, 1993.

INDEX